General Introduction to Empirical Research of Cognitive Linguistics

认知语言学实证研究通论

吴 斐 著

WUHAN UNIVERSITY PRESS
武汉大学出版社

图书在版编目(CIP)数据

认知语言学实证研究通论/吴斐著 . —武汉:武汉大学出版社,2012.8
ISBN 978-7-307-10030-5

Ⅰ.认… Ⅱ.吴… Ⅲ.认知科学—语言学—研究 Ⅳ.H0-05

中国版本图书馆 CIP 数据核字(2012)第 169417 号

责任编辑:叶玲利　　　责任校对:黄添生　　　版式设计:韩闻锦

出版发行:**武汉大学出版社**　　(430072　武昌　珞珈山)
　　　　　(电子邮件:cbs22@ whu. edu. cn 网址:www. wdp. com. cn)
印刷:湖北睿智印务有限公司
开本:787×1092　1/16　　印张:26.25　　字数:682 千字　　插页:1
版次:2012 年 8 月第 1 版　　2012 年 8 月第 1 次印刷
ISBN 978-7-307-10030-5/H · 924　　定价:47.00 元

前　言

认知语言学是活跃在当前国际理论语言学界一种新兴的研究方法,它建立在经验主义的哲学基础之上。这种经验主义的认知观强调思维的概念——形体结构、思维的想象空间以及思维的完形特征。因此,认知语言学是一门实验性很强的科学,研究方法对获得数据以检验种种认知语言学假设至关重要,使用非常广泛,涉及言语信息的感知、解码和编码、存储和提取。实验是认知语言学常用的一种研究方法,从本质上讲,它是一种有控制的观察。一种语言行为往往是多种因素共同作用的结果,为了研究某一因素在这一语言行为过程中所起的作用,通过实验控制其他的相关因素,在它们保持不变的状态下,发现需要研究因素的变化和状态,研究这一因素的作用,是认知语言学实证研究的主要特点。《认知语言学实证研究通论》根据中国学生的第二语言习得规律,从语言技能(language skills)、语义和句法(semantics and syntax)的概念接面——包括象似性(iconicity)、标记性(markedness)和语法化(grammaticalization),以及隐喻(metaphor)和转喻(metonymy)三大部分讨论了认知语言学近年来热门课题的实证研究方法。

第一部分共四章,主要研究听、说、读、写语言技能的实证研究范式。

第一章论述了听力理解认知过程中的实证研究方法。听力理解是一个复杂的认知心理活动过程。听者不仅要对语音、词汇、语法等语言知识进行表层加工,还要利用社会和文化背景知识进行联想、推理和判断等一系列深层语义的综合分析。在第二语言习得的研究中,听力理解在语言输入方面的重要性受到普遍关注。本章主要考察话语熟悉程度和语言水平对中国英语学习者听力理解能力的影响,揭示这一群体的听力理解认知过程。

本研究对武汉大学水利专业三年级本科生和政管一年级学生进行了两组听力测试,一组是受试者熟悉的话题"年",另一组是受试者陌生的话题"日式茶道"。实验采用撰写回想的方法检验学生的听力理解。为弥补学生在撰写回想过程中回避无把握答案,对两种实验分别补充了三个问题作为定性分析的依据。测试结果用 SPSS 软件进行独立样本、配对样本和ANOVA 等统计检验,在图示理论和关联理论框架下解释和说明话语熟悉程度和语言水平对非英语专业本科生听力理解的影响。

研究结果表明,话题熟悉程度对中国学生的听力理解呈显著影响态势。熟悉语篇对听力理解起着促进作用,高水平和中等水平的受试者对熟悉的语篇均比对陌生的语篇理解更好。语言水平对中国学生的听力理解呈显著意义,无论是熟悉的语篇还是陌生的语篇,高水平受试者均比中等水平受试者理解更好,高水平受试者更能利用语言知识激活大脑中的相关图式,获取顺畅的信息理解通道。但话题熟悉程度和语言水平的交互意义并不明显。在处理模式上,高水平受试者和中等水平受试者在熟悉语篇下趋于"自上而下"的听力处理模式,而在陌生语篇下趋于采用"自下而上"的听力处理模式。听力理解信息处理可用图 1 说明:

第二章研究中国英语学习者话语标记语的使用情况与习得规律。话语标记语是语言中普遍存在、用来标记话语信息的词语或结构。对话语标记语功能和意义的普遍研究存在两种倾

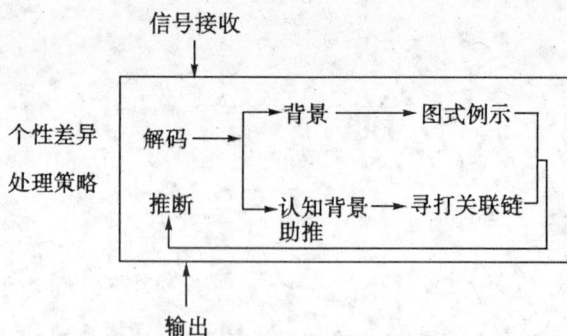

图 1　听力理解处理模型

向:在语篇连贯理论框架下,静态研究话语标记语表达的概念意义及其对加强话语连贯性的作用;在关联理论框架下,动态研究话语标记语表达的程序意义及其在话语生成和话语理解中的作用。对话语标记语使用与习得的研究分为两个方面:本族语使用者对话语标记语的使用与习得,包括年龄、性别以及社会阶层等个体因素和话语语境等外部因素;二语习得者对话语标记语的使用与习得,主要研究与本族语使用者在话语标记语使用中的异同及其影响因素等。

　　本研究首先对空间复合理论和关联理论框架下的话语标记语使用和习得进行整合。然后运用录音、转录方式,收集 65 名受试者在小组讨论活动中的语料,62 名受试者在看图说话活动中的语料,分析统计语料中话语标记的使用类型、使用次数,以及各类占总使用次数的比例。在此基础上,通过完形填空和话语理解两组测试,分别获取 61 名受试者对话语标记语的使用情况,以及对话语标记语 well 语用功能的元语用意识的有关数据。本研究对以上数据进行了各种分析对比,包括与本族语使用者话语标记语使用的对比,得出中国英语学习者话语标记语的使用与习得规律:对话语标记语的使用呈书面化倾向、使用僵化;对话语标记语的习得遵循从字面意义到语用意义的规律。话语标记语在话语理解动态过程中的作用和话语标记语语用含义的演变过程可以形成以下话语标记语的空间复合模式:

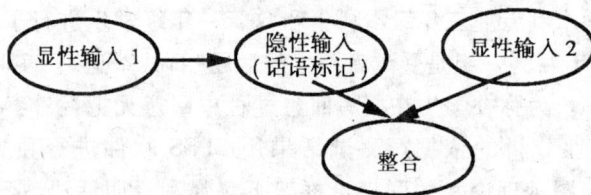

图 2　话语标记在言语表达中的整合模型 1

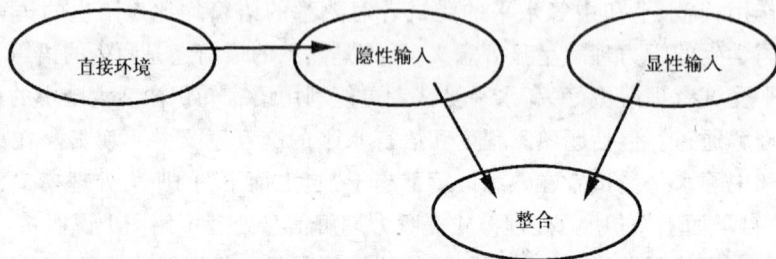

图 3　话语标记在言语表达中的整合模型 2

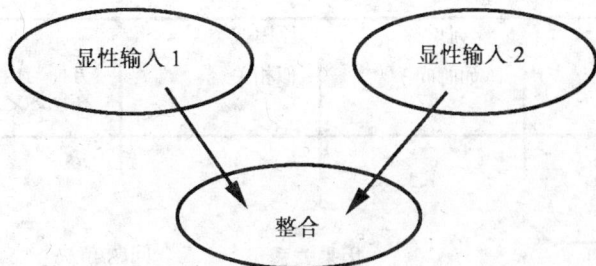

图 4　话语标记在言语表达中的整合模型 3

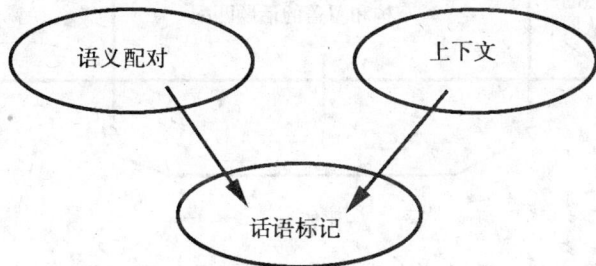

图 5　话语标记独立参数整合模型

第三章研究修辞结构对中国英语学习者阅读理解的影响。修辞结构在本研究中被定义为篇章语言学和话语分析中组织文章或话语的潜在结构。图式理论指理解语言时,人们激活相关图式,快速、高效地加工和阐释新的知识。图式往往被用做一种参考存储,人们可以从中提取现存的相关知识。图式理论在第二语言阅读理解时起着重要作用,常常被用来揭示某种阅读现象。图式可以分为两种形式:内容图式和形式图式。前者是关于话题的一般性背景知识,而后者是关于语言修辞结构和读者关于某一特定类型结构的知识。就阅读理解而言,形式图式是读者对不同文体文本的结构、修辞等方面的篇章结构知识。

本研究采用了四种最基本的修辞结构(列举描述、因果关系、解决问题和对比关系)和三种最为常见的文体(说明文、议论文和记叙文),如图 6 所示。

为了探讨上述四种修辞结构对中国英语学习者阅读是否产生影响,以及上述三种文体对阅读是否产生影响,研究采用"阅读回忆"等研究工具。研究对象为武汉大学非英语专业二年级的 50 名学生。测试结果用 SPSS 的 ANOVA 和 Scheffe Multiple Comparison 等统计方法检验。研究结果显示,在说明文和记叙文中,英语学习者更能驾驭修辞结构较为紧密的因果关系、解决问题和对比关系语篇;但在议论文中,解决问题式的修辞结构较之列举描述式的修辞结构更容易被学习者理解。其次,不同文体对学习者的二语阅读影响各异。但在解决问题的修辞结构中,学习者在三种文体的表现中不存在显著差异。最后,学习者对母语较高层次阅读技巧的掌握(如使用背景知识)对阅读理解产生正迁移,同时也可以弥补基本语言技能的缺失。

第四章研究读写结合法对读写能力产生的效果。阅读和写作是语言能力表现的重要组成部分。"输入假设"(Krashen,1985)认为"可理解的语言输入"是语言习得的唯一途径,学习

联想聚合	序列聚合 （如时间）	原因或类 似相关	至少解决问题的一个 方面与内容相符，并 在问题之前停止

1   2   3   4

因果关系   问题/解决

聚集

描述

通过联想的分组 类型：联想的一 种成分是从属联 想的另一分类	至少有一类与相关结 构和覆盖的话题匹配

1   2   3   4

比较

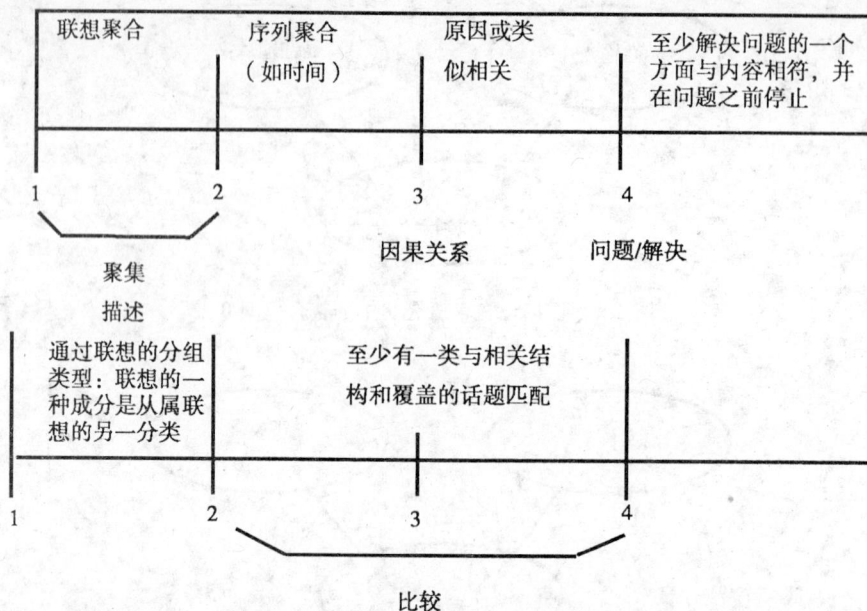

图 6　文本结构的成分（Meyer and Freedle, 1984）

者只要接触大量的可理解输入，语言习得就自然而然地发生。"输出假设"（Swain, 1985）认为学习者在语言习得过程中不仅需要"可理解输入"，更需要"可理解输出"，以达到第二语言使用的流利度和准确度。"输入假设"和"输出假设"验证了输入和输出的互补，为构建"输入—构建—理解—输出—输入"循环模式奠定了基础。"整体法"（Widdowson, 1978）从交际角度阐释语习得过程，提倡将听、说、读、写四项语言技能相结合从而促进语言习得。"读写过程认知模型"（Kucer, 2005）引入读写平行概念观；分析了影响读者、文本和作者三者之间互动过程的五个因素：语言体系、策略运用的有效性和灵活度、背景知识、使用语言的目的、同化和顺应能力，并指出读写过程共享以下特征：探寻、生成和整合意义，积极使用语言资源和认知资源，运用并构建背景知识，依赖语境，修订意义，以目标为导向。研究以上述理论为框架，结合中国 21 世纪大学英语读写教学现状，探讨一种读写结合的教学模式。

本研究受试者为武汉大学 09 级三个班的 98 名本科生（包括信息管理专业的 31 名学生，测绘专业的 33 名学生，水质科学与技术专业的 34 名学生）。在为期 12 周的实验中，对三个班分别采用读写结合、强化阅读输入和强化写作输出的英语教学方法进行英语教学。实验测量工具包括读写水平测试试卷和读写结合策略问卷。实验数据采用 SPSS 软件进行配对样本 T 检验和单向方差分析等统计检验。实证研究数据显示：读写结合法对提高中国英语学习者的写作水平具有显著效果，强化阅读输入法对中国英语学习者的写作水平产生促进作用，但强化写作输出法对写作水平的促进作用并不明显。此外，上述三种教学法在提高中国英语学习者的阅读水平方面均无显著效果。本研究构建了"输入—构建—理解—输出—输入"循环模型，论证了阅读和写作的复杂心理过程，有着共同的认知基础和相同的处理模式，二者可以相互结合，相互促进。

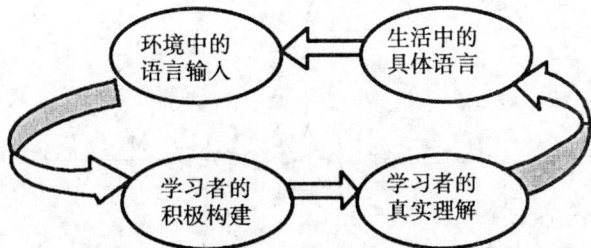

图7 "输入—构建—理解—输出—输入"循环模型

第二部分共四章,主要研究词汇和语法在使用过程中的实证数据统计和模型。

第五章研究中国英语学习者对英语多义动作动词的习得。多义性是一种普遍的语言现象。一词多义指一个词具有两个或两个以上互相联系的语义。传统的语义理论如成分分析和语义场理论将一词多义置于同形异义的框架下分析,从而忽略了多个意义之间的语义联系。认知语言学家运用原型理论、意象图示、隐喻和转喻理论对一词多义现象进行了新的阐释。原型理论认为范畴的边界是模糊的,范畴成员之间表现出家族相似性;范畴成员在范畴中的地位不相等,同一词中某些意义比另一意义更具有典型性。意象图示是一种基本的概念结构,它建立在人类身体运动经验及其与外部世界相互作用的物理经验基础之上,可以用来组织和理解更复杂、更抽象的语义概念。隐喻和转喻不仅是修辞手段,而且是两种重要的认知模式。隐喻是源域的图示结构向目标域的映射,而转喻则是同一理想认知域中一个概念实体为另一个概念实体提供心理通道的认知过程。一词多义是以多义词的核心义或基本义为中心,通过隐喻或转喻的认知方式向其他意义延伸的过程,是人类认知范畴化和概念化的结果。本章研究以上述理论为基础,考察中国英语学习者对六个英语多义动作动词 draw, fix, hit, hold, move, run 的基本义、引申义及搭配义的习得状况。

本研究的受试者为36名武汉大学医学专业的大一学生。实验采用单项选择、英译汉、汉译英三种测试工具。收集的数据用 SPSS 软件进行分析。研究结果表明:(1)中国英语学习者对英语多义动作动词的基本义把握较好,因为人体与客观世界相互作用的经验构成了理解基本义的有利基础。(2)基本义与引申义、基本义与搭配义的习得之间基本上没有呈现显著的正相关关系,但中国英语学习者对单个多义词不同引申义的习得情况不同。(3)在多个引申义中,中国学生对熟悉或常用的意义有较好的把握;他们对不同引申义的习得水平与引申义理据性的强弱程度有关,理据性更明显的引申义习得更好。然而,中国英语学习者即使在对基本义习得较好的情况下,理解和掌握比较抽象的引申义依然有较大的困难,他们在多义动作动词习得过程中的隐喻和转喻能力有待提高。研究建立了 draw, fix, hit, hold, move, run 六个英语多义动作动词的意义延伸模型和图式。选用 move 一词作为示例,如图8、图9所示。

第六章研究中国英语学习者英语介词的空间象似性习得。介词及介词短语多义性是英语学习过程中难以掌握的要素。介词通过空间象似性——语言形式和它所表达的意义之间的象似或相像关系——把本来的空间意义投射到更为抽象的概念意义域中,形成介词的多义性。在语义学层面,介词及介词短语多义性折射出象似性的三大原则:距离象似性(语符距离象似于概念距离)、数量象似性(语言单位的数量与所表示的概念量和复杂度成正比象似,与可测

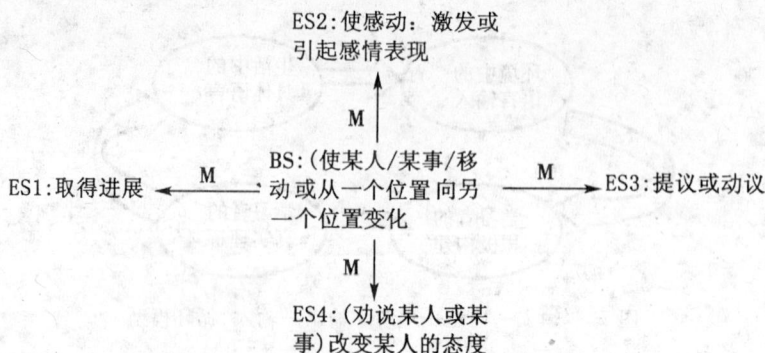

图 8　多义动作动词 move 的语义延伸模型

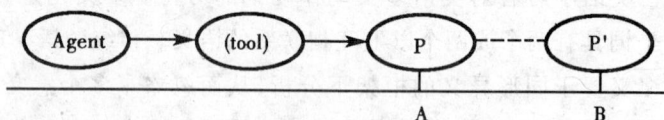

图 9　多义动作动词 move 的语义力量图式

注:A 和 B 代表语义延伸路径的两端,P 指代接受者的初始位置 A 点,P′指代接受者的新位置 B 点,(tool) 表示工具可有可无。箭头显示语义力量的流向。

度成反比象似)和顺序象似性(思维顺序与语言单位排列的顺序象似)。空间象似性将现实生活中各种事物之间的相互依存关系归纳为相对应的语言形式的两个层次:物理空间象似性和心理空间象似性。介词正是借助空间象似性由空间语义域向时间、数量、状态、目的/原因以及方法/手段等语义域延伸。本章研究运用认知语言学的研究方法,从象似性的角度观察介词及介词短语的多义性,研究象似性原则在介词语义中的生成,空间象似性在介词语义域中的延伸和语言结构上的投射。

Type	Static		Dynamic	
ZD	$\cdot$ X (at)	$\cdot$ X (from)	$\longrightarrow$ X (to)	X$\longrightarrow$ (from)
OD	___$\cdot$___ (on)	(before) $\longleftarrow\longrightarrow$ (after)	_____$\longrightarrow$ (along)	$\uparrow$ (up) $\downarrow$ (down)
TWD	(on)	(off)	(onto)	(off)
THD	(in)	(out of)	(into)	(out of)

ZD = zero-dimensioned　OD = one-dimensioned　TWD = two-dimensioned　THD = three-dimensioned

图 10　英语介词的位移

　　本研究主要考察中国英语学习者在习得介词多义性的过程中，象似性三大原则的认知发展和空间象似性在语义域中的认知发展。本研究对低、中、高三个层次的 163 名中国英语学习者(包括武汉市洪山中学的 46 名高一学生，武汉大学法学专业和化学专业的 78 名二年级学生，以及武汉大学外语学院英语专业 39 名一年级研究生)进行了介词多义性的象似性认知调查。实验采用句子正误判断、图片描述、完形填空、多项选择、英汉互译和翻译选择六种研究工具。测试结果用 SPSS 的 ANOVA 和 Scheffe Multiple Comparison 等统计方法检验，从介词的象似性原则和语义域两个方面进行分析，深层次探讨语境对介词多义性的象似性原则以及基于空间象似性延伸的介词语义域的认知习得影响。

　　研究结果表明，中国英语学习者在介词多义性的习得过程中，对象似性原则的认知随着英语水平的提高呈不均衡上扬趋势：从初级阶段向中级阶段的认知发展强势增长，从中级阶段向高级阶段的认知发展明显减弱，对数量象似性原则的认知甚至呈停滞状态。中国英语学习者在习得介词语义域延伸的过程中，空间象似性认知发展随着学习者英语水平的提高呈不均衡上扬趋势：从初级阶段向中级阶段的认知发展强势增长，从中级阶段向高级阶段的认知发展明显减弱，其中介词数量语义域的认知发展呈停滞状态。

　　第七章研究中国英语学习者 wh-移位的发展阶段。移位是转换生成语法的理论之一，主要分为论元移位和非论元移位。作为非论元移位的 wh-移位一直是语言学习者难以逾越的一道障碍。在句法学层面，wh-词或短语在移位时受到论旨理论、界限理论和移位岛等条件的限制。功能学派认为 wh-移位时受其功能差异的影响，属于功能提前的移位；认知语法学家着重解读学习者 wh-移位习得的复杂认知过程；应用语言学家从中介语层面进行实证研究，认为二语习得者在进行 wh-移位时受母语影响，并提出语法现象的习得顺序和发展阶段。本章研究以上述理论为基础，考察母语为 wh-词位于句中的中国英语学习者 wh-移位过程的习得顺序和发展阶段。

　　本研究的受试者为武汉大学建筑工程学院的 31 名学生。实验采用单项选择、连词成句和汉译英三种研究工具。测试结果用 SPSS 进行统计检验，将 wh-移位习得的发展阶段和 wh-移位的句法特征结合起来对 wh-移位习得程度进行分析。研究结果表明：根据 Mackey(1999) 的理论，中国英语学习者在大学阶段对 wh-移位的整个阶段已经基本掌握，但在实际操作中依然会出现很多句法错误。每一阶段 wh-移位的习得并不以完全掌握前一个或几个阶段为前提。除语法规则外，动因、负迁移以及低效输入均对 wh-词置位规则习得产生影响。尽管语言习得发展阶段规划了基本的习得过程，但学习者的个人差异仍然对习得结果产生显著影响，母语并不具有决定性的影响。

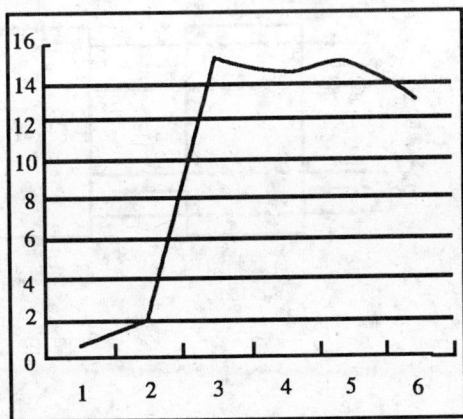

图 11　中国英语学习者 wh-移位总体发展趋势

中国英语学习者对于 wh-移位规则中的语法特例掌握依然十分欠缺，难以准确把握规则中区别于一般性的特殊用法。图 11 显示了中国英语学习者 wh-移位总体发展趋势。

　　第八章研究语言标记性对形态和句法习得的影响。语言标记项习得是语言学习者语言能力的重要表现。语言学界对语言标记性的研究主要有两大倾向：一、在普遍语法理论框架下研究语言标记性对语言学习者习得语言项目顺序的影响;二、在语言类型学理论框架下研究语言标记性对语言迁移和学习难度的影响。乔姆斯基(1986)的语言标记理论围绕核心和边缘概念展开,核心法则可以通过使用语言结构普遍抽象原理获取,无标记性;边缘法则不受普遍原则的支配,是特殊的语言,反映了语言的历史起源,具有标记性。埃克曼(1986)的语言标记理论将类型标记概念并入鉴别两种语言之间的语音体系难度的中间语框架,提出标记差异假设。凯勒曼(1987)通过研究语言标记性与语言迁移之间的关系,提出"心理距离"概念,即学习者是否实现迁移,部分取决于他们认为这种形式在另一种语言中被接收的可能性。目前对语言标记性的研究集中在两个方面:(1) 在自然环境下,研究二语习得者如何习得语言中的标记项,以及语言标记性对语言习得者习得各语言项顺序的影响;(2) 在课堂教学环境下,研究语言标记性对语言学习者造成的语言迁移和习得障碍。

对中国英语学习者形态和句法习得的考察基于语言类型学标记理论。研究采用翻译、写作和完形填空三种测试工具,收集了初级、中级和高级三组共90名不同水平的中国英语学习者使用一般过去时动词曲折变化和疑问句词序的数据,统计了有标记项和无标记项在不同水平和不同任务中的错误类型、错误数量和各类错误所占比例。实证研究数据分析显示了语言标记性对第二语言习得的显著影响、语言水平和标记项/无标记项迁移的相互关系:在课堂教学环境下,语言标记性仍然是造成学习困难和语言迁移的重要影响因素,特别是当目的语为有标记项,而母语为无标记项时影响更为显著;标记程度与学习难度成正相关,即目的语标记程度越高,学习者的学习困难越大;低水平学习者在习得过程中对有标记项和无标记项的迁移呈显著分布状态,但随着英语水平的提高,这种迁移倾向逐渐减弱。

本研究论证了标记性差异度假说的普遍意义,部分验证了语言水平对语言迁移的相关影响,提出对附有标记项目的语的教学可以采用选择性注意假说模型,提高学习者对目的语形式和内容统一的注意力,从而为语言标记项习得打开新思路。

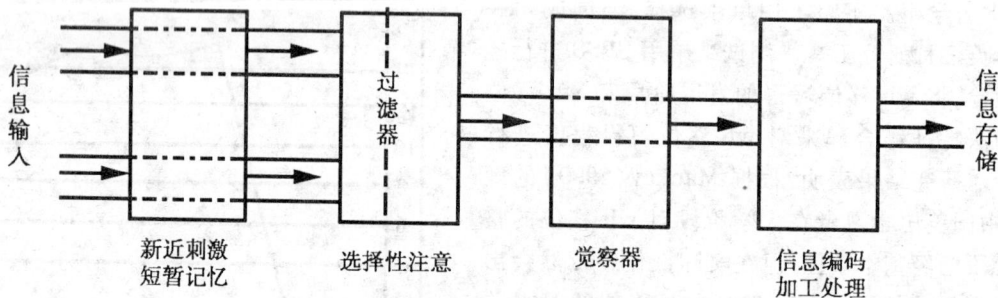

图 12　选择性注意假说模型

第三部分共两章,主要研究隐喻和转喻习得过程中的认知理据。

第九章研究英语量词的隐喻习得。量词在人们日常口语表达和书面表达中起着重要的作用。量词隐喻是中国英语学习者量词习得的主要障碍,对量词隐喻内部工作机制的研究能有效促进量词及量词隐喻的习得。认知语言关于隐喻内部工作机制的研究存在两个不同的方向:概念隐喻理论认为,从规约隐喻中抽象而来的概念隐喻反映人们对世界的认识;概念整合理论通过概念空间形式阐释新奇隐喻的理解和产出,提出相应的概念模式反映隐喻的合成过程。

本章从语言习得顺序的角度对量词隐喻习得进行了两个实验。实验一根据概念隐喻理论和概念合成理论,对量词隐喻进行定性分析,探索隐喻内部工作机制的合成模式。实验二以武汉大学和中国地质大学英语专业在读研究生为研究对象,采用词义选择、选词填空、句子翻译和完形填空四种研究工具,首先考查不同类型量词隐喻的正确使用率,其次描述各类量词隐喻的习得顺序,最后排列隐喻合成模式在量词隐喻中的顺序,定量分析研究各合成模式在中国英语学习者量词隐喻习得中的顺序。

　　实验结果表明,量词隐喻存在四种合成模式:最简合成模式、潜概念合成模式、规则两步合成模式和不规则两步合成模式。四种合成模式在中国英语学习者量词隐喻习得过程中存在下列顺序:(1)最简合成模式;(2)潜概念合成模式;(3)规则两步合成模式;(4)不规则两步合成模式。实验结果还显示,在语篇环境下学习者对量词隐喻的理解最充分。本研究建立了中国学生英语量词隐喻的习得模式和习得顺序,提出量词隐喻习得的语境概念,为中国英语教育者和学习者更为有效地习得量词和量词隐喻提供了行之有效的方法和途径。

图 13　最简合成模式

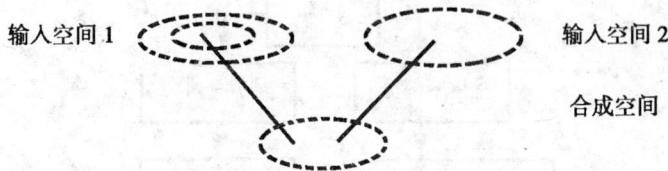

图 14　潜概念合成模式

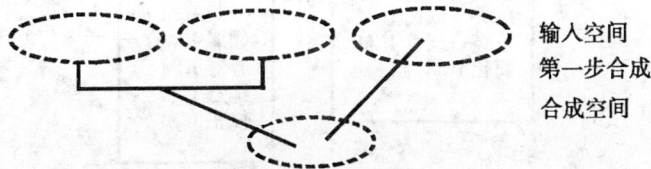

图 15　规则两步合成模式

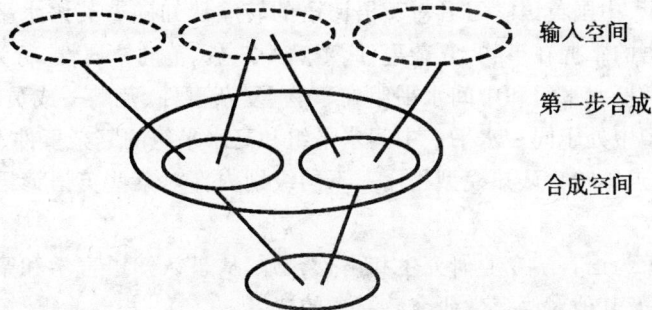

图 16　不规则两步合成模式

第十章从理想化认知模式角度研究英语谚语转喻习得理据。转喻是认知的基本思维方式之一。根据理想化认知机制(Lakoff,1987),转喻分为两类:整体—部分模型和部分—部分模型。前者包括事物、等级、构成、复杂事件、范畴—成员、范畴—属性、简化等认知转喻关系,后者包括行为、感知、使役、产品、控制、领属、容器、地点以及修饰等认知转喻关系。作为语言基本组成部分之一的谚语是各民族在不同历史时期集体智慧的结晶,它具有语言形式简洁、语言结构稳定、地域文化浓郁等特征。因此,英语谚语的习得对中国学习者造成了一定程度上的障碍。

本章在理想化认知模型框架下研究中国英语学习者对以转喻为理据的英语谚语的习得状况。理想化认知模型 ICM(Idealized Cognitive Model)是人们在认识事物、理解世界的过程中对某领域中经验和知识所形成的抽象的、统一的、理想化的组织和表征结构(Lakoff,1987)。意象图示 IS(Image Schema)构成认知模型 CM(Cognitive Model),多个 CM 构成 ICM,它们是形成原型、进行范畴化和概念化的基础。本实验的受试者共 97 人,来自武汉大学(35 名非英语专业一年级学生,31 名非英语专业硕士研究生和 31 名英语专业硕士研究生)。实验材料包括根据转喻理据设计的英语谚语试卷。实验采用英译汉、汉译英和选词填空三种研究工具。实验结果用 SPSS 的 ANOVA 和 Scheffe Multiple Comparison 等统计方法检验,测量不同组别的受试者对各类英语谚语转喻的认知差异。

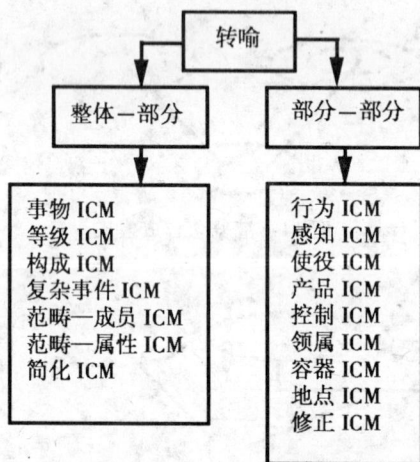

图 17　理想化认知模型中的转喻认知机制

实验结果显示,中国英语学习者对英语谚语的转喻认知随着英语水平的提高而发展。高水平组对英语谚语的掌握在事物、复杂事件、范畴—成员、范畴—属性、行为以及地点等领域明显优于低水平组。低水平组和中间水平组在事物、复杂事件、范畴—成员、范畴—属性以及地点等转喻认知模型中处于同一水平。中间水平组和高水平组的复杂事件、范畴—成员、范畴—属性、行为以及地点等转喻认知模型相同。不同级别内部对某些英语谚语转喻的认知存在显著性差异。

本书读者对象为语言学专业研究生和高校教师,从事认知语言学和第二语言习得研究的专业研究人员,以及其他对语言学研究感兴趣的读者。

Contents

Part One

Language Skills

Chapter 1

The Effects of Topic Familiarity and English Proficiency on Listening Comprehension

Listening comprehension is a complex cognitive process during which listeners have to use different elements of their knowledge of language such as phonetics, vocabulary and grammar to do surface processing. They also have to take advantage of their social and cultural background knowledge to do deep-level processing semantic analysis, such as association and inference. In the studies of SLA, listening has aroused great concern among researchers and language teachers due to its important function in absorption of language input. A great number of studies have confirmed the effect of listening comprehension on second language acquisition and research in this area abounds both at home and abroad, yet most of those research focuses on the study of listening procedures and on the various macro and micro listening skills by which a better performance on listening comprehension could be achieved. The present study attempts to investigate the effects of topic familiarity and the proficiency level on the Chinese non-English majors' listening comprehension, and attempts to reveal their cognitive processing in the field.

The study took as its subjects from the Hydraulic Engineering Department and freshmen from political science department of Wuhan University. The subjects were required to take two tests: one test adopted the familiar passage "Nian" as the listening comprehension test passage and the other adopted "Japanese Tea Ceremony—Cha-Nu-Yu" as the unfamiliar passage. The testing instrument is the recall protocol with three supplementary questions for each passage which allow gaps in comprehension to surface and the results are used for qualitative analysis. The data collected underwent an independent sample test, a paired sample test and an ANOVA test. Discussions and explanations are then carried out from schemata and relevance theory perspectives to illustrate the effect of topic familiarity and the proficiency level on the listening comprehension of learners.

Statistical results indicate that topic familiarity exerts a significant effect on the subjects' listening comprehension. Familiar topics enhance the learners' listening comprehension; learners at both high and intermediate levels did much better on the familiar topic than on the unfamiliar topic. Language proficiency levels have a great influence on learners' listening comprehension; high-proficiency subjects outperformed intermediate proficiency subjects on both familiar and unfamiliar topics. High proficiency subjects are better than intermediate level subjects in activating the relevant schema in their mind to enhance the comprehension of listening materials. The interactive effects of both topic familiarity and the proficiency level are not significant. As regard to the processing model, learners at both proficiency levels tend to use "top-down" processing when the listening passage is familiar to them and "bottom-up" when they are dealing with an unfamiliar topic.

1.1 Information processing and components of listening comprehension

Information processing is the term used to describe "the activities of the mind in extracting, processing, storing and retrieving the meaning of verbal and nonverbal communication" (Rivers 1981). Within schemata theory, the process of information processing is oriented by the principle that all data must be accounted for (Adam& Collins, 1979). Stated differently, every input event or datum must be mapped against certain schema, and all aspects of that schema must be compatible with the incoming information (Huang, 1998). There exist two basic models of information processing, which shed light on the schemata operation in the process of listening comprehension. They are the "bottom-up" and "top-down" processing (Chaudron & Richards, 1986).

1.1.1 Bottom-up processing

As far as listening comprehension is concerned, the bottom-up processing refers to the form of processing in which listeners attempt to derive meaning from novel textual information by analyzing individual word meanings or grammatical characteristics of the text (O'Malley & Chamot, 1990: 421). It posits that human comprehension is driven by the listener's need or desire to process "input data" accurately.

This processing model is used to explain how information, initially in the form of phonological signals, is transformed in the listener's memory as it undergoes storage and retrieval conversions. A central tenet of this model is that listening is a sequential process initiated by incoming data:

> *First, Listener takes in raw speech and retains a phonological representation of it in working memory. Then, Listener immediately tries to organize phonological representation, identifying its content and function. As listener identifies each constituent, listener uses it to construct underlying propositions, building continually into a hierarchical representation of propositions. Once listener has identified the propositions for a constituent, listener retains them in working memory and at some point purges memory of the phonological representation.*

(Clark& Clark, 1977: 49)

The listener uses the incoming data as a source of information about the meaning of a message. The process of comprehension begins with the message received, which is analyzed at successive levels of organization—sounds, words, clauses, and sentences—

until the intended meaning is arrived at. Comprehension is thus viewed as a process of decoding. The listeners' lexical and grammatical competence in a language provides the basis for bottom-up processing. A person's lexical competence serves as a mental dictionary to which incoming words are referred for meaning assignment.

The bottom-up processing has been the dominant theory in research and teaching for a long time. However, it has been repeatedly questioned in recent years on the basis of insights from psychological research. For example, research into human memory has shown that the serial decoding from sound to meaning should take a long time. Thus, it would slow comprehension down and be quite difficult for meaning to be retained.

1.1.2   Top-down processing

The top-down processing in listening comprehension, on the other hand, refers to the special form of mental processing in which individuals attempt to comprehend textual information by making use of schemata based on real-world knowledge. This model tends to be "top-down" in that comprehension is said to be goal-driven: listeners pay attention only to information which seems to them relevant to their purposes or needs. The newly activated schema, no matter if right or wrong, serves as a basis for the listeners to infer meaning and make predictions using personal knowledge, experiences, and strategies.

In the top-down processing process, the listeners tend to employ the knowledge relevant to the listening material to comprehend the text and the knowledge acts like an outline which guides the listeners in organizing the text during the process of listening. This is usually done unconsciously. When the conceptually driven process starts, listeners hypothesize about the content of the text, make interpretations and judgments based upon what they know, assess what more they need to know and then selectively sample the text to confirm or disconfirm the hypothesis, verify and revise their predictions. Information is often added, subtracted, ignored, or transformed depending on different schema possessed by different people. The schema operates in a top-down manner to facilitate comprehension or interpretation of the world. It can be used to explain how language users find relevance in situations and texts through activation of expectations and use of selective attention. The central tenet of schemata and relevance approaches in listening comprehension will be further elaborated upon later.

1.1.3   Interactional processing

Deficiencies of both the above-mentioned models in listening would naturally result in a third model: the "interactive-compensatory" model, in which both bottom-up and top-down processes operate simultaneously or alternately, with information from each processing feeding into the other and influencing the course of one another.

Many researches have proved that accurate and efficient listening comprehension is neither a purely bottom-up nor top-down process. A bottom-up processing is evoked by the incoming linguistic data; the features of the data enter the system through the best fitting bottom-level schemata (Adam & Collin, 1979; Carrel & Eisterhold, 1983). Schemata are hierarchically organized, from specific at the bottom, to most general at the top. As these bottom-level schemata converge in higher levels, more general schemata will be activated. An interactive model recognizes the interaction of bottom-up and top-down processes simultaneously throughout the listening practice. Top-down listening processes, which are sometimes referred to as macro processing, involve activation of schematic knowledge and contextual knowledge. The bottom-up listening process involves the knowledge of a language system that allows the listener to segment and interpret the acoustic signals as sounds that form words, words that form phrases or clauses with intonation, and phrases or clauses that form cohesive and coherent texts such that all levels of language analysis come into play. Celce-Murcia (1999) combines the two models together as an interactive model of listening comprehension:

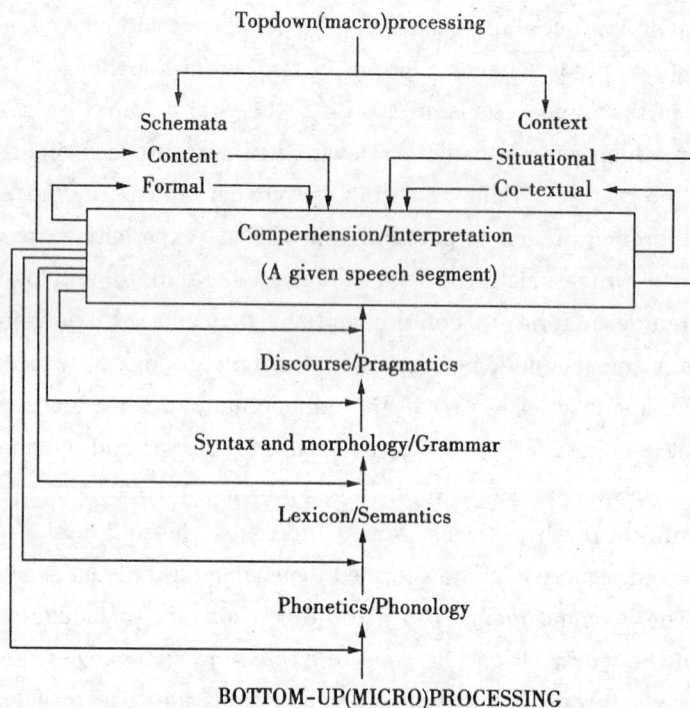

Figure 1.1　The interactive model of listening comprehension (Celce-Murcia, 1999)

Two types of knowledge are activated in the two models of processing: linguistic and non-linguistic knowledge. It is generally postulated that while linguistic knowledge is activated in the bottom-up manner of processing, constraining the accessing of general knowledge, non-linguistic knowledge is used in a top-down manner, facilitating the interpretation of the incoming input.

1.1.4　Components of listening comprehension

Listening to spoken language has been acknowledged in second language acquisition theory to consist of active and complex processes that determine the content and level of what is comprehended (Bynes 1984; Richards 1983). The processes use utterances as the basis for constructing meaning-based propositional representations that are identified initially in short-term memory and stored in long-term memory. Anderson (1983, 1995) differentiates comprehension into three interrelated and recursive processes necessary for compre-hending the aural text—perceptual processing, parsing, and utilization.

In perceptual processing, attention is focused on the oral text and the sounds are retained in echoic memory (O'Malley, Chamot & Küpper, 1989). The echoic memory is distinctive for its limited capacity, which prevents specific word sequences from being retained longer than a few seconds, so the new information which the listener attends to replaces the former information almost immediately. The initial analysis of the language code may begin and the encoding process may convert some of the text into meaningful representation (Anderson, 1995). During this stage, the factors which focus attention on oral text to the exclusion of other competing stimuli also selectively focus on certain key words or phrases that are important in the context. Furthermore, the above-mentioned factors also concentrate on pauses and acoustic emphases which may provide clues to the segmentation and to meaning, and at the same time, the same factors also attend to contextual elements that may coincide with or support the interpretation of meaning such as the listener's goals, expectations about the speaker's intent, and types of speech interaction involved.

In the second listening comprehension process—parsing, words and phrases are used to construct meaningful mental representations (O'Malley, Chamot & Küpper 1989). During this phase, listeners use words and phrases to construct a meaningful unit that can be stored in short-term memory. In other words listeners segment the information into smaller units. This representation is an abstraction of the original word sequence, but can be used to recreate the original sequences or at least their intended meaning. The unit or segment of information processed is called a "chunk". The size of the chunk that listeners retain depends on several factors: including the learner's knowledge of language, general knowledge of the topic and how the information is represented (Richards, 1983).

The third process, utilization, consists of relating a mental representation of the text meaning to existing knowledge (O'Malley, Chamot & Küpper, 1989). Existing knowledge is stored in long-term memory in the form of schemata, scripts or interrelated concepts. During the phase, knowledge in the long-term memory is activated to some degree to relate the new information in the short-term memory. As Faerch and Kasper (1986: 264) note, "Comprehension takes place when input and knowledge are matched against each other."

Listeners make use of two kinds of information to identify the meaning of propositions: real world knowledge and linguistic knowledge (Richards, 1983). Real world knowledge is stored either in propositions or schemata. Listeners may augment existing propositions or schemata with new information instead of being required to build entirely new knowledge structures. The listener elaborates on the new information by using what is known or in some cases by connecting interrelated portions of the new text. "The more additional processing one does that results in related, or redundant proportions, the better will be memory for the material processed. " (Reder, 1980: 7) In some cases existing knowledge is stored in terms of scripts, which are special schemata consisting of situation-specific knowledge about the goals, participants, and procedures in real-life situations, and in story grammars, which are special schemata representing the discourse organization of fables, stories, narratives, and so on. The advantages of these schemata are that they enable the listener to anticipate what will occur next, to predict conclusions, and to infer meaning where a portion of the text was incompletely understood.

1.2 Schema theory and its listening comprehension model

Schema theory is basically a theory about how knowledge is represented in a comprehender's mind and about how that presentation facilitates the use of knowledge in particular ways (Rumelhart, 1983).

The basic premise of schema-based learning theory is that an individual comprehends material by using prior knowledge to produce an anticipated meaning (Rumelhart, 1983). Thus, comprehension depends on an interaction between the structure and content of the material and on what the individual's previously acquired repertoire of background experience is. It follows that schemata, as "organized background knowledge" (Brown and Yule, 1983), can be considered as an important source in comprehension. They "lead listeners to expect or predict aspects in the interpretation of discourse" (Brown and Yule, 1983, 248).

1.2.1 Schema theory

Anderson and Lynch (1988: 13) refer to schematic knowledge as one of the "information sources in comprehension" and suggest that it is the lack of such information that impedes comprehension. Listeners probe long-term memory to connect what they hear with what they already know. Prior knowledge stored in long-term memory appears undoubtedly to be very important in language comprehension.

Prior knowledge can exert its influence on the "retrieval" of a message in at least three ways. First, the propositions of a message can be integrated with the listeners' knowledge. Second, knowledge permits the listeners to select the correct sense of a word. Third, knowledge provides the listeners with expectations about what the message might state. These expectations might facilitate understanding. Important as the prior knowledge is, the question of how prior knowledge is structured should be discussed with the help of schema theory.

There have been several attempts to provide conventional or stereotypical representations of "prior knowledge" as a basis for the interpretation of discourse. These representations, found in psychological and computational approaches to discourse understanding, are mainly used to account for the type of predictable information that a speaker can assume his listener has available whenever a particular situation is described. As knowledge of a particular situation is treated as being stored in memory as a single easily accessible unit, rather than as a scattered collection of individual facts which have to be assembled from different parts of the memory each time the situation is mentioned, an important direction of the research in this area has consequently been towards finding the best storage concept for handling pre-existing conventional knowledge and how it relates to discourse processing.

Minsky (1975) proposes that our knowledge is stored in memory in the form of data structures, which he called "frames", and which represent stereotyped situations. The basic structure of a frame contains labeled slots which can be filled with the expressions and fillers. Formulated in this way, a frame is characteristically a fixed representation of knowledge about the world, or a process of fitting what one is told into the framework established by what one already knows. By analogy, the notion of a "script" was developed, which is "specialized to deal with event sequences" (Schank & Abelson, 1977). Whereas a frame is generally treated as an essentially stable set of facts about the world, a script is more programmatic in that it incorporates a "standard sequence of events that describes a situation" (Brown & Yule, 1983: 238-241).

Sanford & Garrod (1981: 110) choose the term "scenario" to describe the extended domain of reference which is used in interpreting texts, since one can think of knowledge of settings and situations as constituting the interpretative scenario behind a text. For example, a text concerning going to a restaurant automatically brings a "waiter" slot into the representation. The success of scenario-based comprehension is dependent on the text-producer's effectiveness in activating appropriate scenarios (1981: 129). Although Sanford & Garrod prefer the term "scenario", they indicate that their notion of text-processing involving prior knowledge representations has much in common with other studies in which the term "schemata' is more generally used.

Schemata are said to be "higher-level complex knowledge structures" (van Dijk, 1981: 141), which function as "ideational scaffolding" in the organization and interpretation of experience. The concept believes that our memory for discourse is not based on straight reproduction, instead it is constructive. This constructive process uses information from the encountered discourse, together with knowledge from past experience relating to the discourse at hand, to build a mental representation. Therefore, the past experience cannot be an accumulation of successive individuated events and experiences: rather it must be organized and made manageable. What gives structure to that organized mass is the schema.

Representing stereotypes of concepts, schema is believed to have a general assumption underlying it: "Human behavior is determined by a far greater knowledge of environment than afforded by the current pattern of visual or audio stimulation. It takes a great deal of information processing using much real world knowledge for humans to comprehend the images, which the eye detects or the sounds that the ear receives. Our actions are addressed not only to interacting with the environment in some instrumental way, but also to updating our "internal model of the world." In a new situation we can recognize familiar things in new relationships and use our knowledge of those things and our perception of the relationships to guide our behavior in that situation. It thus seems reasonable to posit that the internal model of the world must be built of units, in a more technical term, schemas. What is more, schemas may be combined to form new schemas (Arbib et. al. , 1987: 9).

As an abstract structure of knowledge stored in semantic memory, schema is structured in the sense that it indicates relations among constituent concepts, and is abstract in the sense that one schema has the potential to cover a number of texts that differ in particulars. In linguistic study, learners are considered to be active processors of linguistic input; therefore it is the listener who constructs schemata from past experience relating to the discourse to build a mental representation.

One thing that has to be noted is that every listener does not come to a given text with the same background knowledge or schemata. Personal histories and interests contribute to the creation of higher-level schemata which cause them to see messages in certain ways. Schema theory highlights the fact that more than one interpretation of a text is possible. In short, the schema that will be brought to bear on a text depends on the listener's age, sex, race, religion, nationality, occupation, personal histories and so on (Wilson&Anderson, 1984: 34).

The advantage of activating listener's existing schemata is obvious in foreign language teaching. Foreign language learners usually have imperfect control of linguistic codes so they find it difficult to identify key inputs and often just give up when the velocity of incoming speech is rapid. Being able to instantiate an appropriate schema provides a framework of reference into which listeners can fit the bits and pieces that they have comprehended (Long, 1989: 33). Specific functions schemata may serve were summarized by Wilson and Anderson (1984: 35-36):

(1) A schema provides ideational scaffolding. A schema embodies structural organization and incoming text information can fit into places called slots within the schema.

(2) A schema directs allocation of attention. Skilled listeners may use their schemata to judge how familiar information is and then pay attention to what is more important or less familiar.

(3) A schema enables inferential elaboration. The listener's schema provides the basis for making inferences that go beyond the literally stated information to ensure comprehension.

(4) A schema allows orderly searches of memory. As a structured system, the schema can guide the listener to the kind of information that need to be recalled.

(5) A schema facilitates editing and summarizing. A schema contains criteria for the relative importance of different information which a listener can draw on in order to compose summaries that include significant propositions and omit trivial ones.

(6) A schema permits inferential reconstruction. The listener's schema helps to generate hypotheses about the missing information when there are gaps in understanding.

Although there is a general consensus, application of schema theory to L2 listening remains largely unexplored, just as Pearson and Fielding (1982: 24) have noted: " … little has been written about listening from this more active cognitive perspective, even though much of the cognitive research supporting this view has been done using listening as the mode through which information has been transmitted to subjects. " It seems that schema-theoretic models of comprehension can apply even more to the listening process than to reading.

1.2.2   Listening comprehension model on schema theory

The listening comprehension model from schema-theoretic perspective is closely connected with the information-processing model. According to Carrell & Eisterhold (1983:554), bottom-up processing is started by the concrete information coming into the cognitive comprehension system. The concrete information activates the schema of the lowest level, the instantiation of which leads to the comprehension. Thus, bottom-up processing, also called data-driven processing, works upwards from input to the sense receptors to higher perceptual analysis. On the other hand, in top-down processing the listeners begin from the higher level of schemata (knowledge system of past experience) with which they predict, infer, select, intake or assimilate the sensory input to form abstract mental representation. As far as listening comprehension is concerned, the bottom-up processing is form-oriented with listeners employing lexical, syntactic and grammatical knowledge, while the top-down processing is the process in which listeners predict and extract the meaning using their world and contextual knowledge as well as their personal interactive information. The schemata theory listening comprehension model developed from the schemata theory in cognitive science is basically "top-down":

> *First, comprehending language requires processing structures larger than sentences; then comprehending an extended text consists of using knowledge about the world and schemata about what a normal, plausible text should include; third, understanding involves filling in gaps, introducing consistencies, and eliminating implausible interpretations, with a steady use of inference to assemble the different elements in the story into a congruent structure.*
>
> (Flores d'Arcais and Schreuder, 1983 in Rost, M. 1990: 18)

According to the model, familiar knowledge structures are triggered by the recognition of a sequence of related lexical items and propositions that cannot be interpreted clearly then assume a default value in the particular schema that is activated. "Meaning occurs as a result of the interaction between the listener's prior knowledge about the world and the speech text, and the internal schemata in listeners' minds are the essence to decide whether the listening comprehension will succeed or fail. " (Chiang & Dunkel 1992:351)

1.3   Relevance theory and its listening comprehension model

The relevance theory holds that every utterance in natural language has a wild array of interpretations. The correct understanding of the intended meaning could be realized by the search for relevance through context, and inference from the relevance between information and context. Information processing is an inferential process which starts from a set of premises and results in a set of conclusions which follow logically from, or are at least warranted by, the premises, in other words, "any conceptually represented information available to the listener can be used as a premise in this inferential process" (Sperber & Wilson. 2001, 65), and all this happens in the cognitive environment. The very reason that communication among people could go smoothly is rooted in people's inference and judgment on the basis of their behaviors and utterance.

Sperber and Wilson point out that the process of reaching valid comprehension is generally broken down into two distinct stages: hypothesis formation and hypothesis confirmation. The former is a matter of creative imagination; the latter, on the other hand, can be seen as a purely logical process governed by inferential rules (2001:68). This assumption well illustrates the view that listening is a top-down process in the sense that the various types of knowledge involved in understanding language are not applied in any fixed order-they can be used in the order of relevance.

1.3.1　Relevance theory

Relevance theory is a pragmatic theory about how communication occurs in social contexts. The theory holds that understanding a text involves an "encoding-decoding" process of mutual acknowledgement as well as "cognition-inference" process of mutual manifestation between the interlocutors. In their book *Relevance: Communication and Cognition* (2001: 260), Sperber and Wilson made two fundamental claims, the "principle of cognition", and the "principle of communication", that is, human cognition tends to be geared to the maximization of relevance and every act of ostensive communication communicates a presumption of its own optimal relevance.

The human brain is a complicated mechanism for information storage and processing. It requires maximum efficiency from the minimum cognitive effort. Starting from the old information on hand, it handles the incomplete incoming information from which it concludes new information and realizes the contextual effect. The process of perceiving the world for human beings follows almost the same route, i. e. , in cognitive processes people try to withdraw the maximum cognitive effect from the minimum exertion. To achieve the goal, people have to focus on the most "relevant" information. Therefore, the "principle of cognition" is the core of the relevance theory.

According to Sperber and Wilson, an act of "ostension" from the perspective of speakers provides two layers of information. First, there is the information which has been pointed out or "locution" layer of information; then there is the information that the first layer of information has been pointed out, or roughly termed as the "illocution" layer of information. Any "ostension" of the speaker would activate the corresponding cognitive context, resulting in the assumption of the optimal relevance automatically. Understanding the ostensive act is an inferential process of finding a relevant link between the two layers of information.

Yet, any utterance in natural language can be interpreted in different ways: it is not necessarily that people can fully understand the various kinds of implied meanings under any circumstance, rather they would interpret the utterance according to their own cognitive mode and standard, excluding all the other possible interpretations. As there is no procedure for ensuring mutually acceptable and unambiguous understanding between interlocutors, communication is the process in which a listener attempts to find the relevant link via his own context; to conduct inference to manifest the speaker's possible communicative intention, and to achieve contextual effect. The more relevant the context and the utterance are, the easier the inference and the understanding would be. In contrast, if the relationship between the context and the utterance is distant, inference and understanding will be more difficult.

Sperber and Wilson fully revised the original presumption of optimal relevance, indicating that the ostensive stimulus is relevant enough for it to be worth the addressee's effort to process it, and that the ostensive stimulus is the most relevant one compatible with the communicator's abilities and preferences (2001: 270). This means that a rational communicator must intend the stimulus s/he uses to appear relevant enough to the addressee to attract his attention and make him willing to spend the effort needed for comprehension, and a rational addressee will not expect more relevance than the communicator is willing and able to achieve. Therefore, relevance can be taken as a natural selection as it reflects the natural reflexive tendency of human verbal communication and comprehension. Relevance has its automatic, unconscious side as well as conscious side when the addressee attends to the ostensive stimulus and succeeds in understanding it. The characteristic of relevance would endow the listening comprehension with both conscious and unconscious facets (Huang, 1998:21).

1.3.2   Listening comprehension model of relevance theory

According to the principles of relevance theory, listeners work out meaning through finding the optimal relevance between the discourse heard and contextual assumptions. Rost was one of the first linguists who put forward the listening comprehension model based on the relevance theory. In his *Listening in Language Learning* (1990: 33), Rost concludes that "understanding is an inferential process of finding a relevant link between the information rather than straightforward matching of sound to meaning". The model can be used to explain how language users find relevance in situations and texts through the activation of expectations and use of selective attention. Rost summarizes the key tenet of the model as follows, the stages of which are overlapping and interdependent:

(1) Listener activates probable knowledge base needed to interpret incoming utterances.

(2) Listener attends to utterances selectively, interpreting the propositional meaning of utterances through phonological-syntactic-lexical analysis.

(3) Listener interprets a possible pragmatic meaning for utterances, that is, a plausible intention for the speaker in making the utterances in a particular context.

(4) Listener orders interpreted propositions into a hierarchical representation to be retained in long-term memory (Rost, 1990: 95).

This placement of responsibility for interpretation on the hearer is a direct departure from the information-processing view of understanding. The model also suggests that understanding involves both decoding processes and inferential processes based on the speaker's actions.

1.4   Research methodology of listening comprehension

Senior subjects of this study were randomly chosen from two classes of hydraulic engineering majors, their proficiency level was implied by their course level, but considering the situation of language learning for non-English majors, two other criterion were imposed to differentiate advanced from intermediate level English users. Their language proficiency was judged by whether they passed CET-6 and by what grades they were in. The freshmen were randomly chosen from two classes of political science majors. They were categorized as subjects with intermediate proficiency level. Altogether there were 126 subjects who took part in the study, among which there were 67 freshmen and 59 senior learners. The after-test questionnaire indicated that there were some learners who had prior knowledge of the unfamiliar topic, so they were excluded from the statistics. Senior subjects who hadn't passed CET-6 were excluded from the data analysis. Freshmen who had passed CET-4 or PETS-4/5 were excluded from the analysis. 59 learners met all our criteria and were selected as our subjects for statistical analysis. Among these, 31 belonged to the intermediate proficiency and 27 belonged to the advanced proficiency level.

1.4.1   Research materials and tools

To meet the purpose of this study, two texts are deliberately revised and recorded by a British teacher with neutral accent. In order to study the effects of topic familiarity, two distinct topics were chosen. One was "Nian" and the other was "Japanese Tea Ceremony". It was assumed that Chinese students are familiar with the first text and know very little about the second one. Different textual factors which are believed to influence listening comprehension, such as syntax, speech rate, pauses, hesitation were controlled in the process of text revision and recording. The detailed information about the texts is as follows:

Table 1.1   **Details of two listening passages**

Factors/ Topics	Nian	Japanese Tea Ceremony
Length of passage in words	289	309
Recording time	2'37"	2'49"
Speech rate in WPM (Words per minute)	122 wpm	124 wpm
Number of sentences	12	15
Number of short pause	32	38

续表

Factors/ Topics	Nian	Japanese Tea Ceremony
Number of long sentences	5	5
Number of hesitation *	1	2
Text type	narrative	narrative
Quality of the recordings	clear	clear
Unfamiliar vocabulary * * Intermediate level Advanced level	1. 38% 0. 7%	1. 29% 0. 6%

* Long sentence refers to the sentences that are more than 20 words long, $1 \leqslant$ number of pauses $\leqslant 4$, $2 \leqslant$ number of clauses $\leqslant 4$.

* * Unfamiliar vocabulary rate means the proportion of words in the passage failing to appear in the *College English Syllabus for Non-English Major Students in Institutions of Higher Learning*. Intermediate level = College English Band 4; Advanced level = College English Band 6.

The experiment was conducted in a regularly scheduled fifty minute class session. Prior to listening to the experimental passages, the subjects participated in a warming-up exercise that was designed to familiarize them with the speaker's voice and to have them practice writing a recall protocol.

The subjects were informed that they were to listen to two passages, try to understand it, and then recall the passages in English or Chinese. Because it was important for subjects to clearly understand what level of detail and original sentence structure they were expected to reproduce, the instructions were to write as much information as they could remember, retaining as much detail as possible. They were not given information about the content of the experimental passages, other than that they dealt with customs or culture. Each recording was played twice. Students were instructed not to write any information during the first playing of the recording. After the second playing, they wrote what they could remember. After completion of the recall, 4 questions concerning the passages were given, and learners were required to underlie their answers in their recall or to complement their recall with the questions in mind. After completion of the second recall, students were asked to complete a post-listening survey in order to determine their prior familiarity with the topics.

The recall protocol is adopted as the assessment of comprehension. Recall protocol is widely practiced in L2 listening research. It involves having students listen to an orally spoken target language text and write down, in English or their native language, everything that they can remember about the text. It is considered to be the most straightforward assessment of the result of test-testee interaction (Johnston, 1983:29). The recall protocol reveals something about the organization of stored information, about some of the retrieval strategies used by the listener, and reveals the method of reconstruction which the listener employs to encode information in a text. Hayes (1989: 69) describes protocol analysis as

" cognitive psychology's most powerful tool for tracking psychological process ". Berkemeyer (1989:132) points out that the immediate recall protocol demands that the learner comprehend the text well enough to be able to recall it in a coherent and logical manner, and more importantly, it allows misunderstandings and gaps in comprehension to surface, a feature that other methods of evaluation cannot offer.

There are several advantages of using immediate recall protocol. First, generating recall data does not influence a learner's understanding of a text. A free recall provides a pure measure of comprehension uncomplicated by linguistic performance and tester's interference. It also provides qualitative information which is critical for new insights into the comprehension processes of L2 learners, which seems to be more pertinent to the present study.

However, there are no perfect approaches for analyzing the listening process. The disadvantage of immediate recall is that memory effects are too strong. Few people possess a "phonogrammic" memory which permits them to retain in and replay from their short-term memory what they hear from a recording.

Considering this minor inconvenience, the method was modified slightly to make it more suitable for the current purpose. In order to control the memory effects, the time duration of each passage was limited to no more than 3 minutes, and the subjects were allowed to listen to the texts twice, which would certainly reduce the workload on the memory of the subjects. Besides this, it was also stressed in the experiment that the subjects could write their recalls in either Chinese or English, i. e. to use the language that they felt most comfortable with. Last but not least; subjects were given enough time to write their recalls to ensure the completeness of their reports.

Three questions were asked about each of the listening passages in case subjects shied away from writing down what they were not sure of and to further tap the students' processing strategies. The answers to the questions were used in qualitative analysis.

In the actual scoring of recall protocol, propositions were credited from the original passages and each recall was scored based on the percentage of the possible proposition contained in the protocol. Credit was given based on sufficient gist of the meaning of proposition rather than verbatim recall. The proposition defined in each text received one of three scores: 2 points for gist of proposition (i. e. the relation was mentioned along with both argument) and 1 point for fragment of proposition (i. e. the relation was mentioned along with one argument). Subjects got nothing without mentioning the proposition. The criterion to determine "gist" centered on the predicate not being substantially different in meaning from the relation used in the original text, and resulted in a proportional score that represented the match between the semantic content of the text and the listener's recall of that content. The more scores the subjects could obtain, the better the subjects comprehended the passage.

1.4.2 Research questions and hypotheses

The key in this scoring is how to identify what a proposition is. The basic unit of listening comprehension is a proposition, which consists of a relation followed by an ordered list of arguments (Anderson 1985; Kintsche 1974). A proposition deals with what the sentence is about, rather than with the precise words used. It is, therefore, a way of stating relationships between two or more concepts. Thus, there may be many different sentences that could be used to state "Maggie watered the flowers in the backyard", or "The flowers in the backyard are watered by Maggie". A proposition, therefore, is a structure that holds together different parts of the mental lexicon in interaction. In order to understand how to break a sentence into proposition, an example is cited here:

The coach gave a beautiful Cadillac to Jack, who is the winner of the match.

This sentence can be constructed as including the following simpler sentences which closely correspond to the propositions that underlie the meaning of the original sentence.

The coach gave a Cadillac to Jack.

The Cadillac was beautiful.

Jack is the winner of the match.

Therefore, a condition each proposition must satisfy is that it expresses a primitive unit of meaning. A proposition consists of one relation and one or more arguments (Anderson, 1985; Gui, 1991)

Thus, it is necessary to further explore the possible effect of the two factors on the listening comprehension processes of Chinese non-English majors, and the following research questions are raised: Does topic familiarity affect the recall measures of learners' listening comprehension? If so, how? Does language proficiency level affect the recall measures of learners' listening comprehension? If yes, how? Does the effects of topic familiarity vary with learners' proficiency level? In the process of listening comprehension, how do learners use "top-down" and "bottom-up" strategies?

Accordingly, four hypotheses are proposed:

Hypothesis 1: Topic familiarity would have considerable influence on recall measures of listening comprehension.

Hypothesis 2: Higher level of overall language proficiency would positively affect listening comprehension.

Hypothesis 3: There shouldn't be any significant difference in recall measure of listening comprehension on familiar topics between freshman and senior subjects, but a significant difference on unfamiliar topics.

Hypothesis 4: Subjects adopt "bottom-up" processing on unfamiliar topics and "top-down" processing on familiar topics.

1.4.3   The operational definition of variables

From the research questions put forward, two independent variables are defined: topic familiarity and proficiency level. The dependent variable of the present study is recall measure of listening comprehension. The operational definition of these variables is as follows:

Proficiency level: Language proficiency level is defined as the overall English competence of the subjects implied by their course level. For the current study, the subjects are randomly chosen among which the senior students who passed CET-6 are assumed to have high proficiency level and freshmen who haven't taken CET-4 are assumed to have intermediate proficiency level.

Listening comprehension is operationalized as the scores the subjects get after finishing the required task. As far as the present experiment is concerned, it refers to the recall protocols they wrote after listening to the passage.

Topic familiarity in the present study consists of two levels which are determined by previous exposure to the information contained in the passage according to cultural experience and a questionnaire following the listening tasks. It is assumed that the subjects are familiar with "Nian" since the Chinese celebrate it every year and stories about "Nian" are told from childhood. Anyone indicating no prior familiarity was excluded from the data analysis. The novel topic, " Cha-No-Yu—Japanese tea ceremony" was selected because the researcher hypothesized that subjects would have no knowledge of this. As with the familiar topic, if a subject indicated in the post-listening questionnaire that they had prior knowledge, they were excluded from the data analysis.

1.5 Empirical approaches to listening comprehension

The research employs both quantitative and qualitative analysis. The quantitative analysis is to ensure the ability to generalize the results, while the qualitative analysis is needed to show the vividness and richness of the data with a potential to reveal the complexity of the real context—in this case the complex psychological processes happening within the mind of the subjects.

1.5.1 Quantitative statistics and description

After careful scoring of the test papers, the scores of 27 advanced proficiency level students and 31 intermediate proficiency level students are as follows:

Table 1.2   **Level of topic familiarity and language proficiency**

PL \ TF	N	Familiar topic	Unfamiliar topic
Intermediate	31	13.56	8.26
Advanced	27	18.92	12.07

Note: TF = Topic Familiarity PL = Proficiency Level

The results indicate that there are differences between the means under four combinations of proficiency level and topic familiarity ($13.56 < 18.92$, $8.26 < 12.07$, $13.56 > 8.26$, $18.92 > 12.07$). Their scores on familiar topics are much higher than on unfamiliar topics. However, we don't know whether these differences are significant or not, so to further verify the issue the results were subjected to paired-sample T-test and independent

T-testing. The outcomes are as follows:

Table 1.3 　　　　　　　**Inferential statistics—Paired sample**

Pair	t	sig. (2-tailed)
F+I U+I	6. 287	.000
F+A U+A	5. 895	.000

Note: F = Familiar topic　U = Unfamiliar topic　I = Intermediate level　A = Advanced level

　　Table 1.3 shows that the paired T-test value of 6. 287 with 30 degrees of freedom is significant at 0. 05. So at the 95% significance level, learners at intermediate level perform significantly better in doing familiar passages than in doing unfamiliar passages.

　　Similar results are found for advanced level subjects. The paired t-test value of 5. 895 with 27 degree of freedom is significant at 0. 05 level. So at 95% significance level, learners at advanced level perform significantly better in doing familiar passages than in doing unfamiliar passages.

Table 1.4 　　　　　　　**Inferential statistics—Independent sample**

Pair	t	sig. (2-tailed)
F+I, F+A	−4. 556	.000
U+I U+A	−4. 326	.000

Note: F = Familiar topic　U = Unfamiliar topic　I = Intermediate level　A = Advanced level

　　Table 1.4 shows that the t-test value for learners' performance in doing a familiar passage is −4. 556 with 55 degrees of freedom. The probability of 2-tailed t-test significance is 0. 000 <0. 05, so at 95% confidence level, learners at advanced level performed better than intermediate level students.

　　This is also true for the unfamiliar passage. The t-test value for students' performance in unfamiliar passage is—4. 326 with two tailed significance 0. 000 <0. 05. It is concluded that the t-test value −4. 326 is significant at 95% confidence level. That's to say, subjects at advanced level performed better than those at intermediate level in listening to unfamiliar passages.

　　Both Table 1.3 and Table 1.4 demonstrate that whether listening to familiar or unfamiliar topics, high-proficiency students always performed better than intermediate-proficiency students. Is the difference the result of topic familiarity or their proficiency level, or the interactive effect of both? The subjects' score underwent ANOVA test, and the results are as follows.

Table 1.5   **Inferential statistics—Summary of scores**

Source	SS	df	M S	F	Sig.
Corrected model	1688.113(a)	3	562.704	34.197	.000 * *
Intercept	20213.305	1	20213.305	1228.407	.000 * *
PL	608.477	1	608.477	36.978	.000 * *
TF	1070.248	1	1070.248	65.041	.000 * *
PL * TF	17.558	1	17.558	1.067	.304
Error	1842.948	112	16.455		
Total	23527.000	116			
Corrected total	3531.060	115			

* * $p < .01$

Note: PL = Proficiency Level TF = Topic Familiarity

Table 1.5 reveals the main effects of topic familiarity and proficiency level are both significant, but their interactive effect is not significant ($0.304 > 0.005$). According to Hatch & Farhady (1982: 160), whenever we have a strong interaction effect, we can be more confident about the significance of the main effect. So, the conclusion could be drawn that so far as the main effects are concerned the topic familiarity has a significant effect on students' success in listening comprehension.

1.5.2 Qualitative statistics and description

According to Miles and Huberman (1994), quantitative research aims primarily at larger numbers of context-stripped cases when seeking statistical significance. It guarantees the generalization of the research results. The strength of qualitative data is that it is rich and holistic with strong potential for revealing complexity nested in real context. The qualitative statistics followed calculated the performance of subjects under two different topics. Two questions are posed in order to tap into subjects' listening processes.

Performance under the familiar topic

In order to give a clearer picture of subject's performance on familiar topic, their answers are further analyzed under two different question types identified by Shohamy and Inbar (1991). The first one is a local question which is used to tap subjects' ability to locate details and their ability to make reasonable and appropriate elaborations.

According to the schema theory, comprehending a text is an interactive process between the subjects' background knowledge and the text. Efficient comprehension requires the ability to relate the textual material to one's own knowledge. Comprehending words, sentences, and entire texts involves more than just relying on one's linguistic knowledge. As the opening quote from Anderson, et al. points out, " Every act of comprehension involves one's knowledge of the world as well. " (Anderson et al. 1977: 369)

Familiar topic equipped subjects with necessary schema to identify the details and make appropriate elaborations; the subjects are expected to perform better and give more reasonable and appropriate elaborations than unfamiliar topics. The following table is the subjects' performance under familiar topic to answer the question: How was "Nian" described in the passage?

Table 1.6   **Performance of subjects under familiar topic (local question)**

Performance of the subjects	Number of subjects (58)
Making reasonable and appropriate elaborations	43
No elaborations	15
Making distorted elaborations	0

Table1.6 shows that the answers to the familiar topic "Nian" is full of reasonable and appropriate elaborations. There is no sign of distorted elaborations; their recall testifies again that familiar topics aid listening comprehension.

Above is a description of subjects' performance on local questions under familiar topic. How would they perform on global questions? As global questions require subjects to listen to the text and get the gist of the text or draw inferences or make inferential reconstruction. Inference involves in the process of instantiating slots within a selected schema. A listener typically make inference when deciding that a particular item mentioned in the text is intended to fill in a particular slot. Furthermore, a listener may fill a particular slot in a schema by assigning default values in the absence of any specifically substantiating information in the text.

Theoretically speaking, under familiar topic even if the text didn't provide the candidate with direct answer, subjects could infer it out with the schema in their head. Familiar topic would facilitate the understanding of the passage. The following table is the subjects' performance on the global question under familiar topic: Why do Chinese people use fireworks on Spring Festival?

Table 1.7   **Performance under familiar topic (global questions)**

Performance of the subjects	Number of subjects (58)
Making reasonable inferential reconstruction	52
Making unreasonable inferential reconstruction	6

Table1.7 shows that under familiar topic, 52 out of 58 subjects are able to make reasonable interferential reconstruction. There are still 6 subjects who made unreasonable inferential reconstruction. The schema theory could explain those who made reasonable inferential construction, while the relevance theory is referred to explain why subjects made unreasonable inferential reconstructions.

Performance of the subjects under the unfamiliar topic

When deprived of schema, how would subjects perform under unfamiliar topic?

The local question which as discussed above is designed to tap into subjects ability to locate details and make elaborations. Their answers had fewer reasonable elaborations than in the familiar text. Some of the subjects get too far away from the source text, and some seriously distort the original meaning. Here the question put forward is: Where are the guests supposed to wash their hands before going to the tea room?

Table 1.8　　　**Performance under unfamiliar topic（local question）**

Performance of the subjects	Number of subjects（58）
Making reasonable and appropriate elaborations	17
No elaborations	24
Making distorted elaborations	7

Table1.8 shows that 17 subjects made reasonable elaborations, 24 didn't make any elaborations, and there were 7 subjects who made distorted elaborations. It appears that the unfamiliarity with the topic to some degree hinders the listening comprehension of Chinese non-English majors. Their difficulty could be explained by schema theory.

As it is summarized above, unfamiliar topic pose a serious obstacle to subjects ability to make elaborations. Deprived of schema, would subjects to make no inference or inferential reconstruction at all?

According to the relevance theory, inference is a necessary process for the hearer to understand the speaker's ostensive act. Understanding or comprehension is an inferential process of finding the optimal relevant points between the forthcoming information and the old assumptions about the world that existed in the hearer's cognitive environment. The task of the hearer in comprehension is to search the optimal relevant premises from his or her cognitive environment to form a context for inference.

The procedure of transactional listening comprehension is an inferential process in which listener uses his or her encyclopedic, logical and lexical knowledge to process the forthcoming new information. When deprived of the world knowledge, the listener could still figure out the answer by relying on the text. Now look at their performance on the global questions: What is the main purpose of Japanese Cha-No-Yu?

Table 1.9　　　**Performance under unfamiliar topic（global questions）**

Performance of the subjects	Number of subjects（58）
Making reasonable inferential reconstruction	29
Making distorted inferential reconstruction	15
Not mentioned or never mentioned	8
Making no answer	6

The statistics in Table 1. 9 indicates that even though subjects were not familiar with the topic, there were still 29 subjects who made reasonable inferential reconstructions, the rest of the subjects either made distorted inferential reconstructions, gave no answer at all or claimed the passage did not give the answers. According to the schema theory, the unfamiliarity should seriously hinder the listening comprehension. It can explain the phenomenon of subjects making wrong answers, but can't explain why there were still subjects who made the right answers. The relevance theory could help people fill this gap. The following are detailed explanations from two theoretical frameworks of Chinese non-English majors' performance on two listening topics.

1.6   Topic familiarity and its effects on listening comprehension

Both the quantitative and the qualitative statistics demonstrated that topic familiarity exerts great influence on listening comprehension. Here are two explanations, from the schematic and relevance perspective respectively.

1.6.1   Explanation from schematic perspective

Statistical results of Tables 1. 2, 1. 3 and 1. 5 clearly indicate that topic familiarity has a significant effect on EFL listening comprehension. That's the answer to the first research questions "Does topic familiarity have any effect on Chinese EFL learners' listening comprehension? If so, how?" More specifically, being familiar with the topic or theme of a listening text, facilitates the listening comprehension of subjects. The results undoubtedly verify what had been found by Chiang & Dunkel (1992), Schmidt-Rinehart (1994) and Huang Zidong (1998), that is, subjects' background knowledge or familiarity with the topic of the listening text to a great extent facilitate the EFL listening comprehension.

The effect of topic familiarity on EFL listening comprehension for Chinese EFL learners can be explained from the perspective of the schema theory, because the schemata are composed of generic or abstract knowledge used to guide encoding, organization, and retrieval of information. The schemata reflect prototypical properties of experiences encountered by an individual, integrated over many instances. Although the schemata are assumed to reflect an individual's experience, they are also assumed to be shared across individuals. One important characteristic of the schemata is that it is created through experience with people, objects, and events in the world.

The learners are able to activate the proper schemata stored in their minds which are relevant to "Nian". Considering the functions of a schema, providing ideational scaffolding, directing allocation of attention, enabling inferential elaboration, allowing orderly searches of memory, facilitating editing and summarizing and permitting inferential reconstruction, the schema-theoretic models of comprehension apply even more to the listening process than to reading (Huang Zidong, 1998). Though reading and listening both have similar comprehension process, listening requires phonological decoding and interpretation as it is impossible for the listener to control the pace, whereas reading depends on the orthographic interpretation of written symbols that the reader can pause and look around for contextual cues. Actually, schema theory posits that in listening comprehension it is often unnecessary for a listener to distinguish every flowing phoneme in order to create mental representation for every word, or to parse every syntactic structure in the listening discourse. As long as the listener is able to build up a harmonious match between the schemata existing in his mind and the input information, the listening text would make sense to him, and he should find it easier to comprehend the listening text and remember important points mentioned in the listening discourse.

With their schemata, learners can easily activate their sub-schemata. An important aspect of the organization of the schemata is that the simpler schemata can be embedded within the more complex schemata, i. e. the schemata can be hierarchically structured. This means under the general schema of "Nian" they have stored the schemata relevant to "Nian" in their long-term memory including the sub-schemata of "firecrackers", "fireworks", "monster", etc. Therefore, in the listening process those schemata are constantly activated and the listener doesn't have to go to great lengths to get every detail in order to comprehend the whole text. This can be proved by the quantitative and qualitative results presented in tables 4. 1, 4. 5 and 4. 6. Also, not every listener comes to a given text with the same background knowledge or schemata so more than one interpretation of a text is possible. This can explain the fact that even though they are quite familiar with the text, many of them elaborate and extend the idea beyond the text. Take the following examples to illustrate:

A. How was Nian described in the passage?

(1) Zhang (freshman): 嗜血、丑陋的动物。

Blood-thirsty, ugly animal. (Literal Translation)

(2) Lin (freshman): 凶猛,在冬天不好觅食的时候到村里吃人。

Ferocious, when food is scarce in winter it comes to the village to hunt humans.

Wu (senior): 虚构的一种凶猛的动物,长得很丑,好像长得既不像龙也不像……

A mythological figure which is fierce, ugly, it doesn't look like a dragon or … (literal translation)

Here is another example:

B. According to the text, how did the practice of playing fireworks on spring festival originate?

(1) Wang (freshman): 传说中"年"很怕噪声,为了保护自己的人身不受"年"的伤害,人们放鞭炮吓跑"年"。

"Nian" in the legend is scared of noise. People play fireworks in order to protect him/herself from the harm of "Nian". (Literal Translation)

(2) Ji(freshman): 鞭炮声很像炸竹子的声音,传说中人们用炸竹子和放鞭炮的方法驱赶年。

The crack of fireworks resembles the cracks of bamboo. People burned bamboo and played with fireworks to drive away"Nian" in the legend. (Literal Translation)

(3) Liao (freshman): "年"怕火光和炸响。

"Nian" is scared of fire and the sound of crackers. (Literal Translation)

（4）Wen（senior）：一个聪明的老人鼓励人们勇敢一些,合作起来战胜"年",放鞭炮是为了驱赶"年",并让他累得筋疲力尽,最后杀死他。

A wise man in the village encourages people to be brave and to work together to fight off "Nian". They play with fireworks to drive "Nian" away. Wherever it went, there was noise so it would be exhausted, giving people the opportunity to kill it. （Literal Translation.）

These examples demonstrate that even though the listening discourse didn't provide these details, the subjects could reasonably infer them. The explanation would be that the schemata were appropriately activated and the listeners made reasonable elaborations and inferential reconstructions in order to improve comprehension. These reasonable inferences are evidence for the existing of the sub-schemata and default values that have been activated and added by the listeners in the listening process.

According to the statistical results in Table 1.8, the unfamiliar topic "Cha-No-Yu" has a negative effect on the listening comprehension. The same group of learners performed very differently with many distorted responses. This can also be explained by the schema theory. In the process of listening comprehension, Chinese learners generally lack the relevant schemata of "Cha-No-Yu—Japanese tea ceremony", meaning comprehension activities such as summarizing, generalizing, elaboration, meaning reconstruction and inference would be hindered, which in turn obstruct general comprehension. Some examples are illustrated here:

C. Where are the guests supposed to wash their hands before going to the tea-room according to the passage?

Ji（freshman）:桶 water bucket （Literal Translation）

Chen（freshman）:花园的池子里 in the pond in the garden

Duan（senior）:主人准备的脸盆里 basin provided by the host

Xu（senior）: basin

Wei（senior）: basing

As the subjects don't have the relevant schema about Japanese tea ceremony and the sub-schemas, so some incomplete segments, distorted inferences and elaboration of the answers appear. Obviously, most of the learners rely heavily on the acoustic stimuli they hear with little help from their world knowledge, so they give answers deviated from the original sentence meaning but similar in wording. Now, turn to global questions:

D. What's the main purpose of the Japanese Cha-No-Yu?

Guan（freshman）: to strengthen the friendship between the hosts and the guests （Distorted Inferential Reconstruction）

Wang（freshman）: to let guest appreciate the decorations in the tea-room （Distorted Inferential Reconstruction）

Liu（senior）: to let the guests try some good tea （Distorted Inferential Reconstruction）

Wei（senior）: to kill time （Distorted Inferential Reconstruction）

The above examples illustrate that lacking relevant schemata of Japanese tea ceremony, the processing activities such as elaboration, inference and reconstruction are hard to conduct, thus obstructing overall comprehension of the text.

1.6.2 Explanations from relevance theory

Even though subjects have reported being familiar with the first text "Nian" there were 6 subjects who made unreasonable inferential reconstructions (Table 1. 7). Schemata theory can be used to explain 52 subjects who made the right inferential reconstruction but can't be used to why those 6 failed to make inferential reconstruction. The relevance theory, on the other hand, can be applied to fill the gap.

Though the subjects are familiar with the topic "Nian", s/he fails to find the relevant link between the listening text and the cognitive context through the analysis of the contextual elements. According to the relevance theory, cognitive context refers to the pragmatic knowledge coming from the concrete contexts which are systemized and internalized through experience, and it is dynamically constructed during the whole process of comprehension rather than being pre-determined. Therefore, the subjects have to extend the context to extract the needed information in order to attain optimal relevance. If the subjects couldn't effectively withdraw the proper world knowledge from their minds and the logical semantic information provided by the listening text in the process of inference, the effort of finding the optimal relevance failed and the comprehension broke down.

Lacking proper schemata for the second text, some subjects can still make reasonable inferential reconstruction. As we can see from Table1. 9 there are 6 subjects who didn't answer the question, and 8 subjects who indicated in the answer sheet that it is not mentioned or never mentioned it in the answer sheet. 15 subjects gave distorted elaborations, yet there are still 29 subjects offering reasonable inferential reconstructions. Let's take one subject's answer as an example:

It didn't mention it directly, I think the host wants to entertain the guests and let them enjoy a moment of peace and calm.

Though the passage didn't mention directly the purpose of inviting the guests for Cha-No-Yu, after listening to the passage twice, the subjects possibly have got in their mind the information for their logical inference: " ... take off the street shoes and put on their bamboo shoes...", "...the guests are not supposed to drink the tea at one go...", "They sip bit by bit...appreciate the design of the bowl. " "When they leave the room, they feel happy and peaceful. "

To sum up, when listeners are familiar with the listening text, the comprehension would still be discounted if they fail to find the optimal relevance between the listening text and the contexts through the analysis of the contextual information. Or on the other hand, when listeners are not familiar with the listening text, they can still successfully comprehend the listening passage by attaining the optimal relevance through the analysis.

1.7   English proficiency and its effects on listening comprehension

The second research problem in the study is "Does language proficiency level have any effect on EFL listening comprehension? If so, how?" The statistical results of Table 1.2, Table 1.3 and Table 1.4 clearly show that the effect of language proficiency is significant. Generally speaking, in spite of the degree of topic familiarity, scores of the high-level proficiency subjects are obviously higher than those of the intermediate subjects. The findings confirm, to a certain extent, the results of Dunkel (1992), Schmidt-Rinehart (1994) and Huang (1998), that is, higher-proficiency level learners will always do better than intermediate proficiency-level learners. The result, though, goes against the third hypothesis: that subjects would do equally well on a familiar text.

Therefore, the impact of language proficiency in listening comprehension should be reconsidered. From the perspective of the schema theory, schemata reflect protypical properties of experiences encountered by an individual, integrated over many instances. It is formed and used without the individual's conscious awareness. However, although schemata are assumed to reflect an individual's experience, they are also assumed to be shared across individuals. Once formed, schemata are thought to be relatively stable over time.

With similar schemata, why did higher proficiency level learners outperform intermediate level learners? To answer this question, another very important psychological process—activation of schemata should be examined. Although higher proficiency level learners and intermediate level learners have shared schemata, their activation of the schemata is not the same. According to the research design, learners at higher proficiency level are superior to learners at intermediate proficiency in their overall English ability. With their rich vocabulary and grammar as well as good sense of the target language, they can easily activate their existed schemata in the brain and as a result, they comprehend the listening passage much better.

From the perspective of the relevance theory, in the listening comprehension process the listeners are expected to undergo a series of complicated and interweaving psychological stages including acoustic input, acoustic decoding, comprehending, processing, summarizing and answering questions, etc. In order to successfully accomplish the task, the process of seeking relevance is inevitable, which requires a series of complicated stages mentioned above. During this process, listeners have to rely on their linguistics knowledge to fulfill all these tasks so as to find the relevance link successfully. Learners at advanced level, with their strong language ability, are able to effectively employ their language ability at word, sentence and discourse level as well as all the other logical, semantic or related knowledge to help them achieve optimal relevance efficiently. More sophisticated linguistic knowledge enables the senior learners to target more effectively the logical and semantic information provided by the listening text; their own world knowledge and other useful information helping in the process of listening comprehension, thus enhancing the success rate in finding optimal relevance.

On the contrary, the freshman are relatively poor at English compared to senior learners, they don't have as large a vocabulary as senior learners, and some even are not familiar with some basic words or phrases that are crucial in comprehending the listening text. As a result they could not analyze the cognitive context effectively to find the relevant link so as to ensure comprehension. Their comprehension of the passage as well as elaboration or inferential reconstruction is somewhat lacking.

However, the interactive effects of independent variables should not be ignored. So as for the third research question: "will the effect of topic familiarity change with the proficiency level?" the statistical results in Table 1.4 show that their interactive effect is not significant. Subjects always do better on familiar topics in spite of their proficiency level. The results denied the original hypothesis that senior subjects' comprehension score on unfamiliar topics would be more or less the same as the familiar topic. Therefore topic familiarity exerted greater influence than proficiency level in listening comprehension. Drawing a conclusion from relevance theory, the senior subjects do not have their "own world knowledge" that is essential for the comprehension, thus the success rate of seeking optimal relevance decreased compared with the familiar topic. The overall comprehension of the passage bore the brunt.

1.8　Bottom-up and top-down processing in listening comprehension

Now to the fourth research question: "In the process of listening comprehension, how do subjects adopt different processing strategies?" In other words, under what kind of circumstances do they tend to use "top-down" more frequently than "bottom-up" processing strategies, and in what kind of situation do they tend to use "bottom-up" more than "top-down" processing strategy?

Based on the research results, it is not hard at all to infer the answers due to the effect of topic familiarity: subjects are more inclined to use top-down processing strategies when dealing with familiar topic and "bottom-up" with unfamiliar topics. Generally speaking, as subjects have schemata and sub-schemata to be activated when listening to "Nian", they pay more attention to content and gist and allocate less attention to individual words and minor points.

From the perspective of relevance theory, when the listening texts are familiar to the subjects, it is much easier for the subjects to form relevant links between their encyclopedic, logical and background knowledge and the forthcoming information, thus they generally pay more attention to meaning and the main points of the listening materials, and try to reach optimal relevance between the two by predicting and searching for the most relevant information from the forthcoming information in order to complete the lack of premise for the making of inferences. They pay less attention to the detailed forms of the listening materials.

When listening to the second passage, as subjects don't have the relevant schemata they have to pay more attention to details and individual words in order to get the whole picture of the listening text. This means they are more inclined to use bottom-up processing strategy. This could be illustrated by their answers to the two local questions regarding the two passages:

Q: What did the wise old man suggest people beat in order to drive off "Nian"?

Key for reference: drums and gongs

Li(freshman): 敲锣打鼓 beating drums and gongs (Literal Translation)

Zheng(senior): drums and gongs

All the 58 subjects have got the right answer of drums, 49 subjects wrote"锣", and 7 wrote "gong" and 2 subjects got the wrong answer.

Though gong is a new word for all the subjects, but they could resort to their mother tongue to make the correct answer, which testifies that subjects adopt concept-driven approach with familiar topics. Look at the unfamiliar text:

Q: What is used to decorate Japanese tea-rooms?

Key for reference: flowers, porcelain tea sets of ancient times, landscape paintings, national costumes

No one got all the correct answers. 11 subjects (among which 8 were freshmen and 3 seniors) wrote national customs as their answer. 8 subjects (5 freshmen, 3 seniors) wrote "porcelain, porcelain sets…" here are samples of their answers:

Zhu (freshman): national customs, flowers

Xu (freshman): land painting

Wei (senior): porcelain sets and paintings

Guan(senior): cauliflower

The above examples demonstrated that they paid more attention to details when they have no schemata to refer to. From relevance theory perspective, they have to pay more attention to the individual words or the detailed forms of the listening texts in order to find the relevant information from the listening material, and try to make assumptions that they deem are relevant. So they adopt a data-driven approach when dealing with the unfamiliar topic.

To sum up, subjects at two proficiency levels are more inclined to use "top-down" processing with familiar listening text while using "bottom-up" with unfamiliar text. The findings verify the claim of Van Dijk & Kintsch (1983).

1.9 The transactional listening comprehension model

The present research probes the listening process of Chinese non-English majors. The two main independent variables were listeners' language proficiency and background knowledge. The schema theory and the relevance theory as a framework help explain the process. Both quantitative and qualitative methods were employed to analyze and interpret the results.

Topic familiarity enjoys the most significant main effects. Subjects score more highly when they are familiar with the topics of listening text. When the recorded passages are unfamiliar to them, they score comparatively lower. This result can be explained by the schema theory. The schema theory can't explain all the listening processes and phenomenon; but the relevance theory can fill in the gap. The research indicates that when the listener failed to reach optimal relevance between the listening texts and their cognitive contexts, the subjects still cannot reach successful understanding though the recorded text is familiar. On the contrary, when the recorded text is not familiar, if subjects can find the optimal relevance between the listening texts and their cognitive contexts, they can achieve successful listening comprehension.

Language proficiency also has a significant main effect on learners. The mean scores of the senior learners are much higher then those of the freshman no matter if they are familiar with the listening text or not. This result reminds people that language proficiency is the basis of listening comprehension.

The interaction between language proficiency and topic familiarity is not significant. In other words, the main effect of topic familiarity does not change with language proficiency levels. The main effect of topic familiarity is greater than that of language proficiency on the listening comprehension of Chinese non-English major students. From the relevance theory perspective, the quickness of finding the effective relevant link between the listening text and cognitive context rely more on topic familiarity rather than language proficiency.

The more greatly significant main effect enjoyed by topic familiarity and the qualitative data analysis, we draw the following conclusion: when listening texts are familiar to the subjects, both the advanced level and intermediate level students tend to use the "top-down" processing strategy. Conversely, when the listening texts are unfamiliar to the subjects, they more frequently tend to use the "bottom-up" processing strategy.

Based on the theoretic framework and the findings of the study, a transactional listening comprehension model of for Chinese non-English major learners has been put forward.

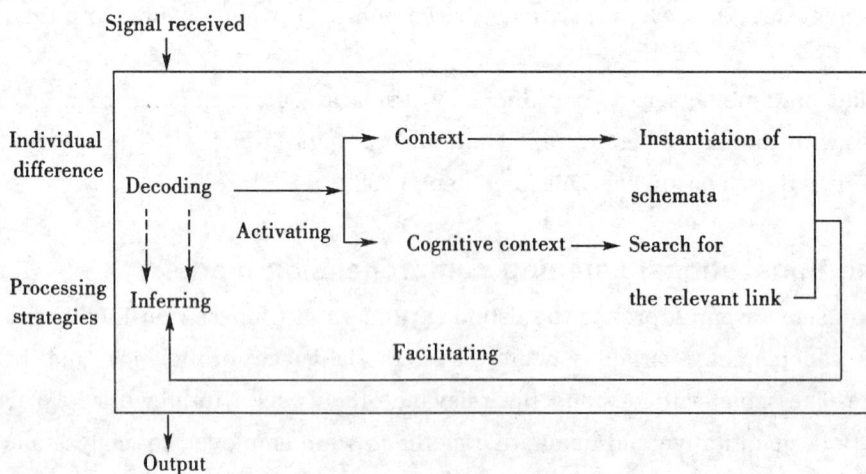

Figure 1.2　The transactional listening comprehension model

The model posits that foreign language listening comprehension is not a process of receiving information with the knowledge of that language, rather it is a reconstructive psychological process consciously or unconsciously controlled by the listener. At the same time, the process of comprehension is also a process of "decoding—inferring" which is conditioned, to a certain extent, by both the instantiation of the schemata and the finding of the relevant link in a cognitive context. The processing strategies and the individual differences also restrain the process. The former explicates the tendency of using top-down and bottom-up processing strategies. The latter contains several layers of implications: the higher the foreign language proficiency level, ability to seek relevant links and ability to instantiate the schema the listener has, the better chance the listener stands of finding the optimal relevance and therefore achieve better understanding of the listening materials. Schemata instantiation, relevant link and searching for optimal relevance are both an automatic and conscious process. They depend on each other and restrain each other.

Chapter 2

A Cognitive Approach to the Acquisition of Discourse Markers

Discourse Markers are words or expressions commonly used in language to mark utterance information. They are very important for the pragmatic competence of a speaker. Research on L2 learners' use and acquisition of DMs can help us learn the patterns so as to increase their acquisition efficiency and thus improve their pragmatic competence. The general research on the functions and meanings of DMs has taken two approaches: the coherence-based approach holding that DMs express conceptual meaning and help enhance discourse coherence, which is a static approach; the relevance-theoretic approach holding that DMs express procedural meaning and play an important role in utterance generation and interpretation, which is a dynamic approach. The research on DM use and acquisition falls into two directions: on the one hand, DM use and acquisition by native speakers, including exploring its influencing factors, such as individual differences in age, gender and social class and exterior factors like speech context; on the other hand, DM use and acquisition by L2 learners, mostly focusing on the differences and similarities as compared to native speakers and their contributing factors.

Based on the relevance-theoretic approach, the present study investigates the patterns in the use and acquisition of DMs by Chinese EFL learners and puts forward corresponding solutions to facilitate the learners' acquisition of DMs. The study collects data by recording and transcribing speeches from a group discussion task by 65 subjects and a picture description task by 62 subjects, and calculates the types and frequencies of the DMs used and the percentages of each type out of the total occurrences of DMs. In addition, the study investigates respectively the learners' knowledge about the use of some DMs, and their metapragmatic awareness of the pragmatic function of the DM *well* by executing two tests to 61 of the subjects: a cloze test and an utterance interpretation test. Through analysis and comparison of the data, including comparison with native speakers' use of DMs, some patterns concerning these learners' use and acquisition of DMs are revealed: the use of DMs is writing-oriented and fossilized, and the acquisition of DMs follows a "literal-to-pragmatic" pattern. It is also proved that context does have some influence on the learners' use of DMs. Apart from that, the study puts forward three blending models for the analysis of DMs in terms of their role in the dynamic process of utterance interpretation, and a blending model for the evolution of their pragmatic meanings, based on the integrative study of the relevance theory and the space blending theory.

2.1   The oral characteristics of Discourse Markers

Being an important topic in the research of language use, the research on DMs has borne fruitful results during the last two decades. DMs are an open class of syntactically optional, non-truth-conditional connective expressions (Schourup, 1999). They are seen as a separate functional class that consists of words or expressions from many different grammatical categories. Included are some conjunctions (e. g., *and, but, because*), adverbials (e. g., *therefore, well*), prepositional phrases (e. g., *as a result*), interjections (e. g., *oh*), clauses (e. g., *you know*), etc. For example:

(1) A: I like him. B. *So*, you think you'll ask him out then.

(2) John can't go. *And* Mary can't go.

(3) Will you go? *Furthermore*, will you represent the class there?

(4) Sue left very late. *But* she arrived on time.

(5) I think it will fly. *After all*, we built it right.

(6) There was considerable flooding. *As a result*, farmers went bankrupt.

(7) Jim is ready for the exam. *In contrast*, Jack is quite unprepared.

Although numerous studies have been done to specify the meanings, functions or classifications of this group of linguistic items, there are no universal agreements on several issues concerning DMs. Agreement has never been reached as to how they should be labeled. The term DMs used here is merely the most popular one of all those competing terms ever used in previous research. A wide variety of other terms (but not limited to these) are: cue phrases (Knott & Dale, 1994), discourse connectives (Blakemore, 1987, 1992; Rouchota, 1996), discourse operators (Redeker, 1990, 1991), discourse particles (Schourup, 1999), pragmatic connectives (Van Dijk, 1979; Stubbs, 1983), pragmatic formatives (Fraser, 1987), pragmatic markers (Fraser, 1988, 1990; Schiffrin, 1987), and pragmatic operators (Ariel, 1994), etc. Each term only partially overlaps with others. Even when the same term "DMs" is used in two studies, items included in one may be excluded in another, for they may emphasize different characteristics of DMs. For example, Schiffrin (1987) refers to *well*, *oh* as DMs, while Fraser (1999) excludes them by labeling them as "pause markers". Apart from that, there is no agreed definition of DMs so far. Most definitions focus on connectivity and non-truth-conditionality, but no definition is likely to win universal acceptance. This is because these definitions are based on different theories and varying background assumptions (Schourup, 1999). Neither is any universal agreement reached as to how DMs function in discourse. The coherence theory claims that DMs are used to connect units of discourse and make the implicit coherence relations explicit. In contrast, in the relevance-theoretic framework, DMs guide the listener in utterance interpretation. By using DMs, the speaker clearly indicates the right way of interpreting his or her utterance so as to save the listener's processing efforts. As some scholars (Blakemore, 1987; Rouchota, 1996; Sperber & Wilson, 2001) suggest, DMs encode procedural information, rather than conceptual. They contribute nothing to the content of the proposition expressed by the utterance.

Despite all those disagreements, some characteristics of DMs can be observed. According to Schourup (1999), there are seven characteristics of DMs, two of which are most often mentioned as criteria to identify a DM status: connectivity and non-truth-conditionality. Connectivity is considered a necessary criterion for DMs. DMs are used to connect the host utterance with its context locally or globally. They ensure the right interpretation of the utterance by guiding the hearer in the choice of appropriate context, or to help achieve discourse coherence by making the implicit relationship between discourse units explicit, according to two approaches to DMs. Non-truth conditionality refers to the belief that DMs do not contribute anything to the truth-conditions of the proposition expressed by an utterance, that is, they do not affect the propositional content of utterances in which they occur. Considering the second characteristic, DMs can be removed without influencing either the propositional content or the grammatical structure of the utterances they introduce. This characteristic is referred to as optionality. "If a DM is omitted, the relationship it signals is still available to the hearer, though no longer explicitly cued"(Schourup, 1999). Since they are said to introduce discourse, most DMs occur in initial position. This is the characteristic of initiality. However, some do occur in other positions. Therefore, this characteristic must be understood as referring to "the position of DMs in relation to the central clause elements rather than to the position of the first word in an utterance" (Schourup, 1999). Weak clause association refers to the characteristic that DMs have a detached relationship with the clause in which they occur. Since early research predominantly focused on DMs in spoken discourse, items categorized into DMs are those primarily found in speech. This constitutes the characteristic of orality. Yet, as long as some written items share the same characteristics of connectivity, non-truth-conditionality and optionality, the denial of such items into the class of DMs is not justified. So, orality cannot be a criterion for DM status. The last characteristic is multi-categoriality. As DMs are seen as performing pragmatic functions, they form a functional rather than grammatical class. As a result, this class includes words from different categories. Nonetheless, specific items in the DM class vary depending on different definitions. Schourup (1999) thus holds that "the class must be regarded as more or less open". However, DMs are often described to show a particular characteristic only to a certain extent, like *always*, *often* or *sometimes*. On the other hand, few DMs , if any, show all of them (Müller, 2004).

2.2　Two approaches to Discourse Markers

According to Rouchota (1996), there are two approaches to DMs: the coherence-based approach and the relevance-theoretic approach. The two approaches are introduced respectively, followed by a comparison of both approaches. The comparison suggests that the relevance-theoretic approach outweighs the coherence-based approach in that it reveals the psychological motivation for the use of DMs in speech. This conclusion justifies the relevance-theoretical framework on which the present study is based.

2.2.1   The coherence-based approach

Research on DMs has begun since the 1970s. Most early researches take the coherence-based approach discussing the general issues such as the classifications, functions or meanings of DMs. Halliday & Hasan (1976) hold that these expressions are cohesive devices and belong to the category of "conjunctions". Levinson (1983) mentions that there are many words and phrases in English and most languages that indicate the relationship between an utterance and the prior discourse, and mentions as examples the utterance-initial usages of *but, therefore, in conclusion, to the contrary, still, however, anyway, well, besides, actually, all in all, so, after all,* and so on. He holds that "what they seem to do is indicate, often in very complex ways, just how the utterance that contains them is a response to, or a continuation of some portion of the prior discourse".

Schiffrin's (1987) approach to DMs is based on, and elaborates on both Levison's (1983) and Halliday and Hasan's (1976) remarks. In her book entitled *Discourse Markers,* Schiffrin claims that all markers have indexical functions, i. e. they index adjacent utterances to the speaker, the hearer, or both and also to prior and/or subsequent discourse. She proposes a model of discourse coherence containing five planes and holds that DMs locate utterances on one or more planes of the model. Coherence is then defined in relation to the overall model. As Fraser (1990) remarks, Schiffrin "sees DMs as serving an integrative function in discourse and thus contributing to discourse coherence. They serve as a kind of ' discourse glue' ". In addition, Schiffrin (1987) proposes a notion of "core meaning" for DMs and analyzes in detail the 11 expressions: *and, because, but, I mean, now, oh, or, so, then, well,* and *y' know.*

Redeker (1991) calls DMs "discourse operators" and holds that the primary function of DMs is bringing to the listener's attention a particular kind of linkage of the upcoming utterance with the immediate discourse context. Redeker approves of Schiffrin's notion of "core meaning" for DMs and suggests, "the core meaning should specify the marker's intrinsic contribution to the semantic representation that will constrain the interpretation of the utterance" (cited in Fraser, 1999). Redeker critically revises Schiffrin's model of discourse coherence and comes up with a three-component model. She proposes "any utterance … in a discourse is then considered to always participate in all three components, but one will usually dominate and suggest itself as the more relevant linkage of this utterance to its context" (cited in Fraser 1999: 936). DMs are to signal linguistically textual coherence links, and the links can be described and classified in terms of the three components mentioned above.

Fraser approaches DMs from a grammatical-pragmatic perspective. He once used different terms to refer to DMs: Pragmatic Formative (1987), Pragmatic Markers (1996) and Discourse Markers (1999). He distinguishes DMs from other Pragmatic Markers and classifies them as one type of Pragmatic Markers. According to Fraser (1999), DMs have a core meaning that can be enriched by the context and signal the relationship that the speaker intends between the utterance the DM introduces and the foregoing utterance.

Thus, DMs are seen as a grammatical category connecting textual elements. Fraser's approach is in common with the relevance-theoretic approach in the claim that DMs contribute nothing to the representative meaning or the propositional content of the utterance.

Knott & Sanders (1998) examine to what extent the classifications of coherence relations and DMs (called "cue phrases") converge in a comparative study of a set of DMs in English and Dutch and find interesting similarities. Hansen (1998) focuses on the semantic status of DMs and proposes an approach, which is said to belong to the function-cognitive paradigm in linguistics, to account for the meanings and functions of DMs. Kroon (1998) sketches an outline of a theoretic framework for the analysis and description of DMs and applies this framework to some Latin DMs. Central to this framework is the insight that DMs (called "connective particles") play a role in signaling or maintaining discourse coherence and that discourse coherence obtains on three levels. Tree & Schrock (2002) study the basic meanings (an equivalent of "core meaning" supported by Schiffrin and Redeker) of the two DMs *you know* and *I mean* and conclude that the basic meanings of the two DMs are different. They propose that the wide range of possible functions for *you know* and *I mean* can be reanalyzed in terms of their basic meanings.

2.2.2 The relevance-theoretic approach

The above researches focus on the role of DMs in signaling discourse coherence and the core meaning of DMs in discourse. Other studies focus on the pragmatic meaning of DMs in languages other than English and provide cross-linguistic evidence for the pragmatic interpretation of DMs.

Fraser and Malamud-Makowski (1996) contrast English and Spanish "contrastive DMs" and find that in both languages they signal similar interpretations of the utterances they introduce. Schwenter (1996) examines the Spanish DM *o sea* and argues that the pragmatic meanings of DMs cannot be analyzed without reference to the content meanings of their lexical sources. Archakis (2001) describes and accounts for the functions of four Modern Greek expressions and argues that only if the dynamics of grammaticalization is taken into account, is it possible to arrive at a principled explanation of the differences and similarities between the four markers. Horne, et al (2001) study the Swedish DM *men* (*but*), which is said to mark the boundary between both different topic units and topic-internal units in spontaneous speech. The study shows that DMs "along with their prosodic correlates and co-occurring lexical items constitute a constellation of important information for understanding how segmentation of spoken discourse is produced and understood" (2001). Chen & He (2001) examine the form *dui bu dui* in Chinese classroom discourse as a "pragmatic marker" and propose that besides functioning as an A-not-A question, this marker can also be used for pragmatic purposes to signal transitions of interactional sequences at different levels of discourse and to help the speaker maintain the addressee's attention in given activities. These studies show that DMs are used for pragmatic purposes and the pragmatic meanings of DMs should be analyzed with reference to their "lexical sources" and "co-occurring lexical items".

It can be observed that there has been a shift of focus from the semantic-pragmatic functions of DMs to the pragmatic interpretations of DMs. The relevance-theoretic approach takes a step further to study the cognitive-pragmatic functions of DMs. This approach is based on the Relevance Theory (hereafter, RT), which is proposed by Sperber and Wilson (2001). According to RT, every act of ostensive communication communicates a presumption of its own optimal relevance; that is to say, an utterance is presumed to be able to yield adequate contextual effects without unnecessary processing efforts. Within the RT framework, DMs are seen as semantic constraints on relevance (Blakemore, 1987). They facilitate the hearer's processing by indicating the direction in which relevance is to be sought by virtue of the inferential connections they express. DMs only carry procedural information, rather than conceptual, about the inferential phase of communication. With the instructions that DMs indicate, the hearer can choose the right contextual assumptions without extra effort and arrive at the intended interpretation of the utterance. According to RT's three ways of achieving relevance, Blakemore (1992) classifies DMs into three main types.

After Blakemore's pioneering work, the focus of the research on DMs has shifted from semantic-pragmatic functions of DMs to the cognitive motivation of using DMs. Two other studies can be found analyzing DMs within the framework of RT. Murillo (2004) discusses the role that "reformation markers" such as *that is, that is to say, in other words, namely, i. e.* and *viz.*, play in linguistic communication. Matsui (2002) analyzes a Japanese DM *dakara* (*in other words/so*) the same as Murillo (2004) does. Both studies claim that such DMs encode procedural information instructing the hearer to identify the utterance that follows it as a reformulation or a contextual implication of another utterance, and that they assist in the inferential processes that are involved in the interpretation of an utterance by contributing to the recovery of different higher-level explicatures.

2.2.3　Differences between the two approaches to Discourse Markers

A comparison of the coherence-based approach (CBA) and the relevance-theoretic approach (RTA) shows the differences between them (shown in Table 2.1) and arrives at the conclusion that the relevance-theoretic approach is more plausible because it provides the psychological motivation for the use of DMs in communication.

Table 2.1　　　　　　　**Differences between the two approaches to DMs**

CBA	RTA
Textual coherence	Optimal relevance
DMs link discourse units	DMs link discourse unit and context
DMs indicate coherence relations	DMs constrain inferential processes
DMs encode conceptual meaning	DMs encode procedural meaning

First of all, the theoretic presumptions of the two approaches are different. CBA is based on the presumption that texts are coherent. What holds a text together is a set of implicit coherence relations. The recovery of such coherence relations is essential for text comprehension. DMs are used to link two discourse units and make the implicit coherence relations explicit. In contrast, RTA is based on the presumption of optimal relevance. According to RT, communication is a dynamic inferential process. DMs are seen as expressing the inferential connection. They facilitate the dynamic process of utterance generation and interpretation. When producing an utterance, the speaker usually has a specific interpretation in mind and expects the hearer to arrive at that interpretation. The hearer has to process the utterance in the right context in order to come to the intended interpretation. The selection of context is determined by the search for relevance. DMs link an utterance and a context, i. e. the speaker uses DMs to constrain the hearer's selection of context "by making a certain set of contextual assumptions immediately accessible" (Rouchota, 1996), and thus may be able to ensure the intended interpretation and save the hearer some processing effort.

The second and very important difference lies in the answer to the question of whether DMs encode conceptual meaning or procedural meaning. According to coherence theorists, DMs indicate coherence relations and thus they are "relational conceptual representations". In other words, DMs encode conceptual meaning, which deals with the question of what the representation is. Some DMs contribute to the content of propositions; others do not. In contrast, for relevance theorists, DMs encode procedural meaning, which deals with the question of how to process, or how to "take" conceptual representations. They do not contribute to the truth-conditional content of propositions. Wilson and Sperber (1993) provide one piece of direct evidence that DMs express procedural meaning rather than conceptual. They believe that DMs are "notoriously hard to pin down in conceptual terms" and attribute the difficulty in the acquisition of DMs to the procedural account of DMs: DMs encode procedural meaning. Procedural meaning cannot be brought to consciousness.

The last but most striking difference concerns the psychological explanation for the speaker's use of DMs in communication. According to Rouchota (1996), RT provides an explanation for the speaker's use of DMs. The motivation for the use of DMs is expressed in two aspects. First, the speaker wants the hearer to interpret the utterance in the right way. To ensure the right interpretation, the speaker uses DMs to guide the hearer to select "the appropriate contextual assumptions and arrive at the appropriate conclusions" (Rouchota, 1996). Second, the speaker wants to minimize the hearer's processing effort. The speaker uses DMs to clearly indicate as to "how she intends her utterance to achieve relevance and thus she saves the hearer some processing effort in arriving at the intended interpretation" (Rouchota, 1996). However, the coherence-based approach does not provide any motivation for the existence of DMs. There is no psychological explanation, in other words, why a speaker would try to indicate the right coherence relation by choosing a DM (Rouchota, 1996). In conclusion, the relevance-theoretic approach to DMs reveals the psychological motivation for the speaker's use of DMs and provides an explanation for some phenomena that the Coherence Theory has failed to account for. The relevance-theoretic approach has become a new trend in the research on DMs and is seen as more powerful in explaining DMs' role in communication.

However, the relevance-theoretic approach is far from being a perfect approach to the explanation of DMs' role in the cognitive process of utterance generation and interpretation. The claim that the speaker uses DMs to guide the process of contextualization so as to ensure the intended interpretation of her utterance seems so superficial. How on earth do DMs guide the process? And how does the result of the contextualization process feed back on the ultimate interpretation? The relevance-theoretic approach fails to provide an accessible and operative model to explain the concrete and detailed on-line inferential processes.

2.3   Researches on the use and acquisition of Discourse Markers

Researches on the use and acquisition of Discourse Markers fall into three categories: DM use and acquisition by native speakers, by non-native speakers, and by Chinese learners. But the third category is relatively less traveled so far, which makes it possible for the present study to make new findings in this area.

2.3.1   The use and acquisition of Discourse Markers by native speakers

Research on the acquisition of DMs by young children reveals that the acquisition of the literal meanings is prior to that of the pragmatic meanings of DMs. Montes (1999) examines the emergence of seven Spanish interjections in the speech of a young child acquiring Spanish as a native language and analyzes them as "information management markers". The study traces the development of these interjections longitudinally in the speech of one child and sees a development from the more literal, contextual uses to the more elaborated functions. Andersen, et al (1999) study early acquisition of DMs as register variables in American, French and Spanish-speaking children and find striking cross-linguistic parallels in the way children learn to use DMs. They find that by the time they enter school, children are sensitive to the social meanings conveyed by the use of different DMs. By age six, children can consistently mark speaker roles with DMs in role-playing tasks and children as young as four show some ability to do this. There is a fair amount of evidence that other (textual) functions of these forms are acquired somewhat earlier than their register function. Based on these findings, the present study investigates the use and acquisition of DMs by Chinese learners of English and hopes to test the hypothesis that their acquisition of DMs develops from the literal meanings to the pragmatic meanings of DMs.

There is evidence in some previous studies that age and speech context are possible factors influencing the use of DMs by native speakers. Evidence for age being one of the factors is provided in the following two studies. Macaulay (2002) analyzes the use of *you know* in two sets of transcribed speeches from Scotland. The first is a set of interviews and the second is a set of same-sex conversations. The analysis shows that age is one of the three factors (the other two being gender and social class differences) that influence the use of the DM *you know*. Erman (2001) classifies the principal function of DMs to monitor discourse in three domains: the textual domain, the social domain and the metalinguistic domain. Based on this classification, it has been found from the corpus-based study of the use of the DM *you know* by two groups of speakers—adolescents and adults—that adult speakers primarily use the marker as a textual monitor to build up a text and create coherence; while young speakers use it as a metalinguistic monitor and as a social monitor. The results of the study show that there are clear indications of differences in the use of *you know* by adult and adolescent speakers, and that speakers from later periods use the item in new functions and contexts. The implication of the study is that "the doors are open" for meaning shift of such items to take place and "further pragmaticalization may eventually lead to the marker becoming fully grammaticalized" and ending up as a grammatical morpheme.

Two other studies provide evidence for speech context being another influencing factor. Norrick (2001) demonstrates that *well* and *but* function as a special sort of DMs in oral narratives, and that their functions within the oral narrative context follow neither their usual meanings nor their usual DM functions in other contexts. Instead, both *well* and *but* are keyed on participant expectations about narrative structures and storytelling procedure. Fuller (2003) studies the influence of speaker roles on the use of DMs. The general research question addressed in his study is: how do native speakers of English alter their patterns of DM use in different speech contexts? The study examines the use of DMs *you know, like, oh, well, yeah,* and *I mean* in two speech contexts—interviews and casual conversations—to determine the role of these DMs in marking and negotiating speaker roles. The data show that in conversations the DMs *oh* and *well* are used significantly. In interviews, the same speakers use *oh* and *well* less frequently because their role as interviewee does not require as much response to the other interlocutor's utterances. The DMs *you know, like, yeah* and *I mean* are used at similar rates across contexts, indicating that their functions are more universal. In conclusion, this study has shown that the role of speakers in an interaction, as well as the relationship of the interlocutors, play a role in the use and distribution of certain DMs. Kyratzis and Ervin-Tripp (1999) adopt Schiffrin's approach and examine to what extent young children use DMs at different levels of talk in two activity contexts: pretend play with a scenario toy, and story-telling. They find that both age and context are factors influencing the use of DMs. Based on the above findings, the present study analyzes the influence of speech context and speaker roles on the use of DMs by Chinese learners of English and tests the hypothesis that they are factors influencing DM use by L2 learners.

2.3.2　The use and acquisition of Discourse Markers by L2 learners

Studies on DMs used by non-native speakers of English find that their acquisition and use of particular DMs are influenced by the amount of instruction on and/or exposure to these DMs. Müller (2004) investigates the use of the DM *well* by German EFL speakers as compared to its use by American native speakers. The analysis is based on 70 conversations in which pairs of university students retold and discussed a short silent movie they had been shown. All instances of *well* in these conversations were categorized according to the function *well* assumed in the interaction. Of the twelve functions found in the data, nine were used more by the EFL speakers than by the native. The EFL speakers also used *well* more frequently than native speakers did in comparison to the DM *so*, especially in the comparable functions of the two markers. Several possible explanations for these results are discussed in the paper; the most likely ones are the respective frequencies of *well* and *so* in German textbooks of English and an overuse of *well* in an attempt to avoid the German-sounding *so*. The study indicates that exposure and instruction are possible factors contributing to the acquisition of certain DMs by L2 learners.

Trillo (2002) explores the use of "pragmatic markers" in the speech of native and non-native speakers of English at two different ages: children and adults. The aim is to see to what extent their exposure to spoken pragmatic information in a foreign language is sufficient to acquire pragmatic markers coherently. The hypothesis is that L2 learners follow a "binary track" in their linguistic development: the formal vs. the pragmatic track. Contrary to native speakers' "function-to-form" developmental process, L2 speakers follow a "form-to-function" process. The findings of Trillo's study are as follows. Firstly, there is a different rate of development for the grammatical and the pragmatic aspects of language in L2. While native and non-native children show a similar pattern in the use of DMs, proficient non-native adult speakers do not show a competent use of DMs in speech. Secondly, the lack of competent use of markers leads to pragmatic fossilization and possibly to communicative failure in many cases. Thirdly, if pragmatic functions were introduced in the teaching process, foreign children might pick up the pragmatic value of linguistic elements in the same way as native children. This knowledge is neglected in the curriculum and thus the use of DMs becomes fossilized both in the quantity and the diversity of elements used.

2.3.3 The use and acquisition of Discourse Markers by Chinese learners

Not until the end of last decade did the research on DMs begin in China, with He Ziran and Ran Yongping (1999) and Ran Yongping (2000) being two of those contributing to the pioneering work on this topic. Theoretical research on DMs in China takes different perspectives. Some studies view DMs as constraints on relevance within RT framework. He Ziran & Ran Yongping (1999) make a tentative study of DMs focusing on their pragmatic constraints on utterance production and interpretation and conclude that DMs can reveal the short-circuited information and minimize the hearer's processing efforts. Along the same line are the pragmatic functions of DMs analyzed by He Ziran & Mo Aiping (2002), Ma Yulei & Yao Lan (2002) and Li Yongzhong (2003). Chen Kai-ju (2002) presents a contrastive pragmatic analysis of discourse end markers (e. g. , *ne, ma* and *ba* in Chinese) in Chinese and English conversations following the relevance-theoretic approach and demonstrates the influence of such markers on the strength of utterance proposition.

Others study DMs in translation. Xue Yuan (2003) focuses on how to deal with DMs in translation and their enrichment of functions. Ma Xiao (2003) conducts a contrastive study of DMs between English and Chinese and points out that while showing some differences, DMs in both languages perform a common function of pragmatic marking. He thus suggests that in translation of DMs we should focus on their pragmatic functions in the source text and represent them appropriately in the target text.

There are also studies exploring the pragmatic meanings and functions of DMs. Ran Yongping (2002) focuses on the DM *you know* and claims that it is used as an adaptive device helping to manage and maintain the on-going interaction. It serves as a meta-knowledge indicator and its function of calling attention leads to the increasing of shared knowledge between the participants. Ran Yongping (2003) studies the pragmatic functions of another DM *well* and claims that it can act as a mitigator of face-threatening acts, hesitation or delay marker of some speech acts, insufficiency marker and repair marker in different contexts. Li Yongzhong (2003) shows that speakers use pragmatic markers not only to organize discourse, to attract hearers' attention, but also to express speakers' attitude and maintain discourse coherence. Wu Yaxin & Yu Guodong (2003) focus on DMs' function of reflecting language users' metapragmatic awareness and explore the relationship between DMs and metapragmatic awareness as well as five types of metapragmatic information conveyed by DMs. Their studies focus on analyzing the pragmatic meanings and functions of individual DMs like *well* and *you know* as well as DMs in general. However, these studies are only theoretical efforts and cannot provide empirical evidence for whether Chinese learners of English use DMs in these functions and whether particular learners have acquired individual DMs.

There are indeed empirical studies on DMs, but the number is surprisingly small; there are no systematic studies on the acquisition of DMs by Chinese learners of English, but rather some sporadic studies focusing on various aspects. Liu Lijin (2002) studies the role of sequential markers (e. g. , *and, then*) in discourse production and comprehension. According to him, sequential markers serve to highlight continuity and discontinuity of propositions in discourse. These markers can be *signals* to improve discourse comprehension, and also *traces* of discourse-production difficulty when a topic shift occurs. The data obtained in this study support the hypothesis that the proportion of sequential markers increases as the discourse structure becomes hierarchically higher, and the more difficult the discourse production becomes, the more frequently the markers appear, especially *and* as a trace, though its function as a signal of proposition continuity is not affected. This study illuminates the role of DMs, in particular sequential markers, in signaling hierarchies of discourse structure so as to improve discourse comprehension, and the positive correlation between the frequency of the use of DMs and the difficulty in discourse production. Although the present study focuses on the use of DMs in speech, the above findings may be able to account for the use of such DMs as *and* and *then* in speeches of the learners.

Chen Xinren (2002) investigates fourth year English majors' argumentative writing and finds that on the one hand they are aware of the necessity of DM use in order to help readers to understand their writing correctly and easily; on the other hand their use of DMs tends to fossilize. Classroom instruction on the use of DMs may account for this finding. L1 interference and obvious individual differences—some overuse DMs while others rarely use DMs—can be found in some subjects' DM use. He also finds that some DMs are misused and thus cause misunderstanding and waste of reader's processing effort. This study reveals that the use of DMs by Chinese learners of English in writing tends to fossilize. Whether such fossilization also exists in Chinese EFL learners' speech will be explored in the present study and the overuse or the rarity in the use of certain DMs will be revealed. Furthermore, the influence of classroom instruction or formal instruction on the use of DMs is also discussed later in the present study in terms of its role in facilitating the acquisition of DMs.

He Anping & Xu Manfei's (2003) study highlights the functions of "small words" (an overlapping term of DMs) in developing speaking fluency and their contribution to EFL teaching and learning. Their study investigates a group of "small words" in different corpora and analyzes them in terms of their types, ranges, frequency and discoursal functions. The investigation finds that Chinese EFL learners as well as EFL learners from other nations use DMs differently from native speakers in terms of either frequency or type. And then a comparison is made between more fluent and less fluent Chinese EFL learners, associating their degree of fluency with their use of "small words". It is found the more fluent learners use more types and use them more frequently than the less fluent learners. The findings from He & Xu's study provide the present study with a clue to the influence of oral English proficiency of Chinese learners of English on the use of DMs in speech.

2.4   Cognitive approaches to Discourse Markers

Cognitive approaches presented by SLA theories derive from four aspects: Schmidt's (1990) construct of noticing; Skehan's (1998) information-processing approach to task-based instruction; Van Pattern's model of processing and acquisition. These theories will be applied to the analysis of factors contributing to EFL learners' acquisition of DMs from three aspects: noticing, instruction and processing of DMs, and thus justify the solution to DM acquisition proposed in the present study.

2.4.1   Schmidt's construct of noticing and the information-processing approach

Schmidt (1990) holds that not all input has equal value and that only the input that is noticed then becomes available for intake and effective processing. Therefore, a degree of awareness is important before material can be incorporated into a developing interlanguage system. Schmidt proposes a construct of noticing. There are six influences operating upon noticing. Frequency of input influences the possibility for a form to be noticed. Other things being equal, the more frequent a form, the more likely it is to be noticed and then become integrated in the interlanguage system. Perception salience plays a similar role in influencing noticing. Other things being equal, the more a form stands out in the input stream, the more likely it is to be noticed. Instruction can work in a more complex way by making salient the less obvious aspects of the input, so that it is the learner who does the extraction and focusing. The role that instruction plays is that it channels attention and brings into awareness what otherwise would have been missed. Processing ability concerns the learner's capacity to deal with the range of forms in input. Readiness refers to the current state of the interlanguage system. A prediction can be made about what the learner can notice and incorporate into the interlanguage system, because it is the "next" thing to be acquired. Task demands concerns what is expected of the language user at any given moment as a result of the activity he or she is engaged in. Overloading the limited capacity system with one task will result in less noticing available for another.

Formal instruction is claimed by many scholars to be important in SLA, for it facilitates the development of explicit knowledge. Bialystok (1982) proposes a model of L2 learning, which allows for the interaction between the two types of knowledge: the implicit knowledge, developed through exposure to communicative language use, and the explicit knowledge, developed when learners focus on the language code (Ellis, 1994: 357). This model justifies the possibility for EFL teachers to facilitate L2 learners' acquisition by means of formal instruction. Skehan (1998), Ellis (1994) and Spolsky (1989) review in detail the studies on the value of formal instruction. According to them, there is considerable evidence in the literature that "SLA instruction does make a difference"; many studies prove the positive effects of instruction on SLA process. Matthews et al. (1998) argue that the most effective learning develops an implicit knowledge base and then generates an explicit model of the material. This implies that explicitness is beneficial later in linguistic development. In contrast, Ellis (1994) argues that this is especially important with more complex material, since the function of explicit instruction is to make aspects of the input salient.

As to how such instruction imposes influence on SLA process, Schmidt (1994) proposes that it channels attention in selective and beneficial ways and brings into awareness what otherwise would have been missed. Unlike in previous surveys where the term "formal instruction" has been understood to refer to grammar teaching, Ellis (1994) takes a broader view of the role of formal instruction, classifying instruction into two types. One type of formal instruction is directed at cognitive goals, focusing on developing linguistic or communicative competence. The other type is directed at metacognitive goals, attempting to train learners to use effective learning strategies.

Having justified the necessity and the role of formal instruction in SLA, scholars explore the approaches to formal instruction. There are two contrasting approaches to task-based instruction: the structure-oriented and the communication-oriented. They represent extreme positions. The quality they share is that both concentrate on one aspect of language performance at the expense of others. The structure-oriented approach emphasizes form while neglecting meaning. And the communication-oriented approach focuses very much on meaning but not on form.

To achieve balanced interlanguage system, an intermediate approach is necessary. On such an approach, a balance is kept between form and meaning, and alternative attention is paid to both of them. Skehan (1998) proposes an information-processing approach to task-based instruction, which can achieve a balance between communication and form. This approach is justified in two aspects of processing perspective: information-processing capacities and selective channeling of attention; more demanding tasks consume more attentional resources for task transaction, and then less attention is available for focus on form. Therefore, Skehan (1998) proposes the principle for task-based instruction— maximize the chances of focus on form through attentional manipulation. This principle proposes the most effective opportunity available for a focus on form in the context of meaningful language use.

2.4.2   VanPattern and input processing

Skehan (1998) presents VanPattern's (1996) principles for input processing and the model of processing and acquisition. The principles relevant to the present study are that learners process content words in the input before anything else and that for learners to process form that is non-meaningful, · they must be able to process information or communicative content that costs no or little attentional resources. VanPattern (1996) also proposes a processing approach to input. He claims that " there is a crucial contrast between comprehension-based and processing-based approaches to input", and that the latter is "more concerned with the control of attention during comprehension and the way different cues can be focused on" (Skehan, 1998). The processing approach suggests "the usefulness of training language learners in effective processing, to make them more able to notice relevant cues in the input so that form-meaning links are more likely to be attended to" (Skehan, 1998). Figure 2. 1 shows VanPattern's model of processing and acquisition:

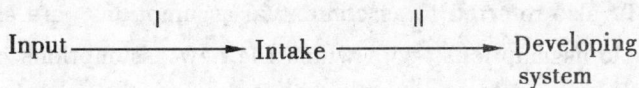

$$\text{Input} \xrightarrow{\quad I \quad} \text{Intake} \xrightarrow{\quad II \quad} \text{Developing system}$$

Figure 2. 1   Van Pattern's model of processing and acquisition (From Skehan, 1998: 47)

The first arrow focuses on the stage where input is processed to make form more salient, so that the learner can deliberately attempt to attend to aspects of form. The second arrow concerns explicit attempts by the learner to incorporate those elements in the input that have been attended to into a developing interlanguage system. The focus of instruction in input processing is at Stage I: the input-to-intake stage. What such instruction aims to do is to maximize the efficiency of this stage in the information-processing flow so that acquisitional processes can work more effectively. Subsequently, output processes can have access to the product of such acquisition.

2.4.3 Relevance Theory and Space Blending Theory: two cognitive theories

Since the relevance-theoretic approach alone to DMs fails to provide an accessible and operative model to explain the concrete and detailed on-line inferential processes despite its importance in the analysis of DMs, the present study is going to create blending models for the analysis of DMs in utterance generation and interpretation, based on the integrative study of the space blending theory (SB) and the relevance theory. Therefore, it is necessary to draw an overall picture of the two theories. Furthermore, the notion of pragmaticalization of DMs suggested by Erman (2001) prompts a blending model for the analysis of the process of pragmaticalization.

Relevance Theory (RT)

Sperber and Wilson propose the relevance theory (RT) in their book *Relevance: communication and cognition* (2001). It is a new approach to human communication and utterance interpretation. In this theory, they put forward the ostensive-inferential communication model, in which human communication is a cognitive activity involving two sides of the same communicative act: ostension on the part of the speaker and inference on the part of the hearer.

Ostension of the speaker conveys two layers of information. The first layer of information is what the speaker has made manifest; the second layer of information is the speaker's intention to make manifest the first layer of information. The former is the speaker's informative intention and the latter the communicative intention. Only when the hearer arrives at the communicative intention can the communication be successful.

Inference is a process of figuring out the speaker's intentions in appropriate contexts. RT holds that it is a two-phase process: the decoding phase and the inferential phase. At the decoding phase, the hearer decodes the information that has been encoded linguistically in an utterance and thus gets input to the inferential phase. At the inferential phase, the hearer constructs hypotheses of the speaker's intentions by contextualizing the decoded information (Wilson & Sperber, 1993).

Contexts in RT, also referred to as contextual assumptions, are essentially "a subset of the individual's old assumptions, with which the new assumptions combined to yield a variety of contextual effects" (Sperber & Wilson, 2001). Unlike the traditional notion, RT's notion of context is not limited to linguistic contexts or physical settings of the utterance. Instead, it refers to an individual's cognitive environments, in which a set of facts are manifest and accessible to him at the moment of processing new information. Neither is it fixed and determined before the producing of the utterance. On the contrary, it is selective and dynamic. In other words, the hearer chooses the appropriate contextual assumptions, tests them and constructs new assumptions during the process of communication.

The choice of context is determined by the search for relevance. Sperber and Wilson define relevance in the following statement: an assumption is relevant in a context if and only if it has some contextual effects in that context (Sperber & Wilson, 2001). Contextual effects result from the interaction of new and old information. When the new information conveyed in an utterance combines with the old contextual assumptions and yields contextual implications, strengthens the old contextual assumptions, or contradicts with the old contextual assumptions, it is said to have contextual effects and thus is relevant in the context.

Relevance is only a problem of degree. It is determined by the contextual effects achieved and the processing efforts used in the interpretation of an utterance. " The relevance of an input for an individual at a given time is a positive function of the cognitive benefits that he would gain from processing it, and a negative function of the processing efforts needed to achieve these benefits" (Sperber & Wilson, 2002), i. e. the greater the contextual effects, the more relevant the utterance is to the hearer; on the other hand, the greater the processing efforts, the less relevant the utterance.

According to the relevance theory, there are two principles of relevance. The first principle is the cognitive principle, which is a claim about the general tendency of human cognition. It is stated as follows: human cognition tends to be geared to the maximization of relevance. The cognitive principle is the principle of maximal relevance, defined as the greatest contextual effects for the least processing efforts. However, this concept merely reveals the universal cognitive tendency towards the greatest cognitive efficiency in communication. Actual successful communication is achieved by searching for optimal relevance.

The second principle is the communicative principle, defined as: every act of ostensive communication communicates a presumption of its own optimal relevance: adequate contextual effects for enough processing efforts, reaching a balance between the two aspects (Sperber & Wilson, 2001). That's to say, in utterance interpretation, the hearer is entitled to believe that, within the limits of the speaker's abilities and preferences, the speaker will make her utterance as relevant as possible or at least relevant enough to attract the hearer's attention, and as easy as possible to understand, so that her utterance will yield adequate contextual effects without unnecessary extra processing efforts.

Sperber and Wilson (2002) suggest that the communicative principle of relevance motivates the use of the following comprehension procedure in interpreting the speaker's meaning: that is when interpreting an utterance the hearer follows a path of least effort and stops when her expectations of relevance are satisfied.

Space Blending Theory (SB)

Fauconnier & Turner (1998) propose the space blending theory (or the conceptual integration theory) for the on-line dynamic cognitive work people do to construct meaning. According to them, language itself does not have meaning but rather prompts the construction of meaning in particular contexts with particular cultural models and cognitive resources. Visible language is only the "tip of the iceberg" of invisible meaning construction. The main task of cognitive linguistics is to reveal the "invisible part of the iceberg"—the cognitive mechanism behind linguistic phenomena. What the language form is doing is prompting us to build mental spaces. Mental spaces are "small conceptual packets constructed as we think and talk, for purpose of local understanding and action" (Fauconnier & Turner, 1996). They are set up as the result of activation of partial information in our cognitive domains, such as time, space, belief, reality and so on. In other words, spaces represent particular scenarios, which are structured by given domains. For example, "that surgeon is a butcher" involves a space in which a surgeon is performing an operation on a patient. The space only contains a small subset of knowledge of the domain of surgeon. In short, a mental space is a short-term construct informed by the more general and more stable knowledge structures associated with a particular domain. Mental spaces do not exist in isolation, nor are they stable. They are interconnected and can be modified as discourse and thought unfold. To put it into simple words, in everyday thinking and talking, we are constantly setting up spaces and creating new ones and performing cognitive operations on them. The construction of meaning is the result of those cognitive operations.

Conceptual integration (or blending) is one striking case of such cognitive operations. It is based on the blending of spaces. In blending, structures in mental spaces map onto each other and blend into new spaces. A basic conceptual integration network (CIN) consists of four spaces: two input spaces, a generic space and a blended space. In conceptual integration, a cross-space mapping is established between the two input spaces with partial structure mapped onto each other. This mapping represents the counterpart connections between two input spaces. As conceptual projection unfolds, whatever structure is recognized as belonging to both of the input spaces constitutes a generic space. At any moment in the construction, the generic space maps onto each of the inputs. It defines the current cross-space mapping between them. A given element in the generic space maps onto paired counterparts in the two input spaces. The fourth space, the blend, is established by selectively projecting structure from both input spaces, that is, not all elements from the inputs are projected to the blend. The blend not only contains the generic structure captured in the generic space, but also develops emergent structure of its own. Figure 2.2 shows a minimum conceptual integration network.

In Figure 2.2, the circles represent mental spaces; the dots in the circles represent elements in spaces; the solid lines represent cross-space mapping; the dotted lines represent selective projection between spaces; the square in the blend represent emergent structure. Emergent structure in the blend is not copied from the inputs, but rather constructed in three ways: composition, completion and elaboration. The structure and inferences developed in the blend can then project back to the other spaces in the network. People work over all four spaces simultaneously and this results in a dynamic process of the CIN.

This model is applied to the analysis of metaphor. For example, the blending model can account for how the incompetence inference is made from "that surgeon is a butcher". As is shown in Figure 2.3, we first build two input mental spaces by obtaining partly structure from two domains: the Surgeon domain, and the Butcher domain. Then a cross-space mapping is set up between the two spaces with the following counterpart connections: surgeon/butcher, patient (person)/ commodity (animal), scalpel/cleaver, operating room/abattoir, surgery/butchery and so on. These counterpart connections are projected to the blend. The generic space contains this shared frame: a person does something to another living creature with sharp instruments with a certain goal. And this frame maps onto the two input spaces and the blend as well. Blending makes it possible for the hybrid surgeon-butcher to perform surgery on a human in the same manner a butcher might operate on a cow carcass, holding a butcher knife and cutting a patient's body with the

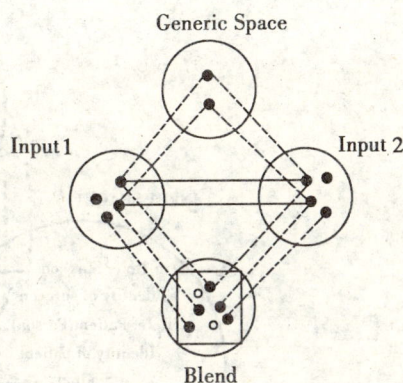

Figure 2.2 A conceptual integration network

butcher's techniques, which are commonly thought to have no mercy. This leads to the unpleasant thought that the result of the operation might be tragic. Therefore, the incompetence inference arises from the composition of the butcher's techniques and instruments with the surgeon's goal in the blend. (In Figure 2.3, solid lines represent the cross-space correspondences that constitute the mapping between the input spaces. The dotted lines represent projections between spaces. And the dashed line between the Surgeon role in Input 1 and the Butcher role in the blend represents the fact that the butcher in the blend is associated with the surgeon in Input 1.)

However, these cognitive operations are not unique to metaphor comprehension. All language comprehension involves the construction of meaning shown in CIN. According to Fauconnier & Turner (1998), most of our thinking, even in the simplest circumstances, is unbelievably complex but completely unconscious. Conceptual blending operates largely behind the scenes and the vast networks of mental spaces are quite beyond the reach of our conscious awareness. Our conscious experience is merely the cognitive products at the conscious level that appear so straightforward. Conceptual blending with emergent structures shows up in all areas of human behavior; cultures develop successive blends and the ones that become " entrenched ", i. e. established, can be transmitted to new generations. Some of the things that we often take to be the most basic in everyday living and thinking are the result of creative successive blends evolved by cultures over time. These entrenched blends can be learned by new generations as "knowledge"; learning does not necessarily involve consciously apprehending the full networks of blending. This can account for the fact that communicating with language seems so straightforward and natural that no one is ever aware of what is happening behind the scenes.

In China, the space blending model has recently been studied and applied to the study of various linguistic phenomena, such as metaphor, humor, translation or poetry. Chinese scholars have been studying the SB theory since 2000. Some of them focus on the theoretical studies of SB. Wang Shaohua (2001) introduces the theory itself and its

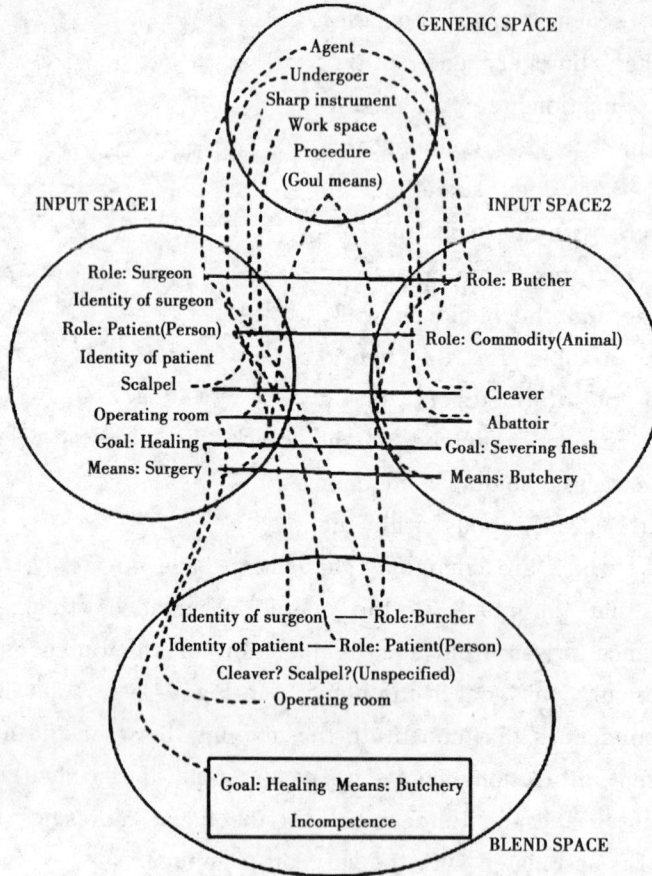

Figure 2.3   Conceptual integration network: surgeon as butcher (From Grady, et al 2005)

application in linguistics as well. Liu Zhengguang (2002) challenges certain ideas in this theory. A comparison is made in Huang Hua (2001) between the SB theory and the conceptual metaphor theory. While, Jiang Yong & Ma Yulei, (2003) and Jiang Yong, (2003) compare the SB theory with the RT and try to integrate the two most influential inferential theories. Others apply the theory to in a variety of fields, for example, the analysis of metaphor, humor, translation, poetry and the interpretation of idiomatic expressions or other linguistic phenomena (Wang Shaohua, 2002; Sun Ya, 2001; Wang Bing, 2001; Yu Weishen & Dong Pingrong, 2003). Their studies show that the SB theory has great explanatory power in various fields. However, the blending model has never been applied to the analysis of DMs.

2.4.4   Integrative study of Relevance Theory and Space Blending Theory

Based on a review of the development of the space blending theory and the contributions of this theory to cognitive linguistics, Wang Wenbing (2004) points out several problems with this theory. He says that since this theory is developed on the basis of the conceptual metaphor theory, it is somewhat metaphor-oriented. It proposes that only partial structure from the input spaces are selectively projected to the blend. But this cannot be the case with natural everyday discourse, for everyday discourse is always in a flow and the on-line interpretation goes on and on with linguistic units of all length following one another. Furthermore, the space blending theory seems unable to effectively explain the on-line interpretation of humor. He then proposes an interpretation process, which involves six types of cognitive operations on mental spaces and two forms of thought: inference and relevance. The introduction of inference and relevance into cognitive operations on mental spaces is undoubtedly an integration of RT and SB.

Integration of RT and SB is based on the similarities of both theories. According to Jiang Yong & Ma Yulei (2003) and Jiang Yong (2003), both theories are based on cognitive linguistics, which views the construction of meaning as the products of cognitive processing and emphasizes the importance of the backstage cognition. Jiang Yong (2003) highlights the similarities in three aspects: the metonymic function of language, the on-line inferential process and the blending of information. The metonymic function of language refers to the fact that language form itself can be very brief but some implicit information can be activated through metonymic mapping between explicit language form and implicit backstage information. This idea emphasizes the least effort principle in human cognition. The speaker tends to spend the least effort in providing as much information as is needed. As a result, the information that is encoded in language form is incomplete. Much of our understanding process relies on human capacity to activate contextual information and make inferences. The inferential process involves the blending of explicit information and the activated backstage information. A formulation is used to illustrate the blending process: $y = F(x+k)$, in which x stands for explicit information; k stands for the activated information, including personal experience, encyclopedic knowledge or other information stored in long term memory; y is the inference or conclusion and F is the total of all kinds of cognitive operations.

Jiang Yong (2003) then comments on the drawbacks of both theories. He says that RT only deals with the general communicative principle and a three-phase deductive inferential model and does not explain the detailed on-line cognitive processes involved in inference. SB can deal with the very problem by drawing a picture of conceptual blending to show the dynamic inferential process. But, according to him, SB neglects the role of contextual assumptions in cross-space mapping and blending. So he puts forward a pragmatic triangle inferential model, as he calls, the implicit space blending model, which is an integration of SB and RT. This model is illustrated in Figure 2. 4. In this model, there are two input spaces. One is called Explicit Input Space and only contains partial relevant contextual assumptions. The other is called the implicit input space and can provide all the contextual assumptions that are relevant. Contextual information from any domain can come into this space.

The blending model for the analysis of DMs put forward in the present study is based on the integrative study. It is proposed that DMs function as space-builders. They trigger the building of implicit input spaces.

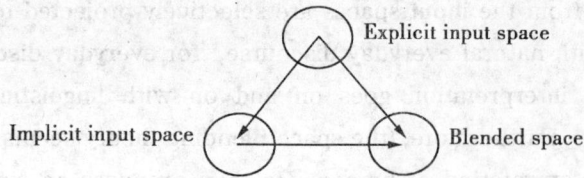

Figure 2.4　Implicit space blending mode 1

2.5　Research methodology of and empirical approaches to Discourse Markers

Subjects in the study were 65 freshmen from two intact classes in Wuhan University. They were engineering students, aged from 17 to 19. Among them were 15 female students and 50 male students. They were the first students in this university to use the *New Era Interactive English*, which is a kind of on-line English study package developed by Qinghua University. The primary function of the package is to provide students with authentic English and help them acquire native-like spoken English. They were required to self-study the on-line oral course in the autonomous study center whenever it was convenient for them. They were also required to finish some off-line exercises before they attended the "class meeting" twice a week, where they had the chance to participate in face-to-face communication in English.

The study collected three types of data: the oral data collected by recording and then transcribing the learners' speeches from a picture description task and a group discussion task; the test data collected by executing a cloze test and an utterance interpretation test and the input data collected from the 13 videos in the *New Era Interactive English* (Level One). All the data were processed by using Excel.

Two oral tasks were designed in order to investigate the use of DMs by the learners. The descriptions and discussions were recorded and later transcribed. Picture description was done two weeks before the end of the first term. Every subject was asked to describe a set of pictures in English to form one story. They were allowed three to five minutes to prepare before they began. Most subjects finished their description in about one minute or so. The longest took about three and a half minutes. For some reason, only 63 attended this task and one of them did not do the task as required. So the data included only transcripts of 62 descriptions. Group discussion done at the end of the first term as an oral test. The subjects were divided into groups of four and altogether there were 16 groups, with one group having one more subject. Each group got 1 from 8 topics for discussion by drawing lots. First, each subject was asked to state his or her opinion on this topic within one minute. Then, they exchanged opinions with their group members. Most groups finished the task in about 10 minutes. The time spent varied from 6 minutes to 13 minutes across groups. The recording lasted for about 160 minutes.

The data collected from the two tasks can cover two basic types of oral discourse: narrative and negotiation, these two types of data will hereafter be referred to as the "description data" and the "discussion data". There are two reasons for covering both. First of all, it is predicted that in describing things the learners may use some DMs more often while in stating and negotiating opinions they may use others more often. So, the data collected from both types may form an overall picture of their use of DMs and thus yield relatively more objective results than those from only one type alone. Secondly, if any differences do exist, the hypothesis that context difference influences L2 learners' use of DMs can be checked.

DMs in the transcripts were identified according to these criteria: connectivity and non-truth conditionality, with some consideration for optionality and initiality. Frequencies and percentages of DMs were calculated and presented in tables or figures. A comparison was made between the findings of this study and those presented in He Anping & Xu Manfei (2003) and in Trillo (2002).

Two tests were executed 10 days after the group discussion task was done. (For some reason, only 61 subjects attended the test.) The cloze test was intended to investigate the learners' knowledge about the usage of DMs. There are 15 blanks in the test, Each blank is given an item number. The subjects were required to fill in the blanks with the most appropriate DMs (This term "DMs" was not used in the directions of the test. Instead, a sample of different types of DMs was given). The utterance interpretation test was aimed at revealing the learners' metapragmatic awareness of the use of the DM *well*, i. e. the awareness of the DM's pragmatic use. In this test, the subjects were asked to write down their interpretations of the utterances, each containing a *well*. For ease of reference, the data from these two tests will hereafter be referred to as the "cloze data" and the "interpretation data".

Since the above data were collected during the first term, during which the subjects were supposed to self-study *New Era Interactive English* (Level One) and finish it by the end of the term, all the 13 units in Level One were taken as the oral input material. DMs used in 13 videos in Level One were counted.

The results of data collection are presented in tables and figures followed by discussion of the results. Presentations and discussions of results follow the same line as data collection procedure: oral data, test data and input data. Specifically, the oral data will be discussed in the following sequence: the description data and the discussion data respectively; a comparison of the two types of data; a comparison with findings from the native corpora, with a focus on IPU and frequencies of four DMs: *well, you know, I mean* and *you see*.

2.5.1   Data in the picture description

Table 2. 2 shows the percentages of DMs used by all the subjects in the picture description. Of the 17 types, *and* ranks first in the list with a total of 118 tokens, taking up about 34.6% of the sum of DMs. The first three DMs *and, so* (99 tokens) and *but* (47 tokens) altogether take up about 77% out of 343, which indicates that they are overwhelmingly used by the learners. There are relatively less tokens of the DMs *then* (27) and *because* (22), taking up 7.87% and 6.41% respectively. Still less tokens of the other 11 DMs can be found in the data (9 tokens of *now*, 6 tokens of *even*, 4 tokens of *oh*, 2 tokens of *of course* and 2 tokens of *in fact*). Seven of these DMs (*ok*, *besides*, *you know*, *I think*, *although*, *also* and *after all*) are used only once, each taking up only 0.29% of the total.

Table 2.2   **Frequencies (F) and percentages (%) of 17 DMs in the picture description**

DM	F	%
and	118	34.40
so	99	28.86
but	47	13.70
then	27	7.87
because	22	6.41
now	9	2.62
even	6	1.75
oh	4	1.17
of course	2	0.58
in fact	2	0.58
OK	1	0.29
besides	1	0.29
you know	1	0.29
I think	1	0.29
although	1	0.29
also	1	0.29
after all	1	0.29
Sum	343	100.00
Type	17	

A further analysis of these tokens reveals a striking pattern of the learners' use of DMs: most of the DMs used are those occurring frequently in written discourse. Except for *oh*, *OK* and *you know*, the other 14 DMs are used most frequently in written discourse. The three DMs, *oh*, *OK* and *you know*, occur almost always in spoken discourse. There are only a total of 6 tokens of these three DMs, accounting for 1.75% of the 343 tokens.

The data show another marked pattern that the learners use less or few DMs that have elaborative pragmatic meanings, such as *well*, *you know*, *you see*, and *I mean*. This pattern is illustrated in the following analysis. Usually, conjunctions, adverbials or adverbial phrases and prepositional phrases do not convey much elaborated pragmatic meaning. On the contrary, interjections and clauses are more likely to develop a wide variety of pragmatic meanings. When classified into their grammatical categories, most of these DMs are found to belong to conjunctions, adverbials or adverbial phrases and prepositional phrases, with the exception of 4 DMs (*oh*, *OK*, *you know* and *I think*, with a total of 7 tokens).

Table 2.3   **Classification of 17 DMs in the descriptive data**

Category	DM
Conjunction	and, so, but, because, although
Adverbial (phrase)	then, now, even, also, besides, after all, of course
Prepositional phrase	in fact
Interjection	oh, OK
Clause	you know, I think

According to Blakemore (1992), there are three main types of DMs in accordance with three kinds of contextual effects. DMs listed as typical examples of the three types in Blakemore (1992) all belong to the above categories except for one (*that's to say*), which is a clause. These three types of DMs either introduce contextual implications, or strengthen, or deny the old assumptions. Blakemore (1992) mentions that there are other types, for example, DMs that indicate what kind of contextual implications the hearer is expected to derive. However, she does not provide any detailed illustration of them. The reason for her not illustrating in detail may lie in the difficulty in classifying definitely these types of DMs due to their developed pragmatic meanings, which might be far away from their literal meanings, such as *well* and *you know*. For example, in sequence (1), *well* no longer means fine or good. It expresses the short-circuited information that there is some reason for the speaker to kill his wife. In sequence (2), *you know* is not a subject-predicate structure followed by a that-clause, but rather a DM that "separates constitutes that are usually contiguous" (Macaulay, 2002). There are also prosodic features of *you know* as a DM. "It is generally uttered as a single unit with a falling intonation and often at a slightly lower pitch and volume than the surrounding speech" (Macaulay, 2002). Prosodic features are especially important for interjections (*oh*, for example) to express various pragmatic meanings.

(1) —Did you kill your wife?

　　—*Well*, yes.

(2) I could see *you know* the hunted look on his face.

In the descriptive data, except for the DM *you know*, the DMs used by the learners do not show obvious pragmatic elaboration, that is, the development of pragmatic meanings away from the literal meanings. In sequences (3) to (7), the meanings of these DMs are relatively easier to recognize. The two DMs, *and* and *then*, are used as sequential markers (Liu Lijin, 2002) to mark the continuity of narration. The DMs, *so* and *because*, indicate the clause-effect relationship between adjacent discourse units. The DM *but* indicates a contrastive or unexpected result. There is only one instance of the DM *you know* as is shown in sequence (8), and not a single instance of *well*. Although there are 4 instances of the DM *oh*, the use of this DM falls into a single pattern, as is shown in sequence (9). In sum, DMs that the learners use frequently are those with less elaborative pragmatic meanings. On the contrary, those DMs that express a variety of pragmatic meanings are very rarely used.

(3) One day a man was ill. *So* he went to hospital and had a test.

(4) *But* after a few days, another test report was given to him.

(5) When he went home he had a lot of pills, *because* he wanted to be healthy again.

(6) Some days later, he went to the hospital again. *And* the doctor checked him carefully again.

(7) *Then* the doctor discovered they had made a mistake.

(8) Because, *you know*, he knew he was going to die.

(9) *Oh*, it's very terrible!

2.5.2 Data in the group discussion

Table 2.4 shows the percentages of DMs in the group discussion. Altogether 32 types of DMs are identified in the data. Only 17 DMs are shown in the table in order to compare with the data in the picture description, in which the other 15 DMs do not occur. The 15 DMs are: *in conclusion, in addition, in my mind, in that case, in other words, that means, or, on the one hand, on the other hand, first/first of all, second(ly), third, at last, we know/as we know,* and *I know*.

Table 2.4 shows that four DMs (*I think, but, and,* and *so*) are dominantly used. There are a total of 158 tokens of *I think*, with the highest percentage of 31.29%, followed by *but* (95 tokens, taking up 18.81%), *and* (90 tokens, taking up 17.82%), and *so* (69 tokens, taking up 13.66%). All of the four DMs together occur 81.58% out of 505. The other 13 DMs as a whole occur only 18.42%. This pattern is very similar to that in the data description. It will be discussed in detail in the comparison between both data.

There are uses of DMs that are obviously influenced by the nature ofthe discussion task itself. In the discussion task, it is usually necessary to state personal opinions, provide reasons or examples for these opinions and then make a conclusion. Therefore, such DMs as *I think, in my opinion* or *in my mind, for example, in a word* or *in conclusion*, etc. find their way in the data in the group discussion.

Table 2.4   **Frequencies (F) and percentages (%) of 17 DMs in the group discussion**

DM	F	%
I think	158	31.29
but	95	18.81
and	90	17.82
so	69	13.66
because	22	4.36
for example	18	3.56

续表

DM	F	%
in my opinion	13	2.57
also	10	1.98
although	7	1.39
OK	6	1.19
in fact	4	0.79
now	4	0.79
in a word	3	0.59
oh	2	0.40
then	2	0.40
of course	1	0.20
after all	1	0.20
Sun	505	100.00

Surprisingly, there is a lack of the use of DMs that show interaction between the interlocutors. To account for this pattern, the present author studied the way the subjects behaved in the discussion task. It was found that there was indeed a lack of negotiation between group members. They stated their opinions the way they wrote a composition. As a result, even at the opinion exchanging stage of the task, they only paid attention to what was expressed instead of how to involve their listeners in the process of speech. That may be part of the reason why they rarely use DMs like *you know*, *you see*, *I mean* and *well*, categorized as "involvement markers" by Trillo (2002).

2.5.3　Comparison of the two kinds of data

A comparison was made between the picture-description data and the group-discussion data to see what DMs were used more frequently in which context. There are striking similarities in DM use across contexts. First of all, the learners tend to overuse the 4 DMs (*but*, *and*, *so* and *because*) in both contexts. As is shown in Figure 2.5 and Figure 2.6, 4 out of the top 5 DMs used in both tasks are the same, i.e. *but*, *and*, *so* and *because*. In the description data, where the sum of the percentages of its top 5 DMs is 91.25%, the percentages of the 4 DMs can amount to 83.38%. In the discussion data, the total percentage of its top 5 DMs is 85.94% and the same 4 DMs can amount to 54.65%. Another similarity is that there is not too much variation in types of DMs that the learners use, despite the different speech contexts. As is shown in Table 2.5, of the 17 DMs, 14 are the same. Only three DMs (*even*, *besides* and *you know*) occur in the picture-description data but not in the group-discussion data. This strongly leads to the conclusion that DMs used by the learners are limited to such types as *but*, *and*, *so*, *because*, etc.

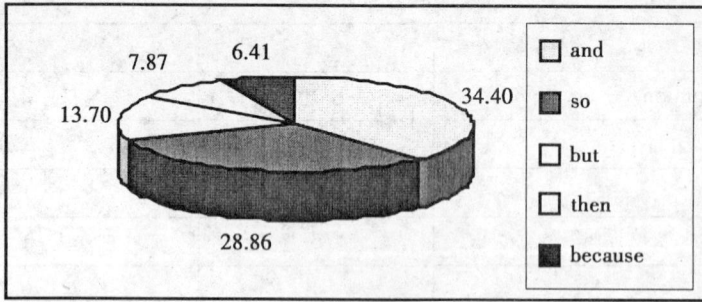

Figure 2.5 Percentages of the top 5 DMs in the picture description data

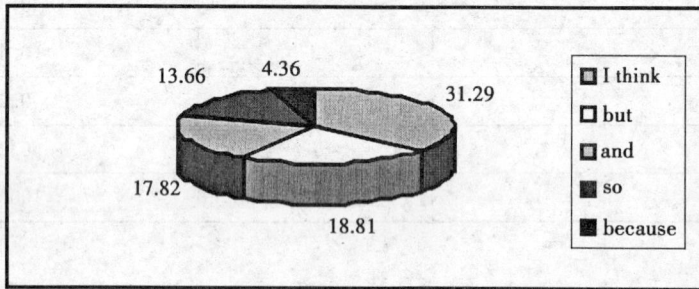

Figure 2.6 Percentages of the top 5 DMs in the group-discussion data

Table 2.5 **Comparison of types and frequencies of 17 DMs in the two kinds of data**

DM	Picture-description	Group-discussion
I think	1	158
but	47	95
and	118	90
so	99	69
because	22	22
also	1	10
although	1	7
OK	1	6
in fact	2	4
now	9	4
then	27	2
oh	4	2
of course	2	1
after all	1	1
even	6	0
besides	1	0
you know	1	0
in a word	0	3
for example	0	3
in my opinion	0	13

Some differences in DM use can be attributed to context differences. On the whole, a wider variety of DMs are used in the group-discussion task than in the picture-description task. 32 types of DMs are used in the group-discussion task, but only 17 types in the picture-description task. Three DMs (*in a word, for example* and *in my opinion*), together with 15 other DMs occur in the group-discussion but not in the picture-description data. This difference may be caused by different task requirements. In the picture-description task, the pictures keep the subjects from elaborating. In contrast, the group-discussing around some topics allows for more personal views and various ways to express such views, and thus DMs are more likely to be used to introduce utterances that express these views. Meanwhile, differences in the use of specific types of DMs are obviously caused by context differences. The most striking difference in type is that, the occurrences of *I think* increase significantly in the group-discussion, in contrast to the single instance of it in the picture-description. However, the most frequently used DM in the picture-description task is *and*. This difference can be easily attributed to context difference. The picture-description task requires primarily narration. In narrative discourse, it is necessary to make clear the sequential order of what happens first and what happens next. So sequential DMs like *and* or *then* are more often used than others. Since there is less need to state personal opinions and the reasons for such opinions in narration, DMs like *I think* or *in my opinion* are rarely used. By contrast, in the discussion task, which includes mostly negotiation of opinions, stating personal opinions, challenging others' opinions and coming to a conclusion are the main types of discourse. Therefore, the use of such DMs as *I think* or *in my opinion*, *but* and *so* is unavoidable.

However, as the most salient dimension of speech context, the speaker role does not show any influence on the learners' use of DMs, not in accordance with Fuller's (2003) findings about the influence of speaker roles on DM use by native speakers. In theory, the group-discussion task will induce the use of "involvement markers" (Trillo, 2002) such as *well* and *you know*, for this task requires the subjects to take turns in speech and negotiate meaning with each other. But this is not the case in the learners' speech. Reflections on how the oral data were collected reveal one thing in common concerning these subjects' role in the two tasks: performing the oral tasks at the presence of the researcher (in their eyes, the teacher). Therefore, sometimes these subjects were addressing the researcher instead of their group members. Since the researcher was not acting as a participant, but rather an outside controller, these subjects tended to use few DMs showing interaction and response. In a word, the design of the present study might have influenced the results. Whether the learners are able to mark the speaker role by using certain DMs remains unclear. Therefore, the influence of the speaker role on the learners' use of DMs needs to be further studied.

2.5.4   Comparison with the native corpora

Another finding concerning both tasks is that the learners very rarely use DMs like *well, you know, I mean* and *you see*, which occur most frequently in native corpora.

Trillo (2002), in the study of DMs in non-native speakers of English, calculates the Index of Pragmatic Use (IPU), which shows the degree of pragmatic use of an element in a corpus. This index is calculated as follows: number of pragmatic realizations divided by the overall presence of an element. According to Trillo (2002), IPU is very helpful for stylistic and pedagogical purposes, because it shows the probability of an element being used as a DM. The higher the number, the more often this element is used as a DM. Also, since different styles of speech show different patterns of use of DMs, for which both Fuller's (2003) and Norrick's (2001) studies provide some evidence, the IPU can be used in comparative analysis of DMs in different styles of speech.

Trillo (2002) calculates the IPU of 6 DMs (*look, listen, you know, I mean, well* and *you see*) in the London-Lund Corpus—the adult corpus, and finds that four DMs have very high IPU (*you know* 90.9%, *I mean* 95%, *well* 87.4%, *you see* 86.1%), which indicates that they are very often used by native adults as DMs. In the child corpus, the percentages are very much similar to the adult corpus (*I mean* 100%, *well* 97.8%, *you see* 86.1%), with the exception of *you know*, the IPU of which is only 53.4%. Despite the slight difference, a conclusion can be made that these four elements are very frequently used as DMs by both adults and children.

Another set of statistics points to the same conclusion. According to Trillo (2002), of the totals of DM use in the London-Lund Corpus, *you know, I mean, well, you see* show the highest percentage in native speakers, except for *yes, yeah* and *no*. Specifically, *well* occurs 10.33%, *you know* 9.27%, *I mean* 3.18% and *you see* 2.73%.

Table 2.6   **Percentages (%) of 4 DMs in the London-Lund Corpus**

DMs	%
well	10.33
you know	9.27
I mean	3.18
you see	2.73

In sharp contrast to these findings, the Chinese learners rarely use these DMs. There is only a single instance (*you know*, the percentage of which is 0.29%) of the four DMs. Instead, the learners overuse a limited range of DMs (*and, but, so, I think*). This results in the high percentages of these DMs. In other words, the uses of DMs are much too concentrated. On the one hand, the learners frequently use those DMs that not usually occur in native speech. On the other hand, DMs that seldom occur in the learners' speech happen to be those most frequently used in native data. So, even though the learners do use many DMs, there are great differences between what they use and what should be used. They fail to use DMs the way native speakers do. Therefore, we can come to the conclusion that their acquisition of DMs is not successful.

He & Xu (2003) present the frequencies of 19 "small words" in different corpora. Some of the small words are what the present study refers to as DMs. Table 3. 6 shows the frequencies of 8 DMs out of the 19 presented in He & Xu (2003).

Table 2. 7   **Frequencies (per 10000 words) of 8 DMs in three corpora**
(Adapted from He & Xu, **2003**)

DM	ICE-GB	COLT	CHIN
well	68	23	7
oh	59	75	26
I mean	42	14	18
you know	36	36	20
I think	34	11	63
OK	15	15	24
I know	0	9	0
you see	5	2	2

Note: ICE-GB is a native adult corpus and COLT is a native teenager corpus.

CHIN is a spoken English corpus of advanced Chinese learners.

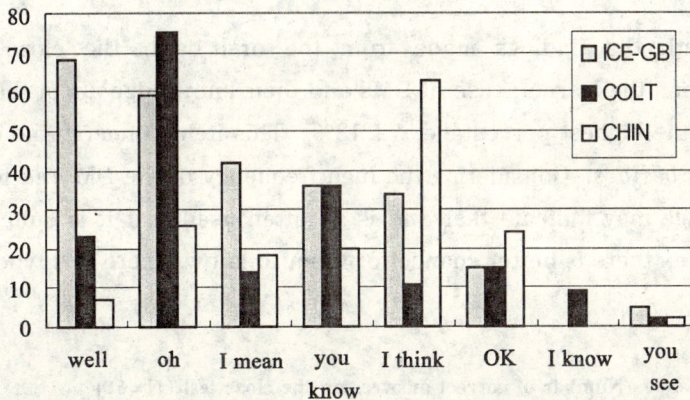

Figure 2. 7   Presenting frequencies (per 10,000 words) of 8 DMs in three corpora

As is shown in Figure 2. 7, Chinese learners' uses of these 8 DMs differ from those of both native adults and teenagers. Chinese learners use *I think* the most frequently. But neither adults nor teenagers in the native corpora use the DM as often as they do. This is consistent with the finding presented earlier in the present study that the DM *I think* is overused by the subjects. In addition, He & Xu (2003) have found that both the high proficiency group and the low group use this DM very often. This might be the clue that all Chinese learners tend to overuse the DM *I think*.

On the other hand, there is a lack of the use of the DM *well* in the Chinese learner corpus. The DM *well* is the most frequently used DM in native adult corpus, 68 per 10,000 words. But it does not often occur in native teenagers and Chinese learners (7 per 10,000 words). According to He & Xu (2003), *well* might be one of the indexes to oral proficiency. So they compare the high oral proficiency group and the low group to see whether the use of such words differs between the groups. They find that 80% of 43 instances of *well* occur in the more proficient learners. The high group use *well* far more often than the low group, 34 verses 1. The finding holds true in the case of *you know* and *I mean*. Therefore, oral proficiency level is another part of the reason why the learners in the present study use very few DMs like *well*, *you know* and *I mean* (see the discussion of the discussion data on p. 34). Even advanced Chinese learners (English majors in their junior or senior years) use the DM *well* so rarely; it is not surprising to find that the subjects (non-English-major freshmen) never use this DM, for they are less likely to have developed higher oral proficiency in English than senior English majors.

2.5.5 Data in the cloze test

The results of the cloze test are shown in Table 3.7. The second column shows the number of correct answers out of 61 for each item. The corresponding percentages are shown in Figure 3.4. The average percentage is 40.22%, 368 (the sum of correct answers) out of 915 (15 items by 61 subjects). On the whole, more than half of the blanks do not have the correct answers. This may indicate that the learners lack the knowledge about the use of these DMs.

Compared with the findings made from the oral data, the cloze data reveal a relationship between the learners' use of DMs and their knowledge about the corresponding DMs. Item 1 has the highest percentage, 72.13%. This item concerns the use of DMs like *and*, *moreover* or *besides*. Considering the high frequency of the DM *and* in the oral data, this high percentage may indicate that *and* is so often used that it is quite familiar to the subjects, therefore, there is better chance for them to know where this type of DMs should be used.

Table 2.8   **Number of correct answers on the cloze test (N=61)**

Item	Correct
1	44
2	4
3	15
4	29
5	13
6	17
7	14
8	33
9	25

续表

Item	Correct
10	33
11	24
12	14
13	43
14	17
15	43
Sum	368

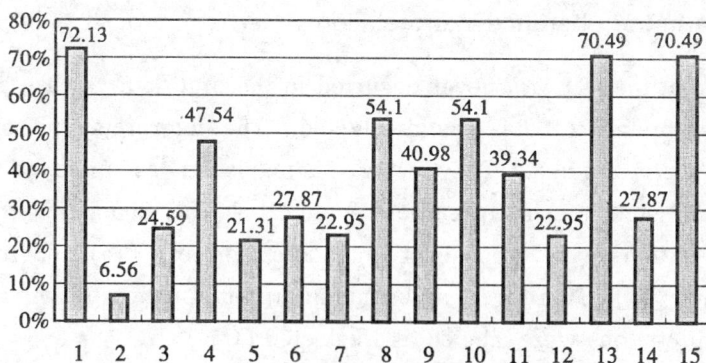

Figure 2.8　Percentages of correct answers on the cloze test

Second to Item 1, Item 13 and Item 15 have a percentage of 70. 49% . Item 13 concerns the use of *but* and Item 15 *I think*. This result is not surprising. The indication of this percentage is similar to that in the case of Item 1. In the oral data, *but* is one of the first five most frequently used DMs in both tasks and *I think* is dominantly used in the discussion task. Therefore, the subjects are more likely to use the two DMs correctly.

Item 8 and Item 10 go next with the same percentage, 54.1% . Item 8 concerns the use of *you know* and Item 10 the use of *well*. This result seems contradictory to the finding about *well* and *you know* in the oral data, where there is no single instance of the DM *well* and only one instance of *you know*. One distinction can account for this contradiction: communicative competence verse linguistic knowledge. Knowing where to use a particular item in a cloze test does not follow that the person will use it in actual discourse, because the former reflects the linguistic knowledge while the latter communicative competence. Communicative competence and linguistic knowledge usually do not develop in balance in EFL learners (Trillo, 2002 on the "binary track" of function and form). Despite the relatively high percentages on Item 8 and Item 10, the percentages are quite low (only more than 20%) on Item 12 and Item 14, which also test the use of *well* and *you know*. Moreover, there are several instances of *well* used in the wrong places. The uncertainty about use of *well* in the learners will be discussed in the case study of this DM that follows soon.

Both Item 4 and Item 9 test the use of *so*. The percentages are respectively 47.54% and 40.98%, both being a little higher than the average. This result is a little surprising considering that *so* is very frequently used by the learners in the oral tasks, ranking fourth and second respectively. On the other 6 items (Item 2, *oh*; Item 3, *furthermore/I mean*; Item 5, *but*; Item 6, *you know/after all*; Item 7, *therefore*; Item 11, *I mean*), the percentages are all below the average. Except for Item 5, all the other 5 items concern the use of DMs that either occur rarely (e.g., *oh*, *after all*, *you know*) or never occur (e.g., *I mean*, *therefore*) in the learners' speech in both oral tasks. To conclude, there is a relationship between the learners' use of DMs and their knowledge about the usage. The more the learners use a DM, the better they know how to use it, or vice versa.

2.5.6 Data in the utterance interpretation

Considering that the DM *well* never occurred in the oral data, a case study of *well* in the utterance interpretation data was conducted. The interpretations of 6 utterances containing *well* were studied. They were distinguished as pragmatic or semantic interpretations. The semantic interpretations were labeled as Semantic (S). The correct pragmatic interpretations were labeled as Pragmatic Correct (P+) and the incorrect as Pragmatic Incorrect (P-). There were still some interpretations totally avoiding interpreting *well*. These interpretations were labeled as Neglected (O).

Table 2.9 and Table 2.10 show the numbers and percentages of each type of interpretations of *well* in six utterances by 61 subjects. The Sum column in Table 2.9 presents the total number of each type of interpretations on all six utterances, and the Overall (%) column in Table 210 presents the corresponding percentages of the sums in a total of 366 interpretations (6 utterances by 61 subjects).

Table 2.9 **Number of four types of interpretations of *well* (N=61)**

Type	No.1	No.2	No.3	No.4	No.5	No.6	Sum
P+	7	23	10	13	14	3	70
P-	32	18	13	30	7	27	127
S	5	11	2	1	6	4	29
O	17	9	36	17	34	27	140

Table 2.10 **Percentage (%) of four types of interpretations of *well* (N=61)**

Type	No.1	No.2	No.3	No.4	No.5	No.6	Overall (%)
P+	11.48	37.70	16.39	21.31	22.95	4.92	19.13
P-	52.46	29.51	21.31	49.18	11.48	44.26	34.70
S	8.20	18.03	3.28	1.64	9.84	6.56	7.92
O	27.87	14.75	59.02	27.87	55.74	44.26	38.25

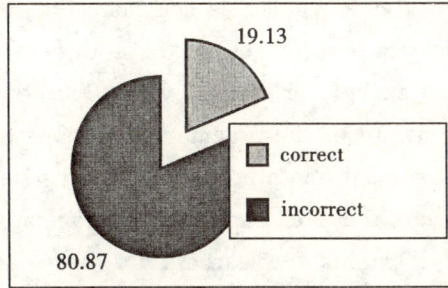

Figure 2.9   Percentages of correct and incorrect interpretations

A detailed study of the figures in Tables 2. 9 and 2. 10 shows that most of the interpretations are incorrect. There are very few instances of semantic interpretations on each utterance and the overall semantic interpretations on all the six utterances add up to only 29, taking up 7. 92% of the total of 366. But more than 1/3 of the interpretations neglect the DM *well* and provide neither pragmatic nor semantic interpretations. The overall instances of interpretations neglecting *well* are 140, taking up 38. 25% of the total. Neglecting instances even amount to 36 (59. 02%) on No. 3 and 34 (55. 74%) on No. 5. Although pragmatic interpretations (P+ and P-) account for a large proportion (53. 83%) of the total, only 70 (19. 13%) are correct and 127 (34. 7%) are incorrect. Three out of the four types of interpretations: Semantic (S), Pragmatic Incorrect (P-) and Neglected (O), are all considered incorrect, adding up to 80. 87% of the total. The percentages of correct and incorrect interpretations are presented in Figure 3. 5.

Further study of the pragmatic interpretations and the neglecting instances points to the fact that to a large extent, the learners are aware of the pragmatic meanings of DMs, although they do not necessarily know the meanings exactly. Figure 2. 10 presents the percentages of pragmatic interpretations, i. e. the sum of Pragmatic Correct (P +) and Pragmatic Incorrect (P-). It is shown that on three of these utterances most of the learners are aware that the DM *well* functions pragmatically. The percentages of pragmatic interpretations are all higher than 60% on No. 1, No. 2 and No. 4. Specifically, No. 4 has the highest percentage 70. 49%, followed by No. 2 (67. 21%), and No. 1 (63. 93%). But fewer learners are aware of the pragmatic functions of *well* on the other three utterances. The percentages of pragmatic interpretations do not amount to 50%, specifically, 49. 18% on No. 6, 37. 7% on No. 3 and 34. 43% on No. 5. The percentages of neglecting instances are relatively high. The reason for the learners to neglect the DM *well* may be that they are not aware of its functions and thus regard it as unimportant, or that they are aware of its functions but are not sure what exactly its pragmatic meaning is. Considering that the word *well* as an adverb must be very familiar to the learners, they are very likely to notice that *well* is not used as an adverb in the six utterances. So, the latter account sounds more reasonable, that is, the neglecting instances show the learners' awareness of its pragmatic functions. Therefore, the three types of interpretations (P +, P- and O) all indicate that these learners are aware of the pragmatic functions of *well*. Figure 2. 11 shows the percentages of the three types as a whole, as contrasted to the percentages of semantic interpretations (S). The overall percentages of these three types on five utterances all amount to more than 90% (except for No. 2, with 81. 97%). This indicates that the majority of the learners are aware of the pragmatic functions of *well*. On each utterance there are a few instances of semantic interpretations. This suggests that only a small part of the learners are still unaware that *well* can function pragmatically in utterance.

In conclusion, to a large extent, the learners are aware of the pragmatic use of the DM *well*, but most often are either incorrect or uncertain about their pragmatic meanings. In other words, despite the learners' metapragmatic awareness of the use of *well*, they lack the knowledge or the certainty about the exact pragmatic meanings.

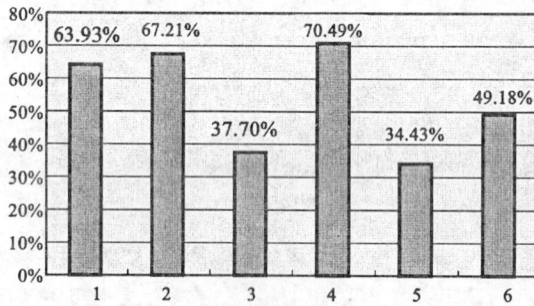

Figure 2. 10   Percentages of pragmatic interpretations (P+ and P–)

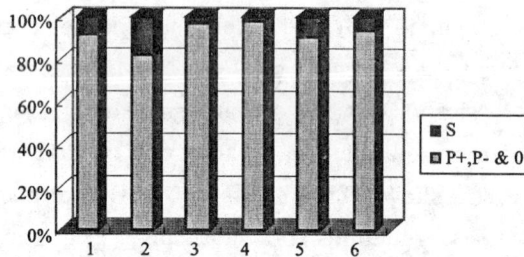

Figure 2. 11   Contrasting the three types of interpretations (P+, P- & O) as a whole
and semantic interpretations (S) in percentage

This finding explains why the DM *well* does not occur in the oral data. Receptive language skills (understanding speech or written text) usually develop prior to productive skills (speaking or writing) (Spolsky, 1989). Since the learners have not acquired the pragmatic meanings of this DM and thus are not able to interpret it correctly, they cannot be expected to use it. And according to Trillo (2002), unlike native speakers, non-native learners do not develop the "formal track" and the "pragmatic track" simultaneously. They follow a "form to function process" in their linguistic development. Therefore, simply knowing that it functions pragmatically in interpretation of an utterance does not result in the actual use of this DM in the learners' own speech.

2.5.7   Data in the sufficiency of the input

New Era Interactive English (Level One) consists of 13 units. Each unit has a short video on a particular topic. It is observed that the characters in these videos use a number of DMs. The present study thus investigates the sufficiency of the input.

Table 2. 11   **Frequencies (F) and percentages (%) of 8 DMs occurring in the 13 videos**

DM	F	%
oh	29	35. 37
well	16	19. 51
OK	15	18. 29
and	5	6. 10
but	5	6. 10
so	4	4. 88
yeah	4	4. 88
you know	4	4. 88
SUM	82	100. 00

Table 2. 11 shows the frequencies and percentages of the 8 DMs occurring in these videos. It is shown that *oh, well* and *OK* are used very often, with relatively higher percentages, specifically, *oh* occurring 35. 37% , *well* 19. 51% and *OK* 18. 29% . *Yeah* and *you know* each occurs 4 times, i. e. 4. 88% of the total use of DMs. There are altogether 14 instances of *and, but* and *so* in 13 videos. The percentages of *and* (6. 1%), *but* (6. 1%) and *so* (4. 88%) are far too low, considering the results from the oral data presented earlier. The percentages of these three DMs in the input data add up to only 17. 08% , while in the oral data they amount to 77. 42% and 50. 5% in two tasks respectively. This may indicate that the learners' overuse of the three DMs is not the result of too much exposure to them in spoken discourse, but rather the result of too much input of these elements in written text. The learners' use of DMs may be more influenced by written text rather than spoken. They use more DMs that appear mostly in written text, such as *and, but, so, because, although,* etc. On the contrary, DMs (like *well, oh, OK, you know, I mean,* etc.) that are typical of spoken discourse are very rarely used. If there are instances of such DMs, they occur mostly in those orally proficient learners.

Considering the fact that the learners self-study their oral course and that formal instruction on pragmatic knowledge falls short, more emphases should be laid on formal instruction in order to parallel the "binary track"—linguistic form and pragmatic function.

2.5.8   The patterns and implications of Discourse Markers

The analysis and discussion of the different types of data have revealed in the present study some patterns of DM use by Chinese EFL learners. Firstly, the learners rarely use those DMs that are typical of speech, like *you know*, *you see*, *I mean* and *well*. In other words, they do not use appropriate DMs to involve their listeners in the process of speech. On the other hand, they tend to use many DMs that occur more often in written rather than in spoken English, for example, *in conclusion*, *in a word*, *in other words*, *in addition*, *in that case* and *as we know*, etc. And they carry on their speech the way they write a composition. In a word, the learners' use of DMs is more writing-oriented than communication-oriented.

Secondly, the learners tend to frequently use those DMs with less elaborative pragmatic meanings. On the contrary, those DMs that express a variety of pragmatic meanings are very rarely used. This pattern may indicate that the acquisition of pragmatic use by these learners has not developed hand in hand with linguistic knowledge, although they have achieved intermediate level in written English (between the level of beginners and senior English majors). Their development of pragmatic competence falls behind that of linguistic competence. This pattern supports the notion of the "binary track" (Trillo, 2002) in L2 learners' acquisition of a foreign language, and also the hypothesis that in the acquisition of DMs, Chinese learners of English follow the developmental track from the literal meanings to the pragmatic meanings of DMs.

Thirdly, the learners tend to overuse several DMs and on the other hand rarely use those that appear very frequently in native corpora. The DMs used by the learners are limited in terms of types. This is supported by the findings about the ranking of the most frequently used DMs in the oral data, with *but*, *and*, *so* and *because* being four of the top five DMs in both data. Meanwhile, the total percentage of these most frequently used DMs is surprisingly high. By contrast, the use of DMs like *well* and *you know* is incredibly rare. This pattern answers the question raised earlier concerning the overuse and the rarity of use of DMs in Chinese EFL learners. Moreover, the striking similarities in this pattern concerning both tasks suggest that pragmatic fossilization in DM use does exist in Chinese EFL learners' speech.

Apart from the findings about the patterns, the differences in DMs used in the two tasks shows that context differences impose some influence on the learners' use of DMs. However, there is no evidence that the learners are able to mark their speaker roles in the tasks by using appropriate DMs.

Meanwhile, the present study finds that there is a relationship between the learners' use of DMs and their knowledge about the usage. The more the learners use a DM, the better they know how to use it, or vice versa. It also suggests that the learners are aware of the pragmatic use of the DM *well*, but they have not acquired its exactly use or meaning. This may lead to the implication that formal instruction on DMs might be necessary in order to help the learners acquire the DM *well* and other DMs in general, thus enhance their pragmatic competence.

2.6 Factors contributing to the acquisition of Discourse Markers

Some problems have been found in the above analysis, which suggest that the learners have not succeeded in acquiring DMs despite their development of linguistic competence. Compared to native speakers, these learners show obvious differences in DM use. Those frequently used by native speakers seldom occur in these learners' spoken discourse. Since the use of DMs can contribute to naturalness and interactivity of speech, this deficiency in DM use results in unnaturalness and awkwardness, which are characteristic of the learners' speech. According to Wilson and Sperber (1993), DMs encode procedural meaning and cannot be brought to consciousness. So it is often difficult to notice, let alone to acquire DMs, especially for L2 learners. But this can only be one of the reasons for the learners' difficulty in DM acquisition. Other possible factors contributing to the learners' acquisition of DMs are discussed from the three aspects: noticing of DMs, instruction on DMs and processing of DMs.

2.6.1   Noticing of Discourse Markers

According to Schmidt (1990), only when input is noticed can it become available for intake and effective processing. Therefore, a degree of awareness is important before material can be incorporated into a developing interlanguage system. The acquisition of DMs by L2 learners is first analyzed according to the six influences upon noticing suggested by Schmidt (1990).

Theoretically, other things being equal, the more frequent a DM is in the input stream, the more likely it is to be noticed and then become integrated in the interlanguage system. However, no evidence can be found from the input data that the more frequently occurring DMs have been noticed and integrated into the learners' interlanguage. *Oh, well* and *OK* occur more frequently, but are far less frequently used by the learners than *and*, *but* and *so*. Therefore, frequent use of *and*, *but* and *so* in the learners' speech is not due to frequent exposure to these DMs in spoken discourse, but rather may be because *and*, *but* and *so* occur more often in written discourse. In the case of these learners, neither instruction on nor exposure to spoken discourse is as sufficient as that on/to written discourse. Under such circumstances, the development of spoken interlanguage is not likely to be in balance with that of written. To facilitate their acquisition of DMs, the learners must be exposed more to spoken discourse than now and be instructed on the use of DMs. Then, other things being equal, the more a DM stands out in the input stream, the more likely that it will be noticed. Whereas, according to Wilson and Sperber (1993), DMs express procedural information and cannot be brought to consciousness. In other words, DMs are not perceptively salient because they do not express conceptual meaning. Therefore, there is slim chance for DMs to be noticed and acquired by the learners. Although they are not perceptively salient, the learners' awareness of DMs can be aroused by way of instruction. Instruction can make salient the less obvious aspects of the input. It channels attention and brings into awareness what otherwise would have been missed. Considering that DMs are not easy to be noticed, instruction seems quite necessary in the case of DM acquisition. Otherwise, they would often be neglected. What the present oral course falls short of is the opportunity available for a focus on DMs as well as other forms in spoken discourse in the context of meaningful language use. So, it is advocated here that formal instruction on DMs be introduced. Only when this is done can acquisition of DMs be more efficient and fruitful. Processing ability concerns the learner's capacity to deal with the range of forms in input. A person's processing ability is limited. When part of the capacity is occupied with one task, less is available for another. So when the learners concentrate more on meaning or on the forms other than DMs, they are less likely to notice DMs, and thus the acquisition of DMs is less likely to take place. In order to make the learners fully aware of DM use, tasks should not be too demanding. Other aspects of language should not distract them too much to make sure that enough capacity is available for the processing of DMs. This influence is relevant to the sixth one, task demand, which follows soon. Readiness refers to the current state of the interlanguage system; it shows whether a learner is ready to acquire an item or not. According to two studies on the acquisition of DMs by young children (Montes, 1999; Andersen, et al, 1999), the acquisition of DMs tends to develop from that of the literal meanings to that of the pragmatic meanings. For the learners who have acquired the literal meanings of DMs, a prediction can be made that the noticing and then the acquisition of the pragmatic meanings of DMs will subsequently take place, because it is the "next" thing to be acquired. Finally, according to Schmidt (1990), more demanding tasks consume more attentional resources for task transaction, and then less attention is available for focus on form. When a learner's limited processing capacity system is overloaded, noticing is less likely to take place. So the design of tasks for formal instruction on DMs should take task difficulty into consideration.

In conclusion, the lack of frequent input as well as perceptive salience and instruction may have led to the learners' failure to acquire DMs. To ensure their acquisition of DMs, formal instruction should be adopted so that DMs are frequent and salient enough to be noticed and then acquired. Formal instruction should take into consideration processing capacity and the current state of the learners' interlanguage, and task difficulty as well.

2.6.2　Instruction on Discourse Markers

Trillo (2002) proposes a "binary track" that learners of a foreign language follow in their linguistic development: the formal track and the pragmatic track. Non-native learners develop both tracks through formal instruction, rather than by means of natural language contact, because they are not in a target language environment. However, it is difficult to produce a (pseudo)-natural foreign language context that the development of pragmatic competence demands. Consequently, the pragmatic knowledge is often neglected in the curriculum and thus the use of DMs becomes fossilized both in the quantity and the diversity of elements used (Trillo, 2002). He mentions that there is an urgent need to bring the consistent teaching of DMs to language instruction and the need to investigate the development of DMs in speech in order to monitor pragmatic competence and pragmatic fossilization in non-native speakers.

Instruction can be conducted in various ways. It can be directed at cognitive goals, for example, focusing on drawing the learners' attention to DMs used by native speakers and allowing them to acquire the pragmatic use of DMs and thus developing their communicative competence. Instruction can also be directed at metacognitive goals, attempting to train the learners to use effective learning strategies. It is more desirable for the learners to acquire the pragmatic use of DMs in carefully designed tasks that can "produce a (pseudo)- natural foreign language context". According to the information-processing approach to task-based instruction proposed by Skehan (1998), the balance should be kept between communication and form. Therefore the design of the tasks for instruction should balance the chance for a focus on both the form of DMs and the pragmatic meanings of DMs in communication to maximize the efficiency of the acquisitional process of DMs. Within given information-processing capacities, the tasks should be less demanding, for less attention will be channeled for task transaction and more attention can become available for a focus on DMs. In short, through attentional manipulation in formal instruction on DMs, more attention is available for a focus on DMs in communication. And the acquisitional process of DMs can work more effectively. As a result, the product of such acquisition can facilitate the use of DMs.

2.6.3　Processing of Discourse Markers

According to Van Pattern (1996), learners process content words in the input before anything else, and for learners to process form that is non-meaningful, they must be able to process information or communicative content that costs no or little attentional resources. Since DMs do not express conceptual meaning, they cannot be processed before it is done with content words. What is more, there is a lack of exposure to the use of DMs in the input material, as can be seen from the data analysis presented earlier in the present study. So it is even less likely for the learners to process DMs. Meanwhile, although DMs cannot be seen as non-meaningful, for they do express " procedural meaning", only when the learners are able to process the content without extra attentional resources is it possible for DMs to be processed, because there is a limit to the learners' processing capacity.

It is claimed by the processing approach to input that it is useful to train language learners in effective processing and to make them more able to notice relevant cues in the input so that form-meaning links are more likely to be attended to (Skehan, 1998). According to Van Pattern's model of processing and acquisition, the focus of instruction on the input processing of DMs should be at the input-to-intake stage, where the input is processed to make the form of DMs more salient, so that the learners can deliberately attempt to attend to them. Such instruction can maximize the efficiency of this stage in the processing of DMs so that the acquisitional processes can work more effectively.

2.7　Models for the analysis of Discourse Markers

The relevance-theoretic approach to DMs claims that DMs encode procedural information. They guide the inferential process in utterance interpretation. However, the

RT approach fails to provide a model that can show the concrete on-line inferential process. Beginning with the illustration of the inferential model on the RT approach, this section then suggests the application of space blending model to the analysis of DMs and presents the dynamic inferential process with a focus on DMs' role in the process.

2.7.1 The inferential model of Relevance Theory

According to Blakemore's (1992) classification, there are three types of DMs: (1) DMs that introduce contextual implications (for example, *so*, *therefore*, *that's to say*, *in other words*, etc.) (2) DMs concerned with strengthening (for example, *and*, *after all*, *also*, *besides*, *moreover*, *furthermore*, *indeed*, etc.) (3) DMs that introduce denials (for example, *but*, *still*, *nevertheless*, etc.). The following illustration of the inferential processes in the model is based on this classification. Look at the following example:

a) A: It's raining.

　B. *So*, the grass is wet.

b) (A comes home from shopping laden with parcels)

　B: *So*, you've spent all your money.

c) A: Your clothes smell of perfume.

　B: *So* (what)?

d) You have to have another drink. *After all* it is your birthday.

e) A: Will you make pancakes?

　B: I haven't really got time tonight. *Besides*, there's no milk.

f) David is here. *However*, you can't see him.

The RT account of DMs' role is that DMs express procedural meaning and they guide the hearer towards the choice of the appropriate contextual assumptions. For example, the propositions expressed by a) are: "It's raining" and "The grass is wet". The DM *so* does not contribute to the conceptual meanings. Instead, it indicates that the utterance it introduces, i. e. "the grass is wet" should be processed as a conclusion, or as a contextual implication of the assumption just made accessible by the preceding utterance, "it's raining". In b), the DM *so* functions in the same way as it does in a). The difference is that the speaker B is drawing a conclusion from the assumption made accessible by her own observation of an event. In c), the speaker B is asking A what conclusion she is expected to draw. In a word, the function of this type of DMs is to guide the inferential process by indicating the procedure of drawing a conclusion.

According to Blakemore, *after all* belongs to the second type and the proposition it introduces is relevant as justification for the proposition in the first utterance. In other words, the DM *after all* is used in the second utterance to indicate that this host utterance provides further evidence for, and therefore strengthens the assumption that has been made accessible in the first utterance. For example, in d) *after all* introduces the utterance "it is your birthday". The proposition expressed provides evidence for the proposition that "You have to have another drink". Thus, the hearer can interpret the utterance as the reason for having another drink. In e), B's utterances express the following propositions: "I have not really got time tonight" and "There's no milk". Speaker B uses *besides* to indicate that A is to draw a conclusion from the first proposition and from the second proposition as well. In other words, DM *besides* suggests that the utterance following it provides additional evidence for the assumption derived from the first proposition: B will not make pancakes. Since a conclusion drawn from two premises is stronger than the one drawn from either premise alone, the effect of providing additional evidence is to strengthen the existing assumption. Here, the existing assumption is made accessible by the immediately foregoing utterance "I haven't really got time tonight".

Expressions such as *however*, *but*, *nevertheless*, *still* etc. belong to the third type. According to Blakemore, there are cases in which it is necessary for the speaker to indicate that his or her utterance is relevant as a denial. In example f), the speaker assumes that the hearer has derived a contextual implication from the first utterance "David is here" that the hearer can see David. But the following proposition the speaker is going to present is inconsistent with this implication. So the speaker thinks it is necessary to use such the DM *however* to guide the hearer to the assumption that the coming proposition is a denial of his existing assumption.

2.7.2   Blending models for Discourse Markers' role in utterance interpretation

However convincing the inferential model might be, the detailed on-line inferential processes are not clear. The "invisible part of the iceberg" remains invisible. The aim of the blending models of utterance interpretation is to reveal the "tip of the iceberg" of the inferential process.

It is proposed here that in utterance interpretation process, DMs function as space-builders. They trigger the building of implicit input spaces. This function of DMs will be illustrated in three patterns: **S1 + DM + S2**, **DM + S2** and **S1 + S2**. What is common with the three patterns is the principle for the implicit input spaces to obtain their elements. According to RT, in the inferential phase of utterance interpretation, figuring out the speaker's communicative intentions depends largely on the choice of appropriate contexts, which is determined by the search for relevance. RT claims that it is human cognitive tendency to be as relevant as possible in communication. When processing an utterance, a path of least effort will be followed and stopped when the expectation of relevance is fulfilled. So long as the certain inference could be made from some elements first retrieved, these elements are the most relevant ones, for the retrieval of these elements costs the least effort and can meet the expectation of relevance. Therefore, it is believed here that the implicit input spaces obtain their elements according to the principle of relevance.

In the S1 + DM + S2 blending model, at first S1 prompts the building of Explicit Input 1. The elements and structure of Explicit Input 1 are determined by the activation of a subset of knowledge associated with a particular domain. The DM determines a cross-space connection between Explicit Input 1 and Implicit Input, which is to be set up immediately. According to this cross-space connection, Implicit Input is set up by

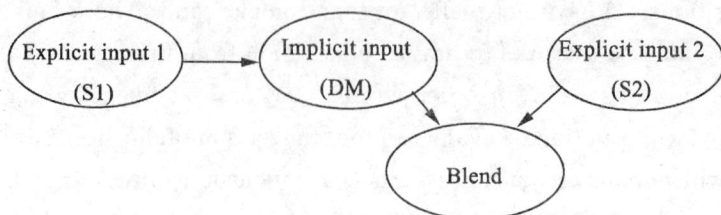

Figure 2.12 S1+ DM + S2 blending model

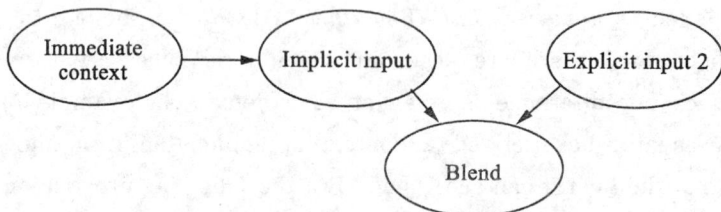

Figure 2.13   DM + S2 blending model

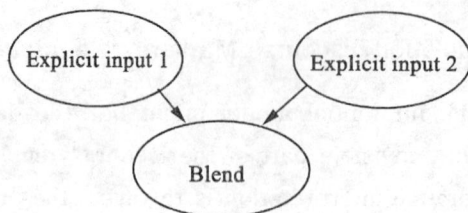

Figure 2.14   S1 + S2 blending model

retrieving information from the hearer's cognitive contexts (a set of facts that are manifest and accessible at the moment of processing new information). In other words, DMs constrain the particular elements that can appear in Implicit Input according to the principle of relevance on the one hand and the cross-space connection on the other. Subsequently, S2 builds Explicit Input 2 and obtains its elements the same way as Explicit Input 1 does. Blending happens between Implicit Input and Explicit Input 2 and results in the blended space where the inference can be made. In the DM + S2 blending model, illustrated in Figure 2.13, usually there is certain immediate physical setting or context manifest at the moment when the utterance is produced. The DM has a stronger power in connecting the utterance it introduces, i.e. S2, with the hearer's cognitive contexts, including the immediate physical context and other background information stored in the long-term memory. Like the S1 + DM + S2 blending model, the DM still determines a cross-space connection, but here this connection exists between the cognitive contexts and Implicit Input. The blending happens between Implicit Input and Explicit Input prompted by S2. In the S1 + S2 pattern illustrated in Figure 2.14, however, the cross-space connection does not exist. The entire cognitive contexts of the hearer play the role of the Implicit Input and work on the blending process.

Take this utterance as an example: *I want to buy a watch, but I have no money*. This utterance falls into the S1 + DM + S2 pattern. When interpreting this utterance we first set up Explicit Input 1: buying a watch. A set of elements and structure from the domain of purchase are activated and come into the Explicit Input 1: *I need some money to pay for it; I want to buy it because I need/like/can afford it*; etc. The DM *but* indicates a counterfactual mapping connection and a counterfactual Implicit Input space is set up. The negative counterparts of those elements in Input 1 are projected to the counterfactual space. These are the structure of the Implicit Input: *If I don't have money, I can't buy the watch; If I don't want/need/like it, I won't buy it; etc.* In Input 2 there is the structure: having no money. What the two Explicit Input spaces have in common derives from the domain of purchase, in which a buyer pays a seller some money for a commodity. This common information constitutes the generic space. In the blend, the conclusion that "*I can't buy this watch*" is drawn as a result of the blending of "*If I don't have money, I can't buy the watch*" and "*I have no money*".

The blending models are a combination of the SB and the RT creatively applied to the analysis of DMs in utterance interpretation. They demonstrate the dynamic inferential processes in light of DMs' role in these processes and can reveal the invisible part of the construction of meaning. This is where these models outweigh the RT's inferential model. From another angle, the following model demonstrates the evolution of DMs themselves from their semantic counterparts to what they are now.

2.7.3   The separate pragmatic blending model of Discourse Markers

According to Fauconnier & Turner (1998), conceptual blending takes place in all areas of human behavior. Once such blending becomes entrenched, it can be transmitted to new generations. Human knowledge is the result of successively established blends that cultures develop over time. These blends can be learned by new generations. Since blending occurs mostly behind the scenes, it is beyond the reach of our consciousness. Learning does not necessarily involve consciously knowing the process of blending. In the case of DMs, by way of conceptual blending, cultures have developed over time pragmatic uses of such words or expressions as established blends.

Studies on the acquisition of DMs provide some evidence for the blending of DMs. In the literature of the research on DMs, studies on the acquisition of DMs by young children (Montes, 1999; Andersen, et al, 1999) reveal that the acquisition of the literal meanings of DMs is prior to that of the pragmatic meanings. Erman's (2001) study shows that young speakers use *you know* as social and metalinguistic monitors, contrast to the elder generation's use of this DM as textual monitor. Such a change in use points to the tendency from literal use to pragmatic and that there is potential for DMs to end up as pragmaticalized items. Therefore, it is claimed in the present study that DMs are evolved from their semantic counterparts by blending the literal meanings of their counterparts with the pragmatic implications in particular contexts (see Figure 2. 15). When the results of such blending processes become established, DMs come into being as a separate pragmatic class.

After that, the pragmatic knowledge about DMs can be transmitted without referring to the process of blending. This blending account of DMs can reinforce the argument that formal instruction on DMs should be introduced into EFL oral class. Formal instruction on the pragmatic knowledge about DMs is more efficient for Chinese L2 learners to acquire DMs than mere exposure to native English. The

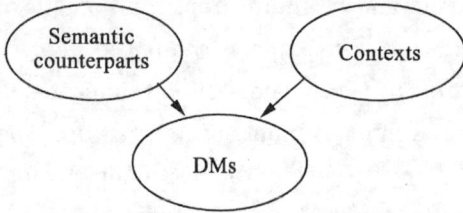

Figure 2.15   Blending of DMs

patterns of the learners' use of DMs and their implications show that most learners fail to acquire DMs in English, even though they have been exposed to native English. For these freshmen learners, mere exposure to native English once or twice a week is far from enough to result in the acquisition of DMs. If the learners are not instructed on DMs, they may neglect such words, because DMs' function of expressing procedural information, proposed by Wilson and Sperber (1993) constrains them from being brought to consciousness. Formal instruction on DMs can help bring to the learners' consciousness the pragmatic use of DMs. Without being instructed on DMs, the learners may have noticed such words and realized their pragmatic use, but they themselves may have to go through the whole process of blending the semantic counterparts of DMs with particular pragmatic meanings over a long time to develop their own understanding of DMs. This is undoubtedly time-consuming and inefficient as far as the acquisition is concerned. Moreover, their understanding of DMs may be quite different from what native speakers have agreed on. In conclusion, the pragmatic knowledge of DMs has to be transmitted to the learners by way of formal instruction. It is a waste of time to let L2 learners acquire DMs only through exposure to native English.

Chapter 3

The Effects of Rhetorical Organization on Reading Comprehension

Current research on discourse comprehension in the first language reading has focused on the relationship between formal schemata and the comprehension of expository text. Formal schemata refer to the background knowledge of the formal, rhetorical organizational structures of different types of texts. A reader needs a good knowledge of formal schemata, for it affects the reader's reading comprehension. There is considerable evidence that how a text influences the comprehension of the text. Formal schemata are also described as abstract, encoded, internalized, coherent patterns of meta-linguistic, discoursal, and textual organization that guide expectations in the attempts to understand a meaningful piece of language.

Central to the research is Meyer's (1975) work that has dealt with what readers remember and retain from a text. Based on his text analysis system, Meyer (1984) specified five types of top-level rhetorical relationships that organize ideas in a passage into hierarchical patterns. They are description, collection, causation, comparison, and problem/solution. The structures of collection and description are often combined forming a type of structure called collection of descriptions. In a study with native English readers, Meyer and Freedle (1984) found that certain types of top-level rhetorical organizations interacted with the reader's formal schemata differently from other types to affect comprehension and memory. Another study (Talyor, 1980) showed that good readers had prior knowledge about the structure and they used that structure to aid comprehension and recall; and the use of text structure was positively related to the amount of information recalled. Carrell (1985) also suggested that formal schemata are important factors in reading comprehension in English as a second language and that different types of rhetorical organization of English expository text differentially affect comprehension of ESL readers of different language backgrounds (Carrell, 1985).

This study explores the relationship of rhetorical organization to reading comprehension, by examining the features presented in Chinese EFL learners' recall of different rhetorical structures in expository text, argumentative text and narrative text. Based on the data from written recall analysis, the study investigates the features and difference of recall from three types of writing (expository text, argumentative text and narrative text) with different rhetorical structures (collection of descriptions, causation, problem/solution and comparison).

In order to investigate whether there are any differences among the four types of rhetorical organization in reading expository text, argumentative text and narrative text and whether different types of writing have effects on reading comprehension and recall of Chinese learners, descriptive statistics, one-way ANOVA and Scheffe were performed to analyze the effects of rhetorical organization on English written recall done by 50 undergraduate non-English majors in the third semester in Wuhan University. Conclusions are drawn as follows: first, the more tightly organized causation, problem/solution and comparison structures tend to be more facilitative of recall of important information from the expository and narrative texts than are the more loosely organized collection of descriptions. The more tightly organized causation, problem/solution and comparison structures tend to be more facilitative of recall of important information from argumentative texts than are the more loosely organized collection of descriptions. Only the problem/solution texts tend to be more facilitative of recall than the collection of descriptions. Second, the Chinese learners experience the differences among the four types of rhetorical organization in expository text, argumentative text and narrative text in written recalls. There is an insignificant difference between types of writing in learners' recognizing and utilizing the rhetorical organization of the original text in their own recall from passages with problem/ solution text. The last is that the higher-level processing skills (the use of background knowledge, for example) can be transferred to a second language, and can compensate for inadequacies in lower-level linguistic skills.

3.1 Rhetorical organization and reading comprehension

There are various interpretations of rhetorical organization. Contrast to traditional grammar, which regards sentences as the largest units for study, rhetorical organization studies such supra-sentential units as sequence of sentences and texts, the relationship between sentences, the structures of texts, etc. A text is almost composed of parts, each of which is separated from the others and has some kind of internal structures. This complex network of relationship within a text is called rhetorical organization. It is the structure of the underlying ideas, and the connections that the writer makes between them. When he begins to write his text, the writer has in his mind a certain body of facts, or a story, or an argument, etc, which he wants to convey to the reader. He has to decide where to start, what sequence to follow, which aspects to emphasize and so on. He knows what he wants to say, but he has to choose the best way to say it. The choices he makes are the choices of text patterns. So finding out the text pattern means perceiving how the writer selects from his raw material, organizes and shapes it, and gives it coherence until it suits his purpose and becomes the text we read.

Rhetorical organization focuses on the organization of a text, that is, how the ideas and concepts in the text are organized. Rhetorical organization can also be called text pattern, text structure, discourse structure, rhetorical structure and organizational pattern.

3.1.1   Organizational components of structures

Discourse can be organized in different ways. Meyer (1975) has gathered empirical evidence for five basic ways to organize discourse: collection, description, causation, problem/solution, and comparison. Most discourse will contain more than one of these basic organizations. For example, folktales contain much description, causation, and events sequenced in time (collection) within an overall problem/solution organization where the protagonist confronts and resolves a problem, folktales may carry an overall comparison organization, such as demonstrating the contrast between good versus evil. Figure 3. 1 specifies the organizational components of the structures that correspond to the five basic types of discourse.

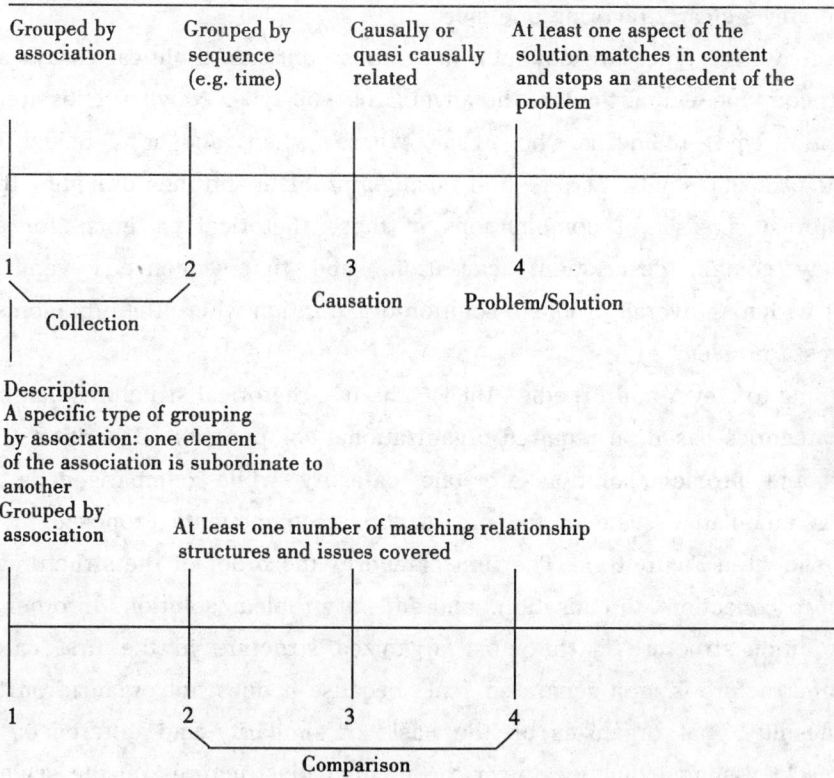

```
Grouped by          Grouped by        Causally or       At least one aspect of the
association         sequence          quasi causally    solution matches in content
                    (e.g. time)       related           and stops an antecedent of the
                                                         problem


  |                   |                 |                 |
  1                   2                 3                 4
        Collection                    Causation         Problem/Solution

  |
Description
A specific type of grouping
by association: one element
of the association is subordinate to
another
Grouped by          At least one number of matching relationship
association         structures and issues covered


  |                   |                 |                 |
  1                   2                 3                 4
                              Comparison
```

Figure 3. 1   Components of text structure (Meyer and Freedle, 1984)

As seen in Figure 3. 1, the collection type represents the loosest organizational type, being merely a grouping or listing of concepts or ideas by association. If the association is by sequence (by time, for example), then the listing becomes more organized (yielding, for example, a historical chronology).

The description type is a specific kind of grouping by association in which one element of the association is subordinate to another, namely to the topic. By presenting a particular attribute, specification, or setting, the description gives more information about the topic. When a number of collections of attributes, specifications, or settings are given about a topic, the structures of collection and description are combined to form a sixth type collection of descriptions.

The causation type represents ideas which are organized not only chronologically, but also causally related. This discourse type is like the if-then statements of logic, or like cause-effect (antecedent-consequence) statements.

The problem/solution type contains all the features of cause-effect, with the additional feature of overlapping content between propositions in the problem and solution. One or more propositional elements of the solution can neutralize a causal antecedent of the problem.

The comparison type is on a different scale from causation and problem/solution. Rather than being organized on the basis of time or causality, it is organized on the basis of opposing viewpoints (either alternative views giving equal weight to two sides, or adversative views clearly favoring one side).

These five basic types are common in various contexts. Political essays are often of the comparison type—in particular, the adversative sub-type. News articles are typically of the description type—telling us who, what, where, when, and how. Scientific texts are often of the problem/solution type—first raising a problem and then providing the solution.

Most prose consists of combinations of these rhetorical patterns; for example, a folktale may contain description, causation, and time-sequenced events (that is, collection) within an overall problem/solution organization where the protagonist confronts and resolves a problem.

According to Meyer and Freedle (1984), the five rhetorical structures can be classified into two categories based on required organizational components. Description, collection, causation, and problem/solution are one category while comparison is in another category. A cumulative scale of the organizational components proposed by Meyer and Freedle is shown in Figure 3.1. The first category, the order of the structures goes from description to collection, to causation, and ends at problem/solution. In other words, the problem/solution structure is the most organized structure in the first category. The comparison structure is on a separated scale because it does not organize on the basis of time or causality, but organizes on the basis of similarity and difference; Meyer and Freedle (1984) assumed that the lower the number of structures on the scale, the more poorly the texts organized by the structures can be recalled.

3.1.2 Features and basic rhetorical structures of different types of text

The three types of writing, expository text, argumentative text and narrative text have their own features and basic rhetorical structures.

Exposition is a kind of text that is most frequently come across by English learners. Exposition means expounding or explaining. An expository paper explains or explores something, such as the process of making a machine, the causes of natural or social phenomenon, the planning of a project, or the solution of a problem. This type or text generally contains more unfamiliar vocabulary and concepts and fewer ideas related to personal experience as well as variety of structures. The unfamiliarity with the types of text structures impedes language learners' reading comprehension. An expository text is generally more difficult to comprehend due to the variety of structures and unfamiliar content.

The rhetorical organization is part of the macrostructure of a text and it contains the logical organization of the text which the writer has used to represent the intended meaning. Meyer (1975) has recognized five groups of rhetorical relations in expository texts: collection, description, comparison/contrast, cause-effect and problem-solution. The structures of collection and description are combined to form collection of descriptive structures. However, Piccolo (1987) identified six types of expository text structures that are useful for teaching purposes and occur in text materials readers may encounter. They are descriptive, enumerative, sequence, cause and effect, compare and contrast, and problem-solution.

Argumentation is a kind of text that the writer adopts to convince other people to agree with his point of view, to approve a policy or a course of action that he proposes, or to do something that he wants to be done. Speeches on policies, editorials of newspapers, articles on political or theoretical questions, are often argumentative.

Argumentation frequently makes use of the other three types of writing: description, narration and exposition. Although they can take different shapes, argumentative essays have certain basic features in common. First, it has a well-defined theme. The theme of an argumentative text is often stated in the first or introductory paragraph. It is called a proposition if it is put in the form of a simple declarative sentence in the affirmative, such as "Practice is the only criterion of truth", or "Smoking is harmful to one's health." For the sake of unity, a short essay needs only one theme or proposition. Second, it provides sufficient evidence. The proposition of an essay has to be backed up with sufficient facts, examples, statistics, reasons, or opinions of reliable authorities. Valid evidence is provided with clearly and directly connected views. Third, it stresses good logic. It is obvious that good logic is even more important to argumentation than to any other type or writing. All the facts and reasons that are given as evidence should be logically connected with the conclusion and proved with each other. Any fallacy in logic or wrong step in reasoning would leave the reader in doubt about the whole argument. Fourth, the organization of the text is very clear. A typical argumentative essay consists of three parts: an introduction which identifies the issue to be discussed and explains the importance of such discussion; a body which presents the evidence; and a conclusion in which the proposition, if it is stated at the beginning, is reaffirmed (Ding Wangdao & Wu Bing, 1997). Therefore, many researchers at home and abroad have developed various kinds of rhetorical structures of argumentative text. For example, Hoey (2001) set up the organization patterns of written discourse as follows: problem-solution pattern, cause-effect, matching pattern and general- particular pattern. While Liu (1999) proposed only three patterns for discourse organization: problem-solution pattern; general-specific pattern and claim-counterclaim pattern.

Narrative writing reports an event or tells the story of something that happened. Many theorists today believe that there is not only a "grammar" of narration but also established patterns of organization for all narrative literary style. "Grammars" of narratives have been studied extensively. Researchers like Stein and Glenn (1979) have noted that stories have internal structures; these structures may be depicted as hierarchical networks of units of information serving different functions in stories; logical relations exist among these units; hierarchical structures correspond to some extent to the ways readers comprehend and store information in stories; and readers more easily remember items higher up in the hierarchical networks. Researches make it clear that stories have a structure. Some imply that the structure of narration, like grammar of the language, built into all people (Rumelhart, 1975).

3.2　Schema theory and reading comprehension

Schema theory is probably the most influential and still prevailing theory about written text processing. It has its origin in the field of psychology in the study of the mental organization for storing and retrieving existing knowledge while dealing with new information. Schema theory is based on the assumption that readers' prior knowledge directly affects new learning situations and is now widely accepted as playing a key role in the process of reading comprehension and inference generation. A schema is an abstract structure of knowledge (Anderson, Spiro, & Anderson, 1978), or a data structure for representing the generic concepts stored in memory (Rumelhart, 1980). It is a description of a particular class of concepts and is composed of a hierarchy of schemata embedded within schemata (Adams & Collins, 1979). Schema theory is currently seen as useful in explaining how human knowledge is structured and used. Schema theory proposes that one's existing knowledge directly influences the content and form of new knowledge (Anderson, 1978). Schema theory provides insights into reading, and in particular explains how inference comes into being. Readers' schemata provide the basis for making inferences that go beyond the literally stated information and thus complete the meaning of a text, which ensures comprehension.

Schemata are abstract structures that represent what one holds to be generally true about the world. Knowledge is organized, as opposed to being simply unrelated bits of information. In addition, schemata include structures for objects, events, and facts; for academic topics; for social situations and routine series of actions; and for how information is typically presented. A particular schema is embedded in other schemata and contains subschemata. Human knowledge about the world is held in long-term memory in a form which is not a direct match to the input and which is abstracted from it. The schema has been proposed as a knowledge structure to store this abstracted information. Schema, also called the building block of cognition (Rumelhart, 1980), is a significant notion in understanding the knowledge structure of the brains. What people know exists in schemata hierarchies and this prior knowledge is activated when they encounter new information. Rinehart defines schema as follows: a schema theory about how knowledge is presented and about how that representation facilitates the use of the knowledge in particular ways. According to schema theories, all knowledge packaged into units is called schemata. Embedded in those packets of knowledge is information about how this knowledge is to be used.

Schema theory is not only used to account for storage of information, but is also a procedural theory of knowledge acquisition. It is assumed that schemata are used to interpret incoming sensory information, retrieve information from memory and guide the sequence of processing. They embody a prototype which is a typical category member or event. When incomplete information concerning an event or object is given, more detail can be filled in using this prototype. Schemata can therefore be used to guide inferences and can also be used to guide the encoding of incoming information by generating expectations for features that are normally present for a given category. Schema theory is a theoretical metaphor for the reader's prior knowledge (Grabe, 1991). In attempt to comprehend text, the reader is building up an internal model of the message or story contained in the text. Relevant schemata are instantiated to determine their goodness of fit to the situation portrayed in the text. Misrepresentation may occur when schemata are incorrectly activated due to ambiguity in the text or incorrect inferences from a poorly developed schema. A reader's failure to activate an appropriate schema during reading results in various degrees of non-comprehension. The failure to activate an appropriate schema may either be due to the writer's not having provided sufficient clues in the text for the reader to effectively use the processing mode to activate schemata the reader may already possess, or it may be due to the fact that the reader does not possess the appropriate schema anticipated by the author and thus fails to comprehend. In both instances there is a mismatch between what the writer anticipates the reader can do to extract meaning from the text and what the reader is actually able to. The point is that the appropriate schemata must exist and must be activated during text processing.

3.2.1   Classification of schema

Carrell, a well-known researcher on schema theory, has written various papers on schema. According to Carrell, there are two types of schema: content and formal (Carrell, 1984). In the process of reading, the two prior schemata in learners' brains interact with the printed words, content and form of a reading passage, which at the end results in learners' comprehension to the material.

Content schemata is the background knowledge of the content area of a text, such as a text about the economy of China, celebrating the New Year's Eve in America, the history of Mexico, problems of nuclear weapons. It involves readers' prior knowledge and experience concerning the reading passage. Schema theory emphasizes that background knowledge affects reading comprehension greatly in that new knowledge is taken in on condition that one has already possessed something related to it, otherwise learning won't take place. As an English language learner, knowledge about the society, the history, the customs and culture, and the people of English-speaking countries are always "The more, the better".

Researchers have found out that reader's familiarity with a topic affects his understanding directly and greatly either in the first language reading or in the second language reading. When a reader familiarizes himself with the topic, he can effectively stimulate the schemata stored in his memory to assist him to make predictions and inferences about the incoming information, even when he meets with linguistic problems, his schemata can guide him to make wise assumptions and judgments. If the reader is unfamiliar with the topic of a text, of course, he cannot make sense of what he is reading. And because language is a reflection of culture, understanding the cultural content of what one reads is also a crucial factor in reading comprehension. A significant problem for EFL learners is that texts sometimes contain unfamiliar concepts or culture-specific elements. In some instances, the cultural schemata needed are not provided by the text because the author assumes, probably tacitly, that the reader already has them. When the cultural background assumed by an author is missing, reading can become a time-consuming and laborious task.

Formal schemata are the background knowledge of the formal, rhetorical organizational structures of different types of texts. The more a reader learns about the formation of an article, the better he will grasp the logical order and get the general meaning. Formal schemata are described as abstract, encoded, internalized, coherent patterns of meta-linguistic, discoursal, and textual organization that guide expectations in our attempts to understand a meaningful piece of language. Many studies suggested that different types of text structure affected comprehension and recall (Carrell, 1984). According to the classification of linguistics, reading materials can be divided into such groups as argumentation, exposition, description and narration. There are actually various types in daily reading like newspaper articles, reports, poems, prose, essays, autobiographies, correspondence, etc. Different reading materials bear different characteristics which pose different reading requests for readers. A proper employment of formal schemata during reading may help to predict the texts' discourse organization and cohesion, which will result in improved comprehension. In language learning, learners will meet with different kinds of reading materials, which call on a good mastery of different rhetorical structures. As a matter of fact, each kind of text structure has its unique components. If learners have a firm command of the characteristics of those types of writing, they will read with ease and interest. Otherwise, they will find it incomprehensible and problematic. For example:

(1)A girl reported to be daughter of the mayor killed herself in car crashes last night.

At first glance, it seems that there is no logic behind this sentence. How could a girl report that she killed herself in car crashes? If the reader is familiar with newspaper language, he will probably have a clue. In fact, this sentence accords with the requirement of the newspaper lead. In English, it is sometimes possible to leave out the first words of a clause that follow a noun. Most often these missing words will be who (or which) and a form of the verb "be". If we put back the missing words, the sentence reads:

(2)A girl who was reported to be daughter of the mayor killed herself in car crashes last night.

But if readers lack this knowledge, they will supposedly take this sentence as wrong. This example convincingly proves that if readers possess knowledge about the rhetorical structure of a given text, they are able to make sense of it.

Thus, formal schemata are claimed to be the background knowledge of the formal, rhetorical organizational structures of different types of texts. A reader needs a good knowledge of formal schemata, for it affects the reader's reading comprehension. There is considerable evidence that knowing how a text is organized influences the comprehension of the text. A good reader appears to make better use of text organization, write better recalls by recognizing and using the same organizational structure as the text is studied, and, generally, recall information better from certain types of text organization such as comparison-contrast. A reader who includes in their prior knowledge information about standard rhetorical organizational patterns tends to more easily reconstruct in their minds what a writer may be trying to say. Writers try to organize what they write as an aid for themselves in writing and as an aid for their readers in comprehending. Readers, however, tend to organize what they read as they read. The structure of a text, no matter how well established in the writer's mind, is ultimately realized by readers. This realization is made easier, when reader's perceptions are guided by well-organized texts; thus when readers may expect a comparison and contrast plan of organization good writers guide them to see it. Text does play a part in comprehensibility.

3.2.2   Schema theory and reading comprehension

Schema theory asserts that reading is an interactive process between the text and the reader (Rumelhart, 1980). Such interaction involves the reader's prior knowledge of schemata, and the actual information in the text. Schemata refer to what the reader already knows about the world, i. e., knowledge stored in memory. Rumelhart (1980) defined schemata as data structures for representing the generic concepts stored in memory. Schemata are thought to aid in the encoding and retrieval of information contained in a text. According to schema theory, a text in itself does not carry meaning. A text provides directions for readers as to how they should construct meaning from their own previously acquired knowledge, or background knowledge. Therefore, comprehending a text is dependent upon the extent to which schemata are available for the text and the extent to which the schemata are actually used during reading.

Schemata are used to interpret a new text by matching incoming data in the text with a particular schema knowledge structure. According to schema theory, the process of interpretation is guided by the principle that every input is mapped against some existing schema and that all aspects of that schema must be compatible with the input information. This principle results in two basic modes of information processing, called bottom-up and top-down processing.

Bottom-up models are proposed by a number of scholars (Gough, 1972). In their models, they hold a passive view toward second and foreign language reading. They believe reading is primarily a decoding process of reconstructing the author's intended meaning via recognizing the printed letters and words and building up a meaning for a text from the smallest textual units at the "bottom" (letters and words) to larger units at the "top" (phrases, clauses, etc.). These are text-driven models of comprehension. The bottom-up reading model is also known as "part to whole model". It is a reading model that emphasizes a single direction, part-to-whole processing of a written or printed text. Bottom-up models operate on the principle that the written text is hierarchically organized (i. e., on the graphic-phonic, phonemic, syllabic, morphemic, word, and sentence levels) and that the reader first processes the smallest unit, gradually compiling the smaller units to decipher and comprehend the higher units (Dechant, 1991). Basically, this model fosters practices in reading instruction which builds up learners' decoding ability from the bottom up, starting from the smallest units, single letters, and build up to words and phrases. Many early pedagogical suggestions focus on the role of vocabulary in reading.

However, gradually, this model began to attract criticism due to its deficiency. Research into human memory provides counterfactual evidence. It has been shown that the serial processing of every letter in a text would slow down the reading speed up to the point where it would be very difficult for meaning to be retained. Given the fact that we can only hold in memory about seven items at a time, readers would, under the bottom-up model, very often forget the beginning of a sentence (and perhaps even a word) before they have reached the end. Therefore, this model exerts a series of problems. With the advent of Goodman's top-down view of reading as a psychological process, the bottom-up view of reading fell into disfavor.

Top-down models are proposed by many scholars. The best known are those proposed by Goodman (1967, 1969) and Coady (1979). According to this model, the role of readers is considered to be quite active: they predict meaning as they read, they take in large chunks of text at a time, they do not attend to separate letters, rather they match what they already know with the meaning they derive from the text. In this view, reading is more a matter of constructing meaning using only partly the graphic, syntactic, and semantic systems of the language.

In the past three decades, EFL reading theory has come under influence of psychologists and Goodman's psycholinguistic model of reading. Goodman (1969) has described reading as a "psycholinguistic game" in which "the reader reconstructs, as best as he can, message which has been encoded by a writer as a graphic display". Goodman views this act of the construction of meaning as being an ongoing, cyclical process of sampling from the input text, predicting, testing and confirming or revising those predictions, and sampling further. In this model, the reader need not (and the efficient reader does not) use all the textual cues. The better the reader is able to make correct prediction, the less confirming via the text is necessary, that is, the less visual perceptual information the reader requires. In a word, Goodman lays a particular emphasis on the guessing behavior in reading comprehension.

Coady (1979) has elaborated on this basic psycholinguistic model (Figure 3.2) and has suggested a model in which the EFL reader's background knowledge interacts with conceptual abilities and process strategies, more or less successfully, to produce comprehension.

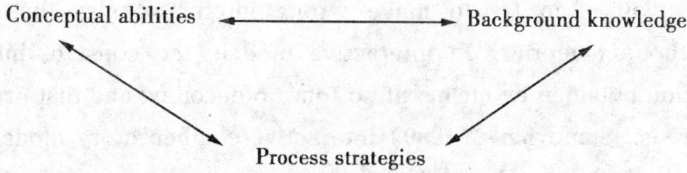

Conceptual abilities ⟷ Background knowledge

Process strategies

Figure 3.2   Model of the ESL (Reade Coady, 1979)

By conceptual ability, Coady means general intellectual capacity. By processing strategies, he means various sub-components of reading ability, such as the ability to recognize lexical meaning and contextual meaning. Coady says little more about the role of background knowledge other than to observe that "background knowledge becomes an important variable when we notice, as many have, that students with a western background of some kind learn English faster, on the average, than those without such a background".

Coady also suggests that background knowledge can compensate for certain syntactic deficiencies: the subject of reading materials should be of high interest and relate well to the background of the reader, since strong semantic input can help when syntactic control is weak. The interest and background knowledge will enable the student to comprehend at a reasonable rate and keep him involved in the material in spite of its syntactic difficulty.

An important aspect of schema-theoretic view of reading is that top-down and bottom-up processing should be occurring at all levels simultaneously (Rumelhart, 1980). Bottom-up processing ensures that readers will be sensitive to information that is new or that does not fit their ongoing hypotheses about the content or structure of the text; top-down processing helps the reader resolve ambiguities or select between alternative possible interpretations of the incoming data. Thus, according to schema theory, comprehending a text is an interaction between a reader's background knowledge and the information in the text.

In practice a reader continually changes from one focus to another, now adopting a top-down approach to predict the probable meaning, then moving to the bottom-up approach to check whether that is really what the writer says. In other words, bottom-up and top-down approaches are used to complement each other. Most current EFL reading comprehension models are interactive in that EFL reading comprehension is considered as a process involving the combination and integration of various kinds of knowledge sources. Interactive models of reading assume that skills at all levels are interactively available to process and interpret the text.

The interactive model of reading views itself as a dynamic balance of two processes-decoding of text (bottom-up) and application to the text of the readers' own elaborations and background knowledge (top-down). Readers construct meaning through some mixture of these processes. However, embracing one process to the exclusion of the other leads to difficulties. On the other hand, over reliance on top-down processing can interfere with attention to syntactic, semantic, and discourse constraints (Hudson, 1982). Low proficient readers will often try to make wrong interpretations, thus corrupting and distorting the author's blueprint. In interactive model, the constant interaction occurs between information obtained by means of bottom-up decoding and that provided by means of top-down analysis. Stanovich's (1980) interactive-compensatory model deals with the shortcomings of both approaches. The bottom-up model assumes that background knowledge cannot be activated before lower-level decoding while the top-down model does not allow lower-level processes to influence or direct higher level ones. The basic premise of Stanovich's model is that reading involves "an array of processes". Therefore, a reader who is weak in one particular skill area will compensate by bringing into effect other reading processes. Grabe's (1991) interpretation of an interactive approach is one that takes into account the critical contribution of both lower level processing skill (identification) and higher level comprehension and reasoning skills (interpretation). The process, then, is reciprocal. The interactive model is not just a compromising between the bottom-up and top-down models. Generally speaking, the interactive model provides a more accurate conceptualization of reading performance than strictly top-down or bottom-up models (Stanovich, 1980). The advantages of the interactive model is quickly recognized and put into practice in the field of English language learning and teaching, where EFL readers, due to their inadequate language competence and/or inadequate background knowledge, have much to compensate for in the reading process. In light of the broad sense of the theory, readers are encouraged not only to resort to various sources of knowledge—lexical, syntactic, semantic and general knowledge of the world, but also to use both carefully-arranged reading skills and expedition reading strategies to cater to different tasks which embody various reading materials and reading purposes. It is clearly seen that interactive approach has a dominant position in the reading comprehension.

3.3 Effects of schemata on reading comprehension

There are two opposing views on EFL reading. Some researchers argue that reading ability is largely a function of proficiency in that language, or that at least some minimal threshold of proficiency needs to be reached in that language before good readers' first language reading strategies can be transferred to reading in the second language (Cziko, 1980). Other groups of researchers, however, argue that reading in a foreign language depends crucially upon the reading ability in one's first language rather than upon the students' level of ability in the second language (Coady, 1979). In this view, learners who read poorly in a second language do so either because they do not have good reading skills in their L1, or because they fail to transfer them.

3.3.1   Effects of reading proficiency

The researchers argue that higher-level processing skills may be transferred to a second language, and may compensate for inadequacies in low-level linguistic skills (Coady, 1979; Hudson, 1982; Johnson, 1981, 1982). Research by Cziko (1980) suggests that a reader's competence in a second language affects the reading strategies. Cziko compared the reading strategies of French learners at advanced English proficiency with those of native English readers as both read in English. French readers performed very much like native English speakers and they showed sensitivity to syntactic, semantic, and discourse constraints in the text; readers at low language proficiency, however, employed poor reading strategies attempting to reproduce the orthographic features of text. Cziko suggested that much of the difficulty in L2 may be due to the inability to use the syntactic, semantic, and discourse constraints because of low language proficiency.

Carrell (1988) also suggests that before L2 readers can transfer L1 reading skills and background knowledge to improve comprehension, they must reach a threshold level of language proficiency. As further evidence for a language ceiling for EFL learners, Carrell (1983) found that they do not employ contextual clues or appropriate background knowledge in the way native speakers do. She also cited the apparent inability of even advanced EFL learners to ascertain whether or not a passage was difficult for them. Subjects were asked to rate their overall comprehension of a text. Performance on the test, as measured by the number of idea units recalled, was compared with the comprehensibility rating. Carrell found no significant correlation between performance and comprehensibility rating for ESL readers, but she reported a positive correlation between those two factors for native readers.

While some researchers argue that difficulties in L2 reading comprehension may be traced back to limited L2 language proficiency, other researchers claim that reading problems in a foreign language are due to inappropriate reading skills in L1 rather than language competence. Therefore, students who read poorly in a second language do so either because they do not have good reading skills in their L1, or because they fail to transfer them. Many researches have shown that reading skills developed in L1 can be transferred to a second language, and may compensate for inadequacies in lower-level linguistic skills (Coady, 1979; Hudson, 1982; Johnson, 1981, 1982). Hudson (1982) has found that some aspects of reading ability are readily transferred from one language to another and that the application of cognitive strategies is not dependent on the English language proficiency of the reader. Two studies by Johnson (1981, 1982) reported on the relationship between cultural background knowledge and second language proficiency. And both of his studies demonstrated that cultural background knowledge could override the effects of limited language proficiency.

3.3.2   Effects of content schemata

The importance of background knowledge in reading is central to schema theory

(Rumelhart, 1980). Schema theory claims that reading a text implies an interaction between the reader's various schemata and the text itself. A number of empirical studies have been conducted about applying schema theory to EFL reading instruction.

The research on the effects of content schemata on reading comprehension of native English readers has been dealt with in several studies. Bransford and Johnson (1972) examined the role of contextual schemata in comprehension. They presented learners with a deliberately vague passage about "washing clothes". Some of the learners were told the title of the passage while others were not. Learners who were told the title of the passage recalled more than learners who did not hear the title. The study has revealed that when subjects are provided with a schema or context against which to understand and recall a passage, they perform better than when they are not given such a schema.

Much of the second language research on content schemata concerns the role of cultural knowledge in reading comprehension. Studies (Johnson, 1981, 1982; Carrell, 1987) have shown that the reader's cultural content schemata influence how a text is interpreted and that the implicit cultural knowledge presupposed by a text interacts with the reader's own cultural background knowledge to make texts whose content is based on one's own culture easier to read and understand than syntactically and rhetorically equivalent text based on a less familiar culture.

3.3.3 Effects of formal schemata

Research in schema theory has shown that reading comprehension is an interactive process between the reader and the text (Rumelhart, 1977; Adams and Collins 1979; Carrell 1983; Meyer and Freedle, 1984). Among other things, this means that reading comprehension is an interaction between a reader's background knowledge and processing strategies for text structure on the one hand, and the rhetorical organization of the text on the other. Meyer (1975; Meyer & Freedle, 1984) has investigated native readers of English interacting with different types of rhetorical organization of expository prose. Her research has shown that certain types of expository organization interact with readers' background knowledge and processing strategies differently from other types. The structures in the form of causation, problem/solution and comparison are more organized than those of collection of descriptions because they have more links that related two or more components of the text to the topic. In the collection of descriptions passage, the only links that occur are between the topic and the listed attributes. That is, the attributes are linked only by association with the topic. They hypothesize that the more organized top-level structures in causation, problem/solution, and comparison affect greater recall than those of collection of descriptions which is less organized.

Carrell (1985) examines the effects of rhetorical organization of different types of expository text. Results showed that recall was better for the texts with the three more tightly organized discourse structures (comparison, causation, and problem/solution) than for those that were more loosely organized. Carrel found that the more highly organized types of discourse are generally more facilitative of recall than the less organized collection of descriptions.

In order to investigate the effects of different top-level structures on recall, Meyer and Freedle (1984) have graduate students listen to passages that contained the same information, but organized in each of the four top-level structures. Analysis of the subject's free recall protocols showed that the collection of descriptions was less effective for recall than the other types and subjects recalled more from comparison, causation, problem/solution structures than from the collection of descriptions structure. This study supported the hypothesis that more tightly organized top-level structures facilitate recall than less organized structure.

Carrell (1985) uses Meyer and Freedle's (1984) four passages on dehydration to examine the effects of rhetorical organizations on reading comprehension of four groups of intermediate ESL readers: Spanish, Arabic, Asian, and a mixed group designated as "Other". Passages contained the same information written according to four different top-level rhetorical structures: collection of descriptions, causation, comparison, and problem/solution. He found that the collection of descriptions was the least effective for immediate recall of idea units. This finding is similar to Meyer and Freedle's finding with native speakers of English. In addition, the study also found significant differences among the language groups according to their L1 as to which English discourse types facilitated better recall. Carrel interpreted the differences as due to interference from the preferred L1 rhetorical patterns.

In a more recent study, Carrell (1994) investigates the relationship between awareness of text structure and recall. Forty-five high-intermediate proficiency ESL students produced written recalls of both comparison and collection of descriptive texts. Two measures of awareness were used: use of structure in written recall and recognition of structure in response to a probe question. The results showed no significant differences in awareness to the two structures, nor were there differences on the two types of text structure in the quantity of information recalled. However, there were differences in the quality of information recall between text structures. Significantly more superordinated ideas were recalled from the comparison than from the collection of descriptions passage. Finally, those subjects who used the structure of the original passage in organizing their recall recalled more total ideas and more of the superordinated ideas of the text.

All these researches illustrated that schemata such as a language schemata, formal schemata and content schemata have great effects on achieving EFL reading comprehension. It is necessary for teachers to help students build up and activate these schemata.

3.4 Research methodology of reading comprehension

The empirical investigation of the present study aims to find the features of Chinese EFL learners experience in students' organization of their recall of the passages in different discourse structures of expository, argumentative and narrative texts. The specific questions that are addressed include:

(1) Are there any differences among the four types of rhetorical organization of

expository text (collection of descriptions, comparison, causation and problem/ solution) in the reading recalls of Chinese learners?

(2) Are there any differences among the four types of rhetorical organization in narrative text and argumentative text in the reading recalls of Chinese learners?

(3) Do different types of writing affect the students' comprehension and recall?

(4) May the higher-level processing skills (use of background knowledge, for example) be transferred to a second language, and compensate for inadequacies in lower-level linguistic skills?

Based on the above linguistic analysis and review of previous studies on the formal schemata, three hypotheses with specific predictions for the present study are put forward as follows:

Hypotheses 1: The more tightly organized comparison, causation and problem/ solution types tend to be more facilitative of recall of main information from a text than the more loosely organized collection of descriptions.

Hypotheses 2: Chinese learners of English experience differences among the four types of rhetorical organization in expository text, argumentative text and narrative text in written recalls.

Hypotheses 3: Higher-level processing skills (use of background knowledge, for example) may be transferred to a second language, and may compensate for inadequacies in lower-level linguistic skills.

The theories mentioned above have lent considerable theoretical and empirical supports for the schema-theoretical view of reading that comprehension is an interaction between the reader's background knowledge and the information in the text. The research in both L1 and L2 has demonstrated the effects of content and formal schemata on comprehension. It has been shown that different rhetorical top-level structures have different effects on a reader's comprehension and recall and that learners' knowledge of text structure influences what they comprehend and recall from a passage.

The subjects involved in the study are 50 students (non-English majors) in Wuhan University in the third semester. They have been studying English for years and have received quite a lot of knowledge on rhetorical organization and types of writing as well. All of these students are of about the same age. Their mother tongue is Chinese and English is a foreign language to them.

The instrument for the present study was collected by administering written recall. There are several reading comprehension measurements in L2 reading research: cloze test, multiple choice, true-false question, open-ended questions and recall. The recall protocol is a free recall measure providing a purer measure of comprehension, uncomplicated by linguistic performance and tester interference. It is more reliable and valid measurement of comprehension because it does not delimit the response or influence comprehension. The most widely used awareness measure has been the written recall, analyzed not for number of ideas recalled, but for the degree to which readers use the same organizational pattern as the author (Taylor, 1980). Researchers have assumed that the more closely the organization of a recall matches the organization of a text, the more likely it is that the reader noted and used (was aware of) text organization while reading and recalling.

The 60 testing materials for the present study were adapted from *College English* (Books 3 & 4) compiled by Li Yinhua which were published by Shanghai Foreign Language Education Press and *CET-4* (reading comprehension). Because very few naturally occurring texts are written that exactly fit text structure patterns, only part of the passages are adopted. In order to establish that each of the passages was representative of the structure it was composed to follow, another two teachers were given the 60 passages to read in random order. They were told to label the overall structure of each passage. Only few passages were not correctly labeled by the teachers. These passages were replaced by other passages to make the structures more salient. The passages include 20 expository texts, 20 argumentative texts and 20 narrative texts. 5 passages with collection of descriptions structure, 5 passages with causation structure, 5 with problem and solution and 5 with comparison structure were selected for expository text, argumentative text and narrative text respectively.

The experiment was conducted within 8 weeks, with two 45-minute session the first 7 weeks and one 45-minute session the last week. In each 45-minute session, students were given the 4 passages randomly selected from the 60 passages, accompanied by written instructions which asked them to read the text to find out what it said about the topic. Students were told to devote approximately equal time and attention to all passages. They were to write down everything they could remember from the text, using their own words or words from the texts. They were asked to try to write in complete sentences and not just to list isolated words or ideas.

Scores were obtained from the recall task according to the percentages of main ideas and how well the students' organization of their recall of the passages resembled the organization. For each structure, a scale (0 to 1) was developed. A score of 1 indicates that main information of the passage was recalled with using the organization in his or her recall that was similar to the organization of the passage; a score of 0 indicates that the student randomly ordered ideas in the recall and little of the main ideas recalled.

All the written recall were coded and analyzed for different types of writing (expository text, argumentative text and narrative text) and different discourse structures (collection of descriptions, causation, problem/solution and comparison). All the data collected at the first step were typed into computer and analyzed in SPSS.

For Research Questions, firstly, descriptive data for each types of writing was drawn. The comparisons of different discourse structures in the same types of writing and the comparisons of different types of writing in the same discourse structures were made by using one-way ANOVA and Scheffe Multiple Comparison to examine whether there are any significant differences in the discourse structures in the same type of writing and whether there are any significant differences in the types of writing with the same discourse structures.

3.5 Empirical approaches to reading comprehension

The following displays the results from the quantitative study. First, it presents the results about students' recognizing and utilizing the discourse organization of the original text in expository text, argumentative text and narrative respectively in order to examine what kind of features shown in Chinese EFL learner' written recall. Then with the purpose to find out whether there are any differences in different discourse structures in the same types of writing, the comparison results are presented by one-way ANOVE and Scheffe Multiple Comparison. Second, it presents the results about learners' recognizing and utilizing the discourse organization of the original text in collection of descriptions, causation, problem/solution and comparison respectively in order to examine what kind of features shown in Chinese EFL learner' written recall. The comparison results are also presented by one-way ANOVE and Scheffe Multiple Comparison to examine whether there are any differences in different types of writing in the same discourse structure.

3.5.1 Data analysis in types of writing

The data analysis started with the descriptive data in different types of writing. The means, standard deviations of expositive text, argumentative text and narrative text produced by learners are displayed in Table 3.1, Table 3.2 and Table 3.3. "Col" stands for collection of descriptions, "Cau" for causation, "P/S" for problem/solution and "Com" for comparison; "Exp" stands for expositive text, "Arg" for argumentative text and "Nar" for narrative text.

Table 3.1   **Means and standard deviations of expository text**

Variable		N	Mean	Std. Deviation	Std. Error	95% Confidence Interval for Mean		Minimum	Maximum
						Lower Bound	Upper Bound		
Exp	Col	50	2.00	1.370	.194	1.61	2.39	0	5
	Cau	50	3.40	1.143	.162	3.08	3.72	1	5
	P/S	50	3.60	1.245	.176	3.25	3.95	1	5
	Com	50	4.14	.948	.134	3.87	4.41	2	5
	Total	200	3.29	1.419	.100	3.09	3.48	0	5

Descriptive data in Table 3.1 shows that the mean of information recalled from the collection of descriptions top-level structure is 2.00, the minimum is 0; the mean for causation is 3.40; the mean for problem and solution is 3.60 and for comparison is 4.14, the std. deviation is 0.948, the minimum is 2. There is a clear distinction between causation, problem/solution and comparison on the one hand, and collection of descriptions on the other. The result in Table 3.1 reveals that subjects recalled much more information, recognizing and utilizing the discourse organization of the original text from passages with causation, problem/solution and comparison structures. The subjects did best when recalling from the passages with comparison structure. It is a little difficult for subjects to remember and recall information from passages with collection of descriptions. Thus, subjects recalled more information from causation, problem/solution and comparison than that from collection of descriptions. The data indicates that most subjects recognized the text structures and used the text structure as an aid for understanding and remembering the main information from the passages with causation, problem/solution and comparison structures.

Table 3.2   **Means and standard deviations of argumentative text**

Variable		N	Mean	Std. Deviation	Std. Error	95% Confidence Interval for Mean		Minimum	Maximum
						Lower Bound	Upper Bound		
Arg	Col	50	3.26	1.291	.183	2.89	3.63	1	5
	Cau	50	3.20	1.125	.159	2.88	3.52	1	5
	P/S	50	4.02	1.059	.150	3.72	4.32	1	5
	Com	50	3.86	1.143	.162	3.54	4.18	1	5
	Total	200	3.59	1.204	.085	3.42	3.75	1	5

The data displayed in Table 3.2 shows that the mean of information recalled from the collection of descriptions top-level structure is 3.26; the mean for causation is 3.20; the mean for problem and solution is 4.02 and std. deviation is 1.059; the mean for comparison is 3.86. There is a clear distinction between problem/solution and comparison on the one hand, and collection of descriptions and causation on the other hand. The result in Table 3.2 reveals that subjects recalled much more information, recognizing and utilizing the discourse organization of the original texts from argumentative text problem/solution and comparison than that from collection of descriptions and causation. It is much easier for subjects to recognize and follow the discourse organization of the original text in their recall from problem/solution.

Table 3.3   **Means and standard deviations of narrative text**

Variable		N	Mean	Std. Deviation	Std. Error	95% Confidence Interval for Mean		Minimum	Maximum
						Lower Bound	Upper Bound		
Nar	Col	50	2.40	1.485	.210	1.98	2.82	0	5
	Cau	50	3.90	1.129	.160	3.58	4.22	1	5
	P/S	50	4.12	1.154	.163	3.79	4.45	0	5
	Com	50	3.36	1.382	.195	2.97	3.75	0	5
	Total	200	3.45	1.448	.102	3.24	3.65	0	5

As to narrative text, data in Table 3.3 shows that the mean of information recalled from the collection of descriptions top-level structure is 2.40; the mean for causation is 3.90; the means for problem/solution is 4.12 and for comparison is 3.36. As shown in the table, there is a significant distinction between causation, problem/solution and comparison on the one hand and collection of descriptions on the other. The figures in Table 3.3 reveal that subjects recalled much more information, recognizing and utilizing the discourse organization of the original text from causation, problem/solution and comparison. The subjects did best when recalling from the problem/solution structure. It is a little difficult for subjects to remember and recall information from passages with collection of descriptions. Thus, subjects recalled more information from causation, problem/solution and comparison than from the collection of descriptions. The data indicates that most subjects recognized the text structure and used text structure as an aid for understanding and remembering the main information in the passages with causation, problem/solution and comparison structures.

Table 3.4   **Descriptive means by discourse structures within types of writing**

Variable	Col	Cau	P/S	Com	Total
Exp	2.00	3.40	3.60	4.14	3.29
Arg	3.26	3.20	4.02	3.86	3.59
Nar	2.40	3.90	4.12	3.36	3.45

The data displayed in Table 3.4 indicates that subjects recalled more information from expository and narrative texts with causation, problem/solution and comparison structure over collection of descriptions. The data shows that it is a little difficult for students to recognize and utilize the discourse organization of the original text and recall more information in their own recall from the collection of descriptions. The data also shows that subjects recalled more information from argumentative text with problem/solution structure and causation structure than that of the collection of descriptions and causation.

The data shows that the effects of discourse structure are not the same for each types of writing although they are not sufficiently strong to have produced an overall significant interaction of types of writing by discourse structure. Thus, depending on the types of writing, different discourse types appear to have different effects on the quantity of information reproduced in recall and on the recognizing and utilizing the discourse organization of the original text.

In order to test if the three types of writing in the tasks would be significantly different in the collection of descriptions, causation, problem/solution and comparison in recall. One-way ANOVA test is conducted on the three types of writing with collection of descriptions, causation, problem/solution and comparison in Table 3.5. The Scheffe post-hoc test shows a significant difference between different discourse structures in Table 3.6, Table 3.7 and Table 3.8.

Table 3.5   **ANOVA test of recall of the types of writing across the discourse structure (N = 50)**

Variable		Sum of Squares	df	Mean Square	F	Sig.
Exp	Between Groups	124.735	3	41.578	29.525	.000
	Within Groups	276.020	196	1.408		
	Total	400.755	199			
Arg	Between Groups	25.935	3	8.645	6.452	.000
	Within Groups	262.620	196	1.340		
	Total	288.555	199			
Nar	Between Groups	88.095	3	29.365	17.478	.000
	Within Groups	329.300	196	1.680		
	Total	417.395	199			

* $p < 0.5$

As shown in Table 3.5, the ANOVA analysis identifies a significant difference among the discourse structures in expository text (sig. $= .00 < .05$), argumentative text (sig. $= .00 < .05$) and narrative text (sig. $= .00 < .05$). Expository text, argumentative text and narrative text are found to be factors significantly associated with students' recognizing and utilizing the discourse organization of the text in their own recall. In order to determine the distribution of difference among the discourse structures, Post hoc multiple comparisons are made as Table 3.6, Table 3.7 and Table 3.8 display.

Table 3.6   **Multiple comparisons of discourse structures of expository text**

Variable	(I) Type	(J) Type	Mean Difference (I-J)	Std. Error	Sig.
Exp	Col	Cau	−1.400(*)	.237	.000
		P/S	−1.600(*)	.237	.000
		Com	−2.140(*)	.237	.000
	Cau	Col	1.400(*)	.237	.000
		P/S	−.200	.237	.871
		Com	−.740(*)	.237	.023
	P/S	Col	1.600(*)	.237	.000
		Cau	.200	.237	.871
		Com	−.540	.237	.163
	Com	Col	2.140(*)	.237	.000
		Cau	.740(*)	.237	.023
		P/S	.540	.237	.163

* $p < 0.5$

As shown in Table 3.6, significant difference at .00 level is discovered between collection of descriptions and causation, at .00 level between collection of descriptions and problem/solution and at .00 level between collection of descriptions and comparison in terms of expository text and at .023 level between causation and comparison. The figures in the table demonstrate that there is no significant difference between causation and problem/solution: for sig. $= .871 > .05$. So the two structures are also the same level in recall. There is also no significant difference between problem/solution and comparison: for sig. $= .163 > .05$. So the two structures are also the same level in recall. For expository writing, an planned comparison between the collection of descriptions on the one hand, and the rest three discourse structures on the other hand, was significant. Thus for expository writing the causation, problem/solution and comparison discourse structures are statistically better recalled than the collection of descriptive ones.

Table 3.7　　　**Multiple comparisons of discourse structures of argumentative text**

Variable	(I) Type	(J) Type	Mean Difference (I-J)	Std. Error	Sig.
Arg	Col	Cau	.060	.232	.995
		P/S	−.760(*)	.232	.015
		Com	−.600	.232	.085
	Cau	Col	−.060	.232	.995
		P/S	−.820(*)	.232	.007
		Com	−.660(*)	.232	.046
	P/S	Col	.760(*)	.232	.015
		Cau	.820(*)	.232	.007
		Com	.160	.232	.924
	Com	Col	.600	.232	.085
		Cau	.660(*)	.232	.046
		P/S	−.160	.232	.924

* p<0.5

As displayed in Table 3.7, significant difference at .015 level is discovered between collection of descriptions and problem and solution; at .007 level between causation and problem/solution; and at .046 level between causation and comparison in terms of argumentative text. As figures in the table show, there is no significant difference between collection of descriptions: for sig. =.995>.05. So the two structures are the same level in recall. There is also no difference between collection of descriptions and comparison: for sig. =.085>.05, which indicates that the two structures are the same level in recall. As to problem/solution and comparison, there is no significant difference between them for sig. =.924>.05, which indicates the two structures are also the same level in recall. Thus, for argumentative writing, only problem/solution structure is statistically better recalled than the collection of descriptions structure.

As shown in Table 3.8, significant difference at .00 was discovered between collection of descriptions and causation. And significant difference at .00 was discovered between collection of descriptions and problem/solution. The significant difference at .004 levels was discovered between collection of descriptions and causation. The significant difference was at .038 level between problem/solution and comparison in terms of the narrative text. There is no significant difference between causation and problem/solution: for sig. =.868 >.05. So the two structures are the same level in recall. There is also no significant difference between causation and comparison: for sig. =.231 >.05. Thus causation and comparison are the same level in recall.

Table 3.8   **Multiple comparisons of discourse structures of narrative text**

Variable	(I) Type	(J) Type	Mean Difference (I-J)	Std. Error	Sig.
Nar	Col	Cau	−1.500(*)	.259	.000
		P/S	−1.720(*)	.259	.000
		Com	−.960(*)	.259	.004
	Cau	Col	1.500(*)	.259	.000
		P/S	−.220	.259	.868
		Com	.540	.259	.231
	P/S	Col	1.720(*)	.259	.000
		Cau	.220	.259	.868
		Com	.760(*)	.259	.038
	Com	Col	.960(*)	.259	.004
		Cau	−.540	.259	.231
		P/S	−.760(*)	.259	.038

* $p < 0.5$

So a comparison between the collection of descriptions and the rest three discourse structures is significant. Thus for narrative writing, the causation, problem/solution and comparison structures are statistically better recalled than the collection of descriptions structure.

3.5.2 Data analysis in discourse structures

In order to give a full-scale investigation on the discourse structure, the means, standard deviations of collection of descriptions, causation, problem/solution and comparison produced by expository text, argumentative text and narrative text were also analyzed (Table 3.9, Table 3.10, Table 3,11 and Table 3.12). The means and standard deviations of collection of descriptions are displayed in Table 3.9. Descriptive data in Table 3.9 shows that, referring to collection of descriptions, the mean of information recalled, recognizing and utilizing the discourse organization of the original text from expository text is 2.00 and minimum is 0. And the mean for argumentative text is 3.26, the minimum is 1. The mean for narrative text is 2.40 and the minimum is 0. The data shows that in terms of collection of descriptions the subjects recalled much more information, followed the structure in their recall of the original argumentative text than they did from expository text and narrative text.

Table 3.9　　　　　**Means and standard deviations of collection of descriptions**

Variable		N	Mean	Std. Deviation	Std. Error	95% Confidence Interval for Mean		Minimum	Maximum
						Lower Bound	Upper Bound		
Col	Exp	50	2.00	1.370	.194	1.61	2.39	0	5
	Arg	50	3.26	1.291	.183	2.89	3.63	1	5
	Nar	50	2.40	1.485	.210	1.98	2.82	0	5
	Total	150	2.55	1.473	.120	2.32	2.79	0	5

Table 3.10　　　　　**Means and standard deviations of causation structure**

Variable		N	Mean	Std. Deviation	Std. Error	95% Confidence Interval for Mean		Minimum	Maximum
						Lower Bound	Upper Bound		
Cau	Exp	50	3.40	1.143	.162	3.08	3.72	1	5
	Arg	50	3.20	1.125	.159	2.88	3.52	1	5
	Nar	50	3.90	1.129	.160	3.58	4.22	1	5
	Total	150	3.50	1.163	.095	3.31	3.69	1	5

Referring to causation, the mean of information recalled, recognizing and utilizing the discourse organization of the original text from expository text is 3.40; and the mean for argumentative text is 3.20; the mean for narrative text is 3.90. The data shows that in terms of causation the subjects recalled much more information following the structure in their recall of the original narrative text than they did from expository text and argumentative text.

Table 3.11　　　　　**Means and standard deviations of problem/solution structure**

Variable		N	Mean	Std. Deviation	Std. Error	95% Confidence Interval for Mean		Minimum	Maximum
						Lower Bound	Upper Bound		
P/S	Exp	50	3.60	1.245	.176	3.25	3.95	1	5
	Arg	50	4.02	1.059	.150	3.72	4.32	1	5
	Nar	50	4.12	1.154	.163	3.79	4.45	0	5
	Total	150	3.91	1.170	.096	3.72	4.10	0	5

Speaking of problem/ solution, the mean of information recalled, recognizing and utilizing the discourse organization of the original text from expository text is 3.60, the minimum is 1; And the mean for argumentative text is 4.02, the minimum is 1and 4.12 for narrative text, the minimum is 0. The data shows that in terms of problem/ solution the subjects recalled much more information and followed the structure in their recall of the original narrative text than they did in expository text and argumentative text.

Table 3.12　　　　　**Means and standard deviations of comparison structure**

Variable		N	Mean	Std. Deviation	Std. Error	95% Confidence Interval for Mean		Minimum	Maximum
						Lower Bound	Upper Bound		
Com	Exp	50	4.14	.948	.134	3.87	4.41	2	5
	Arg	50	3.86	1.143	.162	3.54	4.18	1	5
	Nar	50	3.36	1.382	.195	2.97	3.75	0	5
	Total	150	3.79	1.207	.099	3.59	3.98	0	5

As to comparison, the mean of main information recalled, recognizing and utilizing the discourse organization of the original text from expository text is 3.14, std. deviation is .948 and minimum is 2; the mean for argumentative text is 3.86, minimum is 1 and 3.36 for narrative text with minimum 0. The data shows that in terms of comparison the subjects recalled much more information and followed the structure in their recall of the original expository text than they did from argumentative text and narrative text.

Table 3.13　　　　**Descriptive means by types of writing within discourse structures**

Variable	Expository Text	Argumentative Text	Narrative Text
Col	2.00	3.26	2.40
Cau	3.40	3.20	3.90
P/S	3.60	4.02	4.12
Com	4.14	3.86	3.36
Total	3.29	3.59	3.45

The data displayed in Table 3.13 indicates that the learners did better in passages with causation, problem/solution and comparison structures than collection of descriptions structure. It shows that it is a little difficult for learners to recognize and utilize the rhetorical organization of the original text and recalled more information in their own recall from expository text and narrative text with the collection of descriptions structure. We can see that the recall is better for the texts with more tightly organized discourses. The data also shows that the effects of types of writing are not the same for each discourse structure though they are not sufficiently strong to have produced an overall significant interaction of discourse structure by types of writing.

In order to investigate whether there are any significant differences in expository text, argumentative text and narrative text of Chinese EFL learners in recall in the four different discourse structures, one-way ANOVA test was conducted on the different discourse structures in Table 4.16. Post hoc multiple comparisons are made to see the interactions of discourse structures by types of writing in Tables 3.15, 3.16 and 3.17.

As shown in Table 3.14, there is a significant difference among types of writings with collection of descriptions (sig. =.000<.05), causation (sig. =.007<.05) and comparison (sig. =.004<.05). And there is an insignificant difference in problem/solution (sig. =.061 >.05). Collection of descriptions, causation and comparison are found to be factors significantly associated with learners' recognizing and utilizing the discourse organization of the original text in their own recall. There is an insignificant difference between types of writing in learners' recognizing and utilizing the discourse organization of the original texts in their own recall from problem/solution. It is quite easy for subjects to recognize and follow the problem/solution in their recall of the original passages. The recall is better for texts with problem/solution.

Table 3.14   ANOVA test of recall of the discourse structure across the types of writing (N=50)

Variable		Sum of Squares	df	Mean Square	F	Sig.
Col	Between Groups	41.453	2	20.727	10.819	.000
	Within Groups	281.620	147	1.916		
	Total	323.073	149			
Cau	Between Groups	13.000	2	6.500	5.069	.007
	Within Groups	188.500	147	1.282		
	Total	201.500	149			
P/S	Between Groups	7.613	2	3.807	2.851	.061
	Within Groups	196.260	147	1.335		
	Total	203.873	149			
Com	Between Groups	15.613	2	7.807	5.693	.004
	Within Groups	201.560	147	1.371		
	Total	217.173	149			

* The mean difference is significant at the .05 level.

In order to determine the distribution of difference among the different types of writings, Post hoc multiple comparisons were made as Table 3.15, Table 3.16, Table 3.17 displayed. As shown in Table 3.15, significant difference at .000 level is discovered between expository text and argumentative text in terms of collection of description; significant difference at .009 level between argumentative text and narrative text. There is no significant difference between expository text and narrative text: for sig. =.355>.05. So the two types of writing are at the same level in recall in terms of collection of descriptive structure. Thus for collection of descriptions, the argumentative writing is significantly better recalled than expository writing and narrative writing.

Table 3.15   **Multiple comparisons of types of writing of collection of descriptions**

Dependent Variable	(I) Style	(J) Style	Mean Difference (I-J)	Std. Error	Sig.
Col	Exp	Arg	−1.260(*)	.277	.000
		Nar	−.400	.277	.355
	Arg	Exp	1.260(*)	.277	.000
		Nar	.860(*)	.277	.009
	Nar	Exp	.400	.277	.355
		Arg	-.860(*)	.277	.009

* p<0.5

Table 3.16   **Multiple comparisons of types of writing of causation**

Dependent Variable	(I) Style	(J) Style	Mean Difference (I-J)	Std. Error	Sig.
Cau	Exp	Arg	.200	.226	.678
		Nar	−.500	.226	.091
	Arg	Exp	−.200	.226	.678
		Nar	-.700(*)	.226	.010
	Nar	Exp	.500	.226	.091
		Arg	.700(*)	.226	.010

* p<0.5

Data in Table 3.16 shows that significant difference at .010 is discovered between the argumentative text and the narrative text in terms of causation. There is no significant difference between the expository text and the argumentative text: for sig. =.678>.05. The two types of writing are at the same level in recall. There is also no significant difference between expository text and narrative text: for sig. =.091>.05. Thus the two types of writing are at the same level in recall in terms of causation.

Table 3.17   **Multiple comparisons of types of writing of comparison**

Dependent Variable	(I) Style	(J) Style	Mean Difference (I-J)	Std. Error	Sig.
Com	Exp	Arg	.280	.234	.491
		Nar	.780(*)	.234	.005
	Arg	Exp	−.280	.234	.491
		Nar	.500	.234	.106
	Nar	Exp	−.780(*)	.234	.005
		Arg	−.500	.234	.106

* p<0.5

As shown in Table 3.17, significant difference at .005 level is discovered between expository text and narrative text in terms of comparison. There is no significant difference between expository text and argumentative text: for sig. =.491>.05. Thus the two types of writing are at the same level in recall. And there is also no significant difference between argumentative text and narrative text: for sig. =.106>.05. So argumentative text and narrative text are at the same level in recall in terms of comparison. From the analysis of the learners' performance in discourse structure, there was an insignificant difference between types of writing in learners' recognizing and utilizing the discourage organization of the original text in their own recall from passages with problem and solution structure. For collection of descriptions argumentative writing is significantly better recalled than expository and narrative writing.

Descriptive data of learners' using the structure of the original text in recall in Table 3.18 shows that most subjects are able to identify the top-level structure of the passage and use the structure as an aid in comprehending and memorizing the passage. The identification and utilization of the same structure of original text enable the reader to remember more information from the text.

Table 3.18   **Percentage of learners' utilizing the structure of the original text in recall**

Variable	Utilize the Original Structure in Recall	Not Utilize the Original Structure in Recall
Exp	65.8%	34.2%
Aru	69%	31%
Nar	71%	29%
Total	68.6%	31.4%

3.6 Schema activation of reading comprehension

On the basis of the work described in the preceding part, the implications of the study will be further discussed at length. The picture of Chinese EFL learners' awareness of text structure that emerged from the present study was complex. Learners showed varying degrees of awareness of the reading structures depending upon the rhetoric structures and the types of writing. It produces the information about differences in awareness of the four text structures in expository, argumentative and narrative text.

Implication 1: The more tightly organized comparison, causation and problem/solution types tend to be more facilitative of recall of main information from a text than the more loosely organized collection of descriptions.

The major finding emerged from this experiment is that differences in rhetorical structures affect learning and recalling. Results show the significant differences between the four types of top-level rhetorical structures in the quantity of information recalled by Chinese learners. The mean of important information recalled from the passages with the collection of descriptions structure is lower than that from the passages with the causation, problem/solution and comparison structure in expository text and in narrative text. Data collected indicate that for expository text and narrative text, the comparison, causation, and problem/solution discourse structures are significantly better recalled than the collection of descriptions structure. As to argumentative writing, only problem/solution structure is statistically better recalled than the collection of descriptions structure. Thus the different top-level text structures have effect upon Chinese learners' comprehension and recall. The hypothesis that more tightly organized causation, problem/solution and comparison rhetorical structures are more facilitative of comprehension than the more loosely organized collection of descriptions has been confirmed in expository text and in narrative text but not confirmed in argumentative text.

The previous findings of high awareness of the problem/solution, causation and comparison structure are repeated in expository text and narrative text. Here awareness of the problem/solution, causation and comparison structure are significantly greater than the awareness of collection of descriptions in expository text and narrative text. As shown in Figure 3. 1, the first category, the order of the structures goes from description to collection, to causation, and ends at problem/solution. In other words, the problem/solution structure is the most organized structure in the first category. The comparison structure is on a separated scale because it does not organize on the basis of time or causality, but organizes on the basis of similarity and differences. Meyer and Freedle (1984) assumed that the lower the number of structures on the scale, the more poorly the texts organized by the structures can be recalled. But in argumentative text, awareness of problem/solution is much greater than the awareness of collection of descriptions, causation and comparison.

The data also demonstrate the importance of text structure knowledge in facilitating comprehension and recall. Most subjects are able to identify the top-level structure of the passages and use the structure as an aid in comprehending and memorizing the passages. The structure- aware reader approaches texts with knowledge about how they are conventionally organized (i. e. problem/solution, collection of description, etc.). The structure-aware reader uses this knowledge to select from among a finite numbers of textual schemata the schema that is most appropriate for the text in question. In other words, if a text is written with a comparison top-level structure, the structure aware reader is able to activate her or his comparison schema and to use it to guide the reading of the passage. Later, the structure-aware reader is able to use the same process to retrieve information. The identification and utilization of the same structure of schema of the original text enable the reader to remember more ideas from the text. On the other hand, readers who are not aware of the top-level structure, or who do not have the appropriated schemata to activate during reading will recall less information from the text. Thus, knowledge of the text structure has been shown to aid in encoding as well as in reproduction of the passages.

Implication 2: Chinese learners of English experience differences among the four types in rhetorical organization of expository text, argumentative text and narrative text in written

recalls.

There appear to be significant differences among types of writing as to which English rhetorical structures are more or less facilitative of recall. In the texts with collection of descriptive structures, learners recalled better from the argumentative text and it is a little difficult for learners to recall from the expository text. As to the text with causation structure students recalled better from narrative texts. The data show that it is not difficult for learners to recognize and utilize the rhetorical organization of the original text from problem/solution. The learners recalled better compared with other discourse structures. As to comparison, learners recalled better from the expository text (mean = 4. 14; standard deviation = . 948 and minimum = 2). Data show that there was an insignificant difference between types of writing in learners' recognizing and utilizing the discourse organization of the original text in their own recall from passages with problem/solution. As shown in Figure 3. 1, the first category, the order of the structures goes from description to collection to causation, and ends at problem/solution. In other words, problem/solution structure is the most organized structure in the first category. The study also raises the possibility that discourse structures patterned after the comparison and response organizations with much overlap of issues may be particularly resistant to forgetting over time due to economy of storage in memory. For collection of descriptions, argumentative writing is significantly better recalled than expository and narrative texts.

The features of the differences of the subjects' performance in recall from different types of writing can be explained in several ways. First, because some subjects have had more knowledge about the structures and known quite well about the features of these three types of writing. They may have more experience reading and learning from passages with collection of descriptions etc. They may have more opportunities to develop concepts about the features of certain structures in certain types of writing. Readers may have more prior information about certain passage topics or have a great facility in producing written recall. Second, the subjects who recall more important information are aware of structure in text and they may employ a more effective strategy of using text structure to guide encoding and retrieval of textual ideas. Conversely, the subjects who are not aware of text structure use a less effective strategy of serial and discrete encoding of textual information and random retrieval of ideas.

Implication 3: Higher-level processing skills (use of background knowledge, for example) may be transferred to a second language, and may compensate for inadequacies in lower- level linguistic skills.

The hypothesis that reading strategies may be transferred from L1 to L2 is supported in this study. Some learners have transferred aspects of their ability to read in Chinese to reading in English. Some subjects realize the similarities between the rhetorical patterns in English expository, argumentative and narrative writings and in Chinese writings and these similarities helped them in their comprehension and recall. This seems to indicate that there is a transfer of higher-level reading strategies in Chinese such as structure strategy into the reading of English. Research findings by Hudson (1982) have already proved that reading strategies transfer from one language to another. Block believes that strategy used is not tied to specific language features and that readers of a second language bring with them their knowledge of the reading process and of approaches to specific tasks and apply these to specific language features in the text. The results of Hudson's study indicate that L2 readers are able to apply cognitive strategies to their reading in a second language and that this application of strategies is not dependent on English language proficiency. One reason which may account for the transfer of structure strategy is that certain similarities exist between the rhetorical structures of Chinese writings and those of English writings. Therefore it is likely that there exist in some of the learners' mind similar schemata as those of English writings. A second reason may be that the structure strategy is a skill that is also taught in reading in Chinese. This skill thus becomes a conscious strategy for Chinese learners. This strategy was automatically transferred into the reading of English and assisted in instantiating the learners' schemata.

Chapter 4

The Effects of Integrated Reading-Writing Approach on Reading/Writing Proficiency

Reading and writing are two of the most important components of language performance. Krashen's input hypothesis (1985) maintains that comprehensible input is the sole source of language acquisition and second language acquisition will automatically occur only if L2 learners obtain sufficient comprehensible input. Swain's output hypothesis (1985) argues that only with both comprehensible input and comprehensible output in language acquisition can language learners use a second language fluently and accurately. The two hypotheses verify that input and output complement each other; neither of the two is dispensable. They also lay a solid foundation for an "input-construction-comprehension-output-input" model in which input, construction, comprehension and output constitute a circular developmental sequence. Widdowson (1978) illuminates the language acquisition process from a communicative aspect. Claiming that the four language skills are interrelated and interdependent, he advocates an integrated approach to improve language acquisition. Kucer (2005) puts forward a cognitive model of reading-writing processes which regards reading and writing as parallel or complementary processes instead of inverse or opposite communicative events. He elaborates the five factors impacting the reader-text-writer transaction: systems of language, availability of and flexibility with the strategies, background knowledge, purpose, ability and willingness to assimilate and/or accommodate; and points out that reading and writing processes share the following cognitive features in common: searching, generating and integrating meaning; making use of linguistic and cognitive resources actively; using and building background knowledge; depending on context; revising meaning; being goal/purpose-oriented.

The purpose of this study was to examine the effects of the integrated reading-writing approach on EFL learners' reading/writing proficiency. The subjects involved in the study were 98 non-English major freshmen of three different classes from Wuhan University (31 majoring in Information Management, 33 majoring in Surveying and Mapping, and 34 majoring in Water Quality Science and Technology). During the 12-week experiment, the three classes respectively received three different teaching approaches: an integrated reading-writing approach, an enhanced reading input approach and an enhanced writing output approach. The testing instrument was a reading-writing test paper for revealing subjects' reading and writing proficiency before and after the experiment, together with a supplementary questionnaire of reading/writing strategies. The research data were analyzed via the statistical tools of Paired Samples T-test and one-way ANOVA in SPSS.

The analysis of the data revealed that the integrated reading-writing approach is significantly effective in improving EFL learners' writing proficiency, the enhanced reading input approach also has significant effects on improving their writing proficiency, but the enhanced writing output approach shows no evident effects; in addition, none of the three approaches mentioned above has significantly positive effects on improving EFL learners' reading proficiency, indicating that there exists fossilization in college EFL learners' reading proficiency in China.

4.1 The nature and processes of reading

Reading is a complicated psycholinguistic process, which "starts with linguistic surface representation encoded by a writer and ends with the meaning which the reader constructs". (Carrel, Devine & Eskey, 1988). It has often been said that the one foreign-language skill that learners retain throughout their lives is reading. For many learners, reading is by far the most important of the four skills in a second language, particularly in English as a second or foreign language (Carrell, 1988). Therefore, it is absolutely necessary for teachers to understand the nature and process of reading so that they can teach effectively, since the views they hold of reading are usually revealed in their teaching process.

4.1.1 The nature of reading

Reading is a very important source of language input in language learning and it is a good way for learners to obtain new information and knowledge. Different people use the term "reading" in different ways. The recognition of the nature of reading has experienced a long struggle, in which both linguists and psycholinguists have engaged.

Traditionally, reading has been viewed as a passive decoding process in which the reader reconstructs the author's intended meaning by means of matching sounds to printed letters and words, and accumulating a meaning for the whole text from the "bottom" to the "top" of a hierarchy (Li Li & Chen Zhi'an, 1997: 279). With the development of psycholinguistics and cognitive psychology, people have found that reading is not a passive decoding, but an active process of "predicting and testing" (Goodman, 1971: 135). In other words, reading can be described as a psycholinguistic process in that it starts with a linguistic surface representation encoded by writer and ends with meaning which the reader reconstructs (Goodman, 1979). Given this perspective, reading is a two-way communication process in which the writer encodes thought as language and the reader decodes language as thought. Widdowson (1979) regards reading as the process of combining textual information with the information a reader brings to the text. In this view reading is seen as a kind of dialogue between the reader and the text to be processed, because the reading process is not simply a process of extracting information from the text but a process in which reading activates a range of knowledge in the reader's mind that he or she uses, and that, in turn, may be refined and extended by the new information supplied by the text.

So reading is not a passive process of receiving information, but an active way to think, to infer and to reason, and in fact a communicative and interactive process involving linguistic and psycholinguistic factors, the essence of which is to construct or arrive at meaning.

4.1.2 The reading processes

For second language learners, it is essential to read well in a target language. Reading is probably the most important skill in learning a foreign language. The importance of reading has initiated much research in SLA, and the reading process has been one of the key aspects of reading research. In the L2 reading domain, theories about the mental nature of L2 reading generally fall into three categories: the bottom-up model, the top-down model, and the interactive model.

From the 30s to the 60s of the 20th century, the bottom-up model dominated the reading field because behaviorism took over the mainstream of experimental psychology during this period. The bottom-up theory was proposed by Gough (1972). The main feature of this model is focus on the function of the text itself. Gough believes that reading is a series of discrete stages. He describes the reading process as following: a) When reading starts, the reader's eyes first notice the printed symbols; b) When the symbols form a figure representation on the retina, , the reader begins to identify the letters; c) The words composed by the letters are searched for meaning in the reader's "psychological dictionary" and then added to the sentence to process sentence meaning; d) The words in the sentence are comprehended from the left to the right. All these discrete stages happen within a very short time, and the information is passed on in a linear fashion (Cheng Xiaotang & Zheng Min, 2002).

Cambourne (1979), who uses the term "outside-in" rather than bottom-up, provides the following illustration (Figure 4.1) of how the process is supposed to work:

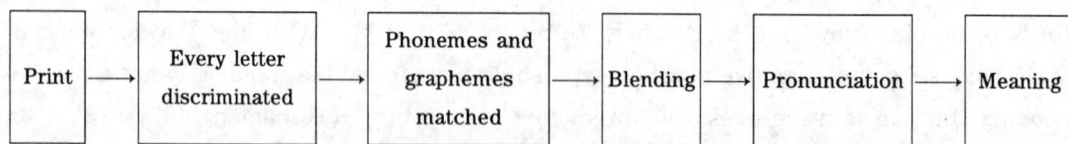

Figure 4.1 Cambourne's (1979) bottom-up model of reading

According to this model, the reader processes every letter as it is encountered. These letters, or graphemes, are matched with the phonemes of the language. These phonemes (the individual units of sound in a language) are blended together to form words. The derivation of meaning is thus the end process in which the language is translated from one form of symbolic representation to another (Nunan, 1991).

Supporters of this model believe that reading is primarily a decoding process of recognizing the printed letters and words and building up a meaning for a text from the smallest textual units at the "bottom" (letters and words) to larger units at the "top" (phrases, clauses, inter-sentential linkages, etc.). In reading, readers analyze small chunks of text and gradually add them to the next chunks until the text becomes meaningful.

Bottom-up models underlie much early work in second and foreign language reading. Cambourne (1979) says it was the basis of the vast majority of reading schemes. Bottom-up approach has a great influence on reading teaching in China. The traditional way of teaching reading in China belongs to a bottom-up model. The teacher guides students to read from the smaller units (letters and words) to the larger units (phrases, sentences, paragraphs and texts). As a result, vocabulary and grammar are highlighted in the teaching. Enlarging vocabulary and reinforcing grammatical knowledge become the main task in reading class. However, gradually, the model began to attract criticism due to its deficiencies. An obvious shortcoming of this model is that it regards reading as a static and passive process, ignoring learners' motivation, interests and attitudes towards the content of the text. The reader needs to do nothing more than manage to get the meaning from the text. Explanation of words and sentences is isolated from their context, cultural background and the reader's prior knowledge of text topic; therefore, both reading speed and reading comprehension are greatly affected.

Bottom-up model pays much attention to the detailed analysis of words, sentences and grammar structure; it is viewed as a text-based decoding process. Word recognition is its essential point. However, sometimes it is difficult for the readers to understand a sentence even if they know every word in the sentence, which indicates that meaning does not merely exist in words. In the middle of the 60s of the 20th century, another reading approach which is opposite to the bottom-up model and based on cognitive psychology came into being. That is top-down model, proposed by Goodman (1967). He suggests, during reading, the reader plays the central and active role; he or she uses his or her previous knowledge to comprehend the whole text. He also calls reading "a psycholinguistic guessing game". According to this opinion, the top-down model is considered as knowledge-based and the reading process operates in a linear fashion, proceeding from the highest level down to the lowest level. Based on Goodman's views, Cambourne (1979) provides the following schematization of the approach (Figure 4.2).

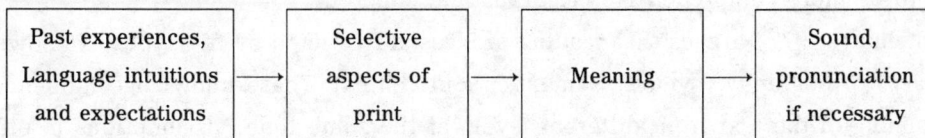

Past experiences, Language intuitions and expectations	→	Selective aspects of print	→	Meaning	→	Sound, pronunciation if necessary

Figure 4.2   Cambourne's (1979) top-down model of reading

The diagram, which goes in accordance with Goodman's model, indicates that the top-down model emphasizes the reconstruction of meaning instead of the decoding of form. In fact, Goodman's theory provides good explanations of this figure. Goodman (1967) argues that readers use their knowledge of syntax and semantics to reduce their dependence on the print and phonics of the text and specifies four processes in reading. first, readers make predictions about the grammatical structure in a text, using their knowledge of the language and supplying semantic concepts to get meaning from the structure. Then, they sample the print to confirm their predictions. They neither see nor need to see every letter or word. The more highly developed the readers' sense of syntax and meaning, the more selective the readers can be in sampling. After sampling, they confirm their guesses of what they see does not make sense or if the graphic input predict is not there. As Goodman (1967) writes, "in all this it is meaning which makes the system go", but the model does allow the reader to move from print to sound to meaning when necessary.

Top-down model has a deep affection on reading and is believed to have greatly helped people to understand the action of reading (Eskey, 1998). However, in contrast with the bottom-up model, the top-down model goes to another extreme. It overemphasizes the role of top knowledge (e. g. background knowledge) while ignores the low skills of accurate identification of words and grammar structure. It tends to emphasize such higher-level skills as prediction of meaning by means of context clues or certain kinds of background knowledge at the expense of such lower level skills as rapid and accurate identification of lexical and grammatical. That is, in making the perfectly valid point that fluent reading is primarily a cognitive process, they tend to de-emphasize perceptual and decoding dimensions of skillful, fluent readers, for whom perception and decoding have become automatic, but for the less proficient, developing readers—like most second language readers—this model does not provide a true picture of the problems such readers must surmount (Clarke, 1979, 1980).

Bottom-up model and top-down model are usually regarded as linearity as they hold that every stage in reading process proceeds separately and passes on its result to the next stage. However, current models of the reading process focus on the interactive relation of reader and text, seeing reading process as an interactive process. In the last thirty years, beginning with Rumelhart (1977), researchers have proposed interactive models of reading which argue that lower-level and high-level processes work together interactively as parts of reading process. The issue is not only the relation of the reader to the text but also the processing relations among various component skills in reading. The interactive models attempt to be more comprehensive, rigorous and coherent.

Rumelhart (1977) argues that reading process is restricted by five types of knowledge: vocabulary, orthography, syntax, semantics and context. These knowledge influences the understanding of the text from different level, at the same time, assumptions in different levels work together to help the reader comprehend the visual information. The information centre is the synthesizer. He views reading process as not only obtaining information from the text, but also a behavior of activating the reader's past experience and knowledge, and also a simultaneous interaction of the text and the reader. Thus, a new and more reasonable model, the interactive model, came into being. Figure 4. 3 (Rumelhart 1977) shows us clearly about its characteristics.

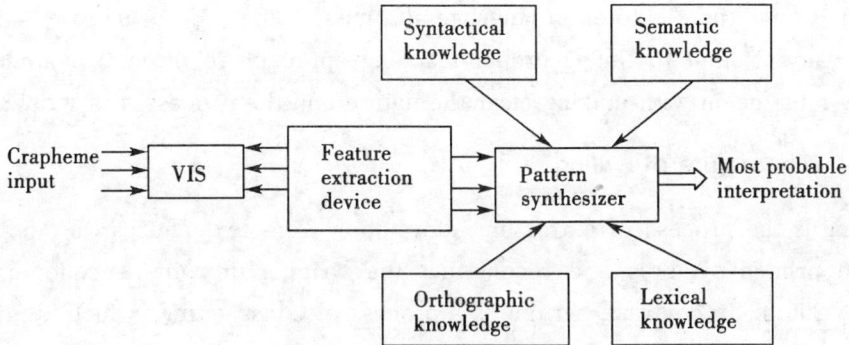

Figure 4.3   Rumelhart's (1977) interaction model of reading

The figure indicates when the reader looks at the words and spelling that are registered in a visual information store (VIS), the feature extraction device pulls out the critical features of these words (with the successful reader sampling only enough of the text to continue) and moves them into the pattern synthesizer. The pattern synthesizer is where all the reader's previous knowledge about the language spelling pattern, vocabulary, syntax, semantics and context comes together to interpret what has been read, "Thus, all of the various sources of knowledge, both sensory and non-sensory, come together at one place and the reading process is the product of the simultaneous joint application of all the knowledge sources." (Rumelhart, 1977)

The interactive model absorbs the quintessence of the bottom-up model and the top-down model by merging them together, so it shows more advantages and flexibility over them. Interactive models of reading assume that skills at all levels are interactively available to process and interpret the text. Unlike the top-down model, this interactive model does not presuppose the primacy of top-down processing skills—the gradual replacing of painful word-by-word decoding with educated guessing based on minimal visual cues—but rather posits a constant interaction between bottom-up processing and top-down processing in reading, each source of information contributing to a comprehensive reconstruction of the meaning of the text. In this view, good readers are both good decoders and good interpreters of texts, their decoding skills becoming more automatic but no less important as their reading skill develops. In their simplest forms, such models incorporate both top-down and bottom-up strategies. At the same time they also incorporate notions of rapid and accurate feature recognition for letters and words, spreading activation of lexical forms and the concept of automaticity in processing such forms—a processing that does not depend on active intentional context for primary recognition of linguistic units.

4.2   The nature and processes of writing

EFL writing is a complex, goal-directed, recursive activity (Flower & Hayes, 1980), and it reflects an ability of comprehensive language using, which leads to the fact that "in terms of skills, producing a coherent, fluent, extended piece of writing is probably the most difficult thing there is to do in language" (Nunan, 2001: 271). Due to this complexity of writing, any attempt to find a proper teaching approach to promote learners' writing proficiency must begin with making clear the nature and the processes of writing.

4.2.1 The nature of writing

Reading is the process of extracting information from text and can be defined as to decode the printed symbols and reconstruct the writer's thoughts encode in the print (McKenna, 2001). In contrast, writing is a process of constructing, which is utilized as a mean through which writers can clarify, analyze and integrate their own thoughts and knowledge to a certain topic. A writing task involves selecting, organizing, and finally encoding one's thoughts into coherent written form, the text. Writing process is a combination of individual cognitive processing, social-context influences, motivation, reading processes, and writer's background knowledge. With one's writing behaviors, it's likely that one starts with an intention one wishes to convey through writing in which one's prior knowledge about the topic may assist to construct new information. In writing process, writers' successful writing depends on their background knowledge, language knowledge. With them they might transfer their intended thoughts through a cognitive process to the audience. Gould and Smith (1989) reveal the nature of writing as follows:

> Writing is a creative act because it requires us to interpret or make sense of something: an experience, a text, and an event. We write largely in order to understand and not just to express ourselves. In fact, most of our writing in college and world of work aims both to reach an understanding and to share that understanding with other people.
>
> Writing is a way of finding out what our ideas, and even our intentions really are. And those discoveries involve a good deal of rereading and rewriting. We state and restate our ideas. Revising our texts, until we are at least reasonable satisfied that "this is what we want to say". Thus writing is also a discovery process.
>
> Writing is a form of social dialogue, a way of talking to someone. And that is true not just because it is pleasant to have conversation with people, or because it is good to be friendly with reader to win them over to our ways of seeing things. The reader is essential to complete the meaning of anything we write.

4.2.2 The writing processes

Though different researchers hold different views on writing, it is widely accepted that writing is a meaning-making activity; people write for different purposes and use various strategies to achieve those purposes. Sperling (1996) notes that "writing, like language in general, is a meaning-making activity which is socially and culturally shaped and individually and socially purposeful". Silva (1993) defines writing as a composing process which consists of three sub-processes as planning, translating and reviewing. Similarly,

White and Arndt view writing as a complex, cognitive process that requires sustained intellectual effort over a considerable period of time (cited in Nunan, 2001: 273).

Beginning at the end of the 1960s and continuing through the 70s and 80s, composition was investigated as a cognitive process (Flower & Hayes, 1981), which led to discussions about the pedagogical role of reading, and the demands of different discourse communities into the process of writing. For example, Collins and Gentner (1980) view writing as a process of generating and editing text within a variety of constraints such as those of structure, content, and purpose. They think that the writing process could be separated into two stages. One is the stage of producing ideas during which the writer is advised to brainstorm or to use adventurous thinking. The other is the text producing stage, which produces a linear sequence satisfying certain grammatical rules at the word level, the sentence level, the paragraph level, or the text level.

The cognitive process theory sees writing as thinking, especially from the pioneering work of psychologists Flower and Hayes. They gathered the findings from many studies of composing practices, and proposed a working model of the writing process (Figure 4. 4). Flower and Hayes (1981) suggested that there are essentially three cognitive writing processes: planning (deciding what to say and how to say it), text generation (turning plans into written text), and revision (improving existing text). This approach stresses the often non-linear cognitive choices that students make during the writing process, which negates the linear model pre-writing, writing, and re-writing. The process approach highlights the awareness of additional factors influencing writing ability such as: anxiety, topic development, content control (a process of controlling topic information), and organization. In place of examining product precision, researchers using the process model now focus on the development of student writing. The emphases on grammatical, mechanical, and lexical accuracy are superseded by emphases on content and organization, suggesting that conveying meaning is more important than sentence-level accuracy.

Dyson & Freedman (1991) stated that the processes in Hayes and Flower's model do not occur in any fixed order but proceed in an organized way that is largely determined by the individual writer's goals. At one moment writers might be writing, moving their ideas and their discourse forward; at the next they were backtracking, rereading, and digesting what had been written. The finding that these processes are recursive, with sub-processes such as planning and editing often interrupting each other represented an important shift in the understanding of the writing process.

A key premise of this model is that writing is hierarchically organized and that it is, above all, a goal-directed, problem-solving process (Flower & Hayes, 1980). Whenever a person writes, he or she poses a problem to be solved on multiple levels. To solve the problem, the writer must set up sub-goals and solve sub-problems. As writers gain experience, many of the lower-level processes (such as forming letters and spelling) become automatic and unconscious. Other processes require planning and skill, no matter how experienced the writer is. Their theory of writing suggests that it is a highly complex,

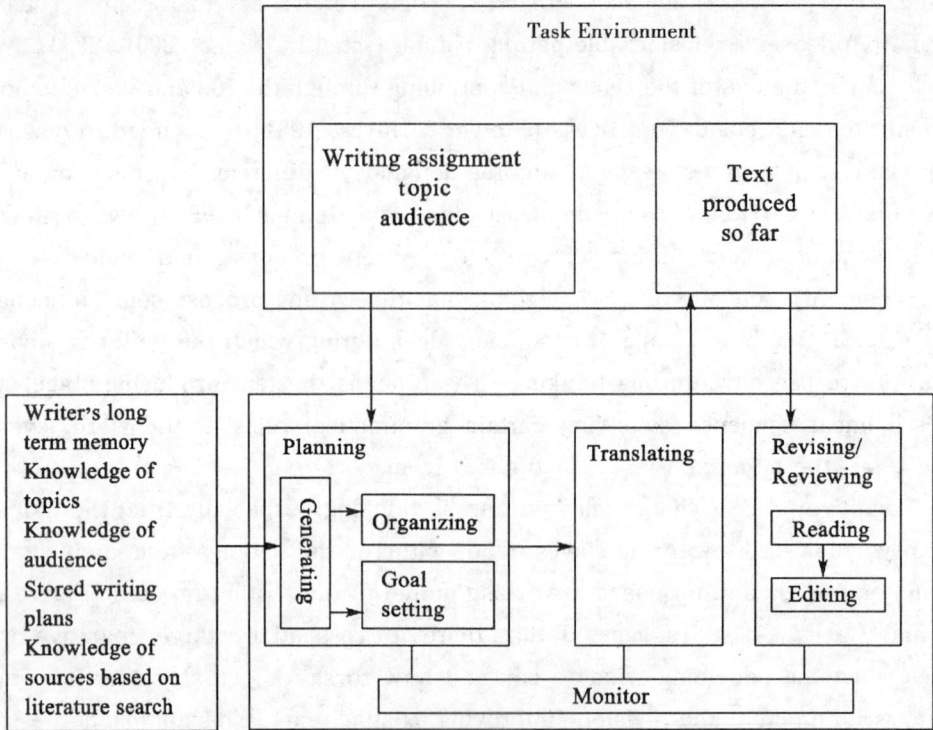

Figure 4.4　The cognitive process model of the composing process (Flower and Hayes, 1981)

goal-directed, recursive activity. It develops over time as writers move from the production of egocentric, writer-based texts (typically, writing everything they know on a topic without thinking of what the reader wants or needs to know) to reader-based texts.

The writing process model produced by Flower and Hayes has served as the theoretical basis for using the process approach in both L1 and L2 writing instruction. Attention to the writing process stresses more of a workshop approach to instruction, which fosters classroom interaction, and engages students in analyzing and commenting on a variety of texts. Despite their implications for classroom instruction, not all the components of the models are appropriate in an L2 context. The Flower model, in particular, does not recognize cross-cultural differences and issues related to sociocultural variation in the functions of the written language (Kern, 2000). Additionally, with native speakers, "writing ability is more closely linked to fluency in and familiarity with the conventions of expository discourse" (Kogen, 1986: 25). L2 writers, however, are in the process of acquiring these conventions and so they often need more instruction about the language itself. Limited knowledge of vocabulary, language structure, and content can inhibit a L2 writer's performance. In addition, the model does not account for growing language proficiency, which is a vital element of L2 writing development. However, this model has had enormous influence on subsequent research and writing pedagogy in EFL.

4.3 Theoretical bases of reading-writing integration

Although the term reading-writing integration is relatively a new concept, people are by no means unfamiliar with reading-writing correlation. In fact, the roles of reading and writing, together with the interrelationship between reading and writing, have already been discussed from several aspects. Among them are three typical representatives: Krashen's input hypothesis and Swain's output hypothesis, Widdowson's integrated approach and Kucer's cognitive model of reading and writing processes.

4.3.1   Krashen's input hypothesis and Swain's output hypothesis

In language learning, reading serves as input while writing as output, hence, it is necessary to have a look at the role of input and output, and then analyze the relationships between input and output before probing reading-writing relationships. Among those studies contributed to the role of input and output in language learning and their relationship with acquisition and comprehension, Krashen's Input Hypothesis and Swain's Output Hypothesis are the representations.

The input hypothesis and the role of input

The input hypothesis attempts to answer a question that is important both theoretically and practically: How is language acquired. In his theory Krashen maintains that humans acquire language in only one-way—by understanding messages, or by "receiving comprehensible input". Second language acquisition will automatically occur only if L2 learner obtains sufficient comprehensible input. Comprehensible input is the sole source of language acquisition while output serves no roles in SLA except possibly as one source of input to the learner (Krashen, 1985). By "comprehensible Input", Krashen (1985) means the language material provided to the learner must contain the structure of "i+1", with "i" referring to the learner's current language level and "i+1" the next level along the natural order. New language structures intended to be acquired by the learner are contained in the part "+1". The gap or the distance between "i" and "i+1" is bridged by information drawn from the situation and from the learner's previous experience. An acquirer's language proficiency can move from "i" to "i+1" by understanding input materials containing "+1". In input hypothesis, two core elements are emphasized by Krashen, one is the quantity of input, namely, large amount of input must be provided to the learner before he can acquire the target language. Only when the acquirer obtains sufficient amount of input, can more rapid SLA be stimulated. The other is the quality of input, namely, the input presented to the learner should be neither too difficult to understand nor too easy. Too complex input which is greatly beyond the learner's current level will frustrate the acquirer, resulting in the learner's inability to understand and intake them. On the other hand, if the material is too simple and easy, the learner's interest and motivation to learn will be diminished.

Ellis (1985) also discusses the importance of input. According to Ellis, input refers to the language that is addressed to the L2 learner either by a native speaker or by another L2 learner. Ellis (1985: 127-129) distinguished three different views about the role of input: the behaviorist view, the mentalist view, and the interactionist view. The behaviorist theorists emphasize the importance of the linguistic environment, which is treated in terms of stimuli and feedback. They hold that the whole process of acquisition can be controlled by presenting learners with input in the right amount and encouraging them to practice the target language forms in it. The mentalist accounts of L2 acquisition emphasize the importance of the learner's "black box". Although input is still seen as essential for L2 acquisition, it is seen as only a "trigger" that activates the learner's internal mechanisms. The interactionist view sees language development as the result of both input factors and innate mechanisms. Language acquisition derives from the collaborative efforts of the learner and his interlocutors and involves a dynamic interplay between external and internal factors. The third view proved more tenable and acceptable.

The output hypothesis and the role of output

Krashen emphasizes the contribution of input to the success of language acquisition, but denies the role of output in language acquisition. As a complement to the input hypothesis, Swain put forward the output hypothesis, in which the learner's production (i. e. output) is regarded as a key factor to language acquisition.

The output hypothesis was first proposed in 1985 (Swain, 1985). Swain argues that learners need the opportunity for meaningful use of their linguistic resources to achieve full grammatical competence. She states that when learners experience communicative failure, they are pushed into making their output more precise, coherent, and appropriate. She also argues that production may encourage learners to move from semantic (top-down) to syntactic (bottom-up) processing. Whereas comprehension of a message can take place with little syntactic analysis of the input, production forces the learner to pay attention to the forms with which intended messages are expressed. In this process, output is hypothesized to promote language acquisition by making learners recognize problems in their interlanguage (IL) and promoting learners to do something about those problems. For example, the learners will seek out relevant input with more focused attention, search for alternative means to express the given intention and stretch their IL capacity, formulate and test a hypothesis, and modify it upon receiving feedback (Izumi and Bigelow, 2000).

Swain (1995) claims that output plays three functions, namely, the "noticing/ triggering" function, the hypothesis-testing function and the metalinguistic function. The first function refers to output contributes to consciousness-raising: output enables learners to "notice a gap between what they want to say and what they can say, leading them to recognize what they do not know, or only know partially." The second function means output encourages hypothesis testing: output provides the opportunity to try out new language structures as L2 learners stretch their language to meet communicative needs; they make experiments with their language just to see what works and what does not. The third function refers to that output facilitates the metalinguistic development: It may encourage learners to discuss explicitly their doubts and questions about language and, enabling them to control and internalize linguistic knowledge (Ding Yanren, 2004).

To sum up, output (production) may "stimulate learners to move from the semantic, open-ended, non-deterministic, strategic processing prevalent in comprehension to the complete grammatical processing needed for accurate production" (Swain, 1995: 128). It is important to recognize that the output hypothesis by no means negates the importance of input. Its intention is to complement and reinforce, rather than replace, input-based approaches to language acquisition so that learners will gain more than what is required for comprehension.

The combination of input and output

The enlightenment Krashen's input hypothesis and Swain's output hypothesis brought is: input and output are both indispensable parts of SLA. For one thing, input is the base and prerequisite for output, it provides language material for output. There will be no output if there is no sufficient comprehensible input. For another, output is the ultimate goal of SLA, input must be converted and internalized by the learner's active use of the language in the form of output activity. Output can enhance the understandability of the input material and it can also add the amount of input. In short, input and output are closely related to and depend on each other so that they should be combined together.

Perhaps constructivism provides the best support to this combination. In constructivist learning theory, knowledge construction is an active and constructive process rather than a passive and static period, which means that the learners really digest these language materials or information and understand them through the construction themselves. Constructivism holds that the learners can get the new knowledge by the way of mutual construction between the subject and the object. In this process, the learners construct the meaning of the new linguistic input on the basis of their learnt knowledge, an in return, the newly-constructed knowledge will change the old information or schema on an object to have the input developed, improved and perfected. Therefore, language learning is not simply the addition of linguistic input and the filtering of new information, but the active construction of the learners, through which the comprehensible input turns into the real comprehension or learning by the learners.

Since the whole process of linguistic input and learning is active and constructive, the language pattern or structure in the learners' mind also does not exist alone in a stalemate. With the unremitting interaction between the old schema and the new language information, the newly-constructed knowledge must move on to the practice—the language use. Even though linguistic input and knowledge construction are important in language learning, the learners still need to practice what they have learnt or constructed and have the opportunities to use the language in concrete circumstances. So apart from the important linguistic input and active learning, language use can reversely strengthen their linguistic input and consolidate their language learning, and the learners should make best use of the sufficient linguistic input and the constructed knowledge to improve their language abilities. What's more, there must be necessary opportunities and a certain environment for the learners to practice what they comprehend and learn about the language. As a whole, linguistic input, active construction and language use (output) are all importantly involved like a circle in the process of language learning.

4.3.2　Widdowson's integrated approach

As a preparation of putting forward the integrated approach, Widdowson (1978) elaborates the four language skills in terms of two levels: linguistic skills and communi-cative abilities. According to Widdowson, linguistic skills include speaking, hearing, composing and comprehending. They refer to the way in which the language system is manifested or recognized to be manifested, as usage. On the other hand, saying, listening and writing belong to communicative abilities. In order to explore the nature of the four skills, Widdowson has established three ways to classify the four language skills. One way is with reference to medium, another way is with reference to mode. The third way is with reference to manner. "With reference to *medium*, the actual physical means whereby the language system is manifested as usage, we can specify speaking and composing as the productive skills using the aural and visual media respectively and, of course, we can also specify hearing and comprehending as their receptive counterparts. With reference to *mode*, the way in which the language system is realized as use in acts of communication, we can distinguish a written mode in which interpretation is expressed productively as writing or conducted receptively in reading and a spoken mode, which is realized productively as saying and receptively as listening. Finally with reference to *manner*, the kind of social activity involved in communication, we can distinguish the reciprocal skills od corresponding in the written mode and talking in the spoken mode and contrast those with the non-reciprocal skill of interpreting, which is the psychological process of understanding which is not made overt through physical or social activity. " (Widdowson, 1978: 65-66) The general idea of the different language skills is also shown in Widdowson's diagram (Figure 4.5). In this Figure those that are defined with reference to mode are in italics. The skills that relate simply to medium appear in ordinary print.

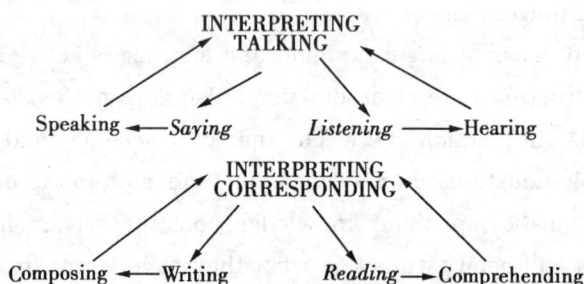

Figure 4.5   Widdowson's (1978) diagram of the four language skills

In this diagram, the sameness of typeface is meant to indicate the sameness of type of the different skills. Therefore, interpreting, talking and corresponding are skills defined with reference to manner; saying, listening, writing and reading are skills defined with reference to mode; and speaking, hearing, composing and comprehending are skills which are defined with reference to medium. The arrows on the diagram are intended to show dependency. Thus, you can speak a sentence without saying anything and you can compose a sentence without writing anything. Similarly, you can hear what a sentence means in terms of its signification without listening to what value it has as an act of communication and you can comprehend the significance of a written sentence without recognizing what it counts as in the context of a particular piece of written discourse. (Widdowson defines "signification" and "value" as the following: sentences have meaning as instances of usage: they express propositions by combining words into structures in accordance with grammatical rules. This kind of meaning is called *signification*. The second kind of meaning is that which sentences and parts of sentences assume when they are put to use for communicative purpose. It is referred to as *value*.) Saying something, however, necessarily involves speaking a sentence, and writing something necessarily involves composing a sentence. Similarly, you can say something without talking, as when you deliver a speech or sermon, but you cannot talk without saying and listening. And you can write something without corresponding, as when you write a report but you cannot correspond without writing and reading. Interpreting is represented here as the highest level skill: it is the ability to process language as communication and it underlies all language use. You cannot talk or correspond without interpreting but you can interpret without talking or corresponding, as when you attend a lecture (where interpreting underlies listening) or read a newspaper (where interpreting underlies reading) or produce an essay (where interpreting underlies writing) or deliver an after dinner address (where interpreting underlies saying). Given this perspective, being communicative activities, saying, listening, reading and writing involve both receptive and productive participation.

The above analysis shows clearly that the four skills are interrelated and interdependent. They can be viewed as both linguistic skills and communicative abilities. When they are defined with reference to medium, they are linguistic skills, for at this level, they refer to the way in which the language system is manifested, or recognized to be manifested, as usage. When they are defined with reference to the mode and manner, they are communicative abilities, for from this perspective, the language system is realized as use.

After analyzing the relationships between the four basic skills, Widdowson (1978) points out that teaching language as communication calls for an approach which brings linguistic skills and communicative abilities into close association with each other, namely, an integrated approach. Since the four basic language skills are interrelated and interdependent, and "all linguistic behavior was related to the underlying activity of interpreting, any approach directed at promoting learners' communicative competence should avoid treating different skills in isolation from each other. What the learner needs to know is to compose in the act of writing, to comprehend in the act of reading and to learn techniques of reading by writing and techniques of writing by reading. If the aim of language learning is to develop the underlying interpreting ability, then it would seem reasonable to adopt an integrated approach to achieve it." (Widdowson, 1978: 143)

In fact, the cases in which different skills are employed at the same time in the daily life. It is not rare for people to read and write or read and speak at the same time. The integration typically involves linking the four language skills together in such a way that what has been learnt and practiced through the exercise of one language skill is reinforced and perhaps extended through further language activities, bringing one or more of the other language skills into use. As Harmer (1991) states that often the learners' activities will have a focus on one particular skill so that at a certain stage the learners will concentrate on reading abilities; but the focus can later shift to one or more of other skills.

4.3.3 Kucer's cognitive model of reading and writing processes

Kucer (2005: 118-122) examines the factors that impact the reader-text-writer transaction and points out there are five variables influencing the transaction among reader, text, and writer (Figure 4.6). The first factor, according to Kucer, is the systems of language of the reader and the writer. The relationship between the reader's language and the writer's language influences the ease with which a text can be processed. Potentially, shared language systems can more easily produce shared understandings. A second factor that influences a reader's and writer's transaction with print is the strategies available to the language user and his or her flexibility in employing them. Both readers and writers use strategies that represent those cognitive processes or behaviors they engage so as to create meaning through written discourse. The third factor is background knowledge; there exists a symbiotic relationship between the knowledge conveyed through a text by the author and the knowledge conveyed through a text by the reader. In general, the more the reader's and author's backgrounds parallel one another, the smoother the construction of meaning is likely to be. The fourth factor is purpose; both reader and writer engage the text for some purposes, these purposes have a direct and significant impact on how and what meaning are ultimately constructed through written discourse. The last factor is assimilation and accommodation; both readers and writers build knowledge through two basic processes of learning: assimilation and accommodation. When the meaning constructed through print fit within the knowledge structures of the reader or writer; the new knowledge is assimilated into what is already known. In this top-down process, the meanings fit within existing cognitive frameworks. When the information to be generated through print does not easily fit into the language user's available cognitive structures, a restructuring or accommodation of what is known is required. This bottom-up process results in a modified cognitive framework from which the reader or writer is then able to assimilate the meanings under construction. In general and to varying degrees, both assimilation and accommodation occur during reading and writing.

READER<—>TEXT<—>WRITER

Systems of language	Systems of language
Availability of, and flexibility with the reading strategies	Availability of, and flexibility with the writing strategies
Background knowledge	Background knowledge
Purpose for the reading	Purpose for the writing
Ability and willingness to assimilate and/or accommodate during reading	Ability and willingness to assimilate and/or accommodate during writing

Figure 4.6   Factors impacting reader-text-writer transaction

On the basis of the above discussion, Kucer (2005: 191-193) analyzes reading-writing relationships and points out that reading and writing share five features: knowledge search, context, goals and plans, strategies, and evolving text. When illustrating the cognitive interrelationships between the reading and writing processes, Kucer (2005) reviews the traditional viewpoint of reading-writing relationship that reading and writing are simply inverse or opposite communicative events, that is, reading is viewed as a decoding process, readers passively take in or abstract the author's meaning from the page, while writers are perceived as more actively engaged in the construction of meaning, their meanings are encoded into print through the use of various cognitive resources (Figure 4.7).

<----------------------------◆----------------------------->

Reading	Writing
Decoding	Encoding
Passive	Active
Less use of cognitive resources	More use of cognitive resources
Meaning abstracting	Meaning generating
Building background knowledge	Expressing background knowledge
Context independent	Context dependent

Figure 4.7   Reading and writing as opposite processes

In contrast with this traditional viewpoint, Kucer argues that a more accurate depiction of the relationship between reading and writing is that of parallel or complementary processes (Figure 4.8). Kucer holds that readers and writers are, in fact, both intensely engaged in the searching for, and the integrating of, meaning. In both processes, "meaning is continually in a state of becoming". This state of becoming involves not only the active use of prior knowledge, but the construction of knowledge as well. Cognitively, both readers and writers can be changed through their transactions with print. Revision, commonly thought as central to the writing process, is also evident during reading. As discussed previously, readers monitor their processing of print and engage in such revision strategies as reflecting, rereading, and reading on and returning, when meaning is disrupted. Finally, although not typically perceived as such, readers as well as writers are impacted by context and purpose. The context and purpose significantly impact the meanings generated by the reader. Both readers and writers are cognizant of for whom and for what text meanings are constructed. In short, Kucer's model expresses how the linguistic and cognitive similarities between the two process support and enhance literacy learning.

To sum up, Kucer examines literacy from the cognitive dimension and reports that both reading and writing involve the mind transacting with written discourse to a large extent. In this transaction, both LTM and STM systems, perception, and various strategies are employed for the creation of meaning. Impacting the creation of meaning are such relational factors as the correspondence between the background of the reader and that of the writer, or the correspondence between the language of the reader and the language of the writer.

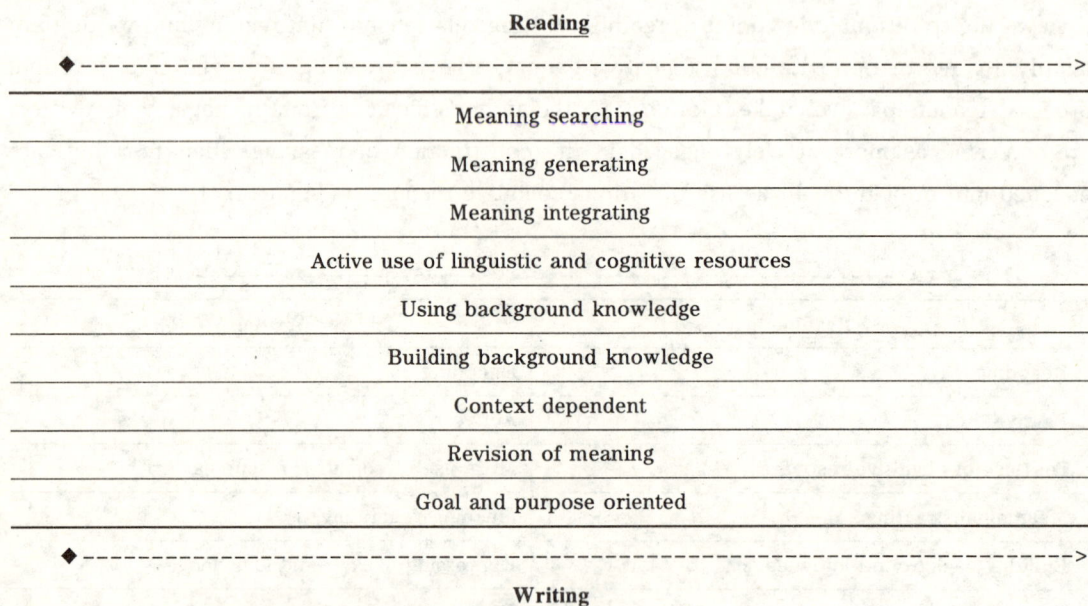

Reading

--->

Meaning searching

Meaning generating

Meaning integrating

Active use of linguistic and cognitive resources

Using background knowledge

Building background knowledge

Context dependent

Revision of meaning

Goal and purpose oriented

--->

Writing

Figure 4.8   Reading and writing as parallel processes

4.4   Theoretical bases of reading-writing correlation

Widdowson (1978) points out that in reading area, the understanding of discourse does not simply involve the recognition of what words and sentences mean but also involves the recognition of the value they take on in association with each other as elements in the discourse. Readers actively work out what the discourse means as they go along, predicting what is to come by reference to what has preceded. Reading, in this sense, is a kind of accomplishment whereby a discourse is created in the mind by means of a process of reasoning. While in writing area, a discourse should be created or constructed for the readers to read, the intended meanings or message of the writer need to be created or, to be exact, recreated. "In this respect, the ability to read and the ability to write are the same and it is neutral with regard to production or reception. " In both reading and writing processes, creation is needed. Widdowson's ideas support the viewpoint that learners can master the writing skills through reading, and at the same time, learners can also learn the reading skills through writing.

Tierney and Pearson(1983) offer the best known of the reading-writing theories in L1. Their model views reading as an act of composing parallel to writing. Both the reading and the writing models have five parallel stages: planning, drafting, aligning, revising, and monitoring. Thus, both reading and writing are viewed as constructive processes. In another influential publication stressing the theoretical links between reading and writing processes, Tierney and Margie (1986) asserts that the general correlation between reading and writing is moderate, but fluctuates with age and schooling, and that selected reading experiences definitely contribute to writing performance and vice versa.

Among efforts to provide empirical verification for these theories of reading and writing connections, the research by Shanahan (1984, 1987) stands out. In studies designed to provide a more comprehensive examination of the reading-writing relationship, Shanahan (1987: 98) used correlation analysis to examine the relationships between a large, multivariate set of reading and writing measures. The correlations between measures of reading (vocabulary, word recognition, sentence comprehension, and passage comprehension) and measures of writing (vocabulary diversity, syntactic complexity, and qualitative and quantitative measures of spelling and organization) all showed that "the idea that reading and writing are identical in terms of underlying knowledge does not appear to be true". However, his results showed that reading and writing were significantly related among elementary school children and that the reading-writing relationship changed with reading development, e. g., increased importance of vocabulary to writing achievement as learners become more proficient as readers.

Flahive and Bailey (1988) similarly investigated reading and writing relationships in ESL, finding a number of significant correlations for a heterogeneous group of learners on holistic writing measures, standardized, native-English speaker reading tests, and other grammatical, as well as reading- experiential, measures.

Hyland (2005: 57) states that "reading and writing are basic resources for constructing our relationships with others and for understanding our experience of the world, and as such they are centrally involved in the ways we negotiate, construct and change our understanding of our society and ourselves".

Xie Weina (1994) describes reading and writing relationships in depth. In her opinion, reading and writing are both acts that imitate each other. Writing imitates reading in that during the process of writing; the writer must predict readers' feedback and imitate readers' reading process so as to make sure what he/she wrote can be easily understood by readers. By saying reading imitates writing, Xie means that during the reading process the reader must imitate the writer's writing process, project and conjecture the writer's meaning and intention, and only in this way can the reader understand what the writer mean exactly. In other words, Xie holds that the reader acts the roles of both a reader and a writer in the reading process. By the same token, the writer performs the functions of a writer as well as a reader. Therefore, Xie points out that as two acts closely related to each other and influence each other in a lot of ways, reading and writing should not be separated but be combined; teachers should teach reading in writing and vice versa.

4.5   Research methodology of the effects of reading/writing proficiency

Despite that the previous studies have touched reading-writing interrelationships more or less, they were mostly carried out to testify the effects of reading on writing (reading-to-write) or the effects of writing on reading (writing-to-read), In this sense, those studies still let reading or writing each goes its own way. Even some other studies have gone a little bit further, touching the reading-writing correlation; empirical studies on the integration of reading and writing are rare. However, a large amount of evidence from the input hypothesis, the output hypothesis, the integrated approach and the cognitive model of reading-writing process support such a viewpoint: Reading and writing are two of the language skills that go together; they not only have the same linguistic knowledge but also share common cognitive bases; reading ability and writing ability are closely interrelated and either of the two can be used to facilitate the other.

In short, previous studies are more or less partial, seeing the picture of reading-writing relationship from just one side. Therefore, it is of necessity to probe an approach that can see the whole picture and grasp the essence of reading-writing relationships so as to supply the gap left by the previous studies. Perhaps McKusick et al. (2001) gave a more accurate statement of this necessity, by regarding efforts integrating reading and writing as a venture, they said, "We are still in the beginning stages of this venture. Many questions remain unanswered. What is clear, however, is the positive influence that knowledge of theory and research has had on our practice. In turn, we believe that conducting research on our efforts to integrate reading and writing instruction will continue to inform our practice in an ongoing cycle of theory to research to practice."

4.5.1　Research design

The purpose of the present study is to carry out an experimental research integrating reading and writing into one, putting the same emphasis on both reading-to-write and writing-to-reading, i. e., to explore whether the integrated reading-writing approach is beneficial for improving English learners' reading/writing proficiency. In order to make the effects of the integrated reading-writing approach convenient for observation, the researcher takes two other approaches as the point of reference: an enhanced reading input approach and an enhanced writing output approach. Concretely, the enhanced reading input approach refers to regular English classroom instruction plus large amount of reading practice after class, the enhanced writing output approach refers to regular English classroom instruction plus enhanced writing output practice after class, and the integrated reading-writing approach refers to regular English classroom instruction plus both enhanced reading input practice and enhanced writing output practice.

Based on the findings of previous studies, and in consideration of the relations between input/output and the reading/writing proficiency, a general hypothesis is proposed that the integrated reading-writing approach will help facilitate development of EFL learners' reading and writing abilities. With this hypothesis, two predictions can be made as follows:

Prediction 1: Learners under the integrated reading-writing approach might show progress in their reading proficiency and the progress would be greater than that of those under the enhanced reading input approach or the enhanced writing output approach.

Prediction 2: Learners under the integrated reading-writing approach might show progress in their writing proficiency and the progress would be greater than that of those under the enhanced reading input approach or the enhanced writing output approach.

4.5.2　Subjects

According to the present educational situation, although most students begin their English learning as early as primary school, the English knowledge they learnt in primary school are pretty limited; many students actually can not receive formal English instruction until in junior middle school. Thus learners' English proficiency and ability will not be adequately developed until they finish their high school. To guarantee a truthful reflection of the complicated English reading and writing processes and accordingly guarantee the reliability of analysis of factors influencing these processes, college students will be more appropriate for the present study.

There are 98 students participating in this study in total. Subjects in the study are all native speakers of Chinese and learners of English as a foreign language. They are freshmen from 3 natural classes randomly selected from Wuhan University in their first semester. The three experimental classes received three different English teaching programs: A) an enhanced reading input program—regular English classroom instruction plus large amount of reading practice after class, B) an enhanced writing output program— regular English classroom instruction plus enhanced writing output practice after class, and C) an integrated reading-writing program—regular English classroom instruction plus both enhanced reading input practice and enhanced writing output practice. The class receiving program A was called Reading Class (hereinafter referred to as RC), the class receiving program B was called Writing Class (WC), and the class receiving program C was called Integrated Class (IC). The number of students in RC was 33, and the number in WC and IC was 31 and 34 respectively. The English proficiency of all these subjects could be described as moderate high in the context of China since all the subjects have received English instruction for more than 6 years and entered Wuhan University which is a famous university with high scores in the National College Entrance Examination. Therefore, these subjects are expected to be easily motivated and cooperative.

4.5.3　Instruments

In the study, a quantitative research containing a pretest and a posttest was employed to obtain statistics to reveal application of the reading-writing integration program and its relationship with reading and writing proficiency, as well as the difference between the integrated reading-writing program and the other two programs. Moreover, a qualitative research (a questionnaire) was also adopted to supply in-depth and detailed information about learners' strategies used in their reading and writing processes, and thus the factors functioning in these processes can be explored.

A reading-writing test was conducted as pretest in the first week, and then another reading-writing test was held in the last week as posttest. The same test paper was employed in both pre-test and post-test. This test paper consisted of two parts, one was reading comprehension part and the other was writing task part. The former was further divided into two sections, that is, a section of skimming and scanning, including only one fast-reading passage; and a section of reading in depth including four careful-reading passages. The latter was simply a writing task designed to trigger learners' opinions on a certain topic. In the section of skimming and scanning, ten questions were attached to the fast-reading passage, among which seven were multiple choice questions and three were blank-filling questions. In the section of reading in depth, each passage was followed by five multiple choice questions. As to the writing task, the topic was "some people think that personal happiness is directly related to economic success. Others argue that happiness depends on completely other factors. Discuss both of the views and give your own opinion". This topic was chosen because of its familiarity to every student. Since everyone has his/her own idea about personal happiness, this topic can assure that every student has something to say in their composition. All the reading passages in the reading comprehension part were excerpted from CET-4 and the writing topic from IELTS. Since CET-4 and IELTS are still now the most authoritative proficiency test for college students, it is justifiable to choose and adapt their test items for the evaluation of the growth of the subjects' writing proficiency in the present study.

In addition to reading-writing tests, subjects were also required to fill out a questionnaire. The sources of this questionnaire were based on William Baker and Kamonpan Boonkit's questionnaire "Reading and Writing Strategies Employed in the Questionnaire and Their Classification", which was put forward in their study in 2004. Some adaptations and modifications were made so as to ensure the questionnaire could reflect Chinese English learners' actual situation in using reading and writing strategies. To add internal validity to the questionnaire, a number of the questions were cross-referenced and negative questions were also used to offset overly positive responses and any tendencies to simply agree with everything in the questionnaire. This questionnaire consisted of 69 items written in Chinese version to make sure the students could fully understand and avoid misunderstanding which might be caused by the original English version; each item was a learning strategy. Each item was to be answered on a 5-point Likert scale, ranging from "strongly disagree"(1), "disagree"(2), "neither agree nor disagree"(3), "agree"(4) to "strongly agree"(5). In terms of the form of the 69 items in the questionnaire, they were divided into two sections, the first section dealing with learning strategies in reading and the second section dealing with learning strategies in writing. The former could be further divided into three subsections: pre-reading strategies, during-reading strategies, and post-reading strategies. The latter could also be further divided into three subsections: pre-writing strategies, during-writing strategies, and post-writing strategies. In terms of the nature of the 69 strategies in the questionnaire, the items covered the following categories: cognitive strategies, memory strategies, compensation strategies, meta-cognitive strategies, social strategies, affective strategies, and negative strategies.

4.5.4 Procedures

The subjects in all the classes were administered the pretest. The pretest was given to examine the subjects' English reading proficiency and writing competence before the experiment. The subjects were allowed to finish the pretest in one hour and a half (the time limit was enough for them to finish both the reading comprehension and the writing task). The same test was administered to all four classes; hence there was no test difference to control across classes. In addition, the students were informed that there would be two tests, the first one unmarked until the second one was finished, to compare their improvement throughout the semester. The teachers of each class did not tell them the same test paper would be used and tried to avoid sensitizing them the true purpose of the study.

The study spread over 12 weeks (equivalent to 36 classes). The teaching experiment consists of two parts: regular classroom instruction and special teaching programs. All students in this study received regular English instruction of 45-minute class two to four times per week. The teaching material for all four classes was *New College English* (Book I, second edition) published by Foreign Language Teaching and Research Press. According to the teaching aims and the teaching plan, the teaching tasks (at least 5 units in Book I) lasted about three months.

Apart from regular classroom instruction, different programs were also assigned to the experimental classes as the treatment of this study after the pretest. The RC received regular classroom instruction plus large amount of reading practice after class; the WC received regular English classroom instruction plus enhanced writing output practice after class; and the IC received regular plus both enhanced reading input and enhanced writing output.

In both the RC and the IC, students were assigned 25 reading passages during the whole semester. The reading passages were concerned with the first five units of students' textbook, for each unit, five passages were assigned to students for providing them with large amount of information concerning this unit. These reading materials were carefully selected from web sources by the author and the standards of selecting reading materials were as follows: First, the materials should be closely related to the themes of the five units. Second, the materials should be well-organized. Third, the materials should be concise, interesting and easy to follow. Learners in these two classes were assigned 5 passages at the beginning of every two weeks and required to read them during their own free time within two weeks. As a control of learners' work, at the end of every two weeks the teachers of these two classes checked whether the learners had finished the 5 passages on time by means of asking questions concerning the content details or rhetorical devices of these passages or choosing some learners to summarize the main idea of the passages and so on.

In both the WC and the IC, students were given 8 essay-writing tasks chosen from CET-4 writing topics to complete in 12 weeks, again, during their own free time. The 8 topics consisted of 4 pairs, with each pair having two topics. The 2 topics in each pair were both closely related to the same theme of a unit in the textbook but still standing for opposite opinions to each other so that the writing tasks would demand more efforts from learners. They were required to finish one topic per week and their compositions were collected every two weeks. The compositions were graded by teachers of the two classes and then returned to the learners. The best pieces of writing were selected and the best writers were commended in front of all of the learners so that they could be motivated to continue in the study and exert their best efforts.

At the end of the term, the posttest was carried out to the learners of all three classes (as mentioned above, the posttest paper was completely the same as the pretest paper). The same as last time, one hour and a half was given to students to finish the test paper.

After the posttest was conducted, the questionnaire was administered to all three classes at the end of the study. Before the subjects answered the questionnaire, how to use the 5-point Likert scale was briefly explained so as to avoid misunderstanding and ensure the quality of data.

4.5.5 Data collection and data analysis

All the scores of the students' performances on each test were collected. Each test had two sets of data: the first was the scores of reading test; the second was the scores of composition. There were totally 30 questions in the reading part, 2 points per question; therefore, the total score of reading was 60. There was only one writing task in the writing part, thus the total score of this part was equal to the score of the writing topic which was 15. The scores were so designed according to the general practice of the CET-4 test.

As to scoring, for reading comprehension, multiple-choice questions and short answer questions had only one correct answer, thus fair scoring should be beyond question. However, scoring a composition involved subjective judgment. So the following measures were taken by the study to increase the reliability of scoring: Three scorers who are experienced in scoring CET-4 writing test were invited to participate in the scoring of the students' compositions and the average score of theirs were regarded as the final to the students; The papers of all the classes were mixed up so that the scorers could not show bias to either class in scoring the compositions; The writing papers were sealed up so that subjects' names and classes were kept unknown to the scorers.

The data collected from the reading-writing tests (pretest and posttest) and the results of the questionnaire were analyzed with the aid of SPSS. In order to compare the different effects of different programs within one class and between classes, the data was analyzed with the following statistical procedure: descriptive statistics (mean and standard deviation), then paired-samples t-test, one-way ANOVA and Scheffe Multiple Comparison test. An alpha of 0.05 was chosen as the significant level. The results were reported in the table form.

4.6 Empirical approaches to the effects of reading/writing proficiency

After careful scoring of the test papers, the performance of all learners under the three different teaching programs in reading-writing tests was reflected in their reading and writing scores. These scores will be clearly presented and carefully discussed in the following sections. Three different teaching programs were applied to English instruction in this study. In order to find out whether each program has some effects on subjects' reading and writing proficiency, or in other words, whether each class has made some significant progress after receiving different teaching programs, the descriptive statistics and the results of paired-sample T-test will be discussed first. After that, the results of one-way ANOVA and Scheffe Multiple Comparison will be analyzed so that it can be made clear whether the reading-writing integration program is more effective than the other two.

4.6.1   Results of each class on reading

Of the whole reading-writing test paper, there are 30 items in the reading part, that is, 27 in multiple choice and 3 in blank filling. In this section, subjects' performance on reading will be discussed according to their gains from pretest to posttest. The following discussion falls into four aspects: the general performance on reading of the three groups, the specific performance on reading of the WC, the RC and the IC.

Table 4. 1 shows the descriptive data of the general performance of all subjects on reading. The numbers of participants (N), minimums, maximums, means, and standard deviations of reading scores in pretest and posttest separately according to different programs are all reported in the table.

Table 4. 1   **Descriptive statistics on reading of all three classes**

G		N	Min	Max	M	SD
WC	R1	31	36	54	45.94	4.690
	R2	31	38	56	47.61	4.964
RC	R1	33	22	56	45.52	7.072
	R2	33	34	58	47.33	6.940
IC	R1	34	28	54	42.88	6.193
	R2	34	24	54	44.59	7.378

Note: WC = Writing Class, RC = Reading Class, IC = Integrated Reading-Writing Class,
R1 = Reading score of pretest, R2 = Reading score of posttest

As shown in Table 4. 1, the mean score of the IC on reading part in the pretest is 42. 88 while that of the RC and WC are 45. 52 and 45. 94. The mean score of reading in the pretest of the IC is evidently lower than that of WC and RC. That means, in the pretest, the IC scores the lowest and the WC scores the highest. As for the posttest, the mean scores of the IC, RC and WC on reading are in order as follows: 44. 59, 47. 33 and 47. 61. In other words, in the posttest, the IC scores the lowest and the WC scores the highest again. However, it does not mean that the IC makes no progress in reading proficiency after receiving the integrated reading-writing approach, because it has got a rise in its average score by nearly 2 points. In fact all three groups show a rise in their mean scores from the pretest to the posttest, which can be seen from the mean difference of each group.

Generally speaking, Table 4.1 reveals an interesting trend concerned all of the three classes. That is, there is an ascending tendency in the 98 subjects' reading proficiency. But how much progress they have made and to what extent the progress is significant are not clear yet.

The results of paired samples T-test on reading within the Writing Class are shown in Table 4.2. The statistics indicates that although the mean differences between the pretest and the posttest results exist, they are not statistically significant at 0.05 (the t-value is -1.885, $p = 0.069 > 0.05$). This proves there is no significant difference between the pretest and the posttest on reading, which means that the Writing Class shows no significant growth in their reading proficiency.

Table 4.2 **Results of Paired Samples T-Test on reading for WC**

	Paired Differences			t	df	Sig. (2-tailed)
	M	SD	SEM			
R1–R2	−1.677	4.956	.890	−1.885	30	.069

Note: R1 = Reading score of pretest, R2 = Reading score of posttest

Table 4.3 displays the results of paired samples T-test within the reading class. Although the scores of the learners under the reading program show an ascending tendency in their reading proficiency, Table 4.3 illustrates that the difference between the pretest and the posttest of the RC is not statistically significant (the t-value is -1.681, $p1 = 0.102 > 0.05$). As there is no significant difference between the pretest and the posttest on reading, the RC does not show significant growth in their reading proficiency.

Table 4.3 **Results of Paired Samples T-Test on reading for RC**

	Paired Differences			t	df	Sig. (2-tailed)
	M	SD	SEM			
R1–R2	−1.818	6.212	1.081	−1.681	32	.102

Note: R1 = Reading score of pretest, R2 = Reading score of posttest

As for the Integrated Reading-Writing Class, Table 4.4 shows its performance on reading in terms of results of paired samples T-test. It can be found that there is mean difference between the reading scores of the pretest and the posttest (R1-R2 = −1.706), indicating that the learners under the reading-writing integration program show an ascending tendency in their reading proficiency. Nevertheless, this ascending tendency is not enough for coming to the conclusion that the IC has made progress in reading. As a matter of fact, the mean difference between pretest and posttest on reading for the IC is not significant at 0.05 level ($p2 = 0.061 > 0.05$). This means that the Integrated Reading-Writing Class does not make significant progress in their reading proficiency.

Table 4.4   **Results of Paired Samples T-Test on reading for IC**

	Paired Differences			t	df	Sig. (2-tailed)
	M	SD	SEM			
R1–R2	−1.706	5.120	.878	−1.943	33	.061

Note: R1 = Reading score of pretest, R2 = Reading score of posttest

4.6.2 Comparisons of the three classes' reading performance

The previous section dealt with the subjects' performance on reading under different teaching programs within each class separately, and the results of paired samples T-test shed light on whether the three teaching programs have some effects on learners' reading proficiency. As there are three different programs involved, in order to check out which one of the three programs was more effective than the other two, comparison among the three classes should also be conducted.

Table 4.5   **Results of One-Way ANOVA on reading**

		SS	df	MS	F	Sig.
R1	Between Groups	181.459	2	90.730	2.445	.092
	Within Groups	3525.643	95	37.112		
	Total	3707.102	97			
R2	Between Groups	185.485	2	92.742	2.161	.121
	Within Groups	4076.923	95	42.915		
	Total	4262.408	97			

Note: R1 = Reading score of pretest, R2 = Reading score of posttest

Table 4.5 reports the results of one-way ANOVA for reading scores of all three classes in both the pretest and the posttest. Here, R1 refers to reading scores in the pretest, R2 refers to reading scores in the posttest. It can be noted from the table that before the experiment (in the pretest), there was no significant difference among the three classes in their reading level (pR1 = 0.092 >0.05). However, the three classes were expected to show some difference in their reading proficiency after receiving different programs. Table 4.5 illustrates that even for the posttest, there is no significant difference among the three classes in their reading level (pR1 = 0.121 >0.05). In other words, there is no difference among the effects of the three programs on reading proficiency. Evidently, this finding goes against the author's expectations and needs careful analysis and explanation.

In order to find whether there is difference between any two classes in their reading proficiency, the Scheffe Multiple Comparison was also conducted and the results are shown in the following table.

Table 4.6   **Results of the Scheffe Multiple Comparison on reading**

	(I) G	(J) G	M D (I-J)	S E	Sig.
R1	WC	RC	.420	1.524	.963
		IC	3.053	1.513	.136
	RC	WC	-.420	1.524	.963
		IC	2.633	1.489	.215
	IC	WC	-3.053	1.513	.136
		RC	-2.633	1.489	.215
R2	WC	RC	.280	1.639	.986
		IC	3.025	1.627	.183
	RC	WC	-.280	1.639	.986
		IC	2.745	1.601	.235
	IC	WC	-3.025	1.627	.183
		RC	-2.745	1.601	.235

Note: WC = Writing Class, RC = Reading Class, IC = Integrated Reading-Writing Class,
     R1 = Reading score of pretest, R2 = Reading score of posttest

Table 4.6 proves that there is no significant difference between any two classes in their reading level because all the p values observed from this table are higher than 0.05. This is in accordance with what is revealed by Table 4.5. Thus, it can be concluded from the above two tables that the reading-writing integration teaching approach does not show superiority in improving students' reading proficiency compared with the enhanced reading input program and the enhanced writing output program.

4.6.3 Results of each class on writing

Of the whole reading-writing test paper, there was only one item in the writing part, that is, a writing task requiring subjects to write a composition on a given topic. Subjects' performance on writing will be discussed in this section, again, according to their gains from pretest to posttest. After the general description of the general performance on writing of the three groups, the performance of the WC, the RC and the IC on writing will be described one by one.

The descriptive data of the general performance of all subjects on writing are shown in Table 4.7. The numbers of participants (N), minimums, maximums, means, and standard deviations of reading scores in pretest and posttest can be easily found according to different programs in this table.

Table 4.7   **Descriptive statistics on writing of all three classes**

G		N	Min	Max	M	SD
WC	W1	31	7	12	9.13	1.176
	W2	31	6	11	9.45	1.207

续表

G		N	Min	Max	M	SD
RC	W1	33	7	12	8.97	1.357
	W2	33	7	12	9.39	1.345
IC	W1	34	6	12	8.44	1.418
	W2	34	5	12	9.38	1.652

Note: WC = Writing Class, RC = Reading Class, IC = Integrated Reading-Writing Class,
W1 = Writing score of pretest, W2 = Writing score of posttest

From Table 4.7, the mean scores of writing part of all three classes were bumped up from the pretest to the posttest. Just as in the reading part, the mean scores of writing in both pretest and posttest of the IC are lower than that of the WC and the RC. By the same token, this does not necessarily mean that the IC has not made any progress in writing proficiency because making such an inference needs support from the data produced by paired samples T-test. So far the only thing that can be inferred from Table 4.7 is that all three groups show a rise in their writing mean scores from the pretest to the posttest, and there is an ascending tendency in the 98 subjects' writing proficiency.

Table 4.8 presents the results of paired samples T-test on writing within the Writing Class. The table shows that although the mean differences between the pretest and the posttest results exist (W1 – W2 = –.323), there is no statistically significant difference between the pretest writing score and the posttest writing score at a level of 0.05 (the t-value is –1.885, p = 0.067 > 0.05), which means that the writing class shows no significant growth in their writing proficiency.

Table 4.8 **Results of Paired Samples T-Test on writing for WC**

	Paired Differences			t	df	Sig. (2-tailed)
	M	SD	SEM			
W1–W2	–.323	.945	.170	–1.901	30	.067

Note: W1 = Writing score of pretest, W2 = Writing score of posttest

Table 4.9 displays the results of paired samples T-test within the Reading Class. Though the RC does not show significant progress in reading, things are quite different as far as writing is concerned. Table 4.9 illustrates that the difference between writing scores of the pretest and that of the posttest is statistically significant (the t-value is –2.811, p2 = 0.008 < 0.05), indicating that the reading class shows significant improvement in their writing proficiency.

Table 4.9 **Results of Paired Samples T-Test on writing for RC**

	Paired Differences			t	df	Sig. (2-tailed)
	M	SD	SEM			
W1–W2	–.424	.867	.151	–2.811	32	.008

Note: W1 = Writing score of pretest, W2 = Writing score of posttest

Table 4. 10 shows the performance of the IC on writing in terms of results of paired samples T-test. From Table 4. 10, it can be found that there is mean difference between the writing scores of pretest and posttest (W1–W2 = –. 941), indicating that the learners under the reading-writing integration program show an ascending tendency in their writing proficiency. Furthermore, the difference between writing scores of pretest and that of posttest is statistically significant with no doubt (p2 = 0. 000 < 0. 05). Thus, it can be inferred that the Integrated reading-writing class makes significant progress in their writing proficiency.

Table 4. 10   **Results of Paired Samples T-Test on writing for IC**

	Paired Differences			t	df	Sig. (2-tailed)
	M	SD	SEM			
W1–W2	–. 941	1. 205	. 207	–4. 556	33	. 000

Note: W1 = Writing score of pretest, W2 = Writing score of posttest

So the situation of the IC is quite similar to that of the RC. Both IC and RC show significant improvement in their writing proficiency, while no such significant progress can be found in the WC. Yet one thing that must be pointed out is the growth of IC in writing proficiency is larger than that of RC (. 424 <. 941), that is, the integrated reading-writing program is more effective than the enhanced reading input program or the integrated reading-writing program gives rise to more rapid growth in comparison with the enhanced reading input program. Such a conclusion can never be arrived at unless the results of one-way ANOVA show sufficient evidence for it.

4.6.4   Comparisons of the three classes' writing performance

Comparison within each group demonstrates whether that group has made progress in language proficiency but this comparison is far from enough. So comparison between groups should be conducted as well so that which one of the three programs is more effective than the other two can be checked out.

Table 4. 11 reports the results of one-way ANOVA for writing scores of all three classes in both the pretest and the posttest. W1 refers to writing scores in the pretest, W2 refers to writing scores in the posttest. The table shows that there is no significant difference among the three classes in their writing level before the experiment (pW1 = 0. 093 > 0. 05). In addition to this, even for the posttest, there is no difference among the three classes in their writing level (pW2 = 0. 978 > 0. 05). This data demonstrate that learners have not shown different rate of progress in writing proficiency after receiving the three different programs. Namely, there is no difference among the effects of the three programs on writing proficiency. Again, this finding is in opposition to the author's expectations.

Table 4.11   **Results of One-Way ANOVA on writing**

		SS	df	MS	F	Sig.
W1	Between Groups	8.552	2	4.276	2.435	.093
	Within Groups	166.836	95	1.756		
	Total	175.388	97			
W2	Between Groups	.088	2	.044	.022	.978
	Within Groups	191.586	95	2.017		
	Total	191.673	97			

Note: W1 = Writing score of pretest, W2 = Writing score of posttest

Table 4.12, presenting the results of the Scheffe Multiple Comparison and serving as a supplement to Table 4.11, reveals whether there is difference between any two experimental classes in their writing proficiency.

Table 4.12   **Results of the Scheffe Multiple Comparison on writing**

	(I) G	(J) G	M D (I-J)	S E	Sig.
W1	WC	RC	.159	.331	.891
		IC	.688	.329	.118
	RC	WC	−.159	.331	.891
		IC	.529	.324	.269
	IC	WC	−.688	.329	.118
		RC	−.529	.324	.269
W2	WC	RC	.058	.355	.987
		IC	.069	.353	.981
	RC	WC	−.058	.355	.987
		IC	.012	.347	.999
	IC	WC	−.069	.353	.981
		RC	−.012	.347	.999

Note: WC = Writing Class, RC = Reading Class, IC = Integrated Reading-Writing Class,
　　　 W1 = Writing score of pretest, W2 = Writing score of posttest

Table 4.12 shows that all the p values observed are higher than 0.05. Similar to Table 4.11, Table 4.12 proves that there is no significant difference between any two classes in their writing level. With the support of the two tables presented above, a conclusion can be drawn that the integrated reading-writing program is not superior in improving learners' writing proficiency compared with the enhanced reading input program and the enhanced writing output program.

4.6.5 Results of the questionnaire

Considering that there are 69 items in the questionnaire in total and it is impossible to present all details of each item clearly in this thesis, the researcher classifies the 69 items of the questionnaire into several categories and mean scores of these categories instead of mean scores of all the items are calculated, and the classification of those items falls into two types.

For type 1, the items were put into two categories in terms of the form of strategies: reading strategies (RS) and writing strategies (WS). The first category, reading strategies (RS) were further divided into three subcategories: pre-reading strategies, during-reading strategies and post-reading strategies. In order to make sure each category has a fitting abbreviation and those abbreviations would not be overlapping; three new terms are used to stand for the three subcategories of RS, namely, before-reading strategies (BR), while-reading strategies (WR), after-reading strategies (AR). By the same token, the following three terms are used to refer to the three subcategories of WS: before-writing strategies (BW), while-writing strategies (WW) and after-writing strategies (AW).

For type 2, the items are put into seven categories according to the nature of these strategies, namely, Cognitive strategies (C), Memory strategies (M), Compensation strategies (CP), Meta-cognitive strategies (MC), Social strategies (S), Affective strategies (A), and Negative strategies (N).

To help the readers form a clearer impression of these intricate categories, the components of each category are listed here: for type 1, RS consist of 32 items (item 1-32), WS consist of 37 items (item 33-69), BR are composed of 7 items (item 1-7), WR contain 15 items (item 8-22), AR contain 10 items (item 23-32), BW contain 12 items (item 33-44), WW contain 15 items (item 45-59), and AW consist of 10 items (item 60-69). As for type 2, C consist of 16 items (item 8, 11, 14, 15, 16, 22, 23, 24, 26, 27, 45, 54, 56, 57, 60, 62), M include 4 items (item 29, 34, 65, 66), CP contain 14 items (item 5, 17, 18, 21, 48, 49, 50, 51, 52, 53, 55, 58, 59, 61), MC consist of 21 items (item 1, 2, 3, 4, 6, 7, 10, 28, 30, 31, 33, 35, 36, 38, 39, 40, 41, 43, 46, 47, 67), S contain 3 items (item 25, 37, 63), A contained only 3 items (item 32, 44, 69), and N contain 8 items (item 9, 12, 13, 19, 20, 64, 68).

Based on these two types of classification, Table 4.13 and Table 4.14 demonstrate the descriptive statistics of the within-class results of the questionnaire obtained from the three classes: the WC, the RC and the IC. As this study aims to compare the effectiveness of three different teaching programs and the questionnaire is adopted as a supplement of analysis, the data obtained from questionnaire are compared between classes and within-class comparison is beyond focus here.

Table 4.13   **Overall strategy use by class for type 1**

	Category	RS	WS	BR	WR	AR	BW	WW	AW
Mean	WC	3.67	3.13	4.06	3.63	3.46	3.37	3.21	2.73
	RC	3.46	2.99	3.72	3.47	3.24	3.18	3.04	2.70
	IC	3.44	3.00	3.79	3.41	3.24	3.32	2.96	2.65

Table 4.13 displays the mean score of the three classes on each category according to type 1. The data indicate that the writing class used strategies most frequently in the three classes in general. Concretely speaking, the WC used more strategies in both reading and writing processes, including before-reading process, while-reading process, after-reading process, before-writing process, while-writing process, and after-writing process, compared with the RC and the IC. Meanwhile, there is tiny difference between the enhanced reading input class and the integrated reading-writing class in their strategy use in almost every category.

Table 4.14   **Overall strategy use by class for type 2**

	Category	C	M	CP	MC	S	A	N
Mean	WC	3.72	3.26	3.55	3.23	2.49	1.90	2.61
	RC	3.57	3.15	3.28	3.04	2.26	1.90	2.65
	IC	3.43	3.14	3.29	3.10	2.56	2.03	2.43

Table 4.14 shows the mean score of the three classes on each category according to type 2. The results from the overall strategy use by class for type 2 show that the WC has a higher mean score in nearly every category except in A and N, which means the writing class used more metacognitive, cognitive, compensation and memory strategies than the RC and the IC. As for the affective strategies, the IC used this strategy more than the other two classes. When it comes to the negative strategies, the RC used this strategy more than others.

The analysis above indicates that the WC had a trend of using more strategies in both reading and writing processes than the other two classes, no matter in what kind of categorization, type 1 or type 2. However, although the mean score of strategy use of the three classes for each of the categories are different, a Scheffe Multiple Comparison surprisingly reveals that the differences between all types of strategies are not significant at the 0.05 level. This suggests that there is no significant difference in strategy use between the three classes.

4.7   The "input-construction-comprehension-output" circulation

The data analysis and results indicate that the IC learners' writing proficiency has been improved a lot because there is significant difference between the writing test results before and after the experiment. But IC learners have not made significant progress in reading proficiency. The WC has made no gains in both reading and writing, which means WC learners' reading and writing proficiency have not been improved. RC learners have made progress in their writing proficiency but no such improvement can been observed in their reading proficiency. Furthermore, there is no significant difference between the effects of the three teaching programs, no matter in the case of reading proficiency or in the case of writing proficiency. Thus, Krashen's input hypothesis, Swain's output hypothesis, Widdowson's integrated approach, Kucer's cognitive model of reading and writing are used to explain the findings mentioned above.

Implication 1: Learners under the integrated reading-writing approach might show progress in their reading proficiency and the progress would be greater than that of those under the enhanced reading input approach or the enhanced writing output approach.

As far as reading proficiency is concerned, all learners' development of reading proficiency can be clearly observed from the following figure. It can be found that learners of all three classes show some minor advance in their reading performance, but it can not prove directly whether the reading-writing integration approach has better effects on learners' reading proficiency. Looking back on what has been analyzed, it can be seen that the mean difference between pretest and posttest on reading for each class is not significant at the 0.05 level; furthermore, there is no significant difference between the posttest scores of all three classes. So the wispy advance observed from three experimental classes is not equal to the effectiveness of the three teaching programs. To be more specific, the reading-writing integration teaching approach is not effective in enhancing reading proficiency, not to mention the superiority of this teaching approach over the other two programs.

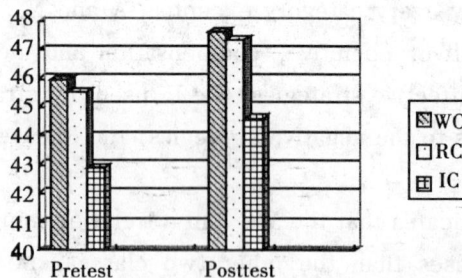

Figure 4.9　The development of learners' reading proficiency

The Writing Class, who received regular English classroom instruction plus enhanced writing output practice after class, did not show significant gain in reading proficiency. The inability of writing program in the present study goes in the opposite direction to Adams and Jager (1994) and Vivian Zamel (1992)'s studies, which hold that writing can be used to improve reading. A possible explanation of this contradiction may be that the writing program in the present study does not take effective forms of "writing-to-read".

Zamel (1992) argues that effective "writing-to-read" forms can be: asking students to keep reading journals or logs in which reactions are recorded and elaborated upon; giving students the opportunity to write about what they find interesting/significant/moving/ puzzling; asking learners to summarize or react to certain passages in one column and then reflect on these reactions in the other; asking learners to write about the associations a text calls forth after they have summarized and reacted to it in separate and self-contained pieces of writing; or asking learners to mark certain passages or insert marginal notations or some other form of reflective comment as they read and then go back to these passages and explore in writing why they think these passages resonate for them; the final suggestion Zamel gives on "writing-to-read" is that teachers sequence assignments around reading so that learners are guided to address these readings from different perspectives. However, in the present study, the writing program laid little emphasis on what forms writing-to-read should take. Although the writing program required learners to write frequently, the learners were just asked to write compositions on given topics and such writing assignments are far from being regarded as an effective form of "writing-to-read".

The Reading Class, who received regular English classroom instruction plus large amount of reading practice after class, did not show significant progress in learners' reading proficiency. This can be analyzed in this way: although reading and writing are both complex processes and hard to be improved, it is obviously noticed from various kinds of test scores that Chinese EFL learners' writing performance lags far behind their reading performance. The subjects of this study are no exception. The underlying meaning of what has been mentioned above is that the subjects' reading proficiency was higher than their writing proficiency. As is known to all that it is comparatively easy to improve one's proficiency in a certain aspect from a quite low level to a higher level, but to improve this proficiency from a relatively high level to a higher level is much more difficult. This may explain why the reading program succeeded in improving learners' writing proficiency but failed in improving their reading proficiency.

The Integrated Reading-Writing Class, who received regular classroom instruction plus both enhanced reading input and enhanced writing output, despite its evident effects on improving learners' writing proficiency, did not show significant effects on learners' reading proficiency. This is against Xie (1994) and Chen's (2001) viewpoints and partially contradictory to Xu's study in 2002. Xu Jinfen conducted a research in 2002 on applying an integrated-skills approach to the teaching of intensive reading and reported that the new approach not only helped improve learners' reading ability, but also contributed to the cultivation of their ability in listening, speaking and writing, thus enhancing learners' overall communicative competence. Apart from the explanation given in the paragraph above (that explanation fit for the case discussed here as well), there are another two possibilities concerned with the reasons for this contradiction.

One possibility is that the control of reading materials was not as rigorous as that of writing tasks. By asking the learners to hand in there compositions and telling them their performance on compositions would be connected to their achievements, teachers of the

WC and the RC could make sure learners would finish the writing tasks. Moreover, teacher's grading process of those compositions surely reinforced this effect. However, it was hard to make sure the learners had finished their reading tasks. The large amount of the reading materials (25 passages in total, with the premise that there were a lot of reading tasks in their textbooks) was one impediment and the single form of checking (teachers of the RC and the IC could only check whether the learners had read the materials by asking them questions concerned with the materials) was another. If the learners had not read the materials carefully at all, their reading proficiency would not have significant gains of course.

The other possibility is that the reading-writing integration program did not take effective forms to insert reading into writing or insert writing to reading despite of its emphasis on the quantity of reading and writing, that is, this program told the learners to read extensively and write frequently but did not tell the learners how to integrate the two into one. Support for this explanation may come from Calkins's (1986) work and Mateos, Martin, Villlalon and Luna's study in 2008. Calkins (1986), whose work is primarily in children's acquisition of literacy, describes how a perspective influences the ways in which writing is now being introduced in reading classrooms like this: "Under the rubric of reading-writing connections, writing is being squeezed, stretched, and distorted to service existing reading programs... In the name of reading-writing connections, writing is being treated as an elaborate ditto." In other words, writing is being inserted into the reading program and is typically viewed as either reinforcing reading or taking away from reading time. By questioning whether these writing activities make a significant contribution to reading because they fail to take into account the genuine connections readers make as they read, Calkins suggests the reading and writing relationship should be explored provocatively enough. Calkins goes further to suggest an effective form of connecting writing and reading, that is, one can find one's reactions and responses to texts by reflecting on them through writing. Mateos et al. (2008) also give suggestions on integrating reading and writing. By elaborating that reading and writing are more powerful tools for learning when used together than when used separately, Mateos et al. point out that tasks such as writing a summary of a single text and writing a synthesis of multiple texts, which both involve writing a new text by selecting, organizing, and connecting contents from the source texts, can be classified as hybrid of reading and writing.

Comparing the reading performance of the three classes, it can be found that none of the three teaching programs (the enhanced reading input program, the extensive writing program and the reading-writing integration program) showed significant positive effects on reading. The reasons for this phenomenon may fall into two aspects. The first reason is the limited duration of the experiment. Anyway, the experiment lasted only one semester, equal to about three months. This length of time is really not enough for a study of the complex processes of English reading and writing.

The second explanation may be given from the perspective of fossilization. Since the term came into being, many modifications and versions of that definition have been developed by SLA researchers, among which Han's (2004) opinion is worth attention. Han argues that even if language learners are constantly exposed to input of the target language, fully motivated to learn the target language and provided with enough opportunities to practice that language, fossilization may still occur (Yang Ling, 2002). With the support of this viewpoint, the general stagnancy of all subjects' reading proficiency in the present study may be explained by fossilization. Although the RC and the IC received sufficient English input (the large amount of reading materials), the WC and the IC had enough chances to practice their English (enhanced writing output assignments), and they are supposed to have high motivation, the three classes showed little improvement in their reading proficiency, this phenomenon is a case in point of fossilization. In fact, in terms of the classification of fossilization into Temporary Fossilization and Permanent Fossilization provided by Selinker, the general stagnancy of all subjects' reading proficiency in this study should be come under the type of Temporary Fossilization. For the EFL learners in China, especially for non-English majors, their fossilization mostly belongs to temporary fossilization, namely, stabilization. Factors causing this stabilization may include negative transfer, misuse of learning strategies, low quality of input, and lack of cross-cultural knowledge.

Implication 2: Learners under the integrated reading-writing approach might show progress in their writing proficiency and the progress would be greater than that of those under the enhanced reading input approach or the enhanced writing output approach.

As with writing proficiency, the situation is quite different from that of reading proficiency, which can be observed clearly from the following figure. Figure 4.10 displays that all three classes show a clear ascending tendency in their writing scores; this is especially clear for the integrated reading-writing class. Besides, the analysis of the data in 4.1.3 indicates that the mean differences between pretest and posttest on reading for both the reading class and the integrated reading-writing class are significant. Therefore, the effectiveness of reading-writing integration approach has been confirmed thereby. The integration program is truly effective in improving writing proficiency. Nevertheless, the evidence from the present study can not prove that reading-writing integration teaching approach is more effective than the reading program because no statistically significant difference can be found between the IC and the RC.

Despite of its tiny rise in the mean scores of writing from pretest to posttest, the writing class did not show significant gains in writing proficiency. This phenomenon can be explained from two aspects: for one thing, the most important implication from Krashen's Input Hypothesis is that comprehensible input plays a very important role in language learning. Without input, output is just like water without a source. However, the writing program was, by virtue of the design, an output-based approach, it may lack the necessary input for writing so that it did not show any significant gain. For another, it was worth noticing that the teacher of the writing class did not give feedback to learners' compositions. The present study draws attention to the fact that frequent writing practice without teacher feedback brought about little improvement in writing of non-native

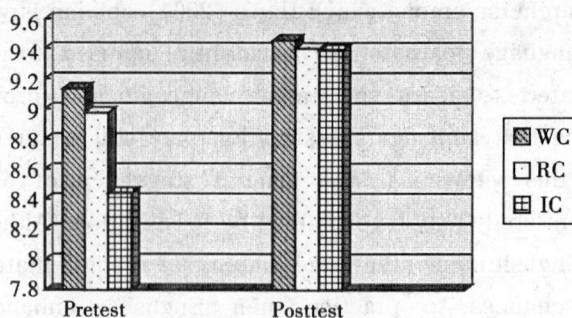

Figure 4.10   The development of learners' writing proficiency

speakers. Though writing for its own sake has been shown to be valuable in L1 contexts as in Smith's (1984) study, conventional writing extension program in L2 with minimal teacher support may not work. It is also possible that the learners in the writing class concerned did not achieve an L2 level where writing practice with little feedback or consultation might be of value.

Although it did not show significant progress in learners' reading proficiency, the reading class showed significant improvement in their writing proficiency. This finding is totally in accordance with the viewpoints of Bracewell and Frederiksen (1982), Elley and Mangubhai (1983), Stotsky (1983), Carrell (1985, 1987), Hafiz & Tudor (1989), Elley (1991), Grabe (1991), Chen Pi-Ching and Chen Chien-Ying (2005) and so on. Therefore, the present study has testified the effects of reading on writing once again. Possible explanations for this may be that the reading program exposed learners to an appropriate model of the target language at an appropriate level (Krashen 1982), it improved general knowledge and thus helped develop content in writing. It also exposed learners to appropriate models of construction, agreement, tense, number, and word order, which strengthened their use of the language.

The integrated reading-writing class was found to be of great progress in writing. In other words, the reading-writing integration program was quite effective in improving learners' writing proficiency although it did not show much influence on learners' reading proficiency. The significant positive effects of this program on learners' writing proficiency lends support to Krashen's input hypothesis (1982), Swain's output hypothesis (1985), Widdowson's integrated approach theory (1978) and Kucer's cognitive model of reading and writing processes (2005). Meanwhile, it strikes a resonant note with Tierney and Pearson (1983), Shanahan (1984, 1987), and Xie Weina (1994) in that it demonstrates the contribution of reading-writing integration to writing. The reasons may fall into four aspects:

First, enough input is beneficial to writing. Due to exposing to a large amount of reading materials, learners got more input in English, which provided them with new language information, ideas that can be used as a basis for writing one's own texts, and matters to write about. That is why learners' writing proficiency improved quickly under the integrated reading-writing program.

Second, transacting information and constructing meaning are really important for writing. Through reading extensively and writing frequently, learners under this program got used to transacting with texts and became good at actively constructing meanings, which is the premise for being a good reader or writer.

Third, integrated language skills can lead to better effects than isolated language skills. For the IC, reading and writing were combined together by the teaching program and thus it made more gains than the WC and the RC, for whom reading and writing were treated in isolation by the concerned teaching programs.

Finally, feedback also plays a role in enhancing writing proficiency. The teacher of IC gave much feedback to the learners' compositions, including giving encouragement to those who had not done a good job and showing satisfaction or rejoice to those who had done well, such as *"I know this one is not your best, you will show me a better one next time, right?" "Frankly speaking, this composition is not good enough, but I know you are always working hard and this one is better than you last one. Keep on making efforts and you will write a fantastic one. " "You have done a good job, next time I hope you can do better. " "Fantastic! I really enjoy your language! " "The structure is great, if the language can be more fluent, it will be wonderful!"* These encouraging words gave learners some confidence and in a way motivated their interests in writing. Therefore, one possible reason for the success of learners under this program may be large amounts of positive feedback from the teacher. This goes in accordance with a research by Ferris (2001), which has shown that teachers' feedback on earlier drafts of work can be quite important in influencing learners' writing processes (Baker & Boonkit, 2004).

According to the results of the comparisons of writing performance between the three classes, there was no significant difference between the effects of the three different teaching programs, which means the integration approach is not superior to the other two approaches. This may be caused by the limited duration of the experiment. Three-month duration was evidently not enough for reflecting the advantage of the integration approach. If a longitudinal research is conducted, the results might be different and the advantage of such an approach might be clearer.

In addition to the discussion of those results displayed in the experiment, there is some other interesting discussion on the results demonstrated in the questionnaire. Figures 4. 11 and 4. 12 separately show the three classes' strategy use according to two sorts of categorization of strategies.

From these two figures that for type 1, the WC uses more strategies than the other two classes in before-reading process, while-reading process, after-reading process, before-writing process, while-writing process, and after-writing process. For type 2, the WC uses more metacognitive, cognitive, compensation and memory strategies than the RC and the IC. According to the perceptual intuition of the above figures, the WC makes more use of reading and writing strategies than the other two classes, in contrast, the RC and the IC are quite similar to each other in language use. However, the results of the Scheffe

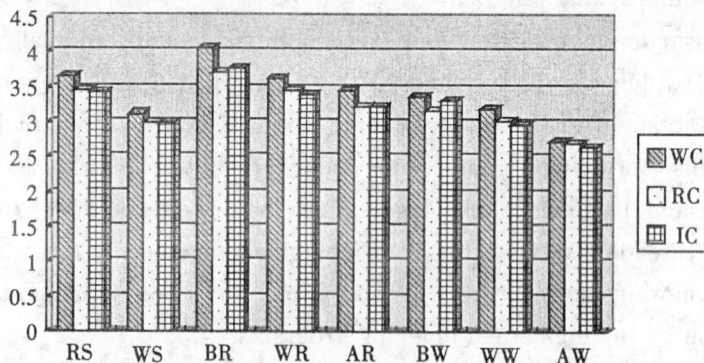

Figure 4.11   The situation of learners' strategy use for type 1

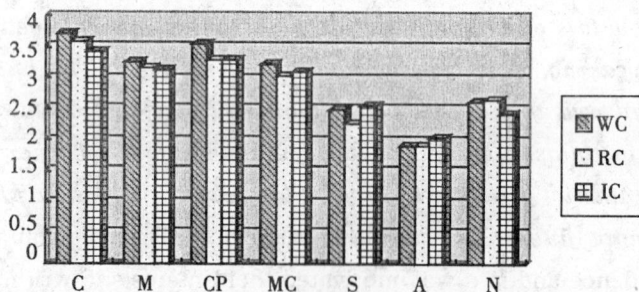

Figure 4.12   The situation of learners' strategy use for type 2

Multiple Comparison show that there is no significant difference in strategy use between any two classes. That is, strategy use has not contributed to the different performance of the three classes in the posttest; learning strategies is not so closely related to language learning. This finding obviously goes in the opposite direction to Baker and Boonkit's viewpoint. In a study aiming to identify the most frequently used strategies and different strategy use between "successful" and "less successful" learners, William Baker and Kamonpan Boonkit (2004) investigated learning strategies employed by undergraduate learners at a Thai university studying EAP reading and writing courses, and pointed out the fact that learning strategies play an important role in second language acquisition (SLA) has been highlighted by numerous writers and studies (Cohen, 1998, 2000; Cook, 2000; Ellis, 1994; Larsen-Freeman and Long, 1991; O'Malley and Chamot, 1990). They also demonstrated that successful and less successful readers and writers showed significant differences in their strategy use. The cause of this contradiction can be justified from two aspects.

First, the reason why subjects of the three classes show no significant difference in their reading and writing strategy use can be discussed in terms of the fact that these students are all freshmen, who entered the university just for a short time. They may still follow the learning habits they have formed in their high school period, which focused on practice and paid less enough attention to strategy use.

Second, this contradiction may be closely related to the high-speed advancement of science and technology, especially that of information technology. Nowadays, the rapid development of the Internet and multivariate and multi-media instruction devices has enormous effects on language learners' learning style. For instance, learners can practice their reading and writing with pen-friends through e-mail, download and store some reading materials in mp3 and so on. And their reading and writing strategies have been imperceptibly influenced by modern technology.

Consequently, the fact that there is no significant difference in strategy use between any two classes in this study does not reduce the importance of teaching and training strategy use. On the contrary, this result implies that strategy use training should be reinforced and be closely related to the new era, the updated learning environment as well as the new characteristics of nowadays language learners.

In conclusion, the study has adopted a constructive viewpoint to analyze the input-output combination. It indicates that linguistic input, active construction and output are all importantly involved like a circle in the process of language learning, which serves as a strong support for Krashen's input hypothesis (1985) and Swain's output hypothesis (1995). According to this viewpoint, a circulation model of "input—construction—comprehension—output" can be set up.

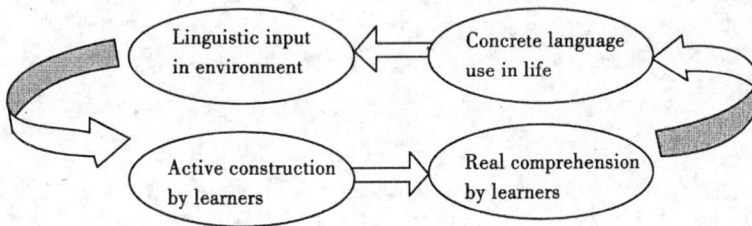

Figure 4.13   An "input—construction—comprehension—output" circulation model

In this model, the input changes into real comprehension through learners' active construction, the real comprehension then leads to concrete language use in life (output), and then the output in turn develops and improves input. The whole process of this circulation model is demonstrated for the convenience of understanding. In the model, the dotted lines are used to mark the boundaries of the two lower boxes while the solid lines are used to mark the boundaries of the two upper boxes. The basic reason lies in that the process of learners' construction and comprehension cannot be observed directly while input and output can be observed directly with ease.

Part Two

Morphology and Grammaticalization

Chapter 5

The Acquisition of English Polysemous Verbs of Motion

Polysemy is ubiquitous in language. It is a linguistic phenomenon of one word having two or more semantically related senses. Traditional semantic theories, such as componential analysis and the field theory, adopt a homonymy approach to lexical polysemy, leading to a neglect of the semantic relatedness between the multiple senses. Cognitive linguists draw on the prototype theory, image schemas, and the metaphor and metonymy theories to account for polysemy. The prototype theory holds the view that the boundary of categories are vague, members of a category display family resemblance; the status of members of a category are not equal, some senses of a word are more central than other senses of it. Image schemas, which are based on human bodily experiences and the physical experiences of the body interacting with the outside world, are a form of basic conceptual structure and can be used to organize and interpret more complex and more abstract concepts, like meanings. Metaphor and metonymy are not only rhetoric devices, but they are also important cognitive models. Metaphor is regarded as the mapping of the schematic structure of the source domain onto that of the target domain, and metonymy is a cognitive process in which one conceptual entity provides mental access to another conceptual entity within the same idealized cognitive domain. Polysemy is the process of meaning extension from the core sense or basic sense of polysemous words to other meanings through cognitive means, such as metaphor and metonymy, and it is the result of cognitive categorization and conceptualization. Based on these above theories, the present study investigates the Chinese EFL learners' acquisition of six English polysemous verbs of motion *draw*, *fix*, *hit*, *hold*, *move*, and *run* in terms of the basic senses, the extended senses and the collocative senses.

Thirty six freshmen majored in Medical Science from Wuhan University are chosen as the subjects of the research. The instruments used in the study include a questionnaire on the strategies for learning of English polysemous verbs and three tests, namely, Multiple Choices, Translation from English to Chinese, and Translation from Chinese to English. The data collected are analyzed via the statistical tool of SPSS. The analysis of the data reveals: Chinese EFL learners generally do better in their acquisition of the basic senses of polysemous verbs of motion, for the human experiences gained from the interaction between the body and the physical world offer a sound basis for the interpretation of the basis senses. In general, there is no significant positive correlation between learners' performances on the basic senses of polysemous verbs of motion and their performances on the extended senses or the collocative senses, but they display unbalanced performances on their acquisition of different extended senses within individual polysemous verbs. Among the multiple extended senses of one polysemous verb, learners can have a good command of the familiar or frequently used senses; the proficiency levels of their acquisition of each of the extended senses vary with the degree of semantic motivatedness, those extended senses that have more obvious and perceivable semantic motivations tend to be better acquired. However, learners still have much difficulty in understanding and grasping the more abstract senses of English polysemous verbs of motion even when they have good performances on the acquisition of the basic senses. They need to improve their metaphorical and metonymic competence in the acquisition of English polysemous verbs of motion.

5.1 Semantic theories related to lexicon

The semantic theories regarding how the meaning of a word is represented and comprehended include componential analysis, field theory, frame semantics, and models of organization of internal lexicon.

5.1.1 Componential analysis of lexicon

Componential analysis, also called semantic feature analysis, has been proposed by structural semanticists. It is a treatment of lexical meaning in which the sense of a lexeme is distinguished from those of other lexemes by a set of semantic features or components. The basic idea is that, analogous to the phonetic analysis, the lexeme can be analysed into smaller units, which are called semantic features or components. Componential analysis involves the analysis of the sense of a lexeme into its component parts. For example, the sense of the word *man* can be analyzed into three components: "human", "male" and "adult"; *women* into "human", "female" and "adult".

Componential analysis originated with the work of Trubetzkoy and the Prague school of linguistics and several versions of componential analysis were developed independently from the 1930s onwards. In the English-speaking countries, the best known version is the one devised by Katz and Fodor in 1963 (Figure 5.1) within the framework of a generative grammar. As is shown in Figure 5.1 below, in the componential analysis of the polysemous word *bachelor*, a set of semantic *markers*, the features that have consequences in grammar and are put in "< >", such as <+animal>, <+human>, <+male>, <noun>, etc., are applied for the sake of analyzing convenience, combined with other features called *distinguishers* which distinguish meanings for only a very limited number of words and do not have grammatical importance and which are put in square bracket [ ], e.g. [who has not married]. The semantic markers are assumed to be substantive universals. Plus and minus (+/−) used in front of the semantic features indicate the presence or absence of the particular feature. Thus, the sense of *man, woman, boy* and *girl* can be analysed respectively as follows:

 man: <+human>, <+adult>, <+male>

 woman: <+human>, <+adult>, <−male>

 boy: <+human>, <−adult>, <+male>

 girl: <+human>, <−adult>, <−male>

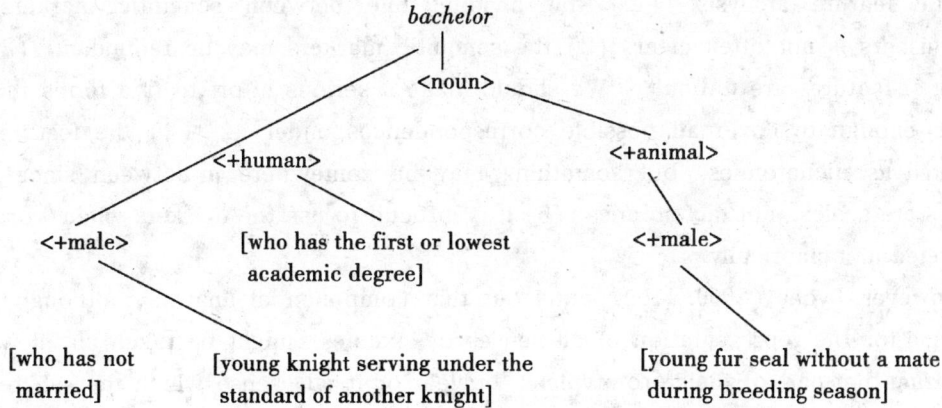

Figure 5.1　Semantic feature diagram for bachelor

(Katz and Fodor, 1963, cited in Hatch and Brown, 2001: 16.)

Some linguists also introduced logical operation symbols into the description of lexical senses. They used the negation operator " ~ " to indicate the absence of certain semantic features, and the propositional connective of conjunction '&' to symbolize the operation by means of which components are combined. The semantic feature of FEMALE thus can be represented as ~MALE. In this case, the sense of *man*, *woman*, *boy* and *girl* can be analysed respectively as follows:

 man =HUMAN & MALE & ADULT

 woman =HUMAN & ~MALE & ADULT

 boy =HUMAN & MALE & ~ADULT

 girl =HUMAN & ~MALE & ~ADULT

The componential analysis of relational words like *father*, *mother*, *son* and *daughter*, is a little bit more complicated, which involves using logical expressions. The sense of *father*, *mother*, *son* and *daughter* may be shown as follows:

 father =PARENT (x, y) & MALE (x)

 mother =PARENT (x, y) & ~MALE (x)

 son =CHILD (x, y) & MALE (x)

 daughter =CHILD (x, y) & ~MALE (x)

(The expression for *father* above means "x is a parent of y, and x is male")

Verbs can also be analyzed in this way, for example, *take* =CAUSE (x, (HAVE (x, y))), which reads "x cause x to have y".

Componential analysis " provides linguists, in principle, with a systematic and economical means of representing the sense-relations that hold among lexemes in particular languages and, on the assumption that the components are universal, across languages (Lyons, 2000: 114)". Despite its advantages, it is not without its defects. Guo Yukai (2005: 187) points out that the theory of componential analysis requires that the meaning of each word be analysed in terms of a definite quantity of semantic components, which is usually impossible. Hatch and Brown (2001: 28-29) summarized five problems for semantic feature analysis: (1) the dividing line between semantic markers and distinguishers is not often clear. (2) the semantic markers may be redundant. (3) the naming of features are difficult. "We should make a serious effort to find terms that are abstract enough to cover all possible correspondences under it." (4) the features are presented as dichotomies, but something may be somewhere in-between since many features are scales, not dichotomies. (5) it is difficult to use the markers when words are interpreted metaphorically.

However, Lyons (2000: 116) points out that componential analysis, although not a technique for the representation of all senses of lexemes, might be taken as "a way of formalizing that part of their prototypical, nuclear or focal, sense which they share with other lexemes". Thus, although componential analysis is no longer popular now, it may still be worthy of the attention and be helpful when dealing with the sense relations among words or among the many senses of a polysemous word. For instance, Taylor (2001: 106-107) analyses the polysemy of the verb *crawl* in terms of the semantic attributes [ascend] and [clamber].

5.1.2 Semantic field theory and polysemous field

While componential analysis tries to define and discern different word meanings by attributing a definite set of semantic features, semantic field theory tries to describe and interpret words of paradigmatic relations in terms of "field". The semantic field theory mainly seeks to explore such sense relations of words like hyponymy, synonymy and antonymy. Generally, semantic field refers to a lexical field consisting of a set of semantically related words defined by some general term or concept. For example, the words *father, mother, son, daughter, brother, sister, aunt, uncle, niece* and *cousin* make up the semantic field of kinship. Semantic field analysis uses semantic features to show relationship of lexical items within a field, one classic example of which is the semantic field analysis of kinship term, as cited in Hatch and Brown (2001: 34-35)).

Field theory holds the view that the vocabulary of a given language is a system of interrelated lexical networks rather than simply a listing of independent items, and is organized into areas, or fields, within which words interrelate and define each other in various ways. For example, the semantic field of *food* includes words such as *fruit, meat, vegetable* and *grain*, etc. And the words *apple, banana, orange, grape, coconut*, etc. make up the semantic field of *fruit*. The words of a semantic field are joined together by a common concept, and they are likely to have a number of collocations in common. Thus, we can detect the cultural differences between two languages through a comparison between the semantic fields in these languages.

According to field theory, a meaning of a word is dependent partly on its relation to other words in the same conceptual area. In other words, a word can have its own meaning only if being viewed as "a part of a whole", that is, only in the semantic field can a word have its own meaning. For example, under the concept of "*week*" there are *Sunday*, *Monday*, *Tuesday*, *Wednesday*, *Thursday*, *Friday*, and *Saturday*. To understand the meaning of "*Sunday*" we have to understand its relations with other words in the semantic field of *week*, that is, its place in the semantic field.

Polysemous field is regarded as a sub-type included in the semantic field in its broad sense. The semantic field theory views polysemy of a word as the polysemous structure, holding that the polysemous field is a semantic network at the synchronic level, underlying which are the diachronic semantic changes of the word. Such a polysemous structure is a paradigmatic semantic continuum which, with a core glosseme (the original or basic sense) as its center, has one or several general semes (which are equal to "semantic components") (Zhang & Zhang, 2001: 78). Such a view is sort of insightful and reasonable. However, the semantic field theory fails to shed much light on the polysemy phenomenon, since neither has it gone deeper into the internal semantic structure of the polysemous word nor does it succeed in accounting for the semantic relations between the multiple meanings of the polysemous word.

5.1.3   Frame semantics and the knowledge of words

Compared with componential analysis and the field theory, frame semantics is a rather new treatment to lexical meanings, which is deeply rooted in the encyclopedic view of meaning interpretation. Frame semantics is developed by Charles J. Fillmore (1982) and is a further development of his case grammar. It is a theory that relates linguistic semantics to encyclopedic knowledge and it "emphasizes the continuities between language and experience (Petruck, 1995)". "A frame is any system of concepts related in such a way that to understand any one concept it is necessary to understand the entire system; introducing any one concept results in all of them becoming available" (Petruck, 1995). A semantic frame is a coherent structure of related concepts that are related such that without knowledge of all of them, one does not have complete knowledge of one of the either. The notion of frame used in frame semantics can be traced back to case frames. Case frames were understood as "Characterizing a small 'scene' or 'situation', so that to understand the semantic structure of the verb it was necessary to understand the properties of such schematized scenes " (Fillmore, 1982: 115).

The basic idea of frame semantics is that one cannot understand the meaning of a single word without access to all the essential knowledge that relates to that word. A most frequently cited example of Frame is the Commercial Transaction Frame which includes such elements as *a buyer*, *a seller*, *goods* and *money*. Each one of the large set of semantically related verbs linked to this frame such as *buy*, *sell*, *pay*, *spend*, *cost* and *charge* indexes or evokes different aspects of the frame. In other words, words specify a certain perspective in which the frame is viewed. For instance, the verb *buy* focuses on the buyer and the goods, while the seller and the money are the background; *sell* focuses on the goods, while the buyer and the money are the background; *pay* focuses on the buyer, the money, and the seller, while the goods is the background; and so on. Thus, the idea is that one cannot understand any one of these verbs without knowing what takes place in a commercial transaction and that, in some sense, knowing the meaning of any one of these verbs means knowing the meaning of all of them. According to Fillmore, the knowledge and experience structured by the Commercial Transaction Frame provide the background and motivation for the categories represented by the words; the meaning of the words are structured by the frame, the words evoke the frame, and the interpreter invokes the frame.

One of the important concepts incorporated into Frame Semantics is that of a prototype, which is understood as "the surrounding culture against which the meaning of a word is defined and understood" (Petruck, 1995). Fillmore (1982) argues that to understand the meaning of the word *breakfast*, one has to understand the institutions and practices of the culture in which the category exists; the variety of contexts in which the *breakfast* category can be used are determined by the word's prototypical use, and the prototypical use of the word is the one it has when conditions of the background situation match the defining prototype. Another example is the word *bachelor*. For Fillmore, the word *bachelor* should be defined against a prototype background frame, but if *bachelor* occurs in contexts which don't match the prototype, it suggests that the prototype frame of the word is extended into a new frame.

Originally as a useful and powerful tool for semantic description of individual words and expressions, frame semantics has now been used to account for various syntactic and semantic phenomena and has, to some extent, been integrated into construction grammar as an important semantic principle.

5.1.4　Organization of the internal lexicon

Psychologists refer to the representation of words in permanent memory as the internal lexicon, or mental lexicon. When a given word in the internal lexicon has been found, the properties associated with the word become available for use, including the meaning of the word, its spelling and pronunciation, its relationship to other words, and related information. With regard to how the internal lexicon is organized, the current main idea is that it is set up as a network of interconnected elements. The elements are concepts or nodes, which are connected to one another by virtue of having various relations with one another. There are two kinds of models regarding the organization of the internal lexicon, namely, the hierarchical network models and the spreading activation models.

In the hierarchical network models, some of the elements stand above or below other members of the network, and concepts similar to the word are represented as distinct nodes in a network of category and property relations. Category relations are those that deal with hyponymy. Property relations indicate what characteristics may be attributed to the items at various levels in the network. In the spreading activation models, in contrast, the organization of the internal lexicon is closer to a web of interconnecting nodes. The distance between the nodes is determined by both structural characteristics such as taxonomic relations and considerations such as typicality and degree of association between related concepts. Activation spreads from one node to neighboring nodes.

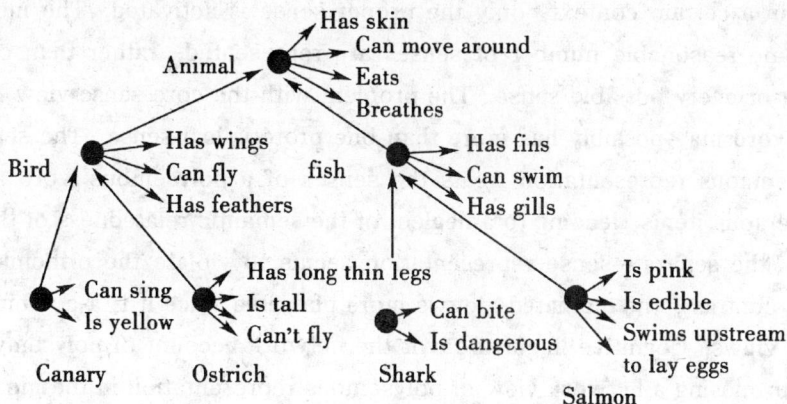

Figure 5.2   A hierarchical network models of semantic information related to animals.
(From "Retrieval Time from Semantic Memory", cited by Carroll, 2000:110)

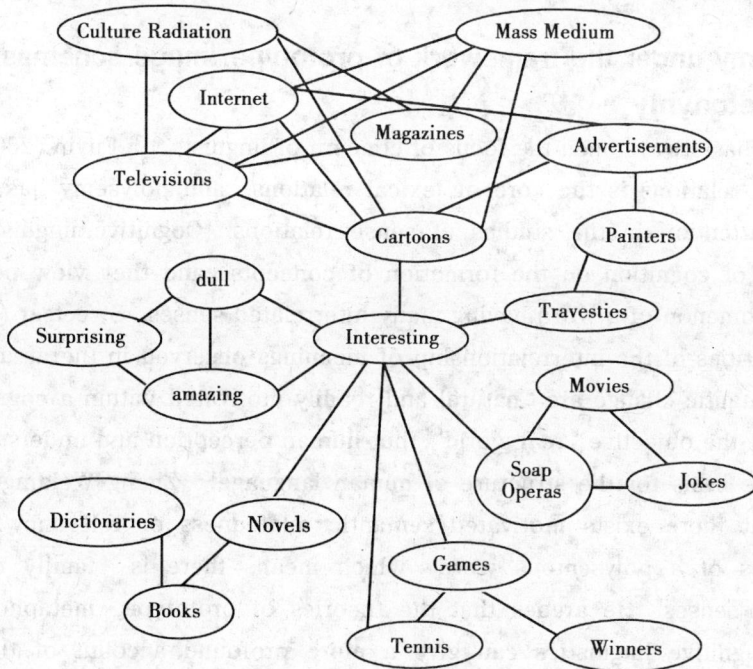

Figure 5.3   A lexical network of *Magazines* according to the spreading Activation Model

Then how are the multiple senses of a polysemous word represented in one's mind? Are they organized in a similar fashion as words are organized in the mental lexical? Zhao

Cuilian (2006) summarizes three main types of views about polysemous representation in the mental lexicon: the core sense view, the separate-sense view and the mediated view. According to the core sense view which is based on the prototype theory, there is only a single, core representation of a word, and all other senses are subsumed under that core representation, which can be derived online in context. The separate-sense view holds that the familiar senses are distinctively represented and that each time a polysemous word is encountered in a certain context, only the proper sense is activated. The mediated view holds that some reasonable number of senses are represented, rather than only a single core meaning or every possible sense. The problem with the core sense view lies in that a polysemous word may possibly has more than one prototypical sense. The separate-sense view on polysemous representation treats the senses of a polysemous word as senses of many monosemous items, leading to a neglect of the semantic relatedness of these senses. What's more, the separate-sense representation seems to violate the principle of storage economy. In contrast, the mediated view is more plausible since it is a combination of the previous two views. Cognitive linguists favor the network account of polysemy, however, they are not proposing a network view of polysemous representation in the mental lexicon; the cognitive linguistic work illustrates one way of making explicit predictions about linguistic behavior from nonlinguistic information. Gibbs and Matlock (1997) point out that both network and monosemy (or separate-sense) views might be needed to fully explain how speakers learn, use and understand words with multiple meanings.

5.2 Polysemy under the framework of prototype, image schemas, metaphor and metonymy

Polysemy has always been the focus of concern of linguists. Li Fuyin (2006: 72) points out that sense relations is the core of lexical relations, and polysemy has received the concentrated attention in the studies of sense relations. Cognitive linguists stress the important role of cognition on the formation of concepts, and they view polysemy as a linguistic phenomenon of a word having many interrelated senses. Sweetser (1990) argues that the regularities of the interrelationship of meanings observed in the area of polysemy and lexical semantic change are "natural and readily motivated within a cognitively based theory that not the objective ' real world', but human perception and understanding of the world to be the basis for the structure of human language". Zhang Weiding (2007: 302) points out that there exists motivated semantic relatedness or relevancy between the multiple senses of a polysemous word, which means there is " family resemblance" between these senses. He argues that the theories of prototype, metaphor and image schemas in cognitive linguistics can give a more profound account of this motivated semantic relatedness which is cognitive in nature. Yan Chensong (2005: 102, 104, 105) contends that semantic motivations of words include metonymy and metaphor, and such motivations are rooted in people's cognitive habit of tending to build up relations between things that are close in nature. In other words, metaphor and metonymy are two vitally important mechanisms of meaning extension of polysemous words. Studies on polysemy from the perspective of cognitive linguistics have shown that polysemy is the process of semantic extension from the core sense or the basic sense of a word to other senses through cognitive means (such as metaphor and metonymy) and that it is the result of cognitive categorization and conceptualization (Zhao Yanfang, 2001:36).

5.2.1 Polysemy and prototype

Categorization is one of the basic ways for human cognition. Cognitive linguists have made attempts to analyze and explain polysemy of words drawing on the main viewpoints of the categorization theories, among which are the prototype theory originally put forward by Rosch, and the idealized cognitive models (ICM for short) advanced by George Lakoff (1987). ICMs are a complex and integral structure, including the propositional structure, schema, metaphor and metonymy, the latter three of which will be accounted in the later sections.

Rosch (1978) demonstrates through a number of experiments that people do not actually categorize objects on the basis of necessary and sufficient conditions but rather on the basis of resemblance of the objects to a prototypical member of the category, which best exhibits the features of the category. Different from the classical categorization theory founded by Aristotle, which defines a category in terms of a set of necessary and sufficient conditions and allocates equal status to all member of a category, the prototype theory holds the brief that the boundary of categories is vague, members of a category will display family resemblance; that the status of members of a category are not equal, some members are more central than others; and that prototype and degree of membership vary with people, and correspondingly, characteristics of syntax and semantics vary across languages.

Prototype theory is a mode of graded categorization in cognitive science, where some members of a category are more central than others. For example, when asked to give an example of the concept *furniture*, *chair* is more frequently cited than *stool*. While a bird may be defined in the classical categorization theory as elements with the features [+feathers], [+beak] and [+ability to fly], prototype theory would view a category like bird as consisting of different elements which have unequal status, for instance, a *robin* is more prototypical of a *bird* than a *penguin* or an *ostrich*.

Cognitive linguists adopt a prototype approach to word meaning. They contend that lexical concepts are categories which are defined by disjunctive set of semantic information that are interrelated by means of a family resemblance structure; in which some semantic information is more salient or prototypical than other information; in which the semantic information need not have a definitional status. This prototype approach to word meaning has been applied to polysemous words (Brugman & Lakoff 1988). In other words, polysemous words are viewed as categories of senses which are interrelated through family resemblance and which possibly center around a prototype. However, while applying the prototype approach to the polysemous category, the central member of a polysemous category (usually the basic sense of it) may not have the same psychological status as the prototype representation of a monosemous category like *bird*.

The term *family resemblance*, an important notion in categorization theory, was originally put forward by Wittgenstein in 1953. It has been widely applied in linguistic studies since then on. Taylor (2001: 99) points out that "many natural language categories, perhaps even the majority, exhibit a polycentric, rather than a monocentric structure, i. e. category membership is a function of similarity to one of several prototype representations. The multiple prototypes associated with the category are themselves related in a family resemblance structure." In other words, polysemy is ubiquitous in language and the multiple senses of a polysemous word are related in a family resemblance structure.

The main idea of the prototype approach to meanings of polysemous words is that the polysemous word has a core sense or a basic sense (usually acting as a prototypical meaning) and other senses are derived or extended from the core sense, and that the multiple senses constitute a semantic network with the core sense as the centre, through the principle of family resemblance. Liao Guangrong (2005) points out that "a polysemous word constitutes a cognitive and semantic category with its primary meaning as the prototype, in which the prototype and non-central members can relate to each other" through several semantic relation models. Traditional semantic relation models of the multiple senses of polysemous words include the meaning train model (Figure 5.4) and the semantic network model. The semantic network model assumes that there is a basic sense from which other senses are derived. The idea of the meaning train model is that meaning A is related to meaning B in virtue of some shared attribute(s), or other kind of similarity; meaning B in turn becomes the source for a further extension to meaning C, which is likewise chained to meaning D and E, and so on. Taylor (2001: 106-108), drawing on Fillmore's analysis of the verb *crawl*, discusses how the multiple senses of the verb are related through "meaning trains". However, Liao Guangrong (2005) points out that the semantic relations within polysemous words are too complicated to be exactly and comprehensively generalized with only one semantic relation model. Although he proposes a combined model of the two traditional models to account for the complexity of semantic relations of the senses of a polysemous word, the starting point of analysis is still the primary sense or the prototype. Thus, it seems obvious that the core or primary sense of polysemous words plays a vital role in the interpretation of their multiple senses.

$$A \longrightarrow B \longrightarrow C \longrightarrow D...$$

Figure 5.4　The meaning train model (Taylor, 2001)

Empirical studies have been carried out to investigate the important role of the core or primary sense in the effective acquisition of polysemous words (Ren Chaohua, 2009; Zhao Qun & Luo Weidong, 2005). Based on cognitive linguistics, Zhao Qun and Luo Weidong (2005) investigate the effect of providing the core sense on guessing and long-term retention of figurative senses of polysemous words. They conduct a series of vocabulary tests involving 40 Chinese EFL learners and the results show that providing a core sense leads to better guessing and long-term retention of figurative senses of polysemous words.

Another thing about the prototype approach is worth mentioning here. In the process of semantic changes, the meaning prototype of a word may undergo prototype shift (in which the central attributes of a category are replaced) and prototype split (in which the prototype of a category changes from a global one to a more local one) (Ungerer and Schmid, 2001). In other words, the prototype of a word may split up or shift, from which the meaning can be further split up or transformed into subcategories or sub-prototypes. Therefore, apart from the basic sense of a polysemous word, which is usually the prototype of its multiple senses, some of its extended senses may be more prototypical than others. In this sense, it is possible that a polysemous word may have more than only one prototypical meaning.

5.2.2 Polysemy and image schemas

Image schemas are an important form of conceptual structure, which is based on human experience gained from the interaction between human body and the physical world. The basic idea is that "because of our physical experience of being and acting in the world—of perceiving the environment, moving our bodies, exerting and experiencing force, etc. —we form basic conceptual structures which we then use to organize thought across a range of more abstract domains" (Saeed, 2000:308). In other words, image schemas of concrete spatial relations and forces are often used to facilitate the understanding of more abstract things, like meanings of words. Image schemas have been used to account for meaning extensions of polysemous words, that is, how image schemas function in the meaning extension of polysemous words. The research into polysemy has shown that extended meanings of a polysemous word can be regarded as derived from the metaphorical extensions of the image schema of the basic sense of that word onto more abstract domains. Image schema is thus a useful technique for describing polysemous meaning extensions.

Image schemas are first proposed by Mark Johnson (1987). In his book *The Body in the Mind: the bodily basis of meaning, imagination, and reason*, Mark Johnson (1987) identifies such schemas as Container, Path, Forces, Balance, Up-Down, Front-Back, Part-Whole and Centre- Periphery. For example, Johnson (1987) uses the Container schema to analyze the various spatial senses of the English word *out*. In his opinion, *out* may be used in cases where a clearly defined trajector (TR) leaves a spatially bounded landmark (LM), as in:

(1a) John went *out* of the room.

(1b) Mary got *out* of the car.

Out may also be used to indicate those cases where the trajector is a mass that spreads out, effectively expanding the area of the containing landmark:

(2a) She poured *out* the beans.

(2b) Roll out the carpet.

(2c) Send *out* the troops.

Out is also often used to describe motion along a linear path where the containing landmark is implied and not defined at all:

(3) The train started *out* for Chicago.

Johnson (1987) argues that the term *out* can also be metaphorically used to describe non-spatial experiences by lending the logic of experientially basic and primarily spatial image schemas such as the Container schema to non-spatial situations:

(4) Leave *out* that big log when you stack the firewood.

(Schema used directly and non-metaphorically.)

(4a) I don't want to leave any relevant data *out* of my argument.

(Schema metaphorically projected onto argumentation.)

(4b) Tell me your story again, and don't leave *out* any details.

(Schema metaphorically projected onto story-telling.)

(4c) She finally came *out* of her depression.

(Schema metaphorically projected onto emotional life.)

Lakoff (1987) views the image schema as a fundamental "building-block" of conceptual structure and argues that our experience and concepts of SPACE are structured in large part by image schemas like Container, Source-Path-Goal, Part-Whole, Up-Down, Front-Back and so on.

Image schemas and their extension by metaphor have been used to describe a number of areas of language which display polysemy. According to Saeed (2000:312), Container schema has been used to investigate the semantics of spatial prepositions in a number of languages including the Cora language of Mexico (Langacker & Cassad, 1985), English (Herkovits, 1986), and French (Vandeloise, 1991). These studies use schemas to explore the typical polysemy of prepositions. Herkovits (1986) analyzes the polysemy of English preposition *in* in terms of the schema of Container and she claims that the multiple uses of the preposition *in* are most satisfactorily described by viewing them as extensions from a central, ideal Container schema which, in her words, is described as "the inclusion of a geometric construct in a one-, two-, or three-dimensional geometric construct". Drawing on spatial schemas such as *Path*, *Above*, *Across*, *Covering*, *Contact* and so on, Brugman and Lakoff (1988) describe and analyze the polysemous meanings of the preposition *over*, three major senses among which are the *above-across* sense, the *above* sense and the *covering* sense. Moreover, Brugman and Lakoff (1988) give a detailed accounting of how these schemas are interrelated in terms of the prototypical schema and the radial category structure which is used to refer to "the characteristic pattern produced by the metaphorical extension of meanings from a central origin (Saeed, 2000:312)". For example, they argue that a central schema such as the prototypical *above-across* schema for *over* could be altered or further specified by other spatial schemas such as whether the trajector (a moving entity) was in contact with the landmark (the background against which movement occurs) or not (as in *the plane is flying over the hill* v. *Sam walked over the hill*); whether the geometric shape of the landmark may be viewed as an extended area or as a vertical form (as in *The bird flew over the yard* v. *The bird flew over the wall*); and the focus may be on the endpoint of the path as in *Sam lives over the hill*. The preposition *over* can also be used metaphorically as in *Harry still hasn't gotten over his divorce* (such use may be viewed as a version of the LIFE AS A JOURNEY metaphor, where problems are seen as obstacles).

Force schemas have been used to describe polysemy in modal verbs (Talmy, 1985, 1988; Sweetser, 1990). Modal verbs typically have both deontic and epistemic senses (the term "root senses" is used by Sweetser instead of "deontic senses"), with the former involving the speaker's attitude to social factors of obligation, responsibility and permission (e. g. the meaning of *must* in *You must pay for your rent when the time is due* is deontic), and the latter signaling a speaker's judgment about the way the real world is (e. g. the meaning of *must* in *Lucy must have cried before she came in* is epistemic). Talmy (1985, 1988) analyzes the deontic uses of model verbs like *must*, *can*, and *may* in terms of forces and barriers. For example, Talmy proposes that a typical use of *may* as permission as in *You may enter the studio when the light goes out* is an example of removing a barrier or keeping back a potential but absent barrier, thus some potential barrier to entering the studio is identified as being negated. Sweetser (1990) adopts and extends this analysis of *may*, and she analyses the epistemic use of modal verbs as a metaphorical extension of their deontic uses. Take *must* and *may* for example. *Must* in its epistemic use can express a reasonable conclusion as in (a) *You've travelled all day. You must be tired* and the epistemic use of *may* express possibility as in (b) *You may feel a bit sick when we take off*. Sweetser argues that such uses of modal verbs for rational argument and judgment are derived from their uses for the real world of social obligation and permission, which fits the usual pattern of metaphorical extension from the external concrete world to the internal world of cognition and emotion. A parallel between barriers in social action and barriers in mental reasoning is drawn. The epistemic use of *may* is thus viewed as representing a lack of barrier. Thus the sentence *You may be right* can be paraphrased as *There is no evidence preventing the conclusion that you are right*. The epistemic use of *must* is interpreted as the extension of the Compulsion Force schema to the domain of reasoning, and the sentence *You must have driven too fast* can thus be paraphrased as *The evidence forces my conclusion that you drove too fast*. For Sweetser, the relationship between the deontic and epistemic use of each modal is not accidental but a further example of polysemy, and what relates these senses is the metaphorical extension of the force and barriers schemas from the social world to the inner reasoning.

Saeed's (2000) argues that "image schemas are proposed as experientially-based conceptual constructs by which we characterize, for example, spatial relations, and which can be metaphorically extended across a range of domains, typically shifting from the external and concrete to the internal and abstract. " Such schemas allow us to have a good understanding of metaphorical use of words. Polysemy is the result of such extension of schemas to form radical categories. Thus, image schemas can serve as a useful tool in the interpretation of the sense relations within a polysemous category. In such interpreting process, however, image schemas can not be separated from another important cognitive model—metaphor.

5.2.3 Polysemy and metaphor

Metaphor is traditionally viewed as a rhetoric device in language, but now most linguists have approved of the idea that metaphor is not a mere language phenomenon, but rather a cognitive model. Just as Lakoff and Johnson (1980: 3) put it, "Metaphor is pervasive in everyday life, not just in language but in thought and action. Our ordinary conceptual system, in terms of which we both think and act, is fundamentally metaphorical in nature". Lakoff and his colleagues (Lakoff, 1987; Johnson, 1987; Lakoff & Johnson, 1980; Lakoff & Turner, 1989) claim that "the locus of metaphor is thought". According to Lakoff and Johnson (1980:5), "the essence of metaphor is understanding and experiencing one kind of thing in terms of another". They believe that metaphor is not only linguistic expression, but more basically a form of thought with their own epistemological functions.

The central idea of the conceptual metaphor theory, founded by Lakoff and Johnson (1980), is that a conceptual metaphor consists of a target domain and a source domain, and that metaphor is the mapping of the schematic structure of the source domain onto that of the target domain. The mapping occurs at the conceptual level and is systematic in that there is a fixed set of correspondences between the structure of the target domain and the structure of the source domain. "Metaphors allow us to understand one domain of experience in terms of another (Lakoff and Turner, 1989:135). " In the LIFE IS JOURNEY metaphor, an often-cited example, the target domain is LIFE, while the source domain is JOURNEY. Why LIFE can be interpreted in terms of JOURNEY lies in that there is a systematicity in the mapping of the two concepts: the person leading a life is a traveler; his purposes are destinations; the means for achieving purposes are routes; difficulties in life are impediments to travel; counselors are guides; progress is the distance travelled; things you gauge your progress by are landmarkers; material resources and talents are provisions (Lakoff and Turner, 1989: 3-4). Thus, one can understand the abstract thing like LIFE in terms of the concrete experience of a journey.

Lakoff (1990, 1993, 1994) argues that metaphorical mapping preserves the cognitive typology (that is, the image-schema structure) of the source domain, in a way consistent with the inherent structure of the target domain. Lakoff and Johnson (1980) assume that a metaphorical mapping of the structure of the source domain onto that of the target domain usually consists of the following: slots in the source domain, relations in the source domain, properties in the source domain, and knowledge in the source domain.

Metaphor is believed to be an important mechanism for meaning extension of polysemous words. One cognitive function of metaphor is to allow us to make motivated semantic associations and extensions (Zhang Weiding, 2007: 303). Sweetser (1990: 8) generalizes that "a great deal of polysemy is due to metaphorical usage". Lyons (2000: 59) also points out that metaphorical extension is one of the principle factors operative in semantic change of words. For example, the word "foot" which means "terminal part of a leg" also comes to mean "lowest part of a hill or mountain". Also, image schemas and their extension by metaphor have been used to describe a number of areas of language which display polysemy (Johnson, 1987; Talmy, 1985, 1988; Sweetser, 1990; etc.).

The powerful metaphor theory has also drawn a lot of attention from applied linguists and practitioners. Based on the modern metaphor theory, Danesi (cited in Chen Wanhui, 2008: 260) put forward the notion of "metaphorical competence" in 1992, and he argues that "metaphorical competence" is the neglected dimension in second language acquisition and second language teaching. In his another article in 1993, Danesi (ibid.) points out that "metaphorical competence" is the hyponym structure of "conceptual fluency" and that a fundamental characteristic of the native speaker's language competence is the ability to speak in a metaphorical way. In another word, metaphorical competence is an important index of mastery of a language. Some researchers (Ijaz, 1986; Biskup, 1992; etc. as cited in Chen Wanhui, 2008) also recognize metaphor as an important factor in the second language vocabulary acquisition. In light of the universality and systematicity of metaphor in languages, to cultivate the metaphorical competence in second language learners is both possible and necessary. Influenced by the cognitive metaphor theories, many scholars in China (Cai Longquan, 2003; Wang Yin, 2001, 2004.) have proposed that second language teachers should emphasize the cultivation of metaphorical competence in Chinese EFL learners in their teaching practice, and they consider the metaphorical competence as an equally important aspect of language ability as are the linguistic competence and the communicative competence.

5.2.4   Polysemy and metonymy

Metonymy has been traditionally viewed as a relationship involving substitution, namely, A STANDS FOR B. Nowadays, it is widely accepted that both metonymy and metaphor are fundamental conceptual mechanisms that have great impact on human thought. Lakoff (1987: 78) views metonymy as a stand-for relation occurring in one ICM. For instance, in the sentence "I have bought a Ford", the name of the car-making company stands for one of its characteristic products.

Langacker (1993: 30) defines metonymy as "a reference-point phenomenon in which one conceptual entity, the reference point, affords mental access to another conceptual entity, the desired target. " For him, metonymic process consists in mentally accessing one conceptual entity via another entity. Croft (1993: 347) defines metonymy with the core concept of "contiguity", based on which he gives a definition that "Metonymy is a shift of word meaning from the entity it stands for to a 'contiguous' entity." However, Croft fails to explain how the cognitive process of metonymy shifts.

Blank and Koch have points to the terms "salient" and "domain highlighting", with Blank's definition (1999: 174) of metonymy as "a linguistic device based on salient conceptual relations within a frame network" and Koch's (1999: 152) as "a conceptual effect of domain highlighting within one domain matrix". Radden & Kovecses (1999: 21) declare that "Metonymy is a cognitive process in which one conceptual entity, the vehicle, provides mental access to another conceptual entity, the target, within the same idealized cognitive model." Barcelona (2000: 32-33) argues that "Metonymy is the conceptual mapping of a cognitive domain onto another domain, both domains being included on the same domain or ICM, so that the source provides mental access to the target."

Metonymy plays an important role in the extension of lexical meanings. Cognitive linguists claim that both metaphor and metonymy "are seen as being conceptual in nature, both can be conventionalized, both are means of extending the resources of a language, and both can be explained as mapping process (Ungerer and Schmid, 2001: 128)". The main difference between metaphor and metonymy is that "while metaphor involves a mapping across different cognitive models, metonymy is a mapping within one model" (ibid.). While metaphor arises due to association by principle of similarity or by principle of good continuation, metonymy is based on association by principle of proximity or by principle of prominence. Types of conventionalized metonymy include Part-for-Whole metonymy as in "We met some new faces around here", Producer-for-Product metonymy as in "I bought a Ford", Tool-for-User metonymy as in "the buses are on strike" and Whole-for-Part metonymy as in "Please fill up my motor". Dirven (cited in Zhang Shaoquan, 2009) identifies three types of metonymy, namely, linear metonymy, conjunctive metonymy and inclusive metonymy, and he points out that linear metonymy will not give rise to polysemy, for example: (1) Moscow is sensitive to the needs of the people. (locality for institution); (2) Shakespeare is easy to read. (producer for product). It is clear that both "Moscow" in (1) and "Shakespeare" in (2) are easy to be understood and do not get multiple meanings. However, conjunctive metonymy and inclusive metonymy can lead to polysemy. *School* and *bank* are examples of conjunctive metonymy, they can both mean "building" and the "institution". *Head* in "He has a good head" means 'intelligence'. It is an example of inclusive metonymy because there is a relationship of inclusion between the shapeless "intelligence" and "head", an objective part of body.

Taylor points out that "the essence of metonymy resides in the possibility of establishing connections between entities which co-occur within a given conceptual structure (2001: 123-124)". Just because of metonymy, people are able to attribute multiple meanings to a single word from different angles. Taylor (2001: 124) even argues that metonymy is one of the most fundamental processes of meaning extension, which is perhaps even more basic than metaphor.

5.3 Polysemy and polysemous verbs of motion

When it comes to the definition of polysemy, a distinction between homonymy and polysemy should be made. Homonyms are traditionally defined as different words with the same form. According to *American Heritage Dictionary* (the 4th edition), a homonym is "one of two or more words that have the same sound and often the same spelling but differ in meaning, such as *bank* (embankment) and *bank* (place where money is kept)." Whereas homonymy is a relation that holds between two or more distinct lexemes, polysemy is a property of a single lexeme which has multiple meanings. Saeed (2000:64) points out that both homonymy and polysemy deal with multiple senses of the same phonological word, but polysemy is invoked if the senses are judged to be related. In dictionaries, polysemous senses are listed under the same lexical entry, while homonymous senses are given separate entries.

Lyons (2000:58) raises two criteria to identify polysemy and homonymy, namely, etymology (the historical source of the words) and relatedness of meaning. He argues that in general, the etymological criterion supports the native speaker's untutored intuitions about particular lexemes. However, the thought-to-be homonyms supported by the native speaker's intuition might or might not come from different source. For example, most native speakers of English would probably classify "bat$_1$" ("furry mammal with membranous wings") and "bat$_2$" ("implement for striking a ball in certain games") are different lexemes, and they do indeed differ in respect to their historical source, "bat$_1$" being derived from a regional variant of Middle English "bakkle", and "bat$_2$" from Old English 'batt' meaning "club, cudgle"; in contrast, the homonyms "sole$_1$" ("bottom of foot or shoe") and "sole$_2$" ("kind of fish") which are thought of as being semantically unrelated have come from the same source. As to the criterion of relatedness of meaning, metaphorical extension is one of the principle factor operative in semantic change. So, an operational definition of polysemy is reached: polysemy is a synchronic linguistic phenomenon of a single word having two or more than two semantically related senses.

According Hatch and Brown (2001:223), Vendler (1976) identified four types of verbs: activities (e. g. run, write, look for), accomplishments (e. g. kill, put, run a mile), achievements (e. g. recognize, find, see, understand) and states (e. g. know, love, have, be). Some divides verbs into three general types: verbs of motion (e. g. run, hold, hit, go), psych verbs (e. g. think, love, hate) and perception verbs (e. g. see, hear. taste), though they may not cover all the verbs.

By verbs of motion, the author means verbs that denote actions which involve body movements, such as *run*, *hold*, *crawl*, *move* and so on. Uses of verbs of motion, such as *crawl* and *run*, are closely related with one's experience of body movements and his or her physical interactions with the outside environments and can be understood in terms of many basic image schemas such as Path, Container, Force, Contact, Up-Down, etc. Since people always depend much on the embodied experiences and the basic image schemas for interpreting abstract things such as meaning, the metaphorical uses of words in particular, verbs of motion have great potential in generating new senses by means of metaphorical extension. In other words, verbs of motion can have a rich set of meanings.

Verbs of motion are one of the most frequently used types of verbs in everyday life, and embodied experiences play an essential role in the interpretation and learning of multiple senses of polysemous verbs of motion. In addition to innumerous studies on the polysemy of nouns, spatial prepositions, adjectives and perception verbs, the polysemy of verbs of motion has also become the research concern of more and more researchers and scholars (Taylor's discussion on polysemy of "crawl", 2001; Hans C. Boas, 2001; Tang Yao, 2007). Many theoretical studies on polysemous verbs of motion are carried out from the perspective of frame semantics and cognitive semantics. However, only a few empirical studies have been conducted to investigate language learners' acquisition of polysemous verbs of motion from the perspective of cognitive linguistics.

5.4 Research methodology of the acquisition of English polysemous verbs of motion

There are motivated sense relations between the multiple senses of a polysemous word, and the basic sense or core sense of a polysemous word is considered both important and facilitative to the interpretation of its extended senses, which requires certain metaphorical and metonymic competence of an interpreter. To interpret and master the multiple senses of a polysemous word well, it is better to view them as a systematic and interrelated semantic network with motivated sense relations. To investigate the Chinese EFL learners' acquisition of English polysemous verbs of motion, the author chooses six polysemous verbs of motion, including *draw*, *fix*, *hit*, *hold*, *move*, and *run*, and the multiple senses of polysemous verbs of motion are classified into three types: the basic senses, the extended senses and the collocative senses. Take the verb *hold* for example, its basic sense is "to have and keep in one's grasp" as in *held the reins tightly*; one of its extended senses is "to cover (the ears or the nose, for example) especially for protection" as in *held my nose against the stench*; one of its collocative senses is "hold back (from sth): hesitate to act or speak because of fear or reluctance" as in sentence *She held back, not knowing how to break the terrible news*, and in sentence *She held back from telling him what she thought of him*. The reason why the six polysemous verbs of motion are chosen lies in the belief that the bodily experience underlying these verbs of motion may be easier and concrete enough for one to draw semantic connections between the basic sense of a polysemous verb of motion and its extended senses.

5.4.1   Research questions and hypotheses

Since the basic sense of the six polysemous verbs of motion selected in the present study are closely related to human bodily experience, the basic senses of these verbs are assumed to be better acquired than other senses. Theoretically speaking, a good acquisition of the basic sense of polysemous verbs of motion may well have beneficial effects on the learners' acquisition of the extended senses and collocative senses of polysemous verbs of motion, provided that the learners have a good metaphorical competence. So, the present research tries to explore four research questions: (1) How do Chinese EFL learners perform on their acquisition of polysemous verbs of motion in terms of the basic sense, the extended sense and the collocative sense respectively? (2) Do they display more difficulty in acquiring the extended senses of polysemous verbs of motion than the basic sense of polysemous verbs of motion? (3) Does the better acquisition of the basic sense of polysemous verbs of motion have any beneficial effects on their acquisition of the extended senses and collocative senses? (4) Have the learners, to some degree, already developed a good metaphorical competence? In order to answer these research questions, two hypotheses are advanced, with the second hypothesis as the central focus of the study:

Hypothesis 1: Chinese EFL learners generally do better in their acquisition of the basic senses of polysemous verbs of motion, and in most cases, they display significant difference between their performances on the basic senses of the polysemous verbs of motion and that on the extended senses.

Hypothesis 2: In general, there is probably some positive correlation between the learners' performances on the basic senses of polysemous verbs of motion and their performances on the extended senses or collocative senses. That is, if Chinese EFL learners do well in their acquisition of the basic senses of polysemous verbs of motion, that will probably facilitate their acquisition of the extended senses or the collocative senses.

Thirty six freshmen from Medical School of Wuhan University are chosen as the subjects of the present research. They are majored in Medical Science. Among the 36 subjects, 20 are female students and 16 are male students. All of them have learnt English for 6 years and are deemed to be acquainted with the seven polysemous verbs of motion which are chosen in the research.

5.4.2   Instruments

In this research, three test papers are designed to test the subjects' performance on the acquisition of the six polysemous verbs of motion in terms of the basic sense, the extended senses and the collocative senses. The six polysemous verbs of motion selected include *draw*, *fix*, *hit*, *hold*, *move*, and *run*. These test papers involve three types of testing items, namely, multiple choices, translation from English to Chinese, and translation from Chinese to English. The purpose of designing testing items of different types is to make the tests more scientific and valid.

The first test takes the form of multiple choices, with the testing items designed in accordance with the paradigm of vocabulary-and-structure items in CET-4 papers. There are 30 items in total, with 5 test items for each verb. 10 of the testing items are selected from the vocabulary-and-structure test items in CET-4 from 1989 to 2005. 14 of them are adapted from sentences selected either from the British National Corpus (BNC) or the American National Corpus (ANC). The rest 6 items are made up using sentences selected from *Oxford Advanced Learner's English-Chinese Dictionary*, *Collins COBUILD Advanced Learner's Dictionary 5th Edition*, and the online Iciba Sentence Bank. The subjects are required to choose the most suitable word that fits the meaning of the given sentence.

The second test is translation from English into Chinese and the third one is translation from Chinese into English. There are 36 test items for translation from English into Chinese with 6 items for each verb, and 24 test items for translation from Chinese to English with each verb having 4 items. Most testing items (48 items) in the second and third test are carefully selected either from the British National Corpus (BNC), the American National Corpus (ANC) or *Oxford Advanced Learner's English-Chinese Dictionary*. Sources of the rest of them include the online *Iciba Sentence Bank*, *Longman Dictionary of Contemporary English*, *Collins COBUILD Advanced Learner's Dictionary* 5th Edition, etc.

Each verb has 15 test items in total in these tests, and the 15 items are designed in terms of the basic senses, the extended senses and the collocative senses. However, the numbers of items assigned to each type of meaning are not equal.

5.4.3 Data collection and analysis

Data will be collected from the three tests and the questionnaire stated above. In the first test of multiple choices, the correct answer will be valued 1, and the wrong answer will be valued 0. In the second and third test of translation, the correct understanding or use of the polysemous verbs of motion in each test item will be valued 1, and the wrong understanding or use of them will be valued 0. For each verb, the values of test items testing either type of the three meanings of the verb are added to get a mean for that meaning. Thus, three means are calculated for each verb, namely, mean for basic sense (BS), mean for extended sense (ES) and mean for collocative sense (CS). SPSS is used to process the means calculated for each verb. For the data of each verb, descriptive statistics of the BS, ES and CS are yielded to see the subjects' overall performance on the three types of meanings of a given verb, which type of meaning is best acquired and which worst acquired. Since the number of items testing the BS, ES and CS are not equal, and for the convenience of comparing the subjects' performance on the BS, ES and CS of a verb, the primary means for BS, ES, and CS are transferred into a 1-point scale.

Correlation between BS and ES, BS and CS are done to see whether and to what degree the subjects' performance on the acquisition of BS of a polysemous verb of motion is positively correlated with their performance on the acquisition of ES or CS of it in a systematic way.

In light of the large quantity of test items in each of the three tests, they were taken in three different periods of the regular English classroom, so as to ensure that their performance on the three tests were least influenced by tiredness. All the test papers were collected right after the subjects finished them within a given period of time.

5.5   The acquisition of the basic senses of English polysemous verbs of motion

The descriptive statistics of the subjects' performance on the acquisition of English polysemous verbs of motion are provided. The data analysis goes in accordance with the steps of research questions. For the three tests (Multiple Choices, E-C Translation and C-S Translation) in which each of the six polysemous verbs has 15 items in total, descriptive statistics for each verb in terms of the basic sense (BS), the extended sense (ES) and the collocative sense (CS) are elicited via SPSS analysis. Table 5.1 shows the subjects' overall performance on the three types of meanings (i.e. BS, ES and CS) of the seven polysemous verbs.

Table 5.1   **Comparison of the means of the six polysemous verbs**

Verbs	N	BS	SD for BS	ES	SD for ES	CS	SD for CS
draw	36	.5847	.16929	.3844	.17676	.1389	.18366
fix	36	.6386	.36054	.5861	.16354	.2361	.17873
hit	36	.5694	.17537	.5236	.13152	.3278	.19215
hold	36	.5972	.26239	.4372	.15784	.6017	.19284
move	36	.7917	.25000	.3881	.09636	.4500	.25014
run	36	.8750	.25000	.5228	.19071	.6111	.22396
Valid N (listwise)	36						

Note: BS stands for the basic sense, ES stands for the extended sense, CS stands for the collocative sense, SD stands for standard deviation, and the means got are based on a 1-point scale.

As is shown in Table 5.1, the mean for BS of each of the six verbs is higher than the mean for ES. For the three verbs *draw*, *fix*, *hit*, the mean for CS is the lowest. To be clearer, the order of means for BS, ES, CS from high to low for *draw*, *fix*, and *hit* is BS>ES>CS, while for *move* and *run*, the order of means is BS>CS>ES, and for *hold*, the order is CS>BS>ES (.6017>.5972>.4372). Such results seem to be supportive of the assumption made in Hypothesis 1 that Chinese EFL learners generally do better in their acquisition of the basic senses of polysemous verbs of motion.

Since the means for BS are higher than the means for ES for all the six verbs, and the degrees of mean difference between BS and ES vary from verb to verb, independent samples tests between the mean for BS and the mean for ES are carried out for each verb so as to see whether the mean differences between BS and ES are significant or not. The results are shown in Table 5.2.

Table 5.2　**Independent samples test between the BS mean and the ES mean for the six verbs**

Verbs		Levene's Test for Equality of Variances		t-test for Equality of Means							
		F	Sig.	t	df	Sig. (2-tailed)	Mean Difference	Std. Error Difference	95% Confidence Interval of the Difference	
									Lower	Upper
draw	Equal variances assumed	.066	.798	4.910	70	.000	.20028 *	.04079	.11892	.28163
fix	Equal variances assumed	32.373	.000	.796	70	.429	.05250	.06598	-.07910	.18410
hit	Equal variances assumed	.455	.502	1.255	70	.214	.04583	.03653	-.02703	.11870
hold	Equal variances assumed	5.618	.021	3.135	70	.003	.16000 *	.05103	.05822	.26178
move	Equal variances assumed	178.974	.000	9.039	70	.000	.40361 *	.04465	.31455	.49267
run	Equal variances assumed	2.237	.139	6.721	70	.000	.35222 *	.05241	.24770	.45674

*Note: The mean difference is significant at the .05 level ($p < .05$). * indicates that the mean difference is significant at the .05 level.*

Table 5.2 demonstrates that the mean differences for *draw*, *hold*, *move*, and *run* are significant at the .05 level, whereas the mean differences for *fix* and *hit* are not significant at the .05 level. The subjects have significantly better performances on the basic senses than on the extended senses with the four verbs (i. e. *draw*, *hold*, *move*, and *run*) , but not with *fix* and *hit*.

In order to test the second hypothesis of the present research, that is, to see whether and to what degree the subjects' mastery of BS of a polysemous verb of motion is positively correlated with their performance on the acquisition of ES or CS in a systematic way, the Pearson r correlation are used to analyze the relationship between the mean for BS and the mean for ES, the mean for BS and the mean for CS for each verb. The results of such data analyses are shown in Table 5.3 and Table 5.4.

Table 5.3 shows that only the verb *fix* shows a significant positive correlation between the mean for BS and the mean for ES at the .05 level (sig. =.014), which means there is only 5 percent probability that the observed correlation of .404 occurred by chance alone. However, the squared value of r=.404 is r^2=.163, suggesting that the variation in the means for BS accounts for about 16.3 percent of the variation among the means for ES for the verb *fix*. Thus the degree of correlation between the mean for BS and the mean for ES in the case of *fix* is weak. So there is no significant correlation between the mean for BS and the mean for ES in terms of other verbs.

Table 5.3   Correlation between BS and ES for the six verbs

Verbs		Value	Asymp. Std. Error[a]	Approx. T[b]	Approx. Sig.
draw	Interval by Interval Pearson's R	.101	.165	.593	.557[c]
fix	Interval by Interval Pearson's R	.404 *	.103	2.579	.014[c]
hit	Interval by Interval Pearson's R	.088	.161	.515	.610[c]
hold	Interval by Interval Pearson's R	−.162	.131	−.959	.344[c]
move	Interval by Interval Pearson's R	.019	.161	.108	.914[c]
run	Interval by Interval Pearson's R	−.207	.126	−1.231	.227[c]
N of Valid Cases		36			

a. Not assuming the null hypothesis.

b. Using the asymptotic standard error assuming the null hypothesis.

c. Based on normal approximation.

*Note: The correlation is significant at the<.05 level (sig. <.05) and * indicates that the correlation coefficient is significant at the<.05 level.*

Table 5.4 shows that only the verb *run* exhibits a significant positive correlation between the mean for BS and the mean for CS at the .05 level (sig. =.048), which means there is only 5 percent probability that the observed correlation of .332 occurred by chance alone. However, the degree of correlation between the mean for BS and the mean for CS in the case of *run* is rather weak, since the squared value of r=.332 is r^2=.11, suggesting that the variation in the means for BS only accounts for about 11 percent of the variation among the means for CS for the verb *run*. There is no significant correlation between the mean for BS and the mean for CS in terms of other verbs.

Table 5. 4 **Correlation between BS and CS for the six verbs**

Verbs		Value	Asymp. Std. Error[a]	Approx. T[b]	Approx. Sig.
draw	Interval by Interval Pearson's R	.311	.098	1.909	.065[c]
fix	Interval by Interval Pearson's R	.068	.184	.397	.694[c]
hit	Interval by Interval Pearson's R	.068	.138	.399	.692[c]
hold	Interval by Interval Pearson's R	.076	.157	.443	.661[c]
move	Interval by Interval Pearson's R	.034	.171	.200	.843[c]
run	Interval by Interval Pearson's R	.332 *	.218	2.050	.048[c]
N of Valid Cases		36			

a. Not assuming the null hypothesis.

b. Using the asymptotic standard error assuming the null hypothesis.

c. Based on normal approximation.

*Note: The correlation is significant at the <.05 level (sig. <.05) and * indicates that the correlation coefficient is significant at the <.05 level.*

The mean for BS in Table 5.1 are higher than the mean for ES in terms of any of the six verbs, suggesting that the subjects generally do better in their mastery of the basic senses of polysemous verbs of motion. The results of independent samples tests between the mean for BS and the mean for ES for the six verbs show that the mean differences between the mean for BS and the mean for ES are significant on the verbs *draw*, *hold*, *move*, and *run*, but not significant on the verbs *fix* and *hit*. To put it another way, the subjects do significantly better in their acquisition of the basic senses of polysemous verbs of motion than in their acquisition of the extended senses with most of the six verbs (i. e. *draw*, *hold*, *move*, and *run*). These results are thus supportive of Hypothesis 1.

Why are the basic senses of English polysemous verbs of motion instead of the extended senses better acquired by Chinese EFL learners? The reason seems not difficult to seek. It's no denying that experience plays an essential role in human cognition. People are inclined to comprehend abstract properties and concepts, for example, meaning, by referring to all kind of experiences, such as the bodily experiences of movement and perception, the physical experiences of the body interacting with the material world, and the social and cultural experiences and so forth. Taking experientialism and embodiment philosophy as its philosophical bases, cognitive linguistics proposes the experiential view of meaning, which stresses the vital role of bodily experiences in the process of meaning interpretation. It is based on the experiential view of meaning that cognitive linguists put forward the theory of image schemas. Image schemas are derived from everyday interaction with the world, and "An image schema is a recurring, dynamic pattern of our perceptual interactions and motor programs that give coherence and structure to our experience (Johnson, 1987: xiv)". The emergence of image schemas is based on the experience of interaction between the human body and the objective world, especially the spatial experience, such as Up-Down, Front-Back, In-Out, etc. Image schemas are "dynamic analogue representations of spatial relations and movements in space (Gibbs & Colston, as cited in Sun Ya, 2008: 46)". Being highly flexible, pre-conceptual and primitive, they can be used for reasoning in an array of contexts (Johnson, 1987:30).

A close examination of the basic senses of the six polysemous verbs of motion, i. e. , *fix*, *draw*, *hit*, *hold*, *move* and *run*, reveals that these basic senses are closely related to the human bodily experiences. Then is it any wonder that Chinese EFL learners have better acquisition of the basic senses of these polysemous verbs of motion? The experiential view of meaning holds the view that meaning comes out of the process of experiencing things, and experiences in turn facilitate the interpretation of meaning. At the sight of these verbs, image schemas such as Path, Force, Container, and Contact can be easily activated in the mind. For example, at laying one's eyes on the verb *run*, the first mental images coming into his or her mind may be the quick movement of legs and the Path image schema which includes path, starting point, end point and direction, thus the basic sense of *run* "move very quickly, by moving your legs more quickly than when you walk" can be easily acquired. When one sees the verb *move*, both the Path image schema and the Force image schema may well be activated in his or her mind, making the basic sense of *move* "(cause sb/sth to) be in motion or change position or place". Thus the concrete human bodily experiences embodied in these basic senses provide the learners with an easy access to the basic senses of polysemous verbs of motion, leading to the learners' good performances on their acquisition of the basic senses of English polysemous verbs of motion.

According to Table 5. 3 and Table 5. 4, at the . 05 level, only the verb *fix* shows a significant positive correlation between the mean for BS and the mean for ES and the verb *run* between the mean for BS and the mean for CS, but with a rather low correlation coefficient for each of the two. While the variation in the means for BS of *fix* accounts for about 16. 3 percent of the variation among the means for ES of *fix*, the variation in the means for BS of *run* accounts for about 11 percent of the variation among the means for CS of *run*. Thus, the results show that the learners' better performances on the acquisition of the basic senses of *fix* and of *run* have facilitative effects on their acquisition of the extended senses of *fix* and of the collocative senses of *run* respectively. However, for most of the six verbs, there is generally no significant correlation between the means for the basic sense of polysemous verbs of motion and the means for the extended senses or collocative senses of polysemous verbs of motion. That is, the results are generally not supportive of the second hypothesis, and it seems that a better mastery of the basic senses of the polysemous verbs of motion doesn't have facilitative effects on the acquisition of the extended senses or the collocative senses of them. One possibility may be that the subjects lack a good metaphorical competence in their acquisition of English polysemous verbs of motion. However, it is too hasty to make such a generalization before looking into the subjects' acquisition of the multiple extended senses of each of these verbs.

5.6　The acquisition of the extended senses of English polysemous verbs of motion

Why Chinese EFL learners' better performances on the basic senses of a polysemous verb seem not significantly facilitative to their mastery of the extended senses? The statistics in Table 5.2 shows that the degrees of mean differences between BS and ES vary from verb to verb. The mean difference (MD) of statistical significance is biggest with the verb *move* (MD =.40361), the second biggest with *run* (MD =.35222), the third with *draw* (MD =.20028) and the smallest with *hold* (MD =.16000). In terms of the mean for BS of these four verbs in Table 5.1, *run* ranks the first with a mean of .8750, *move* the second with a mean of .7917, *hold* the third with a mean of .5972, and *draw* the last with a mean of .5847. Then here comes the questions: why the subjects do so well on the mastery of the basic sense of the verbs *move* and *run* (with a relatively high mean for each of the two verbs) but still display such big mean differences between BS and ES, why doesn't the better mastery of the basic sense of these verbs have a beneficial effect on the mastery of the extended senses? Is it possible that the subjects haven't developed a good metaphorical competence in their acquisition of the polysemous verbs of motion? Do they perform differently on each of the extended senses of individual polysemous verb?

5.6.1　Acquisition of the extended senses of *move*

A close look at the sense relations between the multiple senses of the polysemous verb *move* will give light to the acquisition of English polysemous verbs of motion. The basic sense of *move* is "(cause sb/sth to) be in motion, or change position or place". The extended senses of *move* chosen in the tests include: (ES1) make progress; (ES2) cause sb to have very powerful feelings, esp. of sadness; (ES3) cause or prompt (sb) (to do or not do sth); and (ES4) (cause or persuade sb/sth to) change one's attitude.

The meaning extension of the verb *move* may be interpreted in terms of the following figure (Figure 5.5). As is shown in Figure 5.5, the four extended senses of *move* can be regarded as extended from its basis sense through metaphorical mappings.

Move can be used both as a transitive verb meaning "cause sb/sth to be in motion or change position or place" and as an intransitive verb meaning "be in motion or change position or place". When used as an intransitive verb, the basic sense of *move* (i.e. be in motion, or change position or place) can be interpreted in terms of the Path schema, meaning a trajector's (a moving entity) changing of position from one place to another along a path as in sentence "On reaching the crossroads, we *moved* quickly to the right, and up the very dusty road leading to the village." When the Path schema of physical movement, with an emphasis on the process of changing of physical positions along a

ES2: cause sb to have very
powerful feelings, esp.of
sadness

M ↑

ES1: make progress ←— M —— BS:(cause sb/sth to)be
in motion, or change —— M —→ ES3: cause or prompt
position or place (sb)(to do or not do sth)

M ↓

ES4:(cause or persuade sb/sth
to)change one's attitude

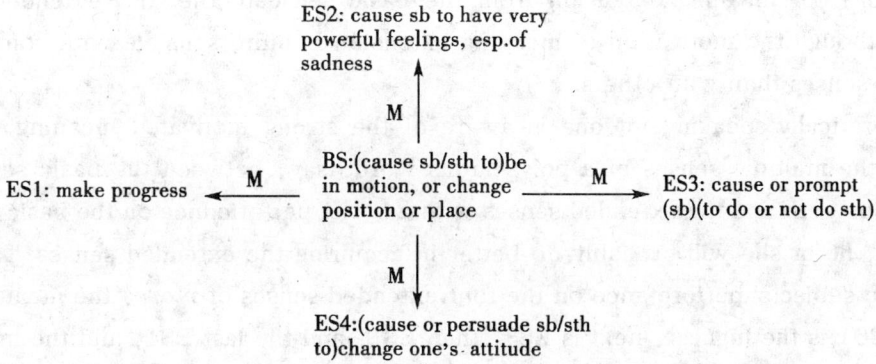

Figure 5.5   Meaning extension of *move*

path, is mapped onto the development of an event through metaphor, we get the extended meaning ES1 (i. e. make progress). Therefore, if a situation or process *is moving*, it is developing or progressing, rather than staying still. For example, *The dispute had also moved against us in another way.*

When used as a transitive verb, the basic sense of *move* (i. e. cause sb/sth to be in motion, or change position or place) can be interpreted in terms of the FORCE schema, that is, the external forces (exerted on a patient by an agent (often animate, say, a person) either by itself or through a tool) causes or forces the patient to change its original position to a new position, as is shown in Figure 5. 6.

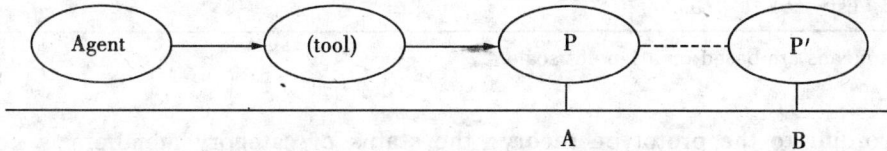

Agent ——→ (tool) ——→ P ------ P'
                              | |
——————————————————————————————
                         A   B

Figure 5.6   Force schema of *move*

Note: A and B stands for two points on a path, P refers to the patient at its original place A, P' refers to the patient at its new place B, (tool) means either with or without a tool. Arrow indicates the direction of the flow of force.

When the Force schema of *move* is mapped through metaphor onto the more abstract domain of emotion, the extended senses of ES2, ES3 and ES4 can be arrived. The forces involved in ES2 can be something spiritual, and such forces "push people's heart" and thus change their mood. However, the metaphorical mappings in ES3 and ES4 are relatively more difficult to sense, which require much elaboration on them since the target domain is more specific than the general domain of emotion. ES3 can be interpreted as "some internal forces (e. g. , curiosity, interest, etc) cause people to take a certain action", and ES4 can be understood as "something exerts forces or influences on people's mind and takes their mind to another place, i. e. change their attitude". Thus, through the analysis of meaning extension of *move*, the strong motivations (metaphor) for meaning extension from the basic sense to the four extended senses emerge, though the motivation of meaning extension is more sensible with some of the extended senses than with others.

Theoretically speaking, if one is aware of the strong motivated meaning relations between the multiple senses of a polysemous word, say, between the basic sense of a polysemous verb and the extended senses with a better performance on the basic sense of that verb, he or she will probably do better in acquiring the extended senses. Table 5.5 shows the subjects' performance on the four extended senses of *move*, the mean for ES2 ($M = .8336$) is the highest, next is ES3, then ES1, and the last ES4, and the means for ES3, ES1 and ES4 are rather low. Such a result indicates that the subjects have unequal performances on their acquisition of the four extended senses, they do well on the acquisition of ES2 (i. e. cause sb to have very powerful feelings, esp. of sadness) of *move*, but have ill performance on that of ES1, ES3, and ES4.

Table 5.5　　　　Descriptive statistics of the four extended senses of *move*

Extended Senses	N	Minimum	Maximum	Mean	Std. Error Mean	Std. Deviation
ES1	36	.00	1.00	.0556	.03872	.23231
ES2	36	.33	1.00	.8336	.04101	.24606
ES3	36	.00	.33	.1742	.02785	.16708
ES4	36	.00	.00	.0000	.00000	.00000
Valid N (listwise)	36					

Note: the means are based on a 1-point scale.

According to the prototype theory, the status of category members is not equal, some members are more central than others. The multiple extended senses of a polysemous verb are members of the polysemous category, and some senses are probably more central than others and thus can be better recognized and acquired by learners. Chinese EFL learners' acquisition of the extended senses of *move* verifies the prototype view of polysemy. The meaning of "cause sb to have very powerful feelings, esp. of sadness (ES2)" has been used so often that it rises up as a prototypical meaning of *move* just as the basic sense of *move* does, which explains the subjects' good performance on ES2.

Thus, on the one hand, the learners exhibit various performances on their acquisition of the extended senses of polysemous verbs of motion in accordance with the degree of prototypicality of the senses of the same polysemous category. Familiar and frequently used senses are likely to become the prototypical meanings of the polysemous category and they can be better acquired than the less prototypical or more peripheral senses. On the other hand, though all the four senses have strong metaphorical motivations, the subjects don't perform well on three of them (ES1, ES3 and ES4). It seems reasonable to assume that the subjects haven't shown a good metaphorical competence in acquiring the polysemous verb *move*.

5.6.2   Acquisition of the extended senses of *run*

How do the subjects' performances on the extended senses vary in the case of *run*? The sense relations between the multiple senses of the polysemous verb *run* should be looked into. The basic sense of *run* is "move very quickly, by moving your legs more quickly than when you walk" as an intransitive verb or "cover (the specified distance) by running" as a transitive verb. The extended senses of *run* chosen in the tests include:

ES1: vi. (of buses, ferries, trains, etc) travel to and fro on a particular route

ES2: vi. move, esp. quickly, in the specified direction

ES3: vt. cause (sth) to move in the specified direction. For instance, *She ran her fingers nervously through her hair*.

ES4: vt. make (a service, course of study, etc) available to people; organize

ES5: vi. function

ES6: vi. be a candidate in an election (for a political position)

Table 5.6 displays the subjects' performances on each of the six extended senses of the verb, it indicates that the subjects have good performances on ES1, ES2 and ES4, with a mean of 1.00, .75 and .86 respectively. In contrast, the means on ES3, ES5 and ES6 are low, suggesting that they have worse performances on these extended senses. In other words, the statistics show the unbalance of the subjects' performances on the extended senses of *run*.

Table 5.6 **Descriptive statistics of the extended senses of *run***

	N	Min.	Max.	Mean	SEM	SD
ES1	36	1	1	1.00	.000	.000
ES2	36	0	1	.75	.073	.439
ES3	36	0	1	.58	.083	.500
ES4	36	0	1	.86	.058	.351
ES5	36	0	1	.42	.083	.500
ES6	36	0	1	.14	.058	.351
Valid N (listwise)	36					

Note: The means are based on a 1-point scale.

Semantic motivations are a graded notion in that the multiple senses differs in the degree of opacity or opaqueness in terms of their association with the basic or primary senses. Some senses have stronger semantic motivations than others and are thus likely to be better interpreted by a learner if he or she has known the basic or primary senses. Thus, even if the extended senses are derived from the basic sense through the same cognitive means such as metaphor or metonymy, some senses have more obvious or perceivable semantic motivations than others. As a result, some senses may be easier to be acquired than others. The polysemous sense relations of *run* can be illustrated with Figure 5.7. ES1 and ES2 are extended from the BS1 through metaphor in that the physical moving action of an animate object (esp. a human being) is metaphorically mapped onto the domain of transportation to refer to the moving of vehicles like buses or trains on certain routes (ES1) or onto the physical moving of inanimate things (e. g. a ball, eye, etc) in the specified direction (ES2). Such metaphorical associations are quite obvious and thus easy to be made sense of, which explains the subjects' good performance on ES1 and ES2.

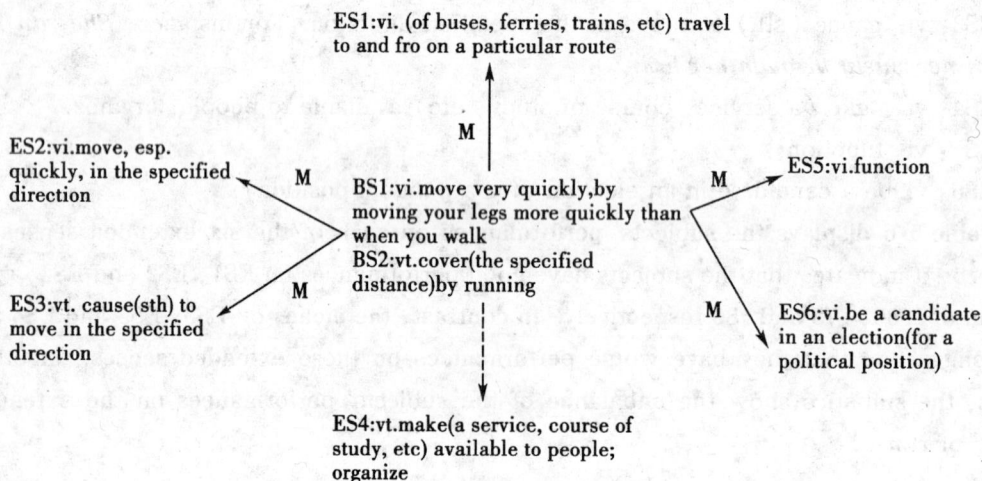

Figure 5.7   Meaning extension of *run*

ES3 may be seen as shifted from ES2 in terms of transitivity of a verb. As a result, the sense relation between BS and ES3 are not as close as that between BS and ES2. Thus it may be understandable that the subjects perform better on ES2 (M =. 75) than on ES3 (M =.58). ES5 and ES6 are also extended from BS1 through metaphor. However, the metaphorical mappings are of a more hidden nature than in the case of ES1 and ES2. The metaphorical mapping between BS1 and ES5 is based on the similarity between the implied conditional relation in BS1 and that in ES5. BS1 may imply the conditional proposition that if a person runs well, probably, he is in a good health condition and his body functions well. Similarly, if a machine or a car runs well, it is in a good condition and functions well. Extension from BS1 and BS6 is based on the similarity of the main features of the running event and the event of a political election. When you run, you move fast and always try to reach a destination; when you make preparation for an election, you get busy going here and there spreading propaganda and your purpose is to get yourself elected to the political position in the end. Thus the common semantic attributes of BS1 and ES6 may be summarized as [move at a faster pace than usual] and [attempt to reach a destination or achieve a goal], which are the basis for metaphorical extension from BS1 to ES6. With a comparison between meaning extensions from BS1 to ES1 & ES2 and that from BS1 to ES5 & ES6, the latter process is more complicated and more opaque than the former process. Thus, the sense relations between BS1 and ES5 & ES6 are less likely and more difficult to be recognized, which may reasonably explain why the subjects have a much better performances on ES1 and ES2 than on ES5 and ES6.

The analysis of *run* made so far seems to suggest that, among the extended senses, those extended senses that have more obvious and perceivable or less opaque semantic motivations tend to be better acquired. However, the acquisition of ES4 seems to be an exception to this general rule. In Figure 5.6, the dotted arrow between BS and ES4 indicates that the sense relation between them is rather weak. However, Table 5.6 notes that the mean for ES4 is .86 which is high, suggesting the subjects have a good performance on this extended meaning. The semantic connection between BS and ES4 seems so distant that BS and ES4 may have been treated and memorized as the senses of two homonyms. That may partly explain why the subjects can still acquire ES4 of *run* so well even though it has a practically insensible semantic relation with the basic sense of the verb. Such result proves that although the core-sense view of polysemous representation seems more advantageous than the separate-sense view, both views explains how learners learn and understand words with multiple meanings. Sometimes, separate-sense treatment to polysemy, as a complement to the prototype approach to lexical polysemy, may aid learners in their acquisition of polysemous categories.

To sum up, the subjects display unevenly in their performances on the extended senses of the verb *run*, their performances on the extended senses vary with the degree of obviousness of the semantic motivations underlying them. Those extended senses that have more obvious and perceivable or less opaque semantic motivations are probably better acquired, though the extended senses that are too semantically distant from the basic sense may be better acquired, too.

5.6.3   Acquisition of the extended senses of *draw*

The basic senses of *draw* include BS1: pull (sb/sth) into a new position; take sth out; BS2: move in the specified direction; and BS3: make (pictures or a picture of sth) with a pencil, etc. The subjects are only tested on BS1 and BS2 in the study. The five extended senses of *draw* selected in the tests include: ES1: attract; ES2: produce (a reaction or response); ES3: become closer (in time or space); ES4: take (money) from a bank account; and ES5: depict.

The meaning extension of the verb can be illustrated by Figure 5.8, ES3 can be considered as metaphorically extended from BS2 and ES5 from BS3. ES3 is derived when the movement of physical objects along a path as denoted by BS2 is mapped onto the abstract domain of time or space. For instance, *draw* in the sentence "*It is already December 23th. Christmas is drawing near*" means "become closer in time". ES1, ES2 and ES3 can be viewed as extended from BS1 through metaphorical mappings of the image schema of Container. BS1 (pull (sb/sth) into a new position; take sth out) can be interpreted in terms of the image schema of Container. To pull sb/sth into a new position or take sth out means to pull sb/sth out of the container where it originally stays into a new place or position. ES1 (attract sb) can be understood as "pull one's attention or interest out of the container of sb/sth (sb or sth can be seen as a container) to a new person or thing" as in the sentence *I felt drawn to this mysterious stranger*; ES2 can be understood as "get a reaction or response from somebody (a container)" ES4 as "take money out from a 'container' of money, i. e. a bank account".

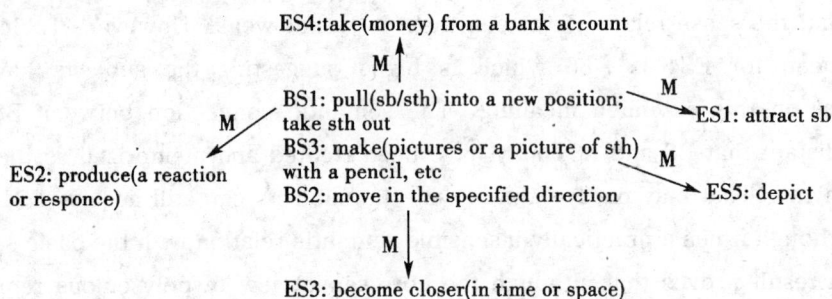

Figure 5.8　Meaning extension of *draw*

Table 5.7 shows the subjects' performances on the basic senses and the extended senses of the verb *draw*. Among the means for the five extended senses, the subjects do best on ES4 (M = .6111) and worst on ES3 (M = .3333), while having similar performance on ES1 (M = .4167), ES2 (M = .4722) and ES5 (M = .4722).

Table 5.7　**Descriptive statistics of the basic senses and the extended senses of *draw***

	N	Min.	Max.	Mean	SEM	SD
ES1	36	.00	1.00	.4167	.05455	.32733
ES2	36	.00	1.00	.4722	.08438	.50631
ES3	36	.00	1.00	.3333	.06299	.37796
ES4	36	.00	1.00	.6111	.08240	.49441
ES5	36	.00	1.00	.4722	.08438	.50631
BS1	36	.50	1.00	.8611	.03785	.22713
BS2	36	.00	1.00	.0278	.02778	.16667
Valid N (listwise)	36					

Note: The means are based on a 1-point scale.

Since ES3 is metaphorically extended from BS2, it seems reasonable to attribute the subject's ill performance on ES3 (M = .3333) partially to their bad performance on BS2 "move in the specified direction", with a rather low mean of .0278. Although ES1, ES2 and ES4 are metaphorically extended from BS1 in the same fashion, ES1 and ES2 are more abstract than ES4. Metaphors, like image schemas, are also deeply rooted in human experiences which include both the bodily experiences and the social or cultural experiences. Metaphor is the mapping of the structure of the source domain onto that of the target domain, and metaphors allow people to understand one domain of experience in terms of another. However, if the target domain of experience is the familiar and concrete life experiences, the metaphorical mapping between the source domain and the target domain can be easily understood. Thus, since the learners are quite familiar with the concrete experience of drawing money from an ATM, they may well feel easier to make metaphorical associations between BS1 and ES4 than between BS1 and ES1 or ES2. The fact that learners perform better on ES4 than on ES1 or ES2 supports the assumption that the extended senses with more obvious semantic motivations tend to be better acquired.

5.6.4 Acquisition of the extended senses of *hold*

The multiple senses of *hold* chosen in the study and their sense relations are demonstrated in Figure 5.9. The extended senses of *hold* from ES1 to ES5 are deemed as extended from BS through metaphor, and the extended senses of ES6 and ES7 are extended from BS through metonymy. The meaning extension from BS to ES7 is more complex than that from BS to ES6 in that ES7 of *hold* (remain unchanged, last), as in the sentence *If their luck holds, they could still win the championship*, is derived from BS through metonymy for at least two times. To elaborate, ES7 is metonymically extended from the sense "keep (oneself/sb/sth) in the specified position or condition" (as in *Hold yourself still for a moment while I take your photograph*) which is also extended from BS through metonymy.

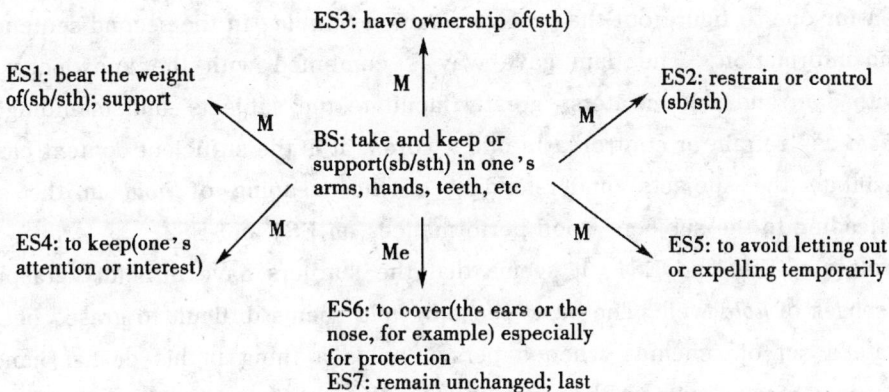

Figure 5.9   Meaning extension of *hold*

Table 5.8 shows the subjects' performance on these senses of *hold*, it proves that the means for most of the extended senses are low, though the subjects perform especially well on ES4 with a mean of .9722 and on ES2 with a mean of .7222.

Table 5.8   **Descriptive statistics of the basic sense and the extended senses of *hold***

	N	Min.	Max.	Mean	SDM	SD
ES1	36	.00	1.00	.1111	.05312	.31873
ES2	36	.00	1.00	.7222	.07571	.45426
ES3	36	.00	1.00	.4444	.08399	.50395
ES4	36	.00	1.00	.9722	.02778	.16667
ES5	36	.00	1.00	.5000	.08452	.50709
ES6	36	.00	1.00	.1944	.06690	.40139
ES7	36	.00	1.00	.1111	.05312	.31873
BS	36	.00	1.00	.5972	.04373	.26239
Valid N (listwise)	36					

Note: The means are based on a 1-point scale.

The low means for most of the extended senses of *hold* are due in part to the subjects' quite moderate or average performance on BS (M = .5972) and in part to the subjects' failure to make a good sense of the metaphorical connections between its basic sense and its extended senses, however, the pretty good performances on ES4 and ES2 should be investigated:

ES4: I was numb and sick from not eating, not sleeping, and crying; I couldn't even *hold* my attention enough to read one sentence.

ES2: The dam gave way; it was not strong enough to *hold* the flood waters.

Both sentences provide a fairly good context for the interpretation of the meaning of *hold*. In the first sentence, the background context information "I was numb and sick from not eating, not sleeping, and crying" and "my attention" used after *hold* is far sufficient information for one to figure out the precise meaning of *hold*; in the second sentence, the background information " The dam gave way", combined with the knowledge of the relation with dam and flood waters, greatly facilitate the subjects' understanding of the sense of *hold* as "refrain or control". In other words, it is the sufficient context clues that greatly facilitate the subjects' understanding of the meaning of *hold* in the specific sentence, leading to the subjects' good performances on ES4 and ES2.

Regardless of ES2 and ES4, it seems that the learners have difficulty grasping the extended senses of *hold* well. The basic sense of *hold* seems difficult to grasp, because it may activate a set of schemas when a person holds a thing in his or her hand. For example, it may mean "support the thing with hand under it in a palm-up fashion" as in "She held an egg in her hand carefully", which can be metaphorically extended to mean "bear the weight of something"; it may just mean "carry something with hands" as in "Can you hold the handbag for me for a while?" The complexity of schemas of the basic sense of *hold* complicates the understanding of its extended senses by drawing on its basic sense. Thus, with a lack of metaphorical competence, the learners exhibit much difficulty in acquiring the abstract senses of *hold*.

5.6.5   Acquisition of the extended senses of *fix*

The basis sense (BS) of *fix* is "fasten (sth) firmly to sth", and the following four extended senses of it are chosen: ES1: direct (esp one's eyes) on sb/sth with steady attention; ES2: set or determine; ES3: repair or mend (sth); ES4: remember (sth) well. Figure 5.9 is the figure of meaning extension of *fix*. As is shown in Figure 5.10, ES1, ES2 and ES4 are extended from BS through metaphor and ES3 is extended from BS through metonymy.

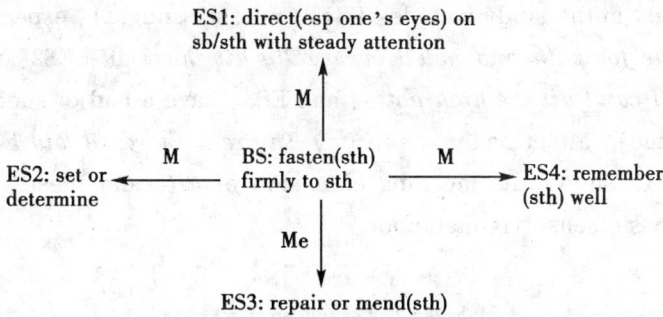

Figure 5.10   Meaning extension of *fix*

Table 5.9 is the descriptive statistics of the learners' performances on the meanings of *fix*. It shows that the means for ES1 (M =.7144) and ES3 (M =.7361) are much higher than the means for ES2 (M =.3472) and ES4 (M =.3889), suggesting that the learners perform better on ES1 and ES3 than on ES2 and ES4.

Table 5.9   **Descriptive statistics the basic sense and the extended senses of *fix***

	N	Min.	Max.	Mean	SEM	SD
ES1	36	.33	1.00	.7144	.03559	.21353
ES2	36	.00	1.00	.3472	.05202	.31212
ES3	36	.50	1.00	.7361	.04219	.25315
ES4	36	.00	1.00	.3889	.08240	.49441
BS	36	.00	1.00	.6386	.06009	.36054
Valid N (listwise)	36					

Note: The means are based on a 1-point scale.

ES3 is regarded as metonymically extended from BS in that to repair something involves fastening loosened parts. ES1 is considered as metaphorically extended from BS because ES1 can be understood as " 'fasten' one's eye firmly to somebody or something by means of looking at it and not directing one's attention away from it". The similarity between ES2 and BS lies in that the thing being fixed in terms of ES2 (e.g. the time of meeting or the rent of a house) is precise and definite and the thing being fixed in terms of BS (e. g. a shelf fixed to the well) is in a determinate position or condition. ES4 can be interpreted as "attach a mental image of sth or sb in one's mind or memory". So the sense relation between the ES and BS are more obvious and perceivable on the sense ES1 and ES3 than on ES2 and ES4. Thus the statistical results as reflected by Table 5. 9 prove that the extended senses of *fix* which have a more obvious or more perceivable sense relation with BS are better acquired by the learners.

5.6.6　Acquisition of the extended senses of *hit*

The basic sense (BS) of *hit* is "strike sb/sth with a blow, missile, etc" and extended senses chosen for test in the study include: ES1: find (sth sought), especially by chance, as in (a) *Follow the footpath and you'll eventually hit the road*; ES2: reach a level or number, as in (b) *I can't hit the high notes*; and ES3: have a bad or sudden effect on (a person, thing or place), affect badly, as in (c) *The rent increase will hit the pockets of the poor*. Figure 5. 11 shows the meaning extension of *hit*, and these three senses are extended from the basic sense via metaphor.

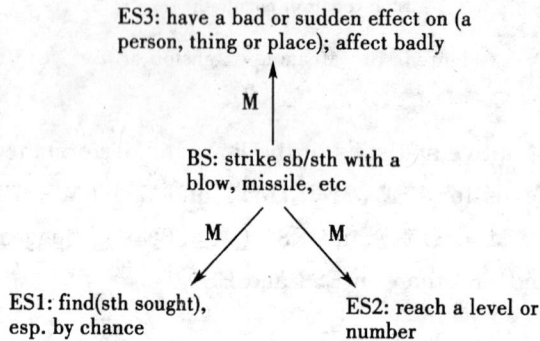

ES3: have a bad or sudden effect on (a person, thing or place); affect badly

M

BS: strike sb/sth with a blow, missile, etc

M　　M

ES1: find(sth sought), esp. by chance

ES2: reach a level or number

Figure 5. 11　Meaning extension of *hit*

Table 5. 10 indicates that the mean for ES1 is fairly high (M = . 9444) and the mean for ES2 (M = . 2222) is quite low, which suggests that the subjects have a good performance on ES1 and a bad performance on ES2.

Table 5. 10　**Descriptive statistics of the basic sense and the extended senses of *hit***

	N	Min.	Max.	Mean	SDM	SD
ES1	36	. 00	1. 00	. 9444	. 03872	. 23231
ES2	36	. 00	1. 00	. 2222	. 04648	. 27889
ES3	36	. 25	1. 00	. 6944	. 03607	. 21639
BS	36	. 50	1. 00	. 5694	. 02923	. 17537
Valid N (listwise)	36					

Note: The means are based on a 1-point scale.

　　To account for this result, we'd better make an analysis of the senses relations between the extended senses and the basic sense of *hit*. All the three extended senses can be considered as the extended from BS by means of metaphor. The basic sense of *hit* can be interpreted in a frame that includes an agent who performs the act of hitting usually through a tool (which can be a part of the agent, say, hand.), an patient on whom the act is performed, the force received by the patient resulting from the sudden contact between the tool and patient. ES1 and ES2 may be interpreted as the metaphorical extension of the contact schema of BS, and ES1 is easier to be understood than ES2 because the "patient" in ES1 (e. g. road) is more concrete than the "patient" in ES2 (e. g. high notes, a record, etc.). ES3 can be regarded as extended from BS by a metaphorical mapping of the frame of BS: the agent is something with a potential damaging power (e. g. an earthquake, the rent raise), the patient is a person, a thing or a place, the force is the bad effects afflicted on the patient resulting from the abstract "contact" between the agent and the patient. Thus, the semantic motivations of ES1 and ES3 are more obvious than that of ES2, which may partly explain the learners' performances on these extended senses. Another reason for the good performance on ES1 may be that the context in which the verb occurs (*Follow the footpath and you'll eventually hit the road*) facilitates the learners' understanding of the sense of it.

　　To sum up, the research reveals that the prototype theory, image schemas, and the metaphor and metonymy theories have shed light on the acquisition of English polysemous verbs of motion.

Chapter 6

The Acquisition of English Spatial Prepositions

The polysemy of prepositions and prepositional phrases is a very important yet difficult part in the acquisition of English language vocabulary for the EFL learners, which is realized by spatial iconicity via projecting the original spatial meaning of prepositions onto more abstract conceptual domains. Iconicity refers to the iconic relation or similarity between linguistic form and the meaning it conveys. The polysemy of prepositions or prepositional phrases can fully prove the projection of the principles of iconicity on the linguistic structure, including distance iconicity (the distance of linguistic form is iconic to conceptual distance), quantity iconicity (the quantity of linguistic forms is iconic to the quantity and complicatedness in direct proportion and to measurability in inverse proportion) and sequence iconicity (the sequence of iconicity is iconic to conceptual sequence). Spatial iconicity refers to the dependence of the objects in reality being parallel to that of their corresponding linguistic signs, which actually involves two kinds of special iconicity: iconicity of physical space and iconicity of mental space. The meanings of prepositions are extended through spatial iconicity to more abstract conceptual semantic domains of time, quantity, state, purpose/cause and method/instrument.

The study is to investigate the development of Chinese EFL learners' cognition of the principles of iconicity when they are learning the polysemy of prepositions, and to probe into the development of their cognition of spatial iconicity, the media of the realization of the semantic extension of prepositions and the five semantic domains of prepositions. 163 subjects of three levels, the primary, intermediate and advance levels, selected from the 46 students in Hongshan high school of Wuhan, 78 undergraduates majoring in Law and Chemistry, and 46 graduates majoring in English in Wuhan University, take part in the experiment. The data of the test are analyzed, via the statistical tools of ANOVA and Scheffe Multiple Comparison in SPSS.

The analysis of the data reveals that the learner's cognition of the principles of iconicity develops along with the promotion of learners' English levels in an uneven way, which develops rapidly at the earlier stages from the primary to the intermediate and slows down its progressing pace when approaching the advanced level, and the learners' cognition of the principle of quantity iconicity event stops to progress. Also, the learner's cognition of the semantic domains of prepositions which is extended via spatial iconicity develops along with the promotion of learners' English levels.

6.1   Iconicity and human cognition

As an important attribute of cognitive linguistics, iconicity has been attached great importance to by the researchers of both abroad and home. Iconicity refers to the iconic relation or similarity between linguistic form and the meaning it conveys, which is one of the concepts that are central to the study of the word-world relation, to explain why language is the way it is and why it means what it means. Unlike other attributes to linguistics which assume that there is no or nearly no relationship between the meaning and form it takes, iconicity, strictly conceived in Peircean terms, indicates one of the relationships in which a representation (expression) may stand to its object (content or referent) and which may be taken as the "ground" for their forming a sign. At the other extreme, iconicity has been variously conceived as a similarity, or identity, between the expression and the content of a sign, or as a particular variety of conventional coding.

The structure of language is iconic to human cognition. The simplest definition of cognition is the acquisition and employment of knowledge. It involves psychological activities such as thought, memory, comprehension, recognition, categorization, etc., and we seek to use general cognitive operation such as conceptual mapping, profiling, and selective attention, knowledge structure or schemas and mental imagery in describing linguistic phenomenon. It is not a "simple" matter of resemblance between form and meaning but a sophisticated process in which the allowable phonetic resources of language are built up into an "analogue" of an image associated with the referent. Iconicity only exists through the mental efforts of human beings; it is dependent on our natural and cultural conceptual association. According to Croft (2000), "the structure of language reflects in some way the structure of experience", and "the structure of the language is therefore motivated or explained by the structure of experience to the extent that the two match". Iconicity of linguistic structure to external or experiential structure can be divided into two parts: the correspondence of parts and the correspondence of relation between parts". Haiman (1983) calls these "isomorphism" and "motivation". Givon (cited by Croft, 2000) also suggests that "linguistic forms are often the way they are because they resemble the conceptual structure they are used to convey and they often resemble each other because the different conceptual domains they represent are thought of in the same way. These relations of resemblance are, respectively, phenomena of isomorphism and automorphism." For example, the word "argument" is organized and expressed to the war although they are in different conceptual domains:

Your claims are indefensible.

He attacked every weak point in my argument.

His criticisms were right on target.

I demolished his argument.

I've never won an argument with him.

(Lakoff & Johnson, cited by Lan (b), 2005)

The universal principles of iconicity are cognitively based. Givon (cited by Shen, 2005) believes that the principle of iconicity of distance is the result of the need of cognitive associative memory and spreading activation. If one concept activates adjacent concepts (For example, the concept of "flower" activates the concepts of "red, fragment, rose", etc.), the adjacency of corresponding linguistic structure in time and space will accelerate the process of information. The principle of iconicity of sequence tends to put at the beginning of the sentence the information with more importance yet lower predictability because the important and unpredictable information is "figure" not "ground", needing more attention in the recognition of "figure and ground" and the location of the beginning of the sentence is the best place to attach importance and can receive the best memory effect. What is more, the principle of iconicity of quantity is obviously related to cognitive complexity and processing time. Cognitively complicated information certainly needs more attention and more time to process.

6.2 The principles of iconicity

The concept that language directly maps human thought and the exterior reality reflected by thought in some way or another can be dated back to ancient Greek. The ancient Greek philosopher Plato has recorded two different kinds of opinions in his *Cratylus*: one is that names and things are naturally related, and the right imitation reveals the essence of things, while the opposite maintains that the names of things are justified by nothing more than rule and custom, that is, words with similar meanings have arbitrarily different forms. Simone called the former the Platonic Paradigm and the latter the Aristotle (or Aristotelian-Sausurean) Paradigm. According to the former, language and reality resemble each other to some extent, while in the light of the latter, language and reality are quite independent respectively.

Although the theory of arbitrariness is the main trend in linguistic study, the study on iconicity attracted the constant attention of semiotic linguists. Semiotic researchers have studied the signal behavior in human artistic activities such as religion, literature, art, etc., of which the nature of iconicity is very obvious. These researches involve human language inevitably. They find that there exist complicate yet universal non-arbitrary relationships even in the single linguistic sign which can not be analyzed any more.

6.2.1 The categorization of iconicity

Peirce is the first one to universally categorize the iconic signs, pointing out that "there exist logical icons assisted by conventional rules in the semantics of every language" (cited by Croft, 2000). Peirce divides the signs in relation to their objects into three types: icons, indices and symbols based on the degree of abstraction. Based on the degree of abstrac-tion, a sign that represents an object by virtue of some similarity with it is an icon; a sign that represents an object by virtue of some factual, esp. causal connection with it is an index; a sign that represents an object by virtue of a convention is a symbol. Then icons are further divided into three subtypes: images, diagrams and metaphors in term of abstraction and similarity. In line with the classification of icons, iconicity is categorized into three types: imagic iconicity, diagrammatic iconicity and metaphorical iconicity. In imagic iconicity there is a "direct" one to one relation between the sign and the meaning, or signifier and the signified; in diagrammatic iconicity, there is a link between the relations on the level of the signifier and the relations on the level of the signified; and with regard to metaphorical iconicity, metaphors are different from images and diagrams in that they require an existence of "something else", i. e. a third thing in addition to a sign and the object.

According to Haiman (cited by Croft, 2000), diagrammatic iconicity can be further developed into three subtypes: isomorphism, automorphism and motivation. Isomorphism refers to the signifier of diagrammatic icons and the signified are one to one correspondent, that is, each point in the diagram is correspondent to the point of its signified in spite of any difference that these points may have in any characteristic. This kind of iconicity is the tendency of "a form correspondent to a meaning" in linguistics. Automorphism refers to the two or more parts in one system are correspondent to each other. Greenberg (cited by Zhang Hui, 1998) finds that the same group of indexes can be used to refer to time, space or conversation. He thinks it is the result of the projection of the spatially perceived structure to the real time and conversational time in terms of iconicity. As for motivation, it refers to this kind of iconic feature: the relations between the constituents of the diagram are correspondent with the relations between the constituents of the signified. Croft (2000) thinks isomorphism which is a mathematic term includes the first two kinds of correspondent relations while motivation can be iconic or economic which is obviously not iconic.

6.2.2   The levels of iconicity

Taub (2001) points out that iconicity is common in both signed and spoken languages, and it is present at all levels of linguistic structure, including morphology and syntax as well as individual words. Haspelmath (2003) depicts 7 kinds of iconicity at different levels, iconicity of sound, sequence, adjacency, scope, syntagmatic isomorphism, correspondence of markedness/complexity, and cohesion. Wang (2001) defines the term iconicity as "a kind of phenomenon that linguistic form in way of its pronunciation, form and structure is projectingly iconic to the meaning it conveys", which generalizes the current study on iconicity from four levels.

The first level is phonetic iconicity. The pronunciation of a linguistic form and its referent is naturally iconic to a much degree, such as onomatopoeia. What is more, a lot of phonemes have a direct relation with the meaning it conveys. For example, gr- shows a kind of grave and unpleasant sound: *groan, grow, gruff*, etc. Wang called it as a "diagrammatic iconicity". people of many languages tend to use rising tone to show a kind of inquisition or uncertain because we feel safe and sound when we are standing to our feet, and feel instable when we up in the sky. The second level is morphemic iconicity. There are a lot of iconic phenomenon between the written form and its meaning. Chinese is a typical example of ideogram, showing the meaning directly corresponding to the form.

There are similar phenomena in English too, such as T-shirt, V-belt. The third level is structural iconicity. Linguistic structure in some respects may reflect the real world structure or human experience, directly projecting human conceptual structure, which is the major thought of syntactic iconicity. There are three widely-accepted syntactic iconicity principles: distance iconicity, quantity iconicity and sequence iconicity. Besides that, Wang (2001) adds one other iconicity principle: markedness iconicity. The fourth level is discourse iconicity. Besides all the above three levels of iconicity, we can find iconic phenomenon in discourse, too, especial in literature. Literary works are divided into realism and romanticism based on the iconic relations between the content and the social reality. Especially, poets, both oral and literate, often exploit and even create in discourse a form or semantic relationship, so that the layout of some poems even takes the shape of the things they depict.

6.2.3 Four iconicity principles

Newmeyer (1998) discusses the principles of iconicity from the perspectives of "distance", "independence", "order", and "complexity" and "categorization". Wang (2004) thinks that there are six types of iconicity, that is, iconicity of linear, iconicity of distance, iconicity of quantity, iconicity of symmetry, iconicity of asymmetry and iconicity of categorization. Shen (2005) categorizes the iconicity of distance, iconicity of sequence and iconicity of quantity, while Wang (2001) categorizes the principles of iconicity into four: the principle of distance iconicity, the principle of quantity iconicity, the principle of sequence of iconicity and the principle of markedness iconicity.

Distance iconicity can be defined as distance of linguistic sign is iconic to conceptual distance. When the concepts are close in distance, belong to the same meaning group or semantic field or are narrating coherent information, they are likely to put together while thinking, then the possibility of juxtaposition will be higher and the distance of linguistic signs of expression will be close too. Lakoff & Johnson (cited by Wang, 2001) regard this principle as the result of the cognition of metaphor of spatial concept: Closeness is the strength of effect. "If the meaning of form A affects the meaning of form B, then, the CLOSER form A is to form B, the STRONGER will be the EFFECT of the meaning of A on the meaning of B." For example, the different locations of "only" in the following three sentences actually emphasize different part of the form:

Only I want two apples.

I *only* want two apples.

I want *only* two apples.

The principle of quantity iconicity refers to that people need more time to process the more complicate concepts, and correspondingly they use more linguistic units to express them. The larger and the more complicate the quantity of concepts, the more the numbers of linguistic units. Plural form in English is more complicated than singular form, and they express a larger quantity. Anaphoric ellipsis is much more wide-spread than cataphoric ellipsis according to the principle of quantity iconicity and the economic principle because the deictic part has come previously and becomes a known information. What's more, the frequent usage of repetition in language is a perfect example to indicate a more complicate concept. For example, "He ran and ran and ran" compares to "He ran". The previous sentence conveys more activity than the latter and the sense of emphasis is much stronger.

The principle of sequence iconicity refers to that the arranging order of the linguistic units is iconic to the sequence of events in the world or the perception of the world, quite closely related to culture. Many languages in the world, such as English, Chinese, etc., are basically arranged in the order of "subject-predicate-object" (SVO), which in fact reflects an order of human thinking, starting from the doer, action out, and then to the receiver of the action. The most often cited example is what Caesar said "Veni, vidi, and vivi (I come, I see, and I conquer)" (Jacobson, cited by Nesset, 2000), in which the order of the words are coherent with the sequence of things happened. What's more, the principle of sequence of iconicity is influenced by people's thinking tendency and cultural conventions as well as people's cognitive sequence. For example, English people say "Ladies and Gentlemen" when giving a speech, which are directed by social convention. Another important aspect underlying sequencing iconicity is "Me-first principle". According to Birdsong (cited by Kong, 2005), the ego "Me" is the center of the speaker's conceptual space. The perception of oneself as being at the center of the universe and as being the measure of all things pervades human language inevitably. For example, directionality in the vertical dimension establishes the differences between upwards and downwards, such as English expressions "up and down", "head and foot", "heaven and earth", "high and low", "from top to toe" in English and 上下,手脚,天地,高低,从头到尾 in Chinese, etc.

The principle of markedness iconicity can be defined as iconic to extra meaning while unmarkedness is iconic to predictable information. The unmarked term is the constituent of ordinary, universal and general meaning and usage; it is often predictable in communication and relatively simpler in structure and cognition; and it needs less time of processing. On the contrast, the marked term is the one with irregular and distinctive features and related to special meaning; it is usually unpredictable in communication, more complicate and needs more time to process. The marked linguistic constituent with distinctive features, comparing to its corresponding unmarked counterpart, indicates extra and unusual meaning. For example, plural form is marked opposite to singular form and it shows extra meaning. The unmarked term is used to represent predictable information; therefore it can be simplified or even omitted in communication. For example, the same constituent in comparative sentence is predictable, so it can be substituted by a pronoun or omitted.

6.3 The philosophic foundation of iconicity

Iconicity presents itself in a semiotic fashion, the essence of iconicity, however, is of the relationship between form and meaning, i. e. the relationship between language and reality, in this sense, it is more a philosophical issue than a linguistic one. Therefore, the philosophical foundation of iconicity can be traced in terms of traditional philosophy, cognitive philosophy and embodied philosophy.

The relation between language and reality is the central notion of traditional philosophy. Researchers are trying to prove that there is a natural relationship between linguistic structure and human experiential or conceptual structure. The debate whether linguistic signs are governed by nature or convention, i. e. whether there is any logical connection between the form of a word and its meaning is from the first a part of philosophy. Actually, the debate of form and meaning began with ancient philosophers, such as Plato's discussion in *Cratylus* and Chinese "*Debate of Name and Entity*". The ancient Greek philosopher Plato has recorded two different kinds of opinions in his *Cratylus*: one insists that names and things are naturally related, and the right imitation reveals the essence of things, while the opposite opinion maintains that the names of things are justified by nothing more than rule and custom, words with similar meanings have arbitrarily different forms. Simone called the former the Platonic Paradigm and the latter the Aristotle (or Aristotelian-Sausurean) Paradigm. Many linguists and philosophers prove that linguistic structure mirrors the conceptual structure, linguistic structure is the external representation of reality. And Peirce's notion of icons, indices and symbols directly proves the existence of iconicity philosophically.

The undeniable progress made in the study of iconicity is closely tied up with the development of cognitive philosophy. The aim of cognitive linguistics is to build a theory of language that is consistent with current knowledge about the mind and the brain. Cognitive linguists draw on results from cognitive psychology, sensory perception and the neural underpinnings of thoughts. Thus, cognitive linguistics based on their experience in the world, and the way in which the human beings perceive and conceptualize the world is not only an approach to language but also the result of the combination of cognitive philosophy and linguistics. It observes language in a comprehensive way, taking into account the factors of reality, perception, and linguistic signs. In respect of language mirroring reality, cognitive philosophy at least faces the following two questions being shunned traditionally. Firstly, to say that language stands for reality is not to say that language is reality itself. Linguistic signs are not the direct mirror image of reality, but with cognition the intermediate between them. When human maps his experience onto signs, he consciously or unconsciously imposes something subjective on the result of his own observations. What language reflects is a conceptualized world, not the real world as it is. In other words, the conceptual structure is formed on the basis of human perceptual experience and cognition process. Secondly, linguistic structure complies with experiential structure. As a means of thinking, language is inevitably in correspondence with the conceptual structure and experiential structure in many aspects, which is a natural and handy way to express the world. The correspondence of linguistic structure to external or experiential structure is thus iconically motivated.

The theory of iconicity is also based on embodied philosophy, maintaining that cognition is embodied in the restriction of human body and experience. Cognitive linguists think language is formed by way of cognitive processing on the basis of the embodiment of the real world. Wang (2001) insists that there is a medium of cognition between reality and language, which can be demonstrated in "reality—cognition—language". The meaning of the form is determined by the conceptualization process of human body and experience rather than location in the structure. The meaning and the form are closely and inevitably related, thus it is natural for the appearance of iconicity. Iconicity is an essence of linguistic sign since embodied philosophy emphasizes the metaphoric nature of human thinking, while from Peircean theory of iconicity, metaphor is the third type of iconicity. Concerning the statistics of Lakoff & Johnson (cited by Wang, 2005), 70% of expression in English are from metaphor, which is an indispensable aspect of human life. All in all, the principles of iconicity are correspondent to the experiential and conceptual world.

6.4 Spatial iconicity of prepositions

The polysemy of prepositions is extended on the basis of the original spatial concept of prepositions. The semantic derivation of prepositions is achieved based on the spatial iconicity (the iconic associations) between concrete objects and abstract conceptual domains. It follows the rule in the process of the transference of conceptual domains, from domains of the familiar, tangible, concrete, and frequent to the unfamiliar, intangible, abstract and infrequent. Through the spatial iconicity, the original spatial domain can be extended to the five semantic domains of time, quantity, state, purpose/cause and method/instrument.

6.4.1 The constitution of spatial concepts

Spatial concepts are one of the basic concepts formed in the process of human cognition in virtue of the development and depth of human cognition, extending to new conceptual areas. One of the core opinions of embodied philosophy and cognitive linguistics is that human perception and meaning construction is based on physical embodiment. Human bodies are used to embody the space first, such as location, direction, movement, etc. All these are the sources of human concept and language. Human knowledge is based on the understanding of himself and the space, developing from near to far, from concrete to abstract, then from body and space to other semantic fields. In the process of human perception and embodiment, body and space are the first thing to be the primary basis of some other concepts (including abstract concepts), the starting point of human thinking, the basic source of imagination and creation.

Thus spatial concept is of great importance in the conceptual system and human embodiment. We understand the real space through bodily perception, and construct a spatial image schema and attain an inner spatial logic and then develop some new conceptual meanings and linguistic expression through human rational thinking and imagination. This can be proved by some language evidences. Many words originally used to show space (including preposition, adverb, verb, nouns, etc.) can be extended to many other semantic fields, just as Regier put it, "The primacy of space, its privileged status, stems from the fact that space serves as a fundamental conceptual structure device in language. This makes itself apparent in two ways. The first is that spatial terms are not often expressed by linguistic forms of the sort that generally carry core conceptual structure. The second is that spatial terms are often used in nonspatial domains, through metaphor, lending a form of spatial structure to these nonspatial domains. Thus, the nature of a language's spatial system will reflect much more of the language than simply its capacity for purely spatial description, and any insights gained into the working of the spatial system may eventually have ramifications throughout the conceptual system of the language".

There are three kinds of representation of subject to spatial location. Vertical referents may take precedence over horizontal referents because verticality information may be processed more easily than horizontal information by human organism. In the process of human embodiment, restricted by human physical structure, neuro-bio organs and G-force, verticality is the most significant space level physically and mentally. Linguistically, verticality is the basic level of space concept. Comparing to verticality, human's horizontal level is not fixed as verticality. Human body structure has the front and the back part, so we perceive the world through the front and back side. Linguistically, horizontality is a relatively subordinate level.

Apart from orientation perception, symmetric perception exercises great influence on linguistic signs as well. Human body is thought to be bilaterally symmetric: such organs as two eyes, two hands, two legs, etc. The bodily symmetry has been intensively perceive and at the same time has been perceive to be perfect structure. As a result, human beings manipulate the outside world according to their own image by imposing their bodily configuration on linguistic expression, and deal with linguistic structure at their disposal. Symmetry is a shaping force in thought which guides human thoughts and actions to an unaware extent.

This kind of anthropocentrism and anthropomorphism of space concept obviously are embodied in human language structure. Language, though, is really a relatively independent commutative system; it is restricted by the brain and the reality of observation and perception. Spatial concept as a basic embodiment certainly influences linguistic structures.

6.4.2　Spatial concept of prepositions

Prepositions are a complicated class of lexicons. As far as functions are concerned, prepositions indicate the relations between two or more objects, of which spatial relations are the most basic.

Spatial relations are often expressed by close-class forms, such as prepositions. They present only certain categories, such as space, time perspective point, and etc. In linguistic system, prepositions belong to closed class, their forms and numbers are quite stable, and although their numbers are not very many, the frequencies of usage are very high because it can be easily used together with other words to form prepositional metaphor. The metaphoric use of preposition is more expressive and visualized by concreting the abstract things. As far as English learners are concerned, understanding the spatial concept of prepositions and its metaphoric meanings can make their study more efficient.

The original senses of most prepositions are to indicate spatial relationship. Wood (1983) collects 105 prepositions in his *English Prepositional Idioms*, of which the use of 67 prepositions, two thirds, is related to space. These prepositions can be divided into four types in terms of their spatial relations: zero-dimensioned (points), one-dimensioned (line), two-dimensioned (surface) and three dimensioned (body). Besides that division, there are some prepositions that can be used to refer to these four types of relations, and some prepositions don't belong to spatial relations and are categorized as the last type. Zero-dimensioned type refers to point relations, that is, the subject is at some location or moving towards or away from some point, such as *at, to, from, by, past, beyond, opposite, between*, etc. One-dimensioned type indicates linear relations, indicating on the "line", along the "line" or before or after the "line", such as *along, across, near, off, on, onto, before, after*, etc. Two-dimensioned type refers to that subjects or the movement of subjects is related to surface, in other words, the subject is on or not on the surface, or around the surface, such as *above, across, below, beneath, up, down, off, on, over, under, underneath, through*, etc. Three-dimensioned type indicates a subject is in or moving in or out of a volume or a domain, such as *in, into, inside, out, outside*, etc. Prepositions can also be divided through dynamic and static states. Dynamic prepositions show the change in a spatial area, usually with direction, such as *to, towards, into, onto, across, out of, off, along*, etc., while static prepositions indicate a relatively stable or a static state, such as *above, at, before, behind, between, in, on, near, out, under, within*, etc. However, many prepositions show both static and dynamic states, such as *in, on, over*, etc. The following is indicating the location or the movement of the prepositions of the four types and also static and dynamic states.

Table 6.1   **The location or the movement of the prepositions**

Type	Static		Dynamic	
ZD	·X (at)	·X (from)	—— →X (to)	X- - - → (from)
OD	–·– (on)	(before) ←—→ (after)	·······→ (along)	↑ (up) ↓ (down)
TWD	 (on)	 (off)	 (onto)	 (off)
THD	 (in)	 (out of)	 (into)	 (out of)

ZD = zero-dimensioned, OD = one-dimensioned, TWD = two-dimensioned, THD = three-dimensioned

In the process of human perception, the first thing perceived is his movement and spatial environment surrounding him, thus it is natural that humans forms a series of concepts concerning space, such as up-down, in-out, front-back, left-right, etc. and then form an abstract image schema—spatial schema. Image schema is the simplest and most basic cognitive structure, and when a kind of image schema is formed in human brain, it will be used unconsciously to cognize those new, complicate and abstract things or phenomenon. Spatial concept is the basic image schema and it is the basis of understanding other concepts. This kind of physical spatial image schema is projected to other experience, and other abstract experience has the iconic image structure, then the original meaning of the word develops metaphoric meaning in terms of projection. For example, the original spatial concept of preposition "in" is "inside of something" (She is in the house), and it can be extended to new and metaphoric concept of "inside of a kind of state" (She is in good condition).

Therefore in virtue of spatial concept of prepositions, humans develop the polysemy of prepositions with colorful metaphoric meanings. The multiple meanings of prepositions are the expansion and extension of original semantic meaning based on their spatial concepts, and these expanded and extended meanings are indiscerptibly related to the original meaning.

6.4.3　Spatial iconicity of prepositions

Spatial iconicity refers to the dependence of the objects in reality being parallel to that of their corresponding linguistic signs. In other words, the contiguity or togetherness of the objects in the real world is conceptually close, thus their corresponding linguistic signs are naturally placed together. There are two major types of special iconicity: iconicity of physical space and iconicity of mental space.

The cognitive foundation of iconicity of physical space is that the objects or features being contiguous are easily to be considered as a unified unit. Since the concept of physical space is central to human thinking, conditioned by such cognitive tendency, the adjacent objects in reality are easily coded adjacently in linguistic structure, and the neighboring concepts are thus put together. For example:

(a) He wrote a letter to me.

(b) He wrote me a letter.

In these two sentences, "wrote" and "me" is closer in distance in sentence (b) than in sentence (a), implying a more emphasis on "me" in sentence (b) than in sentence (a). This simple example displays that the distribution of the elements in a linguistic structure is an iconic reflection of the togetherness or separateness of the entities perceived in reality.

Linguistic signs to a great extent iconically mirror the way of human perception and thus represent the mental or psychological space of human beings. Croft (2000) argues that "the intuition behind iconicity is quite simple: the structure of language reflects in some way the structure of experience, that is, the structure of the world, including (in most functionalists' view) the perspective imposed on the world by the speaker". Iconicity of mental space, also termed iconicity of perception, will be spelt out under the head of iconicity of self-centered perception and iconicity of society-centered perception. Humans tend to interpret the world exclusively in terms of human values and experience, regarding human being as the center of the universe. The speaker, who initiates and dominates the verbal process, is the most active and central participant, so it is natural and of course subjective for him to focus on what he has perceived. Thus self-centered perception is apparently characterized by orientation perception and symmetric perception. People tend to say "my left" or "come here, please", showing that "The ego (me) is the center of the speaker's conceptual space".

Society-centered perception is concerned with the social regulations and conventions accumulated in human society. In society-centered perception, what functions in human cognition and experience is "collective ego", which is gradually fossilized in the recognizant framework, serving as a way of communication, thereby as a way of mastering the world. For example, the sequence "father and son" follows the iconicity of mental space of nature in our perception, while the sequence "ladies and gentlemen" follows the iconicity of mental space of convention.

The spatial iconicity of prepositions refers to the expression of prepositions is iconic to the reality of the world. Humans perceive and describe the world through spatial relations which are often expressed by prepositions, thus, as far as spatial iconicity of prepositions is concerned, it is a kind of relational iconicity. In other word, prepositional expressions are not isomorphic to the real world, but isomorphic in their inner parts or iconic to the real world through some known and easy concepts. For example, Greenberg (cited by Zhang Hui, 1998) finds that the same deictic word used to refer to time, space and discourse can be used in the first person, near to the speaker and the nearest future, because the two domains are iconic in structure. In the process of human cognition, there is such a rule that it is mapping from the basic, familiar and concrete domain to the advanced, unfamiliar and abstract, thus a new conceptual domain, as well as interrelations between different conceptual domains, is constituted in terms of the projection of iconicity when conceptual domains are transferring from one to the other. Therefore, spatial iconicity of prepositions can be extended metaphorically to other domains such as time or discourse space because this iconicity is iconic to human conceptual structure rather than the real world. Danesi (1993) thinks that units of perception (size, shape, etc.) can be transformed into mental iconic unit is the crux of iconicity hypothesis.

Prepositions, indicating the interrelations between objects, especially the spatial relations, are generally employed to express more abstract concepts. Jackendoff (1990) finds out that the formalism for encoding concepts of spatial location and motion, suitably abstracted, can be generalized to many other semantic fields. For example the spatial location and movement can be transferred to the fields of possession, ascription of properties, and schedule of activities. The original sense of preposition mainly refers to spatial domain, but by way of metaphor, a kind of iconicity according to Peirce, it has a strong ability to extend itself to many other abstract domains such as time, quantity, state, purpose/cause and method/instrument.

The mapping of prepositions from spatial domain to the domain of time shows how the concrete meaning of those spatial prepositions transfers to describe the invisible and abstract time. As early in ancient Greek times, time was thought like a river without boundary which moves forever forward. Time is now always thoughts as a one-side arrow since it always goes in one side and can not be turned back, which gives time a meaning in terms of spatiality. Based on that kind of relational iconicity, time can be described as an integration of the past, the present and the future just like the division of the river or an arrow. Thus when referring to time, the concept of point (zero-dimensioned) to describe an exact time point appears, or the concept of line (one-dimensioned) to show a part of time, or the concept of surface (two-dimensioned), when time is treated as a surface, such as *on time* or *through July*, and finally time can be treated as a volume or a domain, such as "in July" or "out of time". Different dimensions of spatial meaning of time are shown in the following examples from zero-dimensioned to three-dimensioned relations:

(a) He gets up at 7:30 every morning.

(b) He went to school before 1980.

(c) I shall stay through the summer season.

(d) He has lived in the small village for thirty years.

Based on the same way of projection of iconicity, the original meaning of prepositions can be easily transferred to other conceptual domains.

a. Domain of time

Prepositions used to express time show the relationship between things and time which things exist or happen. In terms of its relation with space, time may be classified into four types including simple time, relative time, the beginning and ending of time, the experienced period of time. The prepositions expressing time mainly include *in, on, at, above, below, over, under, before, after, behind, by, between, within, inside, around, out of, for, through, till*, etc.

b. Domain of quantity

Prepositions used to express quantity refer to calculation and measure usually for price, rate, pressure, temperature, volume, altitude, speed etc. The prepositions for quantity mainly include *at, by, from, in, minus, off, plus, to, around, below, through, with, for, of, over, within*, etc.

c. Domain of state

Domain of state refers to the various conditions in which things exist or happen. It includes a wide range such as status, circumstances, appearance, mind, health, psychological expression, quality, occupation, order and sequence, process of activity. The prepositions to express state mainly include *at, on, in, above, below, over, under, before, behind, outside, beyond, past, beside*.

d. Domain of purpose/cause

Domain of purpose refers to purposes, goals and objects or the cause and reasons that things exist or happen. The prepositions used to express purpose mainly include *at, on, toward(s), for, against, after, at, by, for, from, of, on, out of, over, through, with*.

e. Domain of method/instrument

Domain of method/instrument refers to ways by which things exist or happen. The prepositions used to express method or instrument mainly include *by, on, after, through, over, under, with, without*.

6.5   Research methodology

In order to investigate Chinese EFL learners' cognition of iconicity and spatial iconicity in the polysemy of prepositions, the present research is carried on to explore the development of learners' cognition of iconicity through the test of polysemy of prepositions from two aspects: the principles of iconicity—distance iconicity, quantity iconicity and sequence iconicity, and the five semantic domains—time, quantity, state, purpose/cause and method/instrument, which are extended in terms of spatial iconicity of prepositions. Some research questions are raised as follows:

a. Do the EFL learners have the cognition of spatial iconicity of prepositions, and is there any difference in the cognition of the learners' cognition at different levels?

b. Do the EFL learners have the cognition of the principles of iconicity in the process the prepositions? What is the developing trend of the cognition of the principle of iconicity concerning the preposition?

c. Do the EFL learners have different degrees of mastery of the semantic extension of prepositional domains in terms of spatial iconicity according to their different levels of English acquisition?

In the process of the study, two hypotheses are put forward attempting to answer these questions, and statistical analysis of the data attained from an empirical study is carried out to testify the hypotheses. The hypotheses are as follows:

Hypotheses 1: In the process of the acquisition of prepositions, EFL learners have some cognition of the three principles of iconicity—the principle of distance, the principle of quantity, and the principle of sequence, and the development trend should go in accordance to the development of English levels.

Hypotheses 2: The cognition of the semantic extension in terms of spatial iconicity of prepositions influences the acquisition of English prepositions, that is, the cognition of semantic extension facilitates the acquisition of English prepositions.

6.5.1   Subjects

The subjects for the present study are 163 students from four natural classes of Hongshan Senior High School in Wuhan and Wuhan University, representing three levels of English acquisition. An overall account of the subjects' information is shown in Table 6.2.

Table 6.2   **Subjects information**

Level	Age	N	Average Years of Study	Grades
One	15-17	46	3-4	First Year Senior High
Two	19-21	78	7-8	University Sophomore
three	22-30	39	10-12	First Year Postgraduate

Note: Level one stands for the lower level; level two stands for the intermediate level and level three stands for the advanced level.

The 163 subjects attending the experiment are picked from the first year students of Hongshan Senior High School (n = 46), sophomores from the Law School and Chemistry School of Wuhan University (n = 78), and first year postgraduates of English major in Wuhan University (n = 39). The age of the subjects of level one range from 15 to 17, who have studied English systematically for three and a half years and have attained some basic knowledge of those most acquainted prepositions, so they are considered as lower level of English learners on prepositions. After succeeding in College Entrance Examination one year ago and preparing for taking part in Band 4 examination, those 78 sophomores of non-English majors from Wuhan University have received quite a lot of the grammatical knowledge on English as well as prepositions, thus they are considered as the intermediate level. As for the representative of advanced level, the postgraduates of English majors are chosen because they have studied English particularly for at least four years and they are receiving even more sophisticated training. Since there has no standard criteria for judging whether a group of subjects are really at their lower, intermediate or advanced level but not at different level, these three groups are labeled as Level One (L1), Level Two (L2), and Level Three (L3), from the lower to the advanced.

6.5.2 Instruments

The experimental design is based on the theory of the principles of iconicity and the extension of semantic domain of prepositions, with the purpose to find out the answers to the questions put forward. Therefore, a questionnaire and a test paper are designed to probe English learners' cognition of prepositions, and then data is collected in terms of the classification of the principles of iconicity of prepositions and the extension of the semantic domains of prepositions.

The selection of testing words is important in that only appropriate test words will bring about reliable test results that go with research questions. The prepositions tested should be rich in meanings as well as among the most frequently used English words that every testee knows them. Thus, the subjects are required in questionnaire to list the most frequently used twenty words, from which 11 prepositions are picked out with highest frequency. These prepositions with highest cognition (*of*, *in*, *for*, *to*, *by*, *on*, *with*, *from*, *about*, *at*, *as*) are selected as testing words.

The test paper is composed of two parts, among which the first part (Picture description) is designed to test Chinese EFL learners' cognition of the spatial concept of the original meaning of prepositions; and the second tests from three aspects, including Right or Wrong Judgment, Cloze, Multiple Choices, Translations and Translation Choices.

Since the original meaning of most prepositions expresses specific spatial relationship and their extended meaning is projected from known concrete domain to unknown abstract domains in terms of spatial iconicity, the precondition of understanding the extended meanings of these prepositions is to understand their original. Therefore, a test of Picture Description is designed as a kind of pretest to test the learners' cognition of the original spatial concept of the prepositions. In Picture Description, ten pictures are designed to test subjects' spatial perception of prepositions as a kind of pretest.

In order to investigate whether learners are developing their cognition of the three principles, the principle of distance, the principle of quantity, and the principle of sequence, in different ways, the data will be analyzed respectively from the aspect of decontext and context. Sentences are chosen from *American Heritage Dictionary* (4th Edition), *A Modern English-Chinese Dictionary*, *A Dictionary of Current English Usage*, and *Oxford Advanced Learner's English-Chinese Dictionary* (the 3rd edition); and the passages are selected from the test papers of Band 4 test. Right or Wrong Judgment and Multiple Choices try to investigate subjects' knowledge on decontextual prepositions, while Cloze and Translations, including translations of English into Chinese and that of Chinese into English, as well as Translations Choice aim to study learners' cognition from the perspective of discourse both from the least and larger context.

Data are also collected with respect to the classification of the extension of semantic domain of prepositions, according to the five kinds of extension of the domains extended through spatial iconicity of prepositions, that is, domain of time, quantity, state, purpose/cause, and method/instrument. After the respective analysis of the five domains of the prepositions, the development of the learners' cognition of the five domains in terms of spatial iconicity are studied in the aspect of context and decontext in order to probe into whether the context has any influence in the acquisition of the cognition of the five extended semantic domains of prepositions.

Since the research design adopted for the present study is to investigate the cognitive sense of the spatial iconicity of the prepositions at the three different proficiency levels, the subjects' score can be analyzed by ANOVA (both one-way and multiple comparisons) and Scheffe Multiple Comparison test. All these analyses are made with the help of SPSS, statistic computer software. The iconicity cognition test of the prepositions were carried out in the form of written test in regular class of 45 minutes, and after the test papers are collected, the subjects' performance is scored. Each correct answer of the test items is given 1 point. Adding all scores of the test together, the scores of the subjects can be attained.

6.5.3   Picture description

The part of picture description is aimed to investigate whether the learners have some cognitions of spatial concept of prepositions, which are the basic sense of the preposition and the foundation of the extension of other semantic domains in terms of spatial iconicity. The results show that the subjects of the three levels can get more than a half score in recognizing what pictures indicate which preposition even though they are in a lower level of English. However, after a hopeful increase in their performance for the spatial concept of prepositions, the mean score of the higher level of this part unexpectedly falls down a little, from 8.3 of the intermediate level down to 7.7 in advanced level. In other words, all the learners have some cognition of the basic spatial concept of prepositions, and the learners' spatial concept of prepositions develops greatly when reaching the intermediate level, but there seems a "retrogress" in their cognition when reaching the higher level of English.

Table 6.3   **The mean score of Picture Description**

Level	Mean Score
1	6.6
2	8.3
3	7.7
Mean of the Total	7.5

This phenomenon shows that the early perceptual stages of language processing may be the most affected by the visual-gestural modality, although even the effects are not dramatic (Greimas & Courtâes, 1982). The high school learners are just like the native children starting learning the first language, so it is natural they depend more no visual aid then higher level learners and their respondence to the picture will be active and positive. The advanced learners are unconsciously predicting (and sometimes mispredicting) as they read. Even more noticeable is the fact that proficient readers are much more likely to notice and try to correct the misuses that don't fit with the context. In fact, even when they were taking test, the learners at advanced level tried to tell that there were some problems with the test design. Such monitoring and correction demonstrate that the learner is thinking about what was being read. Furthermore, the more proficient readers made more misuses on the little, so-called "sight words" than less proficient readers, because the good readers predict words and even grammar that fit the context and don't change the essential meaning. From such observations as these, it can be seen that proficient learners automatically use context to predict when something doesn't sound right or isn't making sense. In other words, they use context to think about what they are reading. Furthermore, proficient learners use context-based strategies more than less proficient learners, for the most part, though not necessarily for the precise identification of words. Proficient learners use such strategies not only to comprehend, but also to get at least an approximate meaning for individual words. For example, learners draw upon such contextual aids as prior knowledge and experience.

6.6 An analysis of the principles of iconicity from the perspective of cognition

In linguistic system, though the form and numbers of prepositions are relatively stable, they have the capability of being used together with other words or used in different contexts to form all kinds of derivative meaning based on the original spatial meaning, thus the polysemy of prepositions is achieved through the spatial·iconicity (similarity) between the source domain and target domain. When the original spatial meanings of prepositions is transferred from domains of the familiar, tangible, concrete, and frequent to the unfamiliar, intangible, abstract and infrequent, the new meanings of the preposition come into being. The following provides descriptive statistics of the principles of iconicity respectively, investigating the cognition of different levels of Chinese EFL learners concerning the three principles of iconicity, the principle of distance, the principle of quantity and the principle of sequence. The data analysis goes in accordance with the steps of the research questions. Statistics shows that the EFL learners' cognition on the principles of iconicity as a whole projects itself in an ascending curve, yet with some exceptions.

6.6.1　The principle of distance

Of the whole test paper, there are 26 items on the principle of distance, 11 in Right or Wrong Judgment, 3 in Cloze, 5 in Multiple Choice and 7 in Translation.

Table 6.4 shows the descriptive data of the subjects' performance on the principles of distance. 163 subjects of three levels have taken part in the test, receiving a mean score of about 16. Of the three groups, Level 1 scores the lowest, about 7, and Level 3 has the highest score of nearly 22, Level 2 is in the middle, 18. From the range of the minimum and maximum score, the subjects' performance varies greatly, of which Level 1 is greatest, ranging from 0 to 16, and Level 3 is the smallest, from the lowest 18 to highest 24. The F ratio ($F = 427.867$) in Table 6.5 indicates that the mean comparison of the principle of distance between groups is of significant difference.

Table 6.4　　　　　　**Descriptive data of the principle of distance**

Level	N	Minimum	Maximum	Mean	Std. Deviation
1.00	46	.00	16.00	7.0217	3.44796
2.00	78	12.00	23.00	18.3462	2.31779
3.00	39	18.00	24.00	21.8718	1.41755
Total	163	.00	24.00	15.9939	6.33771

Table 6.5　　　　　　**F Ratio of ANOVA concerning the principle of distance**

	Sum of Squares	df	Mean Square	F	Sig.
Between Groups	5482.003	2	2741.001	427.867	.000
Within Groups	1024.991	160	6.406		
Total	6506.994	162			

Table 6. 6 shows the Scheffe Multiple Comparison of means between groups in terms of principle of iconicity. Though Levels 1, 2 and 3 vary greatly in their means, the difference are not the same, one is about 11 and the other is about 15, while the difference between group 2 and 3 are not so great, only 3.5. This data indicates that the EFL learners' cognition on the principle of distance does not go in a linear way.

Table 6. 6   **The Scheffe Multiple Comparison concerning the principle of distance**

(I) group	(J) group	Mean Difference (I-J)	Sig.
1.00	2.00	−11.32441(*)	.000
	3.00	−14.85006(*)	.000
2.00	1.00	11.32441(*)	.000
	3.00	−3.52564(*)	.000
3.00	1.00	14.85006(*)	.000
	2.00	3.52564(*)	.000

* $p < 0.5$

6.6.2 The principle of quantity

Of the whole test paper, there are 18 items on the principle of quantity, 7 in Right or Wrong Judgment, 2 in Cloze, 4 in Multiple Choice and 5 in Translation.

According to Table 6. 7, learners' performance goes in accordance to their levels, with a mean of about 12, a little lower than the mean score of Level 2. Level 3 certainly attains highest mean score of about 15 while Level 1 only gets a mean of about 6, and its standard deviation is obviously greater than the other groups. On the other hand, the distributions of the three levels concerning their minimum and maximum score, there is no much difference, with respectively close scores of 8 of Levels 1, 9 of Levels 2 and 7 of Level 3. And the F ratio ($F = 331.752$) in Table 6. 8 indicates that the mean comparison of the principle of quantity between groups is of significant difference. The higher the level, the better they perform.

Table 6. 7   **Descriptive data of the principle of quantity**

Level	N	Minimum	Maximum	Mean	Std. Deviation
1.00	46	2.00	10.00	5.5217	2.10543
2.00	78	8.00	17.00	13.4615	1.84948
3.00	39	11.00	18.00	14.6154	1.59960
Total	163	2.00	18.00	11.4969	4.21838

Table 6.8 **F Ratio of ANOVA concerning the principle of quantity**

	Sum of Squares	df	Mean Square	F	Sig.
Between Groups	2322.655	2	1161.327	331.752	.000
Within Groups	560.094	160	3.501		
Total	2882.748	162			

Table 6.9 is the Scheffe Multiple Comparison of means between groups in terms of principle of iconicity. Its developing curve is not quite the same as what presumed. The mean differences between Levels 1 and 2, 3 are quite significant, with the significance of .000 (p<.05), while the difference between 2 and 3 is not significant, with the significance of .008 (p<.05), which indicating that as far as the principle of quantity is concerned, the EFL learners' cognition almost has no difference in their medium and higher levels. Comparing to the cognition of the principle of distance, the cognition of the principle of quantity unfolds a quite different developing state.

Table 6.9   **The Scheffe Multiple Comparison concerning the principle of quantity**

(I) group	(J) group	Mean Difference (I-J)	Sig.
1.00	2.00	−7.93980(*)	.000
	3.00	−9.09365(*)	.000
2.00	1.00	7.93980(*)	.000
	3.00	−1.15385(*)	.008
3.00	1.00	9.09365(*)	.000
	2.00	1.15385(*)	.008

* p<0.5

6.6.3 The principle of sequence

The principle of sequence iconicity is tested with a total item of 37 items through Right or Wrong Judgment (12 items), Cloze (6 items), Multiple Choices (11 items) and Translation (8 items).

The 163 subjects altogether attain almost 24 scores in average, a little lower than Level 2, which is 27. Level 3 win the highest mean score of almost 31 and Level 1 still lies in the lowest position of average 12. The distribution of range of minimum and maximum scores is quite great too. Level 1 is the greatest 13, from the lowest 7 to highest 20, and Level 2 is very great too with a difference of 12, ranging from 20 to 32, while the lowest difference between individuals exist in Level 3, with a range of 8 from 26 to 34. The F ratio (F = 512.456) in Table 6.11 justifies the significance of difference between the mean comparison in terms of the principle sequence iconicity.

Table 6.10   **Descriptive data of the principle of sequence**

Level	N	Minimum	Maximum	Mean	Std. Deviation
1.00	46	7.00	20.00	12.1739	3.53588
2.00	78	20.00	32.00	27.0256	2.98905
3.00	39	26.00	34.00	30.9487	2.03843
Total	163	7.00	34.00	23.7730	8.02412

Table 6.11   **F Ratio of ANOVA concerning the principle of sequence**

	Sum of Squares	df	Mean Square	F	Sig.
Between Groups	9022.146	2	4511.073	512.456	.000
Within Groups	1408.455	160	8.803		
Total	10430.601	162			

Table 6.12 shows the significance of multiple comparisons of the means between the three groups by way of the Scheffe Multiple Comparison. The means of different groups have great significance of .000. However, the difference between Levels 1 and Levels 2, 3 is much greater than that between Levels 2 and 3. this means that the difference of learners' cognition is great between Levels 2 and 3, but it is much greater in their difference of cognition between the first level than the other two groups.

Table 6.12   **The Scheffe Multiple Comparison concerning the principle of sequence**

(I) group	(J) group	Mean Difference (I-J)	Sig.
1.00	2.00	−14.85173(*)	.000
	3.00	−18.77480(*)	.000
2.00	1.00	14.85173(*)	.000
	3.00	−3.92308(*)	.000
3.00	1.00	18.77480(*)	.000
	2.00	3.92308(*)	.000

* $p < 0.5$

According to the respective statistic results of the three principles of iconicity, the learners' cognition develops along with the level of their English standard, their traces of development are not in a linear way but rather in a curving way which firstly goes up more quickly, and slower down its developing pace in higher levels. And there is one exception that learners make little or almost no advance in their cognition of the principle of quantity iconicity.

6.7   The cognitive networks formed by the principles of iconicity of prepositions

The principles of iconicity, as the fundamental principles in syntactic structure, are the projection and embodiment of grammar and semantics, which reveals the relationship between the human universal cognitive mechanism and linguistic structure. The principles of the distance iconicity, the quantity iconicity and the sequence iconicity are the three most widely accepted ones. Thus, how the EFL learners develop their cognition of the principles of iconicity and what are the justified reasons of the developing rules will be analyzed by the discussion of hypothesis 1.

Hypothesis 1: In the process of the acquisition of prepositions, EFL learners have some cognition of the three principles of iconicity—the principle of distance, the principle of quantity, and the principle of sequence, and the development trend goes in accordance to the development of English levels.

As far as the acquisition of the three principles of iconicity is concerned, the basic developing rule is that the EFL learners' cognition increases along with the increase of their English level, but their proceeding paces are not well-proportioned. In other words, EFL learners in the rough make rapid progress when they begin studying English and they keep such a fast pace till they reach the intermediate level, but after that, their proceeding pace slows down obviously and the cognition of the principle of quantity iconicity even stops to make significant progress.

The following three figures are the developing graphs of the three principles, from which the tendency of the cognition can be clearly observed. Though the developing trends are not all the same, there is obviously a same tendency as a whole. The development of cognition of the principles of iconicity firstly increases fast from the primary stage to the intermediate stage, and when the learners arrive at a higher stage of English level, they don't make a rapid increase as expected.

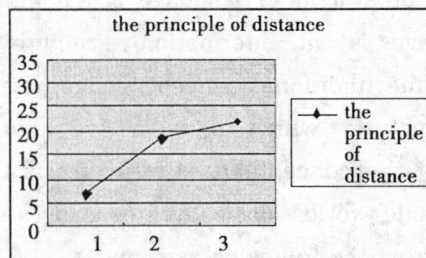

Figure 6.1   The cognitive network of the principle of distance iconicity

This phenomenon can be justified from external and internal perspectives. It is widely accepted in second language learning that the high school students have finished all their basic knowledge of grammar which including the basic semantic meaning of prepositions and they have built a rather sophisticated spatial concept of the world; the college students have finished learning more complicated grammar including the extended semantic meaning

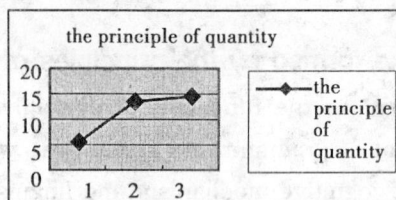

the principle of quantity

Figure 6.2　The cognitive network of the principle of quantity iconicity

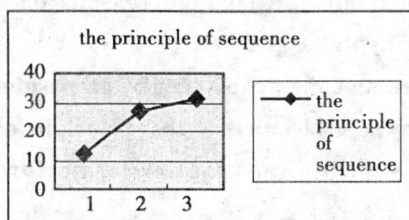

the principle of sequence

Figure 6.3　The cognitive network of the principle of sequence iconicity

of the prepositions and their cognition of the world develops from the basic visual concept to a more complicated and abstract conceptual world; and the graduates of English majors have received much more cultural and contextual training of the English language and as grown-ups, they have built a quite integrate conceptual world, so they will utilize all the cognitive instruments when they are dealing with linguistic forms. In fact, many English learners have the same kind of experience: they have learned English for many years, reading textbooks, memorizing words, grasping grammatical rules, but still don't making much progress, and they feel that they have been stagnated. That could be the main cause of the changeable paces of the cognition of the three principles of iconicity.

The main cause of the uneven development of the cognition of the principles of iconicity can be analyzed internally from the cognitive aspect. According to cognitive linguists, the internal rules or system of language is a kind of thinking state, and the meaning of natural language is an information structure with the meaning being symbolized. Different from the traditional concept, language meaning is interpreted as a form of conceptualized structure, which is evolved a kind of thinking called image mapping. The foundation of the conceptualized structure is the accumulation of human brains' cognition to the outside world. Basically, the causes of the uneven development can be cognitively justified from the following aspects.

First, language learning and performance is an information-processing which centers on the brain (information-processor), joins input and output. Information processing includes perception, representation, memory, comprehension, consciousness, thought, strategy making, problem solving and other mental representations. Bloom (2000) points out that children's word learning actually draws extensively on their understanding of the thoughts of others—on their theory of mind. That is, the child learns the meaning of a word based on his own cognitive system. As it's known to all, children learn to speak their native language only when their cognitive system has developed into a certain period. In addition, the maturation of their brain is the fundamental cause of the changes in their language. In Level 1, the high school learners' cognitive system is not very complicated and sophisticated though they have built a certain conceptual structure of English language. Compared to the adults, they tend to depend more on the teaching program because of their age. They will remember exactly what the teacher says when attaining the grammatical knowledge since their cognitive mechanism and their language structure of the target language are not perfect and sophisticated yet. But along with their growing up, their knowledge of the world and of the language becomes sophisticated, and they are gradually skillful at dealing with the linguistic problems based on their own conceptual structure. Thus, there is a very rapid improvement for them in their performance of the principles of iconicity in finding the motivated similarities efficiently between the linguistic forms and the conceptual structures.

Second, the reason why the learners make little progress when approaching advanced level is closely related to the fossilization of the interlanguage and the transfer from the declarative knowledge and the procedural knowledge. The notion "interlanguage" is put forward by Larry Selinker in his paper *Language Transfer*. According to Selinker (cited by Luo & Liu, 2005), the fossilization of the interlanguage refers to that in the process of the IL (interlanguage) approaching TL (target language), some of the linguistic item, grammatical rules and sub-systematic knowledge tend to be stagnant. And the growing-up of the learner's age, the change of the amount of language learning and the knowledge of target language do not have much help to change the situation. Selinker (cited by Tao, 1997) attributes the causes of the fossilization to five processes: language transfer; transfer of training; strategies of second language learning; strategies of second language communication; and overgeneralization of TL linguistic material. In the process of acquiring English, the learners are affected both from the external and internal factors, which prevent learners from approaching the target language by stagnating them in some grammatical items when they reach some degrees. It is the same for the cognition of the principles of iconicity.

The fact that the learners do not successfully transfer their declarative knowledge to procedural knowledge directly causes the learners' stagnancy or lowers developing pace in their performance even when they are labeled as advanced level. In the theory of cognitive science, there are two types of knowledge: declarative and procedural. The declarative knowledge refers to the facts, anecdotes, and so forth about the world, whereas the procedural knowledge is knowledge of "how to do". There is certainly distinction between the declarative knowledge and the procedural knowledge, just like that you "have some knowledge of driving" is definitely different from that you know "how to drive". Johnson (1996) suggests there are two pathways to the mastery of a foreign language, one of which is called the "learning pathway" and the other is the "acquisition pathway". For Chinese learners, the typical pathway to master a language starts with the declarative knowledge of getting to know the grammatical structure and knowledge and moves to the procedural knowledge of language usage. The process itself is very useful but there is a problem that the declarative knowledge and the procedural knowledge are not equivalently procedural, that is, their procedural knowledge is insufficient. At the declarative stage, there are both the familiar native language system and the ready-to-be-developed second language system in the second language learner's brain. If the learner is familiar with a specific second language item, he will make use of it to acquire a new second language item and build up his own second language system, so the overgeneralization errors like "goed" will be produced. If the learner is not familiar with any second language knowledge and has not enough second language, when he needs to learn the new second language items, he will associate the knowledge from his own native language with the new knowledge and thus language transfer will be brought about and lead to fossilization. Besides overgeneralization, oversimplification and hypercorrection are easy to appear at the procedural stage along with native language interference, language performance errors and vague language uses, etc.

6.8　An analysis of the extension of the semantic domains of prepositions

Spatial iconicity, the medium of semantic extension of prepositions, refers to the dependence of the objects in reality being parallel to that of their corresponding linguistic signs, which actually involves two kinds of special iconicity: iconicity of physical space and iconicity of mental space. Since the original meanings of most prepositions are formed on the basis of human spatial concept, one of the most basic concepts of human beings, the polysemy of prepositions can represent how spatial iconicity constructs relationship through similarity existing between linguistic form and human conceptual system. Prepositions extend their original semantic domain of space to other abstract and conceptual domains, such as time, quantity, state, purpose/cause and method/instrument via spatial iconicity. The extension of semantic domains based on the spatial iconicity of prepositions are investigated: the domain of time, the domain of quantity, the domain of state, the domain of purpose/cause and the domain of method/instrument.

6.8.1　The domain of time

There are altogether 19 items in the test paper checking the learners' cognition of the extension of the domain of time based on spatial iconicity, 6 items in Right or Wrong Judgment (1, 9, 10, 13, 14, 18), 2 in Cloze (15, 16), 1 in Multiple Choices (8), 10 in Translation Choices (3, 7, 8, 9, 14, 15, 19, 20, 24, 25).

As far as the domain of time from Table 6.13 is concerned, the rang of the minimum and maximum score is from 3 to 20, of which each level is ranging separately from 9 (Level 1), 10 (Level 2) to 7 (Level 3), which means the two levels have the same differences within groups except for the advanced level. The mean score shows that the gap between Level 1(about 8.0) and Level 2 (14.3) is about 6.3, while the difference is not so great between Level 2 (14.3) to Level 3 (16.5), only about 2.2. And the F ratio (F = 198.812) indicates the mean comparison between the groups is significant.

Table 6.13   **Descriptive data of domain of time**

Level	N	Minimum	Maximum	Mean	Std. Deviation
1.00	46	3.00	12.00	7.9783	2.12382
2.00	78	9.00	19.00	14.2949	2.31376
3.00	39	13.00	20.00	16.5128	1.60381
Total	163	3.00	20.00	13.0429	3.91633

Table 6.14   **F Ratio of ANOVA of domain of time**

	Sum of Squares	df	Mean Square	F	Sig.
Between Groups	1771.760	2	885.880	198.812	.000
Within Groups	712.940	160	4.456		
Total	2484.699	162			

The Scheff Multiple Comparison (Table 6.15) indicates the mean differences between different groups are significant ($p<.05$). For the domain of time, the developing trend of learners' cognition of the semantic extension of prepositions can be found out. The mean difference of Level 1 and Levels 2 is 6.3, while the mean difference between Levels 2 and 3 is 2.2, becoming much smaller comparing to that of the first two. The results of the data prove that the learners' cognition of the domain of time goes up in a curving way, developing fast in the beginning and the slowing down to the advanced level.

Table 6.15   **The Scheffe Multiple Comparison of domain of time**

(I) Group	(J) Group	Mean Difference (I-J)	Sig.
1.00	2.00	−6.31661(*)	.000
	3.00	−8.53456(*)	.000
2.00	1.00	6.31661(*)	.000
	3.00	−2.21795(*)	.000
3.00	1.00	8.53456(*)	.000
	2.00	2.21795(*)	.000

* $p<0.5$

6.8.2 The domain of quantity

20 items are designed to test EFL learners' cognition of domain of quantity in terms of spatial iconicity of prepositions, 5 items in Right or Wrong Judgment (7, 23, 24, 25, 27), 1 in Cloze (4), 2 in Multiple Choices (5, 13), 2 in Translations (5, 10), and 10 in Translation Choices (2, 5, 10, 12, 16, 17, 18, 21, 23, 26).

Table 6.16 shows the development of the learners' cognition concerning the domain of quantity. the scores of the subjects in Level 1 range form 5 to 12, with the mean of 8.4;

the scores of Level 2 have a variety from 10 to 18, with the mean of 13.8; and Level 3 are from 12 to 19, with the mean of 12.6. There is not much difference concerning the range of the scores·except that their starting points and ending points are getting higher and higher according to the ascendance of the levels. However, the mean score is not much different between Level 2 and Level 3, about 1.2, which shows that the learners progress very fast from the beginning to the intermediate level but makes little increase in the higher levels. The F ratio in Table 6.35 ($F = 200.601$) indicates the significance of the mean comparison between groups.

Table 6.16　　　　　　　　**Descriptive data of domain of quantity**

Level	N	Minimum	Maximum	Mean	Std. Deviation
1.00	46	5.00	12.00	8.4783	1.65649
2.00	78	10.00	18.00	13.7564	1.61314
3.00	39	12.00	19.00	14.9744	1.75450
Total	163	5.00	19.00	12.5583	3.08940

Table 6.17　　　　　　　　**F Ratio of ANOVA of domain of quantity**

	Sum of Squares	df	Mean Square	F	Sig.
Between Groups	1105.372	2	552.686	200.601	.000
Within Groups	440.824	160	2.755		
Total	1546.196	162			

The Scheff Mean Comparison in Table 6.18 shows that the mean difference is significant between the comparison of Level 1 and 2, which is 5.3, while the mean difference is not significant between the comparison of Level 2 and 3. The data shows that the subjects of Level 2 performs much better than that of Level 1, meaning that the learners make great progress in this stage, while the subjects of Level 3 perform almost the same as that of Level 2, demonstrating the progress of Level 3 has not qualitative difference from Level 2.

Table 6.18　　　　　**The Scheffe Multiple Comparison of domain of quantity**

(I) Group	(J) Group	Mean Difference (I-J)	Sig.
1.00	2.00	−5.27815(*)	.000
	3.00	−6.49610(*)	.000
2.00	1.00	5.27815(*)	.000
	3.00	−1.21795(*)	.001
3.00	1.00	6.49610(*)	.000
	2.00	1.21795(*)	.001

* $p < 0.5$

6.8.3   The domain of state

The learners' cognition of extended semantic domain of state by way of spatial iconicity is examined via 35 items, 10 items in Right or Wrong Judgment (5, 8, 12, 15, 17, 20, 23, 27, 28, 29), 4 items in Cloze (2, 5, 7, 9), 10 items in Multiple Choices (2, 3, 4, 9, 11, 12, 16, 17, 18, 19), and 11 items in Translations (2, 3, 4, 6, 7, 8, 9, 11, 12, 15, 18).

The minimum and maximum scores in Table 6.19 present an obvious scalar progress from the elementary level to the advanced level, with Level 1 the greatest distance of 18, from 4 to 22, the medium distance of levels 2 of 10, from 23 to 33, and the smallest distance of only 7, from 28 to 35 for Level 3, indicating that the advanced level performs in general better than the other groups. The mean score of the three levels shows that the learners' cognition of domain of state in terms of spatial iconicity of prepositions makes great progress at the beginning, and when it comes to the relatively higher stage, their progress is not as big as the previous stages. The F ratio ($F = 744.031$) in Table 6.20 proves the significance of the mean comparison between different groups.

Table 6.19   **Descriptive data of domain of state**

level	N	Minimum	Maximum	Mean	Std. Deviation
1.00	46	4.00	22.00	11.3261	3.41925
2.00	78	23.00	33.00	28.0385	2.74189
3.00	39	28.00	35.00	32.2821	1.71600
Total	163	4.00	35.00	24.3374	8.79620

Table 6.20   **F Ratio of ANOVA of domain of state**

	Sum of Squares	df	Mean Square	F	Sig.
Between Groups	11317.551	2	5658.775	744.031	.000
Within Groups	1216.891	160	7.606		
Total	12534.442	162			

The significance of mean difference between groups is checked through Scheffe Multiple Comparison in Table 6.21. The results show that there is significant difference between each group to the other two in their means. However, the mean difference is not developing in a linear way with a balanced speed. Actually, there is much greater difference between Level 1 and Level 2, with the statistic of 16.7, and a much smaller difference between Levels 2 and 3, with the statistic of 4.2, illustrating that there is a rapid progress in the learners' cognition of domain of state in terms of spatial iconicity of prepositions between Level 1 and Level 2, and the progress between Level 2 and 3 is much slower comparing to the trend of the first two groups.

Table 6.21 **The Scheffe Multiple Comparison of domain of state**

(I) Group	(J) Group	Mean Difference (I-J)	Sig.
1.00	2.00	−16.71237(*)	.000
	3.00	−20.95596(*)	.000
2.00	1.00	16.71237(*)	.000
	3.00	−4.24359(*)	.000
3.00	1.00	20.95596(*)	.000
	2.00	4.24359(*)	.000

* p<0.5

6.8.4 The domain of purpose/cause

24 items are involved in the examination of the learners' cognition of domain of purpose/cause extended by way of spatial iconicity of prepositions, 5 items in Right or Wrong Judgment (3, 11, 16, 22, 26), 2 in Cloze, (9, 17), 6 in Multiple Choices (1, 6, 7, 10, 15, 20), 1 in Translation (16), and 10 in Translation Choices (1, 4, 6, 11, 13, 22, 27, 28, 29, 30).

This kind of relative balance can be seen from the descriptive data of the subjects' score of each item. Firstly, the ranges of the subjects' minimum and maximum scores are not very different from each group. Among the three groups, Level 1 is from 1 to 13, while Level 2 from 8 to 21, indicating that learners in Level 1have lower cognition of domain of purpose and cause than Level 2, and Level 3 ranges from 13 to 23, a distance that apparently a little smaller than that of Level 1 and 2, but still quite large comparing to other domains of prepositions extended in terms of spatial iconicity. Secondly, the mean distance of separate groups also shows the learners' cognition concerning domain of purpose and cause develops quite balanced, from 6.1 (7.9 of Level 1 to14.8 of Level 2) to 4.4 (14.8 of Level 2 to 19.1 of Level 3). And F ration in Table 6.23 (F=249.043) indicates that the mean difference between each group is significant.

Table 6.22 **Descriptive data of domain of purpose/cause**

Level	N	Minimum	Maximum	Mean	Std. Deviation
1.00	46	1.00	13.00	7.9348	2.22513
2.00	78	8.00	21.00	14.7436	2.54536
3.00	39	13.00	23.00	19.1282	2.07972
Total	163	1.00	23.00	13.8712	4.74296

Table 6.23   **F Ratio of ANOVA of domain of purpose/cause**

	Sum of Squares	df	Mean Square	F	Sig.
Between Groups	2758.259	2	1379.130	249.043	.000
Within Groups	886.035	160	5.538		
Total	3644.294	162			

The Scheffe Multiple Comparison in Table 6.24 proves the significance of the mean difference comparison. The data shows that the mean difference between Level 1 and Level 2 is 6.8 and the mean difference between Levels 2 and 3 is 4.4. Besides the indication of the significance of the mean difference, the difference between each group is not so big, which suggests that the development of the learners' cognition of domain of purpose/cause is quite balanced, not so changeable as other domains of extension in terms of spatial iconicity.

Table 6.24   **The Scheffe Multiple Comparison of domain of purpose/cause**

(I) Group	(J) Group	Mean Difference (I-J)	Sig.
1.00	2.00	−6.80881(*)	.000
	3.00	−11.19342(*)	.000
2.00	1.00	6.80881(*)	.000
	3.00	−4.38462(*)	.000
3.00	1.00	11.19342(*)	.000
	2.00	4.38462(*)	.000

* $p < 0.5$

6.8.5   The domain of method/instrument

As for the learners' cognition of domain of method/instrument in terms of spatial iconicity of prepositions, 11 items are applied to the subjects and the data of their performance are analyzed, 3 items in Right or Wrong Judgment (6, 19, 30), 2 items in Cloze (1, 20), 1 in Multiple Choices (14), and 5 in Translation (1, 6, 13, 17, 19).

The descriptive data in Table 6.25 show that the ranges of minimum and maximum scores get smaller from the lower level to the higher level, 6 from Level 1 to Level 2, and 4 from Levels 2 to 3, indicating that Level 3 gets a better score in general. The subjects in Level 2 and Level 3 can both attain the full mark of 11, indicating that a few subjects in intermediate level can have a level of cognition of the domain of method and instrument similar to the advance level. The mean score of the three groups also indicates the developing trend. The mean distance between Levels 1 and 2 is 5.1 while only 1.3 between Levels 2 and 3. The ascending line goes obviously slower at a higher stage. And the F ratio in Table 6.26 justifies the mean comparison between groups.

Table 6.25　　　　　　　　**Descriptive data of domain of method/instrument**

Level	N	Minimum	Maximum	Mean	Std. Deviation
1.00	46	1.00	7.00	3.4130	1.59967
2.00	78	5.00	11.00	8.5769	1.36295
3.00	39	7.00	11.00	9.8718	.95089
Total	163	1.00	11.00	7.4294	2.90799

Table 6.26　　　　　　　　**F Ratio of ANOVA of domain of method/instrument**

	Sum of Squares	df	Mean Square	F	Sig.
Between Groups	1077.389	2	538.695	294.621	.000
Within Groups	292.550	160	1.828		
Total	1369.939	162			

The Scheffe Multiple Comparison is done in order to examine the significance mean difference. The result shows that the comparison of mean difference of each group is significant at $p<.05$ level. And the developing trend of the learners' cognition of domain of method/instrument can be found out. The comparison of the mean difference between Levels 1 and 2 is 5.1 while the comparison of the mean difference between Levels 2 and 3 is about 1.3, suggesting that the curve of the learners' cognitive development goes up quickly from the elementary stage to the medium stage, and then it slows down when approaching the advanced level.

Table 6.27　　　　**The Scheffe Multiple Comparison of domain of method/instrument**

(I) Group	(J) Group	Mean Difference (I-J)	Sig.
1.00	2.00	−5.16388(∗)	.000
	3.00	−6.45875(∗)	.000
2.00	1.00	5.16388(∗)	.000
	3.00	−1.29487(∗)	.000
3.00	1.00	6.45875(∗)	.000
	2.00	1.29487(∗)	.000

∗ $p<0.5$

As far as the five extended semantic domains on the spatial iconicity of prepositions are concerned, the development of the learners' cognition proceeds in an irregular way, it first increases very fast from the primary stage, then slows down its progressive pace when approaching to the advanced level. However, the development of the domain of quantity almost stops their development in the higher level although it also improves fast at the early stage.

6.9   The cognitive networks formed by semantic extension of prepositions

The original meaning of most of the prepositions is to express different spatial concept and new meanings are endued in the process of exploration based on their spatial concept, and thus the semantic network of prepositions is formed. Langacker (1997) suggests that the relations between the meanings of polysemous words are not arbitrary but develop from a particular mechanism of semantic extension, and the relations between each meaning are motivated. The extension of the meaning of preposition is based on spatial iconicity—the similarities existing between human basic spatial concepts. In terms of spatial iconicity, spatial concept is projected to other abstract concept on human embodiment. For example, the abstract changes of objects such as nature, quantity, state, etc. or even more abstract changes of concept of feeling, cognition, treasure, etc. can be analogous to the displacement of concrete objects.

Although spatial concept and ability of semantic domains is universal to humans, the law of the development of EFL learners' cognition of the extended domains of preposition is to be found by Hypothesis 2 in the analysis of the data from the perspectives the five semantic domains of prepositions—domain of time, quantity, state, purpose /cause, and method/instrument, and in the decontextual aspect and contextual aspect as well.

Hypothesis 2: The cognition of the semantic extension in terms of spatial iconicity of prepositions influences the acquisition of English prepositions, that is, the cognition of spatial iconicity in semantic extension facilitates the acquisition of English prepositions.

The learners' cognition of the extended semantic domains of time, quantity, state, purpose/cause, and method/instrument develops in almost the same way: Learners improve their cognition of the extended domains of prepositions which is achieved by spatial iconicity of prepositions very quickly at the early stages from the primary level to the intermediate level, but at the later stages, they don't make much progress. The following five figures serve as the networks of the five respective domains of preposition, from which the Chinese EFL learners' development of cognition of the extended domains of preposition can be observed in terms of spatial iconicity.

The polysemy of prepositions is extended on the basis of the original spatial concept of prepositions, which is indispensably related to the original spatial meanings. The semantic extension of prepositions is a kind of metaphorical projection, which is achieved on two things: human experience and the similarity (spatial iconicity) between the source domain and target domain. Humans are capable of projecting one conceptual domain to another, and thus interrelations between different conceptual domains are established, which actually is the iconic associations between objects and human cognitive domains. It follows the rule in the process of the transference of conceptual domains, from domains of the familiar, tangible, concrete, and frequent to the unfamiliar, intangible, abstract and infrequent. When the concept of the source domain is completely transferred to the associated objects and concept in target domains, the new meanings of the preposition come into being.

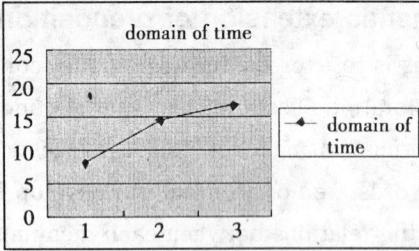

Figure 6.4   The cognitive network of semantic extension in domain of time

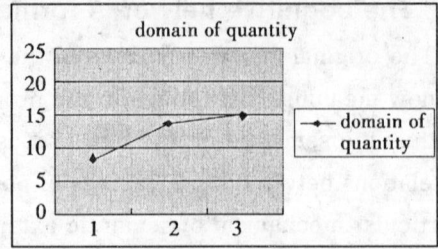

Figure 6.5   The cognitive network of semantic extension in domain of quantity

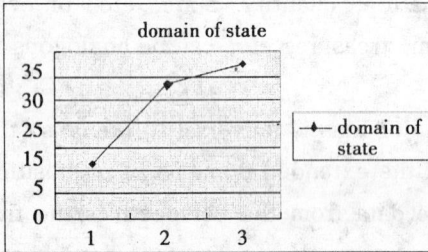

Figure 6.6   The cognitive network of semantic extension in domain of state

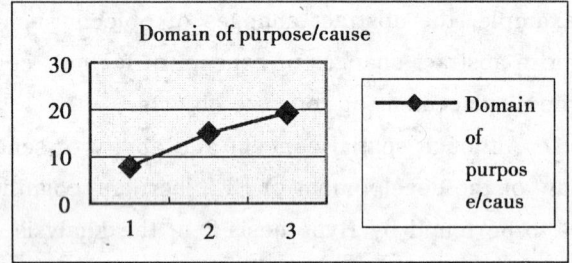

Figure 6.7   The cognitive network of semantic extension in domain of purpose/cause

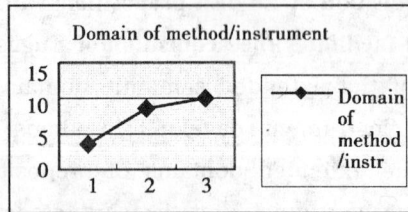

Figure 6.8   The cognitive network of semantic extension in domain of method/instrument

The acquisition of the vocabulary can be put into two stages which are circular from one to the other: the semantization, the stage where the form and the meaning are correlates, and consolidation, where new words are stored in learner's long term memory, together with their pragmatic, social and contextual features (Mondrain, cited by Zhao & Luo, 2005). In the process of vocabulary acquisition, derivative meaning is extended from the core meaning of the word, but since one derivative meaning can be the core meaning of another derivative meaning, the conceptual relations between linguistic expressions are not constrained to the core meaning and the derived meaning although these meanings are certainly interrelated. Mistakes and misunderstandings of the meaning of words occur when the derivative meanings in a radiate semantic domain are not directly related to each other and the learners fail to retrieve correctly the earlier related knowledge about them, or the learners are wrongly elaborate the network of the words. This can be regarded as one of the most important reasons that the learners fail to get the correct meanings of extended domains of prepositions especially at their early stage due to lack to adequate cognition of the interrelations between the core meaning and derived meaning.

The acquisition of prepositions can be achieved successfully by projecting the spatial concept to other abstract domains, which is the reason why the learners can make rapid progress along with the development of their cognitive ability and their English levels because the growth and maturation of both mechanisms are vital to the extension of the derivative conceptual domains of prepositions. But the process of semantic cognition is very complicated, and the learners find that they can not acquire the semantic meaning of words with a steadily elevated speed as the previous stages, but rather struggle in a state of stagnation. As we know, the process of semantic cognition virtually is the process of semantization, which is made up of two circular stages semantization and consolidation, and fossilization of semantic cognition arises in this process, which generally occurs in two aspects: the learner forms a rigid understanding of the word meaning at the first stage or they lack of systematic cognition of the semantic meaning at the second stage. At the first stage of semantic cognition, the learners mainly try to establish relations between the form and meaning. While in the process of foreign language, the conceptual meaning of word is mastered through the semantic system of native language due to lack of authentic EFL learning environment and the influence of vocabulary and semantic system of native language. That is to say, when the learners are learning the word, they try to remember the pronunciation and spelling of the word on the one hand, and on the other, they seek the word in their native semantic system which is similar in meaning to the foreign word, and then a relation between the form, the sound and the meaning of the foreign word is established. However, this kind of learning approach is doubtful by establishing rigid relationship between source language and target language in that it is impossible for learners to understand the meaning of the word completely and to improve their semantic network. Furthermore, even when the learners have mastered the reference of the word and developed their knowledge related to the word, such as derivations, collocations of words, etc., there is a fossilization of semantic cognition at the second stage. For example, the learners are likely to treat the synonyms, derivations and collocations of words as separate words, failing to consciously relate them to the core meaning or the semantics. In fact, the learners are satisfied in enlarging the vocabulary, with no intent to construct a semantic network of what are learned, which results in the fossilization of semantic cognition at the stage of getting to know polysemy.

In summary, the learner can make rapid progress at the early stage of their acquisition as their basic spatial concept schemata help them to understand the extended meaning of words, and a correspondent relation of the word meaning can be established between the source language and the target language according to the universal nature of language. However, when the learners move to a higher stage, they can not make rapid progress as they do at the early stage. One reason is that, it becomes difficult to parallel the target language to the source language because the derived meanings of prepositions which are achieved in terms of spatial iconicity become more and more complicated and farther away from the core meaning. The other reason is that the learners fail to construct an effective semantic network that can be activated by new propositions, which results in the expansion of the number of the vocabulary, not the richness and depth of vocabulary and thus their progress is definitely slowed down despite of their great effort.

Chapter 7

The Developmental Stages of Wh-movement Acquisition

As one of the significant theories of Transformational-Generative grammar, movement mainly consists of argument movement(A-movement) and non-argument movement (A-bar movement). Wh-movement, which is a non-argument movement, has long been a large obstacle for EFL learners. Syntactically, wh-movement is constrained by thematic theory, subjacency theory, wh-islands, and other conditions. Functionalists do many researches on wh-movement from the functional perspective and believe that wh-movement belongs to a kind of "fronting" movement; cognitive grammarians put emphasis on the complex cognitive process of wh-movement acquisition of EFL learners; applied linguists conclude the above theories, analyze wh-movement from the perspective of interlanguage, and argue that second language learners are influenced by their mother tongue during wh-movement acquisition. They put forward the theories of acquisition orders and developmental process of second language acquisition. Based on these theories, the study investigates the acquisition orders and developmental stages during wh-movement acquisition of Chinese EFL learners, whose mother tongue belongs to a kind of wh-in-situ language.

Thirty-one subjects from Civil Engineering School of Wuhan University took part in the experiment of the wh-movement acquisition research. A test paper consisted of multiple choice questions, sentence sequence task and translation from Chinese into English was designed and the data collected were analyzed via the statistical tool of SPSS to investigate the wh-movement acquisition proficiency, from the perspective of combining developmental stages with syntactic rules. The analysis of the data reveals that learners have grasped all the rules of six stages of wh-movement following the guideline of Mackey's theory (1999); however, they have still made all kinds of syntactical mistakes. Each stage does not clearly depend on mastery of the operations that characterize the previous stage(s). Except for syntactical grammars, learners' motivation, negative transfer, and low quality of input all prevent them from acquiring wh-movement rules. Even though developmental acquisition orders do map out learners' acquisition in general, individual differences among learners still play a significant role in obstructing learners' second language acquisition. The characteristics and syntactical structures of L1 cannot necessarily explain or predict L2 acquisition. It is a regular pattern for learners to master those exceptional grammatical rules.

7.1　Wh-movement phenomenon

Wh-movement is obligatory in English, which changes a sentence from affirmative to interrogative. This term comes from the analyses in Generative Grammar where a wh-word begins at some other place in a sentence and moves to the front. The details of wh-movement are very complex, particularly when English is compared to other languages with wh-movement. All modern theories of syntax have some part of the theory which deals with the correct formulation of the rules of wh-movement.

7.1.1　Wh-phrases

Wh-phrases are non-referring expressions. In order to explain the transformation of grammatical and meaningful sentences, Chomsky (1965) forwarded the acronyms DS and SS to stand for *deep structure* and *surface structure* respectively. Unlike names such as *John*, they do not pick out a specific individual or entity in a given world (or domain of discourse). The wh-phrase *which problem* in (1a), for example, does not refer to a specific problem. The speaker knows that John solved a problem, but does not know which one. The same is true of simpler wh-phrases such as *who*, *what*…etc.

(1) a. which problem did John solve?

b. DS: $[_{CP}$ e $[_{IP}$ Mary $[_{I'}$ did $[_{VP}$ solve which problem$]]]]$

c. SS: $[_{CP}$ which problem$_i[_{C'}$ did$_j[$ John $[_{I'}$ $t_j[_{VP}$ solve $t_i]]]]]]$

The nature of wh-phrases as non-referring expressions, and therefore non-arguments, raises an interesting problem relating to the argument structure of the verb *solve* in (1). The verb *solve* is a two-place predicate, and therefore expected to have two arguments. Yet in (1) it apparently has only one argument, namely *John*. The object *which problem* is a non-argument because it is a wh-phrase. It appears that the argument structure of the verb is not properly reflected in the syntactic representation. This state of affairs, if ture, should result in excluding the sentence. Notice, however, that in the SS representation (1c), the wh-phrase does not occupy the object position of the verb. The latter is occupied by the trace of the wh-phrase. Traces of wh-phrases (or wh-traces) are said to have the status of logical variables. Logical variables can generally be assigned a value, i. e. they can be translated as a referential expression in a given domain of discourse. Using the terminology of Logic, the wh-question (1a) can be translated as in (2), where the expression "for which problem" corresponds to the wh-phrase *which problem* and the variable x corresponds to the wh-trace. The expression "for which problem" corresponds to the wh-trace. The expression "for which problem" is said to be the operator binding the variable:

(2) for which problem x [John solved x]

If the answer to the question is "John solved the Maths problem", the variable in the object position of the verb is assigned the value MATHS (PROBLEM). Wh-traces are therefore (potential) arguments by virtue of being variables.

In view of this, the requirement that the argument structure of the verb be accurately reflected holds of the SS representation (1c). To solve the problem identified above, it appears that all we need to say is that the requirement in question does not hold of DS representations such as (1b). However, there is evidence that the requirement in question does not hold of SS representations either. The evidence partly has to do with wh-questions which have more than one wh-phrase called multiple wh-questions. (3a) is an information-seeking multiple wh-question with one wh-phrase in [Spec, CP] and the other in situ at SS, as shown in (3c):

(3) a. Who solved which problem?

b. DS: [$_{CP}$ C [$_{IP}$ who I [$_{VP}$ solved which problem]]]

c. SS: [$_{CP}$ who$_i$[$_{IP}$ t_i I [$_{VP}$ solved which problem]]]

In view of (3c), it appears that the requirement that a two-place predicate such as *solve* has two arguments does not hold of SS representations. The predicate *solve* has only one argument at SS, namely the wh-trace of *who* in the subject position. The requirement must therefore hold of a subsequent level of representation. Whatever the exact nature of this level of representation, something must happen that would result in removing the wh-phrase *which problem* from the object position and leaving a variable trace behind. In other words, the required representation must have the form shown in (4a), where the object wh-phrase is moved to [Spec, CP] leaving a variable trace behind:

(4) a. LF: [$_{CP}$[who]$_i$[which problem]$_j$ did [$_{IP}$ t_i I [$_{VP}$ solve t_j]]]

b. for which person x and which problem y [x solved y]

While LF component gives the syntactic meaning, PF component presents the s-structure as sound. The need for the representation in (4a) is suggested by the logical translation in (4b), where the operator that corresponds to the wh-phrase *which problem* is placed at the beginning of the clause and the object position of the verb *solve* is occupied by a variable.

Movement of *which problem* in (4) does not have a "visible" effect on word order, contrary to movement of *which problem* in the mapping form DS onto SS. The model of grammar branches off at the level of SS into the separate levels PF and LF. PF is the "visible" level and LF the "invisible" level. Any recording (movement) process which takes place prior to or at the level of SS will be "visibly" reflected (at PF) (Ouhalla, 2001). However, any recording (movement) process which takes place in the mapping from SS onto LF will not be "visibly" reflected. It follows that movement of the wh-phrase *which problem* which derives representation (4a) applies in the mapping from SS onto LF. The order in the PF representation of the multiple wh-question (3a) is as it is in the SS representation (3c), with *which problem* in the direct object position of the verb.

Movement processes which take place prior to or at the level of SS are called overt movement. Movement processes which apply in the mapping onto LF are called covert movements. Given that process which derives the LF representation (4a) involves movement of a wh-phrase to [Spec, CP], it is tempting to call it wh-movement. However, because wh-movement is substitution movement, which is not the case in (4a) the [Spec, CP] targeted by movement of *which problem* is already filled with the wh-phrase who, moved there overtly. The movement involved in (4a) must therefore be an adjunction movement, the only other type of movement allowed. This movement process adjoins the moved wh-phrase to the wh-phrase already in Spec, CP, deriving the adjunction structure shown in (5):

(5)

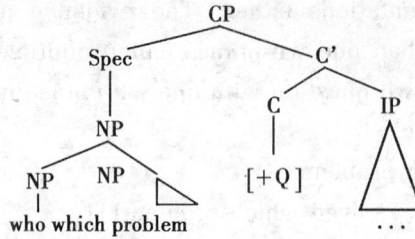

In this way, the process which moves categories in the mapping from SS onto LF is called Quantifier Raising (QR). Wh-phrases are sometimes called quasi-quantifiers.

To conclude, wh-phrase is a constituent that is somehow characterized as a question operator. No matter when it is a simpler word such as "what" or an entire phrase as "which books", it plays an important role during wh-movement transformation from a deep structure to a surface structure.

7.1.2 Wh-trace

As one of the basic terminologies of wh-movement, wh-trace (also named as variable) explains how wh-phrases are transformed during the process of wh-movement. For a better understanding of wh-trace, two important terms which are connected with wh-trace closely, empty category and trace should firstly be focused on.

An empty category is a nominal element which does not have any phonological content and is therefore unpronounced in syntax; they may also be referred to as covert nouns, in contrast to overt nouns which are pronounced. There are four types of empty category: NP-trace, wh-trace, PRO, and pro. The types of empty category are differentiated by their two binding features, namely the anaphoric feature (a) and the pronominal feature (p). The four possible combinations of plus or minus values for these features yield the four types of empty category. In generative-binding theory (GB theory), the empty category which is left behind when a word or phrase is moved and which is coindexed with the moved item is named as trace. In transformational grammar, a trace is an empty (phonologically null) category that occupies a position in the syntactic structure. According to the trace theory, when an element is moved in the course of a derivation, it leaves behind a trace in its original position. For example, in the following sentence (i) since *who* has been moved from subject position in a lower clause, a trace is left behind in that position.

(i) Who did you say [$t_i$left] (Richards J, Schmidt R, et al, 2005)

And the trace is often indicated in a syntactic diagram of the sentence as *t* (for trace) or *e* (for empty) in analyzing a sentence surface structure (see the following example 7). In some theories of syntax, traces are used in the account of constructions such as wh-movement and passive.

Since traces are important theoretical devices in some approaches to syntax, so wh-trace is the trace what wh-movement leaves because of moving. For example,

What did he say?

The D-structure of this sentence is:

He *past* say what

The specifier (spec) of this sentence lacks as shows in the following diagram (6):

(6)

```
              CP
           /      \
   (specifier)     C'
                 /    \
                C      IP
                      /  \
                he past say what
```

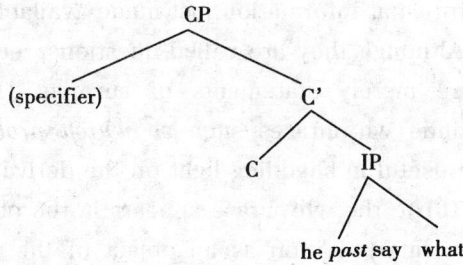

The S-structure after wh-movement becomes:

(7)

```
              CP
           /      \
   (specifier)     C'
        |         /   \
      What       C     IP
                      /__\
                he past say t
```

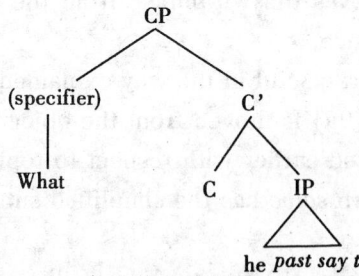

The wh-trace in this way is a variable, and the syntactic function is a specifier. To sum up, as one of the basic terminologies, wh-trace explains how a wh-phrase is transformed during the process of wh-movement, and it is quite important to understand better the movement rules in syntax.

7.1.3 Wh-questions

Wh-questions are interrogatives whose outsets are wh-words, such as *who/whom*, *what*, *when*, *where*, *why*, *which*, and *how*, and at the same time, people cannot answer the questions just with *yes*, or *no* simply. For example:

(8) a. He sold all his English books to Mary after the test.

   b. what did he sell to Mary?

   c. To whom did he sell his English books?

   d. When did he sell his English books?

In each of the above interrogative sentences, a wh-word moves out of its "normal" position uniformly in a leftward manner to the sentence initial-position, which indicates that wh-preposing is syntactically required when the sentence changes from a statement into a question (Mei, 2003). Compare the pair of question-answer (9a) and (9b) to the pair of statements in (10a) and (10b):

(9) a. Question: Which problem did you solve?

   b. Answer: I solved the problem.

(10) a. Statement: I solved the problem.

b. Statement: You solved which problem!

The sentence (9a) is a wh-question, used to ask for new information. The answer (9b) provides the information asked by the wh-question. While (10b) is an echo-question, usually used to express surprise at information just made available to the speaker, such as the information in (10a). Although they are called questions, echo-questions do not seek new information. They are merely statements of surprise. However, they resemble questions in that they include wh-phrases such as *which problem* in (10b). For this reason, echo-questions are useful in shedding light on the derivation of wh-questions.

In the echo-question (10b), the wh-phrase appears in the object position of the verb, which is consistent with its interpretation as an object of the verb. In the wh-question (9a), however, the wh-phrase appears in the initial position of the sentence. Now, if the position occupied by the wh-phrase in the echo-question (10b) is assumed to be the DS position of the wh-phrase in the wh-question (9a), the latter can be said to be derived by a transformational rule which moves the wh-phrase from the object position of the verb to the initial position of the sentence.

Although echo-questions are useful in the way explained, as a matter of fact, that the wh-phrase in the wh-question (9a) is moved from the object position of the verb is still in suspense. The reasoning adopted earlier with respect to topicalised objects also applies to the wh-phrase in (9a). The verb *solve* has the simplified subcategorisation frame shown in (11a). (11b) and

(11c) show the *solve* takes an NP object obligatorily:

(11) a. solve: [V; — NP]

b. I solved the problem.

c. * I solved.

It follows from the information in (11a, b & c) that the verb *solve* must have an object in the wh-question (11a). Otherwise, the example should be excluded for the same reason as (11c). The object of the verb in (9a) is the wh-phrase base-generated in the object position of the verb and subsequently moved to the initial position of the sentence. The derivation of this example is as outlined in (12a, b & c):

(12) a. Which problem did you solve?

b. DS: [$_S$ you [$_{Aux}$ Tense] [$_{VP}$ solve [$_{NP}$ which problem]]]

c. SS: [$_{S'}$ [$_{NP}$ which problem]$_i$ [$_S$ you [$_{Aux}$ Tense [$_{VP}$ solve [$_{NP}$ t]$_i$]]]]

In this way, the transformation responsible for movement of the wh-phrase to the sentence-initial position is called wh-movement.

However, the derivation in (12b & c) ignores the Aux element *did*. This is the case in sentences where it applies within the embedded clause called indirect questions. The following sentence (13a) is an example of an indirect question where the wh-phrase is wh-moved from the direct object position of the verb to the initial position of the embedded clause:

(13) a. I wonder which problem Mary solved.

b. I wonder [$_{S'}$ [$_{NP}$ which problem]$_i$ [$_S$ Mary [$_{Aux}$ Tense] [$_{VP}$ solved [$_{NP}$ t]$_i$]]].

As far as topicalisation is concerned, the conclusion that topicalised categories are attached to the left of S was somewhat dictated by the fact that the topicalised phrase occurs to the right of the complementizer *that* and to the left of the subject in embedded clauses. Moved wh-phrases also occur to the left of the subjects, but there is no point of reference to the left of the moved wh-phrase as there is with topicalised phrases. This is because interrogative clauses are incompatible with the complementizer *that*. As a working hypothesis, that moved wh-phrases are placed in all clauses irrespective of whether they include a complementizer. Accordingly the embedded wh-question in (13) has the more articulated representation shown in the following diagram (14).

(14)

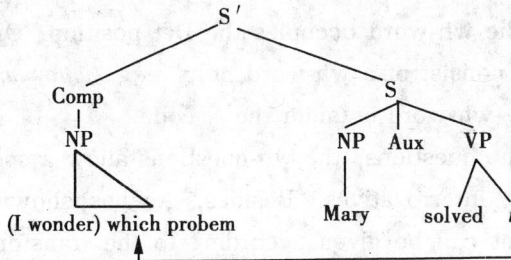

Having identified the landing site of the moved wh-phrase, wh-movement can simply be defined as in the following wh-movement, that is, move wh-XP to comp. The use of the variable XP in the definition is intended to capture the fact that wh-phrases other than NP can also undergo wh-movement. (15) involves wh-movement of an adjectival wh-phrase and (16) wh-movement of an adverbial wh-phrase:

(15) a. I wonder how difficult the problem was.

   b. I wonder $[_{s'}[_{AP}$how difficult$]_i[_s$ the problem was $_{AP}t]_i]]$

(16) a. I wonder when Mary solved the problem.

   b. I wonder $[_{s'}[_{ADV}$when$]_i[_s$ Mary solved the problem $[_{ADV}t]_i]]$

PPs can also undergo wh-movement, as shown in (17). In English, the preposition has the option of staying behind, as in (18). The latter phenomenon is known as preposition stranding. Movement of the whole PP, seen in (17), is said to involve pied piping of the preparation along with the wh-phrase. The actual wh-phrase in this example is an NP object of the preposition:

(17) a. I wonder to whom Mary gave the book.

   b. I wonder $[_{s'}[_{PP}$ to whom$]_i[_s$ Mary gave the book $[_{PP}t]_i]]$

(18) a. I wonder whom Mary gave the book to.

   b. I wonder $[_{s'}[_{NP}$whom$]_i[_s$ Mary gave the book $[_{PP}$to$[_{NP}t]_i]]]$

Before moving on to discuss other issues relating to wh-movement, a word about the internal structure of wh-phrases should be made clear. Look at the following example at first:

(19)   a.

```
            NP                                    NP
          /    \                                   |
       Det      N                                  N
        |       |                                  |
      which  problem                              Who
```
b.

In both (19a) and (19b) the wh-phrase is a phrasal category. Wh-movement is an instance of the set of transformations which target phrasal categories. The wh-phrases which consist of both a wh-word and a noun, e. g. *which problem*, have the structure shown in (19a), where the wh-word occupies the Det position. On the other hand, wh-phrases which apparently consist of a wh-word only, e. g. *who, what* have the structure shown in (19b) where the wh-word is under the N code.

For distinguishing echo questions, the wh-questions allow a speaker to find out more information by employing interrogatives. Besides, As has shown in this section, the definition of wh-movement can be given according to the transformational rules of wh-questions as moving a wh-phrase to a complementizer.

7.1.4 Relatives

Except for wh-questions, another result of wh-movement is relatives, a grammar denoting or relating to a clause (relative clause) that modifies a noun or pronoun occurring earlier in the sentence. In this part, the author will introduce relatives with an overt wh-phrase, a null wh-phrase, the recoverability and the doubly filled comp filter. Compare two sentences (20) and (21):

(20) a. John heard the claim that Bill made a cake.

b. John heard [$_{NP}$ the claim [$_{S'}$ that [$_S$ Bill made a cake]]]

(21) a. John heard the claim which Bill made.

b. John heard [$_{NP}$ the claim [$_{S'}$ which [$_S$ Bill made]]]

Both sentences include a complex NP with a clause S′ inside it. In (20), S′ is the complement of the noun *claim* and therefore is a complement clause. In (21), however, S′ is not a complement of the noun *claim*. In this example, S′ has an adjective-like function whereby it modifies the noun *claim* by restricting its reference to a particular instance. Such a clause is called a relative clause, and the noun phrase which includes a relative clause is called a relative noun phrase.

The complement clause in (20) and the relative clause in (21) differ in one other important respect. In (20) the object of the verb *made* appears in its normal position immediately following the verb. However, in the relative clause (21) the object of the verb *made* is missing from its normal position. Instead, it appears in the form of the wh-phrase *which*, apparently situated under Comp. This property of the relative clause groups it together with wh-clauses even though, strictly speaking, the relative clause groups it the type illustrated in (21) also involve wh-movement in their derivation, as shown in the following example (22):

(22) a. John heard the claim which Bill made.

b. DS: John heard [$_{NP}$the claim$_i$[$_{S'}$[$_S$ Bill made [$_{NP}$ which]$_i$]]]

c. SS: John heard [$_{NP}$the claim$_i$[$_{S'}$[$_{NP}$ which]$_i$[$_S$ Bill made[$_{NP}$ t]$_i$]]]

Co-indexation between the moved wh-phrase and its *trace* is an automatic consequence of wh-movement. However, that (22) also shows co-indexation between the noun *claim*, called the head of the relative noun phrase, and the wh-phrase which at both DS and SS. This particular co-indexation is intended to capture the fact that the wh-phrase has the same reference as the head N of the noun phrase. The head N is said to be the antecedent of the wh-phrase, although the two categories are not linked by a movement transformation. This is what is responsible for the impression that the head N is the direct object of the verb *made*. It is important to bear in mind that in relative noun phrases it is the wh-phrase co-indexed with the head N that undergoes movement not the head N itself. If it were the head N that undergoes movement, it would be hard to explain the presence of the wh-phrase, among other things.

The relative clause (22) is called a restrictive relative clause. This is because, as pointed out above, it restricts the reference of the head N it modifies. There are other types of relative clause illustrated in (23) and (24):

(23) a. Mary, whom you will meet soon, is our president.

b. Mary, [$_{S'}$[$_{NP}$whom]$_i$[$_S$ you will meet [$_{NP}$ t]$_i$ soon]], is our president.

(24) a. Whatever they say, we will press ahead with the project.

b. [$_{S'}$[$_{NP}$whatever]$_i$[$_S$ they say [$_{NP}$ t]$_i$]], we will press ahead with the project.

The relative clause in (23) is called an appositive relative clause. Unlike restrictive relative clauses, appositive relative clauses do not necessarily restrict the reference of the head N they modify. They are necessarily a kind of after-thought. The relative clause in (24), on the other hand, is called a free relative clause; mainly because it does not modify N in the sentence in which it occurs (it does not have a head). Appositive and free relative clauses involve wh-movement just as restrictive relative clauses do, although they have certain peculiar properties. Compare the relative noun discussed above, reproduced in (25a), to its synonymous counterparts in (25b) and (25c):

(25) a. John heard the claim which Bill made.

b. John heard the claim that Bill made.

c. John heard the claim Bill made.

The above examples (25b&c) apparently do not include a wh-phrase. Sentence (25b) includes neither the complementizer *that* instead of a wh-phrase, and (25c) appears to include neither a wh-phrase nor a complementizer.

In the discussion of (25a) above, it was pointed out that the wh-phrase functions as the object of the verb, meaning it is base-generated in the object position of the verb *made* and subsequently moved to Comp. The wh-phrase is co-indexed with the head N, and hence the interpretation whereby the object of the verb *made* has the same reference as the head N. The fact that the relatives in (25b & c) have exactly the same interpretation implies that they also include a wh-phrase with the same function. In other words, for the head N to be linked to the object position of the verb position of the verb *made*, it needs to be co-indexed with an element which occupies the object position of the verb *made* at DS. Moreover, from a formal point of view, the system forces an analysis for (25b&c) which assumes the presence of an object for the verb *made*. The latter is a transitive verb, and therefore requires an object: *Bill made* ∗ (*a claim*). It follows that the verb *made* must have an object in (25b&c). Otherwise, (25b&c) should be excluded for the same reason that ∗ *Bill made* is excluded.

Sentences (25b&c) must therefore include a null object. Since the equivalent of this category in the synonymous relative clause (25a) is a wh-phrase, it is plausible to conclude that the null object in (25b&c) is also a wh-phrase. This null wh-phrase is base-generated in the object position of *made* and moved to Comp by wh-movement. Accordingly, the derivation of (25b&c) is as shown in (26), where the null wh-phrase is represented with the symbol Op (erator). When a null wh-phrase is moved to a Comp which already dominates the complementizer *that*, the Comp has the structure shown in (26c) where it dominates two categories.

(26) a. ... the claim (that) Bill made.

b. ... $[_{NP}$ the claim $[_{S'}[_{NP}$ Op$]_i$(that) $[_S$ Bill made $[_{NP}$ $t]_i]]]$

c.

```
        Comp
       /    \
     Op      that
```

According to the analysis outlined in (26), relatives with a null wh-phrase are identical to their counterparts with an overt wh-phrase. They differ only in that they include a null wh-phrase instead of an overt one. Although the similarity with relatives with an overt wh-phrase is sufficient to justify the analysis, it is desirable to seek further evidence. If relatives without an overt wh-phrase indeed include a null wh-phrase which undergoes wh-movement, the island effects are expected to be shown. Recall that island effects are a reflection of some of the conditions on wh-movement incorporated into its definition, and a wh-island and/or a complex NP island inside the relative clause should be embedded. (27) includes a wh-island inside a relative noun phrase. Its ungrammatical status is due to extraction of the null wh-phrase out of the wh-island.

(27) a. ∗ I know the way (that) John wonders why Bill went.

b. ∗ ... $[_{NP}$ the way $_i[_{S'}[$ Op$]_i[_S$ John wonders $[_{S'}$ why $[_S$ Bill went$[t]_i]]]]]]$

Island conditions are essentially conditions on wh-movement irrespective of whether the moved wh-phrase is overt or null. Island violations are good indicators for the presence of wh-movement, and for this reason they are often used as diagnostic criteria for the presence of wh-movement in the derivation of sentences which do not include an overt wh-phrase.

However, two questions arise from the analysis of relatives without an overt wh-phrase. First, why can't wh-questions have a null wh-phrase on a par with relatives? In other words, why is (28a) excluded with the analysis outlined in (28b&c) which assumes the presence of a null wh-phrase?

(28) a. ＊ Did Mary solve? (with the meaning: What did Mary solve?)

b. DS: $[_{S'}[+Q][_S$ Mary solved Op$]$

c. SS: $[_{S'}[_{NP}Op]_i$ did $[_S$ Mary $[Aux][_{vp}$solve $[_{NP}t]_i]]]$

Note that the reason (28a) is excluded cannot be attributed to a possible violation of the subcategorisation requirements of the verb *solve*. These are satisfied by the null wh-phrase Op in the same way they are in the relatives with a null wh-phrase discussed above.

The difference between the wh-question in (28) and the relatives with a null wh-phrase is that in the latter the null wh-phrase has an antecedent in the sentence, namely the head N is co-indexed with. The head N is the antecedent of the null wh-phrase in the sense that it identifies the content of the null wh-phrase it is co-indexed with. In contrast, the null wh-phrase in the wh-question (28) does not have an antecedent in the sentence, with the consequence that its content remains unidentified or non-recoverable. (28) illustrates a general condition on the occurrence of null categories called the recoverability condition. The version of this condition is called Recoverability Condition, and assume that the content of a null category must be recoverable (from a co-indexed overt category in the sentence).

The other question which arises from the analysis of relatives without an overt wh-phrase is the following: if a wh-phrase can co-occur with the complementizer *that* in Comp, as in (26) above, why is (29) excluded?

(29) a. ＊ I know the problem which that Mary solved.

b. ＊ I know $[_{NP}$ the problem $[_{S'}[_{NP}$which$]_i$ that $[_S$ Mary solved$[_{NP}t]_i]]]$.

Sentence (29) differs from sentence (26) only in that the wh-phrase which co-occurs with the complementizer *that* under Comp is overt instead of null. For some reason, an overt wh-phrase cannot co-occur with the complementizer *that* under Comp, although a null one can. There are various ways to exclude examples such as (29). However, imposing a condition on wh-movement preventing it from placing an overt wh-phrase under a Comp filled with *that* is not one of them. This is because this measure would render wh-movement sensitive to whether the wh-phrase is null or overt, and therefore would undermine the idea that null and overt categories are treated equally by movement rules. In other words, transformational rules are not expected to discriminate between overt and null categories, on the grounds that they are not sensitive to whether a given category has or does not have a phonetic realization.

A more plausible alternative is to formulate a condition on the co-occurrence possibilities in Comp, irrespective of whether the elements involved are base-generated there or moved to it. This condition will have the effect of excluding sentences where an overt wh-phrase co-occurs with *that* under Comp, that is sentences where Comp is "doubly filled" in the intended sense. A possible way of defining the condition in question is Doubly Filled Comp Filter as showed in (30).

234 | 认知语言学实证研究通论
General Introduction to Empirical Research of Cognitive Linguistics

(30) * [Comp wh-XP that], if wh-XP is overt (non-null).

Sentence (30) acts as a "filter" on (SS) representations derived by wh-movement, and has the effect of excluding phrase markers with a Comp filled by an overt wh-phrase and *that*.

To conclude, unlike the conditions of transformations, the Recoverability Condition and the Doubly Filled Comp Filter are not conditions on (the application of) transformations (Jamal Ouhalla 2nd; 1999). Rather, they are conditions on representations (i. e. phrase makers) derived by transformations. The idea underlying conditions on representations such as these is that transformations can be allowed to overgenerate to a limited degree. The undesirable representations can then be excluded by conditions or filters which apply to the output of transformational rules. Thus, the Recoverability Condition and the Doubly Filled Comp Filter are new conditions which previously consisted exclusively of rules.

7.2 Conditions on wh-movement

Even though wh-phrases can experience a long-range movement, wh-movement, however, does have its constraints (Ross, 1967). Based on some theories and examples, the wh-movement constraint and the forms leading to the phenomenon will be analyzed. Then the conditions on wh-movement will be drawn as the conclusion.

7.2.1 Thematic theory

Thematic theory, also named as theta theory, is one of the subsets forwarded by linguists as a generative grammar which was then developed into government binding theory. Some aspects of the role played by lexical argument structure in syntactic representations, the array of thematic roles encoded on a word as a function of its lexical interpretation have been considered as an increasingly important role in generative grammar (Clark, 1990).

Predicate and entity are the basic elements of a sentence, and we define predicate as a relation, which is described as the relationship between individual and reality; the entity involved in the relation is named as argument. For instance,

(31) Mary solved the problem.

There are two arguments in the above sentence, *Mary* and *the problem*, which are the main elements, involved the movement of the verb *solve*, which is the predicate to describe the relationship between the two arguments. That is to say, the verb *solve* shows the movement the first argument *Mary* to the second one *the problem*.

The above analysis pattern can be used to describe the argument structure of every predicate, which refers to the numbers of arguments a predicate needs. In English, the predicates which only need one argument, such as *smile*, *arrive*, *run* and other intransitive verbs, are called one-place predicate in argument structure theory. In this way, the transitive verbs which need two argument structure, like *hit*, *kill*, *love* and *see*, are called two-place predicate. Besides, there are some three-place predicates since some predicates need three arguments, such as *give* and *put* which are named as double transitive verbs in traditional grammar theory.

The thematic relation is the main form indicating the argument relations; it aims to describe the function of arguments between argument structures and predicates. The argument and it do not necessarily follow the role of one-to-one correspondence. However, the special structure of theta role asks for the one-to-one correspondence between them, and the thematic role is the set of all thematic relations. *Mary* in the above example can show two thematic relations (agent and source), but it only takes one thematic role including these two thematic relations. The wh-words or phrases are far away from the positions assigned by the verbs of theta roles. For example,

(32) Mary bought a new cell phone.

(33) What did Mary buy?

In English, the verb *buy* has two theta roles, the external agent and the internal theme. In the above example (32), *Mary* is the agent and *a new cell phone* is the theme; while in the sentence (33), *Mary* is also the agent and *what* is the theme. In the first sentence, the theme is the object of the verb, while the next theme *what* appears at the initial position of the sentence. Furthermore, let us see another example, the position of whose theme is still confusing,

(34) What did John say Mary bought?

In this sentence, *what* is still the theme of the verb *bought*, but it appears at the initial position of the main clause, which seems to disobey the locality condition of theta role assignment.

On the other hand, the Case Theory requires that the object should be acquired by NP in the sister position (Mei, 2008). For instance,

(35)John beat him.

However, the object of a wh-question is far away from the sister position of the verb. For instance,

(36) Whom did John beat?

The above analysis indicates that the wh-words are neither at the theta role position nor at the case position. Obviously, the wh-words are moved in the sentences based on the above analysis. The goal of the wh-movements [Spec, CP] is a maximal projection position, supposing that wh-words are moved to the referential position of CP, as the following diagram (37) shows:

(37)

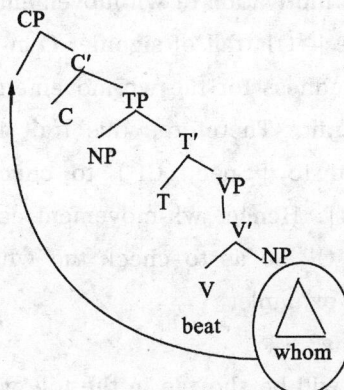

In the above example, the whole NP phrase is moved, which will be showed more clearly in the following more complex wh-questions:

(38) [To whom] did Mary send the mail?

(39) [Which box] did Mary finally choose?

Since the whole phrases are moved, they cannot be the head-to-head movements (For example, the T→C movement is one of the head-to-head movements). Therefore, the goal of this kind of wh-movement is not the head but the empty specifier's position of CP. The wh-movement to [Spec, CP] also explains the sentence sequence orders of wh-questions to some degree, i. e. the movements include the T→C movement of main clauses. As one of the head-to-head movements, the motivation of T→C movement lies in the [+Q] trait of specifier C, which attracts markedness of T that lies before, such as the auxiliary, tense and inflection, and therefore, the movement to C can be used to check the trait. In the following example (40), the auxiliary *are* is moved, or the sentence would be ungrammatical because the [+Q] trait cannot be checked, as showed in (41)

(40) What are you reading?

(41) * What you are reading?

In the above sentence (40), the wh-phrase appears on the left of the auxiliary, which means that wh-phrase has to be moved to a higher position above C, [Spec, CP] will be the only one, which will be showed in the following diagram (42):

(42)

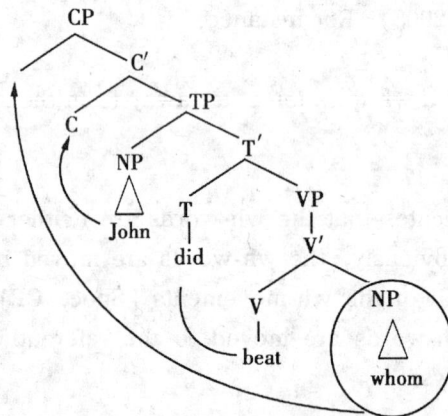

Following the above, the motivation of wh-movement will be checked out. The reason of T→C movement lies in the [+Q] trait of signifier C in wh-questions, and NP movement is required by the case markedness for the wh-movement. Wh-questions move to [Spec, CP] to approach [+WH] trait. Therefore, this trait is used to check the movement process. Wh-word is moved to [Spec, CP] to check [Subjective Case] or verbal complement to check [object]. Hence, wh-movement can also be defined as moving wh-words to the Specifier C of CP so as to check the wh-trait of C. Take the generation process of sentence (43) for example:

(43) What is John reading?

The D-structure of (44) will be showed in the following diagram (44):

(44)

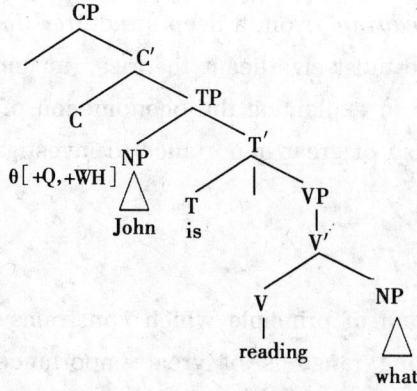

In the above diagram, both *John* and *what* get their own theta roles and the relative case positions in the same place. In order to meet [+Q] trait of C, the auxiliary of T, *is*, is moved as T→C movement:

(45)

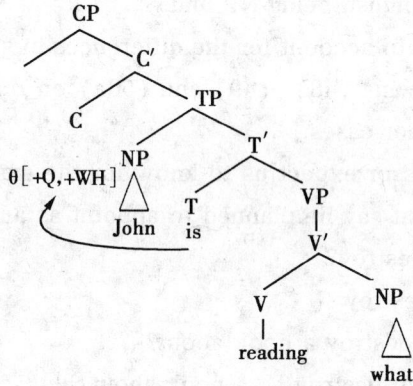

Following that, wh-word what is moved to check [+WH] trait of C in the following diagram :

(46)

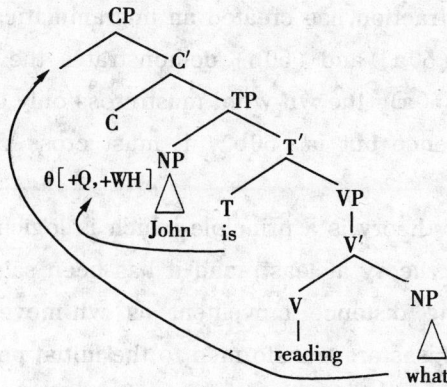

And the above operations finally generate wh-question (47)

(47) What is John reading?

At this time, the process of wh-movement is quite a complex syntactical transformation. From the above figures (44), (45), and (46), the wh-movement is manifested clearly following the rules of wh-movement by elaborating the transformation process of wh-questions "*what is John reading*" from a deep structure "*John is reading what*".

To sum up, as one of the most significant theories, in universal grammar, thematic theory plays an important role in explaining the phenomenon of syntactical rules of many kinds of language, and it is also of great importance to investigate the movement rules of wh-words and phrases.

7.2.2 Subjacency theory

Subjacency theory is a kind of principle which constrains the movements, and this constraint of wh-words' moving range is of great importance for wh-movement. The subjacency principle is a universal and innate principle of universal grammar; its effects vary from language to language depending on the kinds of movement the language allows.

Subjacency has been formulated as a constraint on movement rules at the level of S-structure. The principle itself is that no application of a movement rule can cross more than a single barrier, barriers for English being NP and S.

This condition allows one to account for the differences in grammaticality between the sentences such as in the following (48), (49) and (50a) on one hand and (50b) on the other, as well as for many other cases.

(48) What does the professor expect us to know for the exam?

(49) Who did the President say he planned to appoint as ambassador?

(50) a. What did Susan destroy?

What [$_s$ did Susan destroy t]

b * What did Susan destroy a book about?

* What [$_s$ did Susan destroy [$_{NP}$a book about$t$]]

Sentences (49) and (50) demonstrate that wh-words can be extracted from embed clause object position and moved to the front of the sentence in English. (50a) demonstrates that wh-words can be moved from a main clause object position as well. In (50b), however, the wh-extraction has created an ungrammatical sentence. The contrast in grammaticality between (50a) and (50b) demonstrates the effect of the subjacency principle on extraction. In (50a), the wh-word must cross only one barrier (s) in order to get to the front of the sentence but in (50b), it must cross two (NP, S) and is thus ungrammatical.

To sum up, subjacency theory is a principle which is logically dependent upon other properties in a language, in theory at least, and it has been said to apply vacuously in a given language without long distance movement as wh-movement. This theory does constrain a lot when wh-phrases are transformed to the initial position of a sentence.

7.2.3 Other conditions on wh-movement

Based on semantic theory and subjacency principle, other conditions on wh-movement which are also very important for wh-movement constraint will be given in the following section. Among them, /+Q/ -Comp Condition, wh-island condition, complex noun phrase condition, cyclicity condition and transformational cycle will be showed and a conclusion about another definition of wh-movement can be drawn.

To begin with, let's compare two pairs of sentences (51) to (52):

(51) a. I wonder which problem Mary solved.

   b. I wonder [$_{S'}$ [$_{NP}$ which problem] $_i$ [$_S$ Mary Aux[$_{VP}$ solved [$_{NP}$ t] $_i$]]]

(52) a. * I believe which problem Mary solved.

   b. * I believe [$_{S'}$ [$_{NP}$ which problem] $_i$ [$_S$ Mary Aux [$_{VP}$ solved[$_{NP}$ t] $_i$]]] .

Together, these examples show that wh-movement cannot move a wh-phrase to any Comp position, contrary to what is implied by the preliminary definition of wh-movement. Wh-movement to the embedded Comp is allowed in (51) but not in (52). The definition of wh-movement therefore has to be revised to take into consideration the fact that not all Comps are legitimate targets for wh-movement.

The difference between (51) and (52) lies in a difference in the subcategorizes properties of the verbs in the root clause. The verb *wonder* subcategorizes for an interrogative clause. The verb *believe*, however, does not subcategorize for an interrogative clause. Instead, it subcategories for a declarative clause, as in *I believe that Mary solved the problem*. The difference in the subcategorization properties of the two types of verb can be encoded in terms of the feature [+/-Q(uestion)] associated with the Comp of the clause they subcategorize for. Interrogative clauses are marked with the feature specification [+Q] and declarative clauses with the negative feature specification [-Q]. Accordingly, the subcategorization frames of the verbs in (51) and (52) are roughly as shown in (53):

(53) a. wonder: [— S': [+ Q]]

   b. believe: [— S': [–Q]]

In (51), the Comp of the embedded clause is marked with the feature [+Q] as required by the subcategorization properties of the root verb *wonder*. In (52), however, the Comp of the embedded clause is marked with the feature [-Q] as required by the subcategorization properties of the root verb *believe*. Now, if wh-movement can move a wh-phrase only to a Comp which is [+Q], (52) will be excluded on the grounds that it involves wh-movement to a [-Q]-Comp. The condition in question is called the [+Q]-Comp condition, and in corporate it onto the definition of wh-movement as moving wh-XP to Comp provided Comp is [+Q].

The idea that interrogative clauses are marked with the feature [+Q] plausibly extends to root interrogatives such as *which problem did Mary solve?* Like embedded clauses, root sentences can also be interrogative or declarative, among other possibilities. It is natural to assume that root sentences are distinguished in terms of the same mechanism as subcategorized clauses, so that root wh-interrogatives are marked with the feature [+Q] and root declaratives are marked with the feature [-Q]. Consequently, movement of the wh-phrase to Comp in root sentences is also consistent with [+Q]. In (54), which is the direct question counterpart of (52), the root Comp is marked with the feature [+Q] and the embedded Comp with the feature [-Q]. This is the reason why the wh-phrase moves to the root Comp instead of to the embedded Comp, although there are complications that will need to be sorted out later on:

(54) a. which problem do you believe that Mary solved?

b. $[_{S'}[_{NP}$which problem$]_i$ do $[_S$ you believe $[_{S'}$ that $[_S$ Mary solved$[_{NP}\ t]_i]]]$

The feature [+/-Q] can also be used to distinguish between genuine wh-questions and echo-questions such as *John solved which problem!* discussed above. Echo-questions can be said to be [-Q], meaning they are not wh-questions even though they include a wh-phrase. Marking echo-questions with the feature [-Q] accounts for why the wh-phrase does not move to Comp in them. The wh-phrase remains in-situ in echo-questions. Thus, the fundamental difference between genuine wh-questions and echo-questions relates to the feature encoded in their Comp and not to whether the wh-phrase they include moves or does not move to Comp. whether the wh-phrase moves to Comp is a consequential property which depends on the feature of Comp. Compare examples (55) and (56):

(55) a. How do you think that Mary solved the problem?

b. $[_{S'}[how]_i$ do $[_S$ you think $[_{S'}$ that $[_S$ Mary solved the problem $[t]_i]]]]$

(56) a. * How do you wonder whether Mary solved the problem?

b. * $[_{S'}[how]_i$ do $[_S$ you wonder $[_{S'}$ whether $[_S$ Mary solved the problem$[t]_i]]]]$

Both sentences involve movement of a wh-phrase out of the embedded clause to the root Comp, which differ in that the Comp of the embedded clause dominates the complementizer *that* in (55) and the wh-phrase *whether* in (56). This difference is the consequence of the difference in the type of the root verb discussed above.

The contrast between (55) and (56) illustrates the fact that it is generally more difficult to extract a wh-phrase out of a clause with a wh-phrase in its Comp position than it is from a clause without a wh-phrase in its Comp position. This fact is further illustrated by the contrast in (57) and (58). The Comp of the embedded clause dominates a wh-phrase in (57) but not in (58):

(57) a. Which way do you think that John went.

b. $[_{S'}[_{NP}$which way$]_i$ do $[_S$ you think $[_{S'}$(that) $[_S$John went $[t]_i]]]]$

(58) a. * Which way do you wonder why John went?

b. * $[_{S'}[_{NP}$which way$]_i$ do $[_S$ you wonder $[_{S'}$ why $[_S$John went $[t]_i]]]]$

Because it is difficult for a wh-phrase to escape out of a clause the Comp position of which dominates a wh-phrase, these clauses are called wh-islands. The condition on wh-movement they illustrate is called the wh-Island Condition. Continuing the strategy of incorporating conditions on transformation into their definitions, wh-movement can now be defined as in moving wh-XP to Comp provided Comp:

   ⅰ) [+Q]

   ⅱ) not included in a wh-island that excludes the targeted Comp.

The revised version of wh-movement excludes (56) and (58) on the grounds that they involve wh-movement out of a wh-island, and therefore a violation of one of the conditions on wh-movement.

The following example (59) illustrates another condition on wh-movement called the Complex Noun Phrase Condition (CNPC). Sentence (59) involves movement of a wh-phrase out of a complex noun phrase, where a complex noun phrase is a noun phrase which includes a clause (S') in addition to N and Det. The noun *claim* is of the type that subcategories for a clausal complement:

(59) a. * which way did you hear the claim that John went?

    b. * $[_{S'}[_{NP}$which way$]_i$ did $[_S$ you hear $[_{NP}$ the claim $[_{S'}$that $[_S$John went $[t]_i]]]]]]$

The fact that it is difficult to extract a wh-phrase out of a complex noun phrase is further illustrated in (60). The noun *rumour* resembles *claim* in that it also subcategorises for a clausal complement:

(60) a. * which way did Mary spread the rumour that John went?

    b. * $[_{S'}[_{NP}$which way$]_i$ did $[_S$ Mary spread $[_{NP}$ the rumour $[_{S'}$that $[_S$John went $[t]_i]]]]]]$

Incorporating CNPC into the definition of wh-movement yields the more complex but more restrictive version in wh-XP to Comp provided Comp:

   ⅰ) [+Q]   (the [+Q]-Comp Condition)

   ⅱ) not included in a wh-island   (the Wh-island Condition)

   ⅲ) not included in a complex NP   (the Complex NP Condition)

One important characteristic of wh-movement is that it seems to be unbounded, in the sense that it can operate across any number of clausal boundaries. This is partly illustrated in (61), where wh-movement crosses at least three clausal boundaries:

(61) a. Which problem do you think (that) Jane believes (that) Bill claims (that) Mary solved?

    b. $[_{S'}[_{NP}$which problem$]_i$ do $[_S$ you think $[_{S'}$(that) $[_S$Jane believes $[_{S'}$(that)

$[_S$ Bill claims $[_{S'}$(that) $[_S$Mary solved $[t]_i]]]]]]]]]$

There is a sense in which the impression that wh-movement is completely free (unbounded) is false. Two contexts where it is restricted, namely the contexts where the wh-phrase is included inside a wh-clause or a complex NP have already been seen. Wh-movement is not allowed to operate out of these two contexts. The Wh-island Condition and the CNPC are often called locality conditions on wh-movement, insofar as they define certain local domains out of which wh-movement in (61) applies in a series of local steps rather than in one step (or one swoop).

Compare examples (62) and (63). Both sentences include the verb *know* which subcategories for either a [+Q] or a [-Q] clause. The complement clause is interrogative in (62) and declarative in (63). In (63), it is the root sentence which is interrogative:

(62) a. John knows which problem Mary solved.

    b. John knows $[_{S'}[_{NP}$ which problem$]_i[_S$ Mary solved $[_{NP}t]_i]]$

(63) a. Which problem does John know Mary solved?

    b. $[_{S'}[_{NP}$which problem$]_i$ does $[_S[$John know $[_{S'}[_S$Mary solved $[_{NP}t]_i]]]]]$

The example (62) is an indirect question and (63) is a direct question. However, let us assume for the sake of the argument that the derivation of (63) is partially similar to that of (62). The wh-phrase in (63) moves first to the position occupied by the wh-phrase in (62), i. e. the Comp of the embedded clause, then to the Comp of the root clause. This more detailed derivation is shown in (64):

(64) a. Which problem does John know Mary solved?

    b. $[_{S'}[_{NP}$which problem$]_i$ does $[_S[$John know $[_{S'}t_i'[_S$Mary solved $[_{NP}t]_i]]]]]]$

The *trace* in the embedded Comp position, marked with a prime, is called an intermediate trace to distinguish it from the initial trace in the original object position of the wh-phrase. Just as the initial trace marks the position from which the wh-phrase has been extracted, the intermediate trace marks the position through which the wh-phrase has passed on its way to the root clause. Traces are sometimes said to encode the "history of movement".

Nothing in the system developed so far that forces the derivation in (64b). A condition on wh-movement will force it to move an embedded wh-phrase first to the Comp of the embedded clause before it moves it to the Comp of the root clause. The condition in question has to do with the notion transformational cycle. The latter is a domain within which a transformation can apply exhaustively. For example, S' is a transformational cycle because wh-movement can apply within it (without leaving it). In (62), for example, wh-movement applies exhaustively within the embedded clause. wh-movement is cyclical in nature, meaning it applies within the cycle that includes the wh-phrase before leaving it to the next cycle up, and so on. This condition on wh-movement is called the Cyclicity Condition. The consequence is that apparently unbounded instances of wh-movement such as in (61) and (64) apply in successive cyclic steps, that is wh-movement moves the phrase to the nearest Comp position and from there to the nearest Comp position up till it reaches the target Comp position marked with the feature [+Q]. The derivation outlined in

(64b) becomes the only legitimate derivation for (64a). The one swoop derivation in (63b) is illegitimate on the grounds that it violates the Cyclicity Condition on wh-movement.

There are various ways the Cyclicity Condition can be incorporated into the definition of wh-movement. A simple way of doing this which achieves the desired results if shown in moving wh-XP to Comp provided Comp:

    ⅰ) [+Q]   ([+Q] – Comp Condition)

    ⅱ) not included in a wh-island   (Wh-island Condition)

    ⅲ) not included in a complex NP   (Complex NP Condition)

    ⅳ) the nearest to the wh-phrase   (Cyclicity Condition)

The ungrammatical sentences would be excluded by the revised definition but not by the previous one. In other words, there is some empirical evidence that wh-movement indeed applies successive cyclically rather than in one step. The point to keep in mind is that the Cyclicity Condition imposes a relatively severe locality condition on wh-movement, so that wh-movement is not, strictly speaking, unbounded.

Finally, note that the newly introduced condition seems to clash with the condition that the Comp targeted by wh-movement must be [+Q] ([+Q]-Comp Condition). Consider the examples in (65) and (66). (65) illustrates the familiar fact that belief does not subcategorise for a [+Q]-clause. In view of this, the first step of wh-movement involved in the derivation of (66) appears to target a Comp which is [-Q]:

(65) a. ∗ I believe which problem Mary solved?

     b. ∗ I believe [$_{S'}$[$_{NP}$which problem]$_i$[$_S$ Mary solved [$_{NP}$$t$]$_i$]]

(66) a. Which problem do you believe Mary solved?

     b. [$_{S'}$[$_{NP}$which problem]$_i$ do [$_S$ you believe [$_{S'}$$t_{i'}$[$_S$Mary solved [$_{NP}$$t$]$_i$]]]]

It is possible to solve the problem in such a way as to refer to the Comp position where the wh-phrase finally rests, with the intermediate Comp positions exempted. It is no doubt that there are still other conditions, such as pied piping, extraction islands, adjunct islands, or the coordinate structure constraint, to constrain wh-phrases transform freely. However, the conditions, especially for the subjacency theory, wh-island are the most referred by linguistics to explain the phenomenon of wh-movement.

7.3　Interlanguage theories on wh-movement

Interlanguage is defined as the language produced by a non-native speaker of a language. In 1960s, language learners' proficiency was measured by the degree of correctness in certain formal aspects of L2. In the late 1970s, language testers began to argue that correctness did not indicate much about the learner's ability to use L2. The commonality among these orientations is to document and describe the acquisitional or developmental process of L2 learners, or compare it with that of native speakers. wh-question is an important pattern to check the learners' development of acquisition. For

China EFL learners, English wh-questions, especially for the clauses with wh-words are difficult to be mastered since Chinese is a Wh-in-situ language and there is no wh-movement in general.

7.3.1 The differences between English and Chinese on wh-movement

Languages differ as to where they plan the wh-phrase in simple wh-questions. English obligatorily moves the wh-phrase to [Spec, CP] in overt syntax. Chinese differs radically in that it apparently never moves the wh-phrase to [Spec, CP] in overt syntax.

The movement rules in English to be considered are those of "raising", "lowering", "fronting", and "backing". Wh-movement is the clearest example of a fronting rule that is simultaneously a raising rule. A raising rule will be defined as one that moves some constituent from a lower clause into a higher one, while a fronting rule is one that moves some constituent to clause-initial position. The fronting rule is the one responsible for the surface position of Wh-words in questions and relative clauses. For example:

(67) Tell me which elephant you said Joyce believes Helen tried to tickle.

(68) I fondled the elephant which you said Joyce believes Helen tried to tickle.

Which elephant in (67) originates as the object of *tickle*, as does *which* in (68). The constituent marked with Wh is moved over an essential variable; it is raised and fronted as far as possible consistent with the requirement that it remains in an asymmetric command relationship with the controlling element. The controlling element is a head noun in the case of a relative clause; the governing predicate in the case of an embedded question; and the deleted performative predicate in the case of a direct question (Ross, 1970; Langacker, 1999). While on the other hand, Chinese varies in the extent to which it allows the kind of movement that subjacency is said to apply to and it shows considerably more limited subjacency effects.

Researches on wh-movement have occupied a central place in generative grammar since Chomsky (1977), Rizzi (1990) and Ross (1967) has led to important insights into the nature of transformational operations. In languages like Chinese and Japanese, however, wh-phrases have not to be displaced in overt syntax, as can be seen from comparison between an English sentence (69) and a Chinese example (70):

(69) John wonders [what$_i$ Mary bought t_i].

(70) Zhangsan xiang-zhidao [Lisi mai-le shenme]

      Zhangsan wonder   Lisi bought what

      "Zhangsan wonders what Lisi bought."

Huang (1982a, 1982b) has extended the domain of inquiry by treating wh-in-situ in terms of LF wh-movement. According to Huang's proposal, the wh-phrase in (70) undergoes LF movement after mapping to PF to produce the following LF representations:

(71) Zhangsan xiang-zhidao [$_{CP}$ shenme$_i$ [$_{IP}$ Lisi mai-le t_i]]

      Zhangsan wonder   what   Lisi bought.

Note that the LF represention (71) is parallel to the structure in (69).

Huang's LF movement approach to wh-in-situ in languages like Chinese makes it possible to directly compare wh-in-situ languages with English-type languages where wh-phrases are overtly displaced. One immediate consequence, Huang argues, is that the parallelism can be captured in scope and selection between English-type languages and wh-in-situ languages by looking at the LF representations. Consider the following Chinese examples:

(72) a. Zhangsan yiwei Lisi mai-le shenme?

Zhangsan think Lisi bought what

"What does Zhangsan think Lisi bought?"

b. Zhangsan xiang-zhidao Lisi mai-le shenme?

Zhangsan wonder   Lisi bought what

"Zhangsan wonders what Lisi bought?"

Sentence (72a) must be interpreted as a direct question, whereas (72b) has only the reading of an indirect question where the wh-phrase takes the embedded scope. The situation is analogous to what in English-type languages, as shown in (73):

(73) a. What does John think Mary bought t?

b. * John thinks what Mary bought t.

c. John wonders what Mary bought t.

d. * What does John wonder Mary bought t?

Example (73b) is ungrammatical because the verb *think* selects a declarative clause and is incompatible with a wh-phrase in Spec of its complement CP. (73d) is ruled out because *wonder* takes an interrogative clause and requires a wh-phrase in Spec of its complement CP. Now, if wh-phrases in (72) undergoes LF movement, we have the following possibilities to consider:

(74) a. [$_{CP}$ shenme$_i$] [$_{IP}$ Zhangsan yiwei [$_{CP}$[$_{IP}$ Lisi mai-le t_i]]]]

What   Zhangsan think   Lisi bought

b. Zhangsan yiwei [$_{CP}$ shenme$_i$[$_{IP}$ Lisi mai-le t_i]]

Zhangsan think what Lisi bought

c. Zhangsan xing-zhidao [$_{CP}$ shenme$_i$[$_{IP}$ Lisi mai-le t_i]]

Zhangsan wonder   what   Lisi bought.

d. [$_{CP}$ shenme$_i$[$_{IP}$ Zhangsan xiang-zhidao [$_{CP}$[$_{IP}$ Lisi mai-le t_i]]]]

what   Zhangsan wonder   Lisi bought

Of these, (74b) and (74d) are ruled out for the same reason as (73b) and (73d) are ungrammatical: violation of selectional requirements. Notice that the LF representations in (74) display the same structural pattern as the visible effects of wh-movement in (73). The advantage of the LF movement approach to wh-in-situ is that the selectional restrictions can be stated as straightforward formal conditions on LF representations, applications as straightforward formal conditions on LF representations, applicable to English-type languages as well as to Chinese-type languages. The two types of language simply differ in whether wh-movement takes place in overt syntax or at LF.

The significance of Huang's proposal is, of course, not limited to the statement of selectional properties. His discussion of restrictions on LF movement generated a series of important works dealing with locality of movement (Aoun & Li 1993c, Lasnik & Sanito 1992).

7.3.2   The universal stages of EFL learners' development

The ZISA Project originated the idea that acquisition could be "neatly" divided into six developmental stages. Descriptions and English examples utterances typical of each of these stages are provided below.

Stage 1: The first stage is characterized by the production of single words and formulaic chunks, such as "I don't know". Learners at this stage have not broken chunks into constituents and often use formulaic chunks for a wider range of functions than native speakers. For example, "*I don't know*" means "*I can't*", "*I don't know*" and "*I don't understand*". The emergence of "*do*" in the learners' grammar means almost inevitably through the utterance "*do(n't) know*". It is produced very early and is clearly formulaic. Forms can enter a system before the functions that they ultimately come to index. "*Don't*" shows that formulaic language can serve as a seedbed of propositional language. This implies that the acquisition of chunks is a necessary step in being able to analyze and acquire a grammar.

Stage 2: At this stage learners produce strings of elements, but continue not to be able to recognize the differences between the constituents. The simple strings that the learners produce will be ordered according to meaning or information they focus. As shown in "*The boys throw the shoes?*" or "*It's a monster in the right corner?*"

Stage 3: learners in the third stage are able to identify the beginning and end of the string and can perform operations on the elements in those positions. An example string might be, "*Yesterday, I sick.*" as well as "*I sick yesterday.*" showing the learner's ability to move the element from the end of a string to the beginning and vice versa.

Stage 4: This stage marks the beginning of syntactic operations. Learners at this stage are able to move an element within a string, which she/he has identified to be of a particular type, to either the beginning or the end of the utterance. An example of the learner's production at this stage is "*Can you tell me?*" where the learner has fronted the verb in this yes/no question.

Stage 5: Learners at the fifth stage are now capable of identifying various elements within a string and they begin to shift these elements around in an ordered way inside the string, also called *sentence internal inversion*. An example of this type of operation is the use of inversion in wh-questions, as in "*What are you studying at tech?*" or "*What can you tell me about this course?*" which demonstrate that the wh-word has been fronted and the Auxiliary verbs and modals are in the second position before the subject.

Stage 6: At the final developmental stage learners are able to break down elements within a string of substrings and attach them to other elements. An example of this would include double subject complement constructions like "*He asked me to go*". Other Stage 6 utterances include negative questions, "*Doesn't your cat look black?*" and Tag questions, "*It's on the wall, isn't it?*"

Table 7. 1   **The acquisition orders of questions**

STAGE	DESC RIPTION
1	Single Words
2	SVO? W/Intonation
3	Do-front/ Wh-front
4	Wh-Fronting across Verb/Sub/Aux Inversion for Y/N
5	Aux 2th/Suppletion
6	Tag Question

As described above, acquisition orders apply to many types of syntactic structures as a learner's grammar develops. Given that the focus of the analysis will be solely on questions, Mackey's (1999) expansion of Pienemann and Johnston's descriptions and criterion will provide the basis for assessing the data collection.

Table 7. 2   **The description of the wh-movement stages**

Stage	Description of stages	Example
2	SVO Canonical word order with question intonation	It's a monster? Your cat is black? I draw a house here?
3	Fronting: Wh/Do/Q-word Direct questions with main verbs and some form of fronting	Where the cats are? What the cat doing in your picture? Do you have an animal? Does in this picture there is a cat?
4	Pseudo Inversion: Y/N, Copula In yes/no questions an auxiliary or modal is in sentence initial position. In wh-questions the copula and the subject change positions.	(Y/N) Have you got a dog? (Y/N) Have you drawn the cat? (Cop) Where is the cat in your picture?
5	Do/Aux-second Q-word→Aux/modal → subj(main verb, etc) Auxiliary verbs and modals are placed in second position to wh-questions and (Q-words) and before subject (applies only in main clauses/direct questions)	Why (Q) have (Aux) you (subj) left home? What do you have? Where does your cat sit? What have you got in your picture?

续表

Stage	Description of stages	Example
6	Cancel Inv, Neg Q, Tag Q Cancel Inv: Wh-question inversions are not present in relative clauses. Neg Q: A negated form of do/Aux placed before the subject. Tag Q: An Aux verb and pronoun are attached to the end of main clause.	(Canc Inv) Can you tell me where the cat is? (Neg Q) Doesn't your cat look black? (Neg Q) Haven't you seen a dog? (Tag Q) It's on the wall, isn't it?

Additionally, Mackey (1999) interprets Pienemann et al., as suggesting that "two different usages of two different structures is sufficient evidence that a stage has been acquired" (Mackey, 1999). While there is still debate as to how determine whether or not a learner has acquired a stage, the data analysis will follow Mackey's assumption (1999) that two different structures imply the acquisition of a stage. Hopefully, this issue will ultimately gain consensus with the field of SLA research.

7.3.3　Stages of wh-movement comprehension and production

Based on the classification of English sentences of ZISA project which originated the idea that acquisition of English learning could be "neatly" divided into six developmental stages, and of the one about Question Formation of Mackey's (1999), there will be six stages of development for wh-movement acquisition:

Stage 1. The first stage is characterized by the production of single words and formulaic chunks, and is deeply influenced by the L1. For example, *You like which book?*

Stage 2. The second stage is called wh-fronting stage, in which the direct questions with main verbs and some form of fronting happen. Such as, *where the cats are?/What the cat doing in your picture?*

Stage 3. In this stage, the learners use pseudo inversion: the copula and subject change positions are employed in wh-questions. For example, *Where is the cat in your picture?*

Stage 4. The learners in the fourth stage are capable of identifying various elements within a string and they begin to shift these elements around in an ordered way inside the string, also called sentence internal inversion. The wh-word has been fronted and the Auxiliary verbs and modals are in the second position before the subject which can be shown as wh-word→Aux/modal→subj. For example, *Why have you left home?/What do you have?*

Stage 5. At Stage five, learners are able to break down elements within a string of substrings. For the wh-movement sentences, the cancel inversion is applied, i. e. wh-question inversions are present in relative clauses, such as *Can you tell me what the time it is?*

Stage 6. At Stage six, some special wh-sentences will be grasped by the English learners, i. e. the inversion should not be cancelled as the wh-words are the subjects in a clause, such as *Can you tell me which is the most popular book?* On the other hand, some other wh-sentences, a wh-question without auxiliary word or an interjection sentence, are able to be acquired by the learners eventually. For example, *Why not send me an E-mail? What terrible weather it is!*

As for Chinese university sophomores, most of them have learned English for more than ten years. All six stages of wh-movement have been taught before they entered the university. So supposedly, they would have grasped all six stages of wh-movement. Besides, does each stage clearly depend on the mastery of the operations that characterize the previous stage? Based on the syntactic theories and Mackey's explanation (1999), the study proposes the following hypotheses:

Hypothesis 1: The Chinese EFL learners have grasped all six stages of wh-movement acquisition development when they entered the university.

Hypothesis 2: The effective wh-movement acquisition of each stage clearly depends on the mastery of the operations that characterize the previous stage(s).

7.4 The general tendencies of wh-movement acquisition developmental stages

According to the present educational situation in China, most of the students begin their English learning as early as in the primary school. However, the English knowledge they acquired at school is pretty limited. Many students actually cannot receive formal English instruction until entering the middle school. With the competition of the College Entrance Examination to the University, learners try their best to grasp the grammatical rules systematically. However, because of the complexity of wh-movement rules, most of the Chinese EFL learners still can not arrive at the wh-movement proficiency.

Subjects in this experiment are 31 sophomores from Wuhan University. They are from one natural class of the School of Civil Engineering. They have acquired quite a lot of grammatical knowledge, including wh-movement rules. The experimental design is based on the theory of stages of wh-movement, and a test paper including three kinds of tasks is designed to probe English learners' cognition of wh-movement rules: Multiple Choice Questions (MCQ), Sentence Sequence Task(SST), and Translation from Chinese into English, and there are 20 items in each task. The materials consist of items of six different stages of wh-movement. The items were collected from the Senior High School Entrance Examination, College Entrance Examination, College English Test Band 4 (CET-4), and CET-6 for the past few years.

The data were handled right after the correction of the test. The data collected were input into and processed immediately by SPSS. The following table shows the descriptive statistics of wh-movement developmental stages accuracy for all subjects, including the mean and deviation of each category of developmental stage.

Table 7.3　　　　**Descriptive statistics of wh-movement developmental stage accuracy**

	N	Min	Max	Mean	S D
Stage 1	31	0	2	0.60	0.67
Stage 2	31	0	5	1.80	1.69
Stage 3	31	13	17	15.17	1.18
Stage 4	31	12	17	14.47	1.28
Stage 5	31	11	18	14.93	1.57
Stage 6	31	11	14	13.03	0.80
Valid N	31				

Table 7.3 shows the order of wh-movement acquisition developmental stage accuracy, the sequence from the highest to the lowest is: stage 3, stage 5, stage 4, stage 6, stage 2, and stage 1. Among six developmental stages, Stage 3 is the most preferred by EFL students for Chinese college students (mean = 15.17), and Stage 5 follows closely in the second place (mean = 14.93), and then Stage 4 (mean = 14.47). Stage 6 (mean = 13.03) is quite far away from the first three stages. Stage 2 and Stage 1 got the two lowest scores whose means are 1.8 and 0.6 respectively. Moreover, Stage 1 has the lowest SD (SD = 0.67) among all the developmental stages, which means that the learners are homogeneous to each other as far as this developmental stage is concerned. Stage 2 has the highest SD (SD = 6.925), which indicates that the learners are the most heterogeneous with regard to this developmental stage.

Table 7.4　　　　**Descriptive statistics of the multiple choice questions**

	N	Min	Max	Mean	S D
Stage 1	31	0	1	0.30	0.466
Stage 2	31	0	2	0.33	0.547
Stage 3	31	5	7	5.4	0.621
Stage 4	31	3	7	4.7	0.877
Stage 5	31	3	7	5.97	1.13
Stage 6	31	3	4	3.3	0.466
Valid N	31				

Table 7.4 shows the mastery of wh-movement stages for multiple choice questions. The order of developmental stages accuracy from the highest to the lowest is: stage 5, stage 3, stage 4, stage 6, stage 2, and stage 1 respectively. Among the six developmental stages, Stage 5 (mean = 5.97) and Stage 3 (mean = 5.4) are the two most preferred by learners. Stage 4 and Stage 6 follows them with the means equal 4.7 and 3.3. Stage 2 (mean = 0.33) and Stage 1 (mean = 0.3) get the two lowest scores which are quite far away

from the first four stages. Moreover, both Stage 1 and Stage 6 have the lowest SD (SD = 0.466) among all the developmental stages, which means that the learners are homogeneous to each other as far as these two developmental stages are concerned. Stage 5 has the highest SD (SD = 1.13), which indicates that the learners are the most heterogeneous at this developmental stage.

Table 7.5   **Descriptive statistics of the sentence sequence task**

	N	Min	Max	Mean	S D
Stage 1	31	0	1	0.17	0.397
Stage 2	31	0	3	0.77	0.898
Stage 3	31	3	6	4.63	0.765
Stage 4	31	4	5	4.77	0.43
Stage 5	31	4	5	4.77	0.43
Stage 6	31	4	5	4.9	0.305
Valid N	31				

Table 7.5 indicates the results of the sentence sequence task, the order of developmental stage accuracy from the highest to the lowest is: stage 6, stage 5, stage 4, stage 3, stage 2, and stage 1, which is quite different from the data of the comprehensive test paper and the multiple choice questions. The table indicates that Stage 6 (mean = 4.9) gets the highest score, Stage 5 and 4 have the equal means of 4.77. Stage 2 (mean = 0.77) and Stage 1 (mean = 0.17) get the two lowest scores. Moreover, Stage 6 has the lowest SD (SD = 0.305) among all the developmental stages, which means that the learners are homogeneous to each other as far as this developmental stage is concerned. Stage 2 has the highest SD (SD = 0.898), which indicates that the learners are the most heterogeneous at this stage.

Table 7.6   **Descriptive Statistics of Translation from Chinese into English**

	N	Min	Max	Mean	S D
Stage 1	31	0	1	0.13	0.346
Stage 2	31	0	3	0.70	0.988
Stage 3	31	4	7	5.13	0.507
Stage 4	31	3	7	5.00	0.743
Stage 5	31	2	7	4.20	0.997
Stage 6	31	3	5	4.83	0.461
Valid N	31				

Table 7.6 shows the descriptive data of translation from Chinese into English task of

the six stages for the subjects. The order of developmental stages accuracy from the highest to the lowest is: stage 3, stage 4, stage 6, stage 5, stage 2, and stage 1. The data are quite different from the comprehensive results.

The above data indicate that among the six developmental stages, Stage 3 is the best mastered by the subjects with a mean which equals 5. 13. Stage 4 follows closely in the second place (mean = 5. 00), and then followed by stage 6 (mean = 4. 83) and stage 5 (mean = 4. 20) whose means are not quite far away from each other. Stages 2 and 1 get the two lowest scores whose means are 0. 70 and 0. 13. Moreover, Stage 1 has the lowest SD (SD = 0. 346) among all the developmental stages, which means that the college students are homogeneous to each other as far as this developmental stage is concerned. Stage 2 has the highest SD (SD = 0. 997), which concludes that the learners are the most heterogeneous with regard to this developmental stage.

The reasons of the phenomenon will be explored and elaborated based on the above data in order to answer the hypotheses.

Hypothesis 1: The Chinese EFL learners have grasped all six stages of wh-movement acquisition development when they entered the university.

If the data is analyzed according to the guideline "two different usages of two different structures is sufficient evidence that a stage has been acquired" (Mackey, 1999), it seems that the learners all have grasped the rules of six stages of wh-movement since nearly all of them can use two different structures of the every stage. Even though there are some mistakes or ungrammatical sentences during the processes, most of them can accurately choose, compose or translate different structures of wh-movement sentences at all stages. For instance, at Stage 3, the simple structure " *how-the-much-are-rooms* " can be composed by subjects as "*How much are the rooms?*". Besides, for the more difficult one "*kind-job-you-searching-for-are-of-what*", it is also rewritten as the correct structure "*what kind of job are you searching for?*" At Stage 4, in the multiple choice question task, nearly all of them can choose the right answers from the wrong ones, which are formed by different structures, such as "*Why do you suggest us buy a new machine?*" "*With whom will you go to the cinema?*" More mistakes appear at Stage 5 and 6; however, the learners still have some knowledge about two different usages for two different structures. At Stage 5, they can choose the right sentences for different structures: "*Do you know when the train will arrive?*" and "*Could you tell me who you are waiting for?*" At stage 6, they can compose different sentence structures, for example, "*Why not send me an E-mail?*" and "*How to solve the problem is very important*", and "*What terrible weather it is!*" The data from 7. 1 to 7. 4 in the four instrument-column diagrams elaborate and support Hypothesis 1.

Figure 7. 1 shows the mean score of *wh-movement developmental stage accuracy*. For the whole test paper, the highest score 15. 17 comes from stage 3, and the smallest score is 13. 03, 14. 93 of Stage 4 and 14. 47 of Stage 3. For the three tasks of the test paper, 5 items for each stage. So it is possible that the learners have performed quite well at all developmental stages. Figure 7. 2 shows the mean score of the multiple choice question

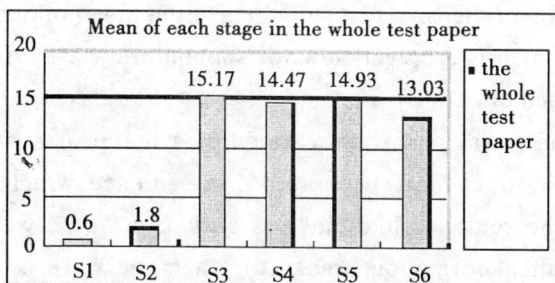

Figure 7.1   The mean score of wh-movement developmental stage accuracy

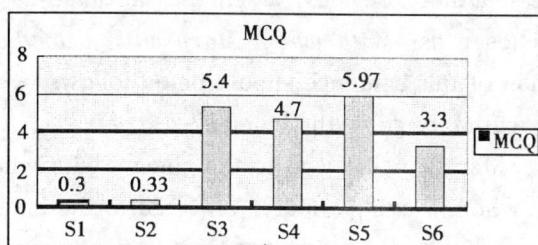

Figure 7.2   The mean score of wh-movement developmental stages in multiple choice question task

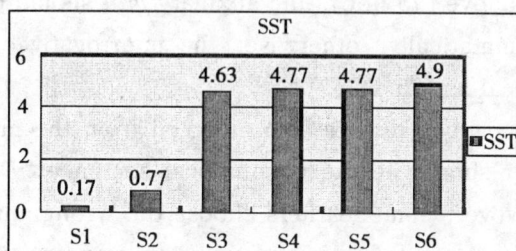

Figure 7.3   The mean score of wh-movement developmental stage in the sentence sequence task

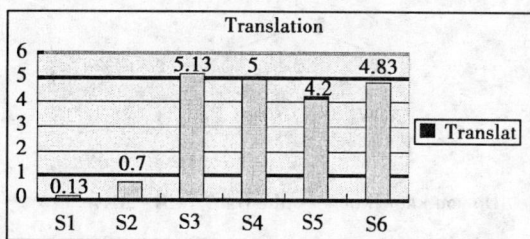

Figure 7.4   The mean score of wh-movement developmental stage in the translation task

task from 5.4, 4.7, 5.97 to 3.3, among which the highest score lies at Stage 5. Figure 7.3 explores the mean score in the sentence sequence task from 4.63, 4.77, and 4.77 to 4.9, indicating the relatively balanced statistics. Figure 7.4 proves the result of the translation task from 5.13, 5, 4.2 to 4.83, among which the highest score is at Stage 3.

The above analysis shows that the learners have all grasped the rules of six stages of wh-movement. However, if the accuracy rate is taken into consideration, the problem is quite evident. For the comprehensive test (60 items), the mean of accuracy is 52, with the accuracy rate 86.7%, which is relatively low for sophomores based on the requirements of the college English curriculum.

However, the learners still make many kinds of syntactical mistakes. For example, "*that-who-speaking-is (who is that speaking?)*", a sentence which belongs to Stage 3, several subjects wrote the sentence like "*who is speaking that?*" which is the mistake at Stage 2. The ungrammatical formation breaks the thematic roles as well. Some learners consider "*speak*" as a transitive verb with two theta roles, the external agent *who*, and internal role *that*. However, as an intransitive verb in this sentence, *speak* cannot be followed with *that* in the sentence. Besides, a sentence at Stage 4 "*With whom will Mary go to the cinema*" was chosen as "*With whom Mary will go to the cinema*" (stage 2). Actually the transformation of this sentence should be as follows:

(75) a. With whom will Mary go to the cinema?

b. DS: $[_{CP}$ e $[_{NP}$ Mary $[_{I'}$ will $[_{VP}$ go to the cinema with whom$]]]]$

c. SS: $[_{CP}$ With whom$_i$ $[_{C'}$ will$_j$ $[_{NP}$ Mary $[_{I'}$ t_j $[_{VP}$ go to the cinema $t_i]]]]]$

d. $*[_{CP}$ With whom$_i$ $[_{NP}$ Mary $[_{I'}$ will $[_{VP}$ go to the cinema $t_i]]]]$

As is showed in the above (75 b&c), the auxiliary *will* should be transformed in front of the subject *Mary* grammatically, otherwise, the interrogative without auxiliary *will*-movement is ungrammatical as (75 d).

Apart from that, some mistakes are also emerged from the multiple choice question task. The correct answer should be the grammatical sentence "*Do you know when the train will arrive?*", however, some learners choose the wrong answer "*∗ Do you know when will the train arrive?*" and the tree diagram of this grammatical sentence should be as follows.

(76)

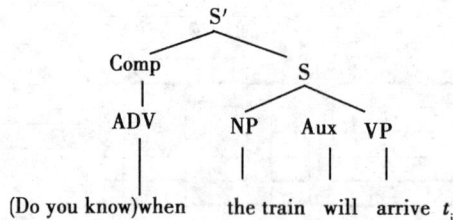

Following the above diagram, the transformation of the sentence can be shown in the following examples:

(77) a. Do you know when the train will arrive?

b. $[_S$ Do you know $[_{S'} [_{ADV}$ when$]_i$ $[_S$ the train will arrive$[_{ADV}$ $t_i]]]]$

c. $*[_S$ Do you know $[_{S'} [_{ADV}$ when$]_i$ $[_S [_{AUX}$ will$]_j$ $[_{NP}$ the train $t']_j$ arrive$[_{ADV}$ $t_i]]]]$

The transformation cannot be processed if the auxiliary *will* miss the subject *the train*, because the sentence could not be formed grammatically when *will* were placed in front of the subject as in the above example (77c).

The reasons of the above phenomena may fall into two aspects. To begin with, while developmental acquisition orders do map out the learners' acquisition in general, there are some individual differences between learners, particularly due to their mother tongues (L1). Additionally, while influential, the characteristics and syntactic structures of the L1 cannot necessarily explain or predict L2 acquisition. According to the data collected in the SAMPLE and ZISA projects, the Spanish speakers have to pass through several developmental stages before mastering German inversion, despite its existence in their L1. However, Polish learners of English are shown not to omit "to be" before adjectives, a pattern which also occurs in Polish. The Vietnameses language, on the other hand, does not use any equivalent of "to be" before adjectives, and the Vietnamese learners in the SAMPLE study omit *be* in the preverbal position nearly 80% in some cases and the number of cases was never low (Pienemann & Johnston, 1987). Meisel and Pienemann (1981) describe this phenomenon of variability as vulnerability of interlanguage due to characteristics of L1.

Another reason of this phenomenon lies in the perspective of fossilization. The term "fossilization" is introduced by Selinker (1972). He defines fossilization as "the long term persistence of plateaus of non-target-like structure in the interlanguage of non-native speakers (even those who are fluent speakers of L2) has been called fossilization". Since he first put forward this definition, many modifications and versions of that definition have been developed by SLA researchers, among which Han's (2000) opinion is one worth attention. He argues that even if language learners are constantly exposed to the input of the target language, fully motivated to learn the target language and provided with enough opportunities to practice that language, fossilization may still occur (cited by Yang Ling, 2002). Since the learners have had less pressure on studying English after their enrolling to the college, they do not practice grammar rules systematically any more, and no training on the wh-movement. In particular, the college English teaching strategies and methods are quite different from that of the middle school, but the listening and speaking abilities are much more emphasized. So it is possible for them to forget some special rules about wh-movement and the fossilization happens. As a matter of fact, in terms of the classification of fossilization into Temporary Fossilization and Permanent Fossilization provided by Selinker, the general stagnancy of learners' wh-movement rules should come under the type of Temporary Fossilization. For the EFL learners in China, especially for non-English majors, their fossilization mostly belongs to temporary fossilization, namely, stabilization. Factors causing this stabilization may include negative transfer, misuse of learning strategies, low quality of input, and lack of cross-cultural knowledge.

Hypothesis 2: The effective wh-movement acquisition of each stage clearly depends on mastery of the operations that characterize the previous stage(s).

The results of data analysis confirm that the tendency of the learners' acquisition on wh-movement developmental stages may depend on mastery of operations that characterize the previous stage(s). The tendencies of the learners' cognition of the wh-movement are manifested from Figures 7. 5 to 7. 8.

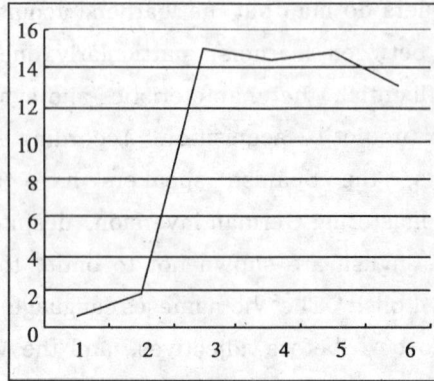

Figure 7. 5   The tendency of wh-movement developmental stages

The results of Figure 7. 5 show that the curves of the learners' acquisition of the wh-movement are in an extremely unbalanced way. The mean of Stage 3 is the highest among the stages, followed by Stage 5, Stage 4 and Stage 6. It shows that there is no even tendency of increase or decrease progressing pace during the learners' wh-movement acquisition process.

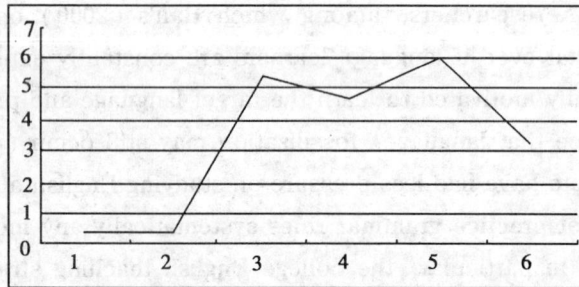

Figure 7. 6   The tendency of wh-movement developmental stages in the multiple choice question task

Figure 7. 6 manifests the tendency of wh-movement developmental stages in multiple choice question task. The mean of Stage 5 is the highest, Stage 3 and Stage 4 followed closely, while Stage 6 is the lowest. The curve in Figure 7. 6 is similar with that in Figure 7. 5, while the curve in Stage 3 is a little higher than that of Stage 5 in Figure 7. 5 and the curve in Stage 3 is much lower than that of Stage 5 in Figure 7. 6.

Figure 7. 7 shows the tendency of wh-movement developmental stages in the sentence sequence task. The mean of Stage 6 is the highest, followed by Stage 5, Stage 4 and Stage 6, which is quite different from the curves in Figures 7. 5 and 7. 6.

Figure 7. 8 manifests the tendency of wh-movement developmental stages in the task

Chapter 7 The Developmental Stages of Wh-movement Acquisition

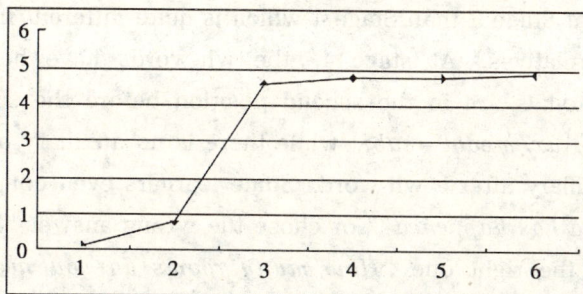

Figure 7.7 The tendency of wh-movement developmental stages in sentence sequence task

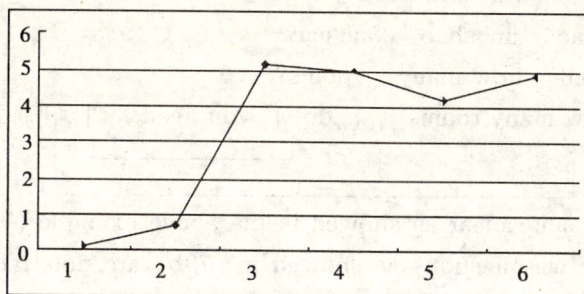

Figure 7.8 The tendency of wh-movement developmental stages in the translation task

of translation from Chinese into English. The mean of Stage 3 is the highest, which is the same as the data in Figure 7.5, however, different from that figure, Stage 4 follows Stage 3 closely and then Stage 6 and Stage 5. So there is no even tendency of increasing or decreasing progressive pace of the learners during their wh-movement acquisition process.

The results are influenced by the different tasks. The multiple choice question task is the very task that has the most mistakes, in which the error-rate is 62%. Translation task has the error-rate 21%, and the sentence sequence task consists of the error-rate 12%. From the above data, it is evident that different tasks influence the result to a great degree. For the sentence sequence task, it is much easier for the learners to write grammatical sentences in accordance with the wh-movement rules. But for multiple choice questions, the learners will make mistakes when they have to do a comparison. For example, most of them can rearrange the sentence "*The important thing is who can help me now*". However, for the multiple choice question "*Excuse me, can you tell me _____*", the majority of them cannot distinguish the right sentence "*which is the most popular book*" from the wrong ones "*how can I use the telephone*", "*where is the washing room*" and "*when is the shop closed*".

Secondly, the results are influenced by their mother tongue-Chinese. The learners have done much better if the sentence pattern is similar with that of the Chinese. For example, the tendency of Stage 3 in the sentence sequence task is higher than that of Stage 4 compared with the other three figures. That's because of the transference of the Chinese language. Stage 3 is the pseudo inversion, the copula and subject change positions are employed in wh-questions. The copula also exists in Chinese that's why the learners can perform much better at Stage 3 than Stage 4 which is quite different from Chinese rules of wh-questions or wh-relatives. At stage 4, the wh-words have been fronted and the auxiliary verbs and modals are in the second position before the subject which can be shown as *wh-word →Aux/modal→subj*, while there is no auxiliary or modal in Chinese, let alone that DO auxiliary after a wh-word. Some learners even composed the sentences like this *"What I asked has happened?"* or chose the wrong answer *"You need how many rooms?"* rather than the right one *"How many rooms do you need?"* The distinction between Chinese and English in the transformation process of wh-movement just as follows:

(78) How many rooms do you need?

(79) a. Ni   xuyao   duoshao   fangjian?

     b. You   need   how many   rooms?

     c. "[$_S$[$_{NP}$how many rooms]$_i$[$_{Aux}$do]$_j$[$_{S'}$you need$t$, t']$_{i, j}$] ?"

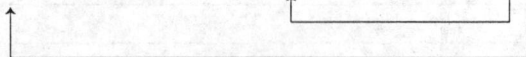

The difference is quite clear as showed in the above example (78) and (79a, b&c). The words in Chinese wh-questions as showed in (79b) are not transformed at all from (79a), while two phrases in the English wh-questions as showed in (79c) are transformed since the noun phrase *how many rooms* and auxiliary *do* are all transformed in the initial position of the sentence respectively to from a syntactically grammatical English wh-question sentence.

Thirdly, it is very difficult for the learners to master some special English sentence patterns at any developmental stages. The complex transformation process of the wh-movement that many learners make mistakes is *"What have I done makes you feel so unhappy?"* Both sentences (80) and (81) include the verb *know* which subcategorises for either a [+Q] or a [-Q] clause. The complement clause is interrogative in (80) and declarative in (81). In (80), it is the root sentence which is interrogative:

(80) a. I have done what does make you feel unhappy.

     b. I have done [$_{S'}$[$_{NP}$what]$_i$[$_S$[$_{NP}$ t]$_i$ does make you feel unhappy]]

(81) a. What have I done make you feel unhappy?

     b. [$_{S'}$[$_{NP}$what]$_i$ have I done [$_{S'}$[$_{NP}$$t$]$_i$[$_S$ make you feel unhappy]]]

The sentence (80) is an indirect question and (81) is a direct question. The derivation of (81) is partially similar to that of (80). The wh-phrase in (83) moves first to the position occupied by the wh-phrase in (80), i. e. the Comp of the embedded clause, then to the Comp of the root clause. This more detailed derivation is shown in (82):

(82) a. What have I done make you feel so unhappy?

     b. [$_{S'}$[$_S$[$_{NP}$what]$_{i,j}$ have I done[$_{NP}$$t$]$_i$][$_S$[$_{NP}$$t'$]$_j$ make you feel unhappy]]]]

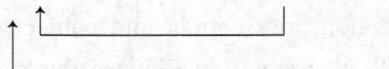

The trace i in the embedded Comp position is marked to distinguish the initial trace in the original object position of the wh-phrase j. Just as the initial trace j marks the position from which the wh-phrase has passed on its way to the root clause, traces are sometimes said to encode the "history of movement". The complex transformation in (82) gives an example to obstruct the wh-movement acquisition for Chinese EFL learners to some degree.

There are some special sentence patterns that do not follow the general rules of wh-movement development, and this kind of phenomenon will mislead the learners to follow the normal rules, the wh-phrases such as preposition + wh-word seem beyond the understanding of the learners. For example, some learners chose the wrong answer *"Will Mary with whom go to the cinema?"* since the preposition mislead them to judge the right sentence pattern *"With whom will Mary go to the cinema?"* Syntactically, the transformation of this sentence is shown in the following diagram (83):

(83)

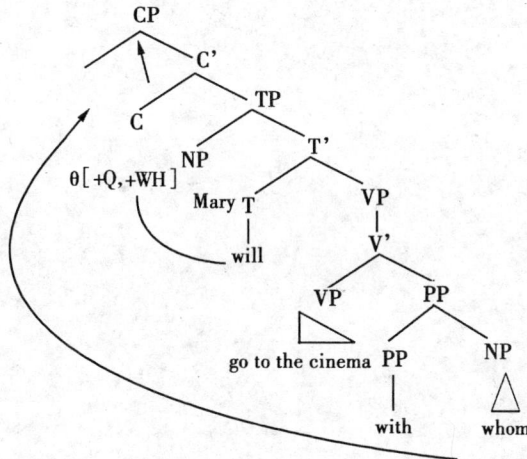

Another distinct example is the *"do you think"*-sentence- pattern. It is ruled that, in a wh-question with *do you think* as a parenthesis, the interrogative sentence should follow the declarative sentence words order. For example, *"Where do you think ＿＿ ·he ＿＿ the computer?"*, the right answer should be "/, bought" since the sentence should be "where do you think he bought the computer?" which follows the declarative sentence words order. But nearly all of the subjects chose the wrong answer, because they believe that the sentence should follow the rules that "wh-word→Aux/modal→subj". This is also the wh-island phenomenon. The transformation of that wh-question is as follows:

(84) a. Where do you think he bought the computer?

　　 b. [s[Where i do [s you think [s·(that)[s he bought the computer t_i]]]]]

　　 c. *[s[Where i do [s you think [s·did j[s he [$t_j$buy the computer t_i]]]]]]

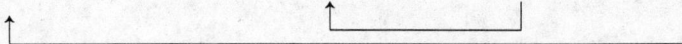

Based on the theories of wh-island in wh-movement process, wh-phrases should be moved to Comp provided Comp is [+Q], and the (84b) follows the rule, while the sentence (84c) is ungrammatical since the auxiliary phrase does obstruct wh-word that is moved to the Comp position.

The conclusion may be safely drawn that there is no rule on the trend of each stage, and the effective wh-movement acquisition of each stage does not clearly depend on the mastery of the operations that characterize the previous stage(s). The phenomenon mainly falls into the factors of different tasks during testing; interlanguage, especially the great gap between Chinese and English wh-movement, and the complex syntactical structures of wh-questions or embeded wh-clauses.

Chapter 8

Markedness Effects on Morphology and Syntax Acquisition

The acquisition of linguistic marked features is an important indication of language learners' linguistic competence. Research on the acquisition and use of marked features can help learners better understand the role and effects of markedness so as to enhance their efficiency in acquiring those marked features and improve their linguistic competence. There are two tendencies in markedness research: one is in the framework of Universal Grammar (UG), with its focus on the markedness effects on the acquisitional order of different linguistic features, and the other is in the framework of linguistic typology, focusing mainly on the markedness effects on learning difficulty and language transfer. Such studies have been carried out in two areas: research on how second language learners acquire linguistic marked features and linguistic markedness effects on the acquisitional order of different linguistic elements in a natural environment; and research on linguistic markedness effects on the learning difficulty experienced by foreign language learners and language transfer in formal instruction settings.

The research on the acquisition of morphology and syntax by Chinese learners of English is based on the typological markedness theory. The present study investigates the use of marked features by 90 Chinese EFL learners and the learning difficulty they experience, and provides possible strategies to enhance their learning efficiency. Employing a translation test, a writing test and a cloze test, the study collects the data of verb inflection and word order use by three groups of Chinese EFL learners with different language proficiency levels (low level, intermediate level and advanced level), and analyzes the types of errors, the number of errors and the ratio of errors in different tasks by different groups. The statistic analyses of the data show a significant effect of linguistic markedness on second language acquisition and a correlation between language proficiency and language transfer of marked/unmarked features.

8.1　Linguistic analysis of markedness

Inflection is an important concept in language, which is expressed by various devices. English is one of the inflective languages in which the form of a word changes to show a change in meaning or grammatical function. In morphology, inflection refers to the process of adding an affix to a word or changing it in some other ways according to the rules of the grammar of a language. Verb inflection is an inflection on verbs that indicates the tense or aspect. The tense system marks time, and in English, it is marked on the first verb in a tense verb group. With most English verbs, the -s inflection marks the present tense; the -ed inflection marks the past tense; the -ing marks the aspect. Verbs using -ed forms are known as "regular" verbs in that those verbs employ the most common, most "productive" inflection to mark the simple past tense, as in *help/helped*, *walk/walked*, *ask/asked*. "Irregular verbs," on the other hand, fall into some classes employing no particular inflections at all, such as *go/went*, *take/took*, *put/put*.

Most morphological theories distinguish between inflectional and derivational processes. Inflectional processes generally involve elements of word structure that are related to grammar such as marking for tense, number, gender, and case. Languages vary in the extent to which this grammatical information is morphologically encoded. In French, verbs are marked for tense, number, gender, and argument structure, resulting in a complex and highly regular verbal inflectional system. In English, verbs are only marked for tense, number and aspect, and in Chinese, verbs are marked for neither tense nor number. Inflectional processes apply in accordance with sentence structures (in English, the subject noun of a sentence has to agree in number with the verb; a failure to do so results in ungrammaticality) and do not alter the core meaning or grammatical class of the inflected stem. Inflectional processes can be viewed as generating classes of systematically related word forms from a basic stem/root form via a small set of morphological operations. Inflectional processes are also highly productive in the sense that they apply to all the words in a language with new words "automatically" receiving a so-called regular "default" treatment. For example, all verbs in English are marked for tense and new verbs generally receive the regular -ed past tense suffix (e. g. *faxed*, *emailed*).

In contrast, derivational processes are more open-ended and involve the creation of new words from other words and morphemes, often resulting in changes in grammatical category. For example, in English, the suffix -ly can be used to form adverbs from adjectives: *glad/gladly*, *poor/poorly*, etc. and derivational processes do not apply across the board (e. g. the suffix -ly cannot be added to adjectives such as *tall*, *old*, *young*). Historically, the more regular nature of inflectional processes suggests that the relation among morphemes, meanings, and word forms can be more easily explained in the area of inflectional morphology than in the area of derivational morphology.

Word order refers to the arrangement of words in a sentence, and the position of a word in a sentence often specifies its function. Languages often differ in their word orders, but some word orders are considered to be basic in languages, such as SVO and SOV (Greenberg, 1966, as cited in Yu, 2004). In English interrogative sentences, the word order follows this pattern: an interrogative word—an auxiliary verb—the subject. The first word is either an interrogative word (e. g. *what*, *who*, *when*, *where*, *how*, etc.) or an auxiliary verb (e. g. *is*, *are*, *do*, *shall*, etc.). The subject comes after the interrogative word or the auxiliary verb, except when the interrogative word is the subject or part of the subject, for example, *Who broke the cup? Which cup is yours?* In contrast with English,

Chinese interrogative sentences have the same word order as the declarative sentences, having the question word "*ma*" at the end of the sentence, and the position of interrogative words is flexible, while wh-movement is English-specific as wh-words are invariably at the beginning of a sentence to indicate an English interrogative sentence.

There have been different definitions of markedness. One definition of markedness derives from Chomsky's theory of Universal Grammar, which distinguishes the rules of a language that are core and periphery. Core rules are those that can be arrived at through the application of general, abstract principles of language structure, which Chomsky and other generative linguists have held to be innate. Basic word order SVO, for example, is considered part of the core. Peripheral rules are rules that are not governed by universal principles; they are idiosyncratic, reflecting their unique historical origins. For example, the structure "*the more... the more...*" is an example of a peripheral rule in English. It can be seen that this notion of "markedness" is defined in terms of complexity, relative infrequency of use or departure from something that is more basic, typical, or canonical in a language. One argument for treating masculine members of pairs like *man/woman* and *waiter/waitress* as unmarked forms is the fact that English adds forms to produce the morphologically more complex feminine form. The feminine form is therefore marked. Similarly, morphemes are added to distinguish past from present, plural from singular, and so on, suggesting that present and singular are unmarked, past and plural are marked.

Another definition of markedness is found in language typology. Markedness can be ascertained typologically when cross-linguistic comparisons of languages show that the presence of some linguistic feature implies the presence of another feature. The identification of typological universality has also been used to make claims about which features are marked and which ones are unmarked. The broad claim is that those features that are universal or present in most languages are unmarked, while those that are specific to a particular language or found in only a few languages are marked. Some languages have a specific feature, whereas some other languages do not have such a specific feature, suggesting that languages with the specific feature are marked, and languages without such a specific feature is unmarked. In other words, typological markedness refers to the linguistic features which are in one language, but not in another (Rutherford, 1982; Gass, 1984; Hyltenstam, 1990).

Underlying the two markedness definitions is the notion that some linguistic features are special in relation to others which are more basic. Thus the core of the markedness theory is that in the languages of the world certain linguistic elements are more basic, natural, and frequent (unmarked) than others which are referred to as "marked". Typological markedness calls for a systematic comparison of the target and native language and of the universal markedness relations. In contrast with English, there is no verb inflection to mark temporal relationship in Chinese, and Chinese verbs do not inflect for number, tense or aspect as they do in English (Liu, 2000). The temporal references in Chinese are most commonly made through context, temporal adverbials or functional words such as *zhuo*, *liao*, and *guo*. In addition, even if Chinese learners are aware of the grammatical constructions needed, they may not be able to physically produce verb inflections correctly. Teaching and learning practice has shown that many Chinese EFL learners, even at the advanced level, seems to have repeated difficulties in perceiving and producing correct verb infections, especially when attempting a fluent conversation. It is, therefore, worth noting that the above problems are frequently associated not only with L1-L2 differences but with the effects of L2 markedness. On the other hand, the word order in Chinese interrogative sentences is different from that in English interrogative sentences. As for the simple interrogative sentences (*yes/no* questions), Chinese interrogative sentences have the same word order as the declarative sentences, having the functional word *ma* at the end of the sentences; in special interrogative sentences (wh-questions), the position of interrogative words is flexible in Chinese as they can be at the beginning, in the middle or at the end of the sentences, for example, *shen me shi hou kai shi bi sai? ni wei shen me da ta? ni xi huan chi shen me?* While wh-movement is English-specific as wh-words are invariably at the beginning of the sentences to indicate an English interrogative sentence. Drawing on the above analyses, it can be found that English is more marked than Chinese on both the verb inflection of the simple past and the word order in interrogative sentences.

8.2 Markedness theories

Markedness generally refers to the theory that in the languages of the world certain linguistic elements are more basic, natural, and frequent (unmarked) than others which are referred to as "marked". In English, sentences which have the word order SVO, such as *I dislike such people*, are considered to be unmarked, whereas sentences which have the word order OSV, e. g. *Such people I dislike*, are considered to be marked. The concept of markedness has been discussed in several ways, and different linguists have proposed different theories on the basis of the implications of markedness. Among them are three typical representatives: Chomsky, Eckman and Kellerman.

8.2.1 Chomsky's markedness theory

How do learners distinguish the input they receive and relate it to their existing knowledge? One of the possible explanations is that they may possess a special linguistic faculty that enables them to operate on the input data in order to discover the L2 rules in maximally efficient ways. Chomsky (1965) describes this linguistic faculty as a "language acquisition device" (LAD) that contains knowledge of linguistic universals. The study of linguistic universals has contributed to explanations of SLA in two ways. First, it has been proposed that the properties of the target language vary in how difficult they are to acquire, according to whether they are universal or language-specific. That is, those properties of the target language which are common to many or all languages are easy to learn in comparison to those properties that are found in few languages, or only in the target language. This approach involves a consideration of just the target language. The second approach involves a comparison of the target and native languages. Chomsky (1965, 1986) seeks to identify linguistic universals by the in-depth study of a single language. He argues that only in this way is it possible to discover the highly abstract principles of grammar that constrain the form of any specific grammar. He refers to these principles as Universal Grammar (UG). His explanation for the innateness of UG is that without a set of innate principles it would not be possible for a child to learn the grammar of his mother tongue. Those rules that the child discovers with the aid of UG form the core grammar of his language. However, not all rules are core rules. Every language contains elements that are not constrained by UG. These consist of peripheral rules.

Related to the concepts of core and periphery is Chomsky's theory of markedness. Core rules are those that can be arrived at through the application of general abstract principles of language structure. Peripheral rules are rules that are not governed by universal principles; they are language-specific, reflecting their unique historical origins. Core rules are unmarked; that is, they accord with the general tendencies of language. Peripheral rules are marked; that is, they are exceptional in some way. Abundant researches on UG-based definition of markedness have been carried out and provided robust evidence for the relationship between markedness and L2 acquisition order, suggesting that learners acquire the unmarked structures earlier than the marked ones, and the level of accuracy in the marked pattern increases with rising proficiency (Mazurkewich, 1985; Kellerman, 1987; Flynn & O'Neill, 1988; Hawkins, 1987; White, 1992).

Chomskyan accounts of the markedness theory state that L2 learners find it easier to learn core rules than language-specific rules, and it has also been suggested that the effect of L1 transfer may be restricted to non-core features. That is, if learners discover that an L2 rule is not in agreement with a universal rule, they will seek to interpret that rule in terms of the equivalent rule in their L1.

8.2.2   Eckman's markedness theory

Differences in the success of L1 learners as opposed to L2 learners have been documented in the literature for over two thousand years (Gass, 1989). However, it wasn't until recently that researchers made a lasting impact on how we view these differences. As early as the 1940s, Fries (1945) proposed the Contrastive Analysis Hypothesis (CAH) (later refined by Lado, 1957, as cited in Rod Ellis 1985), in which he introduced success in a learner's second language proficiency as a matter of the similarities and differences between the native and target languages. Those aspects of the second language that are similar to those in the native language are more easily acquired, while those dissimilar would prove more challenging. But later on, some empirical studies showed that L1-L2 differences do not always result in learning difficulty. In an attempt to reconcile the Contrastive Analysis Hypothesis (CAH) with the findings in empirical research since the 1940s and 1950s (more specifically Dulay and Burt, 1974), markedness, especially typological markedness, has been incorporated as a viable tool in explaining learning difficulty in SLA (Jordens, 1980; Bailey, 1989; Eckman, 1977, 1985;

Mazurkewich, 1985; Larsen-Freeman & Long, 1991). One of the most interesting studies dealing with markedness in SLA is that of Eckman (1977), who incorporates the notion of typological markedness as an interlingual framework of identifying phonological difficulty between two languages and puts forward the Markedness Differential Hypothesis (MDH). According to his theory, not only is native language interference a factor in determining the extent to which a second language is acquired, but he also proposes that inconsistencies in language acquisition not accounted for by CAH are the result of markedness relationships between the two languages; those aspects of the target language (TL) which are more marked than those in the native language (NL) will prove more difficult, while those aspects which are less marked will prove less challenging for the second language learners. The predictions made by the MDH were identified in a number of empirical studies of second language acquisition involving markedness relationships in phonological acquisition and morphological as well as syntactic acquisition (Thomas, 1989; Schachter, 1973, 1988; Zobl, 1983). Eckman's notion, the Markedness Differential Hypothesis (MDH), has since been employed as a theoretical basis for a variety of studies (Anderson, 1985; Berent, 1985; Rutherford, 1982, 1983).

In the first of these studies, Greenberg (1966) (as cited in Eckman, 1985) looks at how universal empirical generalizations can be linked to adult language learning. His findings, in support of Eckman's (1977) Markedness Differential Hypothesis, show a direct relationship between marked features of language phonology and their relative ease, or difficulty of acquisition. Similarly, Schachter (1973) argues for a markedness relationship in the process of first language phonological acquisition, and is able to extend the scope of this influence specifically to the same process in second language acquisition. This is explained in the "theory of opposition", in which he claims that it is not single sounds that are important, but rather, sound distinctions, moving in an order from those least marked to those most marked. These sound distinctions will again have to be discerned by the learner when acquiring the phonological system of L2, proceeding in the same fashion, from least to most marked. He asserts that the markedness relationships revealed in first language phonological acquisition, therefore, mirror those in second language acquisition. In response to this theory, Eckman (1977) extends this idea to general SLA: "Through the incorporation of markedness, the MDH can account for why some L2 errors resemble errors made during the acquisition of TL as an L1".

To support the prediction, Eckman (1985) reanalyzes the data on interlanguage syntax in Schachter (1973), showing that the degree of difficulty with English relative clauses experienced by each of the four groups in that study—Farsi, Arabic, Chinese and Japanese speakers — reflects the relative distance of their L1 from English. There have been some developments of Eckman's proposal. In a related but independent study, Gass (1984) sets out to study language transfer and linguistic markedness, looking for evidence of the effect of universal grammatical relations independent of L1 transfer. She shows that when the L2 rule is marked, the learner will turn to his L1, particularly if his L1 has an equivalent unmarked rule. In SLA there is plentiful evidence suggesting that transfer is most likely to occur when the L1 construction is unmarked. (Hammarberg, 1979; Zobl, 1980, 1983; Kellerman, 1987; White, 1987; Doughty, 1991).

8.2.3 Kellerman's markedness theory

From the perspective of psycholinguistics, Kellerman (1979, 1987) investigates the relationship between markedness and transfer, and shows that whether or not learners actually transfer a form depends in part on how likely they think it to be acceptable in another language, or their perception of the L1-L2 "distance", i. e. how marked its use in their own L1 appears to them. He presents adult Dutch speakers with grammatical English sentences which contain twenty Dutch idiomatic expressions in translation, and asks them which usages they think are acceptable and unacceptable in English. He finds that they improve in their ability to identify acceptable and unacceptable idioms with increasing proficiency but, especially at lower proficiency levels, are conservative in their judgments. In another study, Gass and Selinker (1983) find that ESL learners judge sentences illustrating core uses of progressive aspect, such as *He is working now*, as more acceptable than sentences containing more peripheral uses, such as *He is leaving tomorrow*.

In a second experiment, Kellerman (1979) tests the hypothesis that core and unmarked meanings of a word will be transferred before others. For example, learners will expect *blue* to be more likely to signify a *color* in a second language than *depression*, *jazz* or *pornographic*. Kellerman concludes from his studies, combined with those of other linguists, that transfer is a strategy available to compensate for lack of L2 knowledge. However, its use with idioms, lexis and syntax, at least, and probably with all aspects of language except phonology, will be constrained by the learner's perception of L1-L2 distance, with marked forms being potentially less transferable than unmarked ones.

A learner's proficiency level also seems to be a relevant factor in determining when transfer will occur. Kellerman (1983) notes interesting examples in his and Jorden's (1980) data of the so-called "U-shaped behavior". Beginners are more willing to transfer marked items along with unmarked ones, perhaps recognizing general typological similarities between L1s and L2s. Intermediate learners are more conservative about transferring marked uses, possibly because they have committed enough errors by this stage to know that, while similar, the languages really differ in detail a great deal. Finally, advanced learners once again become willing to assume transferability. Error frequency in the three phases, consequently, is initially low, then rises, and finally falls again. Accuracy, conversely, is initially high, and then falls, finally rises again, giving the "U" shape to a graphic representation of the performance data.

Markedness theory provides a basis for solving some of the problems of the CAH. In particular, it can help to explain why some differences between the native and target language lead to learning difficulty, while other differences do not. Learning difficulty generally results from L1-L2 differences involving greater L2 markedness, not from differences involving less L2 markedness, with the degree of difficulty reflecting the degree of markedness. When L1 transfer occurs, it seems to be constrained by linguistic markedness: Transfer of L1 unmarked forms is more likely than transfer of its marked ones; and transfer of marked forms may occur, however, if the L2 form is also marked.

The present study focuses on Eckman's typological notion of markedness and Kellerman's notion of markedness and transfer. Because, on the one hand, Chinese and English belong to different language families and it is appropriate to make a contrastive analysis on the basis of the elaborate comparisons of Chinese and English; on the other hand, learners often possess a set of perceptions about the distance between their native language and the target language, and it is their perception that triggers or constrains transfer.

8.3　First language transfer in second language acquisition

The term "transfer" is initially borrowed from educational psychology where it has served for many years to describe the human tendency to generalize what has been learnt in one situation to other situations. Kellerman (1987) suggests that the term be restricted to "those processes that lead to the incorporation of elements from one language into another". Odlin (1989) has broadened the definition of language transfer and offers that transfer is the influence resulting from the similarities and differences between the target language and any other language that has been previously acquired. Much effort has gone into identifying the conditions under which transfer is likely to occur.

In the field of Second Language Acquisition (SLA), the influence of L1, so-called L1 transfer or cross-linguistic influence, has been debated for about half a century. It first gained a full acceptance in the 1950s and 1960s, but the next decades saw a downplayed role of L1 in SLA. However, interest in language transfer revived and was re-recognized in the late 1970s and early 1980s. Such an unusual development of L1 transfer has been driven by theoretical issues of language and language acquisition. The main theories of language transfer are summarized below with more attention given to the first one and the third one.

8.3.1　The behaviorist position

The role of L1 in SLA was first recognized in the 1940s and the 1950s with Fries' and Lado's works. Within a behaviorist framework, Lado regards L2 learning as the development of a new set of habits, and believes L1 learning habits interfere with L2 learning habits. Therefore, L1 takes on great significance because it appears to be a major cause for lack of success in L2 learning. Lado's conception of transfer is reflected in the famous Contrastive Analysis Hypothesis (CAH). This hypothesis claims that all areas of difficulty in L2 acquisition can be predicted in terms of the structural differences between the target language and the native language.

Contrastive Analysis Hypothesis (CAH) believes that it is assumed that the learner who comes in contact with a foreign language will find some features of it quite easy and others extremely difficult. Those elements that are similar to his native language will be simple for him, and those elements that are different will be difficult (Lado, 1957: 2, as cited in Larsen-Freeman & Long, 1991). The CAH holds that L1-L2 differences are both necessary and sufficient to explain the difficulties arising in L2 learning. According to this view, all difficulties in L2 acquisition should occur only in areas of difference between L1 and L2, and thus L1 interference is paramount as an explanatory principle in L2 acquisition theories.

In the early 1970s, the CAH was challenged both conceptually and empirically. On the conceptual side, the theoretical foundation of the CAH, namely structuralism, came under severe attack from generative grammar, and on the empirical side, much counterevidence to the CAH was reported (Richards, 1971; Zobl, 1980) and many of predictions of the hypothesis were simply not borne out. In order to reconcile the CAH with those disappointing results of the empirical investigation, Wardhaugh (1970) proposed a distinction between a strong version and a weak version of the CAH. The strong version is the original proposal by Lado. In the weak version, however, researchers start with learner errors and explain at least a subset of them by pointing to the similarities and differences between the two languages. Thus, although the CAH might not be a priority, it still has some explanatory power.

Another approach to conquer the weakness of the CAH is evident in the Markedness Differential Hypothesis (Eckman, 1977, 1985). In his definition, markedness is defined as: a phenomenon X in some language is more marked than Y if the presence of X in a language implies the presence of Y; but the presence of Y does not imply the presence of X (Eckman, 1977: 320). Given this definition, Eckman (1977: 321) proposed the Markedness Differential Hypothesis (MDH): Those areas of difficulty that a second language learner will have can be predicted on the basis of a comparison of the native language (NL) and the target language (TL), such as: those areas of the TL that are different from the NL and are relatively more marked than the NL will be difficult; the degree of difficulty associated with those aspects of the TL that are different and more marked than in the NL corresponds to the relative degree of markedness associated with those aspects; and those areas of the TL that are different from the NL but are not relatively more marked than the NL will not be difficult.

The goal of the MDH is the same as that of the CAH: to explain difficulty in L2 acquisition. The MDH, however, is capable of accounting for some facts that the CAH cannot: (1) Why some NL-TL differences do not cause difficulty; (2) Why some differences are associated with the degree of difficulty and others are not (Gass, 1989).

8.3.2   The mentalist position

1960s saw some challenges to the behaviorist theory of language and language learning. Chomsky (1965) argued that language should not be seen as a set of automatic habits, but as a set of structured rules. These rules are learned not by imitation, but are formulated on innate principles through exposure to the language to learn. Under Chomsky's attack, the behaviorist position did not seem to be tenable any longer. In this condition, Dulay and Burt (1974) proposed a mentalist account of how L2 is learned, which is called Creative Construction Hypothesis (CCH). Creative construction is the process in which children gradually reconstruct rules for speech they hear, guided by universal innate mechanisms which cause them to formulate certain types of hypotheses about the language system being acquired, until the mismatch between what they are exposed to and what they produce is resolved. Taking a mentalist position, Dulay and Burt advocated that children reconstructed L2 in similar ways regardless of their L1 or the language being learned, and this is summarized as the "L1 = L2" hypothesis. In one word, they held that L1 plays no role in L2 learning.

In order to verify this hypothesis, some studies such as the morpheme order studies were conducted (Dulay & Burt, 1974; Bailey et al, 1989). On the basis of their research results, Dulay & Burt posited a "natural order" of the acquisition of English morphemes, which discredits the role of L1.

However, the morpheme order studies have some problems (Wang, 2000). First, their methodology invites criticism. Various morpheme studies used the same test of Bilingual Syntax Measure in collecting data, so this same test may be partly responsible for their similar results. The second problem with the morpheme studies also comes from the findings. Despite a more or less invariant order, these studies also discovered some evidence for the role of L1 (Larsen-Freeman, 1976; Hakuta, 1976). The last problem concerns their conclusions. The morpheme studies investigated a limited number of grammatical morphemes, but researchers extended the implications to acquisition in general based on these results. Such a generalization has been criticized by Gass & Selinker (1983).

8.3.3　The cognitivist position

The late 1970s and early 1980s saw a revived recognition of the importance of L1 in L2 learning. This recognition results from the extension of the cognitive approach to transfer. From a cognitive point of view, it makes sense to assume that learners make use of any prior linguistic knowledge as "input" to the creative construction process, one important knowledge source being their L1 (Ervin-Tripp, 1974; Ellis, 1985). L1, thus, is seen as a kind of input, and transfer is not interference, but a cognitive process. Within a cognitivist framework, language transfer should be seen as a creative process as any other part of acquisition (Schachter, 1973; Faerch & Kasper, 1986). L1 functions primarily as communicative strategy for filling in gaps in the learners' competence. In cognitive accounts, L1 is viewed as a resource on which the learner actively draws in L2 learning (Kellerman, 1987). The use of L1 in L2 learning, thus, has come to be seen as a strategy available to compensate for lack of L2 knowledge, because L1 knowledge helps learners to form hypotheses about L2 rules. It is obvious that learners' L1 also has positive effect on SLA besides negative effect, and the problem facing the researchers is to find out when and how negative transfer occurs and what L1 knowledge can be utilized.

The learner's L1 is an important determinant of SLA, as it is a resource of knowledge which learners will use both consciously and subconsciously to help them sift the L2 data in the input and to perform as best as they can in the L2. When and how this resource is put to use depends on a whole host of factors to do with some linguistic factors on the one hand, and some psycholinguistic and sociolinguistic factors on the other hand.

To summarize, among the three theories of language transfer, the mentalist position does not seem convincing enough. On the contrary, both the behaviorist position and cognitivist position emphasize the importance of L1 in L2 learning, but within different frameworks, for the behaviorist framework stresses the differences between L1 and L2, and the cognitivist position regards language transfer as a strategy in language learning.

8.3.4   Transfer research on morphology and syntax

In the 1970s, a number of studies were carried out to investigate the morphological acquisition from the perspective of language transfer (Dulay & Burt, 1974; Bailey, 1989; Larsen-Freeman, 1976; Corder, 1978). They found that the acquisitional order for a group of English morphemes such as articles and inflectional features such as plural -s, etc. remained the same to the English speakers irrespective of the learners' L1. That is, the learners' mother language made little difference in the acquisition order of a group of morphemes the learners obtained. A different order occurred only when the learners were able to focus on the form rather than on the meaning of their utterances. However, later cross-sectional morphological studies revealed clear evidence for L1 transfer in learners with different language backgrounds (Pica, 1983; Flynn & O'Neill, 1988; Carroll & Swain, 1993; Gundel, 1993; Bhela, 1999).

In terms of linguistic transfer at the syntactical level, Hakuta (1976) documented that the learner's NL played a certain role in the formation of his second language syntax. Larsen-Freeman (1976) also demonstrated that there is a firm relationship between L1 transfer and the emergence of structure in second language acquisition. In addition, Andersen (1984) evidenced such a relationship through the learner's learning of English grammatical morphemes. To Gass (1984), transfer helped us to see the grammatical element universal in human languages. Syntactic comparisons and contrasts include Chen (1985), Tang (1990), Ge (1991), Liu (1992), Ding (1993), Jin (1991) and Chen (1992) (as cited in Yu, 2004). Chen (1985) reported that negation in Chinese and English were different in logical meaning, at the level of phrase and sentence. Tang (1990) looked at the differences in terms of principles and parameters. Ge (1991) pointed out that Chinese is different from English also in sentence group and sequence of sentences. Ding (1993) illustrated the Chinese-English differences in the subject of a sentence. Both Jin (1991) and Chen (1992) displayed the influences of Chinese topic-prominence structures in the learners' English.

In traditional accounts of language transfer, the research focus was placed on the errors that learners produce. Errors occurred as a result of the negative transfer of L1 patterns into the learner's L2. Current discussions of transfer involve the study of errors (negative transfer), facilitation (positive transfer), avoidance of target language forms, and their overuse.

A substantial amount of empirical work in SLA research has been devoted to establishing to what extent errors are the results of transfer (i. e. interference). Ellis (1985) illustrates the considerable variance in the proportion of transfer errors reported by different investigators. Whereas Dulay and Burt (1974) report that transfer accounted for only 3 percent of the errors in their corpus of Spanish-speaking learners' L2 English, Tran-Chi-Chau (1975) reports 51 percent in adult Chinese-speaking learners' English. One of the main reasons for this variation is the difficulty in determining whether an error is the result of transfer or intralingual processes.

The learner's L1 can also facilitate L2 learning. Odlin (1989) pointed out that the facilitative effects can only be observed when learners with different native languages are studied and learner comparisons are carried out. Kellerman (1979, 1987) investigated transfer and found that the facilitative effect of L1 can be adduced by certain types of U-shaped behavior. Gass (1984, 1989) investigated 17 adult learners of L2 English with diverse language backgrounds. Data relating to a number of structural aspects of relative clauses were collected, but only one-pronoun retention—provided clear evidence of transfer effects. The facilitative effect of L1 is evident in some cases where languages share a large number of cognates, such as English and French. Chinese learners of L2 Japanese have an enormous advantage over English learners because of the similarity in the Chinese and Japanese writing systems.

Learners also avoid using linguistic structures which they find difficult because of differences between their native language and the target language. The classic study of avoidance is Schachter (1973), who found that Chinese and Japanese learners of English made fewer errors in the use of relative clauses than Persian and Arabic learners because they produced far fewer clauses overall. The difficulty for the Chinese and Japanese learners may lie in the fact that their mother tongues are left-branching (i. e. nouns are pre-modified), while English is primarily right-branching (i. e. nouns are post-modified). Seliger (1979) points out that it is only possible to claim that avoidance has taken place if the learner has demonstrated knowledge of the form in question, and if there is evidence available that native speakers of L2 would use the form in the context under consideration. In other words, it only makes sense to talk of avoidance if the learners know what they are avoiding.

The overuse or "over-indulgence" (Levenston, 1979) of certain grammatical forms in L2 acquisition can occur as a result of intralingual process such as overgeneralization. For example, L2 learners have often been observed to overgeneralize the regular past tense inflection to irregular verbs in L2 English. Overuse also results from transfer and there is substantial evidence which shows that overuse as a result of transfer can be seen at other linguistic levels.

All transfer scholars emphasize the necessity of considering the multiple ways in which L1 influence can exert itself, and they are also looking for evidence of negative transfer, positive transfer, avoidance and overuse (Ellis, 1985; Dulay and Burt, 1974; Tran-Chi-Chau, 1975; Odlin, 1989; Kellerman, 1987; Gass, 1984, 1989). They recognize, however, that all these aspects of L2 use are likely to demonstrate a variety of factors at work, one of which is L1 knowledge, and it is important to look for when and how L1 transfer occurs.

Previous studies have proved that a number of differing constraints on transfer that incorporate linguistic, psycholinguistic, and sociolinguistic factors. These constraints are: language level including phonology, lexis, grammar, and discourse; social factors such as the effect of the addressee and of different learning contexts on transfer; markedness—the extent to which specific linguistic features are "special" in some way; prototypicality—the extent to which a specific meaning of a word is considered "core" or "basic" in relation to other meanings of the same word; language distance and psychotypology—the perceptions that speakers have regarding the similarity and difference between languages; non-structural factors such as individual learner differences (e. g. personality and age).

8.4　Markedness and transfer

Studies on markedness claim that marked structures are more difficult to acquire or appear later in development (Eckman, 1977, 1985; Gass, 1984, 1989; Hyltenstam, 1984, 1990). The studies also predict that marked structures in the first language (L1) do not transfer to the second language (L2) in the early stages of acquisition (Gass, 1984; Kellerman, 1979; Rutherford, 1983). In addition, studies, such as Gass (1989) and Hystenstam (1984), claim that the presence of marked features of a given structure implies the presence of less or unmarked related structures. In L2 teaching, it has been claimed that learners might be taught marked structures which might then have a domino effect and "push" the acquisition of less marked or unmarked structures (Doughty, 1991; Eckman, 1985; Gass, 1989; Zobl, 1983).

Transfer is more likely to occur when the L1 construction is unmarked. That is, if a particular L2 rule is obscure, so that it cannot be easily derived by means of the learner's projection device, the learner falls back on his L1 and may be prepared to transfer even a marked rule to solve his learnability problem. The condition for transfer to take place is not where L1 has a marked construction, but where L2 has.

Zobl (1983) argues that transfer functions only as an "auxiliary evaluation measure". That is, learners fall back on their L1 knowledge when the L2 rule is obscure. Learners solve the problem by turning to their L1, particularly if the equivalent L1 rule is unmarked. They are likely to resort to their L1 to solve the learnability problem. Eckman (1985) also argues that transfer effects are most in evidence when the L1 setting is unmarked and the L2 setting marked. He illustrates this with reference to the distribution of voice contrast in pairs such as /t/ and /d/ in English and German. English learners of German have no difficulty in mastering the unmarked form in final position, but German learners of English do experience problems in mastering the marked target language contrast. Kellerman (1987) proposes that where the L1 pattern corresponds with a universal developmental stage in SLA, the learner might proceed to that stage faster than learners whose L1s do not have the pattern. He cites Hammarberg (1979), who suggests that English learners of L2 Swedish are likely to miss out the early preverbal negation stage because their L1 does not contain this pattern. Thus, as Kellerman puts it, learners can get a "leg up" the developmental ladder with the help of their L1.

There are arguments and evidence to support the non-transfer of L1 marked forms. Kellerman (1979) suggests that learners tend to avoid one-to-one correspondences between L1 and L2 when meanings are considered far from prototypical, even though errors can result. His work on the semantics of *break* provides a good example. Dutch and English share both transitive and intransitive uses of *break*. Dutch-speaking learners of L2 English accept both uses in the early stages of development. This might be because they are transferring from Dutch, or it might be because they are responding to evidence of both uses in the L2 data. Later, however, they reject English sentences exemplifying the more marked, intransitive use of *break*, while later still they once again accept both marked and unmarked uses. This study shows that learners may initially transfer both marked and unmarked features, while in more advanced interlanguage they resist transferring marked features. Thus the acceptance or rejection of L1 peripheral features may be complicated by developmental factors.

Zobl (1983) investigates L1 French/L2 English learners' use of *how many* ... construction and finds the avoidance of marked forms in L1 transfer. He argues that non-extraction represents the unmarked rule, and extraction the marked one. A group of low-level French learners of English show a strong preference for the non-extracted rule. In other words, they resist the possibility of transferring the marked L1 rule. Liceras (1985) investigates preposition stranding (e. g. *who did John give the book to?*) in English-speaking learners of L2 Spanish. Although preposition stranding is possible in English, it is not possible in Spanish. Liceras finds that 43 percent of her English-speaking subjects accept stranding in Spanish at the beginning level (i. e. are prepared to transfer a L1 marked form), although at intermediate and advanced levels the marked constructions are generally rejected. White (1987, 1992) argues strongly that learners may have difficulty in "unsetting" marked parameters in L1 when they learn L2, and she claims that learners carry over marked constructions from L1 to L2. Furthermore, she suggests that once the marked L1 form has been established in interlanguage, it may be difficult to dislodge it, with the result that fossilization occurs.

8.5 Research methodology of markedness effects on morphology and syntax acquisition

The empirical investigation aims to examine the difficulty Chinese learners of English experience in acquiring and using the verb inflection of the simple past and the word order in interrogative sentences and the effects of language proficiency on language transfer. The research tries to give an explanation of how and why linguistic markedness exerts effects on second language acquisition and how language proficiency interacts with language transfer. Based on the above linguistic analysis and the review of previous studies on the Markedness Differential Hypothesis and U-shaped behavior, two hypotheses with specific predictions for the present study are put forward as follows:

Hypothesis 1: Chinese learners of English experience more difficulty in acquiring past verb forms than present verb forms, and they also experience more difficulty in acquiring the word order in interrogative sentences than in declarative sentences.

Hypothesis 2: **The low-level learners tend to transfer both marked features and unmarked features in L2 and the intermediate-level learners are conservative about the transfer of marked features. However, the advanced-level learners may show a tendency to transfer unmarked features in L2 again.**

8.5.1   Subjects

The subjects in the present study were 90 students representing different language proficiency levels in English, and they were divided into three groups: the low level, the intermediate level and the advanced level. The first group of participants were 30 EFL learners from a junior middle school in their 5th semester English course (the low level); the second group of participants were 30 EFL learners from a senior middle school in their 5th semester course (the intermediate level); the third group of participants were 30 non-English majors from Wuhan University in their 3rd semester (the advanced level). Grade 3 junior middle school students were chosen as the low-level group for several considerations. Generally English textbooks would introduce language features step by step from simple to complex. For Grade 1 junior students, only the simple present was taught, and the simple past was not introduced until in the last few lessons of Grade 2. Thus, it is believed that Grade 3 is a good starting point for the present study.

The 30 participants in the low level were chosen from 64 junior middle school students through the Entrance Examination to Senior High School; the 30 participants in the intermediate level were chosen from 78 senior middle school students through the National College Entrance Examination; the 30 participants in the advanced level were chosen from 67 non-English majors through the College English Test (CET-4). All the participants had received English instruction for two and a half years, five and a half years and seven and a half years respectively, and their language proficiency was thus presumed to be different. The middle school students used the English textbooks that are cooperatively published by People Education Press and Longman Press, and the college students used *New Horizon College English* as their textbooks published by Foreign Language Teaching and Research Press. Thus their English learning experience was mainly based on classroom instruction.

8.5.2   Instruments

All the proficiency tests were predetermined for the purpose of selecting appropriate participants. To select the subjects, a revised Entrance Examination to Senior High School, a National College Entrance Examination and a CET-4 Test were administered to 64 junior students, 78 senior students and 67 college students respectively. 30 participants in each level whose scores were around the mean took part in the present study.

The data for the present study were collected by administering a translation test, a cloze test and a writing test, each containing two tasks, to all the 90 participants, and the six tasks took six weeks with one administered each week. In the E-C-E translation tasks, the participants were required to translate the sentences into Chinese first, and a week later, the Chinese version of the same English sentences was translated by them back into English. The E-C-E translations of the English sentences reflected the participants' thinking process of translating in English; therefore, their performance could reflect their understanding of tenses and interrogative sentences used in the obligatory contexts.

The testing materials for the present study were adapted from *A New English Grammar Coursebook* compiled by Zhang Zhenbang. The translation test consisted of two tasks: the first one was to translate 40 English sentences varying in tense and pattern into Chinese and the second one to translate the Chinese version of those sentences back into English. The cloze test contained two tasks: the first task was to fill in the blanks with the appropriate word forms; the second task to ask questions about the underlined parts of the sentences. The writing test also included two tasks: the first task was to write a 100-word composition with the given verbs on the topic *My Childhood*; the second task to make a dialogue with the given verbs. Each task took about 40 minutes. The vocabularies used in the testing materials were made sure to be within the capacity of all the participants, and Chinese meanings were provided for the supposedly unfamiliar words. English verbs are more marked for both the simple past and the 3rd singular simple present than Chinese verbs, so the 3rd singular simple present marker *-s* may also cause difficulty for the participants in applying the simple present tense, thus affecting their performance. To solve this problem, the researcher excluded the 3rd singular simple present from the data and made full use of the temporal adverbials as a clue to indicate an obligatory context. Time reference was established through the use of contexts or time adverbials. In this regard, the temporal adverbials provided the participants with a useful aid disambiguating the use of the tenses. All the verbs in the testing materials included regulars and irregulars, frequent verbs and infrequent verbs, and all the sentences included simple sentences and complex sentences.

8.5.3 Coding procedures

To begin with, the proficiency tests were carried out so as to select subjects available, and 30 participants in each level whose scores were around the mean took part in the present study. Secondly, the participants were provided with the translation tasks, the cloze tasks and the writing tasks within six consecutive weeks with each task in each week. Thirdly, the data of the present study were collected from these tasks taken by the participants. Finally, the errors the participants made in the verb inflection and word order were collected, classified and analyzed step by step.

In the first step of data coding, all types of errors were annotated, and the tags related to inflectional errors and word order errors were selected and classified respectively. To make the data manageable, all the errors were coded in the obligatory contexts for the verb inflection of the simple past and the word order in interrogative sentences. Basically, the rules of forming the simple past regular verbs can be classified into the following ways:

(1) The simple past verbs are formed by adding *-ed* to the base form. If the base form ends with *-e*, then *-d* is added, e. g. *talk/talked, phone/phoned*.

(2) If the base form ends with a consonant and consists of only one syllable or is accented on the last syllable, the final consonant is doubled, e. g. *stop/ stopped, prefer/ preferred*.

(3) If the base form ends with a consonant followed by a "y", the "y" is replaced by "I" and then *-ed* is added, e. g. *cry/cried, carry/carried.*

Irregular verbs are different from regular verbs, as there is no simple rule for them and their forms vary from one to another, e. g. *go/went, make/made, stand/stood*. Chinese has no verb inflection to indicate grammatical functions, and its grammatical function is shown by the use of functional words. For example, in the Chinese sentence, *zuo tian wo mai le yi ben ying yu shu (I bought an English book yesterday)*, *le* is a functional word showing completion. Therefore, Chinese learners of English tend to have difficulty in applying the verb inflection of the simple past. The following are common inflectional errors made by Chinese EFL learners:

Table 8. 1   **Inflectional errors**

Error type	Inflectional errors
A1. Use of bare verbs	*I arrive* * *in Beijing yesterday.*
A2. Simplification of regular verbs	*rob/robed* *, *stop/stoped.* *
A3. Overgeneralization of regular verbs	*stay/staied* *, *pray/praied.* *
A4. Overgeneralization of regular forms	*make/maked* *, *cut/cutted.* *

The word order in English interrogative sentences is also different from that in Chinese interrogative sentences. Chinese interrogative sentences do not change the word order (SVO), and only have the functional word *ma* at the end of the sentences, whereas English interrogative sentences are formed by putting auxiliary verbs in front of the subject, and the word order in English simple interrogative sentences is VSO, So L1-L2 difference causes difficulty and leads to errors.

Table 8. 2   **Word order errors in interrogative sentences**

Error type	Word order errors
B1. Overuse of linking verbs	*Is your brother is busy?* * *Are you finished your homework?* *
B2. No fronting of wh-words	*You say what?* * *We will go where?* *
B3. wh- questions	*Why you went there alone?* * *How I can get there?* *
B4. Overgeneralization of inversion	*I wonder where did she go.* * *Would you please tell me how can I go to the zoo?* *

The data analysis was conducted in three steps. First, distributions of inflectional error types and word order error types were counted respectively with regard to the simple past and the word order involved. Second, inflectional errors and word order errors were examined separately in different contexts in terms of regulars/irregulars and yes/no questions and wh-questions. Finally, the two types of errors in different categories were compared in terms of their mean.

The process of coding variables was carried out in two phases: coding language proficiency levels and coding error distributions of the verb inflection of the simple past and the word order in interrogative sentences. All errors in the obligatory contexts for the simple past or interrogative sentences were coded into the above-mentioned categories based on the results yielded in the subjects' performance.

In the present experimental materials, the verbs included regulars and irregulars, frequent verbs and infrequent verbs, and the interrogative sentences included *yes/no* questions and wh-questions. Three tests with six tasks were applied for each of the dimensions: regular verbs/irregular verbs, frequent verbs/infrequent verbs, yes/no questions and wh-questions. During the course of coding variables, the verb inflectional errors of the simple past and the word order errors in interrogative sentences were identified as dependent variables, whose values were mainly determined by two independent variables—the degree of linguistic markedness and the participants' language proficiency levels.

The study employed three statistic methods: Chi-square test, T-test and One-way ANOVA test. Chi-square test was used to determine whether the relationship between two or more different variables was independent and it measured whether a particular distribution of observed values was sufficiently different from an expected distribution to indicate that it could not be explained as a chance occurrence. T-test was used to determine the significance of the difference between the means on two sets of scores. ANOVA (analysis of variance) test was used to test whether the difference among the means of the three groups was significant.

8.6 Empirical approaches to morphology and syntax acquisition

The data analysis starts with the summary of the errors in the tasks. A first summary sorts out the verb inflectional errors of the simple past (VIE) and the word order errors in interrogative sentences (WOE) made by the low-level group (LL), the intermediate-level group (IL) and the advanced-level group (AL). Table 8.3 provided the numbers and the percentages of different types of errors yielded in all the tasks administered to the subjects.

Table 8.3　　　　**Distribution/percentage of VIE and WOE (N=30)**

Group	VIE				WOE			
	A1	A2	A3	A4	B1	B2	B3	B4
LL	112(9.9)	29(2.6)	85(7.5)	354(31.2)	25(3.8)	60(9.2)	59(9.0)	185(28.3)
IL	53(4.7)	16(1.4)	34(3.0)	202(17.8)	17(2.6)	48(7.3)	42(6.4)	121(18.5)
AL	44(3.9)	14(1.2)	23(2.0)	167(14.7)	8 (1.2)	14(2.1)	19(2.9)	57(8.7)
Total	209(18.4)	59(5.2)	142(12.5)	723(63.8)	50(7.6)	122(18.6)	120(18.3)	363(55.5)

Error types A1, A2, A3 with similar properties would be treated as one category in the following analyses for the sake of manageability as they all represent regular verb inflectional errors; similarly, error types B2, B3, B4 would be taken together as one group representing word order errors in wh-questions, thus reducing the error types to only four—regular/irregular verb inflectional errors, word order errors in yes/no and wh-questions.

Then a second summary of the errors in different tasks was carried out, resulting in the following Table, which reveals the verb inflection errors (VIE) and the word order errors (WOE) yielded in the translation test (TT), the writing test (WT) and the cloze test (CT).

Table 8.4　　　　　　**Distribution/percentage of VIE and WOE (N＝30)**

Group	TT	WT	CT
Low level (LL)			
VIE	152(13.4)	225(19.9)	203(17.9)
WOE	104(15.9)	111(17.0)	114(17.4)
Intermediate level (IL)			
VIE	89(7.9)	116(10.2)	100(8.8)
WOE	73(11.1)	76(11.6)	79(12.1)
Advanced level (AL)			
VIE	67(5.9)	95(8.4)	86(7.6)
WOE	29(4.4)	36(5.5)	33(5.0)

According to Table 8.4, the errors in the three groups are ordered as such: the low level >the intermediate level >the advanced level, and concerning error types, VIE >WOE. Among these errors, the low-level learners make much more inflectional errors (580) and word order errors (329) than the intermediate (305, 228) and advanced learners (248, 98), implying that the simple past marker -*ed* and the word order marker VSO cause more difficulty for the beginning learners as they has made too many non-targetlike forms. With improved proficiency, however, the learners' accuracy of the use of L2 marked features is enhanced. Therefore, it could be concluded that formal instruction appeared to result in faster learning and higher levels of grammatical competence because plentiful studies identified the effects of formal instructions on the rate/success of SLA. (Seliger, 1979; Krashen, 1981; Chihara & Oller, 1978)

8.6.1 Analysis of verb inflectional errors

This section analyzes how markedness affects the targetlike use of verb inflection, especially with regard to the simple past.

Table 8.5　　　　　Distribution/percentage of VIE in the tasks (N=30)

Group	Simple past	Simple present
LL	580(37.6)	184(11.9)
IL	305(19.8)	144(9.3)
AL	248(16.0)	83(5.4)
Total	1,133(73.4)	411(26.6)

Table 8.6　　　The association between the errors and the existence of markedness

	Value	df	Sig.
Pearson Chi-square	16.53	2	.00
Likelihood Ratio	18.79	2	.00
N of Valid Cases	1,544		

Tables 8.5 and 8.6 illustrate that non-targetlike use of the simple past verb inflection is very popular among the three groups. According to the error distribution, the errors of the simple past verb form made by the three groups are 580, 305 and 248 respectively, in sharp contrast with only 184, 144 and 83 for verb form errors of the simple present. The low rate of errors (26.6%) of the simple present verb form is probably determined by the absence of the tense marker because of the similarity between English and Chinese. As mentioned above, the simple present is often easily acquired due to its unmarkedness, and its easiness to learn is mainly due to the learners' unawareness of the difference between English and Chinese, which, however, results in the overuse of the simple present verb form at the same time. To put it simpler, the finding that the simple past verb form is often replaced by the simple present verb form could be accounted for by the fact that the learners often use unmarked verb forms, like the simple present verb form, to express the meaning of such a marked tense as the simple past verb form. It shows that the first hypothesis is undoubtedly supported that the verb inflection of the simple past is more difficult to be acquired than that of the simple present because of the presence of the simple past marker -ed.

Table 8.7　　　　　Comparison of VIE in the simple past (N=30)

Group	Min	Max	M	SD
LL	18	22	19.27	12.20
IL	10	19	11.77	8.38
AL	2	2	5.60	1.64

Table 8.8　　　　　Comparison of VIE in the simple present (N=30)

Group	Min	Max	M	SD
LL	3	5	4.67	1.06
IL	1	3	2.10	0.19
AL	0	2	1.57	0.03

Table 8.9　　**Mean difference in the simple present and the simple past (N = 30)**

Group	Existence of markedness	N	M	SD
LL	Unmarkedness	30	4.67	1.06
	Markedness	30	19.27	12.20
	T = 2.40	df = 29		Sig = .00
IL	Unmarkedness	30	2.10	0.19
	Markedness	30	11.77	8.38
	t = 2.69	df = 29		Sig = .00
AL	Unmarkedness	30	1.57	0.03
	Markedness	30	5.60	1.64
	t = 1.13	df = 29		Sig = .00

From Tables 8.7, 8.8, 8.9, it could be seen that the low-level group makes at least 18 errors in the simple past verb form and at least 3 errors in the simple present verb form, the intermediate-level group makes 10 errors in the simple past and 1 error in the simple present, and the advanced-level group makes 2 errors in the simple past and 0 error in the simple present. All the participants make about 16 errors on average in the simple past while they made only 2 errors in the simple present, with a gap as wide as 14 errors. It would be easy to conclude that the presence of the simple past marker -ed significantly hinders the targetlike use of the verb inflection as the learners tend to make far more errors in the simple past verb form than in the simple present verb form (P = .00). Zobl (1980) argues that transfer effects are most in evidence when the L1 setting is unmarked and the L2 setting marked, and that the condition for transfer to take place is not where the L1 has a marked construction, but where the L2 has. That is, the verb inflection of the simple past is more difficult to acquire than the simple present verb form because of the negative transfer of unmarked features, and therefore the first hypothesis is once again supported.

Table 8.10　　**VIE of the simple past and the simple present (N = 30)**

		Sum of Squares	df	Mean Square	F	Sig.
Simple past	Between groups	33.36	2	16.68	10.55	.00
	Within groups	137.53	87	1.58		
	Total	170.89	89			
Simple present	Between groups	1.50	2	0.75	0.71	.49
	Within groups	90.73	87	1.04		
	Total	92.23	89			

As Table 8.10 indicates, the simple present verb form has much higher rates of appropriate use than the simple past verb form. In order to test if the three groups in the tasks would differ significantly in their likelihood of using targetlike verb forms, one-way ANOVA test was conducted on the verb form errors in all the three groups. The analysis has identified a significant difference among the three groups in the targetlike use of the simple past verb form (P =. 00) and an insignificant difference among them in using the simple present verb form (P =. 49). The simple past marker *-ed* is found to be a factor significantly associated with the error occurrence. There is a significant difference between their language proficiency levels and their performance in the targetlike use of the simple past verb form, but there is an insignificant difference between their language proficiency levels and their performance in the use of simple present verb form. The advanced-level group shows significantly lower proportions (21.9%) of the non-targetlike use of the verb inflection of the simple past than the low-level (51.2%) and the intermediate-level groups (26.9%). Therefore, language proficiency is one of the factors influencing the targetlike use of the L2 marked features as the low-level learners are more inclined to transfer both L2 marked and unmarked features, and with increasing language proficiency, learners have realize that, though similar, native and target languages really differ a lot from each other, so that they may pay more attention to the use of the marked features in L2 and raise their awareness about form-meaning consistency.

Table 8.11　　　　**Comparison of the regular VIE in the simple past (N=30)**

Group	Min	Max	M	SD
LL	2	15	12.57	8.21
IL	4	10	6.27	4.75
AL	0	5	3.59	1.31

Table 8.12　　　　**Comparison of the irregular VIE in the simple past (N=30)**

Group	Min	Max	M	SD
LL	8	19	13.13	8.26
IL	7	9	8.20	5.72
AL	3	5	3.64	1.04

Table 8.13　　　　**Mean difference in VIE between regulars and irregulars (N=30)**

Group	Verb types	N	M	SD
LL	Regulars	30	12.57	8.21
	Irregulars	30	13.13	8.62
	t=5.78	df=29		Sig=.00
IL	Regulars	30	6.27	4.75
	Irregulars	30	8.20	5.72
	t=5.19	df=29		Sig=.00
AL	Regulars	30	3.59	1.31
	Irregulars	30	3.64	1.04
	t=4.37	df=29		Sig=.00

As was shown in Tables 8.11, 8.12, and 8.13, verbs are analyzed in two categories: regular/ irregular and frequent/infrequent, the low-level group makes at least 2 regular verb inflectional errors and at least 8 irregular verb inflectional errors in the simple past, the intermediate-level group makes 4 and 7, and the advance-level group makes 0 and 3 errors, showing that irregular verb inflectional errors are made twice more than regulars though irregulars are sparse in number. Furthermore, the inflectional errors in irregulars are reflected by highly frequent overgeneralizations of the simple past formation rule. In the tasks the most frequent inflectional errors are in irregulars, such as *go/goed* *, *have/ haved* *, *say/sayed* *, *feel/*feeled *, *tell/telled* *, *think/thinked* *, and so on. Hence, irregular verbs, though sparse in number, are of specially significant difficulty due to rule-based grammar learning. It is natural that learners are likely to overuse the inflectional rules in morphological processing, and transfer of the marked features occurred. Just as the rule-based single-mechanism model indicates, morphological processing is a procedure where all inflected words are formed by morphological rules, and memorization of inflected words are avoided as much as possible. This model proves to be unconvincing as the associative single-mechanism model does, because the associative single-mechanism model claims that all inflected words are stored and processed within a single associative system using distributed representations. The field of cognitive science has identified some more efficient learning mechanisms, and the most influential and convincing model is the dual-mechanism model holding that morphologically complex word forms could be processed associatively both through stored full-form representations and by rules that are decomposed or parsed inflected word forms into morphological constituents (Pinker & Prince, 1999).

Table 8.14   **Comparison of the frequent VIE in the simple past (N = 30)**

Group	Min	Max	M	SD
LL	4	8	6.82	5.31
IL	3	9	6.93	3.72
AL	1	5	3.47	1.65

Table 8.15   **Comparison of the infrequent VIE in the simple past (N = 30)**

Group	Min	Max	M	SD
LL	6	9	7.50	4.47
IL	5	6	5.30	2.53
AL	3	5	2.47	1.33

Table 8.16   **Mean difference in VIE between frequent verbs and infrequent verbs (N = 30)**

Group	Verb types	N	M	SD
LL	Frequent verbs	30	6.82	5.31
	Infrequent verbs	30	7.50	4.47
	t = 3.03	df = 29		Sig. = .01
IL	Frequent verbs	30	6.93	3.72
	Infrequent verbs	30	5.30	2.53
	t = 3.05	df = 29		Sig. = .01
AL	Frequent verbs	30	3.47	1.65
	Infrequent verbs	30	2.47	1.33
	t = 2.98	df = 29		Sig. = .01

Tables 8.14, 8.15, 8.16 reveals the inflectional errors of the frequent verbs and the infrequent verbs in the simple past, illuminating which type of verb is more likely to be overgeneralized and more difficult to acquire because the number of errors show that some infrequent verb inflectional errors are more likely to occur than frequent verb inflectional errors. It is found that the learner tend to apply the simple past inflectional rule to form verbs in the obligatory contexts, which possibly result from the grammar instruction they have received. This phenomenon reflects that Chinese-speaking learners tend to transfer the past tense marker -ed on the basis of the rote-learning mechanism. From the outset of practicing the English simple past, learners are normally instructed to add suffix -ed to a bare verb to form a past tense predicate, and this rule is repeatedly stressed from then on. Therefore, in practicing the verb inflection of the simple past, the learners prefer to use this rule throughout the formation, especially, when meeting some infrequent verbs that they are unfamiliar with, for example, *shed* and *vary*. This is why overgeneralizations occur. Talyor (1975) suggests that transfer involves the use of the learner's L1 as a basis for forming hypotheses about L2, while overgeneralization, as a result of transfer, involves the use of existing L2 knowledge by extending it to new interlanguage forms. Both strategies could be seen as manifestations of the same basic strategy of relying on prior knowledge to facilitate new learning. Richard (1978) also identified overgeneralization as a device used when the items do not carry any obvious contrast for the learner. For example, the past tense marker -ed often carried no meaning in the context, since pastness can be indicated lexically by such words as *yesterday*, *last week*, etc.

In conclusion, the simple past tense marker -ed has caused more difficulty for the learners than the unmarked simple present tense, and markedness effects on irregulars and infrequent verbs are stronger than on regulars and frequent verbs. Learners are likely to transfer both marked and unmarked features, but the transfer tendency has become weaker in unmarked features with increasing language proficiency, while the transfer tendency in marked features has recorded no significant change.

8.6.2   Analysis of word order errors

This section attempts to investigate the influence of syntactic markedness on the acquisition of English interrogative sentences. The first step is to discover the general syntactic errors (GSE) made by the participants, and the second step is to compare the word order errors (WOE) in declarative sentences with those in interrogative sentences.

Table 8.17   Distribution/percentage of WOE (N=30)

Group	Interrogative sentences	Declarative sentences
LL	329(47.4)	23(3.3)
IL	228(32.9)	11(1.6)
AL	98(14.1)	5(0.7)
Total	655(94.4)	39(5.6)

Table 8.18   **The association between the errors and the existence of markedness**

	Value	df	Sig.
Pearson Chi-square	17.09	2	.00
Likelihood Ratio	17.98	2	.00
N of Valid cases	694		

The two tables above demonstrate that word order errors in interrogative sentences are more popular than in declarative sentences among the three groups. The result of Chi-square test suggests that the existence of syntactic markedness is significantly associated with the non-targetlike use of the word order in interrogative sentences (P=.00), implying that the word order errors are distributed differently when the word order is tested in the declarative sentences and the interrogative sentences. The finding that the word order in interrogative sentences is often replaced by the word order in declarative sentences can be accounted for by the fact that the learners often use unmarked forms like the word order in declarative sentences (SVO) to express the meaning of such a marked form as the word order in interrogative sentences (VSO). The word order in declarative sentences is often correctly used due to the similarity of L1-L2 and its unmarkedness; its overuse is mainly caused by the learners' perception to keep sentence meaning consistent with the form of the sentence at the same time as EFL learners would usually think in their mother tongue in the process of learning.

Subsequently, an independent-sample T-test is carried out to examine the mean differences of the non-targetlike word order between the interrogative sentences and the declarative sentences. The unmarkedness of the word order in declarative sentences is shown to have significantly facilitated the subjects' targetlike word order acquisition (P=.00). The result reveals that syntactic unmarkedness has caused less difficulty for the subjects in using declarative sentences, while syntactic markedness causes more difficulty in applying interrogative sentences.

Table 8.19　　　　　Comparison of WOE in interrogative sentences (N=30)

Group	Min	Max	M	SD
LL	5	9	5.20	3.38
IL	2	5	2.61	2.44
AL	0	4	1.04	2.68

Table 8.20　　　　　Comparison of WOE in declarative sentences (N=30)

Group	Min	Max	M	SD
LL	2	5	2.75	3.13
IL	0	3	0.98	3.07
AL	0	2	0.34	2.12

Table 8.21　　　T-test of mean difference in WOE across the existence of markedness (N=30)

Group	Existence of markedness	N	M	SD
LL	Unmarkedness	30	2.75	3.13
	Markedness	30	5.20	3.38
	t=2.47	df=29		Sig. =.00
IL	Unmarkedness	30	0.98	3.07
	Markedness	30	2.61	2.44
	t=2.62	df=29		Sig. =.00
AL	Unmarkedness	30	0.34	2.12
	Markedness	30	1.04	2.68
	t=2.28	df=29		Sig. =.00

Table 8.22　　WOE in interrogative sentences and declarative sentences across the groups (N=30)

		Sum of Squares	df	Mean Square	F	Sig.
Interrogative sentences	Between groups	10.16	2	5.08	5.21	.01
	Within groups	84.83	87	0.98		
	Total	94.99	89			
Declarative sentences	Between groups	0.69	2	0.34	0.20	.82
	Within groups	151.27	87	1.74		
	Total	151.96	89			

The ANOVA analysis identifies a significant difference among the groups in the targetlike use of the word order in interrogative sentences, but an insignificant difference among them in the targetlike use of the word order in declarative sentences. The analysis shows that the targetlike use of word order in interrogative sentences differs significantly among the three groups (P =.01), but the targetlike use of word order in declarative sentences is insignificantly different among the groups (P =. 82). When the markedness effect on word order acquisition is investigated, similar findings are obtained for those with non-targetlike use of the verb inflection of the simple past. Linguistic markedness is found to be a major factor significantly associated with the non-targetlike use of linguistic marked features. Considering the use of both morphological and syntactic marker, there is a significant difference among the low-level group, the intermediate-level group and the advanced-level group. As to the use of the unmarked morphological and syntactic features, there is an insignificant difference among the three groups. That is to say, both language proficiency and markedness affect the targetlike use of the L2 marked features. The low-level learners make 329 word order errors in interrogative sentences, the intermediate-level and the advanced-level learners make 228 and 98 errors respectively, and the error ratios are 50.2%, 34.8% and 15%. The reason might be that formal instruction accelerates the acquisition of L2 marked features and enhances their learning efficiency.

Table 8.23   **Comparison of WOE in yes/no questions (N=30)**

Group	Min	Max	M	SD
LL	2	11	9.57	6.31
IL	2	8	5.46	3.75
AL	0	5	3.43	1.54

Table 8.24   **Comparison of WOE in wh-questions (N=30)**

Group	Min	Max	M	SD
LL	9	21	16.83	11.46
IL	7	15	10.20	9.16
AL	3	7	5.28	3.71

Table 8.25   **Mean difference in WOE between yes/no questions and wh-questions (N=30)**

Group	Interrogative sentences	N	M	SD
LL	Yes/no questions	30	9.75	6.31
	wh-questions	30	16.83	11.46
	t=1.76	df=29		Sig. =.00
IL	Yes/no questions	30	5.46	3.75
	wh-questions	30	10.20	9.16
	t=1.48	df=29		Sig. =.00
AL	Yes/no questions	30	3.43	1.54
	wh-questions	30	5.28	3.71
	t=1.53	df=29		Sig. =.00

After the comparison of mean difference between the word order errors in the interrogative sentences and those in the declarative sentences, all of the word order errors in interrogative sentences are analyzed in yes/no questions and wh-questions. According to Tables 8.23-25, the learners made more word order errors in wh-questions than in yes/no questions and the mean difference between wh-questions and yes/no questions is significant (P = .00). When word order errors and language proficiency are considered together, the error rates among the groups have narrowed down. The maximums of the word order errors made by the low-level group in yes/no questions and wh-questions (11 and 21) are larger than those of the errors made by the intermediate-level group (8 and 15) and the advanced-level group (5 and 7). Both yes/no questions and wh-questions seem to present difficulty for the participants in applying the targetlike word order, for word order VSO and wh-movement in English interrogative sentences are of markedness in English. The wh-movement, however, shows more significant difficulty than the word order VSO in the process of L2 learning (P = .00) as wh-movement is English-specific while the word order VSO, like SVO and SOV, is viewed as basic word orders from the perspective of linguistic universal (Greenberg, 1966, as cited in Yu, 2004).

Table 8.26   **Distribution of WOE in yes/no questions and declarative sentences (N=30)**

Group	*Yes/no* questions	Declarative sentences
LL	25(3.8)	23(3.3)
IL	17(2.6)	11(1.6)
AL	8(1.2)	5(0.7)

A further analysis is undertaken within syntactic markedness to investigate the distribution of word order errors in *yes/no* questions and declarative sentences. The number of errors made by the three groups in *yes/no* questions and declarative sentences are rather close (Table 8.26). It could be seen that learners are less likely to transfer the word order VSO as it belongs to the basic word order family and is less marked than wh-movement. This finding also confirms the results gained by Odlin (1990), who suggests that basic word order is rarely transferred by language learners because they are likely to be highly conscious of the basic word order.

To summarize, the presence of the syntactic marker wh-movement significantly inhibit the learners' targetlike use of the interrogative word order (P<.05). Language proficiency also has significant influence on the targetlike use of the grammatical marker (P<.05). In the acquisition of the word order in interrogative sentences, the low-level learners tend to show the strongest negative transfer of L2 unmarked features and the advanced-level learners show the weakest, while the intermediate-level learners come in between. This phenomenon can be explained by the benefits of formal instruction which claims that formal instruction results in increased accuracy and accelerated progress through developmental sequences and its effects are durable.

Table 8.27   **Distribution of VIE and WOE in TT, WT and CT (N=30)**

Group	Errors	TT	WT	CT
LL		152(13.4)	225(19.9)	203(17.9)
IL	VIE	89(7.9)	116(10.2)	100(8.8)
AL		67(5.9)	95(8.4)	86(7.6)
	Total	308(27.2)	436(38.5)	389(34.3)
LL		104(15.9)	111(17.0)	114(17.4)
IL	WOE	73(11.1)	76(11.6)	79(12.1)
AL		29(4.4)	36(5.5)	33(5.0)
	Total	206(31.4)	223(34.1)	226(34.5)

Table 8.27 shows the verb inflectional errors in the translation task, the writing task and the cloze task are 308, 436, and 389 respectively, and the error rates are 27.2%, 38.5% and 34.3%. Obviously, the errors in the tasks are ordered as such: the translation task<the cloze task<the writing task. Similarly, the word order errors in interrogative sentences in the translation task, the writing task and the cloze task are ordered as such: the translation task<the writing task<the cloze task. It can be concluded that the subjects did better at the sentence level than at the discourse level. The analyses of the tense marker and syntactic marker show that the degree of markedness is found to affect the targetlike use of the grammatical marked features. This finding also support Eckman's (1977) Markedness Differential Hypothesis which holds that the relative degree of difficulty of the areas of L2 which are more marked than L1 would correspond to the relative degree of markedness. The presence of the past tense marker -ed causes significant difficulty for all the three groups in acquiring the verb form of the simple past, and its negative effect on the low-level group is stronger. The presence of the syntactic marker wh-movement shows a significant negative role in both the low-level group and the intermediate-level group, but its effect on the advanced-level group is weaker. The negative role of markedness is more significant at the discourse level, but less significant at the sentence level. This is because at the sentence level, the learners have Chinese temporal adverbials and sentence pattern indications so that they pay more attention to the form-meaning consistency.

8.7 The performance of morphology and syntax acquisition of markedness

On the basis of the work described in the preceding sections, the questions and hypotheses would be further discussed at length. Eckman's Markedness Differential Hypothesis, Odlin's transfer theories, Skehan and Reiss's studies on attention to form and Schmidt's view on language instruction are used to explain the findings for the two hypotheses.

Hypothesis 1: Chinese learners of English experience more difficulty in acquiring past verb forms than present verb forms, and they also experience more difficulty in acquiring the word order in interrogative sentences than in declarative sentences.

The assumption that the L2 feature causes learning difficulty is made under the precondition of L2 markedness effects on L2 learning, which is well described by Eckman's MDH (1977) claiming that the unmarked feature of TL would be easy to learn and the marked feature of TL would be difficult to learn; that the degree of difficulty of the linguistic forms in TL would correspond to their degree of markedness. The present study identifies some significant differences in the transfer of the L2 marked and unmarked features, reflecting both the apparent positive effects of L1-L2 similarities and negative effects of L1-L2 differences. In the use of unmarked features, language proficiency is found to have no significant effect on the subjects' performance on the simple present verb form and the word order in declarative sentences. The verb form of the simple present and the word order in declarative sentences do not cause more difficulty for all the participants, as the absence of the tense and syntactic markers shows significant facilitating role in the acquisition of both the simple present verb form and word order in declarative sentences. Given L1-L2 differences or markedness, the analyses of the different performance of the three groups identify some cases where markedness theories demonstrate evident effects of linguistic markedness on learning difficulty.

Concerning the targetlike use of the simple present verb form, the unmarked simple present verb form shows significant facilitating effects on both regular /irregular verb forms and frequent/infrequent verb forms. As for word order in declarative sentences, the unmarked word order in declarative sentences shows significant facilitating effects on both the simple declarative sentences and the complex declarative sentences. While the simple past verb form is found to be more difficult to acquire for all the participants than the simple present verb form because the simple past marker -ed has significant negative effects on the targetlike use of the simple past verb inflection (P <. 05). Specifically, irregular verb inflectional errors are significantly more popular than regular ones in the present study. Compared with the infrequent verbs, the frequent verb forms are significantly favorable for the targetlike use of the simple past marker -ed (P<. 05).

There is no significant difference in the error ratio in the word order in declarative sentences and the word order in *yes/no* interrogative sentences among the three groups. The present study, however, shows significant markedness effects on the word order acquisition in wh-questions. Compared with the word order error ratio in the declarative sentences, all the three groups exhibit a slightly higher word order error ratio in the *yes/no* questions (7.6%) than in the declarative sentences (5.6%). Only in wh-questions do the word order errors show significantly larger proportions (86. 8%) than in declarative sentences and *yes/no* questions with regard to the targetlike word order use. That is, the degree of markedness corresponds to the degree of learning difficulty. The distribution of different error types across the three groups is more clearly indicated by Graph 8.1.

Graph 8.1 shows an obvious distance between verb inflectional errors of the simple past and word order errors in interrogative sentences across the three groups, and the verb inflectional errors respectively outweigh the word order errors in the three groups. It is revealed that learners' performance is more constrained by the more marked linguistic factor such as the English-specific tense marker -ed than by the less marked one like the word order pattern VSO. Similarly, there is a significant difference between the error ratio (7.6%) in yes/no questions and the error ratio in wh-questions (86.8%), indicating that the learners experience more difficulty in applying wh-questions than yes/no questions. It can be concluded that the more marked the L2 is, the more errors the learners make, and thus more difficult for them to acquire. As Schmidt's (1990) and Odlin's (1989, 1990) studies indicate, more marked patterns are harder to acquire than less marked ones. Gass also (1984: 120) argues that it is universal principles that play a leading role since they are dominant in assigning a relative order of difficulty.

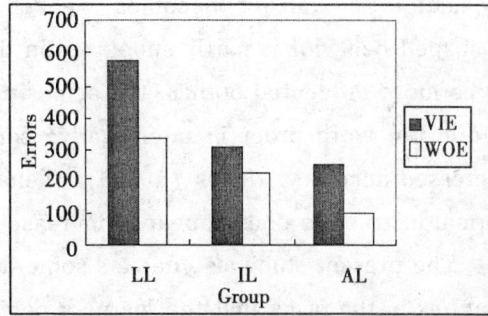

Graph 8.1   Distribution of VIE and WOE

Hypothesis 2: The low-level learners tend to transfer both marked features and unmarked features in L2 and the intermediate-level learners are conservative about the transfer of marked features. However, the advanced-level learners show a tendency to transfer unmarked features in L2 again.

Language transfer is obvious not only with regard to the existence of L2 markedness, but also when this factor interacts with learners' language proficiency. This hypothesis is put forward on the basis of Kellerman's U-shaped behavior which holds that beginners are more willing to transfer both marked and unmarked features; that intermediate learners are more conservative about transferring marked uses; that advanced learners once again become willing to transfer L1 unmarked uses. The learner's language proficiency level is found to significantly influence the targetlike use of the verb inflection. The tense marker -ed brought about the lowest proportion of non-targetlike use of the simple past verb form in the advanced-level group (21.9%), and the highest proportion in the low-level group (51.2%), with the intermediate-level group in between (26.9%). In the acquisition of the simple past marker -ed, the advanced-level group tended to show the strongest benefit from formal instruction as they make the least inflectional errors (248), while the low-level group shows the weakest (580), and the intermediate-level group comes in between (305). In using the word order in interrogative sentences, the advanced-level group makes in total 98 (15%) errors; the intermediate-level group makes in total 228 (34.8%) errors; the low-level group makes 329 (50.2%) errors in interrogative sentences, the phenomenon shows that the low-level learners are most inclined to transfer unmarked features and the inclination to transfer becomes weaker with increasing language proficiency. Thus, U-shaped behavior is partly supported in the present study. Language proficiency is found to be more influential both in the acquisition and use of the simple past tense marker *-ed* and in the word order in interrogative sentences as the formal instruction results in the increased accuracy. Reiss (1985), Skehan (1998) and Schmidt (1990) point out that formal instruction does appear to increase the rate at which the learners acquire language.

The present study also detects some differences in the non-targetlike use of L2 marked features in the tasks that the learners performed. To give a full picture of the acquisition and use of L2 marked features by the Chinese learners of English, it may be helpful to discuss one more factor that causes learning difficulty—the task. The distribution of errors in different tasks across the three groups is more clearly indicated by the following graphs.

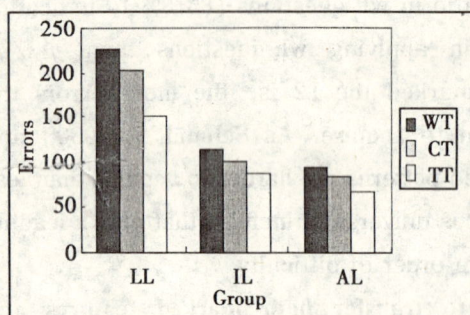

Graph 8. 2   Distribution of VIE in WT, CT and TT   Graph 8.3   Distribution of WOE in WT, CT and TT

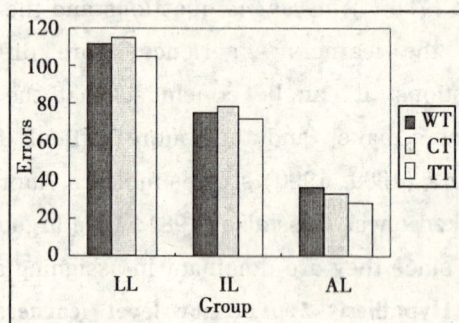

Graphs 8. 2, 8. 3 indicate that different tasks also affect the learners' performance. When the errors in different tasks are analyzed separately, the learners show better performance in the translation tasks than in the cloze tasks and the writing tasks in terms of the targetlike use of the simple past verb inflection; namely, the simple past marker *-ed* causes more difficulty for the subjects at the sentence level than at the discourse level. Reiss (1985) argues that "attention to form" comes out as the most common strategies used by learners whom teachers pick out as good learners. In terms of this argument, it is natural for the errors in the cloze tasks and the writing tasks to predominantly overtake the errors in the translation tasks as the participants pay more attention to the form-meaning consistency in the process of translating than in the process of writing. Spada (1986) also finds that form-focused instruction is a powerful predictor of success on grammar.

However, the syntactic marker VSO seems to play a differential role in the word order errors in the tasks. Graph 8.3 shows that each of the three groups has no sharp difference in the writing tasks, the cloze tasks and the translation tasks with regard to the non-targetlike use of the word order in interrogative sentences. Word order errors in the cloze tasks and the writing tasks exhibit a slightly higher rate than those in the translation tasks. From the two hierarchies, it can be found that the word order in interrogative sentences causes the same difficulty for the participants regardless of the tasks. The reason for this is that the word order in interrogative sentences is acquired mainly by means of communication, while communicative instruction, whose main goal is to develop learners' communicative competence with no focus on form, may be insufficient for word order acquisition. As Higgs and Clifford (1982) suggest, grammarless instruction may lead to fossilization.

The study verifies that the Markedness Differential Hypothesis (MDH) is universal and U-shaped behavior is partly supported. It is proposed that the selective attention hypothesis should be applied to formal instruction for the purpose of increasing learners' attention to the target language form-meaning consistency to open up a new way to make the acquisition of L2 marked features more effective.

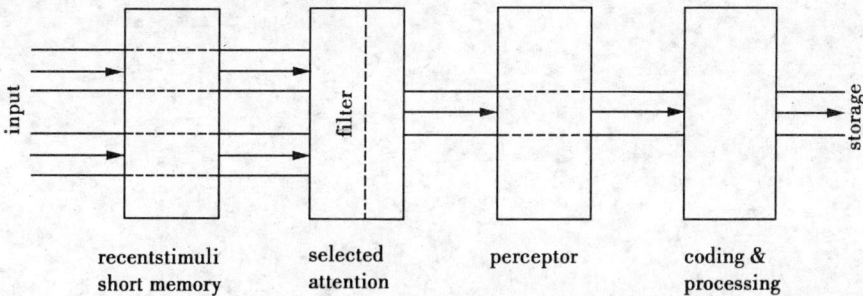

Graph 8. 4   The selective attention hypothesis model

Part Three

Metaphors and Metonymies

Chapter 9

The Acquisition of English Unit Word Metaphors

Unit words play an important role in the communication of oral and written forms of language. The unit word metaphor is the main obstacle in unit word acquisition of Chinese EFL learners. The study on the internal working mechanisms of unit word metaphors can obviously facilitate the acquisition of unit words and unit word metaphors. In cognitive linguistics, there are two different ways to study the internal working mechanisms of unit word metaphors: on the one hand, the Conceptual Metaphor Theory believes that the conceptual metaphor which is generalized from the conventional metaphor reflects people's cognition of the world. On the other hand, the Conceptual Integration Network explains the comprehension and production of the novel metaphors through the conceptual space, and further demonstrates the integration procedures reflected by corresponding conceptual models.

The study contains two experiments, which investigate Chinese EFL learners' acquisition of unit word metaphors from the perspective of language acquisition sequence. Experiment I adopts qualitative methods to analyze unit word metaphors in terms of the Conceptual Metaphor Theory and the Conceptual Integration Theory. It explores the integration networks of the internal working mechanisms. Experiment II invites the graduate students both from Wuhan University and China University of Geosciences as subjects, and takes the multiple choice task, the blank filling task, the sentence translation task and the cloze task as research tools. It first examines the accuracy of different types of the unit word metaphors, and then describes the acquisition sequences of each type of the unit word metaphors, and at last keeps orders the integration models of the unit word metaphors in sequence. This experiment aims at finding out the Chinese EFL learners' acquisition sequences of the integration models in the unit word metaphors by means of the quantitative analyses.

The experimental results indicate that four cognitive models exist in the unit word metaphors, including the simplex integration network, the sub-concept integration network, the regular two-step integration network and the irregular two-step integration network. The sequences of the four integration networks in Chinese EFL learners' unit word metaphors acquisition are as follows: the simplex integration network, the sub-concept integration network, the regular two-step integration network, and the irregular two-step integration network.

9.1 The Conceptual Metaphor Theory

Lakoff and his colleagues (Johnson, 1987; Lakoff, 1987; Lakoff & Johnson, 1980; Lakoff & Turner, 1989) argue that "the locus of metaphor is thought". They believe that metaphor is not only linguistic expression, but more basically a form of thought with their own epistemological functions, otherwise "we would expect different linguistic expressions to be different metaphors" (Lakoff, 1993). Metaphors are ubiquitous, conceptual and systemic from the cognitive perspective. It is a prevalent phenomenon in ordinary language. It is not considered as a figure of speech or a linguistic object. It is a figure of thought, a conceptual or cognitive organization expressed by the linguistic object. One common metaphorical concept may give rise to numerous linguistic expressions. Different metaphorical concepts form a coherent network, which underlies both speeches and thoughts.

9.1.1 The internal structure of the conceptual metaphor

The Conceptual Metaphor Theory states that a conceptual metaphor is composed of two parts: a target domain and a source domain. The cognitive force of the metaphor lies in the mapping of the schematic structure of the source domain onto that of the target domain. This mapping occurs at the conceptual level and is systematic in that there is a fixed set of correspondences between the structure of the target domain and the structure of the source domain. This mapping is not arbitrary but it is constrained by the Invariance Principle. Scholars (Lakoff, 1990, 1993, 1994; Turner, 1990, 1992, 1993) argue that metaphorical mapping preserves the cognitive typology (that is, the image-schema structure) of the source domain, in a way consistent with the inherent structure of the target domain. Take Shakespeare's famous passage as an example:

All the world's a stage,

And all of the men and women merely players.

They have their exits and their entrances;

And one man in his time plays many parts.

(As You Like It 2.7)

The sentences are derived from a basic conceptual metaphor LIFE IS A PLAY. LIFE is the target domain, and PLAY is the source domain. The relation of these two domains is demonstrated in Figure 9.1.

In this conceptual metaphor, PLAY has a rich internal structure with components like actors, make-up, costume, a stage, scenery, setting and lighting, audiences, scripts, parts, roles, cues, prompts, directors, casting, playwrights, and so on. With this conceptual metaphor, a whole set of correspondences is activated, for example: the world corresponds to a stage, people living in the world correspond to players, people's birth corresponds to their entrances onto the stage and their death corresponds to their exits. People may fulfill many functions during the life span of one man, which corresponds to an

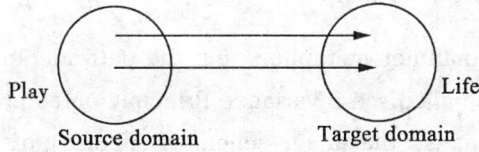

Figure 9.1   The conceptual metaphor mapping

actor playing many parts on the stage.

Consider now some everyday comments cited in Lakoff (1994):

He got a head start in life.

He's without direction in his life.

I'm where I want to be in life.

I'm at a crossroads in my life.

He's never let anyone get in his way.

He's gone through a lot in life.

The basic conceptual metaphor underlying the above idiomatic expressions is LIFE IS A JOURNEY, in which the target domain is LIFE and the source domain is JOURNEY. This metaphor contains the following correspondences or metaphorical mappings (Winter 1995).

Source Domain		Target Domain
JOURNEY	⟶	LIFE
Traveler	⟶	Person
Point of departure	⟶	Birth
Initial conditions	⟶	Personal endowment
Baggage	⟶	Personal problems
Obstacles	⟶	External difficulties
Distance	⟶	Duration
covered	⟶	Accomplishments
Destination	⟶	Life purpose
Termination	⟶	Death

Figure 9.2   The Metaphorical Mappings of *LIFE IS JOURNEY*

Lakoff and Johnson (1980) assume that a metaphorical mapping of the structure of the source domain onto that of the target domain usually consists of the following: slots in the source domain, relations in the source domain, properties in the source domain, and knowledge in the source domain.

9.1.2 The invariance principle

The analyses of the container metaphors and the path metaphors (Lakoff, 1992) lead to the following principle, called the Invariance Principle: Metaphorical mappings preserve the cognitive topology (that is, the image-schema structure) of the source domain, in a way consistent with the inherent structure of the target domain (Lakoff, 1992).

What the Invariance Principle does is to guarantee that, for the container-schema, interiors will be mapped onto interiors, exteriors onto exteriors, and boundaries onto boundaries. For the path-schema, sources will be mapped onto sources, goals onto goals, and trajectories onto trajectories. To understand the Invariance Principle properly, initially the mappings can not be treated as algorithmic processes that start with the source domain structure and closely connect with the target domain structure. Such a mistaken understanding of mappings would lead to a mistaken understanding of the Invariance Principle.

In detail, one first picks all the image-schematic structure of the source domain, and then he copies it onto the target domain unless the target domain interferes. He should instead think of the Invariance Principle in terms of constraints on fixed correspondences. If he looks at the existing correspondences, he will see what the Invariance Principle holds: the source domain interiors correspond to the target domain interiors; the source domain exteriors correspond to the target domain exteriors; etc. As a result, it will turn out that the image-schematic structure of the target domain cannot be violated. One cannot find cases where a source domain interior is mapped onto a target domain exterior, or where a source domain exterior is mapped onto a target domain path. This simply does not happen. The target domain sometimes overrides the character of the source domain. The Invariance Principle operates the mapping in the Conceptual Metaphor Theory as a selective projection from the source domain to the target domain.

The above analyses demonstrate the understandings of the Conceptual Metaphor Theory (CMT). First, in CMT approach, the metaphors have various forms, but these expressions are derived from a number of typological structures, such as LIFF IS A JOURNEY. On the basis of this conceptual metaphor, there are many different ways to express the cognition on LIFE. For example, the sentence, *I'm at a crossroad in my life*, is derived from typology metaphor LIFE IS A JOURNEY, and this typology metaphor is named Conceptual Metaphor. Moreover, the introduction of internal structure of conceptual metaphors and the Invariance Principe emphasizes selective correspondence between target domain and source domain at the conceptual level. In the above example, *crossroad* means traveler has many roads leading to different destinations, and in a certain context, *life* at this time may have some choices to harvest different fruits.

CMT provides important evidence that when the unit word metaphors are analyzed, the conceptual metaphor, which provides image-schema structures stored in people's long-term memory, plays an important role in the metaphorization of unit word metaphors.

9.2 The Conceptual Integration Theory

The centre stone of the working mechanisms of the Conceptual Integration Theory is the conceptual integration network which demonstrates blending procedures of novel metaphors with a graphics. Fauconnier and Turner (2003) argue that with the violation of integration principles, four typical forms related to metaphors are established. They are the simplex network, the mirror network, the single-scope network, and the double-scope network, based on which the integration networks of unit word metaphors are established.

9.2.1 Mapping

Mappings between mental spaces are set up when people think and talk. By and large, such mappings, when they are acknowledged at all, have been confined to phenomena considered peripheral, such as literary metaphor or analogy. But recently, there has been mounting evidence for the central role played by various kinds of mappings at the very heart of natural language semantics and everyday reasoning. There are three kinds of mappings: projection mappings, pragmatic function mappings and schema mappings.

The projection mappings project part of the structure of one domain onto another. The case for metaphorical mappings has been made by Reddy (1979), Lakoff and Johnson (1980), Turner (1987, 1991) Lakoff and Turner (1989), Sweetser (1990), Indurkhya (1992), Gibbs (1994), and many others. This kind of projection means that in order to talk and think about some domains (target domains) the structure of other domains (source domains) and the corresponding vocabulary are used. Some of these mappings are used by all members of a culture—for instance, in English, TIME IS SPACE. People use structure from their everyday conception of space and motion to organize their everyday conception of time, for example, *Christmas is approaching*; *the weeks go by*; *summer is around the corner*; *the long day stretched out with no end in sight*.

The projection of one domain onto another is automatic. Domain projection mappings may also be set up locally, in context, in which case they are typically perceived not as belonging to the language, but rather as "creative" and part of the ongoing reasoning and discourse construction. There is, however, no formal difference between the lexically entrenched cases and the ones that are consciously perceived as innovative.

For the other two mappings, the pragmatic function mappings indicate two relevant domains typically correspond to two categories of objects and are mapped onto each other by a pragmatic function. The schema mappings operate when a general schema, frame, or model is used to structure a situation in context. Concerning the novel metaphors, the projection mapping plays an important role in structuring the base of knowledge and provides means of structuring abstract concept via concrete concepts.

9.2.2 Integration and metaphor

It is known that metaphor is a salient and pervasive cognitive process that links conceptualization and language. It depends on a cross-space mapping between two inputs (the source domain and the target domain). This mapping makes metaphor a prime candidate for the construction of blends, and indeed it has been found that the blended space plays a key role in metaphorical mapping. In addition to the familiar source and target metaphorical projection, blends are constructed in which important cognitive work gets accomplished. Take the notion "computer virus" as an example:

Viruses are programs developed by renegade computer operators who covertly implant them in other programs.

Inflections can spread from computer to computer as fast as the Hong Kong flu.

Files are contaminated by infectious bytes.

Compuserve can never be completely immune to hidden killers.

Data physicians develop vaccines, disinfectants…

The only way users can be assured that their programs are healthy is through safe interface.

(Fauconnier, 1997)

In the examples given by Fauconnier (1997), the vocabulary from the domain of health, biology, and medicine is being used to talk and reason about the domain of computers and programming. The viruses have been mapped onto undesirable, harmful programs, which replicate themselves, erase files, and so on. The vaccines are mapped onto programs that counter the first; physicians map onto computer technicians, attempting to block the action of the harmful programs, and so on. Thus, it is found that the blends on one hand deal with the on-line analyzing; on the other hand this kind of blending is inclined to be conceptualized and typologilized. This trend gives a chance for Conceptual Integration Theory to cooperate with Conceptual Metaphor Theory.

9.2.3 The conceptual integration network

All forms of thoughts are creative in the sense that they produce new links, new configurations, and correspondingly, new meanings and novel conceptualizations. The blending is an important cognitive process that motivates some of this creativity and depends crucially on cognitive mappings between mental spaces. In this process, conceptual blending is studied in some detail in Fauconnier and Turner (1994, 1996), Turner and Fauconnier (1995, 1996), Coulson (1995) and Mandelblit (1995a, 1995b).

It is known that the blending is in principle a simple operation, but in practice the blending gives rise to a myriad of possibilities. It operates on two input mental spaces to yield a third space, the blended space. The blended space inherits partial structure from the input spaces and has emergent structure of its own. Here are some of the conditions that are satisfied when two input spaces I_1 and I_2 are blended (Fauconnier, 1997):

CROSS-SPACE MAPPING: there is a partial mapping of counterparts between the input I1 and the input I2 as shown in the Figure 9.3.

GENERIC SPACE: there is a generic space, which maps onto each of the inputs. This generic space reflects some common, usually more abstract, structure and organization shared by the inputs and defines the core cross-space mapping between them, as in Figure 9.4.

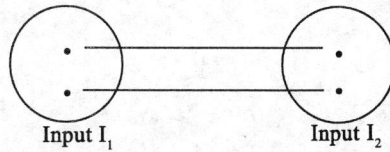

Figure 9.3   Cross-space mapping

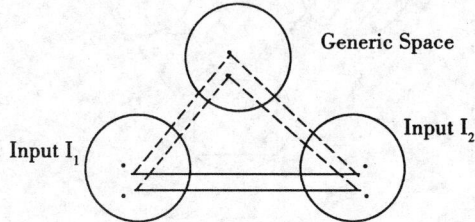

Figure 9.4   Generic space

BLEND: the inputs I_1 and I_2 are partially projected onto a fourth SPACE, the blended space, as in Figure 9.5.

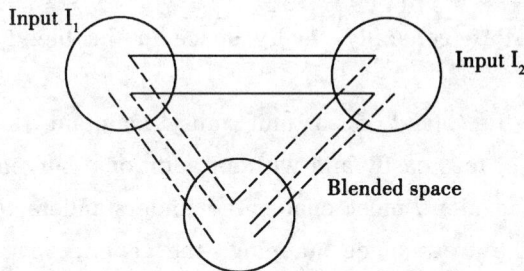

Figure 9.5   Blended space

EMERGENT STRUCTURE: the blend has emergent structure not provided by the inputs. This happens in three (interrelated) ways:

COMPOSITION: Blending composes elements from the input spaces, providing relations that do not exist in the separate inputs.

COMPLETION: Blends recruit a great range of background conceptual structure and knowledge without our recognizing it consciously.

ELABORATION: Elaboration develops the blend through imaginative mental simulation according to principles and logic in the blend.

Schematically, a full four-space blend is shown in Figure 9.6. In this graphics, the square stands for the emergent structure in the blend. The diagram is meant to indicate that when counterparts are projected separately. An additional possibility, not reflected in the diagram, is that one of the counterparts is projected but not the other.

9.2.4   The optimality principles

In addition to the overall structural characterization of conceptual integration network—

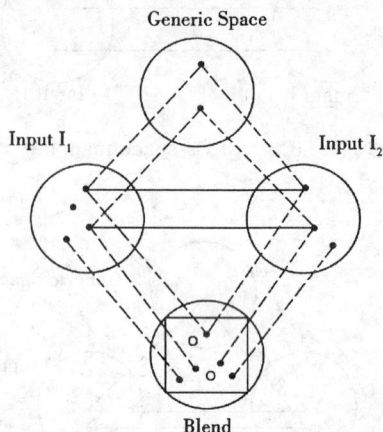

Figure 9.6   Conceptual integration network (Fauconnier, 1997)

cross-space mapping, selective projection in the blend, generic space, emergent structure, and so on—conceptual blending is controlled by an array of competing optimality principles. The principles are the following:

Integration: The blend must constitute a tightly integrated scene that can be manipulated as a unit. More generally, every space in the blend structure should have integration.

Web: Manipulating the blend as a unit must maintain the web of appropriate connections to the input spaces easily and without additional surveillance or computation.

Unpacking: The blend alone must enable the understanders to unpack the blend to reconstruct the inputs, the cross-space mapping, the generic space, and the network of connections between all these spaces.

Topology: For any input space and any element in that space projected into the blend, it is optimal for the relations of the element in the blend to match the relations of its counterpart.

Good reason: All things being equal, if an element appears in the blend, there will be pressure to find significance for this element. Significance will include relevant links to other spaces and relevant functions in running the blend.

Backward projection: as the blend is run and develops emergent structure, avoid backward projection to an input that will disrupt the integration of the input itself (Fauconnier& Turner, 1998).

These principles give rise to specific optimality pressures in the procedures of metaphorization. Practically, the blending does not obey all the principles that cited above. Within one type of blend structure, some blends can be "better" than others because they satisfy more of the optimality pressures, and many blends are ruled out in practice because of excessive violation. A blending process satisfying one principle often violates another principle.

Based on the violation of the optimality principles, Fauconnier and Turner (2003) establish four typical networks to describe the integration procedures. These four typical networks fully conclude the working mechanisms of metaphors.

Simplex Network: one input has a frame and the other has values for its roles. In this model, the relevant part of the frame in one input is projected with its roles, and elements are projected from the other input as values of those roles within the blend. The blend integrates the frame and the values in the simplest way. The frame in one input is compatible with the elements in the other.

Mirror Network: an organizing frame is shared by all spaces. The input spaces mirror each other in the sense that they have the same organizing frame. So does the generic space. The blended space also has that frame.

Single-scope Network: the organizing frame of one input is the organizing frame for the blend. The input provides the organizing frame to the blend, the framing input, is often called "source" which serves as the focus of understanding. Another input is called "target".

Double-scope Network: the organizing frame topology from both inputs is projected to the blend. It has inputs with different organizing frames as well as an organizing frame for the blend that includes parts of each of those frames and has emergent structure of its own.

With the internal and external factors, violation in integration procedure makes the network of integration have the above anamorphosis. As the ubiquity of these networks, the typical networks established by Fauconnier and Turner stimulate two questions. Is there any integration networks existing in unit word metaphors? What are the working procedures of unit word metaphors existing in difference situations?

9.3   The comparison of Conceptual Metaphor Theory and Conceptual Integration Theory

At the first glance, there are many differences between the frameworks of the Conceptual Metaphor Theory and the Conceptual Integration Theory. The differences have led some researchers to treat them as competing theories (Coulson 1995). While the evidence in these two theories tells that there are indeed some differences and similarities between them. The differences between these two theories are shown in Table 9.1:

Table 9.1   **The comparison of Conceptual Metaphor Theory and Conceptual Integration Theory**

Conceptual Metaphor Theory(CMT)	Conceptual Integration Theory(CIT)
Domains	Mental spaces
Two domains	Four spaces
Entrenchment	On-line processing

Metaphors are analyzed as ubiquitous and systematic relationships between the conceptual domains in CMT. In contrast with CMT, the basic unit of CIT is not the domain but the mental space (Fauconnier & Turner, 1994). The mental space is a partial and temporary representational structure which is constructed by speakers when they are thinking or talking about a perceived, imagined, past, present, or future situation. In CMT, language and conceptual structure from the "source" domain of vision is used to depict a situation in the "target" domain of knowledge and understanding. In short, a mental space is a short-term structure informed by the more general and more stable knowledge structures associated with a particular domain. While domains are the knowledge structures stored in long-term memory.

While CMT analyses involve mappings between precisely two conceptual structures, CIT typically makes use of a four-space model. The spaces in the CIT model include two "input" spaces, plus the "generic" space, and the "blend" space. Material in the 4-space model is projected from both the source and target spaces to the blended space. Contrastively, the mapping in CMT is the simple unidirectional projection from the source domain to the target domain. CMT has been primarily concerned with identifying regular, conventional patterns of metaphorical conceptualization, and explained motivated extensions of these conventional structures. On the other hand, CIT has often explicitly addressed itself to novel and unique examples which do not arise from entrenched cross-domain relationships.

Besides the differences cited above, the Conceptual Integration Theory shares many similarities with the Conceptual Metaphor Theory. These two approaches treat metaphor as a conceptual phenomenon rather than a pure linguistic phenomenon. They both involve in systematic projection of language, imagery and inferential structure between conceptual domains, and propose constraints on this projection.

Practically, it is readily assimilated by speakers of the language long before dictionaries and manuals formally record the new meanings that arise. Yet the process is cognitively complex and consists of several nontrivial stages and transitions typical of what goes on in all other areas of the conceptual system under pressure from analogy, metaphor, and real world, and other already available mappings and generic frames. Fauconnier (1997) clarified the following stages:

(1) Analogy and Schema Induction. Generic level features of source domain and target domain are able to be recognized, and can be conceptualized and related to the target domain.

(2) Categorization and New Conceptual Structure. In the second stage, the metaphor develops into categorization of target domain.

(3) Naming and Projected Structure. With the mapping in place and vocabulary transfer operating, the target domain finds itself named and structured.

(4) Blending and Conceptual Integration. Two separate domains blend into a single structure with emergent properties. When a blend gains consistence, it reorganized the categories and allows thought to move in new directions.

(5) Motivated Polysemy. Instead of blending together, the two domains in correspondence may stay apart, and even become increasingly distinguished, but without

losing their analogical and linguistic links.

(6) Divergence and Extinction. The real divergence between domains occurs when the vocabulary remains but the conceptual links disappear, so that the mapping is no longer linguistically transparent.

As illustrated above, novel metaphors are gradually changed into conventional metaphors by people's wide adoption. And it also indicates that the Conceptual Integration Theory seeks to model the dynamic evolution of speakers' on-line expressions.

The main role of unit word metaphors is to describe abstract concept, such as weather, mood of people. This kind of unit word metaphors have been widely adopted by language users. From the first time unit words were used to modify the abstract concept as novel metaphors, till today they are entrenched to conventional metaphors, the metaphorizing procedures of the unit word metaphors are the same as the above demonstration. So unit word metaphors can be investigated from two angles, the Conceptual Integration Theory analyses the procedures of metaphorizing in short-term memory. The Conceptual Metaphor Theory provides conceptual structures stored in long-term memory to structure particular scenarios in the conceptual integration.

9.4   Developmental patterns in second language acquisition

Developmental patterns show that learners pass through stages on route to the target-language rule provides evidence for a sequence of acquisition. It will be used to describe the general regularities which are obvious in language acquisition. The developmental patterns can be used to answer the following two questions in the second language acquisition. Do learners acquire some target-language features before others? And how do learners acquire a particular linguistic feature of the target-language? The first question aims to investigate the order of acquisition, the answer can be found by showing one feature acquired before another. And the second question focuses on the developmental stages of acquisition, it can be answered by showing that learners pass through stages on route to the target-language rule that provides evidence for a sequence of acquisition.

9.4.1   Methods for investigating developmental patterns

Experts set a myriad of different ways to identify developmental patterns in the second language acquisition. Three methods are widely adopted by L2 experts. They are error analysis, obligatory occasion analysis, and target-like use analysis.

The obligatory occasion analysis has the following procedures (Brown, 1973): First, samples of naturally occurring learner language are collected. Second, obligatory occasions for the use of specific target-language features are identified in the data. Third, the percentage of accurate use of the feature is then calculated by establishing whether the feature in question has been supplied in all the contexts in which it is required.

A criterion level of accuracy can then be determined in order to provide an operational definition of whether a feature has been "acquired". Usually, the level is set at 80-90 percent, below 100 percent, to take account the fact that even adult native speakers may not achieve complete accuracy. Brown (1973) considers a feature to be "acquired" if it is performed at the 90 percent level on three consecutive data collection points—a very rigorous definition.

The target-like use analysis is an extension of the obligatory occasion analysis. It is designed to take into account the incorrect use of specific grammatical features in contexts that do not require them in the target language, as well as non-suppliance in contexts that require the feature (Ellis, 1994).

On the other hand, some studies are longitudinal, involving data collection over a period of many months even several years. Such studies provide the strongest evidence in support of developmental patterns. At the same time, there are a number of cross-sectional in design (i. e. data are collected only at a single point of time). In order to make claims about the order of acquisition on the basis of cross-sectional date, researchers resort to a number of statistical procedures. For example, some researchers argue that the accuracy orders with which different features are performed corresponded to their acquisition order (Dulay and Burt, 1973, 1974). If the data show that short plural -s is performed more accurately than long plural -es, then this result indicate that the short plural form is acquired before the long plural form.

9.4.2 Previous researches of developmental patterns

With the purpose of identifying and describing developmental patterns, many experiments, observations are done from the acquisition of individual morpheme, negatives in English and German, relative clauses in English and Swedish, and German word rules. A number of studies are carried to investigate the acquisition order grammatical functions such as articles and inflectional features such as plural -s. the studies adopted obligatory occasion analysis to establish the accuracy with which learners of L2 English perform a range of morphemes. In the case of cross-sectional studies, an accuracy order is calculated and this order is equated with acquisition order by some researchers. The more accurately a morpheme is used, the earlier it must have been acquired.

With the principles of the obligator occasion analysis and the cross-sectional study, Dulay and Burt (1973) studied 3 separate groups of 6-8 years old Spanish-speaking children's oral data with Bilingual Syntax Measure and found that there might be "a universal or natural order" in which L2 children acquire certain morphemes. One year later, they compared oral data of 60 Spanish-speaking children and 55 Chinese-speaking children which were all aged from 6 to 8, with Bilingual Syntax Measure and they found that the acquisition order for both groups of children are basically the same, and learners' L1 does not affect the order development in child L2 acquisition.

Bailey, Madden and Krashen (1974) studied 73 adults aged 17-55 years with their oral data through Bilingual Syntax Measure. They found that adults process linguistic data in similar way to children, and the most effective instruction is that which follows observed order of difficulty.

Larsen-Freeman (1976) investigated 24 adult English learners whose L1 is Arabic, Japanese, Persian and Spanish respectively from University of Michigan. The data were collected with battery of 5 different tests of reading, writing, listening, speaking and imitating. The results show that there is a standard morpheme order for production tasks, and the frequency counts for morphemes on speaking task reflect the actual occurrence in real communication. The frequency in native-speakers' speech is the accuracy orders.

Besides these classical experiments, a number of later morpheme studies have been carried out, including some of languages other than English such as Van Naerssen's (1980) study of L2 Spanish, and Pica's (1983) study of the morpheme order of three separate groups of L2 learners.

One of the problems of these studies is that they distinguished the difference in accuracy between various morphemes. As all morphemes were mixed together, there could not be a strictly boundary to cut accuracy among different kind of morphemes. To overcome this problem, Dulay and Burt (1975) and later Krashen (1977) proposed a grouping of morphemes in experiments. They narrowed down the morpheme studies to a certain kind of morphemes, to constitute a clear developmental stage in that morphemes within it were acquired at more or less the same time. After reviewing the researches in the study of acquisition sequence, scholars propose that there is " a natural order " in acquisition. It can be predicated that there are acquisition orders of unit word metaphors. The acquisition order can be described with the obligatory occasion analysis from the cross-sectional study. The accuracy order of the different types of unit word metaphors can reveal the developmental patterns of unit word metaphors. Going further to the factors influencing the unit word metaphors acquisition sequence, the working mechanisms in metaphors provide evidence for seeking the internal factors that influence unit word metaphors' acquisition sequence.

With the overview of the Conceptual Metaphor Theory and the Conceptual Integration Theory, it is found that the internal and external factors influence the integration procedures of metaphor. Fauconnier and Turner (2003) establish four models in conceptual integration network to indicate different blending procedures in different metaphors. This statement raises questions that: Are there any different forms of integration networks in the unit word metaphors? If so, what are the working procedures of these networks?

With the longitude and cross-sectional experiments, many experts study acquisition sequence in morpheme acquisition, lexicon acquisition, and grammar acquisition etc. They believe that there is a nature order of second language acquisition. What are the acquisition sequences of unit word metaphors? What are the sequences of these cognitive models in the acquisition of the unit word metaphors by Chinese EFL learners? Corresponding to the theoretical assumptions underlying the proposed research questions, two research hypotheses have emerged:

Hypothesis 1: There are four coexisting cognitive models in the unit word metaphors. They are the simplex integration network, the sub-concept integration network, the regular two-step integration network, and the irregular two-step integration network.

Hypothesis 2: In Chinese EFL learners' unit word metaphors acquisition, the four integration networks have the following order: the simplex integration network, the sub-concept integration network, the regular two-step integration network and the irregular two-

step integration network.

9.5 Cognitive models of English unit-word metaphors

With the overview of the Conceptual Metaphor Theory and the Conceptual Integration Theory, it is found that the internal and external factors influence the integration procedures of metaphors. Fauconnier and Turner (2003) establish four models in conceptual integration network to indicate different blending procedures in different metaphors. This statement raises questions that: Are there any different forms of integration networks in the unit word metaphors? If so, what are the working procedures of these networks?

So cognitive models representing working procedures of unit word metaphors will be established with detailed analyzing examples adopted from the six types of unit word metaphors according to Zhang and Xin (1999) in the following table.

Table 9.2　　　　　　　　**The classification of the unit words**

Type	Unit words	Examples
1	Unit words indicating shape	a bale of cotton, a cake of soap
2	Unit words indicating containers	a barrel of beer, a cup of coffee
3	Unit words indicating small quantities	an atom of food, a touch of cold
4	Unit words indicating movement	a flash of lightening, a blast of music
5	Unit words indicating pairs and groups	an army of assistants, a crown of people
6	Miscellaneous unit words	a lot of people, a piece of paper

The first type of unit words describes the number according to the shape of the object, such as *a bale of cotton, a cake of soap*. Take the following phrases as example: *a barrel of beer* and *a cup of coffee*; the second type of unit words describes the quantity of the object according to the container. The third type of unit words counts the small quantities of things, such as *an atom of food, a touch of cold*. The fourth type of unit words describes the quantity of things by movement, such as, *a flash of lightening, a blast of music*. The fifth type of unit words describes the pairs or groups as the following phrases: *an army of assistants* and *a crowd of people*. The last group of unit words indicates the number with the fixed phrases or colloquies, for example *a lot of people* and *a piece of paper*.

9.5.1 Unit word metaphors indicating shape

Some abstract concepts can be described by the shape of objects, this kind of unit words can be treated as unit word metaphors. For example,

(1) He has a drop of pity.

(2) I've got piles of homework to do today.

In these two sentences, *drop* and *piles* are used to indicate shape. In ordinary unit words, they can be used as: *a drop of blood*, and *a pile of books*. Actually, "drop" means a very small amount of liquid that falls in a round shape such as *big drops of rain*, etc. to count any kind of liquid when they fall in a round shape. Pile means heavy column of wood, metal or concrete placed upright in the ground or the sea-bed as a foundation for a building, support for a bridge, etc. For example, *a pile of books* describes a picture that one book covers another and piles very high.

A drop of pity describes human's sympathy. It contains two spaces superficially *drop* and *pity*. The drop space stimulates a concept of liquid or unconsciously flowing things. This concept projects to the blended space. On the other hand, as conceptual metaphor FEELING IS LIQUID (Lakoff, 1992), the pity space provides concept that emotion is like liquid to the blended space. This blending produces the unit word metaphor that pity is quantified by the shape of liquid.

In "*piles of homework*", one input space is *pile*, the things placed upright in the ground. The other space is from the word *homework*. Work means that use of bodily or mental power in order to do or make something. With this definition, homework means somebody makes something at home, so the noun homework can be treated as a concrete entity. The conceptual character of stack from the pile space, and the abstract concept stack which is derived from the homework space, project to blended space to indicate that uncountable and abstract entities can be covered one upon another upright as a foundation of building or bridge.

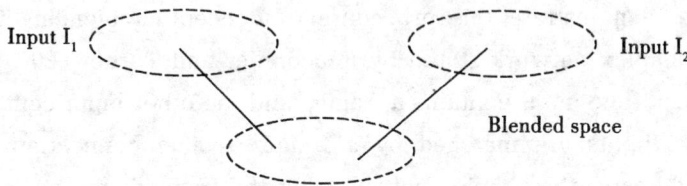

Figure 9.7   The simplex integration network

When some abstract concepts that can be metaphorized as concrete entities are counted, the unit words indicating shape can be used. The processing of metaphorizing is shown in Figure 9.7 which is named simplex integration network. The conceptual features of unit words spaces like *drop* and *pile* and the conceptual features of objects spaces like *pity* and *homework* blend together to denote the meaning of unit word metaphors.

Comparing this model with the typical network established by Fauconnier and Turner (2003), this network in unit word metaphors is similar to the mirror network. The mirror network indicates that the input spaces mirror each other in the sense that they have the same organizing frame. The simplex integration network also shows that the two input spaces have the same organizing frame.

9.5.2   Unit word metaphors indicating containers

The number of unit word metaphors indicating containers is limited, as there are not so many abstract concepts which are metaphorized as concrete entities held by containers. For example,

(3) Tom's got a pot of money.

This sentence means that Tom has made a lot of money, it dose not indicate he has a real pot which is full of money. Pot in the dictionary means round vessel made of earthenware, metal, etc for cooling things in, or any of various types of vessel made for a particular purpose. It is well known that in ancient times, all the money is made of noble metal. As there was not any bank in ancient times, the only way to store treasure is to put metal coins in pots or some other kinds of.containers. Nowadays money is only a number in bank account. The concept of money is transferred from concrete to abstract.

In "a pot of money", one space is *pot*, another space is *money*. The concept of container from the pot space, and the concept of noble metal entities representing money project to the blended space. The meaning of the unit word metaphor, a pot of money, is formed that the abstract number of treasure is contained in a concrete container to indicate that Tom has a lot of money.

Theoretically, when some abstract concepts' quantity or quality is described, the unit word metaphors indicating containers can be used. In this kind of metaphors, the abstract concept is treated as a concrete entity which can be held in container. The abstract concept provides the feature as the frame of metaphor and unit word provides the value. These two concept spaces integrate into the blended space to form the meaning of the unit word metaphor.

The figure to demonstrate this procedure of conceptual blending is similar to the structure of the simplex network stated by Fauconnier and Turner (2003). In unit words indicating container, one input contains a frame, and the other input contains an unframed element, and the inputs are matched by a frame-to-value connection. It is the same integration procedures as the simplex network that the frame from one input space blends with the value from another space.

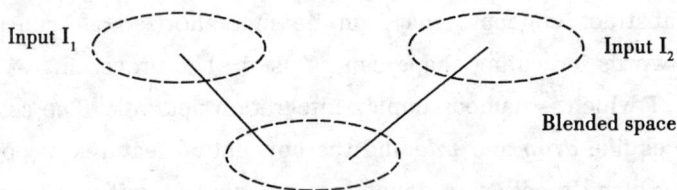

Figure 9.8   The simplex integration network

9.5.3   Unit word metaphors indicating small quantities

This group of unit word metaphors describes the concrete small quantities of things such as *a pinch of salt*, *a scrap of meat*, and *a trickle of water*. On the other hand, it also describes some abstract concepts such as people's sentiment or manner, e. g. *crumbs of learning*, *a fraction of his homework*, *a particle of truth*, and *a touch of cold*. As the objects are too small to be counted by their shape or by containers, it has to be compared with other small things or concepts of small quantities to make readers or hearers understand the concept of small quantity which unit words indicate. The following sentences will be analyzed to establish integration procedure of this type of unit word metaphors.

(4) The team's 2: 1 win on Saturday has provided a small crumb of comfort for their manager after an unsuccessful season.

(5) There is a hint of anger in his voice.

In "*a crumb of comfort*", "*crumb*" means very small piece, esp. of bread, cake or biscuit, which has fallen of a larger piece. From this definition, it is known that crumb is used to modify trivial object, and this kind of things can be cut into smaller pieces. The meaning of this sentence is that with a long time of failure, the manager feels down for a long time. One victory can not provide him with a satisfaction. The comfort lasts a short period of time. The sub-concept behind the "crumb" space is the objects' trivial shape, and this sub-concept of concrete object is extended to trivial shape of time. Thus, comfort denotes meaning from FEELINGS ARE THINGS.

Practically, in "*a crumb of comfort*", the "*crumb*" input chooses trivial things to blend with the comfort input, FEELING IS THINGS. The blending procedure is that the sub-concept of crumb space which implies a short time from a long period of time, and the comfort space integrates into to the blended space. This processing leads to a meaning that comfort is only a flash of time in manager's feeling.

"*A hint of anger*" describes the morale of a person. Anger is not to fly into rage; it is held by the person. He tries to hide it in order not to be mentioned by surrenders. Hint means a subtle way of indicating to somebody what one is thinking or what one wants, or indirect suggestion. The sub-concept of hint infers an indirect or potential expression on things, and these things can be noticed by surrenders' observations. The procedures of "*a hint of anger*" are metaphorizing as the following: the hint space provides a sub-concept that the object is difficult to observe, the anger space projects a concept from FEELING IS THINGS (Lakoff, 1992). With the integration of the two concepts, the character of unobservable anger is metaphorized as a hint.

Generally, unit word metaphors indicating small quantities can be used to modify abstract concepts. It hints that when a noun or verb is used as a unit word to count an abstract concept, the noun or verb has to generalize its concept from its concrete concept. The abstract concept derived from the concrete concept is treated as sub-concept. The integration model in this type of unit word metaphors is called the sub-concept integration network. The integration procedure can be demonstrated in the following figure.

Comparing the single-scope network (Fauconnier and Turner, 2003) and the sub-concept integration network shown in the above figure, the unit word space which focuses on the comprehension of small quantity provides the frame to the integration. The object space blends with the sub-concept space as the similarity between the two networks is that the sub-concept is conventionalized in the process of blending.

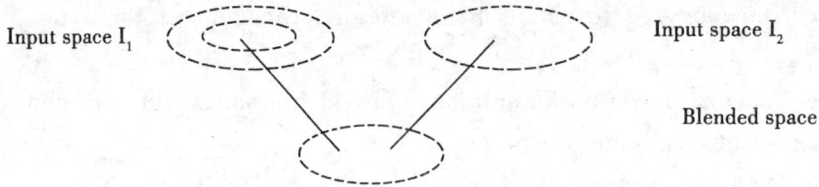

Input space I₁ ... Input space I₂ ... Blended space

Figure 9.9   The sub-concept integration network

9.5.4   Unit word metaphors indicating movement

In modern English, as unit words extend their function of displaying the image and features of objects, more nouns are coming into unit words and even some verbs are converted into unit words. These newborn borrowed unit words are of metaphor and more like adjectives to describe the movement of the object, such as *a blast of cold air, a jet of water*. Accordingly, the working mechanism of the unit word metaphor indicating movement should be analyzed from the meanings of verb which is converted into unit word. For example,

(6) A blast of cold air hit him as he opened the window.

(7) The whale blew a jet of water into the air.

"*A blast of air*" is used to describe the feature of the air. "*Blast*" means to destroy or break apart (esp. rocks) using explosives. This word contains features as destroy and break apart with the explosive as a tool. The sentence means that in a close room the window suddenly opens and the wind strongly blows into the room. When a person faces the cold wind, he will feel strongly cold. There are three input spaces in this metaphor: blast space (which represents the movement), explosive space (which is related to the meaning of blast), and air space. Comparing the definition of blast and the situation described in the sentence, the air or the wind is like a tool to break the close room from airtight to open. The Air space and the explosive space are blended together to form a temporary concept space that the air is used as a tool to break the close room. Then this temporary space is blended with blast space to produce the meaning that the cold wind is strongly blowing into the room.

"*A jet of water*" is used to describe the situation that a stream of water flowing or shooting into the air. Jet means to come out in a jets or jets. This word contains features as coming out, and the container with a narrow opening which can push things out. The sentence describes that a whale pushes a stream of water out of itself from the hole on its back.

Concerning conceptual metaphors LIVING THINGS ARE CONTAINERS (Lakoff, 1992), the whale is the container of the water and the hole on the whale's back is the mouth of this container. There are three input spaces in this metaphor: the jet space (which represents the movement), the tool space (which sprays water out), and the water space. A jet of water is metaphorized as the following steps: First, the water space and the tool space blend together to give receiver a temporary space that the water comes out of the whale through the mouth on the back of it. In the second blending, this blended space blends with the jet space. The state of this metaphor is vivified that the whale is strongly shooting a stream of water out like the trace of jet aircraft leaving in the sky.

With features of the verb, unit word metaphors indicating movement unconsciously emphasizes the movement of the objects. As the framework of the double-scope network stated by Fauconnier and Turner (2003), the input space in the double-space network has different organizing frames as well as an organizing frame for the blend that includes parts of each of those frames and has emergent structure of its own. The cognitive model of the regular two-step integration network in Figure 9.10 completely covers the description of the double-scope network. The difference is that the third input space is derived from one input space and it interacts with two other spaces at different levels of blending.

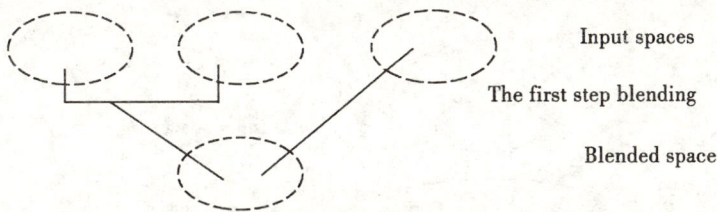

Input spaces

The first step blending

Blended space

Figure 9.10   The regular two-step integration network

9.5.5 Unit word metaphors indicating pairs or groups

Unit word metaphors indicating pairs and groups can express more information of the group than the ordinary unit words indicating groups and pairs. The cognitive model of this kind of unit word metaphors will be investigated through the following examples:

(8) There appeared an army of locusts flying over the land.

(9) He had an army of assistants in his lab.

"*An army of* " is used respectively in sentences (8) and (9). In the sentence (8), "*army*" is used to describe a group of insects, while in the sentence (9) it modifies a group of people. The same word blending in different sentences make different metaphors. From these two sentences, it is easy to predicate that the context of the sentence plays an important role in this kind of metaphors.

"*Army*" means part of a country's military forces that is organized and equipped for fighting on land, or an organized group of people formed for the same purpose. It contains the following conceptual features, such as a large number of well-organized people staying together, people with the same purpose. In sentence (8), the context implies that many insects fly over the land to a certain destination covering the sun and the sky. It has three input spaces in this metaphor, the army space, the locusts space, and the third one is the schema space which provides evidence that these insects fully cover the sky. The metaphorizing procedures in this unit words as the following: Sharing the same feature that a large number of people stay together for the same purpose, the schema space blends with the army space, and this blending leads to a temporary concept space that a group of insects fly to the same destination. Simultaneously, the schema space blending with the insect space produces a temporary space that large quantities of insects are flying on the sky. Blending these two temporary spaces, the metaphor indicates that there are so large a group of locusts flying over a land to some destination that they have covered the sky.

The procedures of metaphorizing in sentence (9) are the same as the procedures in sentence (8). The difference is that the concept which projects to the blended space from the army space is not the high quantity, but the strict organization, because the context stimulates a schema space that different people have different jobs, and they need a strict organization and good cooperation in the lab.

The integration procedures of unit word metaphors indicating pairs and groups are demonstrated in the following figure. It is called the irregular two-step integration network.

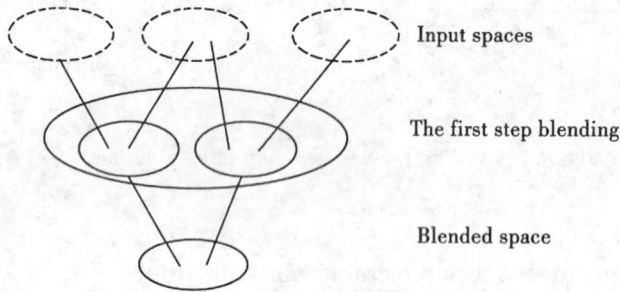

Figure 9.11   The irregular two-step integration network

The double-scope network (Fauconnier and Turner, 2003) demonstrates that the input has different organizing frames as well as an organizing frame for the blend that includes parts of each of those frames and has emergent structure of its own. The irregular two-step integration network established in the above sentences completely covers the description of the double-scope network. The difference between the typical network and the irregular two-step integration network is that the third input space is derived from the context and the schema space blends with two other spaces respectively at the same level of blending.

Therefore, four cognitive models are established in unit word metaphors. They are the simplex integration network, the sub-concept integration network, the regular two-step integration network and the irregular two-step integration network. As is shown in the following table, the simplex integration network is the working mechanism of the unit word metaphors indicating shape and containers. The unit word metaphors indicating small quantities are metaphorized like the sub-concept integration network. The working mechanism of the unit word metaphors indicating movement is the irregular two-step integration network, and the regular two-step integration network is the working mechanism of the unit word metaphors indicating pairs and groups.

Table 9.3   **The cognitive models existing in unit word metaphors**

Type	Model
1. Unit word metaphors indicating shape	The Simplex Integration Network
2. Unit word metaphors indicating containers	The Simplex Integration Network
3. Unit word metaphors indicating small quantities	The Sub-conceptual Integration Network
4. Unit word metaphors indicating movement	The Irregular two-step Integration Network
5. Unit word metaphors indicating pairs or groups	The Regular Two-step Integration Network
6. Miscellaneous unit word metaphors	All the above

Fauconnier and Turner's network theory demonstrates that a blending process can not satisfy all the six optimality principles. To satisfy one principle often involves the violation of another. Blending is often novel and generalized from the concrete concepts, but at the same time, it recruits entrenched mappings and frames. Therefore, the conceptual integration network is an essential one, and the violation of this network brings about the following networks:

(1) Simplex Network: One input has a frame and the other has values for its roles.

(2) Mirror Network: case where all spaces share an organizing frame.

(3) Single-scope Network: Organizing frame of one input is the organizing frame for the blend.

(4) Double-scope Network: organizing frame typology from both inputs is projected to the blend.

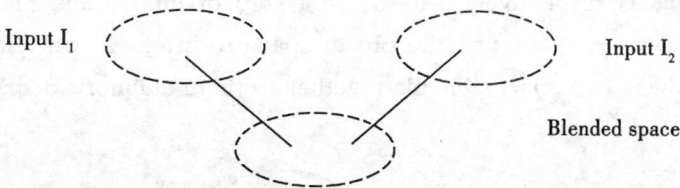

Input I_1 Input I_2

Blended space

Figure 9.12   The simplex integration network

The simplex integration network in Figure 9.12 shows that the frame from one input space is blended with the space in the other domain. These domains are compatible with each other completely. Two alternative situations are contained in this integration. One situation is that one input contains a frame, the other input contains an unframed element, and the inputs are matched by a frame-to-value connection; the second situation is that the two input spaces have the same organizing frame.

The sub-concept integration network in Figure 9.13 works as the following: unit words space is blended with object space indirectly. The unit word space uses its sub-concept to blend with the other input space. The reason of integrating these two spaces together is that the input and the sub-concept share the same frame or value with each other.

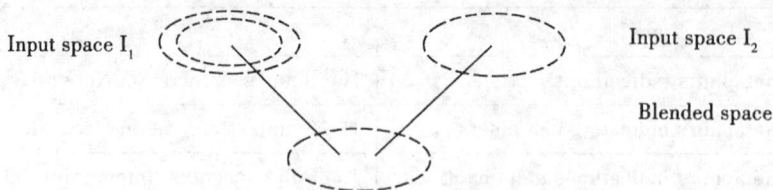

Figure 9.13   The sub-concept integration network

The situations in the fourth and fifth types of the unit word metaphors are different from the above two integration models. The regular and irregular two-step integration networks are originated from the double-space network established by Fauconnier and Turner (2003). The double-space network has inputs with different organizing frames as well as an organizing frame for the blend that includes parts of each of those frames and has emergent structure of its own. In these two networks, both organizing frames make central contribution to the blend.

In the model of regular two-step integration network (Figure 9.14), the context is used to stimulate a related concept from the unit word space, and this concept is treated as the "third space". This "third space" integrates with object space firstly to produce a temporary blended space, and then the temporary blended space integrates with the unit word space. This network reflects the working mechanism of unit word metaphors indicating movement.

The other network derived from the double-space network is the irregular two-step integration network (Figure 9.15). The context has been involved in the blending with the other two input spaces respectively. At the first step of integration, the context space blends with the unit word space and the object space to produce two temporary blended spaces, and then these two spaces blends together to the metaphorical space.

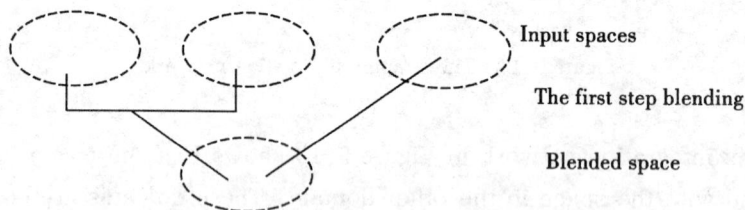

Figure 9.14   The regular two-step integration network

From the above analyses, the four cognitive models completely cover the typical conceptual integration networks established by Fauconnier and Turner (2003). This result completely supports the hypothesis 1 that there are four coexisting cognitive models in the unit word metaphors. With the four cognitive models, it is easy to explain the shift of unit word metaphors from novel to conventional, and with the four cognitive models, the unit word metaphors will be easier to be acquired by Chinese EFL learners.

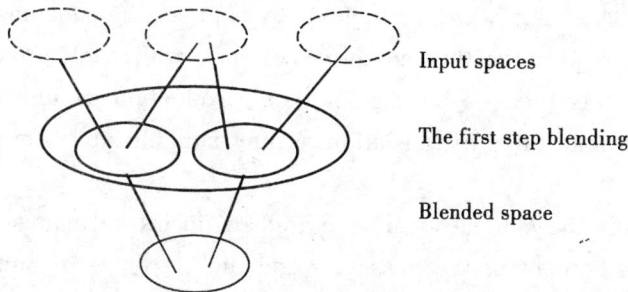

Figure 9.15 The irregular two-step integration network

9.6 The acquisition sequence of English unit word metaphors

The acquisition sequence of the six types of unit word metaphors were described according to the accuracy order of the six types of unit word metaphors. Altogether 44 Chinese EFL learners were tested. All the subjects were postgraduate students from Wuhan University and China University of Geosciences. Their average age was 24.5, ranging from 22 to 30 years old. All of the students majoring in English literature and applied linguistics had passed the Test for English Major Grade Eight (TEM-8). When taking part in the empirical experiment, they were all in the first year study of postgraduate program of English literature and applied linguistics. The English courses that they took in their bachelor program were intensive English, listening comprehension, spoken English, advanced English, lexicography, English literature and western culture. Most of them had read English newspapers, magazines, and novels. On the other hand, none of the subjects had any experience of living in an English-speaking community.

Four tasks were designed to evaluate the hypotheses. The first task was a Multiple Choice Task (MC) to observe the students' mastery of unit words and unit word metaphors. The second task was a Blank Filling Task (BF) to investigate students' comprehension of unit word metaphors at the sentence level. The third task was a Sentence Translation Task (ST) to examine students' comprehension and production of unit word metaphors. The fourth task was a Cloze Task (CT) to test students' comprehension and production of unit word metaphors at the discourse level. Details of these tasks are described in the following:

In the MC task, the subjects were required to choose the best answers that match the Chinese meaning of the given unit word phrase. There were six types of unit words involved, and each type contains five phrases with three choices given. For the details of the MC task, refer to Appendix A. In the BF task, the subjects were required to choose a word from thirty words given in the table to fill in the blank in each sentence. The arrangement of unit words was the same as that of the MC task: it contained thirty sentences with five sentences in each type. In this task, the subjects had to comprehend each sentence so as to get a schema-image of the sentence, and then distinguished the differences among words, and filled in the blanks of each sentence.

In the ST task, the subjects were required to translate thirty Chinese sentences into

English by using suitable unit word metaphors to express the meaning of the sentence accurately. The sentences were divided into six types with each group containing five sentences. The task was focused on the learners' production of unit word metaphors. There were no constraints on the translation as any suitable unit word metaphors were acceptable.

In the Cloze Task, the subjects were required to fill in the blanks with suitable unit words that match the content of the passage. And the six types of unit word metaphors were categorized into 12 blanks.

Each of the four tasks is arranged in an individual paper. Every five consecutive items with the same feature are put together as one group according to the classification of unit words. The choices in the MC task were randomly placed, so that the subjects could not work out a pattern for correct answers merely by guessing. The same layout was adopted for the BF task, in which orders of the words given in the front of the task were listed randomly. The order of the tasks was (1) the MC task, (2) the BF task, (3) the ST task, and (4) the CT task, so the subjects were investigated from the comprehension to the production of unit word metaphors.

9.6.1 The results of the multiple choice task

This task focuses on subjects' mastery of unit word metaphors, and it aims to investigate the comprehension of unit word metaphors at the lexical level. The data are collected in form of subjects' accuracy of each item. And the correctness is also reported in terms of its percentage. The results are shown in the following tables.

Table 9.4   **Accuracy of unit word metaphors indicating shape (N = 44)**

Item	1	2	3	4	5	Total
Total	23	36	31	32	24	146
%	52.3	81.8	70.5	72.7	54.5	66.4

As is shown in Table 9.4, in each item there are more than half of the subjects who chose the correct answer. To be specific, 52.3% subjects chose the right answer in item 1, 81.8% in item 2, 70.5% in item 3, 72.7% in item 4, and 54.5% in item 5. The mean accuracy reaches 66.4% as 146 person-times have chosen the right answers in this type of Unit word metaphors. The highest accuracy is 81.8%, which means 36 subjects in the total number of 44 subjects chose the right answer. Item 1 got the lowest accuracy in the five items as only 23 subjects chose the right answer.

Table 9.5   **Accuracy of unit word metaphors indicating containers (N = 44)**

Item	6	7	8	9	10	Total
Total	24	30	36	39	27	156
%	54.5	68.2	81.8	88.6	61.4	70.9

As is shown in Table 9.5, the accuracy of these five items ranges from 54.5% to 88.6%. The results in detail are: 54.5% subjects chose the right answer in item 6, 68.2% in item 7, 81.8% in item 8, 88.6% in item 9, and 61.4% in item 10. The total person-times of the correct answer of the five items are 156. The percentage of the mean accuracy is 70.9%. The highest accuracy among the five items is item 9 as 39 learners chose the right answer; the lowest one is item 6 as only 24 learners chose the right answer.

Table 9.6   **Accuracy of unit word metaphors indicating small quantities (N=44)**

Item	11	12	13	14	15	Total
N	22	30	34	37	20	143
%	50.0	68.2	81.8	77.2	45.5	65.0

The accuracy of unit word metaphors indicating small quantities is displayed in Table 9.6. In item 11, 22 subjects chose the right answer, in item 12, 30 subjects chose the right answer, and in items 13, 14, 15, the numbers of subjects who chose the right answer were 34, 37 and 20 respectively. The extremes of the accuracy are 45.5% and 81.8%. The mean accuracy of the five items is 65.0% as 143 person-times chose the right answers among the five items.

Table 9.7   **Accuracy of unit word metaphors indicating movement (N=44)**

Item	16	17	18	19	20	Total
Total	21	29	33	27	30	140
%	47.7	65.9	75.0	61.4	68.2	63.6

Table 9.7 shows that the accuracy of item 16 has not passed 50%. 47.7% subjects chose the right answer in item 16, 65.9% in item 17, 75.0% in item 18, 61.4% in item 19, and 68.2% in item 20. Totally, 140 person-times have chosen the right answers in this type of unit word metaphors. The mean accuracy reaches 63.6%. The highest accuracy is 75.0% in item 18 as 33 subjects in the total number of 44 subjects chose the right answer.

Table 9.8   **Accuracy of unit word metaphors indicating pairs and groups (N=44)**

Item	21	22	23	24	25	Total
Total	21	24	31	33	20	129
%	47.7	54.5	70.5	75.0	45.5	58.6

From Table 9.8, it can be seen that the accuracy of these five items ranges from 45.5% to 75.0%. The results in detail are: 47.7% subjects chose the right answer in item

21, 54.5% in item 22, 70.5% in item 23, 75.0% in item 24, and 45.5% in item 25. The total person-times of correct answer of the five items are 129. The mean accuracy is 58.6%. In this type of unit word metaphors, the accuracies of three items are not passed the 50%, but the total accuracy of these five items reaches 58.6%. The highest accuracy among the five items is item 24 in which 33 learners chose the right answer, and the lowest one is item 25 in which only 20 learners chose the right answer.

Table 9.9   **Accuracy of miscellaneous unit word metaphors (N = 44)**

Item	26	27	28	29	30	Total
Total	20	30	32	23	28	133
%	45.5	68.2	72.7	52.3	63.6	60.5

In Table 9.9, the accuracy of unit word metaphors indicating others is displayed. In item 26, 20 subjects chose the right answer, and in item 27, 30 subjects chose the right answer, in items 28, 29, and 30, the numbers of the subject choosing the right answer were 32, 23, 28 respectively. The extremes of the accuracy of the five items are 45.5% and 72.7%. The mean accuracy of the five items is 60.5%.

Table 9.10   **Accuracy of the six types of unit word metaphors (N = 44)**

Type	1	2	3	4	5	6	Total
Total	29	31	29	28	26	27	847
%	66.4	70.9	65.0	63.6	58.6	60.5	64.2

The accuracy of the six types of unit word metaphors are shown together in Table 9.10. The accuracy in type 1, unit word metaphors indicating shape, is 66.4%, and the accuracy in unit word metaphors indicating container is 70.9%. The accuracy in type 3, unit word metaphors indicating small quantities is 65.0%, and the accuracy in type 4, unit word metaphors indicating movement, reaches 36.6%, and in type 5, unit word metaphors indicating pairs and groups, the accuracy is 58.6%, and in the last type the accuracy is 60.5%. The mean accuracy of the multiple choice task is 64.2%.

The data indicate that the accuracy of these six types of unit word metaphors has passed 50%. According to the criterion of accuracy adopted by Brown (1973), a feature is considered to be "acquired" if it was performed accurately at the 90% level. It illustrates that the subjects do not have a good mastery of unit word metaphors. The accuracy of the six types of unit word metaphors is ordered as such: unit word metaphors indicating containers have the highest accuracy, and unit word metaphors indicating pairs and groups have the lowest one. The accuracy order of these six types is in the following: type 2, type 1, type 3, type 4, type 6 and type 5.

9.6.2　The results of the blank filling task

The purpose of this task is to investigate the mastery of unit word metaphors at the sentence level. The data are collected in the form of the subjects' correctness frequency of each item. And this correctness is also reported in terms of percentage. The results are shown in the following tables.

Table 9.11　**Accuracy of unit word metaphors indicating shape (N=44)**

Item	1	2	3	4	5	Total
Total	8	10	8	10	7	43
%	18.2	22.7	18.2	22.7	15.9	19.5

As is shown in Table 9.11, the accuracy of the five items ranges from 15.9% to 22.7%. The results in detail are: 18.2% subjects chose the right answer in both item 1 and item 3, 22.7% in both item 2 and item 4, and 15.9% in item 5. The mean accuracy is 19.5%. The highest accuracy among these five items is item 2 and item 4 as there are 10 learners in 44 choosing the right answer, and the lowest one is item 5 as only 7 learners chose the right answer.

Table 9.12　**Accuracy of unit word metaphors indicating containers (N=44)**

Item	6	7	8	9	10	Total
Total	2	10	17	12	8	49
%	4.5	22.7	38.6	27.3	18.2	22.3

Table 9.12 shows that the accuracy of the five items has not passed 50%. In detail, 4.5% subjects chose the right answer in item 6, 22.7% in item 7, 38.6% in item 8, 27.3% in item 9, and 18.2% in item 10. Totally, 49 person-times have chosen the right answers in this type of unit word metaphors. The mean accuracy reaches 22.3%. The highest accuracy is 38.6%, 17 subjects in the total number of 44 subjects chose the right answer, and the lowest accuracy in the five items is item 6 as only 2 subjects in 44 chose the right answer.

Table 9.13　**Accuracy of unit word metaphors indicating small quantities (N=44)**

Item	11	12	13	14	15	Total
Total	3	6	8	6	15	38
%	6.8	13.6	18.2	13.6	34.1	17.3

As is shown in Table 9.13, only 3 subjects chose the right answer in item 11, and 6 subjects chose the right answer in item 12, 8 subjects in item 13, 6 subjects in item 14, and 15 subjects in item 15. The extremes of the accuracy of the five items are 6.8% and 34.1% respectively. The mean accuracy of the five items is 17.3% as 38 person-times chose the right answers among the five items.

Table 9.14   Accuracy of unit word metaphors indicating movement (N=44)

Item	16	17	18	19	20	Total
Total	16	2	4	5	3	30
%	36.4	4.5	9.1	11.4	6.8	13.6

In Table 9.14, the accuracy of the five items ranges from 4.5% to 36.4%. The results in detail are: 36.4% subjects chose the right answer in item 16, 4.5% in item 17, 9.1% in item 18, 11.4% in item 19, and 6.8% in item 20. The total person-times of the correct answer of the five items are 30, and the mean accuracy is 13.6%. The highest accuracy among the five items is item 16 as 16 learners chose the right answer, and the lowest one is item 17 as only 2 learners chose the right answer.

Table 9.15   Accuracy of unit word metaphors indicating pairs and groups (N=44)

Item	21	22	23	24	25	Total
Total	5	12	2	5	1	25
%	11.4	27.3	4.5	11.4	2.3	11.4

Table 9.15 shows the accuracy of unit word metaphors indicating pairs and groups. In item 21, 5 subjects chose the right answer, and in item 22, 12 subjects chose the right answer. In items 23, 24, and 25, the number of the subjects choosing the right answer were 2, 5, and 1 respectively. The extremes of the accuracy of the five items are 2.3% and 27.3%. The mean accuracy of the five items is 11.4% as 25 person-times chose the right answers among the five items.

Table 9.16   Accuracy of miscellaneous unit word metaphors (N=44)

Item	26	27	28	29	30	Total
Total	14	5	4	8	10	41
%	31.8	11.4	9.1	18.2	22.7	18.6

As is shown in Table 9.16, the percentage of the correct answer in each item has not passed 50%. Only 31.8% subjects chose the right answer in item 26, 11.4% in item 27, 9.1% in item 28, 18.2% in item 29, and 22.7% in item 30. Totally, 41 person-times have chosen the right answers in this type of Unit word metaphors. The mean accuracy of this task reaches 18.6%. The highest accuracy is 31.8% as 14 subjects chose the right answer, and the lowest accuracy in these five items is item 28 as only 4 subjects chose the right answer.

Table 9. 17   **Accuracy of the six types of unit word metaphors (N = 44)**

Type	1	2	3	4	5	6	Total
Total	43	49	38	30	25	41	226
%	19.5	22.3	17.3	13.6	11.4	18.6	17.1

The six types of unit word metaphors are displayed together in Table 9.17. It shows that the accuracy of unit word metaphors indicating shape is 19.5%, the accuracy of unit word metaphors indicating container is 22.3%, the accuracy of unit word metaphors indicating small quantities is 17.3%, the accuracy of unit word metaphors indicating movement reaches 13.6%, and the accuracy of unit word metaphors indicating pairs and groups is 11.4%, and the last type is 18.6%. The mean accuracy of the BF task is 17.1%.

This data show that the mastery of unit word metaphors is not as good as the comprehension of unit word metaphors at the sentence level. The accuracy of the two types of tasks is 64.2% and 17.1% respectively, showing a significant gap. From Table 17, it can be found that unit word metaphors indicating containers have the highest accuracy, and unit word metaphors indicating pairs and groups have the lowest one. The accuracy order of the six types from the highest to the lowest is as such: type 2, type 1, type 3, type 4, type 6 and type 5. The accuracy order of the six types of unit word metaphors in the BF task is the same as the order found in the MC task.

9.6.3   The results of the sentence translation task

The ST task is used to investigate the subjects' comprehension and production of the unit word metaphors. The answers are judged with a standard that if the subjects have used unit word metaphors in the sentence and these metaphors are acceptable according to the dictionary consulting and native speakers' judgments, the answers are treated as the correct answers. The data of this task are demonstrated in the following tables.

Table 9. 18   **Accuracy of unit word metaphors indicating shape (N = 44)**

Item	1	2	3	4	5	Total
Total	26	33	33	26	23	141
%	59.1	75.0	75.0	59.1	52.3	64.1

As is shown in Table 9.18, the correct answer in each item has passed 50%. In detail, 59.1% subjects used suitable answers in item 1, 75.0% in item 2, 75.0% in item 3, 59.1% in item 4, and 52.3% in item 5. Totally, 141 person-times have used suitable unit word metaphors, and the mean accuracy reaches 64.1%. The highest accuracy is 75.0%, as 33 subjects of the total number of 44 subjects used the right unit word metaphors in item 2 and item 3. And the lowest accuracy in these five items is item 5 as only 23 subjects in 44 using suitable unit word metaphors. In each sentence, the most widely used metaphors are: "*a drop of pity*" in item 1, "*a grain of humor*" in item 2, "*a jumble of things*" in item 3, "*a load of complaints*" in item 4, and "*a bar of soap*" in item 5.

Table 9.19   **Accuracy of unit word metaphors indicating containers (N = 44)**

Item	6	7	8	9	10	Total
Total	31	44	38	41	29	183
%	70.5	100	86.4	93.2	65.9	83.2

From Table 9.19, it is clear that the accuracy of the five items ranges from 65.9% to 100%. The results in detail are: 70.5% subjects in item 6 used the suitable answer, 100% in item 7, 86.4% in item 8, 93.2% in item 9, and 65.9% in item 10. The total person-times of using suitable unit word metaphors of the five items are 183, and the mean accuracy is 83.2%. The highest accuracy among these five items is item 7. All of the students in 44 used suitable unit word metaphors in this item. And the lowest one is item 10. Only 29 students used suitable unit word metaphors. In the five sentences, the following are the most widely used in each item: "*a barrel of apples*" in item 1, "*a bottle of wine*" in item 2, "*a houseful of guests*" in item 3, "*a mug of coffee*" in item 4, "*a sachet of shampoo*" in item 5.

Table 9.20   **Accuracy of unit word metaphors indicating small quantities (N = 44)**

Item	11	12	13	14	15	Total
Total	24	32	37	23	22	138
%	54.5	72.7	84.1	52.3	50.0	62.7

The accuracy of unit word metaphors indicating small quantities is indicated in Table 9.20. 24 subjects used suitable unit word metaphors in item 11, 32 subjects use suitable unit word metaphors in item 12, 37 subjects in item 13, 23 in item 14, and 22 in item 15. The extremes of the five items are 50.0% and 84.1%. The mean accuracy of the five items is 62.7%. The following are the most widely used in each item: "*an atom of food*" in item 11; "*a fraction of second*" in item 12, "*a hint of anger*" in item 13, "*a snatch of salt*" in item 14, and "*a scatter of telephone call*" in item 15.

Table 9.21   **Accuracy of unit word metaphors indicating movement (N = 44)**

Item	16	17	18	19	20	Total
Total	36	21	10	26	29	122
%	81.8	47.7	22.7	59.1	65.9	55.5

The correct answers in item 17 and item 18 are below 50% as shown in Table 9.21. 81.8% subjects used suitable unit word metaphors in item 16, 47.7% in item 17, 22.7% in item 18, 59.1% in item 19, and 65.9% in item 20. Totally, 122 persons have chosen the right answers. The mean accuracy reaches 55.5%. The highest accuracy is 81.8%, that is, 36 subjects in the total number of 44 subjects used suitable unit word metaphors, and the lowest accuracy in the five items is item 16 as only 21 subjects in 44 used suitable unit word metaphors. The most widely used metaphors are: "*a barrage of criticism*" in item 16, "*a blast of cold air*" in item 17, "*a fit of coughing*" in item 18, "*a flash of lightening*" in item 19, and "*a gush of water*" in item 20.

Table 9.22　**Accuracy of unit word metaphors indicating pairs and groups (N = 44)**

Item	21	22	23	24	25	Total
Total	10	0	38	18	15	81
%	22.7	0	86.4	40.9	34.1	36.8

The accuracy of the five items ranges from 0% to 86.4% as shown in Table 9.22. The results in detail are: 22.7% subjects in item 21 used suitable unit word metaphors, 0% in item 22, 86.4% in item 23, 40.9% in item 24, and 34.1% in item 25. The total person-times of the correct answer of the five items are 81. The mean accuracy is 36.8%. In this type of unit word metaphors, the accuracy of four items does not pass 50%, and the mean accuracy of the five items only 58.6%. The highest accuracy among these five items is item 23 as 38 learners in item 44 used suitable unit word metaphors in this item, and the lowest one is item 22 as no learners used suitable unit word metaphors. In detail, the following answers are the most widely used ones in each item: "*an army of assistants*" in item 21, "*a bunch of roses*" in item 23, "*a brood of children*" in item 24, and "*a flood of imports*" in item 25.

Table 9.23　**Accuracy of miscellaneous unit word metaphors (N = 44)**

Item	26	27	28	29	30	Total
Total	25	29	31	22	30	137
%	56.8	65.9	70.5	50.0	68.2	62.3

Table 9.23 shows the accuracy of miscellaneous unit word metaphors. In item 26, 25 subjects provided acceptable answers, in item 27, 29 subjects provided suitable answers, in item 28, 31 subjects used the suitable answers. 22 subjects in item 29 used the suitable answers, and 30 subjects in item 30, 30 subjects used the suitable answers. The extremes of the five items are 50.0% and 70.5%. The mean accuracy of the five items is 62.3%. "*An abundance of hair*" in item 26, and "*an article of clothes*" in item 27 are the favorite, "*a belt of trees*" is in item 28, "*a carpet of snow*" in item 29, and "*a myriad of stars*" in item 30 are widely used.

Table 9.24   **Accuracy of the six types of unit word metaphors (N＝44)**

Type	1	2	3	4	5	6	Total
Total	141	183	112	142	81	137	796
%	64.1	83.2	62.7	55.5	36.8	62.3	60.3

The accuracy of the six types of unit word metaphors are displayed in Table 9.24. The accuracy of unit word metaphors indicating shape is 64.1%, the accuracy of unit word metaphors indicating container is 83.2%, the accuracy of unit word metaphors indicating small quantities is 62.7%, the accuracy of unit word metaphors indicating movement reaches 55.5%, and the accuracy of unit word metaphors indicating pairs and groups is 36.8%, and the accuracy in the last type is 62.3%. The total person-times in these thirty items are 796. The mean accuracy is 60.3%, close to the accuracy of the MC task (64.2%). This result demonstrates that in sentence production, learners can use their imaginations to describe numbers or degree of concrete and abstract things.

Unit word metaphor indicating containers has the highest accuracy, and unit word metaphor indicating pairs and groups has the lowest accuracy. The sequence of the six types of unit word metaphors from the highest to the lowest is type 2, type 1, type 3, type 4, type 6 and type 5, which is the same as the sequence in the MC task.

9.6.4 The results of the cloze task

In the CT task, the subjects had to fill in the blanks on the basis of their comprehension about the whole passage. In this task, subjects need to understand the whole passage to get a clear schema-image in their mind. The purpose of this task is to investigate the subjects' comprehension and production of the unit word metaphors at the discourse level. The answers of this task were judged according the dictionary consulting and native speakers' judgments. The answers that were accepted by the dictionary or native speakers were treated as the correct answers. The details of accuracy of the twelve items are revealed in the following tables.

Table 9.25   **Accuracy of blanks in the cloze task (N＝44)**

Item	1	2	3	4	5	6	7	8	9	10	11	12	Total
Total	34	42	38	28	42	34	41	32	38	35	22	27	413
%	77.3	95.5	86.4	63.6	95.5	77.3	93.2	72.7	86.4	79.5	50.0	61.4	78.2

The accuracy of the 12 items which is demonstrated in the above table ranges from 95.5% to 50.0%. Item 5 and item 6 belong to unit word metaphors indicating shape. Unit word metaphors indicating containers contain item 2 and item 7, unit word metaphors indicating small quantities include item 9 and 10. Item 1 and 8 stand for unit word metaphors indicating movement. Item 11 and item 12 represent unit word metaphors indicating pairs and groups. And item 3 and item 4 stand for miscellaneous unit word metaphors.

Table 9.26　　　　　　　　Accuracy of blanks in the cloze task (N=44)

TYPE ITEM	Type 1		Type 2		Type 3		Type 4		Type 5		Type 6	
	5	6	2	7	9	10	1	8	11	12	3	4
Total	42	34	42	41	38	35	34	32	22	27	38	28
%	95.5	77.3	95.5	93.2	86.4	79.5	77.3	72.7	50.0	61.4	86.4	63.6

As is shown in Table 9.26, half of the subjects used suitable unit word metaphors. The six types of unit word metaphors is in the following order: unit word metaphors indicating containers have the highest accuracy, and the lowest accuracy among the six types of unit word metaphors lies in unit word metaphors indicating pairs and groups. The accuracy order of the six types is from the highest accuracy type 2 to type 1, type 3, type 4, type 6 and type 5.

9.6.5　The correlation of the four tasks

After reporting the results of the four tasks respectively, the accuracy of each task is represented in the following table. The accuracy of the Multiple Choice Task is 64.2%, and the accuracy of the Blanks Filling Task is 17.1%. The accuracy of the sentence translation task is 60.3%, and the accuracy of the Cloze Task is 78.2%. The BF task has the lowest accuracy among the four tasks, and the CT task has the highest accuracy among the tasks.

Table 9.27　　　　　　　　Accuracy of the four tasks (N=44)

TYPE	TOTAL	%
Multiple Choice Task (30 items)	847	64.2
Blanks Filling Task　(30 items)	226	17.1
Sentences Translation (30 items)	796	60.3
Cloze Task　　　　(12 items)	413	78.2
Total	2282	50.8

The arrangement of items in the four tasks is that in the MC task, the BF task, the ST task and the CT task, the first five items aim to observe the subjects' comprehension and production of unit word metaphors indicating shape. From item 6 to item 10, the mastery of unit word metaphors indicating containers is investigated. Items 11, 12, 13, 14, 15 concern the mastery of unit word metaphors indicating small quantities. The next five items focus on the subjects' comprehension and production of unit word metaphors indicating movement. Items 21, 22, 23, 24, 25 are for the purpose of investigating subjects' mastery of unit word metaphors indicating pairs and groups. The last five items examine the acquisition of miscellaneous unit word metaphors. In the CT task, the situation is different as the twelve items are randomly arranged and each type of the unit words has two items in this task.

Table 9. 28   **Unit word metaphors in tasks**

Item	Type of unit word metaphors
1, 2, 3, 4, 5	Unit word metaphors indicating shape
6, 7, 8, 9, 10	Unit word metaphors indicating container
11, 12, 13, 14, 15	Unit word metaphors indicating small quantities
16, 17, 18, 19, 20	Unit word metaphors indicating movement
21, 22, 23, 24, 25	Unit word metaphors indicating pairs and groups
26, 27, 28, 29, 30	Miscellaneous unit word metaphors

The Multiple Choice Task examined the subjects' comprehensionat the lexical level, and the Blanking Filling task at the syntactic level. The two tasks above checked subjects from the comprehension aspect. The sentence translation task investigated the subjects' comprehension and production of unit word metaphors at the syntactic level. And the cloze task studied subjects' comprehension and production of unit word metaphors at the discourse level. The two tasks studied subjects from the production aspect.

In terms of the methods of investigating the acquisition sequence, one common method for identifying and describing developmental patterns is obligatory occasion analysis. This has been widely used by L2 acquisition researchers and is clearly described in Brown (1973). The basic procedures are as the following: firstly, samples of naturally occurring learner language are collected. Secondly, obligatory occasions for the use of specific TL features are identified in the data. Third, the percentage of accurate use of the feature is then calculated by establishing whether the feature in question has been supplied in all the contexts in which it is required. The accuracy order of the six types of unit word metaphors reflects the acquisition order of the six types of unit word metaphors.

Statistically, in the MC task, the highest two accuracy among these six types of unit words lies in the unit word metaphors indicating shape and containers. The accuracy is 66. 4% , and 70. 9% respectively (Table 9. 10). In the BF task, the highest two accuracy is 22. 3% and 19. 5% , accuracy of the unit words indicating shape and containers respectively (Table 9. 17). And in the ST task, the highest accuracy of unit word metaphors also lies in the first two types. The accuracy is 64. 1% and 83. 2% (Table 9. 24). In the CT task, the highest accuracy is in the first two types of unit words (Table 9. 25, 9. 26). The data indicate that unit word metaphors indicating shape and containers have the highest accuracy among the six types of unit word metaphors in the four tasks. The two kinds of unit word metaphors are acquired first in the acquisition sequence of unit word metaphors.

Type 2 has the highest accuracy among the six types of unit word metaphors while the accuracy of type 5 is the lowest among the six types of unit word metaphors. The accuracy order of the six types of unit word metaphors from the highest to the lowest is type 2, type

1, type 3, type 4, type 6 and type 5. So the cognitive models existing in the six types of unit word metaphors are shown in Table 9. 29.

Table 9. 29　　　**The cognitive models existing in unit word metaphors**

Type	Model
1. Unit word metaphors indicating shape	The Simplex Integration Network
2. Unit word metaphors indicating containers	The Simplex Integration Network
3. Unit word metaphors indicating small quantities	The Sub-conceptual Integration Network
4. Unit word metaphors indicating movement	The Irregular two-step Integration Network
5. Unit word metaphors indicating pairs or groups	The Regular two-step Integration Network
6. Miscellaneous unit word metaphors	All the above

The simplex integration network is the working mechanism of unit word metaphors indicating shape and containers. Unit word metaphors indicating small quantities are metaphorized following the sub-concept integration network. The working mechanism of unit word metaphors indicating movement is the irregular two-step integration network, and the regular two-step integration network is the working mechanism of unit word metaphors indicating pairs and groups.

With the relationship between unit word metaphors and the four cognitive models, the acquisition of unit word metaphors by Chinese EFL learners follows a certain order: the simplex integration network, the sub-concept integration network, the regular two-step integration network and the irregular two-step integration network. Concerning the results found by Bailey, Madden, and Krashen (1974) that the most effective instruction is that which follows observed order difficulty, the order of these four structures is also from simple to complex.

The Multiple Choice Task examined the subjects' comprehension at the lexical level, the Blanking Filling task at the syntactic level. The two tasks checked subjects from the comprehension aspect. The Sentence Translation Task investigated subjects' production of unit word metaphors at the syntactic level. And the cloze task studied subjects' comprehension and production of unit word metaphors at the discourse level.

In comparison with the accuracy of the four tasks, it is found that the cloze task has the highest accuracy among the Multiple Choice Task, the Blanking Filling Task, the Sentence Translation Task, and the Cloze Task. Before administrating the experiment, the author predicted that the Cloze Task would have the lowest accuracy among the four tasks, but the accuracy order of the tasks completely overthrew the prediction, indicating that the thematic of the passage plays an important role in the comprehension and production of unit word metaphors. Coincidently, Walker and Meyer (1980) demonstrate this understanding by the sentence comprehension experiment. It is evident that the implication of thematic ideas is privileged in comparison to those non-thematic ideas. The role of discourse comprehension of unit word metaphors has been illustrated to be the most useful factor.

Chapter 10

A Study of English Metonymy-motivated Proverbs from the Perspective of Idealized Cognitive Models

Metonymy is a basic way of thinking in cognition. According to a framework of idealized cognitive models (ICMs) put forward by Lakoff in 1987, metonymy can be classified into two types. One type is metonymy caused in the relationship between the whole ICM and its parts, and the other is metonymy caused in the relationship between parts of the same ICM. The former includes metonymy within Thing-part ICM, the Scale ICM, Constitution ICM, Event ICM, Category-and-member ICM, Category-and-property ICM, and Reduction ICM, and the latter includes those within Action ICM, Perception ICM, Causation ICM, Production ICM, Control ICM, Possession ICM, Containment ICM, Location ICM and Modification ICM. As one basic part of language, proverbs are the collective wisdom of all nations of all ages. They are brief in form, stable in structure, but bear national culture and geographical characteristics, and are greatly influenced by political and economic histories. Therefore, Chinese EFL learners may encounter difficulties in acquiring them. Based on the framework of ICMs, this research studies the acquisition of English metonymy-motivated proverbs by Chinese EFL learners from the perspective of idealized cognitive models.

A total of 97 subjects participated in the present study, and they were all from Wuhan University, including 35 non-English major freshmen, 31 non-English major postgraduates and 31 English major postgraduates. A test paper on English proverbs designed according to their metonymic motivations. The items in the test paper were in the form of translation from English into Chinese, translation from Chinese into English and blank filling.

Results of the experiment reveal that in general, the cognition of metonymy in English proverbs goes up with the development of the English proficiency. For metonymy within Thing-part ICM, Event ICM, Category-and-member ICM, Category-and-property ICM, Action ICM and Location ICM, the cognition in the understanding and use of English proverbs goes up from the lower level to the higher level. However, for the lower and the intermediate level, the cognition of metonymy within Thing-part ICM, Event ICM, Category-and-member ICM, Category-and-property ICM, and Location ICM is the same. The difference between the intermediate level and the higher level on the cognition of metonymy within Event ICM, Category-and-member ICM, Category-and-property ICM,

Action ICM, and Location ICM is not statistically significant.

10.1   The nature and definition of metonymy

Traditionally metonymy is viewed as a figure of speech and is studied under the term of metaphor. However, in the recent decades, cognitive linguists hold the view that metonymy, together with metaphor, is a kind of thinking pattern, it is conceptual in nature and it is a cognitive process.

It has been two thousand years since the research on metonymy began. The first appearance of this term can be traced back to ancient Greek philosophy, and more specifically in Platonic debates regarding the arbitrariness and naturalness of signs. Traditionally metonymy is treated as a figure of speech, and is thought basically as a matter of language, especially literary and figurative language. The basic term in traditional views of metonymy used to be "change of names". It is claimed that metonymy operates only on names of things, involves the substitution of name of one thing for that of another and the two things are in certain way associated. Cicero (1967) states that "metonymy is a valuable stylistic ornament; it occurs for the sake of ornament, one proper name is substituted for another." (Cicero, 1967) Besides the view that metonymy's value is restricted to the stylistic ornament of oration, he also believes that metonymy only operates at the lexical level. According to Urgerer and Schimid (2001), as a figure of speech, metonymy involves a relation of contiguity (nearness or neighborhood) between what is denoted by the literal meaning of a word and its figurative meaning. These definitions of metonymy are consistent with what is described in the American Heritage Dictionary: "a figure of speech in which an attribute or commonly associated feature is used to designate something." (*The American Heritage Dictionary*, 1991)

However, since the publication of the influential work of Lakoff and Johnson's *Metaphors We Lives By* in 1980, the study of metaphor and metonymy has made great progress in cognitive linguistics. It is widely accepted that both metonymy and metaphor are fundamental conceptual mechanisms that have great impact on human thought. As for the definition to the term metonymy, researchers now have endorsed no generally accepted one from the perspective of cognitive linguistics. Lakoff (1987) views metonymy as a stand-for relation occurring in one ICM. In other words, metonymy has primarily a referential function by which it allows us to use one entity to stand for another. For instance, in the sentence "*I have bought a Ford*", the name of the car-making company stands for one of its characteristic products.

Langacker (1993) defines metonymy as "a reference-point phenomenon in which one conceptual entity, the reference point, affords mental access to another conceptual entity, the desired target." According to him, metonymic process consists in mentally accessing one conceptual entity via another entity. Croft (1993) defines metonymy with the core concept of "contiguity", based on which he gives a definition that "Metonymy is a shift of word meaning from the entity it stands for to a 'contiguous' entity." However, Croft fails to explain how the cognitive process of metonymy shifts.

Blank and Koch have pointed out "salient" and "domain highlighting", but they both fail to indicate the cognitive process of metonymy, with Blank's definition (1999) of metonymy as "a linguistic device based on salient conceptual relations within a frame network" and Koch's (1999) as "a conceptual effect of domain highlighting within one domain matrix".

Radden & Kovecses (1999) declare that "Metonymy is a cognitive process in which one conceptual entity, the vehicle, provides mental access to another conceptual entity, the target, within the same idealized cognitive model." This definition of metonymy is considered to be the most popular, which is the base for the the terms of domains, schemata or frames.

Barcelona (2000) defines metonymy as "a conceptual projection whereby one experiential domain (the target) is partially understood in terms of another experiential domain (the source)." He declares that "Metonymy is a special case of what Langacker (1987: 385-386) called activation; the metonymic mapping causes the mental activation of the target domain, often with a limited discourse purpose." Later Barcelona (2000) concludes that "Metonymy is the conceptual mapping of a cognitive domain onto another domain, both domains being included on the same domain or ICM, so that the source provides mental access to the target." Li Yongzhong (2004) gives a more comprehensive definition with the consideration of pragmatic function of metonymy. He puts forward the definition that "Metonymy is a mapping of conceptual domain, the source, onto another domain, the target. Both domains belong to the same functional domain (or the same ICM). They are linked by a pragmatic function and the target can be mentally activated by the source."

The definitions of Radden and Kovecses, Barcelona and Li Yongzhong are the development of Langacker's. The notion of "mental access" is the common point of their definitions, and the notion of "ICM" is used to discuss the definition of metonymy.

The new view of metonymy proposed by Lakoff and Johnson challenged all the aspects of traditional rhetoric theory. However, only one single chapter is devoted to metonymy, compared with the dominance of metaphor in the book *Metaphors We Live By*. Since then, although metaphor has been studied as a way of thinking, metonymy has received far less attention. However, the cognitive understanding of metonymy has become increasingly prevalent in the linguistic circles and some linguists hold that metonymy is even more fundamental than metaphor.

In cognitive linguistics, metonymy is claimed to be not just a matter of names of things, but essentially a conceptual phenomenon. Lakoff and Johnson (1980) believes that, metonymy, like metaphor, is part of the everyday way of thinking, grounded in experience and subject to general and systematic principles, and structures our thoughts and actions. Gibbs (1999) holds that the impulse to speak and think with metonymy is a significant part of human's everyday experience. In his opinion, metonymy shapes the way we think and speak of ordinary events and is the basis for many symbolic comparisons in art and literature. Take the following sentences (PART FOR WHOLE) as an example: *We need a couple of strong bodies for our team* (strong people); *There are a lot of good heads in the university* (intelligent people); *We need some new blood in the organization* (new people). These sentences reflect the general cognitive principle of metonymy where people take one well-understood or easily-perceived aspect of something to represent the thing as a whole or for some other aspect of it. All of the sentences relate to the general principle by which part may stand for the whole. Various metonymic models in the conceptual system underlie the use of many kinds of figurative and conventional expressions (e. g. the object for the user, the controller for the controlled and so on). Cai Hui (2006) believes that there are various motivations for the metonymic mode of thinking. Therefore, metonymy in everyday speech reveals systematic character, and it is an inevitable process of human thought and reasoning.

Cognitive linguists declare that models of the concrete world to conceptualize abstract phenomena are what people rely on. For example, the sentence "*I have a temperature*" expresses that someone has caught a fever. The conceptual nature of metonymy is even more clearly manifested in the structure of categories. Lakoff (1987) demonstrates that metonymy is such a situation in which some subcategory or member or sub-model is used (often for some limited and immediate purpose) to comprehend the category as a whole, that is to say, these are cases where a part (a subcategory or member or sub-model) stands for the whole category in reasoning, recognition, etc. Since these salient members may not even have a name, the metonymic transfer merely operates at the conceptual level.

In a word, all metonymies are conceptual in nature. The use of metonymic expressions in language is primarily a reflection of general conceptual metonymies and is motivated by general cognitive principles. Moreover, metonymy is a cognitive process in nature. Metonymy has been traditionally viewed as a relationship involving substitution, namely, A STAND FOR B. However, it does not simply substitute one entity for another, it interrelates them to form a new, complex meaning. According to current cognitive views, metonymy as well as metaphor is more than a linguistic device; actually, it is a fundamental reasoning and inferential process, which structures man's conceptual knowledge (Cacciari & Glucksberg, 1994). It is revealed in the definitions of metonymy by Langacker (1993), Radden & Kovecses (1999) that metonymy is a cognitive process in which one conceptual entity is mentally accessed via another entity. The reference point is taken as the "vehicle" while the desired target simply is the "target". For example, in the sentence *I read Luxun last night*, *Luxun* is not used to refer to the author himself but the work he wrote. A cognitive model "X plus Y" is put forward to substitute the traditional formula "X for Y", in which a more salient conceptual entity is chosen as a reference-point to get to the target entity. This additive notation should more adequately represent metonymic relationships.

10.2   Metonymic categories and models

A lot of metonymic models have been put forward to explain the metonymic thinking and reasoning. For example, OBJECT USED FOR USER (*The sax has the flu today*), CONTROLLER FOR CONTROLLED (*Bush bombed Iraq*). Many of the metonymic models depend on conventional associations, which reflect the general principle that a thing may stand for what it is conventionally associated with (Turner, 1987), and which limits the use of metonymy to certain relationships between entities. For example, people often use the name of any well-known creative artist to refer to his or her work, as in the sentence *He likes reading Chaucer most*, or *Have you ever seen Shakespeare*. However, this function of reference is limited in language use. Not all the creations can be referred to by the name of the creators. For example, *Mary is delicious* can not be used to mean that the dish Mary made is delicious, for any given instance of a referring function needs to be sanctioned by body of beliefs encapsulated in an appropriate frame (Nunberg, 1979; Taylor, 1995). It is generally held that the distinctive value of a work is due uniquely to the genius of the individual who created it while the same relationship between a dish and the person who cooked it is not generally accepted, which proves that conceptual systems are grounded in the bodily experience.

Lakoff and Johnson pointed out that metonymy, like metaphor, is grounded in human experience. Actually, the grounding of metonymy is in general more obvious than that of metaphor, because it usually involves direct physical or causal associations. For example, *She is absent today*, and *I heard she went to hospital this morning*. In these sentences, the speaker wants to express the idea that she went to see a doctor this morning, because according to our experience, people usually go to hospital to see a doctor when they fall ill, so the place refers to the event occurs in it. Look at the sentence *Bush bombed Iraq*. It is not Bush who has dropped bombs on Iraq, but our experience proves that the controller is responsible for the actions of the controlled. Bush was the controller of the American army, so he was sure to be responsible for the action of his army as well as the fact of bombing.

As for the Category-and-member category, it is found that the most prototypical ones are most often used to refer to the category, for example, as for the mother category, housewife mothers are viewed as better examples of mothers than non-housewife mothers. This effect is due to metonymic reasoning, where a salient subcategory has the recognized status standing for the whole category. Extensive research in cognitive psychology demonstrates that people judge certain members of categories as being more representative of those categories than other members. Desk chairs are judged to be more representative of the category chair than are rocking chairs, bean-bag chairs, barber chairs or electric chairs (Rosch, 1978).

Metonymy is a basic mode of thinking, that is, to employ the salient, well-understood or easy-to-perceive part as the source to stand for the whole or the other part of the whole as the target, or to select the whole as the source to represent one of its parts as the target, thus provides a mental access to the target. For the understanding and study of metonymy, it is necessary to draw a distinction between two similar terms, i. e. metonymy and metaphor.

In cognitive linguistics both metaphor and metonymy are believed to be conceptual ways of people's speaking and thinking, based on human experience. The relationship between metonymy and metaphor, as well as the distinction between them, has been the topic of articles by Goossens (1995), Croft (1993), Dirven (1993), Langacker (1993), Kovecses and Gunter (1998), and Shu Dingfang (2004). At first glance, these two tropes appear to be similar, for both of them describe a connection between two things where one term is a substitute for another. According to some theorists, metonymy is a type or subclass of metaphor (Genette, 1980; Searle, 1979), while other theorists argue that metaphor and metonymy are opposed to each other, for they are generated according to opposing principles (Gibbs, 1999; Jakobson, 2002). The former view is from the rhetorical perspective, in which metonymy and metaphor are usually considered to be closely related, without any clear dividing line between them. Ulman (1979) makes a differentiation between metonymy and metaphor with the concept of contiguity opposed to similarity. Contiguity refers to any associative relations other than those based on similarity. As figures of speech, metonymy involves a relation of "contiguity" (nearness or neighborhood) between what is denoted by the literal meaning of a word and its figurative counterpart, while metaphor has traditionally based on the notions "similarity" or "comparison" between the literal and the figurative meaning of an expression. In cognitive views, both metonymy and metaphor are important linguistic phenomena in everyday language. Although metonymy and metaphor are based on opposing principles, the similarities between them can not be overlooked. Both metonymy and metaphor are seen as being conceptual in nature, both can be conventionalized, both can be used by speakers and understood by hearers automatically, unconsciously, effortlessly and generally established as a model of thinking, both are means of extending the resources of a language and both can be explained as mapping processes (Lakoff and Turner, 1989).

Metonymy and metaphor can be best distinguished in making different connections between things (Lakoff and Turner, 1989), which lies in the nature of domains involved. In metaphor, the mapping occurs between two separate conceptual domains, whereas in metonymy there is a domain internal relationship. There are two elements, or entities in metonymy, which are closely related to each other in one conceptual space or ICM. For example, the producer is closely related to the product (PRODUCER FOR PRODUCT); a whole is related to its parts (WHOLE FOR THE PART); effects are closely related to causes that produce them (EFFECT FOR CAUSE); a place is closely related to the institution that is located in that place (PLACE FOR THE INSTITUTION). In the sentence *We need a new glove to play the third base*, "a new glove" is used to refer to a new baseball player who would play the third base in a baseball game as a glove highlights a salient characteristic of one domain (the glove part of the baseball player) as representing the entire domain (the player). In contrast, metaphor involves two concepts that are distinct from each other in the conceptual system. Usually one concept is an abstract one while the other is typically a concrete one. That is, metaphors involve two domains or ICMs. For example, in the sentence *John is a lion*, human behavior is interpreted in terms of animal behavior, the main function of which is to understand one thing in terms of another. Understanding is achieved by mapping the structure of one domain onto another. In terms of function, more differences may be found between metonymy and metaphor (Lakoff and Johnson, 1980). Metaphor is principally a way of conceiving of one thing in terms of another, with its primary function in understanding. Metonymy, on the other hand, has primarily a referential function, with one entity to stand for another.

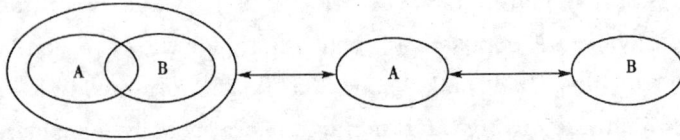

Figure 10.1   Metaphor from metonymy (from Goossens, 1990)

Particular expressions are not always clearly indicators whether they are metonymies or metaphors. Often, an expression is both or two figures are combined in a single expression. Goossens (1995) coins the word "metaphonymy" as "a mere cover term to help to increase our awareness of the fact that metaphor and metonymy can be intertwined". For instance, the sentence *Suddenly the pilot comes over the intercom* may be interpreted metonymically in the sense that the pilot's voice comes over the intercom or it may be interpreted metaphorically in the sense that the pilot announces something over the intercom. The intermediate notion metonymy-based-metaphor overcomes at least part of the problem created by limiting one's study to either particular category. Instead of always separating the two, a metonymy-metaphor continuum with unclear or fuzzy cases in between should be established. Metonymy and metaphor can be seen as prototypical categories at the endpoints of this continuum. Metonymy-based- metaphors take care of much of the fuzzy middle range of the continuum. They may either be closer to the metonymy end or the metaphor end of the metonymy-metaphor continuum.

10.3   The operational mechanism of metonymy

As a conceptual mapping in a domain, metonymy is a cognitive process in which one conceptual entity, the vehicle, provides mental access to another conceptual entity, the target, within the same idealized cognitive model. Through analysis and interpretation on the cognitive principles, operational models and cognitive motivations of conceptual metonymy, its operational mechanism of metonymy is first viewed from the perspective of cognitive linguistics, then cognitive pragmatics, and finally the idealized cognitive models.

10.3.1   Theoretical basis for metonymy in cognitive linguistics

Metonymy can be studied from the perspectives of prototype theory and image schema in cognitive linguistics. The concept of prototype is invented by E. Rosch in the 1970s to mean the goodness of category membership. There are two ways to understand the term "prototype". The term can be applied to the cluster of central member of a category, which one could refer to a particular artifact as the prototype of cup. The term can also be understood as a schematic representation of the conceptual core of a category, it is not a particular entity that is the prototype, but the property that the entity holds. Taylor (1995) claims that there are good reasons for adopting the more abstract approaches to understand the term prototype.

People organize the world through classification, the psychological process of which is called categorization. And the products of categorization are cognitive categories, e. g. the color categories RED, YELLOW, GREEN, and BLUE, etc. The anthropologists Brent Berlin and Paul Kay (1969) find evidence that focal colors are used for color categorization. The main target of Berlin and Kay is to refute the relativist hypothesis, which in its strongest version assumes that different languages carve up reality in totally different ways, by establishing a hierarchy of focal colors which could be regarded as universal. To support the universalistic claim they investigated 98 languages, 20 in oral tests and the rest based on grammars and other written materials. During the investigation, Berlin and Kay are not only interested in the extension of color categories, but also in their best examples. There is compelling evidence that instead of being arbitrary, color categorization is anchored in focal colors. It is found that in categorizing colors people rely on certain points in the color space for orientation. It is revealed that while the boundaries of color categories vary between languages and even between speakers of one language, focal colors are shared by different speakers and even different language communities. Eleanor Rosch in the early 1970s sets out to explore the psychological background of focal colors with the primary aim being to find out whether focal colors are rooted in language or in pre-linguistic cognition. In summary, her experiments lead to the following results:

(1) *Focal colors are perceptually more salient than non-focal colors. The attention of 3 year olds is more often attracted by focal colors than non-focal colors, and 4 year olds match focal colors more accurately to a given display of other colors than non-focal colors.*

(2) *Focal colors are more accurately remembered in short-term memory and more easily retained in long-term memory.*

(3) *The names of focal colors are more rapidly produced in color-naming tasks and are acquired earlier by children.*

(Urgerer and Schimid, 2001)

In Rosch's later experiment, she finds that focal colors are salient no matter where they are located within a given set. Rosch replaces Berlin and Kay's "focus" with "prototype", which is borrowed from earlier research standing for artificially created "best examples". According to Rosch, members of the same category are not in the same position. Prototypical members of cognitive categories have the largest number of attributes in common with other members of the category and the smallest number of attributes which also occur with numbers of neighboring categories. In the same category, good members have many same attributes in common with other members of the same category, while bad or marginal examples share only few attributes with members of the same category. For example, an apple is a fairly good example of fruit whereas an olive is not. The prototype theory provides a way for the understand of metonymy. The most salient, i. e. typical member of a category, tend to be used most to refer to the category. For example, aspirin is used to refer to "any pain-relieving tablet".

Another important term for the understanding of metonymy is image schema, an important form of conceptual structure in Lakoff's ICMs. Lakoff has defined it as relatively simple structures that constantly recur in everyday bodily experience: Containers, Paths, Links, Forces, Balance, Part-whole, Center-Periphery and so on (Lakoff, 1987). These structures are directly meaningful to human being, because they originate from the direct bodily experience. The images emerge as meaningful structures mainly at the level of human movements through space, objects and interactions. According to cognitive linguistics, typical schema will have parts and relations. The parts might consist of a set of entities (such as people, events, states, sources and goals). The relations might include causal relations, temporal sequences, part-whole patterns, relative locations, or instrumental relations (Johnson, 1987). Take the Containment schema as an example, when we see a container, we naturally think about things inside it. So "kettle" can be used to refer to the water in it. As for the Whole-part schema, the part in the same ICM as the whole can be metonymically highlighted to stand for the whole. "Sail" is a part of the ship, which can metonymically denote ship, as in the sentence: *There is no sail in sight*. In the sentence *Light the Christmas tree*, the whole Christmas tree refers to the candles on the Christmas tree.

Image schemata are pervasive in human experience and are instantiated widely in languages. They can be metonymically and metaphorically extended in accordance with human understanding. People make efforts to recognize, understand, organize, and categorize what they have known about the world just via these image schematic structures. Johnson (1987) and Lakoff (1987) make classifications of image schemata, the major types include: Orientational schema, coming out of physical experiences in space; Containment schema, consisting of a boundary distinguishing an interior from an exterior; Whole-part schema and so on.

10.3.2　Interpretation of metonymy in cognitive pragmatics

The study of metonymy from the perspective of cognitive pragmatics has been arousing more and more interest and attention in Grice's relevance theory. According to Grice (1975), metaphor and metonymy can be partially explained by the Cooperative Principle since metaphor and metonymy are often literally and patently false. The interpretation of metaphor and metonymy involves the calculation of implicatures in response to a perceived flouting of the maxims that form part of the Cooperative Principle. Grice assumes that the addressee first computes a literal meaning which corresponds to the proposition expressed by the utterance. He or she then finds it violates the maxim of quality. When the interlocutor hears the sentence *The ham sandwich is waiting for his check*, he or she finds that its literal meaning is abnormal. The speaker seems to say something false, but the hearer assumes that the speaker conforms to the Cooperative Principle and is saying something true. Then he or she can infer that the speaker means to say, "The customer who has ordered the ham sandwich is waiting for his check." Grice's account of metaphor and metonymy attempts to offer a more satisfactory explanation developed within a pragmatic framework. However, he just offers some account of how a metaphoric or metonymic interpretation is triggered and it contributes little to understanding how metaphors and metonymies are interpreted or why they are used.

Relevance theory is one of the most influential theories in cognitive pragmatics and it is characterized in terms of effect and effort. According to Sperber and Wilson (2001), human information processing seeks an optimal balance between consuming mental effort and achieving cognitive effects from a given stimulus or a range of potential stimuli. Within the framework of relevance theory, every utterance is a faithful representation of a thought, but it is not necessarily identical with that thought. It is claimed that a linguistic expression is optimally relevant if it produces maximal contextual effects with a minimum of processing effort.

Metonymy sometimes can enable both the hearer and speaker to expend minimal processing efforts in communication. For example, consider for the situation in a restaurant. When the waiters are talking about one of the customers, these expressions may be used:

A. Table 10 is waiting for his check.

B. The ham sandwich is waiting for his check.

C. John Smith is waiting for his check.

The metonymic expressions table 10 in sentence A and the ham sandwich in sentence B seem to provide the easier access to the target referent than the name of the customer in sentence C. In a restaurant environment, information about customer's table numbers or the food they order is in general more relevant than other features. In this case, it is the metonymy that enables both the speaker and listener to use minimal efforts to achieve successful communication and speak economically. Metonymy can be an efficient way to provide maximal contextual effects with minimal processing efforts.

In essence, pragmatic inference is metonymic. According to Searle (1975), an indirect speech act is a speech act which is performed by means of another speech act. Many indirect speech acts have become conventionalized to such an extent that their indirect force is hardly recognized to the native speakers. Sperber and Wilson (2001) claim that, in the process of cognition, people tend to use the least effort to achieve the optimal contextual effects, which reveals the basic principle of cognitive process, that is, the "principle of economy" in linguistic communication. Therefore, people can understand the world from the surface to the center, from the near to the distant, from the simple to the complex, and from the easy to the difficult. This process can be considered as a cognitive model or schema (Xu, 1993, 2002). Working within the framework of cognitive linguistics, based on the previous studies in the field of speech act studies, Panther and Thornburg

(1997) deal metonymy from a new perspective, with the assumption that illocutionary meaning is represented in the form of illocutionary scenarios. The notion of scenarios can be fruitfully applied to the analysis of conversation. They suggest that the weakness of traditional pragmatic theories can be overcome if metonymy could be represented in the form of illocutionary scenarios. In Thornburg and Panther's view, illocutionary scenarios consist of the felicity conditions for each type of speech act and, in turn, indirect speech acts can be explained via a metonymic process in which one of the felicity conditions refers to the whole scenario.

In cognitive linguistics, the term metonymy goes beyond indirect referring. It is a property of conceptual structure and a relation among concepts and not merely among words. On this base, metonymy can be classified into two basic types as shown in Figure 10.2:

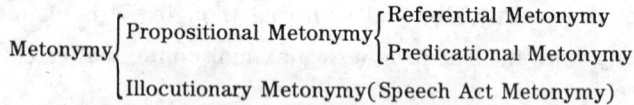

$$\text{Metonymy} \begin{cases} \text{Propositional Metonymy} \begin{cases} \text{Referential Metonymy} \\ \text{Predicational Metonymy} \end{cases} \\ \text{Illocutionary Metonymy (Speech Act Metonymy)} \end{cases}$$

Figure 10.2   Basic types of metonymy

Referential Metonymy is the most typical metonymy, for the case of noun phrases being used referentially is prevailing both in traditional and cognitive analysis. For example, in the sentence *The White House is welcoming a new host next week*, "The White House" is conventionally used to indirectly stand for the executive branch of the American government.

The concept of metonymy applies not only to the referential part of a proposition, but to the predicational part as well. Take the two sentences as an example:

A. She was able to finish her work in time.

B. She finished her work in time.

It is possible to assert A and to deny B without any contradiction, while in some cases, A can be used with the same propositional content as what is expressed in B without any inappropriateness. In this case, the predication is bale to be used metonymically to stand for "finished". Such type of metonymy is called Predicational Metonymy.

Illocutionary Metonymy or Speech Act Metonymy is not that apparent as the previous two. It operates beyond the propositional level and is at the level of illocutionary force, wherein one illocutionary act may represent another illocutionary act. The sentence *I don't know where the salt is* can be literally understood as an assertion about what the speaker does not know, yet in many cases, it is used with the indirect illocutionary force of a question as "Can you pass the salt to me?" In another word, this sentence can stand for the question expressed in "Where is the salt?" But it can also be used as a metonymy, which is called Illocutionary Metonymy or Speech Act Metonymy.

Panther and Thornburg (1999) believe that the speech act metonymy occurs between two illocutionary acts, between which one of the illocutionary acts functions as the metonymic vehicle and the other illocutionary act functions as the metonymic target. In other words, the speech act metonymy can be regarded as a cognitive process, in which one illocutionary act maps on the whole ICM or the other illocutionary act in the same ICM. The speech act metonymy is different from the general metonymy such as the referential metonymy in that the speech act metonymy is related to the speech act theory, which basically holds that language is not always used to inform or to describe things but often used to do things (Levinson, 2001).

It is generally believed that knowledge organization follows four kinds of structuring principles (Lakoff, 1987): propositional principle structure, image-schematic structure, metaphoric mappings (sets of correspondences across discrete conceptual domains) and metonymic mappings (domain-internal conceptual correspondences). In general, the cognitive semantics literature has come to identify propositional ICMs proposed by Lakoff (1987) with Fillmore's frames (1985), image-schemas with Johnson's (1987) analysis of abstract topological structures, and metaphoric and metonymic mappings with the proposals in Lakoff and Johnson (1980) and Lakoff and Turner (1989) (cited by Li Yongzhong, 2004). To some extent, illocutionary knowledge is best organized in the form of propositional idealized cognitive models, although other pragmatic parameters should not be avoided such as the politeness, and power relation.

10.3.3　Metonymy within the same ICM

The idea about cognitive models have developed with cognitive linguistics and come from some sources: Fillmore's frame semantics (Fillmore, 1982), Lakoff and Johnson's theory of metaphor and metonymy (Lakoff and Johnson, 1980), Langacker's cognitive grammar (Langacker, 1999), and Fauconnier's theory of mental spaces (Fauconnier 1985). An ICM, with many other various terms such as scripts, schemata, scenes, scenarios, can be defined as an organized cognitive structure which serves to represent reality from a certain perspective. Lakoff (1987) holds that cognitive models are stored in people's mind in the form of propositions and schema, and they play crucial roles in the communication between human beings and the world as they not only store all kinds of information but also reconstruct the input information. ICMs are valuable for they highly generalize life experiences and behavior patterns, and offer concise and idealized cognitive frames for human to understand the world.

It should be pointed out that ICM is only a concept unless it is used in cognitive processes. That is, "activation" is of vital importance in various contexts and cultures. As a result, ICMs should include at least the following aspects of characteristics. To begin with, an ICM is not a model as those in science, but a combination of different kinds of thoughts involving cultural concepts and having some properties of gestalt. The match between ICM and its corresponding entities in the real world can be graded, depending on the people and culture. Secondly, an ICM is not exhaustive in all the relevant properties, or it is alternative and concerns the prototype of a category, which is greatly influenced by cultures. The adoption of "ICM" is of great help in explaining many linguistic phenomena as it takes "cultural background" into consideration in the explanation of some linguistic phenomena like metonymy. In describing metonymic process, Lakoff's framework of ICMs suggests that both the vehicle and the target are conceptually present when a metonymy is used and this metonymic substitution of one entity for another creates a relation of pragmatic equivalence between the substituting and the substituted entity. Theoretically, either of the two conceptual entities related may stand for the other. Take the following dialogue as an example:

A: How did you get to the harbor?

B: I waved down a taxi.

In fact, B got to the harbor with several actions: (1) B waved down a taxi and got into the car; (2) The car left for the harbor and finally arrived; (3) B paid for the fare and got out of the car. Actually, any part of the cognitive model can evoke the whole event. ICM plays a central role in the generation and understanding of metonymy. Conceptual relationships within an ICM are regarded as "metonymy-generating" relationships. For instance, the conceptual relationship that holds between a container and the things contained may generate the metonymies CONTAINER FOR CONTENTS AND CONTENTS FOR CONTAINER. Generally speaking, a whole ICM is conceptually distinct from its parts, thus metonymy may arise easily from whole to part or vice versa. To a certain extent, distinction between the whole and part is crucial to the generation of metonymy.

To conclude, the framework of ICMs provides the most comprehensive perspective for the study of metonymy, since it takes cognitive, cultural and pragmatic factors into consideration. Based on this framework, metonymy can be classified into two types. One is the metonymic relationship between the whole ICM and its parts and the other is metonymic relationship of different parts of an ICM.

10.4 Metonymic motivations for English proverbs

Metonymy has been used in the studies of various linguistic expressions, including the formation of polysemization, linguistic structures and many fixed expressions as idioms, and euphemisms. As an important part of a language, proverbs are studied on the basis of metonymy.

10.4.1 Metonymic motivations for linguistic expressions

Metonymy is said to be one of the most fundamental processes of meaning extension. Taylor lists three means of meaning extension through metonymy: highlighting different aspects of an entity's constitution; perspectivization of a component of a unitary conceptual structure; and perspectivization of an implication (Taylor, 1989). There are countless instances in the polysemy through metonymic extension by the perspective of a component of an integrated conceptual structure. Take the word "hand" as an example, which is very often used in a metonymic way to stand for the whole person. This conceptual metonymy is called THE HAND STANDS FOR THE PERSON as in the sentence *We are short of hands*. Many of this kind focus on the ability, competence, expertise, experience of a person in general, or in a particular trade, profession or skill, as in the expressions "skilled hand," "good hand", and so on. "Hand" is also closely related with power or control, which always involves skills, means, tactics, etc. Thus it leads to the metonymy called THE HAND STANDS FOR CONTROL and CONTROL IS HOLDING IN THE HAND. For example, the sentence *The firm is at his hands* means that the firm is in his control.

Metonymy also makes effect on linguistic structure. Chomsky's theory involves three levels of conceptualization: (1) a base component made up of "phrase structure rules" that generate (2) a deep structure, which in turn is changed into (3) a surface structure via transformational rules. According to Chomsky, the phrase structure rules represent the internalized and unconscious working of the mind, deep structure determines meaning underlying sentences, and surface structure determines sound. Linguistic structure is the surface structure based on deep structure, and the deep structure is in turn produced by the phrase structure, that is, the internalized and unconscious working of mind. As a result, it is reasonable to say that human thinking patterns determine the linguistic structure of languages. As a cognitive process, metonymy may make much difference on linguistic structures.

Metonymy is a pervasive phenomenon, and metonymic interpretation is a powerful interpretive device, with great impact on grammar. Goldberg (1995) points out that basic sentences of English are instances of constructions: form-meaning correspondences that exist independently of particular verbs. In other words, constructions themselves carry meanings, independently of the words in the sentence. According to Panther and Thornburg (1999), there exist two kinds of interpretation: one is taxonomic reading, and the other is causal reading. Now look at the three sentences:

A. What is that bird?

B. What is that spot on your cheek?

C. What is that smell?

The first question actually is to ask for information that specifies the kind of bird seen, standing for the question *What kind of bird is that?* So the answer may be (It is) *a parrot*, while it can not be my bird, or an animal. This reading of the construction *What's that N?* is actually motivated by the conceptual metonymy GENERIC FOR SPECIFIC. Different from sentence A, sentence B is to ask for the reason for the spot on the hearer's cheek but not for the type of that spot. Thus the reply should be the cause that produced the spot on the cheek. This metonymy is called SYMPTOM FOR ITS CAUSE, which is a subtype of the conceptual metonymy EFFECT FOR CAUSE. Similar to sentence B, C is the PERCEPTUAL EVENT FOR ITS CAUSE metonymy.

Kovecses and Szabo (1996) conclude that the cognitive semantic view can facilitate the learning of idioms for non-native speakers with an informal experimental study. Gibbs (1994) and Kovecses (2002) have studied English idiomatic expressions from conventional knowledge and conceptual metaphors and hold that metaphors play a great role in comprehension of idioms. Many Chinese scholars and linguists have also studied idioms from the perspective of cognitive linguistics. Zhang Hui (2003) investigates into Chinese idioms within the frame of cognitive linguistics from the perspective of metaphor, metonymy, conceptual blending and other. Li Siqing (2005) analyzes the mode and shaping mechanism of metaphor in English and Chinese idioms. All of the studies try to explore the motivation of idioms from different aspects of cognitive linguistics.

Except for idioms, there are also cognitive studies on other forms of expressions, such as proverbs, and euphemisms, which are all basic parts of a language while at the same time are difficult for FL learners to acquire. Li Fuyin (2006) provides an innovative approach to the systematic learning of metaphoric expressions, idioms and proverbs, which bridges the cognitive linguistics and applied linguistics. Since metonymy is considered to be fundamental to human cognition, it will be of great help to language teaching and learning. Thus empirical study on the cognition of metonymy in language learning will be of great value. Proverbs are widely recognized as the crystallization of folk wisdom. Whatever languages they are in, they are much appreciated by the native users, just as the saying goes "learn a new language and get a new soul".

10.4.2 The definition and studies of proverbs

Proverbs have had a long history and have fascinated people around the world. Linguists, cultural anthropologists, psychologists, historians, advertising executives and so on have all studied proverbs, with different views on it. According to *Oxford Advanced Learners' Dictionary of Current English*, a proverb is a short well-known saying that states a general truth to give advice (6th edition, 2005). In *Oxford Concise Dictionary of Literary Terms*, proverb is defined as a short popular saying of unknown authorship, expressing some general truth or superstition. Proverbs are found in most cultures, and are often ancient (Chris Baldich, 1991).

Burton Stevenson (1987) holds the view that a maxim is the sententious expression of some general truth or rule of conduct and it becomes a proverb when it gets its wings by winning popular acceptance. According to Gregory Titelman (1996), proverbs are the collective wisdom of all nations, of all ages, of all times and a proverb typically expresses a commonplace thought in a succinct, often metaphorical way.

To sum up, proverbs are primarily produced in history, consisting of the refining result of experience and wisdom of many people from all walks of life, all nations, all times and all ages, but will never stop developing. They are brief and popular in form and have functions in instruction and persuasion.

Traditional studies on the generation and interpretation of language meaning are based on formal linguistics, semantics and pragmatics. In recent years, there appears rapid development of cognitive linguistics and cognitive psychology which call more attention from many scholars. Cognitive view brings proverbs within the general theoretical scope of cognitive science. The mental structures and processes that subserve proverb learning, comprehension and use are described under the view that focuses on many issues, for example, the cultural background for the creation and production, the mental representation of proverbs, and the phases in their comprehension. Honeck and Kibler (1987) make an attempt to confirm some aspects of the conceptual base theory of the proverb comprehension, occurring in phases that involve getting a literal meaning, recognizing that the literal meaning does not satisfy the communicative context, using the literal meaning and inferences to get a figurative meaning, and then using the figurative meaning for various illustrative purposes. Grice(1975) and Searle (1979) make this kind of study by the standard pragmatic model, based on the same assumption as the conceptual base theory. Nippold, Martin and Erskine (1988) carry out a study illustrating the cognitive view as applied to children's understanding of proverbs. Although the cognitive view can fill in the gaps of traditional views, the studies are far from mature, as Honeck says: "On a large scale, cognitive scientific interest and research on the proverb has lagged behind that of the non-cognitive scientific views, and there has been little rapprochement between the two" (Honeck, 1997).

10.4.3   English proverbs motivated by metonymy

In fact, except for metaphor, metonymy is also an important motivation for English proverbs. A proverb is literally used to refer to a particular situation but metonymically it is often used to stand for a general understanding at hand (Li Yongzhong, 2004). For example, in the sentence *A Jack of all trades and master of none*, Jack is the name of a specific person, while it is used here to stand for a kind of people, which is in turn applied to refer to a person in a specific situation. In the sentence *Love should not be all at one side*, the concept "love" is a feeling with no shape or capacity. But when it is put with the preposition "at", people would regard it as a container with certain shape and capacity, something that can be seen, touched, felt and easily understood. So the abstract concept "love" here is something tangible and no longer so complex and hard to be understood. Take another sentence *Out of sight, out of mind* as an example, the concept "mind" is also an abstract state. But when putting it behind "out of", it is naturally seen as a substantial container. "Out of mind" reminds people that "we" have been released from the constraint or relaxed from some difficulties.

Lakoff and Turner (1989) discuss proverbs from the perspective of GENERIC IS SPECIFIC, while the specific and the generic belong to the same ICM, proverbs are metonymic in nature. For example, in the sentence *Eagles catch no flies*, the verb "catch" refers to the whole event that the eagles aim at flies and begin to run after them and then catch them, which is called SUBEVENT FOR WHOLE EVENT metonymy. There is another metonymy here, eagles refer to the category of things which are powerful while compared with them, and flies refer to those that are minimal, without much effect on others. So this sentence also involves the metonymy MEMBER OF A CATEGORY FOR THE CATEGORY. In the sentence *Even the walls have ears*, "have ears" refers to the effect that walls can make others hear the talk resulting from the fact that they also have ears. Thus it belongs to CAUSE FOR EFFECT metonymy. It is clear that the distribution of motivations is based on different types of metonymy for English proverbs.

10.5 Classification of metonymy within the framework of ICMs

According to Lakoff (1987), the means of structures that organize knowledge is called idealized cognitive models (ICMs), and the category structures and prototype effects are by-products of that organization. Based on the previous research, Radden and Kovecses (1999) have pointed out the existence of a set of "metonymy-producing relationship" or generic principles in their influential paper Towards a Theory of Metonymy (Radden & Kovecses, 1999). There are two types metonymic mechanism. One type is metonymy caused in the relationship of the whole ICM and its parts in which a part of an ICM is accessed with its whole or a whole ICM with one of its part. The other type is metonymy caused in the relationship of different parts of an ICM in which a part is accessed with another part of an ICM, given the whole ICM in the background. The former lays stress on the vehicle as a whole and the target as part of the whole, and vice versa. While the latter emphasizes that both the vehicle and the target are parts of the same ICM. Both of the two types can be divided into subtypes. This cognitive mechanism provides the basis for classification of metonymy, which can be described as the following:

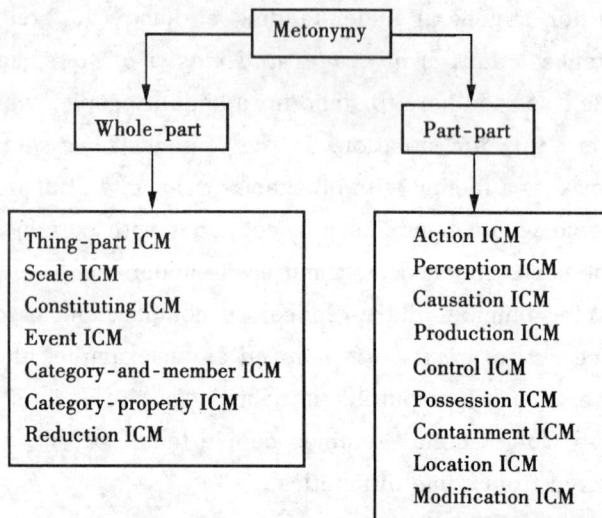

Figure 10.3   Cognitive mechanism of metonymy in ICMs

10.5.1   Whole ICM and its Part(s)

"Whole and its parts" refers to those metonymies in which one part of an ICM is accessed via the whole (THE WHOLE FOR THE PART) or a whole ICM via one of its parts (A PART FOR THE WHOLE). The relationship between a whole and a part typically applies to things and their parts. Things, in particular physical objects, are typically conceived of as a gestalt with well-delineated boundaries and as internally composed of various parts (Li Yongzhong, 2004). According to the cognitive mechanisms of metonymy, the following items are the ICMs that are assumed to be accounted for by the "whole-part configurations".

(1) Thing-part ICM

There are two metonymic variants that this ICM may lead to: a. Whole Thing for a Part of the Thing. For example, in the sentence *He broke the window and was afraid to be blamed*, "window" is used to stand for "the glass of the window". b. Part of a Thing for the Whole Thing. For example, in the sentence *His job is to help those without a roof*, "roof" is used to refer to "house".

The Whole-for-part metonymy is very productive. A typical example is the situation in which parts are used to stand for physical things or body parts such as face, head, hand for the whole person, as in the sentence *We need a couple of strong bodies for our team*, "strong bodies" stands for strong people. Likewise, more abstract things can be metonymically expressed via one of their concrete parts. For example, hand stands control, and tongue for speaking in the following sentences *Things have got out of hand* and *This boy has a smooth tongue*.

(2) Scale ICM

As a special class of things, scales are composed of the scalar units. Typically, a scale as a whole can be used to stand for its positive end and in turn the positive end can be used to stand for the scale as a whole. As a result, the scale ICM may lead to two kinds of metonymies: a. Whole Scale for Positive End of the Scale; b. Positive End of a Scale for Whole Scale.

The former type can be illustrated by the sentence *He is speeding again*. Actually, the word "speed" is defined as the whole scale of velocity while it is used to stand for the positive end of its scale, with the meaning as "running too fast". Conversely, the mention of the positive end of a scale can also evoke the whole scale. In those positive ends of the whole scale sentences *How far is the school from your home? How long is the Nile River?* "old" and "long" refer to the whole scales respectively. People are motivated to use the positive end to stand for the whole scale or the whole scale to stand for the positive end. This phenomenon is regarded as one of the most important cognitive principles "MORE OVER LESS" by Radden and Kovecse (1999: 47), which means that more of something is usually more salient perceptually than less of something. When the negative end of a scale is used, it is usually for the purpose of achieving special effects. Take the sentence *How short is the new member?* as an example, which strongly implies that the new member is short.

(3) Constitution ICM

Constitution ICM involves matter, material or substances that are seen as constituting a thing. The Constitution ICM contains two metonymic variants: a. Object for Material Constituting the Object: *I smell skunk*, in which "skunk" for "the odor of skunk"; b. Material Constituting an Object for the Object: *Let's go for a walk in the wood*, in which "wood" for "forest".

(4) Event ICM

The term "event", is used in a broad sense, including processes, activities as well as states of affairs. Every event is composed of a series of subevents from metaphorical perspective. Thus there exists metonymic relationship between event and its subevents. That is, an event as a whole may stand for one of its subevent and a subevent can stand for the whole event. As a result, there are two variants to this kind of metonymic relationship: a. Whole Event for Subevent; b. Subevent for Whole Event.

The first variant can be illustrated by the sentence: *She smoked a PClady when she was waiting for the bus last night*. The event "smoke" involves a series of subevents: lighting a cigarette, putting it to one's lips, inhaling the smoke and releasing the smoke, etc. Among all the subevents, the inhaling part may be the central and most salient subevent, and then is metonymically used to stand for the whole event. As for the converse variant, look at the example: *She speaks Japanese*. The word "speak" is similar to "read", which is metonymically used to refer to the whole event of "know the language", and should be understood as including the skills of listening, reading, writing and even translating.

(5) Category-and-member ICM

There is a metonymic relation between every category and its members. According to Lakoff (Lakoff, 1987), "each higher-order category is a whole, with the immediate categories being its parts." Category as a whole may be used to refer to any member of it, while the active or salient members may in turn stand for the category to which they belong. Therefore, there are two kinds of metonymies: a. Category for a Member of the Category: e. g. *I hate meat* ("meat" for "pork"); b. Member of a Category for the Category: e. g. *We didn't get paid a penny* ("penny" for "money").

The Category-and-member ICM can invoke a special kind of metonymic relationship between a generic type and a specific token. For example, *Books are friends to people*. The sentence is a generic situation for books, while it can be used to describe a specific book. Conversely, specific tokens may be used to refer to generic types. Look at the sentence: *A dog is obedient to the master*. A dog is generally used to refer to a specific dog while it is metonymically used to stand for the dogs in general. Thus the specific instantiation can call forth the whole class. In fact, a typical example for this kind of metonymies is proverbs. Proverb is literally used to refer to a particular situation but metonymically it is often used to stand for a general understanding, which again is applied to a particular situation at hand (Li Yongzhong, 2004).

(6) Category-and-property ICM

If a category is defined as a set of properties, these properties can be seen as parts of the category. Therefore, between the distinctive properties and a category, there exists a metonymical relation. This relation leads to two kinds of metonymies: a. Category for Defining Property. For example, in the sentence *All is not roses in the firm today*, "roses" stands for "favorable circumstances or ease of success". b. Defining Property for Category. In the sentence *They are considering about how to assist the poor*, "the poor" refers to "poor people".

A common usage of this kind of metonymy can be illustrated by the construction "the

+adjective" which is used to refer to a category the adjective defines. For instance, we often use the rich, the poor, the innocent, etc. to represent a category of people. Among all the defining properties of a category, the most salient ones are often picked out to stand for the whole category. Similarly, some categories are conventionally used to stand for specific properties. For example, Judas is used for "treacherous", Helen for "beauty", and Zhu Geliang for "genius" in Chinese.

(7) Reduction ICM

This kind of metonymy is applied to the reduction of the form of a sign. The specific metonymic relationship is described as: Part of a Form for the Whole Form. For example, "USA" is used to refer to "the United States of America" and in the sentence *Jean is said to be a VIP in our club*, "VIP" represents "very important person". This kind of metonymic relationship is different from the preceding ones, for it is not reversible. Because only a complete form seems to capture the essence of a concept properly, the whole form does not necessarily stand for the one or more of its parts. Such kind of metonymy becomes more and more common now, especially when the internet becomes widespread. For example, UN is used to refer to "the United Nation", OL to refer to "office lady", and KO to refer to "knock out".

10.5.2 Parts of an ICM

Besides the metonymic relationship between a whole ICM and its parts, there exists a metonymic relation between different parts within a whole ICM. The situation "parts of an ICM" may lead to metonymies in which a part of an ICM provides mental access to another, with the whole ICM present in the background. Any type of possible relationship of one conceptual entity to another conceptual entity within an ICM will be understood as an instance of Part-and-Part metonymy. The part-part configuration applies to various parts of ICMs, the details of which are shown in the following part.

(1) Action ICM

An Action ICM involves a variety of participants which may be related to the predicate expressing the action or to each other. Therefore, there are specific relationships between such as the Agent and the Action, the Instrument and the Action, the Instrument and the Agent, etc. Action ICMs includes several variants of metonymic relationships. Here just list some of them: a. Agent for Action: e. g. *to butcher a cow, to author a new book*; b. Action for Agent: e. g. *writer, dancer, liar, singer, driver*; c. Instrument for Action: examples include *to shampoo the hair, to hammer, to ski* and so on; d. Action for Instrument: such as *sharpener* and *screwdriver*.

As is shown in the examples, word-class changes, in particular, noun-verb conversion leads to this kind of metonymy. Noun-verb conversion and nominalization are two common language phenomena which are two complementary morphological processes motivated by metonymic mechanism called grammatical metonymy.

(2) Perception ICM

Perception is very similar to cognition, which can be intentional or unintentional. If the perception ICM is intentional, it may cross-classify with the Action ICM. There are some specific metonymic variants of this type: a. Instrument/Organ of Perception for the Perception: *to eye someone/something*; b. Manner of Perception for the Perception: *She squinted through the mailbox*; c. Thing Perceived for Perception: *There goes my knee* ("knee" for "the pain in my knee"); d. Perception for Thing Perceived: The sunset was a very beautiful sight ("sight" for "thing seen").

(3) Causation ICM

When one thing or event is the cause of another, a cause-and-effect type of relation will appear. Cause and effect are closely interdependent that one of them can easily evoke the other. There are two reversible metonymies in the Causation ICM: a. Cause for Effect: for example, *A: What's the sound? B: The cat in the garden*, "the cat that makes the sound" stands for the "sound"; b. Effect for Cause: the sentence *We can say he is my joy* refers to "he is the cause of my happiness".

While in principle, cause and effect can be used to stand for each other, actually people prefer to choose the effects as the vehicle. Thus the metonymy Effect for Cause is more widespread than Cause for Effect. For example, in daily communication, the construction *She is my pride/joy /pain/...* is often used, "pride/joy/pain" is used to refer to the cause of them.

(4) Production ICM

This type of ICM involves actions in which one of the participants is a product the action creates. The Production ICM is very productive and it will give rise to various metonymic relationships. The most representative one of this type of metonymic relationships is Producer for Product. For instance, in the sentence *We are learning Shakespeare*, what is being learned is not "Shakespeare" but "the works written by Shakespeare". Another sentence *He played Mozart at the party last night* expresses that he played "the music produced by Mozart".

(5) Control ICM

Control ICM involves a controller and a person or object controlled. A controller and a person or object can metonymically stand for each other. There are two variants of metonymy: a. Controller for Controlled: "Bush" for "the US Army", and "Saddam" for "Iraq" in the sentence *Bush defeated Saddam*; b. Controlled for Controller: "the buses" for "the bus drivers" in the sentence *The buses are on strike*.

Generally speaking, the metonymy Controller for Controlled is more often used than the Controlled for Controller metonymy. The latter seems to apply only to situations in which the thing controlled is particularly salient or the controller is unknown.

(6) Possession ICM

The relationship of possession blends into that of control, for the user of an object is at the same time in control of the object used and possesses it. The Possession ICM leads to two reversible metonymies: a. Possessor for Possessed: "I" for "my name" in *I am not in the phone book*, "me" for "my car" in *That is me*, "you" for "your car" in *You have a flat fire*; b. Possessed for Possessor: "money" for "a person who possesses a lot of money" in *She married money*; "blue jeans" for "people who wear blue jeans" in *Mrs. Green frowns in blue jeans*. It is found that people has a preference for choosing the possessor as the vehicle than a possessed object. The Possessor for Possessed is well-entrenched and hardly noticeable.

(7) Containment ICM

The Containment ICM is one of the basic image schemata in human cognition. The image-schematic relationship holds between a container and the things contained in it. The container and content can stand for each other, while we are more interested in the content of a container so that we prefer to use metonymies that target the content via the container rather than the vice versa. Look at the two variants with examples: a. Container for Contents: "kettle" for "water in the kettle" in *The kettle is boiling*; "bottle" for "milk the bottle contains" in *The bottle is sour*; b. Contents for Container: "beers" for "two glasses of beers" in the request *Two beers, please*, "milk" for "the milk container" in *The milk tipped over*.

(8) Location ICM

Places are associated with people living there, well-known institutions located there, events occurring there as well as goods produced or shipped from there. As a result, there are various types of metonymies based on Location ICMs. Just look at some of them: a. Place for Inhabitants: for example, in the sentence *The whole city support the new proposal*, "the whole city" refers to "the people in the city"; b. Inhabitants for Place: "the French" stands for "France" in the sentence *The French hosted the World Cup Soccer Games*; c. Place for Institution: "Beijing" is used for the "Chinese government" in *Beijing has expressed their welcome to the people who will come for the* 2008 *Olympics*; d. Institution for Place: in the sentence *I live close to the Post Office*, "the Post Office" represents "the location of the Post Office".

(9) Modification ICM

This is a kind of ICM mainly applied to variant forms of a sign apart from reduction, which were accounted for by the Part-and-Whole metonymic relationship. The Modification ICM leads to one metonymic relationship: Substitute Form for Original Form. For example,

— Do you want to have some tea? — Yes, I do.

— Has he arrived home now? — I think so.

10.6 Research design of English metonymy-motivated proverbs within ICMs

It has been discussed that metonymy is a cognitive process, thus the appearance and distribution of different types of metonymy in English proverbs can reflect the cognitive processes and preference of people when they want to express their ideas with the help of language. At the same time, the perception and acquisition of English proverbs may also be in accordance with a kind of cognitive process. In other words, when learners confront English proverbs, they may have different achievement as to different types of metonymy-motivated proverbs, since some proverbs are easier for them to acquire than some others. This difference may come from the human cognition as well as the distinctive cognitive processes under different types of proverbs. So an experiment is designed to study on the acquisition of English proverbs by Chinese EFL learners.

Nine kinds of more commonly used metonymy-motivated proverbs are chosen to check the cognition of metonymy in the understanding and use of English proverbs. What is the current situation of the acquisition of English proverbs motivated by metonymy? What is the tendency of the acquisition as well as the reasons for it? These questions are what the research is going to focus on, and the hypotheses are as the following:

Hypothesis 1: Metonymy-motivated proverbs within ICMs have different distribution in English, with some types of them more popular than others.

Hypothesis 2: Chinese EFL learners of different levels have varied mastery of metonymy- motivated English proverbs within ICMs, their cognition of metonymy in English proverbs going up from the lower level to the higher level.

10.6.1　Metonymic proverbs within ICMs

All in all, metonymy-generating relationships can be put under two general conceptual configurations: (a) Whole ICM and its part(s); (b) Parts of an ICM. Based on the processing mechanism of WHOLE- PART, PART-PART ICMs, a classification of metonymic proverbs can be made in the following tables.

Table 10. 1　　**Metonymy within whole ICM and its parts configuration**

Configuration	Samples	Metonymy-generating relationship
Thing-and-part ICM	*False tongue will hardly speak truth.*	"tongue" for "whole person"
Scale ICM	*Forbidden fruit is sweet.*	"sweet" for "the sweetest"
Constituting ICM	*A bird in the hand is worth two in the bush*	"bush" for "forest made up of bush"
Event ICM	*From a little spark may burst a mighty flame*	"burst a mighty flame" refers to "whole development from a small spark to a big fire"
Category-and-member ICM	*A bad bush is better than the open field*	"bush" for "plants"
Category-property ICM	*Boys are boys*	"Boys" have the defining property "boys possess"

Table 10.2　　　**Metonymy within Parts of an ICM configuration**

Configuration	Samples	Metonymy-generating relationship
Action ICM	*From saving comes having.*	action for result
Perception ICM	*Beauty is in the eye of the gazer.*	"eye" for "the perception by the eye"
Causation ICM	*Between friends all is common.*	"all is common" for "friends can share all the things they have"
Production ICM	*The tailor makes the man.*	clothes made by the tailor
Control ICM	*Bacchus has drowned more men than Neptune.*	"Bacchus and Neptune" for "wine and sea"
Possession ICM	*Mickle power makes many enemies.*	"mickle power" for "people who possess it"
Containment ICM	*Better an empty purse than an empty head*	It is better to have no money than any wit
Location ICM	*Life is a battle from cradle to grave.*	"cradle" and "grave" refer to "birth" and "death"

10.6.2　Collection of English proverbs within ICMs

Metonymy-motivated English proverbs are picked out from a collection of English proverbs; the data in the following table are their classification as well as their proportions in the experiment.

Table 10.3　　　**Amount and ratios of metonymy-motivated proverbs**

Type	Action ICM	Category-and-member ICM	Category-and-property ICM	Constitution ICM	Containment ICM	Control ICM	Event ICM
Number	200	146	210	9	34	2	269
Ratio	14.87%	10.86%	15.61%	0.67%	2.53%	0.15%	20%
Type	Location ICM	Causation ICM	Perception ICM	Possession ICM	Production ICM	Scale ICM	Thing-part ICM
Number	19	283	6	46	11	8	102
Ratio	1.41%	21.04%	0.45%	3.42%	0.82%	0.59%	7.58%

Table 10.3 shows the distribution of different metonymy-generating English proverbs within ICMs. Metonymies in Causation ICM, Event ICM, Category-and-property ICM, Action ICM, Category-and-member ICM, and Thing-part ICM are relatively more popular

than those in other ICMs, with the number of 283, 269, 210, 200, 146 and 102, and the ratios compared with the total number of metonymies as 21.04%, 20%, 15.61%, 14.87%, 10.86% and 7.58%. Metonymy-generating relationships in Possession ICM, Containment ICM, and Location ICM are not that common, with only 46, 34, and 19, and the ratios are 3.42%, 2.53%, and 1.41%. The rest types of metonymy are even fewer, with the ratios under 1%.

10.6.3 Subjects

The total number of subjects in this experiment was 97 from Wuhan University. They fell into three groups, freshmen of non-English majors, postgraduates of non-English majors and postgraduates of English majors. They were labeled as Group 1, Group 2 and Group 3 as in the following table.

Table 10.4   **The basic information of subjects**

Groups	Major	N	Average years of study	Grades
1	Non-English	35	About 6 years	Freshman
2	Non-English	31	11-12 years	Postgraduate
3	English	31	11-12 years	Postgraduate

The subjects include both English majors and non-English majors in order that the results can be more comprehensive. The subjects in Group one had the shortest years of experience in English learning (N=35), most of them were learning English only for the Entrance Examination to the university, so their knowledge of English was limited and basic. Group two had a relative longer time of experience of English learning (N=31), and passed the CET-4, CET-6 and the Entrance Examination for Postgraduates, therefore, their experience in learning English should be better than that of Group one. There were 31 subjects in Group three, who were postgraduates majoring in English. Apart from the basic knowledge of English, they also learned other things, such as the culture, history, customs, etc. As a result, their interests in English and their desire to behave like native speakers of English would be the strongest among the three.

10.6.4 Materials

There are nine types of metonymy-motivated proverbs within ICMs as research materials in the experiment, which are organized into three forms of items. The first part is translation from English into Chinese (E to C) in the form of multiple choice (40 items), the second part is translation from Chinese into English (C to E) in the form of multiple choice (40 items), and the last part is blank filling with choices given above each section (85 items), and the distribution of which is shown in Table 10.5.

Table 10.5　　　　　　　　　**The distribution of items in the test papers**

Types of metonymy	E to C	C to E	Blank filling
Within Thing-part ICM	1-5	1-5	1-12
Category-and-property ICM	6-10	6-10	13-23
Category-and-member ICM	11-15	11-15	24-36
Causation ICM	16-20	16-20	37-47
Action ICM	21-25	21-25	48-57
Event ICM	26-30	26-30	58-72
Possession ICM	31-34	31, 32, 40	73-76
Containment ICM	35-37	33, 34, 37, 38, 39	77-78
Location ICM	38-40	35, 36	79-85

In the translation tasks, there are three items for the subjects to choose from for each question, and the choice items are different, with only one right type of metonymy-motivation for the sentence. In the blank filling, the subjects were instructed to choose the best word to each blank from the items provided above each section. The sentences in each section are in the same type according to the metonymy classifications. All English proverbs are frequently used in daily conversations by native speakers. Thus they are the most representative English proverbs that the EFL learners should have a good command of. However, these metonymy-motivated proverbs are not equal in number, with some of them larger in number while some others too small.

10.7　The metonymic motivations of English proverbs within ICMs

The analysis is designed to check the overall mastery of English metonymy-motivated proverbs by the three groups. The accuracy of items in each task of the test paper is calculated and the correctness is presented in the form of percentage, which is shown in Table 10.6.

Table 10.6　　　　　　　　**Accuracy of items the by the three groups**

Groups	E to C (%)	C to E (%)	Blank filling (%)	Total (%)
1	83.4	47.5	41.4	53.0
2	80.2	50.0	48.3	56.0
3	78.5	56.1	58.3	62.6
Total	80.8	50.4	49.0	57.0

As Table 10.4 shows, for the task of the translation from English into Chinese, the accuracy is 80.8%. That means the ratio of right choices is 80.8%. For each group of the subjects, the results are 83.4%, 80.2% and 78.5%. It can be found that Group 1 performs best, while the subjects of Group 3 perform worst. In the task of translation from Chinese into English, the mean accuracy is 50.4%, that is, the ratio of right choices is 50.4%. Group 3 gets the highest accuracy while the subjects of Group 1 get the lowest. As for the task of the blank filling, the mean accuracy is 49.0%, and the results are 41.4%, 48.3% and 49.0% for each group. The mean right choices take up less than half of all the items. Among the three groups, Group 3 perform best while Group 1 remain the lowest. The total accuracy is 57.0%, so the mean right choices of items take up just a little more than half of all the items. The accuracy of each group is 53.0%, 56.0% and 62.6%, with Group 3 perform better, and Group 1 the lowest.

10.7.1 The learners' performance on the translation from English into Chinese

There are 40 items in this task, chosen and organized according to different types of metonymy within ICMs. Table 10.7 shows the descriptive data of subjects' performance on the translation from English into Chinese. The subjects of three groups have received a mean score of about 32.3. Of the three groups, Group 3 scores the lowest, about 31.4, and Group 1 has the highest score of nearly 33.3, with Group 2 in the middle, 32.1. It can be found from the range of the minimum and maximum score that subjects' performance varies greatly, of which Group 2 is the greatest, ranging from 23 to 38, Group 1 is the smallest, from the lowest 28 to highest 38, and Group 3 is in the middle, ranging from 24 to 35. The F ratio (F = 4.337) in Table 10.8 indicates that the mean comparison of the performance between groups is of significant difference.

Table 10.7 **Descriptive data of the translation from English into Chinese**

Groups	N	Min	Max	M	SD
1	35	28.00	38.00	33.3429	2.22212
2	31	23.00	38.00	32.0968	3.12362
3	31	24.00	35.00	31.3871	2.85981
Total	97	23.00	38.00	32.3196	2.83412

Table 10.8 **F Ratio of the translation from English into Chinese**

	SS	df	MS	F	Sig.
Between Groups	65.143	2	32.571	4.337	.016
Within Groups	705.950	94	7.510		
Total	771.093	96			

Table 10.9 　　　　　**Comparison of the translation from English into Chinese**

(I) Group	(J) Group	MD (I-J)	SE	Sig.
1	2	1.2461	.67590	.188
	3	1.9558 *	.67590	.018
2	1	−1.2461	.67590	.188
	3	.7097	.69608	.596
3	1	−1.9558 *	.67590	.018
	2	−.7097	.69608	.596

* $p<0.5$

Table 10.9 shows Scheffe Multiple Comparison of means between groups. It can be seen that it is significantly different between the means of Group 1 and Group 3, while the differences between Group 1 and Group 2, Group 2 and Group 3 are not significant. That is, Group 1 and Group 3 are at different levels in the understanding of English metonymic proverbs. The data show that the subjects of Group 1 perform best while those of Group 3 perform worst.

10.7.2　The learners' performance on the translation from Chinese into English

There are 40 items in this task, chosen and organized according to different types of metonymy within ICMs. Table 10.10 shows the descriptive data of subjects' performance on the items. The subjects of the three groups have received a mean score of about 20.2. Of the three groups, Group 1 scores the lowest of 19, and Group 3 has the highest score of nearly 22.5, with Group 2 in the middle, 19.2. It can be seen from the range of the minimum and maximum score that subjects' performance varies greatly, of which Group 1 is the greatest, ranging from 11 to 30, Group 2 is from the lowest 9 to the highest 26, which is the same with Group 3, ranging from 13 to 30. The F ratio ($F=5.925$) in Table 10.11 indicates that the mean comparison of the performance between groups is of significant difference.

Table 10.10 　　　　**Descriptive data of the translation from Chinese into English**

Groups	N	Min	Max	M	SD
1	35	11.00	30.00	19.0000	4.32503
2	31	9.00	26.00	19.1935	4.57835
3	31	13.00	30.00	22.4516	4.58140
Total	97	9.00	30.00	20.1649	4.71408

Table 10.11 **F Ratio of the translation from Chinese into English**

	SS	df	MS	F	Sig.
Between Groups	238.845	2	119.422	5.925	.004
Within Groups	1894.516	94	20.154		
Total	2133.361	96			

Table 10.12 shows Scheffe Multiple Comparison of means between groups. It is significantly different between the means of Group 1 and Group 3, Group 2 and Group 3, while the difference between Group 1 and Group 2 is not significant. That is, there is no difference between Group 1 and Group 2 in the understanding and use of English metonymy-motivated proverbs. As far as the understanding and use of English metonymy-motivated proverbs are concerned, the learners at different levels perform variedly. The subjects of Group 3 perform best while those of Group 1 perform worst.

Table 10.12 **The Scheffe Multiple Comparison of translation from Chinese into English**

(I) Group	(J) Group	MD (I-J)	SE	Sig.
1	2	-.1935	1.10724	.985
	3	-3.4516 *	1.10724	.010
2	1	.1935	1.10724	.985
	3	-3.2581 *	1.14030	.020
3	1	3.4516 *	1.10724	.010
	2	3.2581 *	1.14030	.020

* $p<0.5$

10.7.3 The learners' performance on the blank filling

There are 85 items chosen and organized according to different types of English metonymy- motivated proverbs for the blank filling. Table 10.13 shows the descriptive data of subjects' performance. The subjects of three groups have received a mean score of about 41.6. Of the three groups, Group 1 scores the lowest, about 35.2, and Group 3 has the highest score of about 49.5, with Group 2 in the middle, nearly 41.1. From the range of the minimum and maximum score, it can be seen that subjects' performance varies greatly, of which Group 2 is the greatest, ranging from 9 to 58, the next one is Group 3, which ranges from the lowest 25 to highest 65, and Group 1 has the least variance, ranging from 21 to 48. The F ratio ($F=17.692$) in Table 10.14 indicates that the mean comparison of the performance between groups is of significant difference.

Table 10.13   **Descriptive data of the blanking filling**

Groups	N	Min	Max	M	SD
1	35	21.00	48.00	35.1714	6.77142
2	31	9.00	58.00	41.0645	13.38640
3	31	25.00	65.00	49.5161	8.35013
Total	97	9.00	65.00	41.6392	11.37631

Table 10.14   **F Ratio of ANOVA of the blank filling**

	SS	df	MS	F	Sig.
Between Groups	3397.787	2	1698.893	17.692	.000
Within Groups	9026.584	94	96.027		
Total	12424.371	96			

Table 10.15   **The Scheffe Multiple Comparison the of blank filling**

(I) Group	(J) Group	MD (I-J)	SE	Sig.
1	2	−5.8931	2.41688	.056
	3	−14.3447 *	2.41688	.000
2	1	5.8931	2.41688	.056
	3	−8.4516 *	2.48904	.004
3	1	14.3447 *	2.41688	.000
	2	8.4516 *	2.48904	.004

* $p < 0.5$

Table 10.15 shows that it is significantly different between the means of Group 1 and Group 3, Group 2 and Group 3, while the difference between Group 1 and Group 2 is not significant. That is, there is no difference between the performance of Group 1 and Group 2. The data show that in the understanding and use of English metonymy-motivated proverbs, EFL learners at different levels perform variedly. The subjects of Group 3 perform best while those of Group 1 perform worst. On the whole the learners' cognition of metonymy in the understanding and use of English proverbs goes up in the process of English learning, while it has almost no change from lower level to intermediate level, which is consistent with the results in the translation from Chinese into English.

10.7.4   The learners' overall performance

There are 165 items altogether as experimental materials, including 40 items in the translation from English into Chinese, 40 items in the translation from Chinese into English and 85 items in the blank filling. Table 10.16 shows the descriptive data of subjects' performance on the whole test. The subjects of the three groups have received a mean score of about 94. 1. Of the three groups, Group 1 scores the lowest, about 87. 5, and Group 3 has the highest score of nearly 103. 4, with Group 2 in the middle, nearly 92. 4. It can be seen from the range of the minimum and maximum score, that subjects' performance varies greatly, of which Group 3 is the highest, ranging from 75 to 125, the following one is Group 2 which ranges from the lowest 56 to highest 110, and the range of Group 3 is relatively smaller, from 75 to 108.

Table 10. 16　　　　　　　　　　　**Descriptive data of the whole test**

Groups	N	Min	Max	M	SD
1	35	75. 00	108. 00	87. 5143	7. 61721
2	31	56. 00	110. 00	92. 3548	14. 66640
3	31	75. 00	125. 00	103. 3548	10. 56267
Total	97	56. 00	125. 00	94. 1237	12. 92628

Table 10. 17　　　　　　　　　　**F ratio of ANOVA of the whole test**

	SS	df	MS	F	Sig.
Between Groups	4267. 579	2	2133. 790	17. 037	. 000
Within Groups	11772. 936	94	125. 244		
Total	16040. 515	96			

The F ratio (F = 17. 037) in Table 10. 17 indicates that the mean comparison of the performance between groups in the whole test is of significant difference. It can be seen from Table 10. 18, the Scheffe Multiple Comparison of means between groups in terms of performance in the whole test is significantly different between the means of Group 1 and Group 3, Group 2 and Group 3, while the difference between Group 1 and Group 2 is not significant. That is, there is no difference between Group 1 and Group 2 in the understanding and use of English metonymy-motivated proverbs. The difference between Group 1 and Group 3 is about 15. 8, which is relatively higher than the difference between Group 2 and Group 3. The data show that in the understanding and use of English metonymy-motivated proverbs, EFL learners at different levels perform variedly. The subjects of Group 3 perform best while those of Group 1 perform worst. On the whole the learners' cognition of metonymy in the understanding and use of English proverbs goes up in the process of English learning, while it has almost no change from the lower level to the intermediate level.

Table 10.18   **The Scheffe Multiple Comparison of the whole test**

(I) Group	(J) Group	MD (I-J)	SE	Sig.
1	2	−4.8406	2.76017	.220
	3	−15.8406 *	2.76017	.000
2	1	4.8406	2.76017	.220
	3	−11.0000 *	2.84258	.001
3	1	15.8406 *	2.76017	.000
	2	11.0000 *	2.84258	.001

* $p < 0.5$

Judging by the learners' performance on the translation from Chinese to English and the blank filling, it can be seen that learners of higher levels perform better than those of the lower and intermediate level. However, the learners' performance on the translation from English into Chinese, learners of the lower level perform better than those of the higher level. For the whole test, subjects of Group 1 and Group 2 perform without difference, which means that in the understanding and use of English metonymy-motivated proverbs, subjects of lower level and intermediate level are at the same level. The data are demonstrated in the following figures.

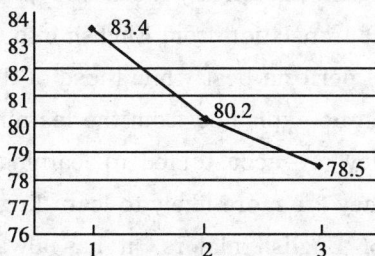

Figure 10.4   Accuracy of translation from English into Chinese

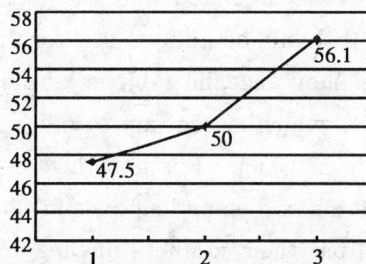

Figure 10.5   Accuracy of translation from Chinese into English

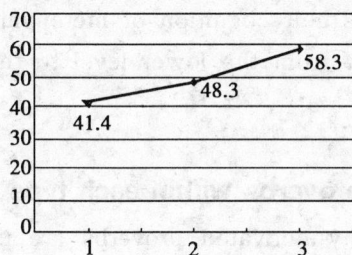

Figure 10.6   Accuracy of blank filling

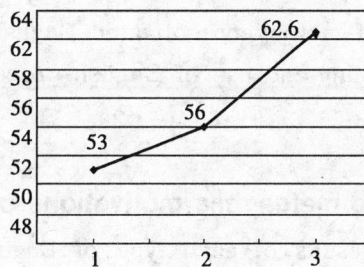

Figure 10.7   Accuracy of all the items

There are some reasons to account for the results. To begin with, learners of non-English majors, no matter undergraduates or postgraduates, pay more attention to the memorization of fixed number of points about English, and their interests and efforts to

English proverbs is limited. However, for English majors, the aim of English learning is integrative, so they are more interested in learning about the culture of English-speaking countries, and are more motivated to be like native speakers of English. According to the great chain metaphor theory (GCMT) growing out of a cognitive linguistics approach developed since 1980 by George Lakoff and his associates (Lakoff & Johnson, 1980; Lakoff & Turner, 1989), much of the mind is structured by conceptual metaphors which allow one domain of knowledge to be understood via another domain. Proverbs are syntactically and semantically generic but they can be used in non-whole ways in utterances. There are four basic concepts that the GCMT relies on: the generic-is-specific metaphor, the great-chain-of-being, the-nature-of-things, and the conventional maxim of quantity. Proverb comprehension depends on the commonly organized work of these, although in some cases not all of these constructs need to be invoked. In order to understand a proverb, the user should invoke many related knowledge systems, including language, cultural and pragmatic points in the mind. As a result, with the accumulation of knowledge, especially that of the target culture, the whole mastery of English proverbs will surely be enhanced. Furthermore, the textbooks and learning materials for English majors and non-English majors also are different, with the former more concerned with the learning of cultural aspects than the latter. The learning of history, literature and other cultural knowledge surely stimulates and enhances the understanding and use of English proverbs. With the process of learning of this kind of knowledge, the learners' cognition of metonymy is more likely to be accumulated and the mastery of English metonymy-motivated proverbs is elevated. It should be noticed that for the task in the translation from English into Chinese, the results show that the subjects of the lower level perform best while those of the higher level worst, which is contrary to other tasks. It can be explained from the learning habits of students in China. For non-English majors, they are accustomed to learning English items with the corresponding ones in Chinese and they are more likely to learn English with the help from their mother tongue. However, for English majors, it has always been emphasized that learning a language is to learn the thinking patterns of the target culture. Consequently, when faced with English proverbs, the lower level is more sensitive to their native Chinese. In conclusion, Chinese EFL learners of different levels have varied mastery of metonymy-motivated English proverbs, their cognition of metonymy in the understanding and use of English proverbs goes up from the lower level to the higher level.

10.8 The metonymic motivations of English proverbs within each type of ICMs

The results of each type of English metonymy-motivated proverbs are presented between the three groups in order to examine if there are any differences between the performances of the learners on each type of proverbs. Table 10.19 shows accuracy of items on different types of metonymic proverbs, the mean percentage of right choices on all the nine types ranges from the highest 61.6 of metonymic proverbs within Location ICM to the lowest 51.3 within Thing-part ICM. In general, the subjects' performance on metonymy-motivated proverbs is just a little bit higher than half of the whole items in the test, with a mean percentage of 57.0.

Table 10.19   **Accuracy of items on different types of metonymic proverbs**

Types of metonymy	Total number of items	Percentage of right choice (%)			
		Group 1	Group 2	Group 3	Mean
Within Thing-part ICM	22	48.8	48.1	57.2	51.3
Category-and-property ICM	21	52.2	58.7	66.7	58.9
Category-and-member ICM	23	53.9	54.8	61.7	56.7
Causation ICM	21	55.9	57.1	60.1	57.6
Action ICM	20	52.7	62.1	66.1	60.0
Event ICM	25	51.5	53.3	59.5	54.6
Possession ICM	11	51.7	55.1	60.7	55.7
Containment ICM	10	61.1	57.1	66.5	61.5
Location ICM	12	53.6	61.0	71.2	61.6
Total	165	53.0	56.0	62.6	57.0

For metonymic proverbs within Thing-part ICM, the subjects of Group 1 and Group 2 get similar accuracy of items, 48.8% and 48.1% respectively, which are smaller than 57.2% by Group 3. For metonymic proverbs within Category-and-property ICM, the subjects of three groups perform quite differently, of which Group 3 gets the highest percentage of 66.7 and Group 1 the lowest, 52.2, with Group 2 in the middle, 58.7. For the accuracy of metonymic proverbs within Category-and-member ICM, the subjects in Group 1 and Group 2 get similar results of 53.9% and 54.8%, which are far from those of Group 3, 61.7%. For the performance of subjects on metonymic proverbs within Causation ICM, the accuracy of three groups has relatively small difference, with 55.9% of Group 1, 57.1% of Group 2 and 60.1% of Group 3. Considering metonymic proverbs within Action ICM, the percentage of right choices by three groups varies greatly, of which the highest is 66.1% by Group 3, and the lowest is 52.7% by Group 1, with 62.1% of Group 2 in the middle. For metonymic proverbs within Event ICM, Group 1 and Group 2 get 51.5% and 53.3% respectively, while Group 3 gets a higher accuracy of 59.5%. Considering metonymic proverbs within Possession ICM, the highest accuracy is got by Group 3, 60.7%, and the following one is 55.1% of Group 2, with Group 1 the lowest of 51.7%. The subjects' performance on metonymic proverbs within Containment ICM varies, with Group 3 the highest of 66.5%, Group 2 the lowest of 57.1% and Group 1 in the middle, 61.1%. For metonymic proverbs within Location ICM, the subjects in three groups get quite different results, the highest is 71.2% by Group 3, Group 2 is in the middle of 61.0% and Group 1 gets the lowest percentage of 53.6.

10.8.1 Metonymic proverbs within Thing-part ICM

Metonymic proverbs within Thing-part ICM include 22 items arranged in the three tasks. Table 10.20 shows the descriptive data of subjects' performance. The subjects of three groups have received a mean score of nearly 11.3, and Group 2 scores the lowest, nearly 10.6, and Group 3 the highest of nearly 12.6, with Group 1 in the middle, about 10.7, which is similar to that of Group 2. It can be seen from the range of the minimum and maximum scores that the subjects' performance varies greatly, of which Group 1 is the greatest, ranging from 8 to 17, the following one is Group 3, ranging from 9 to 17, the range of Group 2 is relatively smaller, from the lowest 6 to 13.

Table 10.20　**Descriptive data of metonymic proverbs within Thing-part ICM**

Groups	N	Min	Max	M	SD
1	35	8.00	17.00	10.7429	2.27961
2	31	6.00	13.00	10.5806	1.87571
3	31	9.00	17.00	12.5806	1.97946
Total	97	6.00	17.00	11.2784	2.23020

The F ratio (F = 9.135) in Table 10.21 indicates that the mean comparison of the performance between groups on metonymic proverbs within Thing-part ICM is of significant difference.

Table 10.21　**F ratio of ANOVA of metonymic proverbs within Thing-part ICM**

	SS	df	MS	F	Sig.
Between groups	77.702	2	38.851	9.135	.000
Within groups	399.782	94	4.253		
Total	477.485	96			

Table 10.22 is the results of Scheffe Multiple Comparison of means between groups, from which it can be concluded that it is significantly different between the means of Group 1 and Group 3, Group 2 and Group 3, while the difference between Group 1 and Group 2 is not significant. That is, there is no difference between Group 1 and Group 2 in the understanding and use of English metonymy-motivated proverbs within Thing-part ICM. The difference between Group 2 and Group 3 is 2, which is slightly higher than the difference between Group 1 and Group 3, about 1.8. The data show that EFL learners at different levels perform variedly. The subjects of Group 3 perform better than those of Group 1 and Group 2. On the whole the learners' cognition of metonymic proverbs within Thing-part ICM goes up in the process of English learning, while it has almost no change from the lower level to the intermediate level.

Table 10.22　**The Scheffe Multiple Comparison of metonymic proverbs within Thing-part ICM**

(I) Group	(J) Group	MD (I-J)	SE	Sig.
1	2	.1622	.50863	.950
	3	−1.8378 *	.50863	.002
2	1	−.1622	.50863	.950
	3	−2.0000 *	.52382	.001
3	1	1.8378 *	.50863	.002
	2	2.0000 *	.52382	.001

* $p < 0.5$

10.8.2　Metonymic proverbs within Category-and-property ICM

Metonymic proverbs within Category-and-property ICM include 21 items arranged in the three tasks. Table 10.23 presents the descriptive data of the subjects' performance. The subjects of the three groups have received a mean score of nearly 12.4. Of the three groups, Group 1 scores the lowest, nearly 11.0, and Group 3 has the highest score of 14, leaving Group 2 in the middle, with a mean score of about 12.3. It can be seen from the range of the minimum and maximum score, that the learners' performance varies greatly, Group 2 ranging from the lowest 7 to the highest of 18 and Group 3 ranging from 9 to 20 are the same, which is slightly greater than Group 1, with the range from 7 to 17.

Table 10.23　**Descriptive data of metonymic proverbs within Category-and-property ICM**

Groups	N	Min	Max	M	SD
1	35	7.00	17.00	10.9714	2.77049
2	31	7.00	18.00	12.3226	3.09179
3	31	9.00	20.00	14.0000	2.75681
Total	97	7.00	20.00	12.3711	3.10685

The F ratio ($F = 9.142$) in Table 10.24 indicates that the mean comparison of the learners' performance between groups on metonymic proverbs within Category-and-property ICM is of significant difference.

Table 10.24　**F ratio of ANOVA of metonymic proverbs within Category-and-property ICM**

	SS	df	MS	F	Sig.
Between groups	150.894	2	75.447	9.142	.000
Within groups	775.746	94	8.253		
Total	926.639	96			

Table 10.25 shows the results of Scheffe Multiple Comparison of means between groups. It can be concluded that it is significantly different between the means of Group 1

and Group 3, while the differences between Group 1 and Group 2, Group 2 and Group 3 is not significant. That is, there is no difference between Group 1 and Group 2, Group 2 and Group 3 in the understanding and use of metonymic proverbs within Category-and-property ICM. The data show that EFL learners of Group 3 and Group 1 perform variedly. The former perform better than the latter. On the whole the learners' cognition of metonymic proverbs within Category-and-property ICM goes up in the process of English learning.

Table 10.25　**The Scheffe Multiple Comparison of metonymic proverbs within Category-and-property ICM**

(I) Group	(J) Group	MD (I-J)	SE	Sig.
1	2	−1.3512	.70852	.168
	3	−3.0286 *	.70852	.000
2	1	1.3512	.70852	.168
	3	−1.6774	.72968	.076
3	1	3.0286 *	.70852	.000
	2	1.6774	.72968	.076

* $p < 0.5$

10.8.3　Metonymic proverbs within Category-and-member ICM

Metonymic proverbs within Category-and- member ICM include 23 items arranged in the three tasks. Table 10.26 shows the descriptive data of the subjects' performance on metonymic proverbs within Category-and-member ICM. The subjects of three levels have received a mean score of about 13.0. Among the three groups, Group 1 scores the lowest, 12.4, and Group 3 has the highest score of nearly 14.2, with Group 2 in the middle, about 12.6, which is slightly higher than that of Group 1. It can be seen from the range of the minimum and maximum score that the subjects' performance varies greatly, of which Group 3 is the greatest, ranging from 8 to 21, the following one is Group 2, ranging from 7 to 17, and Group 1 is relatively smaller, from 9 to 16.

Table 10.26　**Descriptive data of metonymic proverbs within Category-and-member ICM**

Groups	N	Min	Max	M	SD
1	35	9.00	16.00	12.4000	1.95839
2	31	7.00	17.00	12.6129	2.60355
3	31	8.00	21.00	14.1935	3.17720
Total	97	7.00	21.00	13.0412	2.69613

The F ratio ($F = 4.521$) in Table 10.27 indicates that the mean comparison of the performance between groups on metonymic proverbs within Category-and-member ICM is of significant difference.

Table 10.27   **F ratio of ANOVA of metonymic proverbs within Category-and-member ICM**

	SS	df	MS	F	Sig.
Between groups	61.242	2	30.621	4.521	.013
Within groups	636.594	94	6.772		
Total	697.835	96			

Table 10.28 presents the results of Scheffe Multiple Comparison of means between groups. It can be concluded that it is significantly different between the means of Group 1 and Group 3, while the difference between Group 1 and Group 2, Group 2 and Group 3 is not significant. That is, there is no difference between Group 1 and Group 2, Group 2 and Group 3 in the understanding and use of metonymic proverbs within Category-and-member ICM. The data demonstrate that EFL learners of Group 1 and Group 3 perform variedly. The latter outperform the former. On the whole the learners' cognition of metonymic proverbs within Category-and-member ICM goes up in the process of English learning.

Table 10.28   **Scheffe Multiple Comparison metonymic proverbs within Category-and-member ICM**

(I) Group	(J) Group	MD (I-J)	SE	Sig.
1	2	-.2129	.64184	.947
	3	-1.7935 *	.64184	.024
2	1	.2129	.64184	.947
	3	-1.5806	.66100	.062
3	1	1.7935 *	.64184	.024
	2	1.5806	.66100	.062

* The mean difference is significant at the .05 level ($p < .05$).

10.8.4   Metonymic proverbs within Causation ICM

Metonymic proverbs within Causation ICM include 21 items arranged in the three tasks. Table 10.29 is the descriptive data of metonymic proverbs within Causation ICM. The subjects of three groups have received a mean score of about 12.1. Of the three groups, Group 1 scores the lowest, with a mean score of about 11.7, and Group 3 has the highest score of about 12.6, leaving Group 2 in the middle, with a mean score of 12. It can be seen from the range of the minimum and maximum score, that the learners' performance varies greatly, of which Group 2 ranging from the lowest 5 to the highest of 17 and Group 3 ranging from 7 to 19 are the same, which is relatively greater than Group 1, with the range from 7 to 15.

Table 10.29   **Descriptive data of metonymic proverbs within Causation ICM**

Groups	N	Min	Max	M	SD
1	35	7.00	15.00	11.7429	1.97548
2	31	5.00	17.00	12.0000	2.96648
3	31	7.00	19.00	12.6129	2.76499
Total	97	5.00	19.00	12.1031	2.57991

The F ratio ($F = .971$) in Table 10.30 indicates that the mean comparison of the performance between groups on metonymic proverbs within Causation ICM has no significant difference.

Table 10.30   **F ratio of ANOVA of metonymic proverbs within Causation ICM**

	SS	df	MS	F	Sig.
Between groups	12.929	2	6.464	.971	.383
Within groups	626.041	94	6.660		
Total	638.969	96			

Table 10.31 shows the results of Scheffe Multiple Comparison of means between groups. It can be concluded that it is not significantly different between the means of the three groups. That is, there is no difference among the three groups in the understanding and use of metonymic proverbs within Causation ICM.

Table 10.31   **Scheffe Multiple Comparison of metonymic proverbs within Causation ICM**

(I) Group	(J) Group	MD (I-J)	SE	Sig.
1	2	−.2571	.63649	.922
	3	−.8700	.63649	.396
2	1	.2571	.63649	.922
	3	−.6129	.65550	.647
3	1	.8700	.63649	.396
	2	.6129	.65550	.647

* $p < 0.5$

10.8.5   Metonymic proverbs within Action ICM

Metonymic proverbs within Action ICM include 20 items arranged in the three tasks. Table 10.32 shows the descriptive data metonymic proverbs within Action ICM. The subjects of three groups have received a mean score of 12. Of the three groups, Group 1 has the lowest score of about 10.5, and Group 3 has the highest of about 13.2, with Group 2 in the middle, about 12.4. The range of the minimum and maximum scores indicates that subjects' performance varies greatly. Group 2 ranging from 6 to 15 and Group 3 with a range from 9 to 18 are the same, which is slightly greater than Group 1, ranging from the lowest 6 to the highest 14.

Table 10.32   **Descriptive data of metonymic proverbs within Action ICM**

Groups	N	Min	Max	M	SD
1	35	6.00	14.00	10.5429	1.96053
2	31	6.00	15.00	12.4194	2.33487
3	31	9.00	18.00	13.2258	2.20166
Total	97	6.00	18.00	12.0000	2.42813

The F ratio (F = 13.507) in Table 10.33 indicates that the mean comparison of the performance between groups on metonymic proverbs within Action ICM is of significant difference.

Table 10.33   **F ratio of ANOVA of metonymic proverbs within Action ICM**

	SS	df	MS	F	Sig.
Between groups	126.347	2	63.173	13.507	.000
Within groups	439.653	94	4.677		
Total	566.000	96			

Table 10.34 presents the results of Scheffe Multiple Comparison of metonymic proverbs within Action ICM. It is significantly different between the means of Group 1 and Group 2, Group 1 and Group 3, while the difference between Group 2 and Group 3 is not significant. That is, there is no difference between Group 2 and Group 3 in the understanding and use of metonymic proverbs within Action ICM. The difference between Group 1 and Group 3 is nearly 2.7, which is slightly greater than the difference between Group 1 and Group 2, nearly 1.9. The data show that EFL learners at different levels perform variedly. The learners of Group 3 and Group 2 perform better than those of Group 1. The results indicate that the learners' cognition of metonymic proverbs within Action ICM goes up in the process of English learning, while it remains almost the same from the intermediate level to the higher level.

Table 10.34   **Scheffe Multiple Comparison of metonymic proverbs within Action ICM**

(I) Group	(J) Group	MD (I-J)	SE	Sig.
1	2	-1.8765 *	.53339	.003
	3	-2.6829 *	.53339	.000
2	1	1.8765 *	.53339	.003
	3	-.8065	.54932	.345
3	1	2.6829 *	.53339	.000
	2	.8065	.54932	.345

* The mean difference is significant at the .05 level (p< .05).

10.8.6 Metonymic proverbs within Event ICM

Metonymic proverbs within Event ICM include 25 items arranged in the three tasks. Table 10.35 presents the descriptive data of metonymic proverbs within Event ICM. The subjects of three groups have received a mean score of nearly 13.7. Of the three groups, Group 1 scores the lowest, nearly 12.9, and Group 3 has the highest score of nearly 14.9, leaving Group 2 in the middle, with a mean score of about 13.3. It can be seen from the range of the minimum and maximum scores that the learners' performance varies greatly. The scores of Group 3 ranging from the lowest 7 to the highest of 20 are the greatest. Group 1 has the score range from 6 to 18, and the scores of Group 2, which range from 8 to 16, are the lowest.

Table 10.35   **Descriptive data of metonymic proverbs within Event ICM**

Groups	N	Min	Max	M	SD
1	35	6.00	18.00	12.8857	2.76290
2	31	8.00	16.00	13.3226	2.15077
3	31	7.00	20.00	14.8710	3.31403
Total	97	6.00	20.00	13.6598	2.88273

The F ratio (F = 4.519) in Table 10.36 indicates that the mean comparison of the performance between groups on metonymic proverbs within Event ICM is of significant difference.

Table 10.36   **F ratio of ANOVA of metonymic proverbs within Event ICM**

	SS	df	MS	F	Sig.
Between groups	69.972	2	34.986	4.519	.013
Within groups	727.801	94	7.743		
Total	797.773	96			

From Table 10.37, the results of Scheffe Multiple Comparison of metonymic proverbs within Event ICM, it can be concluded that it is significantly different between the means of Group 1 and Group 3, while the difference between Group 1 and Group 2, Group 2 and Group 3 is not significant. That is, there is no difference between Group 1 and Group 2, Group 2 and Group 3 in the understanding and use of metonymic proverbs within Event ICM. The data show that EFL learners of Group 1 and Group 3 perform variedly. The latter outperform the former. The results indicate that the learners' cognition of metonymic proverbs within Event ICM goes up in the process of English learning.

Table 10.37 **Scheffe Multiple Comparison of metonymic proverbs within Event ICM**

(I) Group	(J) Group	MD (I-J)	SE	Sig.
1	2	-.4369	.68628	.817
	3	-1.9853 *	.68628	.018
2	1	.4369	.68628	.817
	3	-1.5484	.70677	.096
3	1	1.9853 *	.68628	.018
	2	1.5484	.70677	.096

* $p < 0.5$

10.8.7 Metonymic proverbs within Possession ICM

Metonymic proverbs within Possession ICM include 11 items arranged in the three tasks. Table 10.38 shows the descriptive data of metonymic proverbs within Possession ICM. The subjects of three groups have received a mean score of about 6.1. Of the three groups, Group 1 scores lowest, nearly 5.7, and Group 3 has the highest score of nearly 6.7, with Group 2 in the middle, nearly 6.1. It can be seen from the range of the minimum and maximum scores that the learners' performance varies greatly, of which Group 3 is the greatest, ranging from 2 to 10, slightly higher than Group 1, from 3 to 10, and Group 2, from 2 to 9.

Table 10.38 **Descriptive data of metonymic proverbs within Possession ICM**

Groups	N	Min	Max	M	SD
1	35	3.00	10.00	5.6857	1.54865
2	31	2.00	9.00	6.0645	1.82456
3	31	2.00	10.00	6.6774	1.93885
Total	97	2.00	10.00	6.1237	1.79848

The F ratio ($F = 9.135$) in Table 10.39 indicates that the mean comparison of the performance between groups on metonymic proverbs within Possession ICM is of no significant difference.

Table 10.39 **F ratio of ANOVA of metonymic proverbs within Possession ICM**

	SS	df	MS	F	Sig.
Between groups	16.327	2	8.164	2.609	.079
Within groups	294.188	94	3.130		
Total	310.515	96			

Table 10.40 is the results of Scheffe Multiple Comparison of metonymic proverbs within Possession ICM. It has no significant difference among the three groups. On the

whole the learners' cognition of metonymic proverbs within Possession ICM has no change during the process of English learning.

Table 10.40   Scheffe Multiple Comparison of metonymic proverbs within Possession ICM

(I) Group	(J) Group	MD (I-J)	S. E	Sig.
1	2	−.3788	.43632	.687
	3	−.9917	.43632	.081
2	1	.3788	.43632	.687
	3	−.6129	.44935	.398
3	1	.9917	.43632	.081
	2	.6129	.44935	.398

* The mean difference is significant at the .05 level (p< .05).

10.8.8 Metonymic proverbs within Containment ICM

Metonymic proverbs within Containment ICM include 10 items arranged in the three tasks. Table 10.41 shows the descriptive data of metonymic proverbs within Containment ICM. The subjects of three groups have a mean score of nearly 6.2. Of the three groups, Group 2 scores the lowest, 4.13, and Group 3 has the highest score of nearly 4.26, with Group 1 in the middle, 4.23. From the range of the minimum and maximum scores, it can be seen that the learners' performance varies slightly, all the three groups with the same range from the lowest 3 to the highest 5.

Table 10.41   Descriptive data of metonymic proverbs within Containment ICM

Groups	N	Min	Max	M	SD
1	35	3	5	4.23	.547
2	31	3	5	4.13	.619
3	31	3	5	4.26	.575
Total	97	2.00	9.00	6.1546	1.53664

The F ratio (F = 3.012) in Table 10.42 indicates that the mean comparison of the performance between groups on metonymic proverbs within Containment ICM is of no significant difference.

Table 10.42   F ratio of ANOVA of metonymic proverbs within Containment ICM

	SS	df	MS	F	Sig.
Between groups	13.654	2	6.827	3.012	.054
Within groups	213.027	94	2.266		
Total	226.680	96			

Table 10. 43 shows the results of Scheffe Multiple Comparison of means between groups in terms of performance on metonymic proverbs within Containment ICM. It can be concluded that the difference among three groups has no significance. That is, there is no difference between three groups in the understanding and use of metonymic proverbs within Containment ICM. On the whole the learners' cognition of metonymic proverbs within Containment ICM remains the same during the process of English learning.

Table 10.43   **Scheffe Multiple Comparison of metonymic proverbs within Containment ICM**

(I) Group	(J) Group	MD (I-J)	SE	Sig.
1	2	.4046	.37129	.554
	3	−.5309	.37129	.364
2	1	−.4046	.37129	.554
	3	−.9355	.38237	.055
3	1	.5309	.37129	.364
	2	.9355	.38237	.055

* $p<0.5$

10.8.9   Metonymic proverbs within Location ICM

Metonymic proverbs within Location ICM include 12 items arranged in the three tasks. Table 10. 44 shows the descriptive data of learners' performance on metonymic proverbs within Location ICM. The subjects of three groups have received a mean score of nearly 7. 4. Of the three groups, Group 1 scores the lowest, about 6. 4, and Group 3 has the highest score of about 8. 5, with Group 1 in the middle, 7. 3. It can be seen from the range of the minimum and maximum scores that the learners' performance varies greatly, of which Group 2 is the greatest ranging from the lowest 1 to the highest 10, slightly greater than the range of Group 1, from 3 to 10 and Group 3, from 4 to 11.

Table 10. 44   **Descriptive data of metonymic proverbs within Location ICM**

Groups	N	Min	Max	M	SD
1	35	3. 00	10. 00	6. 4286	1. 55839
2	31	1. 00	10. 00	7. 3226	2. 39982
3	31	4. 00	11. 00	8. 5484	1. 94660
Total	97	1. 00	11. 00	7. 3918	2. 14843

The F ratio ($F = 9. 436$) in Table 10. 45 indicates that the mean comparison of the performance between groups on metonymic proverbs within Location ICM is of significant difference.

Table 10.45　F ratio of ANOVA of metonymic proverbs within Location ICM

	SS	df	MS	F	Sig.
Between groups	74.090	2	37.045	9.436	.000
Within groups	369.023	94	3.926		
Total	443.113	96			

Table 10.46 shows results of Scheffe Multiple Comparison of means between groups in terms of performance on metonymic proverbs within Location ICM. It is significantly different between the means of Group 1 and Group 3, while the difference between Group 1 and Group 2, Group 2 and Group 3 is not significant. That is, there is no significant difference between Group 1 and Group 2, Group 2 and Group 3. The data show that EFL learners of Group 1 and Group 3 perform variedly, and the latter perform better than the former. On the whole the learners' cognition of metonymic proverbs within Location ICM goes up in the process of English learning.

Table 10.46　Scheffe Multiple Comparison of metonymic proverbs within Location ICM

(I) Group	(J) Group	MD (I-J)	SE	Sig.
1	2	−.8940	.48867	.193
	3	−2.1198 *	.48867	.000
2	1	.8940	.48867	.193
	3	−1.2258	.50327	.056
3	1	2.1198 *	.48867	.000
	2	1.2258	.50327	.056

* p<0.5

The results of the nine types of metonymy-motivated English proverbs indicate that the performances of the learners between groups on those metonymic proverbs within Thing-part ICM, Category-and-property ICM, Category-and-member ICM, Action ICM, Event ICM, and Location ICM are significantly different, while the performances of the learners between groups on some other metonymic proverbs within Causation ICM, Possession ICM and Containment ICM are not. In Causation ICM, Cause and effect are closely interdependent that one of them can easily evoke the other. For example, in the sentence *The fire trucks wailed out of the firehouse*, the typical sound "wail" brought about by an action is used to refer to the action. Metonymy within Possession ICM refers to the relationship between the possessor and the possessed, for example, money can stand for the person who holds money. The container and contents can stand for each other, for example, the container "dish" for holding or serving food can metonymically be used to denote food served in the container in the sentence *My favorite dish is fried steak.*

Therefore, people of different cultures using result to stand for the effect or vice versa, things possessed for possessor or vice versa, or container for the contents or vice versa are very popular, and those metonymic proverbs are widely accepted to express their ideas and to understand the world. As a result, they all hold these kinds of cognition no matter in their daily life or in the process of language learning.

But for the other six types of metonymy-motivated English proverbs, subjects of higher level outperform those of the lower level. The results reveal that the learners' cognition of metonymic proverbs within Thing-part ICM, Category-and-property ICM, Category-and-member ICM, Action ICM, Event ICM and Location ICM during the understanding and use of English proverbs goes up from the lower level to the higher level in the process of English learning. Figures 10.8 to 10.13 demonstrate the tendencies of the acquisition of English metonymic proverbs by Chinese EFL learners.

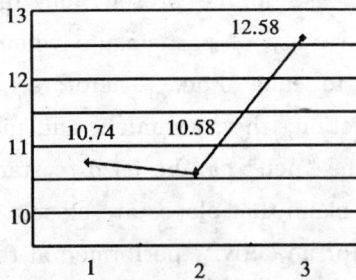

Figure 10.8   Metonymic proverbs within
Thing-part ICM

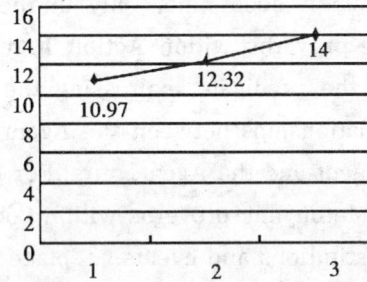

Figure 10.9   Metonymic proverbs within
Category-and-property ICM

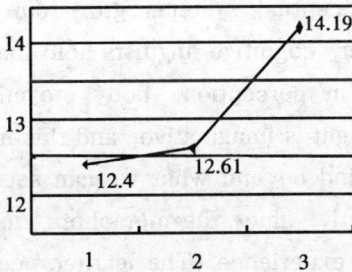

Figure 10.10   Metonymic proverbs within
Category-and-member ICM

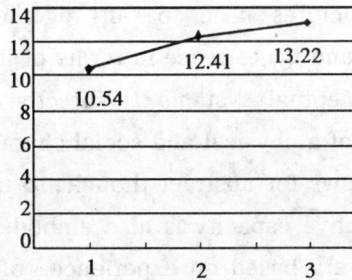

Figure 10.11   Metonymic proverbs within
Action ICM

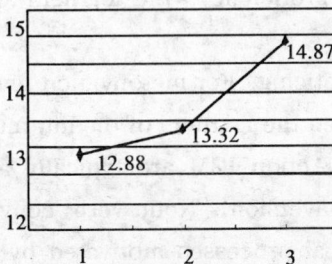

Figure 10.12   Metonymic proverbs within
Event ICM

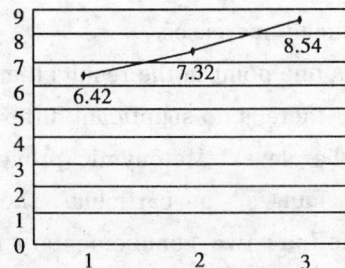

Figure 10.13   Metonymic proverbs within
Event ICM

For metonymic proverbs within Thing-part ICM, the parts can be used to refer to the whole and conversely the whole can be used to refer to the parts. The sentence *The dog bit me yesterday*, actually means that the dog bit the speaker with its teeth. Metonymic proverbs within Category-and-member ICM present the relation between every category and its members. As in the sentence *Two cars crashed into each other and resulted in a traffic block*, "car" refers to the category of "transport". Metonymic proverbs within Category-and-property ICM illustrate a category and its defining properties that can stand for each other, which forms a metonymic relationship. Take this tautology as an example, *kids are kids*. When used in different situations, this sentence may indicates that "kids are innocent, and are easy to be satisfied", "kids are always happy", or "kids are the hope of the future and should be protected", etc. Metonymic proverbs within Event ICM hold that whole and subevent can stand for each other. Such kind of metonymy may be found in the auxiliary system. The habitual event "*She speaks Japanese*" is described by the Present Tense, while it occurs not only in the past, but also in the present and the future. Metonymic proverbs within Action ICM involve a variety of participants which may be related to the predicate expressing the action or to each other. Therefore, there are specific relationships between the Agent and the Action, the Instrument and the Action, the Instrument and the Agent, etc. For example, the "pen" can be used to stand for the "writer". Metonymic proverbs within Location ICM claim that places are closely related to people, institutions and events. A place can stand for an activity performed at that place, as the phrase "*go to the supermarket*" for "*do some shopping*".

According to cognitive linguistics, language is based on our experience of the world and the way we perceive and conceptualize it. It is believed that thought is embodied, that is, the structures used to put together our conceptual systems grow out of bodily experience and make sense in terms of it. Moreover, cognitive linguists hold that the core of our conceptual systems is directly grounded in perception, body movement, and experience of a physical and social character. Thought is imaginative, and this imaginative capacity allows for abstract thought to take the mind beyond what we can see and feel. The imaginative capacity is also embodied, indirectly, since the metaphors, metonymies and images are based on experience, often bodily experience. The learners' cognition of these six kinds of metonymic proverbs is affected by the accumulation of knowledge about both the mother tongue and the target language. As a result, with more access to the target language and gradually elevation of English proficiency, the learners' cognition of them accordingly increases.

There is one point in the results that is worth noticing. For metonymic proverbs within Action ICM, there is no significant difference between the learners of the intermediate level and the higher level. Metonymic proverbs within Action ICM are typically achieved by word-class changes, in particular, noun-verb conversion. Noun-verb conversion and nominalization are two complementary morphological processes motivated by metonymic mechanism which are called grammatical metonymy. As a result of the fact that metonymic proverbs within Action ICM are concerned with grammar and many of the items concerning it have been fixed and accepted by language users, the performance by the intermediate learners and the higher learners may vary little.

To come to a conclusion, some metonymic relationships are common to all learners, including the relationships between cause and effect, possessed and possessor as well as container and contents and the learners' cognition of them has no significant difference between three groups of learners in the understanding and use of English proverbs. However, there are still other six types of metonymic proverbs within Thing-part ICM, Category-and-property ICM, Category-and-member ICM, Action ICM, Event ICM and Location ICM that challenge the acquisition of the Chinese EFL learners.

References

Adam, M. J. & A. Collins, *A Schema-theoretic View of reading*. In R. O. Freedle (eds.). *New Directions in Discourse Processing*. New Jersey: Ablex Publishing Corporation, 1979.

Adams, Marilyn Jager. *Beginning to Read: Thinking and Learning about Print*. Cambridge, Mass. : MIT Press, 1994.

Andersen, E. S. , M. Brizuela & L. DuPuy Gonnerman. Cross-linguistic Evidence for the Early Acquisition of Discourse Markers as Register Variables. *Journal of Pragmatics*, 1999 (31): 1339-1351.

Anderson, A. & T. Lynch. *Listening*. New York: Oxford University Press, 1988.

Anderson, J. R. *Cognitive Psychology and its Implications*. 4th ed. New York: W. H. Freeman and Company, 1995.

Anderson, J. R. *Cognitive Psychology and its Implications*. New York: Freeman, 1995.

Anderson, J. R. *The Architecture of Cognition*. Cambridge, MA: Harvard University Press, 1983.

Anderson, R. The One-to-One Principle of Interlanguage Construction. *Language Learning*, 1985 (34): 77-95.

Anderson, R. C. , R. J. Spiro & M. C. Anderson. Schemata as Scaffolding for the Representation of Information in Connected Discourse. *American Educational Research Journal*, 1978 (3): 433-440.

Anderson, Richard C. The Notion of Schemata and the Educational Enterprise: General Discussion of the Conference. *In Schooling and the Acquisition of Knowledge*, Richard C. Anderson, Rand J. Spiro, and William E. Montague (eds.). Hillsade, New Jersey: Lawrence Erbaum Associates, 1977: 369.

Aoun, J. & Y. Li. On some differences between Chinese and Japanese wh-elements. *Linguistic Inquiry*, 1993(24): 365-372.

Arbib, M. A. , E. J. Conklin, & Jane Hill. *From Schema Theory to Language*. New York: Oxford University Press, 1987.

Archakis, A. On Discourse Markers: Evidence from Modern Greek. *Journal of Pragmatic*. 2001 (33): 1235-1261.

Ariel, M. Pragmatic Operators. *The Encyclopedia of Language and Linguistics*. Oxford: Pragamon Press, 1994: 3250-3253.

Bailey, N. Theoretical Implications of the Acquisition of the English Simple Past and Past Progressive: Putting Together the Pieces of the Puzzle in Gass et al. (eds.), 1989.

Bailey, N. , C. Madden, & S. Krashen. Is There a "Natural Sequence" in Adult Second Language Learning? [J] *Language Learning*, 1974(21) : 235-243.

Baker, W. & K. Boonkit. Learning Strategies in Reading and Writing : EAP Contexts *RELC Journal*, 2004(35) : 299.

Barcelona, A. *Metaphor and Metonymy at the Crossroads : A Cognitive Perspective*. New York : Mouton de Gruyter, 2000.

Barcelona, A. *On the Plausibility of Claiming a Metonymic Motivation for Conceptual Metaphor*. In Barcelona (ed.), *Metaphor and Metonymy at the Crossroad : A Cognitive Perspective*. New York : Mouton de Gruyter, 2000 : 31-58.

Berent, G. Markedness Considerations in the Acquisition of Conditional Sentences. *Language Learning*, 1985(35) : 337-372.

Berkemeyer, U. B. Qualitative Analysis of Immediate Recall Protocol Data : Some Classroom Implications. *Die Unterrichtpraxis*, 1989 (22) : 131-137.

Bhela, A. Native Language Interference in Learning a Second Language Acquisition : Exploratory Case Studies of Native Language Interference with Target Language Usage. *International Education Journal*, 1999(1).

Bialystok, E. On the Relationship Between Knowing and Using Forms. *Applied Linguistics*, 1982 (3) : 181-206.

Blakemore, D. *Semantic Constraints on Relevance*. Oxford : Blackwell, 1987.

Blakemore, D. *Understanding Utterances*. Oxford : Blackwell, 1992.

Blank, A. *Co-presence and Succession : A Cognitive Typology of Metonymy*. In Panther, K. U. & G. Radden (eds.). *Metonymy in Language and Thought*. Amsterdam/Philadelphia : John Benjamins, 1999 :169-191.

Bracewell, R. J. , C. H. Frederiksen & J. D. Frederiksen. Cognitive Processes in Composing and Comprehending Discourse. *Educational Psychologist*, 1982 (17) : 146-164.

Brandsford, J. D. & M. K. Johnson. Contextual Prerequisites for Understanding : Some Investigations of Comprehension and Recall. *Journal of Verbal Learning and Verbal Behavior*, 1972 (11) : 717-726.

Brent, B. & P. Kay. *Basic Color Terms. Their Universality and Evolution*. Berkely, Los Angeles : University of California Press, 1969.

Brown, G. & G. Yule, *Discourse Analysis*. Cambridge : Cambridge University Press, 1983.

Brown, R. *A First Language : The Early Stages*. Mass. ; Harvard University Press, 1973.

Brugman, C. &. L. George . *The Story of Over : Polysemy, Semantics and the Structure of the Lexicon*. New York : Garland, 1988.

Burton, S. *Introduction to the Macmillan Book of Proverbs : Maxims and Famous Phrases*. New York : Macmillan Publishing Company, 1987 :14-29.

Bynes, H. The Role of Listening Comprehension : A Theoretical Base. *Foreign Annuals*, 1984 (17) : 317-329.

Cacciari, C. & G. Sam. *Understanding Figurative Language*. In : M. Gernsbacher (eds.). *Handbook of Psycholinguistics*. San Diego, C. A.: Academic Press, 1994: 447-477.

Calkins, L. *The Art of Teaching Writing*. Portsmouth, N. H.: Heinemann, 1986.

Cambourne, B. How Important is the Theory to the Reading Teacher? *Australian Journal of Reading*, 1979 (2):78-90.

Carrell, P. L. Awareness of Text Structure: Effects on Recall. In A. H. Alister (eds.) *Bilingual Performance in Reading and Writing*. Ann Arbor, M. I.: Research Club in Language Learning, 1994: 23-41.

Carrell, P. L. Content and Formal Schemata in ESL Reading. *TESOL Quarterly*, 1987 (21. 3).

Carrell, P. L. Evidence of a Formal Schema in Second language Comprehension. *Language Learning*, 1984 (34).

Carrell, P. L. Facilitating ESL Reading by Teaching Text Structure. *TESOL Quarterly*, 1985 (19.4): 727-752.

Carrell, P. L. Schema Theory and ESL Reading Pedagogy. *TESOL Quarterly*, 1983 (17. 4): 26-46.

Carrell, P. L. SLA and Classroom Instruction: Reading. *Annual Review of Applied Linguistics*, 1988 (9): 223-242.

Carrell, P. L. The Effects of Rhetorical Organization on ESL Readers. *TESOL Quarterly*, 1984 (18.3): 253-267.

Carrell, P. L. & C. E. Joan, Schema Theory and ESL Reading Pedagogy. *TESOL Quarterly*, 1983 (17.3):553-573.

Carrell, P. L. Facilitating ESL Reading Comprehension by Teaching Text Structure. *TESOL Quarterly*, 1985 (19): 727-752.

Carrell, P. L. & E. J. Carson. Schema Theory and ESL Reading Pedagogy. In Carrell, P. L., J. Devine & D. E. Eskey (eds.). *Interactive Approaches to Second Language Reading*. New York: Cambridge University Press, 1988: 73-92.

Carrell, P. L., J. Devine & D. E. Eskey (eds.). *Interactive Approaches to Second Language Reading*, New York: Cambridge University Press, 1994.

Carroll, D. W. *Psychology of Language*. Beijing: Foreign Language Teaching and Research Press, 2000.

Carroll, S. & M. Swain. Explicit and Negative Feedback: An Empirical Study of the Learning of Linguistic Generalizations. *Studies in Second Language Acquisition*, 1993 (15): 357-386.

Chaudron, C. & J. C. Richards. The Effect of Discourse Markers on the Comprehension of Lectures. *Applied Linguistics*, 1986(7):113-127.

Celce-Murcia, M. *The Grammar Book: An ESL/EFL Teacher's Course*. Heinle & Heinle, 1999.

Chen, Y. Y. & A. W. Y. He. *Dui bu dui* as a Pragmatic Marker: Evidence from Chinese Classroom Discourse. *Journal of Pragmatics*, 2001(33): 1441-1465.

Chiang, C. S. & P. Dunkel. The Effect of Speech Modification, Prior Knowledge, and

Listening Proficiency on EFL Lecture Learning. *TESOL Quarterly*, 1992 (26. 2) : 345-373.

Chihara, T. & J. Oller. Attitudes and Attained Proficiency in EFL: A Sociolinguistic Study of Adult Japanese Speakers. *Language Learning*, 1978(28) : 55-68.

Chomsky, N. *Knowledge of Language: Its Nature, Origin and Use*. New York: Praeger, 1986.

Chomsky, N. Markedness and Core Grammar. In A. Belletti, *et al.* (eds.) *Theory of Markedness in Generative Grammar*, 1965.

Chomsky, N. On Wh-movement. In P. Culicover. T. Wasow & A. Akmajian (eds.). *Formal Syntax*: 71-132. New York: Academic Press, 1977.

Chris, B. *Oxford Dictionary of Literary Terms*. Oxford: Oxford University Press, 1991: 181-182.

Cicero, De Orato. (English Translation). E. W. Sutton. *His Three Dialogues Upon the Character and Qualifications of an Orator*. Cambridge, M. A. : Harvard University Press, 1967.

Clack, R. L. *Thematic Theory in Syntax & Interpretation*. London: Routledge, 1990.

Clark, H. & E. Clark. *Psychology and Language*. New York: Harcourt, Brace Jovanovich, 1977.

Clarke, M. A. Reading in a Spanish and English: Evidence from Adult ESL Students. *Language Learning*, 1979 (29. 1) : 121-151.

Clarke, M. A. The Short Circuit Hypothesis of ESL Reading—Or When Language Competence Interferes with Reading Performance. *Modern Language Journal*, 1980 (64. 2) : 203-209.

Coady, J. A Psycholinguistic Model of the ESL Reader. In R. Mackay, B. Barkman & R. Jordon(eds.). *Reading in a Second Language*, 1979 : 5-12.

Cohen, A. D. *Strategies in Learning and Using a Second Language* . Beijing: Foreign Languages Teaching and Research Press, 2000.

Collins, A. & D. Gentner. A Framework for a Cognitive Theory of Writing. In L. W. Gregg & E. R. Steinberg (eds.). *Cognitive Processes in Writing*. Hillsdale, N. J. : Erlbaum, 1980: 51-72.

Cook, V. J. *Second Language Learning and Language Teaching*. Beijing: Foreign Languages Teaching and Research Press, 2000.

Corder, S. P. Language Distance and the Magnitude of the Learning Task. *Studies in Second Language Acquisition*, 1978(2) : 27-36.

Coulson, S. Analogic and Metaphoric Mapping in Blended Spaces: Menendez Brothers Virus. *The Newsletter of the Center for Research in Language*, 1995(9. 1).

Croft, William. The Role of Domains in the Interpretation of Metaphors and Metonymies. *Cognitive Linguistics*, 1993 (4) : 335-370.

Croft, W. *Typology and Universals*. Beijing: Foreign Language Teaching and Research Press, 2000.

Cziko, G. A. Language Competence and Reading Strategies: A Comparison of First-and

Second-Language Oral Reading Errors. *Language Learning*, 1980 (30): 101-116.

Danesi, M. Vico, Metaphor, and the Origin of Language: Advances in Semiotics. Bloomington, Ind. : Indiana University Press, 1993.

Dechant, E. *Understanding and Teaching Reading: An Interactive Model.* Hillsdale, N. J. : Lawrence Erlbaum, 1991.

Doughty, C. Second Language Instruction Does Make a Difference: Evidence from an Empirical Study on SL Relativization. *Studies in Second Language Acquisition*, 1991 (13): 431-469.

Dulay, H. , & M. Burt. Creative Construction in Second Language Learning and Teaching. *Language Learning*, 1975(24): 37-53.

Dulay, H. , & M. Burt. Natural Sequence in Child Second Language Acquisition. *Language Learning*, 1974(24): 37-53.

Dulay, H. , & M. Burt. Should We Teach Children Syntax? *Language Learning*, 1973(23): 245-258.

Dyson, A. , & S. W. Freedman. Writing. In J. Jensen, D. Lapp, & J. R. Squire (eds.). *Handbook of Research on Teaching in the Language Arts.* New York: Macmillan, 1991: 754-774.

Eckman, F. R. Some Theoretical and Pedagogical Implications of the Markedness Differential Hypothesis. *Studies in Second Language Learning*, 1985(7): 289-307.

Eckman, F. R. Markedness and the Contrastive Analysis Hypothesis. *Language Learning*, 1977(27): 315-330.

Elley, W. B. & F. Mangubhai. The Impact of Reading on Second Language. *Reading Research Quarterly*, 1983 (19): 53-67.

Elley, W. B. Acquiring Literacy in a Second Language: The Effect of Book-based Programs. *Language Learning*, 1991 (41.3): 375-411.

Ellis, R. *The Study of Second Language Acquisition.* Oxford: Oxford University Press, 1994.

Ellis, R. *Understanding Second Language Acquisition.* Oxford: Oxford University Press, 1985.

Erman, B. Pragmatic Markers Revisited with a Focus on *You Know* in Adult and Adolescent Talk. *Journal of Pragmatics*, 2001(33):1337-1359.

Ervin-Tripp, S. Is Second Language Learning Like the First? *TESOL Quarterly*, 1974(8): 111-127.

Eskey, D. E. *An Interactive Approach to the Language Problems of Second Language Readers.* Cambridge: Cambridge University Press, 1998.

Faerch, C. & G. Kasper. The Role of Comprehension in Second Language Learning. *Applied Linguistics*, 1986 (7):257-274.

Fauconnier, G. & M. Turner. Blending as a Central Process of Grammar. In Goldberg, A. E. (eds.). *Conceptual Structure, Discourse and Language*, 1996:113-129.

Fauconnier, G. *Mappings in Thought and Language.* San Diego: Cambridge University Press, 1997.

Fauconnier, G. *Mental Spaces: Aspects of Meaning Construction in Natural Language*. Cambridge: MIT Press, 1985.

Fauconnier, G. & M. Turner. Blending as a Central Process of Grammar. In Goldberg, A. E. (ed.). *Conceptual Structure, Discourse, and Language*. Stanford: Center for the Study of Language and Information (distributed by Cambridge University Press), 1996.

Fauconnier, G. & M. Turner. Conceptual Projection and Middle Spaces. *UCSD Cognitive Science Technical Report*, 1994.

Fauconnier, G. & M. Turner. *The Way We Think*. New York: Basic Books, 2003.

Fauconnier, G. & M. Turner. Conceptual Integration Networks. *Cognitive Science*, 1998 (22.2): 133-187.

Fillmore, C. *Frame Semantics*. In *Linguistic Society of Korea*. *Linguistics in the Morning Calm*. Seoul: Hanshin, 1982.

Fillmore, C. *Frames and the Semantics of Understanding*. Quaderni di Semantica, 1985 (6.2): 222-254.

Fillmore, C. J. Frame Semantics. In Linguistic Society of Korea (eds.). *Linguistics in the Morning Calm*. Seoul: Hanshin, 1982: 111-138.

Flahive, D. E. & N. Bailey. Exploring Reading-Writing Relationships Among Adult Second Language Learners. Paper, Georgia State University. December, 1988.

Flower, L. & G. Hayes. The Dynamics of Composing: Making Plans and Juggling Constraints. In Gregg, L. W. & E. R. Steinberg (eds.). *Cognitive Processes in Writing*. Hillsdale, N. J. : Erlbaum, 1980: 31-50.

Flower, L. & G. Hayes. A Cognitive Process Theory of Writing. *College Composition and Communication*, 1981(32): 365-387.

Flynn, S. & W. O'Neill. *Linguistic Theory in Second Language Acquisition*. Dordrecht: Kluwer, 1988.

Fraser, B. An Approach to Discourse Markers. *Journal of Pragmatics*, 1990(14):383-395.

Fraser, B. M. Malamud-Makowski. English and Spanish Contrastive Discourse Markers. *Language Sciences*, 1996(18):863-881.

Fraser, B. Pragmatic Formatives. In Verschueren, J. and M. Bertuccelli-papi (eds.). *The Pragmatic Perspective*, Amsterdam: Benjamins, 1987: 179-194.

Fraser, B. Types of English Discourse Markers. *Acta Linguistica Hungarica*, 1988 (38): 19-33.

Fraser, B. What Are Discourse Markers? *Journal of Pragmatics*, 1999 (31): 931-952.

Fuller, J. M. The Influence of Speaker Roles on Discourse Marker Use. *Journal of Pragmatics*, 2003 (35): 23-45.

Gass, S. & L. Selinker. (eds.). *Language Transfer in Language Learning*. Rowley, M. A. : Newbury House, 1983.

Gass, S. Language Universals and Second Language Acquisition. *Language Learning*, 1989 (39): 497-534.

Gass, S. Review of Interlanguage Syntax: Language Transfer and Language Universals.

Language Learning, 1984(34): 115-132.

Gass, S. M. & L. Selinker. *Second Language Acquisition: An Introductory Course* (*2nd Edition*). Lawrence: Lawrence Erlbaum Associates, 2001.

Genette, G. *Narrative Discourse: An Essay in Method*. Ithaca, N. Y. : Cornell University Press, 1980.

Gibbs and Matlock. Psycholinguistic Perspectives on Polysemy. In Cuyckens, H. & B. Zawada (eds.). *Polysemy in Cognitive Linguistics: Selected Papers from the Fifth International Cognitive Linguistics Conference*. Amsterdam/Philadelphia: John Benjamins Publishing Company, 1997.

Gibbs, R. W. *Speaking and Thinking with Metonymy*. In Panther, K. & G. Radden (eds.). *Metonymy in Language and Thought*. Amsterdam/ Philadelphia: John Benjamins Publishing Company, 1999: 61-76.

Gibbs, R. W. *The Poetics of Mind: Figurative Thought Language and Understanding*. Cambridge: Cambridge University Press, 1994.

Goldberg, A. E. *A Construction Grammar Approach to Argument Structure*. Chicago and London: The University of Chicago Press, 1995.

Goodman, K. S. Psycholinguistic Universals in the Reading Process. In *The Psychology of Second Language Learning*. Pimsleur, P. & T. Quinn (eds.). International Reading Association, 1971.

Goodman, K. S. & Y. M. Goodman. Learning to Read Is Natural. In L. Resnick & P. Weaver (eds.), *Theory and Practice of Early Reading*. N. J. : Erlbaum, 1979(1): 137-154.

Goodman, K. S. Reading: A Psycholinguistic Guessing Game. *Journal of the Reading Specialist*, 1967(6): 126-135.

Goodman, K. S. Aid of Oral Reading Miscues: Applied Psycholinguistics. *Reading Research Quarterly*, 1969(5): 9-30.

Goossens, L. *Metaphonymy: The Interaction of Metaphor and Metonymy in Figurative Expressions for Linguistic Action*. In Goossens, L. , et al. (eds.) *By Word of Mouth, Metaphor, Metonymy and Action in a Cognitive Perspective*. Amsterdam/ Philadelphia: John Benjamins, 1995:159-174.

Gough, P. B. One Second of Reading. In *Language by Ear and by Eye*. J. F. Kavanagh & I. G. Mattingly (eds.). Cambridge, Mass. : MIT Press, 1972.

Gould, E. , et al. *The Act of Writing*. New York: Random House, 1989.

Grabe, W. Current Developments in Second Language Reading Research. *TESOL Quarterly*, 1991 (25.3): 375-406.

Gregory, Y. T. *Random House Dictionary of Popular Proverbs and Sayings*. New York: New York University Press, 1996:1-2.

Greimas, A. J. & J. Courtâes. Semiotics and Language : An Analytical Dictionary. *Advances in Semiotics*. Bloomington: Indiana University Press, 1982.

Grice, H. P. *Logic and Conversation*. In: Cole, P & J. L. Morgan (eds.), *Syntax and Semantics*, 3. New York: Academic Press, 1975: 41-58.

Gundel, J. K. & E. E. Tarone. Language Transfer and the Acquisition of Pronouns. In Gass, S. & L. Selinker (eds.), *Language Transfer in Language Learning*. Amsterdam: John Benjamins Publishing Company, 1993.

Hafiz, F. M. and I. Tudor. Extensive Reading and the Development of Language Skills in an L2. *ELT Journal*, 1989 (43): 4-13.

Haiman, J. Iconic and Economic Motivation. *Language*, 1983(59.4): 781-819.

Hakuta, K. A Case Study of a Japanese Child Learning English as a Second Language. *Language Learning*, 1976(26): 321-351.

Hammarberg, B. On Intralingual, Interlingual and Developmental Solutions in Interlanguage in Hyltenstam and Linnarud (eds.), 1979.

Han Zhaohong. *Fossilization in Adult Second Language Acquisition*. Multilingual Matters Ltd, 2004.

Hans, C. B. Frame Semantics as a Framework for Describing Polysemy and Syntactic Structures of English and German Motion Verbs in Contrastive Computational Lexicography. In: Rayson, P. , A. Wilson, T. McEnery, A. Hardie, & S. Khoja (eds.), *Proceedings of Corpus Linguistics*, 2001: 64-73.

Hansen, M. B. M. The Semantic Status of Discourse Markers. *Lingua*, 1998 (104):235-260.

Harmer, J. *The Practice of English Teaching*. London: Longman, 1991.

Hasperlmath, M. Against Iconicity and Markedness. Stanford University. http://email. eva. mpg. de/ ~ haspelmt/Iconicity Markedness. pdf. 2003.

Hatch, E. & H. Farhady. *Research Design and Statistics for Applied Linguistics*. Rowley, M. A. : Newbury House, 1982.

Hatch, E. M. ,et al. *Vocabulary, Semantics and Language Education*. Beijing: Foreign Language Teaching and Research Press, 2001.

Hawkins, R. Markedness and the Acquisition of the English Dative Alternation by L2 Learners. *Second Language Research*, 1987 (3): 20-55.

Hayes, J. R. *The Complete Problem Solver*. Hilldale, N. J. : Lawrence Erbaum, 1989.

Higgs, T. & R. Clifford. The Push toward Communication: *Curriculum, Competence, and the Foreign Language Teacher*. National Textbook Co. , 1982.

Hoey, M. *Textual Interaction: An Introduction to Written Discourse Analysis*. London: Routledge, 2001.

Honeck, R. P. *A Proverb in Mind: The Cognitive Science of Proverbial Wit and Wisdom*. *Mahwah*, N. J. : Lawrence Erlbaum, 1997.

Honeck, R. P. , C. Kibler, & M. J. Firment. In Haskell, R. E. (eds.). *Cognition and Symbolic Structures: The Psychology of Metaphoric Transformation*. Ablex Publishing Corporation, 1987.

Horne, M. P. , G. Hansson, J. Bruce, & M. Frid. Filipsson. Cue Words and the Topic Structure of Spoken Discourse: The Case of Swedish *Men* " But ". *Journal of Pragmatics*, 2001 (33): 1061-1081.

Hudson, T. The Effect of Individual Schemata on the"Short Circuit" in L2 Reading: Nondecoding Factors in L2 Reading Performance. *Language Learning*, 1982.

Hyland, K. Representing Readers in Writing: Student and Expert Practices. *Linguistics and Education*, 2005 (16): 363-377.

Hyltenstam, K. The Use of Typological Markedness Conditions as Predictors in Second Language Acquisition: The Case of Pronominal Copies in Relative Clauses in Anderson (eds.), 1984.

Hyltenstam, K. Typological Markedness as a Research Tool in the Study of Second Language Acquisition in Dechert (eds.), 1990.

Indurkhya, B. *Metaphor and Cognition: An Interactionist Approach*. Dorcrecht: Kluwer Academic Publishers, 1992.

Jackendoff, R. S. *Semantics and Cognition—Current Studies in Linguistics Series*, MIT Press, 1983.

Jakobson, R. *The Metaphoric and Metonymic Poles*. In Driven, R. and R. Rorings (eds.). *Metaphor and Metonymy in Comparison and Contrast*. Berlin/ New York: Mouton de Gruyter, 2002:41-47.

Johnson, K. *Language Teaching and Skill Learning*. Oxford: Blackwell, 1996.

Johnson, M. *The Body in the Mind. The Bodily Basis of Meaning, Imagination and Reason*. Chicago, London: University of Chicago Press, 1987.

Johnson, P. Effects on Reading Comprehension of Building Background Knowledge. *TESOL Quarterly*, 1982 (16.4): 503-516.

Johnson, P. Effects on Reading Comprehension of Language Complexity and Cultural Background of a Text. *TESOL Quarterly*, 1981(15): 169-181.

Johnston, P. H. *Reading Comprehension Assessment: A Cognitive Basis*. Newark: DE International Reading Association, 1983.

Jordens, P. Interlanguage Research: interpretation and explanation. *Language Learning*, 1980 (30): 195-207.

Kellerman, E. *Aspects of Transferability in Second Language Acquisition*. Unpublished Ph. D. thesis. University of Nijmegen, 1987.

Kellerman, E. Transfer or Non-transfer: Where We Are Now? *Studies in Second Language Acquisition*, 1979(2): 37-57.

Kern, R. *Literacy and Language Teaching*. Hong Kong: Oxford University Press, 2000.

Kintsche, W. *The Representation of Meaning in Memory*. Hillsdale, N. J.: Lawrence Erlbaum, 1974.

Knott, A. & R. Dale. Using Linguistic Phenomena to Motivate a Set of Coherence Relations. *Discourse Processes*, 1994 (1): 35-62.

Knott, A. & T. Sanders. The Classification of Coherence Relations and Their Linguistic Markers: An Exploration of Two Languages. *Journal of Pragmatics*, 1998 (30):135-175.

Koch, P. *Frame and Contiguity: On the Cognitive Bases of Metonymy and Certain Types of Word Formation*. In, Panther, K. U. & G. Radden (eds.). *Metonymy in Language and Thought*. Amsterdam/Philadelphia: John Benjamins, 1999:139-167.

Kogen, M. The Conventions of Expository Writing. *Journal of Basic Writing*, 1986 (5): 24-37.

Kovecses and Szabo. *Idioms: A View from Cognitive Semantics*. In *Applied Linguistics*, 17(3). Oxford: Oxford University Press, 1996.

Kovecses, Z. & R. Gunter, *Metonymy: Developing a Cognitive Linguistic View*. In *Cognitive Linguistics*, 1998(9).

Kovecses, Z. *Metaphor: A Practical Introduction*. Oxford: Oxford University Press, 2002.

Krashen S. *Principles and Practice in Second Language Acquisition*. Oxford/New York: Pergamon, 1982.

Krashen S. *The Input Hypothesis: Issues and Implications*. London: Longman, 1985.

Krashen, S. *Second Language Acquisition and Second Language Learning*. Oxford: Pergamon, 1981.

Krashen, S. Some Issues Relating to the Monitor Model. In Brown, H., C. Yorio & R. Crymes (eds.) *On TESOL*. Washington, D.C.: TESOL, 1977.

Kroon, C. A Framework for the Description of Latin Discourse Markers. *Journal of Pragmatics*, 1998 (30):205-223.

Kucer, S. B. *Dimensions of Literacy: A Conceptual Base for Teaching Reading and Writing in School Settings*. London: Lawrence Erlbaum Associates, Publishers, 2005.

Kyratzis, A. & S. Ervin-Tripp. The Development of Discourse Markers in Peer Interaction. *Journal of Pragmatics*, 1999 (31): 1321-1338.

Lakoff, G. & M. Johnson. *Metaphors We Live By*. Chicago: The University of Chicago Press, 1980.

Lakoff, G. & M. Tuner. *More than Cool Reason*. Chicago, I. L. : University of Chicago Press, 1989.

Lakoff, G. Metaphor and War: The Metaphor System Used to Justify War in the Gulf. *Journal of Urban and Cultural Studies*, 1992(2,1).

Lakoff, G. The Contemporary Theory of Metaphor. In A. Ortony (ed.). *Metaphor and Thought*. Cambridge: Cambridge University Press, 1993.

Lakoff, G. The Invariance Hypothesis: Is Abstract Reason Based on Image-schema? *Cognitive Linguistics*, 1990(1): 39-74.

Lakoff, G. What Is a Conceptual System? In Overton & Palermo (eds.) *The Nature and Ontogenesis of Meaning*. Hillsdale, N. J. : Lawrence Erlbaum, 1994.

Lakoff, G. *Women, Fire and Dangerous Things: What Categories Reveal about the Mind*. Chicago: University of Chicago Press, 1987.

Lakoff, G., & M. Turner. *More than Cool Reason: A Field Guide to Poetic Metaphor*. Chicago: University of Chicago Press, 1989.

Lakoff, G., & M. Johnson. *Metaphor We Live By*. Chicago: The University of Chicago Press, 1980.

Lakoff, G. The Contemporary Theory of Metaphor. In Ortony, A. (eds.). *Metaphor and Thought* (second edition). Cambridge: Cambridge University Press, 1993: 202-251.

Lakoff, G. The Invariance Hypothesis: Is Abstract Reasoning Based on Image-schemas?

Cognitive Linguistics, 1990(1): 39-74.

Lakoff, G. What Is a Conceptual System? In Overton & Palermo (eds.) *The Nature and Ontogenesis of Meaning*. Hillsdale, N. J. : Lawrence Erlbaum, 1994.

Langacker, R. W. *Foundations of Cognitive Grammar: Theoretical Prerequisites*. Stanford, C. A. : Stanford University Press, 1999.

Langacker, R. W. *Grammar and Conceptualization*. Berlin/New York: Mouton de Gruyter, 1999.

Langacker, R. W. Reference-Point Constructions. *Cognitive Linguistics*. Philadelphia: John Benjamins Publishing Company, 1993(4): 1-38.

Langacker, R. W. The Contextual Basis of Cognitive Semantics. Nutyts, J. , et al (eds). *Language and Conceptualization*. Cambridge: Cambridge University, 1997.

Larsen-Freeman, D. & M. Long. *An Introduction to Second Language Acquisition Research*. New York: Longman, 1991.

Larsen-Freeman, D. An Explanation for the Morpheme Acquisition Order of Second Language Learners. *Language Learning*, 1976(26): 125-134.

Larsen-Freeman, D. & M. Long. *An Introduction to Second Language Research*. London: Longman, 1991.

Lasnik, H. & M. Saito. *Move* α. Cambridge, Mass. : MIT Press, 1992.

Levenston, E. Second Language Lexical Acquisition: Issues and Problems. *Interlanguage Studies Bulletin*, 1979(4): 147-160.

Levinson, S. C. *Pragmatics*. Cambridge: Cambridge University Press, 1983.

Levinson, S. *Pragmatics*. Beijing: Foreign Language Teaching and Research Press, 2001: 226-278.

Li Yongzhong. *A Cognitive Approach to Metonymy in Language*. Shanghai: Donghua University Press, 2004.

Liceras, J. The Role of Intake in the Determination of Learners' Competence. Gass and Madden (eds.), 1985.

Liu, C. Q. Tense Features in Mandarin Verb-le. *Proceedings of Postgraduate Research Forum on Language and Linguistics*. City University of Hong Kong, 2000(99): 93-108.

Long, D. R. Second Language Listening Comprehension: A Schema-Theoretic Perspective. *The Modern Language Journal*, 1989 (73.1):32-40.

Lyons, J. *Linguistic Semantics: An Introduction*. Beijing: Foreign Language Teaching and Research Press, 2000

Macaulay, R. You Know, It Depends. *Journal of Pragmatics*, 2002 (34): 749-767.

Mackey, A. Input, Interaction and Second Language Development: An Empirical Study of Question Formation in ESL. In Valdman, A. & S. Gass (eds.). *Studies in Second Language Acquisition*, 1999(21): 557-587.

Mandelblit, N. Beyond Lexical Semantics: Mapping and Blending of Conceptual and Linguistic Structures in Machine Translation. In *Proceedings of the 4th International Conference in the Cognitive Science of Natural Language Processing*. Dublin, Ireland.

July 1995.

Mandelblit, N. Formal and Conceptual Blending in the Hebrew Verbal System: A Cognitive Basis for Verbal-Pattern Alternations in Modern Hebrew. Cognitive Science Department, University of California, San Diego, 1995.

Mateos, M., E. Martin, R. Villalon & M. Luna. Reading and Writing to Learn in Secondary Education: Online Processing Activity and Written Products in Summarizing and Synthesizing Tasks. *Reading and Writing*, 2008 (21): 675-697.

Matsui, T. Semantics and Pragmatics of a Japanese Discourse Marker *dakara* (*so/in other words*): A Unitary Account. *Journal of Pragmatics*, 2002 (34): 867-891.

Mazurkewich, I. Syntactic Markedness and Language Acquisition. *Studies in Second Language Acquisition*, 1985(7): 15-35.

McKenna, C. M. & D. R. Robinson. *Teaching through Text: Reading and Writing in the Content.* N. J. : Pearson Allyn & Bacon, 2001;20-30.

Meisel, J., H. Clahsen & M. Pienemann. On Determining Developmental Stages in Natural Second Language Acquisition. In Valdman A. & S. Gass (eds.). Studies in Second Language Acquisition, 1981(3.1): 109-135.

Meyer, B. J. F & R. O. Freedle. Effects of Discourse Types on Recall. *American Educational Research Journal*, 1984 (21.1): 121-143.

Meyer, B. J. F. *The Organization of Prose and Its Effect on Memory.* Amsterdam: North Holland Publishing Company, 1975.

Miles, M. & A. Huberman. *Qualitative Data Analysis* 2nd Ed. Beverly Hills: Sage Publishers, 1994.

Minsky, M. A Framework for Representing Knowledge. In Winston (ed.), *The Psychology of Computer Vision.* McGraw-Hill, 1975.

Montes, R. G. The Development of Discourse Markers in Spanish: Interjections. *Journal of Pragmatics*, 1999 (31): 1289-1319.

Müller, S. "Well you know that type of person": Functions of Well in the Speech of American and German Students. *Journal of Pragmatics*, 2004 (36): 1157-1182.

Murillo, S. A Relevance Reassessment of Reformulation Markers. *Journal of Pragmatics*, 2004 (36): 2059-2068.

Nesset, T. Iconicity and Prototype: A New Perspective on Russian Verbs of Motion. http://www. blackwell-synergy. com/doi/pdf/10. 1034/j. 1600-082X. 2000. d01-9. x? cookieSet=1. 2000.

Newmeyer, F. J. *Language Form and Language Function—Language, Speech and Communication.* Cambridge, Mass. : MIT Press, 1998.

Nippold, M., S Martin & B. Erskine. *Proverb Comprehension in Context: A Developmental Study with Children and Adolescents.* In *Journal of Speech and Hearing Research*, 1988(31): 19-28.

Norrick, N. R. Discourse Markers in Oral Narrative. *Journal of Pragmatics*, 2001(33): 849-878.

Nunan, D. *Language Teaching Methodology.* Hertfordshire: Prentice Hall International

（UK) Ltd. , 1991.

Nunan, D. *Second Language Teaching and Learning*. Beijing: Foreign Language and Research Press, 2001:249-273.

Nunberg, G. *The Non-uniqueness of Semantic Solutions: Polysemy*. Linguistics and Philosophy. *Oxford Advanced Learners' English-Chinese Dictionary of Current English* (4*th ed.*). Oxford: Commercial Press & Oxford Press, 1979(3):1192-1193.

O'Malley, J. M. , A. Chamot. *Learning Strategies in Second Language Acquisition*. Cambridge: Cambridge University Press, 1990.

O'Malley, J. M. , A. Chamot. and & L. Kupper. Listening Comprehension Strategies in Second Language Acquisition. *Applied Linguistics*, 1989 (4): 418-437.

Odlin, T. *Language Transfer*. Cambridge: Cambridge University Press, 1989.

Ouhalla, J. *Introducing Transformational Grammar: From Principles and Parameters to Minimalism* (2nd Edition). Foreign Language Teaching and Research Press; Edward Arnold (publishers) Limited, 2001.

Oxford Advanced Learners' Dictionary of Current English. 6th edition. Oxford University Press, 2005

Panther. K. , & L. Thornburg. *Coercion and Metonymy: The Interaction of Constructional and Lexical Meaning*. In: Barbara Lewandowska-Tomaszczyk (eds.). *Cognitive Perspectives on Language*. Frankfurt am Main: Perter Lang GmbH, 1999: 37-51.

Pearson, P. D. & L. Fielding. Research Update: Listening Comprehension *Language Arts*, 1982 (59.6):17-29.

Petruck, M. R. L. Frame Semantics and the Lexicon: Nouns and Verbs in the Body Frame. *Semantics and Pragmatics*. John Benjamins, 1995: 279-296.

Pica, T. Adult Acquisition of English as a Second Language Under Different Conditions of Exposure. *Language Learning*, 1983(33): 465-497.

Piccolo, J. Expository Text Structure: Teaching and Learning Strategies. *The Reading Teacher*, 1987 (40.9): 828-847.

Chen Pi-Ching, & Chien-Ying Chen. Briding Reading and Writing: A Collaborative Task-Based English Instruction. *WHAMPOA—An Interdisciplinary Journal*, 2005 (49): 349-366.

Pienemann, M. & M. Johnston. Factors Influencing the Development of Language Proficiency. In D. Nunan (eds.) *Applying Second Language Acquisition Research*. Adelaide: National Curriculum Resource Center, 1987.

Pinker, S. & A. Prince. Regular and Irregular Morphology and the Psychological Status of Rules of Grammar. *The Reality of Linguistic Rules*. Amsterdam: Benjamins, 1999.

Radden, G. , & 2. Kovecses. *Towards a Theory of Metonymy*. In: Panther, Klaus-Uwe and Gunter Radden (eds.). *Metonymy in Language and Thought*. Amsterdam/ Philadelphia: John Benjamins Publishing Company, 1999:17-60.

Reddy, M. The Conduit Metaphor. In A. Ortony (eds.), *Metaphor and Thought*. Cambridge: Cambridge University Press, 1979.

Redeker, G. Ideational and Pragmatic Markers of Discourse Structure. *Journal of*

Pragmatics, 1990 (14): 367-381.

Redeker, G. Linguistic Markers of Discourse Structure. *Linguistics*, 1991 (29): 1139-1172.

Reder, L. M. The Role of Elaboration in the Comprehension and Retention of Prose: A Critical Review. *Review of Educational Research*, 1980 (50):5-53.

Reiss, M. The Good Language Learner: Another Look. *Language Learning*, 1985 (41): 511-523.

Richards, J. Error Analysis and Second Language Strategies. *Language Sciences*, 1971 (17): 12-22.

Richards, J. Listening Comprehension Approach, Design, Procedure. *TESOL Quarterly*, 1983 (17): 219-239.

Richards, J. C. , R. Schmidt. et al. *Longman Dictionary of Language Teaching and Applied Linguistics* (3rd ED). Pearson Eduacation Ltd. , 2005.

Rivers, W. M. Listening Comprehension: *In Teaching Foreign Language Skills* (2nd edition). The University of Chicago Press, Ltd. , 1981.

Rosch, E. *Principles of Categorization.* In: Rosch E. and B. B. Lloyd, eds, *Cognition and Categorization.* Hillsdale/ N. J. , N. Y. : Lawrence Erlbaum, 1978: 27-48.

Rosch, E. Natural Categories. *Cognitive Psychology*, 1973(7): 532-547.

Ross, J. R. Constraints on Variables in Syntax. PhD dissertation, MIT. Published (1986) as Infinite Syntax! *Norwood N. J. : Ablex*, 1967.

Ross, J. R. On Declaration Sentences. In R. Jacobs & P. Rosenbaum (eds.), *Readings in English Transformational Grammar*(222-227). Waltham M. A. : Ginn, 1970: 222-227.

Rost, M. *Listening in Language Learning.* London: Longman, 1990.

Rouchota, V. Discourse Connectives: What Do They Link. *UCL Working Papers in Linguistics*, 1996 (8): 1-15.

Rumelhart, D. Toward a Interactive Model of Reading. In *Attention and Performance.* New York: Academic Press, 1977.

Rumelhart, D. E. Schemata: The Building Blocks of Cognition. In Spiro, R. J. , B. C. Bruce, & W. E. Brewer (eds.). *Theoretical Issues in Reading Comprehension.* Hillsdale, N. J. : Lawrence Erlbaum Associates, 1980.

Rumelhart, D. E. Notes on a Schema for Stories. In *Representation and Understanding: Studies in Cognitive Science.* Bobrow , D. G. & A. M. Collins (eds.). New York: Academic Press, 1975: 211-236.

Rumelhart, E. E. Understand Understanding. In Flood, J. (eds.), *Understanding Reading Comprehension.* Newark, Delaware: International Reading association, 1983: 1-21.

Rutherford, W. Markedness in Second Language Acquisition. *Language Learning*, 1982 (32): 85-108.

Saeed, J. I. *Semantics.* Beijing: Foreign Language Teaching and Research Press, 2000.

Stanford, A. J. , & S. C. Garrod. *Understanding Written Language.* Chichester: John

Wiley & Sons, 1981.

Schachter, J. An Error in Error Analysis. *Language Learning*, 1973(27): 205-214.

Schachter, J. Second Language Acquisition and its Relationship to Universal Grammar. *Applied Linguistics*, 1988 (9): 219-235.

Schank, R. C. & R. P. Abelson. *Scripts, Plans, Goals and Understanding: An Inquiry into Human Knowledge Structures*. Hillsdale, N. J. : ErlBaum, 1977.

Schiffrin, D. *Discourse Markers*. Cambridge: Cambridge University Press, 1987.

Schmidt, M. Coordinate Structures and Language Universal in Interlanguage. *Language Learning*, 1990(30): 397-416.

Schmidt-Rinehart, B. C. The Effects of Topic Familiarity on Second Language Listening Comprehension. *The Modern Language Journal*, 1994 (78.2): 179-189.

Schourup, L. Discourse Markers. *Lingua*, 1999(107): 227-265.

Schwenter, S. A. Some Reflections on *o sea*: A Discourse Marker in Spanish. *Journal of Pragmatics*, 1996 (25): 855-874.

Searle, J. K. *Expression and Meaning: Studies in the Theory of Speech Acts*. Cambridge: Cambridge University Press, 1979.

Seliger, H. On the Nature and Function of Language Rules in Language Teaching. *TESOL Quarterly*, 1979(13): 359-369.

Selinker, L. Interlanguage. *International Review of Applied Linguistics*, 1972.

Shanahan, T. Nature of the Reading-Writing Relation: An Exploratory Multivariate Analysis. *Journal of Educational Psychology*, 1984 (76): 466-477.

Shanahan, T. The Shared Knowledge of Reading and Writing. *Reading Psychology: An International Quarterly*, 1987 (8): 93-102.

Shohamy, E. & O. Inbar. Validation of Listening Comprehension Tests: The Effect of Text and Question Type. *Language Testing*, 1991(8):23-40.

Silva, T. Toward an Understanding of the Distinct Nature of L2 Writing: The ESL Research and Its Implications. *TESOL Quarterly*, 1993(27): 657-677.

Skehan, P. *A Cognitive Approach to Language Learning*. Oxford: Oxford University Press, 1998.

Smith, V. H. Teaching Beginning Writing vs Nurturing Beginning Writers. Paper Presented at the Fourth *Annual Meeting of the Indiana Teachers of Writing Conference*. Indianapolis, I. N. , September, 1984: 28-29.

Spada, N. The Interaction between Types of Content and Type of Instruction: Some Effects on the L2 Proficiency of Adult Learners. *Studies in Second Language Acquisition*, 1986(8): 181-199.

Sperber, D. & D. Wilson. *Relevance: Communication and Cognition*. Beijing: Foreign Language Teaching and Research Press, 2001.

Sperber, D. & D. Wilson. Pragmatics, Modularity and Mind-reading. *Mind and Language*, 2002 (17): 3-23.

Sperber, D. & D. Wilson. *Relevance: Communication and Cognition*. Blackwell Publishers Ltd./Foreign Language Teaching and Research Press, 2001.

Sperling, M. Revisiting the Writing-speaking Connection: Challenges for Research on Writing and Writing Instruction. *Review of Education Research*, 1996: 66.

Spolsky, B. *Conditions for Second Language Learning*. Oxford: Oxford University Press, 1989.

Stanovich, K. E. Toward an Interactive-compensatory Model of Individual Differences in the Development of Reading Fluency. *Reading in Research Quarterly*, 1980:16.

Stein, N. L. & C. G. Glenn. An Analysis of Story Comprehension in Elementary School Children. In Freedle. R. O. , *New Directions in Discourse Processing* (eds.). Hillsdale, N. J. : Erlbaum, 1979.

Stotsky, S. Research on Reading/Writing Relationships: A Synthesis and Suggested Directions. *Language Arts*, 1983 (60): 627-642.

Stubbs, M. *Discourse Analysis*. Chicago, I. L. : The University of Chicago Press, 1983.

Swain, M. Communicative Competence: Some roles of Comprehensible Input and Comprehensible Output in Its Development. In Gass & Maddent (eds.). *Input in Second Language Acquisition*. Rowley, Mass. : Newbury House, 1985: 235-245.

Swain, M. Three Functions of Output in Second Language Learning. In Cook G. & B. Seidlhofer (eds.). *Principle and Practice in Applied Linguistics*. Studies in Honour of H. G. Widdowson. Shanghai: Shanghai Foreign Languages Press, 1995: 125-144.

Sweester, E. *From Etymology to Pragmatics: The Mind-as-Body Metaphor in Semantic Change*. Cambridge: Cambridge University Press, 1990.

Talmy, L. Force Dynamics in Language and Cognition. *Cognitive Science*, 1988(12): 49-100.

Talmy, L. Lexicalization Patterns: Semantic Structure in Lexical Forms. In Timothy Shopen (ed.) *Language Typology and Syntactic Description*. Cambridge: Cambridge University Press, 1985(3):57-149.

Taub, S. F. *Language from the Body: Iconicity and Metaphor in American Sign Language*. Cambridge: Cambridge, U. K. , New York Cambridge University Press, 2001.

Taylor, J. R. *Linguistic Categorization: Prototypes in Linguistic Theory*. Oxford: Oxford University Press, 1989.

Taylor, J. R. *Linguistic Categorization: Prototypes in Linguistic Theory*. Oxford: Clarendon, 1995.

Taylor, J. R. *Linguistic Categorization: Prototypes in Linguistic Theory* (second edition). Beijing: Foreign Language Teaching and Research Press, 2001.

Tayor, B. Children's Memory for Expository Text after Reading. *Reading Research Quarterly*, 1980 (15): 399-411.

The American Heritage Dictionary. Boston/New York/London. Houghton Mifflin Company, 1991: 792.

Thomas, M. The Interpretation of English Reflexive Pronouns by Non-native Speakers. *Studies in Second Language Acquisition*, 1989(11): 281-303.

Thornburg, L. & K. Panther. *Speech Act Metonymies*. In Liebert W. A. , G. Redeker, et al (eds.), *Discourse and Perspective in Cognitive Linguistics*. Amsterdam/

Philadelphia: John Benjamins Publishing Company, 1997:205-219.

Tierney, R. J. & L. Margie. What Is the Value of Connecting Reading and Writing? *Convergences: Transactions in Reading and Writing.* B. T. Petersened. Urbana, I. L. : NCTE, 1986: 15-29.

Tierney, R. J. & P. D. Pearson. Toward a Composing Model of Reading. *Language Arts*, 1983 (60): 568-580.

Tran-Chi-Chau. Error Analysis, Contrastive Analysis and Students' Perceptions: A Study of Difficulty in Second Language Learning. *International Review of Applied Linguistics*, 1975(13): 119-143.

Tree, J. E. F. & J. C. Schrock. Basic Meanings of *You Know* and *I Mean. Journal of Pragmatics*, 2002 (34): 727-747.

Trillo, J. R. The Pragmatic Fossilization of Discourse Markers in Non-native Speakers of English. *Journal of Pragmatics*, 2002 (34): 769-784.

Turner, M. An Image-schematic Constraint on Metaphor. In Geiger & Rudzka-Ostyn (eds.). *Conceptualizations and Mental Processing in Language.* Berlin: Mouton de Gruyter, 1993.

Turner, M. Aspects of the Invariance Hypothesis. *Cognitive Linguistics*, 1990(1): 247-255.

Turner, M. *Death Is the Mother of Beauty: Mind, Metaphor, Criticism.* Chicago: Chicago University Press, 1987.

Turner, M. Language Is a Virus. *Poetics Today*, 1992(13): 725-736.

Turner, M. *Reading Minds.* Princeton: Princeton University Press, 1991.

Turner, M. , & G. Fauconnier. Blending and Metaphor. In Shen Y. & A. Kasher, (eds.), *Cognitive Aspects of Metaphor.* Amsterdam: John Benjamins, 1996.

Turner, M. , & G. Fauconnier. Conceptual Integration and Formal Expressions. *Journal of Metaphor and Symbolic Activity*, 1995(10.3): 183-204.

Ullman, S. *Semantics: An Introduction to the Science of Meaning.* Happer and Row Publishers, Inc. U. S. A. 1979.

Ungerer, F. , & H. J. Schmid. *An Introduction to Cognitive Linguistics.* Beijing: Foreign Language Teaching and Research Press, 2001.

Van Dijk, T. A Review of R. Journal of linguistics 1981 (17):140-148.

Van Dijk, T. A. *Text and Context: Explorations in the Semantics and Pragmatics of Discourse.* London: Longman, 1977.

Van Naerssen, M. How Similar and Spanish as a First and Foreign Language? In Scarcella, R. & S. Krashen (eds.) *Research in Second Language Acquisition.* Rowley, Mass. : Newbury House, 1980.

Van Pattern, B. *Input Processing and Grammar Instruction in Second Language Acquisition.* Norwood, N. J. : Ablex, 1996.

Walker, C. H. , & B. J. E. Meyer. Integrating Different Types of Information in Text. *Journal of Verbal Learning and Verbal Behavior*, 1980(19): 263-275.

Wang, Wenbin. *Self-negotiation in Metaphor Construction and Interpretation.* Ph. D.

Dissertation. Shanghai International Studies University, 2005.

Wardhaugh, R. The Contrastive Analysis Hypothesis. *TESOL Quarterly*, 1970(4): 123-130.

White, L. Markedness and Second Language Acquisition: the Question of Transfer. *Studies in Second Language Acquisition*, 1987(9): 261-286.

White, L. Universal Grammar: Is It Just a New Name for Old Problems? *Language Transfer in Language Learning*, 1992.

Widdowson. H. G. Teaching Language as Communication. Oxford: Oxford University Press, 1978.

Widdowson. H. G. The Process and Purpose of Reading. London: Oxford University Press, 1979.

Wilson, D. & D. Sperber. Linguistic form and Relevance. *Lingua*, 1993(90): 1-25.

Wilson, P. T. & R. C. Anderson. What They Don't Know Will Hurt Them: The Role of Prior Knowledge in Comprehension. Pearson, P. D. *Handbook of Reading Research*. New York: Longman, 1984:33-52.

Winter, S. L. A clearing in the Forest. *Metaphor and Symbolic Activity*, 1995(10): 223-245.

Wood, F. T. English Prepositional Idioms. Beijing: Knowledge Press, 1983.

Zamel, V. Writing One's Way into Reading, *TESOL Quarterly*, 1992(26.3): 463-485.

Zhao Cuilian. *A developmental model of polysemous representation*. Kaifeng: Henan University Press, 2006.

Zobl, H. Markedness and the Projection Problem. *Language Learning*, 1983(33):293-313.

Zobl, H. The Formal and Developmental Selectivity of L1 Influence on L2 Acquisition. *Language Learning*, 1980(30): 43-58.

蔡辉. 转喻思维产生动因的多元思考[J]. 外语学刊,2006(6).

蔡龙权. 隐喻理论在二语习得中的应用[J]. 外国语, 2003(6).

陈开举. 英汉会话中末尾标记语的语用功能分析[J]. 现代外语, 2002(3).

陈立平. 从阅读与写作的关系看写作教学中的范文教学[J]. 外语与外语教学,2001(4).

陈万会. 中国学习者二语词汇习得研究——从认知心理的视角[M]. 青岛:中国海洋大学出版社, 2008.

陈新仁. 话语联系语与英语议论文写作:调查分析[J]. 外语教学与研究, 2002(5).

程晓堂, 郑敏. 英语学习策略[M]. 北京:外语教学与研究出版社,2002.

丁往道,吴冰,等. 英语写作手册[M] 北京:外语教学与研究出版社,1997.

丁言仁. 第二语言习得研究与外语学习[M]. 上海:上海外语教育出版社,2004.

郭聿楷. 义素分析与原型范畴[A]. 何英玉. 语义学[C]. 上海:上海外语教育出版社, 2005.

韩宝成. 外语教学科研中的统计方法[M]. 北京:外语教学与研究出版社, 2000.

何安平, 徐曼菲. 中国大学生英语口语 small words 的研究[J]. 外语教学与研究, 2003(6).

何自然, 莫爱屏. 话语标记语与语用照应[J]. 广东外语外贸大学学报, 2002(1).

何自然, 冉永平. 话语联系语的语用制约性[J]. 外语教学与研究, 1999(3).

黄华. 试比较概念隐喻理论和概念整合理论[J]. 外语与外语教学, 2001(6).

黄子东. 话题熟悉程度、语言水平和问题类型对 EFL 听力理解的影响:一项基于图式理论和关联理论的实验研究[J]. 现代外语, 1998 (4).

蒋勇, 马玉蕾. SB 与 RT 的整合性研究[J]. 外语学刊, 2003(1).

蒋勇. 从隐性空间复合论看幽默理解时的语义跃迁[J]. 山东外语教学, 2003(1).

孔淑娟. 广告语言的象似研究. 中国优秀硕博士学位论文全文数据库, http://202.114.65.
37/kns50/scdbsearch/scdetail.aspx? QueryID=129&CurRe

蓝纯. 认知语言学与隐喻研究[M]. 北京:外语教学与研究出版社, 2005.

李福印. 语义学概论[M]. 北京:北京大学出版社. 2006.

李力, 陈治安. Language Culture and TEFL [M]. 西南师范大学出版社, 1997.

李四清. 英汉成语中的隐喻模式及其隐喻机制的研究[J]. 上海师范大学学报, 2005(4).

李勇忠. 语用标记与话语连贯. 外语与外语教学[J]. 2003(1).

李勇忠. 言语行为转喻与话语的深层连贯[J]. 外语教学, 2004(3).

廖光蓉. 多义词意义关系模式研究[J]. 外语教学, 2005(3).

刘辰诞. 教学篇章语言学[M]. 上海:上海外语教育出版社, 1999.

刘礼进. 话语生成与理解:语序标记语作用[J]. 外语教学与研究, 2002(3).

刘正光. Fauconnier 的概念合成理论:阐释与质疑[J]. 外语与外语教学, 2002(10).

罗琳, 刘家荣. 介词的语义扩展——through 的个案研究[J]. 重庆交通学院学报, 2005(2).

马萧. 话语标记语的语用功能与翻译[J]. 中国翻译, 2003(5).

马玉蕾, 姚岚. 话语连接词和关联理论[J]. 外语与翻译, 2002(3).

梅德明. 现代句法学[M]. 上海:上海外语教育出版社, 2008.

梅德明. 现代语言学简明教程[M]. 上海:上海外语教育出版社, 2003.

冉永平. 话语标记语 well 的语用功能[J]. 外国语, 2003(3).

冉永平. 话语标记语 you know 的语用增量辨析[J]. 解放军外国语学院学报, 2002(4).

冉永平. 话语标记语的语用学研究综述[J]. 外语研究, 2000(4).

任朝华. 基本义在多义动词习得中促进作用的实证研究[J]. 山东外语教学, 2009(2).

沈家煊. 句法的象似性问题[A]. 语言的认知研究——认知语言学论文精选. 上海:上海外语
出版社, 2005.

束定芳. 隐喻和转喻的差别和联系[J]. 外国语, 2004(3).

孙亚. 心理空间理论与翻译[J]. 上海科技翻译, 2001(4).

唐瑶. 对"move"一词多义的认知阐释[J]. 外语艺术教育研究, 2007(3).

陶文好. 论 over 的空间和隐喻认知[J]. 外语与外语教学, 1997(4).

汪少华. 合成空间理论对隐喻的阐释力[J]. 外国语, 2001(3).

汪少华. 诗歌中视角空间的美学功能[J]. 外语教学, 2002(2).

王斌. 概念整合与翻译[J]. 中国翻译, 2001(3).

王文斌. 概论合成理论研究与应用的回顾与思考[J]. 外语研究, 2004(1).

王寅. 体验哲学和认知语言学对词汇和语法成因的解释[J]. 外语学刊, 2004(1).

王寅. 语义理论与语言教学[M]. 上海:上海外语教育出版社, 2001.

吴亚欣, 于国栋. 话语标记的元语用分析[J]. 外语教学, 2003(4).

谢薇娜. 谈阅读与写作的交融性 [J]. 外语教学, 1994 (4).

徐锦芬. 精读教学中的综合技能集成法——大学英语教学改革实证研究 [J]. 外语教学与研
究, 2002 (11).

徐盛桓. 常规关系与认知化[J]. 外国语, 2002(1).

徐盛桓. 新赖斯会话含意理论和语用推理[J]. 外国语,1993(1).

薛媛. 话语标记语及其在翻译中的语用充实[J]. 外语与外语教学,2003(7).

严辰松. 语言理据探究[A]. 何英玉. 语义学[C]. 上海:上海外语教育出版社,2005.

杨玲. 试论石化现象的成因及应对策略[D]. 南京:南京师范大学硕士学位论文,2002.

余渭深,董平荣. 合成空间与中国古典诗词意象[J]. 外语与外语教学,2003(3).

俞理明. 语言迁移与二语习得——回顾、反思和研究[M]. 上海:上海外语教育出版社,2004.

张辉,论空间概念在语言知识结构中的作用[J]. 解放军南京国际关系学院学报,1998 (10).

张辉. 熟语及其理解的认知语义学研究[M].北京:军事谊文出版社,2003

张绍全. 国外多义性研究综观[J]. 四川外语学院学报,2009(3).

张维鼎. 意义与认知范畴化[M]. 四川:四川大学出版社,2007.

张以文,辛全宝. 英语习语分类词典[M]. 上海:上海外语教育出版社,1999.

张志毅,张庆云. 词汇语义学[M]. 北京:商务印书馆,2001.

赵群,罗炜东. 关注词汇的核心义项——多义词习得的有效途径[J]. 外语教学,2005(6).

赵艳芳. 认知语言学概论[M]. 上海:上海外语教育出版社,2001.